DAMAGES AND HUMAN RIGHTS

Damages and Human Rights is a major work on awards of damages for violations of human rights that will be of compelling interest to practitioners, judges and academics alike. Damages for breaches of human rights is emerging as an important and practically significant field of law, yet the rules and principles governing such awards and their theoretical foundations remain underexplored, while courts continue to struggle to articulate a coherent law of human rights damages. The book's focus is English law, but it draws heavily on comparative material from a range of common law jurisdictions, as well as the jurisprudence of international courts.

The current law on when damages can be obtained and how they are assessed is set out in detail and analysed comprehensively. The theoretical foundations of human rights damages are examined with a view to enhancing our understanding of the remedy and resolving the currently troubled state of human rights damages jurisprudence. The book argues that in awarding damages in human rights cases the courts should adopt a vindicatory approach, modelled on those rules and principles applied in tort cases when basic rights are violated. Other approaches are considered in detail, including the current 'mirror' approach which ties the domestic approach to damages to the European Court of Human Rights' approach to monetary compensation; an interest-balancing approach where the damages are dependent on a judicial balancing of individual and public interests; and approaches drawn from the law of state liability in EU law and United States constitutional law.

The analysis has important implications for our understanding of fundamental issues including the interrelationship between public law and private law, the theoretical and conceptual foundations of human rights law and the law of torts, the nature and functions of the damages remedy, the connection between rights and remedies, the intersection of domestic and international law, and the impact of damages liability on public funds and public administration.

Damages and Human Rights

Jason NE Varuhas

•HART•

OXFORD • LONDON • NEW YORK • NEW DELHI • SYDNEY

HART PUBLISHING
Bloomsbury Publishing Plc
Kemp House, Chawley Park, Cumnor Hill, Oxford, OX2 9PH, UK

HART PUBLISHING, the Hart/Stag logo, BLOOMSBURY and
the Diana logo are trademarks of Bloomsbury Publishing Plc

First published in hardback, 2016
Paperback edition, 2018

A catalogue record for this book is available from the British Library.

Library of Congress Cataloging-in-Publication Data

Names: Varuhas, Jason, author.

Title: Damages and human rights / Jason N.E. Varuhas.

Description: Oxford ; Portland, OR : Hart Pub. Ltd, 2016. | Based on author's thesis (doctoral—University of Cambridge, 2011) issued under title: Damages for breaches of human rights : a tort-based approach. | Includes bibliographical references and index. | Description based on print version record and CIP data provided by publisher; resource not viewed.

Identifiers: LCCN 2016000187 (print) | LCCN 2015049495 (ebook) |
ISBN 9781782252818 (Epub) | ISBN 9781849463720 (hardback)

Subjects: LCSH: Liability for human rights violations.

Classification:LCCK935(print)|LCCK935.V372016(ebook)|DDC342.08/5—dc23

LC record available at http://lccn.loc.gov/2016000187

ISBN: HB: 978-1-78043-157-4
PB: 978-1-50992-444-8
ePDF: 978-1-78043-157-6
ePub: 978-1-78043-157-7

Typeset by Compuscript Ltd, Shannon

Foreword

It has been traditional to regard monetary compensation for violating human rights as a subject to which analytical legal scholarship had little to offer. Legal arguments about the measure of damages for non-pecuniary harms flowing from violations of human rights have tended to be reduced to platitudes about balancing public interests against private interests, or an assumption that monetary compensation for harms of that kind is at most a secondary form of relief because human rights claims have nothing in common with common law claims for which damages traditionally provide a primary remedy. As a result, it has often been thought that the very availability of damages for breaches of human rights is somehow anomalous, and that the search for a principled basis for assessing those damages is pointless because doomed to failure.

In this book, Dr Varuhas subjects those ideas to thorough critical analysis. His exhaustive study shows them to be in need of substantial revision if, indeed, they should not be discarded. He argues that human rights, or at least a number of human rights, are more akin to torts which, in common law systems, are actionable per se, and for which damages at large are available without proof of pecuniary damage, than to public law wrongs or torts in which liability to pay compensation depends on proof of pecuniary damage. Human rights litigation, we are reminded, is principally about vindicating rights, not about compensating for loss. Damages in human rights cases are as important for that purpose as are damages for trespass, defamation or false imprisonment, vindicating the right rather than compensating for loss.

To make out his case, the author ranges far beyond human rights law. He develops the idea of vindication into a normative justification for awarding damages for human rights violations, a philosophical project which draws on but moves beyond the 'law-stuff'. By arguing for a tort-based model of human rights damages, and presenting a pluralistic approach to theories about the nature and purposes of tort law, he contributes to understanding of private law more generally. In challenging the idea that human rights are 'public law' rather than 'private law', he provides a telling critique of that distinction, the significance of which extends to fundamental issues of legal classification. When assessing his own normative arguments by seeing how they map onto legal categories and legal practice in several jurisdictions, he offers a principled critique of current doctrine as well as a potentially viable way forward. All this is done in a way that combines vigorous argument with intellectual rigour, stamina and honesty.

Over a number of years I enjoyed a privileged vantage point from which to watch Dr Varuhas work on the project. I saw him research the subject, and test and refine his own ideas and those of other scholars and judges. As the study of case law grew in depth and scope, normative ideas developed, and challenges were addressed, the work has become steadily richer and more coherent. Public lawyers and private lawyers (if that distinction has real meaning), human rights lawyers and legal theorists, and everyone with an interest in having a principled regime for making *ubi ius, ibi remedium* a practical reality, will find much food for thought in the book; even those who reject the conclusions will benefit from having to confront the manifest strengths of the argument. The book will quickly become the standard point of reference in its field. It is a pleasure to congratulate Dr Varuhas on this sustained, intellectually powerful and practically important piece of legal scholarship, and to commend it to the many readers, in many parts of the world, where it will, I hope, stimulate new approaches to the practice and theory of the subject.

David Feldman
Downing College, Cambridge
27th October 2015

Preface

Damages for breaches of human rights is emerging as one of the most interesting and also challenging subjects across the fields of public and private law. With the proliferation of charters of rights in common law systems, courts have been required to address what remedies ought to be available for breach of enumerated rights, and to articulate rules and principles to govern each such remedy. The remedy of damages is potentially one of the most important remedies available for rights-violations, having the capacity to make victims whole and afford strong protection to and provide a powerful affirmation of the importance of basic rights, as well as promote fundamental principles including government under law and *ubi ius, ibi remedium*. However, the availability of the remedy also gives rise to concerns, including that the making of damages awards may deplete resources set aside to fund public services, have a chilling effect on vigorous public administration, and fuel a damaging public law litigation or compensation culture. To these issues we may add the further complexity that the field lies at the intersection of public law, private law and international law, not being capable of neat compartmentalisation within any one of these fields. These complexities and competing concerns make the remedy a fascinating one for intellectual inquiry. The myriad issues raised by such remedy also helps us to understand why the remedy has posed significant and ongoing problems for courts, which have struggled and largely failed to articulate a coherent, rational and worked-out law of human rights damages, and why the theoretical foundations of this remedy remain obscure. The result has been marginalisation of the remedy, so that it plays a peripheral role in human rights law.

This book seeks to chart a path forward. The book undertakes the first major normative study of human rights damages, focusing on English law and the award of damages under the Human Rights Act 1998, but also considers the law of human rights or constitutional damages of a number of other common law jurisdictions. The book considers the competing approaches to human rights damages and evaluates each. In general English courts have sought to draw a bright line between damages in human rights law and damages in other more established fields of liability, such as the law of torts. They have appealed to an amorphous idea of 'public law' to justify a distinctive conception of damages. They have also looked to international law, with the dominant approach under the Act now being the 'mirror' approach, according to which domestic courts seek to mechanistically replicate the European Court of Human Rights' remedial practices. In general the approaches adopted by English and other common law courts are found to suffer significant weaknesses, as reflected in the unsatisfactory state of human rights damages jurisprudence in England and across common law jurisdictions. The book's central argument is that a vindicatory, tort-based approach ought to be taken to human rights damages, modelled on the approach to damages developed within vindicatory torts, such as trespass, false imprisonment, defamation and battery, which have long performed a constitutional role in affording strong protection to basic rights through damages liability. Such approach gives effect to the underlying functions of human rights law, which are to protect and vindicate basic individual rights and interests, and offers the prospect of development of a coherent and principled law of human rights damages, while not suffering many of the problems that dog alternative approaches. Articulation of this novel approach and its theoretical foundations is one of the major original contributions of this book.

A core theme of this book is that notwithstanding the powerful intuitive appeal of the idea of a fundamental distinction between public law and private law nothing of legal significance should be allowed to rest on this idea. Before I began to research human rights damages I approached the subject similarly to most others: human rights damages are a 'public law remedy', and they ought not to be analogised to damages in private law. As I continued to research and think about this topic I came to realise that this characterisation of the remedy was part of the problem, not the solution, being a significant reason why courts across common law jurisdictions have struggled to articulate a coherent, theoretically sound approach to human rights damages. There is no tradition of a distinctive idea of public law in English law, attempts to delineate public from private have failed, the idea of public law is bound up in interminable disagreement, while public law, as it exists, is a pluralistic field which cannot be reduced to one set of ideas or functions. If we wish to understand the approach that ought to be taken to remedies for breach of human rights we ought to look to the distinctive functions of *human rights law* rather than appeal to abstract notions of public and private.

To answer the difficult question of what approach ought to be taken to human rights damages the book goes beyond this immediate field. The book examines the nature of human rights law, and in particular the nature of the primary legal obligations; one cannot hope to understand what approach should be taken to remedies if one does not understand the nature of the wrongs being remedied. Surprisingly, while much (perhaps too much) has been written on certain topics in human rights law, such as proportionality or deference, very little detailed work has been done on the foundational question of the nature of the primary obligations. In order to understand what can be learned from the law of torts, the book articulates a framework for understanding the approaches to damages across that field, identifying an important vindicatory strand in torts damages which can too easily be lost sight of in an age where the loss-based tort of negligence is dominant. The book considers contextual and empirical research so as to evaluate public policy concerns raised by human rights liability, comparative material from a range of common law jurisdictions as well as the jurisprudence of international courts, and insights from different fields of both public and private law.

Ultimately, this book argues that the field is in need of a major rethink. Axiomatic and longstanding common law rules and principles should be preferred to current approaches characterised by open-ended judicial discretion and a vacuum of principle. Perhaps my criticisms reflect an inevitable divide between academic and judicial perspectives, as recorded by Sir William Wade in a letter to Lord Cooke of Thorndon, written on 12 March 1998. Sir William referred to the academic wanting 'everything clear and sharp and logical and in accordance with principle', whereas the judge's intuition was to resist being driven 'into a corner by ruthless logic and … compelled to decide contrary to what he wants'.[1] However, with Sir William, I maintain that while the judge's perspective may often reflect a 'sound instinct for the administration of justice', as a legal academic 'I am by my cloth obliged to protest when blurring becomes woolly thinking and blasphemy against basics'.

I have sought to write a book that is provocative and presents a novel perspective on an important and challenging field of law. Above all I have sought to maintain the highest standards of legal research, conceptual and analytical rigour, and academic integrity and honesty. Whether the reader agrees or disagrees with the argument made herein, I hope that the book will offer helpful insights into public law and private law, and stimulate new thinking within each field and across fields.

JNE Varuhas
Wellington
11 November 2015

[1] This letter is extracted in the Preface to HWR Wade and CF Forsyth, *Administrative Law* 11th edn (OUP, 2014) xi.

Acknowledgements

The work that has gone into this book has spanned years, institutions and countries. The book developed out of my doctoral thesis on human rights damages, and a great deal more work and thinking has gone into the manuscript since. The final product owes much to the help and support of a number of people and institutions.

I have been privileged to have been a member of several academic communities during the writing of this book. I completed my doctoral thesis at the University of Cambridge, where I was a doctoral student in the Law Faculty and a member of Sidney Sussex College. My doctoral studies were supported by a significant scholarship from the New Zealand Government under the Top Achiever Doctoral Scholarship scheme, for which I am grateful. During my doctoral studies I had the opportunity to spend six months at Yale University as a Fox International Scholar, and I am grateful to the Fox scholarship scheme for their support. Following completion of my thesis the bulk of the work towards this book was completed while I was a Junior Research Fellow at Christ's College and member of the Law Faculty at the University of Cambridge. There can scarcely be a more pleasurable location to work on a book manuscript than Room A6 of the Fellows' Building at Christ's. My work on the book was completed Down Under during my time as Dean's Postdoctoral Research Fellow and then Senior Lecturer at the University of New South Wales. At each institution I have been grateful for the intellectual generosity and fellowship of my colleagues. My different experiences at each institution fundamentally shaped and carried forward my thinking about human rights damages and law and scholarship more generally.

I owe particular thanks to several colleagues with whom I have shared countless stimulating discussions about topics pertinent to this book, and from whom I have learned much: Mark Aronson, James Edwards, Mark Elliott, Nick McBride and P.G. Turner. I am also grateful to several others with whom I have had valuable discussions of specific issues, or who have read material in draft: John Allison, Matthew Kramer, Alistair Mowbray, Rick Rawlings and Jenny Steele. I wish to thank my thesis examiners, Carol Harlow and Stephen Bailey, who provided very helpful comments on the thesis, and have continued to offer valuable advice since. I am grateful to John McGrath, Ian McKinnon and Mark O'Regan for their longstanding encouragement and support. My thanks also to Gia-Yen Luong, Christabel Richards-Nevill and Ian Wilkinson for their research assistance. Aspects of this book have been presented at seminars, workshops and conferences too numerous to mention in the UK, Canada, America, Australia and New Zealand, and I am grateful to the organisers of those events and to participants for their comments. From Hart Publishing I wish to thank Richard Hart, who first commissioned this book, and Bill Asquith with whom I have worked latterly, as well as Helen Kitto for her meticulous copy editing of the manuscript.

I owe special thanks to David Feldman. David was my doctoral supervisor, and he has been a mentor to me, as well as a colleague and friend. I have very much enjoyed our many discussions about human rights damages, and a good many other topics, which have greatly enriched my thinking. I have learned a great deal from him about public law and private law, and what makes good legal scholarship.

Lastly, I wish to thank my family. I thank my grandparents, Peter and Theodora Varuhas, for their love and support. They are an inspiration to me. My greatest thanks are to my mother, Nicola Varuhas. She has had a distinguished career as a senior civil servant, and I have learned much from her of public administration and law's place in it. She has also saved me from many errors through her rigorous proof reading of the book manuscript. For these things I am very grateful. But my gratitude to her goes well beyond this. None of what I have achieved, including this book, would have been possible without her love, support and encouragement. This book is for her.

JNE Varuhas
Coogee
3 December 2015

Table of Contents

Table of Cases

United Kingdom

Australia

Canada

European Court of Justice

European Commission on Human Rights

European Court of Human Rights

Inter-American Court of Human Rights

International Court of Justice

Ireland (Republic of)

New Zealand

South Africa

The Bahamas

Trinidad and Tobago

United States of America

Other Jurisdictions

Table of Legislation

United Kingdom

Statutory Instruments

Australia

Canada

European Union

France

Ireland (Republic of)

New Zealand

South Africa

Trinidad and Tobago

United States of America

Table of International Treaties and Conventions

1

Introduction

IN MANY COMMON law jurisdictions damages are now a recognised remedy for violations of human rights protected by rights-charters. Recognition of a remedy focused on private harm and associated traditionally with individualist fields of private law within public law, often associated with regulation of public power for the collective good through non-monetary relief, has posed significant and ongoing difficulties for common law courts. Courts have, in general, struggled to articulate a coherent, rational and worked-out law of human rights damages, this reflecting that the theoretical foundations of human rights damages remain murky. In turn this state of affairs raises the questions with which this book is concerned: what are the theoretical foundations of human rights damages and what approach ought to be taken to such remedy? For example, should courts apply damages principles derived from established fields of liability in private law? Should novel 'public law' approaches to monetary redress be developed? Or should courts look to the remedial practices of international courts charged with supervising those international human rights treaties which have inspired rights-instruments adopted in municipal law?

This book answers these questions in the context of English law, albeit English law is not its exclusive focus. The book undertakes the first major normative study of competing approaches to human rights damages. It focuses on evaluating those approaches adopted in English law, but also considers approaches developed elsewhere. In general prevailing approaches are found to suffer significant problems, reflected in the generally unsatisfactory state of human rights damages jurisprudence in England and across common law jurisdictions. The book seeks to chart a path forward. The book's central argument is that a 'vindicatory', tort-based approach ought to be taken to the decision whether to award damages, to assessment of quantum and to the kinds of damages available to remedy violations. Such an approach accords with the underlying function of human rights law, which is to protect and vindicate fundamental individual rights, provides a sound basis for a rational, principled and coherent law of human rights damages, and maintains the coherence of English law. Furthermore, such approach does not suffer from many of the serious problems that dog alternatives. One of the book's main contributions is to articulate and explore the theoretical foundations of this original vindicatory theory, and elaborate its defining features.

The Human Rights Act 1998 (HRA) makes the issue of human rights damages relevant in English law. The Act affords legal protection in domestic law to selected European Convention rights, such as freedom of expression and the right to life. Section 7 empowers an individual to initiate legal proceedings against a public authority which he or she alleges has violated their enumerated rights. Section 8 governs courts' remedial jurisdiction and expressly provides that damages may be awarded for proven rights-violations.

So far HRA damages, and the topic of damages for human rights breaches more generally, have, despite the challenges they pose for the higher judiciary, received limited academic attention. In particular there has been little exploration of the theoretical foundations of HRA damages, normative analysis of the possible approaches that courts might adopt and the principles that ought to be applied in deciding whether to make an award and quantum, or in-depth analysis of the possible interaction between common law principles and damages under the Act. More generally, while scholars have examined how human rights law may influence common law fields, very little has been written on how common law rules and principles could enrich human rights law. Reasons for this lack of engagement with human rights damages may include the novelty of this remedy and that the remedy overlaps public and private law, whilst modern scholars tend to specialise in only one field. There is also a tendency among commentators to focus on the law governing primary obligations. This skewed focus has been particularly pronounced in public law, at least since the historically strong link between substantive law and remedy, maintained by separate procedures for different remedies, was broken by enactment of a single procedure for seeking remedies for breach of public law duties.[1] As McLean has observed, the increased focusing of 'judicial and scholarly attention on remedial questions in public law cases' would be 'a development much to be desired'.[2] In private law too commentators lament the 'partiality of tort scholarship', the 'excessive' focus on liability at the expense of damages 'bemus[ing]' practitioners for whom damages is far more often a live and significant issue;[3] albeit, one must note the beginnings of a 'remedies revival' in private law scholarship, which is redressing this imbalance.

[1] See further ch 4.

[2] J McLean, 'Roadblocks, Restraint, and Remedies: The Idea of Progress in Administrative Law' in G Huscroft and M Taggart (eds), *Inside and Outside Canadian Administrative Law* (University of Toronto Press, 2006) 222.

[3] R Lewis, 'Recovery of State Benefits from Tort Damages: Legislating For or Against the Welfare State?' in TT Arvind and J Steele (eds), *Tort Law and the Legislature* (Hart Publishing, 2012) 286.

Despite the lack of scholarly engagement, the issue of what approach ought to be taken to human rights damages is one of importance. Damages can play a central role in protecting and vindicating those individual rights considered fundamental to the maintenance of a civil and democratic society, upholding other fundamental principles such as government under law, and possibly disciplining the exercise of public power, as well as being of great practical significance for individual victims who have suffered loss or injury through violation of their basic rights. The development of this new remedy reflects Sir Alfred Denning's prescient observation, made in the inaugural series of Hamlyn Lectures, that '[j]ust as the pick and shovel is no longer suitable for the winning of coal, so also the procedure of mandamus, certiorari, and actions on the case are not suitable for the winning of freedom in the new age. They must be replaced by new and up to date machinery'.[4] On the other hand the emergence of the new remedy and increased availability of damages against public authorities may give rise to legitimate concerns. For example, awards to individuals may divert public money away from primary governmental functions that benefit the community as a whole in an age of ever-increasing demands on public resources, precipitate defensive administrative practices, or engender or worsen a damaging litigation or compensation culture.

The issue of what approach should be taken has proven complex and difficult to resolve, thus the unsatisfactory, underdeveloped state of human rights damages jurisprudence across common law jurisdictions. As the Chief Justice of New Zealand observes, '[t]he principles upon which damages for breaches of rights are to be assessed are not greatly developed in New Zealand or in comparable jurisdictions'.[5] These difficulties stem in part from the clash of concerns described in the previous paragraph. No doubt they also reflect Lord Halsbury's view that 'the whole region of inquiry into damages is one of extreme difficulty';[6] this is likely why some judges have observed: 'Personally I have a dislike, which I have reason to believe is shared by other judges, to the task of assessing damage'.[7] But the difficulties so far encountered also owe much to human rights damages sitting uneasily on the border of public law and private law. Scholars and courts have tended to view human rights damages as representing a clash of conflicting paradigms, with the answer to what approach should be taken flowing from whether we should view the remedy through the lens of one of public law or private law. Thus, some seek to resolve the issue by asking whether the HRA action for damages can be classified as a 'tort'? More often it has been argued that an approach based in private law is impermissible because human rights law is a field of public law.

[4] A Denning, *Freedom under the Law* (Stevens, 1949) 126.

[5] *Taunoa v Attorney-General* [2008] 1 NZLR 429, [108].

[6] *The Mediana* [1900] AC 113, 116.

[7] *The Greta Holme* [1897] AC 596, 604.

This book eschews this contest of public and private. A viable approach to human rights damages is unlikely to emerge if we frame the issue in terms of an either/or conflict of paradigms which we will likely never be able to resolve satisfactorily; more likely is that the remedy will be caught in a theoretical twilight zone, as it often has been. Importantly, ideas such as 'private law', 'tort' and 'public law' have no settled meaning. Indeed, attempts to identify a general, meaningful and coherent distinction between public law and private law have largely failed, as we shall see in chapter 4. Linked to this, while such categories have often been used for expository purposes, the *normative* implications of classifying an issue or field as one or the other are unclear. Nearly every tort textbook opens by stating there is no settled definition of the field. In any case there is no one approach to damages in tort or across private law: 'loss resulting from a breach of duty has to be measured according to legal rules, and … different rules apply to the breach of different obligations'.[8] Thus, classifying the human rights damages claim as a tort or private law claim would not lead us to any one particular remedial approach. In similar vein, there is no one definition of public law, while the normative implications of classifying a field as one of 'public law' are far from clear; rather, the implications are deeply contested and bound up in intractable theoretical debate which leads into the realm of ordinary politics. There is also a significant danger that by imposing one's favoured conception of public law, one will end up suppressing the distinctive nature of human rights law as its own distinct field of law. Further, by thinking in such strict categorical terms one may close off legitimate debate and blind oneself to important insights: 'Often when we take our knowledge or information or the phenomenon out of its boxes and mix it on the floor, new insight is gained about relationships'.[9]

This book seeks to move beyond this stale contest of public and private paradigms to identify an approach to human rights damages which is normatively defensible *on its merits* given *the distinctive nature of human rights law* including the core functions the field is constituted to perform and the nature of the primary legal norms. Ultimately this book argues for an approach to damages modelled on that developed within certain 'vindicatory' torts such as trespass to land, false imprisonment, battery and defamation. Importantly, it endorses this protective, vindicatory approach not by an appeal to some abstract notion of public or private or what it means for an action to be a tort but because such approach is consonant with and gives direct effect to the underlying functions of *human rights law*, and has certain other important merits over alternative approaches.

[8] *AIB Group Plc v Mark Redler & Co Solicitors* [2014] 3 WLR 1367, [92].

[9] WL Twining et al, 'Ernie and the Centipede' in JA Jolowicz (ed), *The Division and Classification of the Law* (Butterworths, 1970) 17.

By way of background it should be observed that the vindicatory, tort-based approach argued for herein stands in stark contrast to those approaches which have so far characterised damages jurisprudence under the HRA, and which are examined in detail in Part 3 of this book.

While lower courts initially drew upon common law principles in adjudicating HRA damages claims the higher courts have since consistently distanced human rights damages from the law of torts. A bright line has been drawn between damages in 'public law' and those in tort, the strictness of the separation between fields being unparalleled among common law jurisdictions (except those that have followed the English approach). The result has been marginalisation of the damages remedy.

In general the reasons for eschewing established damages principles have not been explored in depth. Lord Woolf in *Anufrijeva*[10] asserted damages should play a different role in respect of 'public law' from that which they play in 'private law'. It was taken to follow from this that human rights damages should be a remedy of last resort, subject to open-ended judicial discretion, and capable of being denied or reduced according to judicial perceptions of what lies in society's best interests. According to this 'public law' paradigm what is of primary importance is bringing an authority's unlawful conduct to an end, while compensation is of secondary, if any, importance. Appeal to an amorphous idea of 'public law' in a jurisdiction which has not traditionally distinguished public from private law does not offer an explanation for eschewing tort nor, once the elaborate and axiomatic corpus of principles developed at common law are ousted, offer a great deal of guidance as to what rules should be applied in their place.

The House of Lords and Supreme Court respectively, in *Greenfield* and *Faulkner*, maintained this strict separation between human rights and tort: the HRA is 'not a tort statute' and damages under it are 'not tortious in nature'.[11] In those decisions the highest court carried forward aspects of *Anufrijeva* but importantly hitched the approach to HRA damages to the European Court of Human Rights' (ECtHR) approach to monetary compensation, under Article 41 of the Convention: 'courts in this country should look to Strasbourg and not to domestic precedents'.[12] This was said to follow from the terms of the HRA though neither the Act nor any rule from Strasbourg requires such approach. One result has been to preclude development of a domestic jurisprudence of human rights damages which is sensitive to English legal tradition and economic conditions, as well as deeper thinking as to the theoretical underpinnings of the remedy. Instead English courts seek to mechanistically replicate Strasbourg remedial practice

[10] *Anufrijeva v Southwark LBC* [2004] QB 1124.

[11] *R (Greenfield) v SOSHD* [2005] 1 WLR 673, [19]; *R (Faulkner) v SOSJ* [2013] 2 AC 254, [29].

[12] *Greenfield*, ibid.

in domestic law. Not only this, but this 'mirror' approach is itself deeply problematic: the Strasbourg Court's approach is influenced by its status as a subsidiary, supranational institution meaning that its remedial practice is not intended as a model for domestic institutions, while its Article 41 jurisprudence is renowned for its lack of principle, consistency and coherence, and 'parsimonious' reasoning. Domestic case law is replete with statements from lower court judges that they have struggled to divine anything of significance from Strasbourg.

The net result of the higher courts' approach has been a stunted, problematic jurisprudence too often characterised by a vacuum of concrete and coherent rules and principles to guide award of damages and quantum. Lower court judges commonly find themselves afloat upon a sea of open-ended discretion with only specks of principle barely visible on the horizon. Fifteen years on from the Act entering force first-instance judges observe, '[t]here is little guidance in the authorities on the approach to be taken when quantifying an award of damages ... If one looks at the authorities for appropriate comparators again there is relatively little assistance'.[13] Similar observations are made in other jurisdictions where the vast institutional learning associated with common law damages has been cast adrift.[14] Incoherence, inconsistency and unfairness are the inevitable result, as are ad hoc breaches of the proscription on looking to common law principles as judges search understandably for any guidance that might aid them. Further, the courts' approach has, in general, been exceptionally restrictive, to the point that even the Government has expressed surprise.[15] Awards have been very rare, though there has been some liberalisation in a few select areas. Scales have been depressed to modest levels, so that awards have been low, often exceptionally low relative to awards for identical losses at common law for breaches of less than fundamental rights. Ultimately, as we shall come back to time and again through the book, the prevailing approach to damages has radically undermined the primary vindicatory and protective goals of human rights law at the remedial stage.

In stark contrast to the prevailing judicial approach are the conclusions reached in the joint report of the English and Scottish Law Commissions, *Damages under the Human Rights Act 1998*, published in 2000.[16] The report is unusual in that it was intended to inform rather than advise upon reform; this itself indicates HRA damages were foreseen as posing tricky

[13] *Re H* [2014] EWFC 38, [84]–[91].

[14] *Taunoa* (n 5) [108]; *City of Vancouver v Ward* [2010] 2 SCR 28, [3] ('Although the *Charter* is 28 years old' authority 'on when damages may be awarded under s 24(1) of the Charter, and what the amount of such damages should be' 'is sparse').

[15] Department for Constitutional Affairs, *Review of the Implementation of the Human Rights Act* (2006) 18.

[16] Law Com 266/Scot Law Com 180 (2000).

issues. In terms of the approach to be taken the Commissions concluded the award of damages in tort is the 'obvious comparator in English law';[17] while care should be taken in reading across principles developed in tort, 'in the majority of cases under the HRA the courts … will find it possible and appropriate to apply the rules by which damages in tort are usually assessed to claims under the HRA'.[18] This advice has fallen on deaf judicial ears.

I. THE STRUCTURE OF THE ARGUMENT

The book is in three parts.

Part 1 propounds the vindicatory, tort-based approach. The law of torts is a natural place to look in considering the approach that should be taken to human rights damages. Tort law has long served to protect important rights through imposition of damages liability, has long been the law's principal mechanism for providing monetary redress for wronged individuals, absent contract, and the common law has developed an elaborate body of norms governing damages.

There is no unitary approach to damages in the law of torts. Rather the approach varies in significant ways from tort to tort. Chapter 2 develops a framework for understanding these variations, which in turn may inform our consideration of human rights damages. Significant variations across tort and the law of damages are explicable by reference to the function that a particular tort performs and the importance of the interests it protects. More specifically, the framework distinguishes torts principally constituted to vindicate and strongly protect basic interests, such as the torts actionable per se, and those concerned principally with compensating for fault-based harms, such as negligence. As discussed in chapter 2, the book uses the term 'vindication' in a specific sense: to attest to, affirm and reinforce the inherent worth of particular interests and the normative importance of those interests within the hierarchy of legal norms, and that they ought to be treated with respect.

In the light of the framework developed in chapter 2, chapter 3 argues for a vindicatory tort-based approach to human rights damages and elaborates the core features of such approach, including the circumstances in which damages ought to be awarded; the range of damages that ought to be available for a rights-violation; the approach that should be taken to assessment; and the interrelationship between human rights damages and other remedies such as specific relief.

Part 2 considers the possible objection that an approach derived from the *private law* of tort is not appropriate in the *public law* context of human

[17] ibid [4.14].
[18] ibid [4.21], [4.26].

rights law. Many find intuitively appealing the idea that there is an important normative distinction between public law and private law which ought to guide legal development. This view has exerted a powerful influence over HRA damages jurisprudence to date.

Part 3 considers alternative approaches to human rights damages, focusing in particular on those adopted under the HRA. Chapter 5 considers the prevailing 'mirror' approach. Chapter 6 considers the interest-balancing approach, propounded in *Anufrijeva* and which has also proven popular in other jurisdictions such as New Zealand and Canada. According to such approach the decision whether to award damages and possibly quantum are subject to a balancing exercise whereby the individual interest in redress is balanced against public interest considerations, such as the importance of protecting public funds. Depending on how a judge strikes the balance on the facts, damages may be denied or reduced below compensatory levels so as to protect community interests, including in cases where loss has been suffered. Chapter 7 considers a series of other principles which might be adopted to limit availability and/or quantum of damages. These include the minimum-loss principle drawn from ECtHR jurisprudence, the 'sufficiently serious' criterion applied in the EU law of state liability, and immunities doctrines which characterise US constitutional tort actions.

The book concludes that the vindicatory, tort-based approach offers a sound basis for development of a principled, rational and coherent law of human rights damages which accords with the underlying functions of human rights law. The distinction between private and public law provides an unsafe basis for legal development; indeed, nothing of legal significance should be allowed to depend on it. The mirror approach is unsound in principle and unworkable in practice; it should be repudiated forthwith. Whatever their intuitive appeal the case for alternative approaches, such as interest-balancing, is by no means straightforward and such approaches suffer significant shortcomings, while there are better ways to address the public interest concerns which underpin such approaches.

Three points remain to be made. First, this book takes a normative approach, considering what the approach to human rights damages ideally ought to be. This normative analysis is not constrained by the specific terms of section 8, HRA. However, to be viable given existing law any approach taken to human rights damages would need to be consonant with the Act's remedial provisions. For this reason the book often relates normative arguments back to the terms of the Act. The book reaches the general conclusion that a vindicatory, tort-based approach is the best approach on a normative level *and* that such approach is supported by the Act. The book treats the other provisions of the HRA as given. It should be noted that the UK Government has announced its intention to replace the HRA with a British Bill of Rights. Whether this will transpire is difficult to predict. However, as discussed in chapter 5, such reform would offer a prime opportunity for the law of human rights damages to be 'reset' and the prevailing mirror approach eschewed. Further, such reform would make a vindicatory approach irresistible, given such approach reflects the longstanding, home-grown approach to protecting basic constitutional rights through imposition of liability.

Second, throughout it is assumed that human rights damages are available in English law. There may be legitimate disagreement over whether such damages should be available or not. However, the fact is such damages are available in England and many other jurisdictions. This fact, by necessity, requires courts and scholars to grapple with what approach should be taken to them, and that is my task. In any case, many of the arguments discussed herein in assessing what approach should be taken are also relevant to the question of whether damages should be available in the first place.

Third, this book is not a comparative study. Its principal concern is the approach that should be taken to human rights damages in English law. However, the book draws on and analyses comparative material where appropriate, particularly from other common law jurisdictions in which damages are available for human or constitutional rights violations including Canada, the US, New Zealand, South Africa, Ireland and the Caribbean states. Comparative material can be relevant as it may, for example, illustrate particular approaches to human rights damages, while the damages case law is more developed in other jurisdictions and can flag important issues which have not yet arisen under the HRA. Though this is not a comparative work, and care should always be taken in applying arguments developed in one jurisdiction in another, the arguments for a tort-based approach and analysis of alternative approaches would have a high degree of relevance in other common law jurisdictions in which human rights damages are available.

Part 1

A Tort-Based Approach to Damages for Human Rights Breaches

2

The Tort Framework

THERE IS NO unitary approach to damages in the law of torts. Different heads of damage and loss are recoverable for different torts, which may be subject to different modes of assessment, and a different range of damages is available for different torts. If we are to model human rights damages on an approach in tort, we must select that which is most appropriate.

This chapter develops a framework for understanding why different approaches are taken to damages for different torts. This will enable us to consider the role damages should play where human rights are infringed, including the kinds of damages that ought to be available for a human rights violation and the approach that ought to be taken to quantification.

Significant variations across the law of torts can be explained by the different functions performed by different torts and the importance of the interests each protects. In this respect, a distinction is drawn between torts that perform primarily a protective, vindicatory function, such as torts actionable per se (TAPS), and those that perform primarily a compensatory function, such as negligence. The chapter explains how variations in function are reflected in the legal structures of different torts, and different approaches to damages.

The chapter's focus is on identifying and explaining the vindicatory function within the law of torts. The function is most clearly evident in TAPS, such as false imprisonment, battery, trespass to land and defamation, which afford strong protection from outside interference to fundamental personal and proprietary interests, such as liberty, physical integrity, exclusive possession of land and reputation. A distinctive and fundamental feature of compensatory damages for vindicatory torts is that they are generally available not only to redress factual losses, that is any negative psychological, physical, emotional or economic effects suffered by the claimant in consequence of the wrongful interference with their interests, but also for the wrongful interference with the underlying protected interest *in and of itself*. Damages for the wrong in itself are assessed objectively and awarded notwithstanding whether the claimant is left factually worse off in consequence of the wrongful interference. These damages are 'normative' in that their availability to redress a wrongful interference with the protected interest in itself, regardless of the suffering of material harms, furthers the normative goals of the law, affording strong protection to the relevant interest in itself, and vindicating its fundamental importance, inherent value, and that it ought to be respected. In addition, for vindicatory torts, a range of damages beyond compensatory damages is available to redress the wrong including nominal and exemplary damages, the availability of a wide range of damages serving the law's vindicatory and protective goals. It is this vindicatory remedial model that I argue, in chapter 3, ought to form the basis of the approach to damages for breaches of human rights.

I. SETTING THE SCENE: VINDICATION, DAMAGES AND TORTS THEORY

Before commencing detailed exegesis of the law of torts it is necessary to undertake some ground-clearing, not only to set up the analysis in this chapter but also because the concepts and ideas introduced herein are important to the book's argument more generally. This section introduces core concepts, specifically the concept of vindication, as well as the concepts of rights and interests. The section goes on to introduce the remedy of damages, and explain why it has been tort law's favoured remedy for redressing past wrongful interferences with basic interests. The section concludes by articulating this chapter's approach to theorising the law of torts, and explaining where the account of torts and damages articulated herein fits into contemporary debates.

A. The Concept of Vindication in the Law of Torts

'Vindication' is accepted by many textbook writers as a function of the law of torts,[1] it is a concept increasingly invoked in case law and commentary within tort,[2] one which has rhetorical appeal particularly when

[1] eg T Weir, *An Introduction to Tort Law* 2nd edn (OUP, 2006) 16–17, 133–35 [Weir 2006]; *A Casebook on Tort* 10th edn (Sweet and Maxwell, 2004) 17–18, 322–23 [Weir 2004]; D Harris et al, *Remedies in Contract and Tort* 2nd edn (CUP, 2002) ch 18; WE Peel and J Goudkamp, *Winfield and Jolowicz on Tort* 19th edn (Sweet and Maxwell, 2010) ch 1; NJ McBride and R Bagshaw, *Tort Law* 4th edn (Pearson, 2012) ch 32; C Harlow, *Understanding Tort Law* 3rd edn (Sweet and Maxwell, 2005) 141–44.

[2] eg *Ashley v Chief Constable of Sussex Police* [2008] 1 AC 962; *R (Lumba) v SOSHD* [2012] 1 AC 245; *Chester v Afshar* [2005] 1 AC 134; D Pearce and R Halson, 'Damages for Breach of Contract: Compensation, Restitution and Vindication' (2008) 28 *Oxford Journal of Legal Studies* 73; Lord Scott, 'Damages' [2008] *Lloyd's Maritime and Commercial Law Quarterly* 465; R Stevens, 'Rights and Other Things' in D Nolan and A Robertson (eds), *Rights and Private Law* (Hart Publishing, 2012); N Witzleb and R Carroll, 'The Role of Vindication in Torts Damages' (2009) 7 *Tort Law Review* 16; K Barker, 'Public and Private: The Mixed Concept of Vindication in Torts' in SGA Pitel et al (eds), *Tort Law: Challenging Orthodoxy* (Hart Publishing, 2013).

coupled with the idea of 'rights', and which has gained increasing currency with emergence of a 'rights'-movement within the law of torts.[3] Yet despite vindication being 'in vogue' the exact meaning of the concept has not been closely examined and remains relatively obscure. It is often run together or equated with other functions such as deterrence,[4] marking society disapproval or redressing societal harm,[5] and/or sanction,[6] and/or distinguished from others, such as compensation[7] and/or punishment.[8] The picture that emerges is more akin to a Kandinsky than a Canaletto.

This chapter argues that a specific conception of vindication is immanent in significant features of the law of torts. In this sense vindication means to publically attest to, affirm and reinforce the importance and inherent value of particular interests, and by association the legal rights which directly protect those interests. Before introducing this definition in more detail, it is important to clarify two concepts central to defining vindication, and to this book's argument more generally: rights and interests.

i. Rights and Interests

The term 'right' may be used in various ways and refer to a range of different phenomena, while in tort (and public law)[9] scholarship a number of not altogether clear or coherent accounts of 'rights' have emerged.[10] When I use the term 'right' in this chapter and book more generally, I shall adopt an orthodox Hohfeldian conception of rights as claim-rights.[11] The main benefit of Hohfeld's conceptual scheme is that it offers analytical clarity, thus why it has stood the test of time and been highly influential and provided a common basis for philosophical debates over rights.[12]

[3] eg Nolan and Robertson, ibid; R Stevens, *Torts and Rights* (OUP, 2007).

[4] eg *Attorney-General of Trinidad and Tobago v Ramanoop* [2006] 1 AC 328, [19]; Peel and Goudkamp (n 1) [1-002]; *Combined Beneficiaries Union Inc v Auckland City COGS Committee* [2009] 2 NZLR 56, [62]; *Taunoa v Attorney-General* [2008] 1 NZLR 429, [255]; *Lumba* (n 2) [180], [217].

[5] eg *Taunoa*, ibid [255], [259], [261], [317]; *City of Vancouver v Ward* [2010] 2 SCR 28, [27]–[28]; *Ramanoop* ibid [19]; *Fose v Minister of Safety and Security* [1997] 3 SA 786, [82].

[6] eg Weir 2004 (n 1) 7, 17–18; *Lumba* (n 2) [100].

[7] ibid; *Watkins v SOSHD* [2006] 2 AC 395, [6]; *Daniels v Thompson* [1998] 3 NZLR 22, 70; *Dunlea v Attorney-General* [2000] 3 NZLR 136, [66], [68]; *Attorney-General v Chapman* [2012] 1 NZLR 462, [30]; *Taunoa* (n 4) [20]; Scott (n 2); *Ward* (n 5) [27]–[28]; *Lumba* ibid [179], [217]; *cf Ashley* (n 2) [22], [60]; *Taunoa*, ibid [109]; *Fose* (n 5) [67]–[68].

[8] *Ramanoop* (n 4) [19]; *Merson v Cartwright* [2005] All ER (D) 144, [17]; Scott (n 2) 471; *Lumba*, ibid [178], [214]; *Fose*, ibid [61].

[9] For critical analysis see: JNE Varuhas, 'The Reformation of English Administrative Law? "Rights", Rhetoric and Reality' (2013) 72 *CLJ* 369. See also ch 4.2.II.

[10] For critical analysis of those accounts see P Cane, 'Rights in Private Law' and NJ McBride, 'Rights and the Basis of Tort Law' in Nolan and Robertson (n 2).

[11] WN Hohfeld, 'Some Fundamental Legal Conceptions as Applied in Judicial Reasoning' (1913) 23 *Yale Law Journal* 16; (1917) 26 *Yale Law Journal* 710. See further ch 4.2.II.A.

[12] See MH Kramer et al, *A Debate Over Rights* (Clarendon Press, 1998).

According to Hohfeld's conception, being endowed with a legal right consists of being legally protected against another's interference or against another's withholding of assistance or remuneration, in regard to some action or state of affairs.[13] The person required to abstain or assist is under a correlative duty to do so. The right is specific to one person and held against another specific person, that individual being subject to the correlative duty. Thus claim-rights are by definition correlative to duties, which mirror the content of the right. So, in Hohfeldian terms the right in false imprisonment might be formulated as follows: X has a right against Y that Y not confine X, while Y has a duty to X that he not confine X. I hold such a right against each other person in society, and each person in society holds an identical right against me, so that there are literally millions of bipolar right-duty correlations.

That claim-rights ground a body of law may tell us something about the nature and function of a field, but this feature cannot by itself offer a full explanation of a field. A right, in the Hohfeldian sense, is the basic form of a legal norm; it is 'definitional'.[14] Legal rights may serve a range of possible normative goals. For example, rights might be bestowed specifically to protect intrinsically valuable individual interests, or individual interests may be the subject of protection because such protection promotes social goals such as facilitation of market competition or distribution of losses.[15]

Whereas rights are prescriptive norms, 'interests' are objectively good aspects of human well-being or flourishing, such as liberty and physical integrity;[16] they have been described loosely as 'assets' or 'resources'.[17] Legal rights within the law of torts afford protection to a range of disparate human interests. Tort protects 'the good things in life', including interests in liberty, bodily integrity, exclusive possession of property and reputation.[18]

Not all interests are equal: 'the Common Law recognizes and affirms a certain scale of values that order themselves in a sort of hierarchy', 'the lesser of which it is ready to subordinate, and on occasion even sacrifice to those of higher rank'.[19] This 'scale' is evident in variations in the structures of torts that protect interests of different 'value', these variations signalling the relative importance of different interests.[20] At the apex of this hierarchy come interests considered fundamental, such as property, physical integrity,

[13] Paraphrasing MH Kramer, 'Rights Without Trimmings', ibid 9.

[14] Kramer, ibid 22.

[15] J Raz, *Ethics in the Public Domain* (OUP, 1994) ch 3; *The Morality of Freedom* (OUP, 2003) 177–80.

[16] Kramer (n 13) 22; Raz, *Morality of Freedom*, ibid ch 7.

[17] P Cane, *The Anatomy of Tort Law* (Hart Publishing, 1997) 66.

[18] Weir 2004 (n 1) 6; see also C Witting, *Street on Torts* 14th edn (OUP, 2015) ch 1; J Steele, *Tort Law* 3rd edn (OUP, 2014) ch 1.

[19] R O'Sullivan, 'A Scale of Values in the Common Law' (1937) 1 *MLR* 27, 35, 38.

[20] Cane (n 17) 90; Weir 2004 (n 1) 6–7.

liberty and reputation: 'the law has always afforded the highest protection to the physical integrity of the person; a lower protection to property rights; and still less protection to economic interests'.[21]

ii. Vindication and Other Functions

This chapter is concerned to identify and explain the conception of vindication which emerges from a detailed consideration of fundamental features of tort doctrine, ie that conception that is 'hard-wired' into the structure of actions in tort and the approach to remedies. Thus, unless context indicates otherwise, where this book refers to the function of vindication—or other functions of tort such as compensation—it is referring to functions that are 'intrinsic' or 'inherent' in, or 'internal' to tort, in the sense that they are 'embedded' in and evidenced by significant doctrinal features of tort doctrine. Such functions are conceptually distinct from 'extrinsic' or 'external' effects which actions in tort may happen to have through their practical operation or the way claimants use them.

Legal rights and obligations may be vindicated in the basic sense that the law affirms the existence of a right or obligation through recognition of a legal claim for breach, and providing remedies such as damages and injunctions to redress breaches. In this sense all torts share a vindicatory function, as do any bodies of law that provide for actions in respect of breach of legal obligations.[22] This sense of vindication is not the focus here. The idea has little explanatory power. It does not tell us anything about the distinctiveness of tort relative to myriad other bodies of doctrine characterised by legal rights and duties, and which provide for remedies for breach. Nor does it help us to understand variations in the structures of and approach to damages across torts, and which cannot be explained by already well-documented functions of tort, such as compensation and punishment.

A more specific, specialised conception of vindication is evident within fundamental features of the law of torts. In this sense vindication means to attest to, affirm and reinforce the importance and inherent value of particular interests, and by association the overlying rights which afford direct protection to those interests.[23] The focus on interests is important because

[21] *Naysmith v ACC* [2006] 1 NZLR 40, [80]; *Murphy v Brentwood DC* [1991] AC 398, 487; *AI Enterprises Ltd v Bram Enterprises Ltd* [2014] 1 SCR 177, [30].

[22] See similarly Witzleb and Carroll (n 2) 42, although not differentiating different senses of vindication.

[23] 'Vindication' is a natural label for the function defined here as the stipulated definition is consonant with the ordinary meaning of that term, one dictionary definition of which is, '[t]he action of asserting or maintaining', while the verb 'vindicate' is defined as '[t]o assert, maintain, make good, by means of action … to defend against encroachment or interference' and '[t]o clear from … doubt, by means of demonstration' (*Oxford English Dictionary Online*, www.oed.com). *What* thing or proposition is being asserted etc, *how*, and *why* is context-dependant.

it is variations in the nature and importance of interests (among other variables),[24] rather than the basic norm being rights, which helps to explain important variations in the structure of torts and the approach to damages among different torts, while recognition of the varying importance of different interests helps us to explain why certain rights carry greater normative weight or value than others.

The vindicatory function is a signalling function. As Cane has said, '[l]aw can be important not only on account of what it practically achieves but also on account of what it symbolically stands for'; those torts with a predominantly vindicatory function embody and reinforce 'values that deserve to be observed and promoted for their own sake such as liberty and physical integrity'.[25] As the authors of one leading textbook observe, the function of the vindicatory torts is 'not to engage in loss-spreading ... but to affirm the fundamental importance of certain interests, such as personal bodily integrity and freedom of movement, *in their own right*'.[26]

The TAPS, such as trespass to land, false imprisonment, battery and defamation, are paradigm examples of torts that evince a primary function of vindication and protection. It has long been recognised that these torts are constituted to afford strong protection from external interference to basic personal and proprietary interests. As we shall see, significant structural features of TAPS, such as liability rules that are very strict relative to those adopted in the context of lesser interests and which afford strong protection from outside interference to the protected interests, signal—attest to, affirm and reinforce—the fundamental importance of these interests. Similarly, that a claimant can establish liability and access powerful remedies for the slightest of interferences with their interests and without having to jump certain hurdles, such as demonstrating actionable, special or material loss (ie factual loss), which are ordinary preconditions of liability for other actions, signals the normative importance and inherent worth of the protected interests.

Remedies have a crucial role to play in vindicating rights and interests. That is because the consequences that flow from the wrong send a signal to individuals, government and society about the nature and importance of the relevant interest and associated right. The approach taken to damages in TAPS serves to strongly affirm and reinforce the importance of the protected interests and their inherent value. That one may establish liability

[24] Variation in the nature and importance of interests is an important explanatory variable in understanding differences across tort, but it is not the only one; countervailing interests (of the public, defendant and third parties), moral and policy concerns, and defendant and claimant conduct, are all relevant. See Cane (n 17).

[25] P Cane, 'Understanding Judicial Review and Its Impact' in M Hertogh and S Halliday (eds), *Judicial Review and Bureaucratic Impact* (CUP, 2004) 41.

[26] S Deakin et al, *Markesinis and Deakin's Tort Law* 6th edn (OUP, 2007) 452.

and recover substantial damages for mere interference with one's interests, regardless of whether the interference has any negative physical, psychological, emotional or economic effects, sends a powerful signal as to the supreme importance of the protected interests within the law's normative hierarchy, their inherent worth and that they ought to be respected in themselves. That such damages are reserved for interference with certain interests—those protected by vindicatory torts—further reinforces that these interests are of fundamental importance within the legal order. Of course damages for consequential factual losses suffered through the wrong are also recoverable, such damages affording the claimant a basic level of protection, by ensuring the claimant does not have to bear the negative effects of the wrong on their material well-being; it would make little sense if such damages were recoverable generally across tort, and for interference with interests of lesser status, but not for wrongful interferences with basic interests. Importantly, that a range of damages, including non-compensatory damages such as exemplary damages, which punish a defendant for outrageous interferences with basic interests, are available to remedy vindicatory torts signals that the protected interests are ones that sit at the apex of the law's normative hierarchy.

Vindication is but one of many functions evident in the law of torts, and the emphasis on or relative priority of vindication varies from tort to tort. For the TAPS vindication is the primary function. For other torts, specifically negligence, their radically different structures and remedial approach suggest a primary function of compensating for fault-based harm. The tort is concerned principally to remedy instances where an individual has been made worse off in fact, for example physically or psychologically, in circumstances where the defendant can be said to be at fault for those factual losses, rather than to serve the expressive function of reinforcing the importance of particular interests and ensuring strong protection of those interests irrespective of whether factual harm is suffered through interference with them. This explains the focus or emphasis within negligence on actionable damage, the nature of the defendant's conduct, and compensation for factual harm, as well as the generalised nature of the concepts governing liability. As Weir argued, 'the difference in rules [between trespass and negligence] is explicable by the difference in roles. To try to effect a synthesis is just a waste of time'.[27]

It is important to emphasise that I have said that the TAPS perform *primarily* a vindicatory function, and negligence performs *primarily* a compensatory function, as I consider that these torts perform other functions as well. For example TAPS perform a compensatory function, affording compensatory damages for damage and loss. But importantly, and as we shall see, the approach to such damages is fundamentally shaped by and gives effect to

[27] Weir 2006 (n 1) 134–35; 2004 (n 1) 321–26.

the primary vindicatory function of the law, so that the compensatory function is put in service of the macro-function of vindication. Negligence obviously affords a degree of protection to various personal, proprietary and economic interests, but that protection is contingent, for example on the claimant's ability to demonstrate that they have suffered actionable material harm. Arguably there are traces of the vindicatory function within negligence. That it is generally easier to establish liability within negligence for damage flowing from interference with personal and proprietary interests than for damage flowing from interference with economic interests, attests to the relative importance of the former.[28] Nonetheless, it is the nature of the defendant's conduct and the element of factual harm that gives negligence its unity across the multifarious situations to which it applies, while the focus of damages is on compensation for material losses.[29] Furthermore, that basic interests, such as liberty, are not afforded direct protection, and only indirectly protected to the extent that an interference makes the claimant worse off—for example where the claimant suffers physical harm as a consequence of being negligently deprived of their liberty[30]—reinforces that vindication is not the law's primary concern.

For completeness it should be recorded that certain torts may perform compensatory and vindicatory functions with neither being dominant or primary. Private nuisance is a paradigm example and is analysed later in this chapter. Further, some actions might not be analysed sensibly in terms of the dichotomy drawn here; indeed it is highly likely that this is the case given the pluralistic and varied nature of the law of torts, comprised as it is of a hodgepodge of disparate actions. For example, it is often argued that one of the central concerns of economic torts is to maintain the integrity of the competitive market process.[31]

As observed above, commentators and courts have equated vindication with, and distinguished it from, other functions which tort is commonly considered to perform, such as punishment, deterrence and compensation. The idea of vindication described here is conceptually distinct from these functions, which are typically associated with different heads of damages, such as compensatory or punitive damages. Nonetheless distinct functions may interact in complex ways; as Glanville Williams said famously, 'the law seems to like to ride two or three horses at once'.[32] For example, within TAPS the 'micro' function of general damages is compensation but the 'macro' vindicatory function of the law shapes the nature and range of

[28] *OBG Ltd v Allan* [2008] 1 AC 1, [99]; *Stovin v Wise* [1996] AC 923, 932.

[29] This is particularly apparent when one considers the tort's historical development: DJ Ibbetson, *A Historical Introduction to the Law of Obligations* (OUP, 1999) chs 9–10.

[30] eg *Sayers v Harlow UDC* [1958] 1 WLR 623; *cf W v Home Office* [1997] Imm AR 302.

[31] S Deakin and J Randall, 'Rethinking the Economic Torts' (2009) 72 *MLR* 519; H Carty, *An Analysis of the Economic Torts* 2nd edn (OUP, 2010).

[32] G Williams, 'The Aims of the Law of Tort' (1951) 4 *Current Legal Problems* 137, 172.

recoverable heads. Similarly, an action which has vindication as its primary intrinsic function may, through its operation, have certain external effects: where damages are awarded for a wrongful interference with basic interests, thereby vindicating the importance of those interests, the effect may be to deter a class of potential defendants from wrongdoing or promote public accountability of public defendants.

B. Damages

In theory the law could respond to a wrong in any number of ways, but there are good reasons why the law of torts has favoured damages as a remedy for redressing past wrongful interferences with basic interests.

Ideally the defendant would perform their primary duty, so the claimant's interests are maintained inviolate as they ought to be and the claimant is not subject to wrongfully inflicted diminutions in their material well-being. In some situations remedies, such as injunctions, can ensure actual performance of the legal duty. If performance is still possible then such remedies ought generally to be granted; it is and ought to be the law's preference that duties are actually complied with, especially where non-performance would result in interference with fundamental interests.

However, where the obligation is, for example, one not to interfere with the claimant's interests, and those interests have been interfered with, it is impossible for the defendant to now comply; injuries caused by the wrong cannot possibly not be suffered, where there is an interference with basic interests there cannot possibly be no interference. In these circumstances damages are the law's favoured remedy. In theory the law could employ any range of responses. For example we could flog a tortfeasor or have them pilloried, but that would be inconsonant with the legal system and society's basic norms and values, including human rights law. We could require the defendant to undertake some specific, less extreme act to somehow 'make good' their wrong. However, it is not clear what that act would be; there is no action now available that could in fact fulfil the defendant's legal obligations. Further, courts are not institutionally well-placed to supervise such acts, thus their preference for money relief where possible. There may be serious problems with requiring the defendant and claimant to interact in the context of a relationship that has broken down. If a defendant refuses to pay a money award, there are straightforward techniques of extracting the money and ensuring fulfilment of the remedial obligation, whereas things may be more difficult if a defendant refuses to do a specific act; a court might hold a non-compliant defendant in contempt but the claimant is still left without remedy. Importantly, damages are a remedy less intrusive on the defendant's freedom of action; where the defendant is a public authority there may also be separation-of-powers concerns associated with courts requiring authorities to exercise their public powers in particular ways, while they may not be empowered under their parent statute to take the required action.

Thus, where actual performance is no longer possible, damages represent the best remaining alternative to actual compliance. Within vindicatory torts damages seek to restore the claimant to the position they were entitled to be in: one in which their interests were maintained inviolate and in pristine form (normative damages) and in which they did not suffer material harms through wrongful interference with their interests (damages for consequential losses). By placing the claimant in a position equivalent to one in which their interests were maintained in pristine form as they ought to have been damages afford strong protection to the relevant rights and interests and affirm and reinforce that these interests are, in themselves, of the utmost importance and that they ought to be maintained inviolate and respected.[33] One level of legal entitlement, which has been wrongfully denied, is substituted for another that is equivalent, at least notionally, and the law's vindicatory and protective policies are ultimately fulfilled. Of course, damages cannot literally place the claimant in a position as if their rights had been respected and they never suffered relevant diminutions in their well-being, and they will in this way always be an inferior, second-best alternative to actual compliance; the law's preference is that basic interests are maintained inviolate while it is clearly preferable for a claimant that they never suffer injury in the first place. However, damages represent the next-best alternative, the best the law can do given the wrong has occurred.

Damages also have much to commend them if we take into account the law's vindicatory function. Damages, as a remedy, are a particularly powerful means of vindication even if they may be a 'crude' means,[34] and within the common law they have traditionally been a remedy reserved for interference with those interests most highly valued by the law. Put simply, 'money talks'; society attaches a particular weight or importance to money, money is a recognised marker of value in a market society. As the Lord Chief Justice said in a defamation case, 'we think it unlikely that [members of the public] will have downloaded the judgment [of the trial judge] and read it with close attention. It is more likely, as in so many cases, that the general public … will be concerned to discover what might be called the "headline" result. What most people want to know, and that includes those who read the judgment closely … is simply "how much did he get?"'.[35] If the only consequence that followed from, say, a wrongful interference with an interest considered basic, was that a judge records this in the terms of his judgment, this could hardly be considered a strong public affirmation of the importance of the rights and interests and that they ought to be maintained inviolate; rather

[33] On this see further ch 6.2.II.
[34] *Broome v Cassell* [1972] AC 1027, 1070–1071; *Cairns v Modi* [2013] 1 WLR 1015, [23].
[35] *Cairns*, ibid [32].

it would undercut the relative importance of that interest, especially within a system of liability in which substantial awards are made routinely for important but less than fundamental interests, such as economic interests. Thus, it is unsurprising that '[h]istorically, damages have been regarded as the ordinary remedy for an invasion of personal interests in liberty'.[36]

C. Torts Theory

My approach to theorising torts is a pluralistic one; that is, I consider no one theory can explain the whole field. Torts and private law are vast fields of law, characterised by significant variation and complexity, and which have been shaped by many hands over many years: 'the Common Law [is] a venerable body of rules, built up slowly in course of centuries, a huge structure, to which has been added new piece here and there ... The causes of action in tort have developed from various sources, unsystematically and with different objects'.[37] It is implausible that the law of torts, or private law more generally, can be explained by reference to one principle, function or idea, unless, perhaps, one operates at an exceptionally high level of abstraction, in which case one's theory is unlikely to be much use to anyone concerned with resolving concrete legal questions, or one commits the error of twisting facts to suit theories and passes over significant variation across the field. The result of the illusive search for unity is perplexing propositions such as, the 'purpose of private law is to be private law',[38] and claims that the ragbag of actions that comprise the field of torts can, it turns out, all be explained by Kantian Right, or Kaldor-Hicks or Pareto efficiency. What a coincidence it would be if these claims were correct.

This is not to say we cannot derive valuable insights from such theories, but that it is unlikely they can satisfactorily explain the entire field. For example corrective justice theories have proven influential as they offer an explanation of the basic idea of compensation which is important within the law of torts, and other fields.[39] But corrective justice also has explanatory limits.[40] While it can explain a duty of repair, it cannot itself explain

[36] *Bivens v Six Unknown Named Agents of Federal Bureau of Narcotics* 403 US 388, 395 (1971).

[37] W Friedman, 'Modern Trends in the Law of Torts' (1937) 1 *MLR* 39, 39.

[38] EJ Weinrib, *The Idea of Private Law* (Harvard University Press, 1995) 5.

[39] EJ Weinrib, *Corrective Justice* (OUP, 2012); J Gardner, 'What is Tort Law For? Part 1: The Place of Corrective Justice' (2011) 30 *Law & Philosophy* 1.

[40] See, eg, Cane (n 10); P Cane, 'Corrective Justice and Correlativity in Private Law' (1996) 16 *Oxford Journal of Legal Studies* 471; J Gardner, 'What is Tort Law For? Part 2: The Place of Distributive Justice' in J Oberdiek (ed), *Philosophical Foundations of the Law of Torts* (OUP, 2014); S Hedley, 'Is Private Law Meaningless?' (2011) 64 *Current Legal Problems* 89; S Steel, 'Private Law and Justice' (2013) 33 *Oxford Journal of Legal Studies* 607; GT Schwartz, 'Mixed Theories of Tort Law' (1997) 75 *Texas Law Review* 1801.

significant structural variations across different actions in tort, particular types of damages such as nominal and exemplary damages, why particular damages are available for certain torts but not others, why the approach to compensatory damages varies from one tort to the next, and why we have the rights that we do, nor why duties of repair are distributed and institutionalised in law in the way that they are. Nor do such theories generally account for statute. Thus, it turns out corrective justice cannot explain a great deal of what we need to explain if we are to fully understand the field.

Of particular relevance for the present inquiry, there is a significant divide among contemporary tort theorists between those that view the law of torts' principal function as determining responsibility for compensation for material losses (loss-based accounts), and others who argue that its function is to vindicate or protect our most fundamental rights or interests (rights-based accounts). As I shall argue herein neither of these theories is satisfactory, in that each overreaches. But each is necessary for the explanation of *certain* aspects of the law of torts. Whereas the compensatory account can convincingly explain certain actions, in particular negligence, it cannot explain others; it has arguably become pervasive as a general theory largely because of the dominance of negligence within the modern law of torts, which makes it all too easy to conflate negligence with the law of torts more generally. The result is regrettable decisions such as *Lumba* (discussed in section III.C.iii below). Vindicatory, rights-based accounts also overreach where they purport to explain tort in general. Albeit, such theories have offered an important challenge to compensatory accounts and a reminder that in respect of certain actions the compensatory account is plainly inapt. Of course, there are aspects of tort that neither account can explain adequately.

We find a similar split among commentators in the province of damages. On the one hand some, such as Stevens, rightly recognise the availability of general damages other than for factual loss within the law of torts.[41] However, Stevens' account overreaches in arguing that such awards are, in principle, available across the field of torts. On the other hand, some commentators continue to resist the proposition that general damages are available other than for factual loss (or gain); such accounts are largely sustained by their protagonists' pinpointing of explanatory and other weaknesses in prevailing accounts of damages in the absence of factual loss, as opposed to their demonstrating conclusively that such awards are not available generally.[42] This chapter offers an account which falls between these

[41] Stevens (n 3) ch 4.

[42] eg A Burrows, 'Damages and Rights' in Nolan and Robertson (n 2) 278–90; 'Are "Damages on the Wrotham Park Basis" Compensatory, Restitutionary or Neither?' in D Saidov and R Cunnington (eds), *Contract Damages* (Hart Publishing, 2008) 181–85; J Edelman, 'The Meaning of Loss and Enrichment' in R Chambers et al (eds), *Philosophical Foundations of the Law of Unjust Enrichment* (OUP, 2009) 218–21.

polarities. Supported by doctrinal exegesis of the law of damages across the TAPS, the chapter argues that normative damages are available within tort but are only generally available for certain actions. We can explain the distribution of such awards across tort by reference to the primary functions of those actions for which they are available.

Ultimately, the key to theorising tort in a way that is sensitive to its complexity and plurality is to begin with a sound understanding of tort doctrine; that is to move from facts to theory. As Weir observes, 'it is surely desirable to become familiar with what that ragbag actually contains; otherwise we shall be like adolescents spending all night discussing the meaning of life—before, perhaps instead of, experiencing it'.[43]

II. DISTINGUISHING VINDICATORY AND COMPENSATORY TORTS

This chapter's focus is on explaining significant variations in the approach to damages across the law of torts. However, in order to understand fully these variations and the different roles damages perform across tort it is important to recognise that different torts perform very different primary functions; a tort's primary function fundamentally shapes remedies.

This section draws a distinction between torts which have as their primary function vindication and protection of fundamental interests, and those which primarily perform a compensatory function. In respect of vindicatory torts, the TAPS are an 'ideal type'; their internal features most obviously evince a primary function of protection and reinforcement of the importance of underlying interests. Roughly speaking, the closer the core features of a tort to those of the ideal type, the stronger the emphasis on vindication. In respect of compensation, the tort of negligence is the 'ideal type', its internal features most obviously evincing a primary function of compensation for fault-based, factual harms. Private nuisance is also analysed, as an example of a tort that straddles vindicatory and compensatory paradigms.

A. Vindicatory Torts: Torts Actionable Per Se

It has long been recognised that the TAPS play an important role in protecting and vindicating those interests fundamental to English civil society. For example trespass to land protects interests in exclusive possession and use of land; battery, interests in physical integrity; false imprisonment, interests in liberty; and defamation, interests in one's reputation. This primary function of protection and vindication of fundamental interests is immanent in the internal structure of these torts.

[43] Weir 2006 (n 1) ix.

i. Prerequisites to Actionability

TAPS are actionable without proof of special or actionable loss;[44] 'damage is not the gist of action'.[45] That an individual may prove a wrong and access remedies for the slightest[46] interference with their protected interests, including where the wrong leaves them factually no worse off, attests to and reinforces the fundamental importance of those interests as well as their inherent value independent of any harm which may flow from the interference, while affording the interests strong protection. As Dicey recorded,

> if in short X interferes unlawfully to however slight a degree with the personal liberty of A, the offender exposes himself to proceedings in a courts of law, and the sufferer, if he can enlist the sympathies of the jury, may recover heavy damages for injury which he has or is supposed to have suffered.[47]

More recently in *Watkins* Lord Walker affirmed that even the 'most trifling and transient physical assault' would give the claimant a cause of action 'sounding in damages (and if appropriate aggravated or exemplary damages)',[48] while in *Ashley* Lord Rodger said 'battery or trespass to the person is actionable without proof that the victim has suffered anything other than the infringement of his right to bodily integrity'.[49]

The highest courts consistently link this feature of TAPS to the importance of the underlying interests. In the false imprisonment context Lord Porter in *John Lewis v Tims* said that '[w]hen the liberty of the subject is at stake questions as to the damage sustained become of little importance',[50] and in *Murray* Lord Griffiths observed that '[t]he law attaches supreme importance to the liberty of the individual and if he suffers a wrongful interference with that liberty it should remain actionable even without proof of special damage'.[51] In the defamation context Lord Hoffmann said that one's 'reputation is a part of his personality, the "immortal part" of himself and it is right that he should be entitled to vindicate his reputation and receive compensation

[44] False imprisonment: *Lumba* (n 2) [64]; Defamation: *Jameel v The Wall Street Journal Europe Sprl* [2007] 1 AC 359, [91]; Assault and battery: *Holmes v Bagge* (1853) 1 El & Bl 782; Trespass to land: *Entick v Carrington* (1765) 95 ER 807, 817.

[45] *Nicholls v Ely Beet Sugar Factory Ltd* [1936] 1 Ch 343, 349.

[46] Defamation: AV Dicey, *Introduction to the Study of the Law of the Constitution* 10th edn (MacMillan, 1960) 211–12; *cf* Defamation Act 2013, s 1, and note restrictions imposed by procedural law: *Tamiz v Google Inc* [2013] EWCA Civ 68, [48]–[52]; Battery: *In re F* [1990] 2 AC 1, 72; Trespass to land: *Entick v Carrington* (1765) 19 State Trials 1030 ('every invasion of private property, be it ever so minute, is a trespass').

[47] Dicey, ibid 211–12.

[48] *Watkins* (n 7) [68].

[49] *Ashley* (n 2) [60].

[50] [1952] AC 676, 680.

[51] *Murray v MOD* [1988] All ER 521, 529.

for a slur upon it without proof of financial loss'.[52] In *Entick v Carrington* the Court observed:

> our law holds the property of every man so sacred, that no man can set his foot upon his neighbour's close without his leave; if he does he is a trespasser, though he does no damage at all; if he will tread upon his neighbour's ground, he must justify it by law.[53]

In a battery claim Lord Goff recalled the 'fundamental principle, long established, that every person's body is inviolate ... the effect of this principle is that everybody is protected not only against physical injury but against any form of physical molestation',[54] in a previous case explaining that '[t]he breadth of the principle reflects the fundamental nature of the interest so protected'.[55]

Similarly, it is a feature of the emergent action for misuse of private information, which protects the basic interest in privacy, that one need not prove actual loss or damage in order to bring a claim.[56] Further, it is increasingly clear that for the interference with privacy to be actionable personal information obtained need not necessarily have been disclosed or published; interference with the private sphere, as through discovering or retaining information, is in itself sufficient to ground the action.[57]

Other actions do not share this feature. For example, for economic torts damage or the threat of damage is in general a necessary element.[58] Within private nuisance the claimant must prove more than mere interference with their interest in quiet enjoyment of their land; they bear the heavier burden of showing that the interference was unreasonable and substantial. These features in turn reflect the lesser value which the common law places on economic interests and those in quiet enjoyment relative to those interests protected by the TAPS. For example, exclusive possession of land, protected by trespass, is more basic than enjoyment of land, protected by nuisance, in that before one may enjoy one's land one must have dominion over it. Reflecting this ranking of interests, the law is less tolerant of interferences with the former interest.

ii. Strictness of Liability

Within TAPS liability is generally strict not fault-based, with the defendant's conduct and blameworthiness not relevant to liability (although they may be

52 *Jameel* (n 44) [91].
53 (n 44) 817.
54 *re F* (n 46) 72.
55 *Collins v Wilcock* [1984] 1 WLR 1172, 1177.
56 eg *Gulati v MGN Ltd* [2015] EWHC 1482.
57 ibid; *Tchenguiz v Imerman* [2011] 2 WLR 592.
58 *Lumley v Gye* (1853) 2 E&B 216; *OBG* (n 28); *Customs and Excise Commissioners v Total Network SL* [2008] 1 AC 1174.

relevant to defences and damages), and the court's inquiry focused firmly on whether the claimant's interests were interfered with.[59] As Pollock recorded, where the 'primary rights to security for a man's person' are at stake 'the knowledge or state of mind of the person violating the right is not material for determining his legal responsibility'.[60] That the underlying interests are afforded such strong protection attests to and reinforces their fundamental importance: the law signals that these interests are of such importance that it is inexcusable to trespass upon them regardless of whether one does so innocently, benevolently or reasonably, and perhaps whether one knows one is trespassing upon them or not.

'Strict liability' here denotes that X may be liable for a voluntary act which infringes Y's protected interests, even though X may not have intended to interfere with Y's interests or cause Y harm, or be said to be 'at fault' through their actions.[61] So, a person may commit trespass to land by walking onto another's property voluntarily, even if she did not know and had no reason to know it was another's and entered in good faith:[62] 'the intention to violate another's rights, or even the knowledge that one is violating them, is not in English law necessary to constitute the wrong of trespass as regards either land or goods, or of conversion as regards goods'.[63] Similarly a defendant may be liable in defamation even if they did not know and had no reason to know that the statement they published was defamatory,[64] if their belief as to the truth of the statement was reasonably held,[65] or if they committed defamation through innocent mistake;[66] it has long been the case that '[p]ersons must often pay heavy damages for giving currency to statements which were not meant to be falsehoods, and which were reasonably believed to be true'.[67]

Liability is not as strict across all TAPS, the peculiar strictness within trespass to land and defamation being linked to the primacy historically placed on property interests[68] and, in the case of defamation, quasi-proprietary interests.[69] More than a voluntary act is required to establish battery.

[59] Weir 2004 (n 1) 322; A Beever, 'The Form of Liability in the Torts of Trespass' (2011) 40 *Common Law World Review* 378; Stevens (n 3) 100–02.

[60] F Pollock, *Law of Torts* (Stevens, 1887) 236.

[61] P Cane, '*Mens Rea* in Tort Law' (2000) 20 *Oxford Journal of Legal Studies* 533, 552.

[62] Cane (n 17) 32–33, 45, 139; *Severn Trent Water Ltd v Barnes* [2004] 2 EGLR 95 (damages awarded for 'trivial, accidental and unintentional' trespass (at [5])).

[63] Pollock (n 60) 7, 218.

[64] Cane (n 17) 45–46, 134; *Cassidy v Daily Mirror Newspapers* [1929] 2 KB 331, 354; *Newstead v London Express Newspaper Ltd* [1940] 1 KB 377; *cf* Defamation Act 1996, s 1.

[65] eg *Peters v Bradlaugh* (1888) 4 TLR 414.

[66] eg *Aktas v Westpac Banking Corporation Ltd* (2010) 241 CLR 79.

[67] Dicey (n 46) 242.

[68] Ibbetson (n 29) 185.

[69] *De Crespigny v Wellesley* (1829) 5 Bing 392, 405–06; O'Sullivan (n 19) 36 (reputation is 'a superior species of inalienable and (so to say) spiritual property').

Recent authority indicates that the defendant must either intend to touch the claimant or be reckless as to whether they would touch the claimant, although significantly it need not be proven that the defendant intended physical harm, or that they intended to touch the claimant against their will.[70] It has been held that '[t]he intention necessary for commission of [false imprisonment] is intentionally to do the act which causes the imprisonment. Added malice towards the imprisoned plaintiff is not necessary'.[71] Though there are competing dicta suggesting more than an intention to do the relevant act is required and that the defendant must either positively intend to confine or be reckless as to whether their actions will result in confinement.[72] Despite representing a somewhat less strict form of liability than that within trespass to land, these liability rules still afford strong protection to the underlying interests. Intentional touching constitutes battery even if it occurred under a mistaken impression[73] or was motivated by a genuine concern for the claimant's best interests.[74] False imprisonment may be established where the interference with liberty was due to a simple error,[75] 'blameless', perpetrated in good faith, or reasonable, or where the defendant was 'clearly conscientious';[76] to hold otherwise would 'reduce the protection currently provided by ... false imprisonment'.[77] Liability may be found where the claimant did not even know they were confined[78] and would have had no occasion to leave the place of confinement;[79] in other words it makes no difference that the interference with liberty leaves the claimant no worse off. Liability will be imposed even if the interference could hypothetically have been justified (but was not);[80] 'the law of false imprisonment does not permit history to be rewritten in this way'.[81] As such, the 'intention' element in trespassory torts is not a 'fault' element.[82]

[70] See FA Trindade, 'Intentional Torts: Some Thoughts on Assault and Battery' (1982) 2 *Oxford Journal of Legal Studies* 211, particularly 219–25; *Williams v Humphrey* (13 February 1975) *The Times*, 20; *Wilson v Pringle* [1987] QB 237, 249–50; *re F* (n 46) 73; *Bici v MOD* [2004] EWHC 786, [67]; *Co-operative Group Ltd v Pritchard* [2012] QB 320, [33].

[71] *Weldon v Home Office* [1990] 3 WLR 465, 470. It is oft-said that the tort has two ingredients: the fact of imprisonment and absence of lawful authority (*R v Deputy Governor of Parkhurst Prison, ex p Hague* [1992] 1 AC 58, 162). This formulation suggests a very strict form of liability, analogous to that within trespass to land.

[72] *Iqbal v POA* [2010] QB 732, [70]–[74].

[73] *Law v Visser* (1961) Qd R 46, discussed in Trindade (n 70) 220; *re F* (n 46) 73.

[74] *re F* particularly 12, 72–73; *Forde v Skinner* (1830) 4 Car & P 239.

[75] *ID v Home Office* [2006] 1 WLR 1003, [120].

[76] *R v Governor of Brockhill Prison, ex p Evans (No 2)* [2001] 2 AC 19; *R (Sessay) v South London and Maudsley NHS Trust* [2012] QB 760, [47].

[77] *Evans* 35; *R (M) v Hackney LBC* [2011] 1 WLR 2873, [100].

[78] *Meering v Grahame-White Aviation Co* (1919) 122 LT 44, 53–54; *Murray* (n 51) 528–29; *Lumba* (n 2) [64]. The position is the same in battery: Trindade (n 70) 227–28.

[79] *Weldon* (n 71) 470.

[80] *Lumba* (n 2); *Sessay* (n 76) [54].

[81] *Lumba* (n 2) [62].

[82] Beever (n 59).

Liability rules are similarly strict within other torts geared towards protecting basic proprietary interests. In conversion the purchaser of goods, who was unaware the sale was made without the true owner's authorisation and acted in good faith, may nonetheless be liable:

> [the common law] has enforced [the rights of the true owner] strictly as against anyone who deals with the goods inconsistently with the dominion of the true owner. Even though the true owner may have been very negligent and the defendant may have acted in complete innocence, nevertheless the common law held him liable.[83]

Liability is not so strict across other nominate torts. In contrast to the 'approving attitude' of the law 'to the protection of rights of property in chattels it is a commonplace that the law has always been very wary of imposing any kind of liability for purely economic loss'.[84] Thus, some economic torts require that the defendant intended to cause the claimant harm, while additional criteria may be imposed, such as that the means adopted to inflict harm were unlawful.[85]

Thus as van Dam observes,

> [s]trict liability protects rights and interests in the best way by holding someone liable for the damage he caused, unless he can invoke force majeure or a similar limited defence. Hence, rules of strict liability generally aim to protect highly valued rights such as personal and property interests.[86]

iii. Onus

Within the TAPS, wherever a protected interest is interfered with the defendant bears the onus of justifying that interference.[87] Thus, the defendant must establish lawful justification for interfering with the claimant's liberty, and in defamation it is for the defendant to prove truth. This approach reflects '[t]he importance which the law places upon the security of the plaintiff's interests'.[88] The position is similar elsewhere in the law, where basic interests

[83] *RH Willis & Son v British Car Auctions* [1978] 1 WLR 438, 441–42; *OBG* (n 28) [95]–[96].

[84] *OBG* (n 28) [99].

[85] ibid; *Allen v Flood* [1898] AC 1; *Total Network* (n 58).

[86] C van Dam, *European Tort Law* (OUP, 2006) 142.

[87] eg *Ashley* (n 2) [24]; *Lumba* (n 2) [65], [88]; *Entick* (n 44) 817. Note, in battery there is authority that the claimant bears the burden of proving he did not consent to the touching. This is premised on lack of consent constituting an element of the tort: *Freeman v Home Office (No 2)* [1984] 1 QB 524, 539, 557. The premise is controversial, not least because consent has been conceptualised as a 'defence' at the highest level: eg *Airedale NHS Trust v Bland* [1993] AC 789. Other jurisdictions consider consent a defence: Trindade (n 70) 228.

[88] RFV Heuston and RA Buckley, *Salmond and Heuston on the Law of Torts* 21st edn (Sweet and Maxwell, 1996) 15. Even if reversing the onus is not always of great practical significance, symbolically it is a significant expression of the importance of the protected interests.

are at stake, such as within the privacy action, and in actions for breach of equality duties.[89]

iv. Defences

While, within TAPS, it is straightforward for the claimant to establish prima facie liability and thereby cast the justificatory onus upon the defendant, defences are subject to careful scrutiny and narrowly construed.[90] For example, to demonstrate that one had statutory authority to detain or touch an individual one must point to 'express', 'explicit' or 'direct' 'authorisation' in statute.[91] In *Lumba* Lord Dyson, after observing that 'the right to liberty is of fundamental importance', said 'the courts should strictly and narrowly construe general statutory powers whose exercise restricts fundamental common law rights and/or constitutes the commission of a tort'.[92] That a breach of statutory condition governing imprisonment is not 'substantial' will not excuse the interference.[93] Administrative convenience or expeditiousness, for example in police operations, will not be sufficient to justify interference with basic interests;[94] '[t]he executive cannot simply assert interests of state or the public interest and rely upon that as a justification for the commission of wrongs'.[95] More generally, claims of justification will 'be examined with very great care',[96] while conditions attached to powers to interfere with basic interests are traditionally 'very closely prescribed by statute and the common law'.[97]

Defences are confined to protecting the 'most important interests—maintenance of public order, enforcement of the law, and preservation of life and property'.[98] Something weighty is required to justify interference with a basic interest. Within those torts with a strong vindicatory flavour, particularly the trespassory torts, defences will, in general, fail if exercised 'unreasonably'.[99] Thus important countervailing interests can be accommodated. But they cannot justify unreasonable interferences with fundamental

89 Equality Act 2010, s 136.

90 Weir 2006 (n 1) 17, 135; *Ruddock v Taylor* (2005) 222 CLR 612, 632.

91 eg *SOSHD v GG* [2010] QB 585; *Morris v Beardmore* [1981] AC 446; *Re Bolton* (1987) 162 CLR 514, 528.

92 *Lumba* (n 2) [53]; *M* (n 77) [100].

93 *Hague* (n 71).

94 *Christie v Leachinsky* [1947] AC 573, 595; *Evans* (n 76) 35.

95 *Bici* (n 70) [86].

96 *Lindley v Rutter* [1981] QB 128, 134; *R (Gillan) v Commissioner of the Metropolis* [2006] 2 AC 307, [1]; *ID* (n 75) [75].

97 *In re SC* [1996] QB 599, 603.

98 Weir 2004 (n 1) 324.

99 Thus, someone who seeks to rely on necessity must only take such action as is reasonable in the circumstances, an individual who seeks to rely on self-defence may only use reasonable force, and in order to effect an arrest without a warrant a police constable must have reasonable suspicion of criminal wrong-doing: *re F* (n 46); *Ashley* (n 2); Police and Criminal Evidence Act 1984, s 24.

interests. This is another consequence of the vindicatory approach, the primacy afforded to the claimant's interests attesting to their relative importance.

Finally, a claimant whose basic interests are interfered with may have recourse to self-help. Thus, for example, if another seeks to arrest you, but they have no lawful authority to do so, you may use physical force to resist the infraction upon your liberty, and in so doing, assuming certain conditions are met, will not be liable in tort or in the criminal law. As Lord Du Parcq observed in *Christie*, 'it strikingly demonstrates to what lengths a man may go in the defence of his liberty',[100] and reiterates the premium the law places on maintaining basic interests inviolate.

v. Other Features

Aside from the foregoing, there are various other features of the TAPS which confirm their vindicatory functions. For example, where in respect of the same act a defendant admits and pays compensation for negligence and false imprisonment, but denies claims in battery and assault, the latter may still proceed to trial despite the parties being agreed that the claimants cannot recover any further compensation.[101] The TAPS are about more than provision of compensation for harm; if an individual suffers wrongful interference with their basic interests they ought to be able to obtain a finding to this effect regardless of whether further compensation is obtainable.

B. Compensatory Torts: Negligence

Negligence has a radically different structure to torts such as false imprisonment and battery. In turn these differences reflect that negligence performs a very different function. In negligence the law's focus is on material or factual loss and determining responsibility for compensating that loss. Put simply, the tort's primary function is to afford compensation for fault-based material losses, rather than to afford strong protection to basic interests in themselves and affirm their inherent importance.

This is not to say that negligence does not afford protection to certain basic interests. It does. But this is not the tort's principal focus or concern. Any protection afforded to such interests is tangential to and dependent upon the primary goal. The tort only protects basic interests so far as interference with those interests causes actionable material harm, and the defendant is at fault for that harm. As Cane says, 'some interests are protected by tort law only to the extent that interference with the interest inflicts some loss, damage or harm on the interest-holder; whereas other interests are

[100] *Christie* (n 94) 600–01.
[101] *Ashley* (n 2).

protected even from interferences which cause no loss, damage or harm beyond the very interference itself'.[102]

Some might contest this conception of negligence on the basis that compensation cannot possibly be the law's function as the tort performs it ineffectively, unfairly and/or inefficiently. It is irrational for tort to perform this function when a state-run compensation scheme or the free market for insurance could perform better.[103] First, it seems entirely plausible that a field could exist to perform function X, but not meet expectations. There may be many reasons why an ineffective body of law remains unreformed, such as lack of political priority. Further, we must not confuse two separate questions: what are the principal concerns of negligence as a matter of law versus what are the extrinsic effects of the operation of negligence. Even those, such as Atiyah, who are staunch functionalist critics of negligence nonetheless consider that *as a matter of doctrine* the tort has developed from the 'basic point that if somebody injures you through his fault he should compensate you'.[104] Second, in some jurisdictions, such as New Zealand, negligence, or significant tracts of negligence liability, *has* been supplanted by alternative means of compensation, such as state-run schemes.[105] In contrast it is difficult to see how vindicatory torts could be adequately replaced by state-run compensation schemes or the market for insurance, given their primary functions transcend compensation for actual loss; those functions include important public, norm-exemplification functions, and delineation of the bounds of our most fundamental rights, which is a quintessentially judicial function.

Let us consider the significant features of negligence which show its primary concern to be compensation for fault-based harm, as opposed to vindication.

i. The Gist: Actionable Loss

Whereas for vindicatory torts any 'infringement [of protected interests] is automatically wrongful'[106] and actionable without more, in negligence it is 'trite law'[107] that damage is the 'gist'[108] of the action.[109] A claimant must demonstrate they have suffered actionable loss before they may mount an

102 Cane (n 17) 90.

103 eg Stevens (n 3) 320–21.

104 PS Atiyah, *The Damages Lottery* (Hart Publishing, 1997) 155.

105 Accident Compensation Act 2001 (NZ).

106 AM Tettenborn and D Wilby, *The Law of Damages* 2nd edn (LexisNexis, 2010) [2.05]–[2.07]. Courts often contrast the actionability requirements of negligence and TAPS: eg *Ashley* (n 2) [60]; *Lumba* (n 2) [64].

107 *Chester* (n 2) [9].

108 Repeatedly stated at the highest level: *Sidaway v Board of Governors of the Bethlem Royal Hospital* [1985] AC 871, 883; *Gregg v Scott* [2005] 2 AC 176, [99]; *Lumba* (n 2) [64]; *Rothwell v Chemical & Insulating Co Ltd* [2008] 1 AC 281, [74]; *Chester* (n 2) [9], [51]; *Admiralty Commissioners v Owners of the SS Amerika* [1917] AC 38, 60.

109 This reflects the tort's origin in case: Ibbetson (n 29) ch 9; 'Consequential damage provided the occasion for, and the foundation of, an action on the case' (*Northern Territory v*

action; 'proof of damage' is an 'essential element'.[110] Damage 'is not a technical requirement. It goes to the foundation of the law of negligence'.[111] Thus, a defendant may act with gross negligence and even disdain for the claimant's most fundamental interests, and negligently interfere with the claimant's physical interests, causing an undesirable physical change in the claimant's body, but if the claimant is not factually worse off in consequence, no action will lie:[112] 'It is not the act but the consequences on which tortious liability is founded'.[113] There shall be 'no cause of action' for an interference with basic interests which 'do[es] not give rise to any harmful physical *effects*'; no liability for 'negligence in the air which has no *effect* on the claimant at all'.[114]

That loss is a basic element of the action reflects the tort's compensatory focus: the court must be sure that there is actual harm to compensate before allowing a claim to proceed. As Lord Hope said in the negligence case of *Rothwell*:

> an injury which is without any symptoms at all because it cannot be seen or felt ... *has no consequences that will attract an award of damages. Damages are given for injuries that cause harm*, not for injuries that are harmless.[115]

In the same case, Lord Hoffmann, in a canonical statement, said, '[d]amage in this sense is an abstract concept of being *worse off*, physically or economically, *so that compensation is an appropriate remedy*'.[116] The focus is on whether the claimant suffered actual negative consequences or effects, so that they are left materially worse off due to the defendant's negligence. It is,

Mengel (1995) 185 CLR 307, 367); '[T]he action on the case ... allowed tortious remedies in damages where harm had been caused in circumstances where the conduct of the authors of the harm had been sufficiently reprehensible to require the conclusion that they ought to be held responsible' (*Total Network* (n 58) [56]).

110 *Law Society v Sephton & Co* [2006] 2 AC 543, [9]; *Wandsworth LBC v Winder* [1985] AC 461, 488; *Hague* (n 71) 34.

111 *In re T & N Ltd* [2006] 1 WLR 1728, [25].

112 eg *Rothwell* (n 108); *Hunter v London Docklands Development Corp* [1996] CLC 197, 209–10 (no action where defendant causes large amounts of dust to be deposited on claimant's land, unless this results in physical damage); *D v Bury MBC* [2006] 1 WLR 917, [88]ff (less than 'significant harm' to a child negligently removed from their parents' care cannot found an action); *Cartledge v E Jopling & Sons Ltd* [1963] AC 758 ('real' or 'material' as opposed to minimal damage required); *Sephton* (n 110) [20], [71]ff (where negligent misrepresentations caused claimant to enter a contract which they would not have otherwise they shall have no action if they suffer no '"actual" damage of a relevant and measurable kind'); *Winder* (n 110) 488 (claimant must 'prove substantial damage').

113 *Overseas Tankship (UK) Ltd v Morts Dock & Engineering Co Ltd* [1961] AC 388, 425; *Sephton* (n 110) [9] ('no cause of action until [the claimant] suffer[s] damage in consequence of [the defendant's] negligence'); *Ely Beet* (n 45) 351 ('the cause of action is not merely that the defendant was negligent, but he was negligent in such a way as to damage the plaintiff').

114 *Rothwell* (n 108) [50]; *Wright v Cambridge Medical Group* [2013] QB 312, [103] (emphasis added).

115 *Rothwell*, ibid [47] (emphasis added).

116 ibid [7]; *Sephton* (n 110) [20].

as we shall see, therefore no surprise that damages in negligence are limited to compensating material harms.

The action's focus on actual loss makes it difficult to conceptualise the tort as one concerned to afford basic rights or interests strong protection in themselves and vindicate their importance, given the loss requirement prevents courts from intervening where there is an interference with basic interests but, as it happens, no loss is suffered.[117]

ii. Fault

Within vindicatory torts liability is *strict*. Damages may be awarded for mere interference with the claimant's *interests*, regardless of whether the defendant can be said to be at fault; the law's focus is on the claimant and maintaining their interests inviolate, rather than the defendant's conduct and whether it can be considered blameworthy. In contrast '[t]he law of negligence is generally fault-based',[118] so that the defendant may only be liable if she is *at fault* for the claimant's *losses*. Thus, the liability inquiry is the inverse of that within vindicatory torts: rather than liability being a reflex of whether basic interests have been interfered with, liability in negligence depends upon an inquiry into whether the defendant 'ought to be held responsible for the harm'.[119] The key questions governing liability are defendant-oriented:

> (a) whether the defendant owed a duty of care to the claimant, to prevent him sustaining the type of harm that was a foreseeable consequence of his careless acts or omissions; (b) whether there was an act or omission by the defendant which was in breach of that duty or care; and (c) for what loss, injury and damages, if any, the defendant is liable.[120]

If the first two questions are answered in the affirmative then the defendant is 'at fault' for relevant loss. Thus the core concepts of duty, reasonable care, breach, causation, remoteness (and defences) are all means by which the court decides whether the defendant ought to be held responsible to compensate the claimant and for which losses.

It is important to record that while fault in negligence was at one time informed predominantly by moral ideas of fault, so that fault connoted personal moral shortcomings, over time the principle has come to reflect a

117 See similarly Witzleb and Carroll (n 2) 41.

118 *Woodland v Essex* CC [2014] AC 537, [5].

119 *Total Network* (n 58) [56]. When courts and commentators state that negligence is 'duty-centric' they seem to be making a similar point: eg *Stubbings v Webb* [1993] AC 498, 508; *Sidaway v Board of Governors of the Bethlem Royal Hospital* [1984] QB 493, 519–20; Weir 2006 (n 1) 30. However, I am not sure focussing on duty is helpful given areas of law which some describe as 'rights-based', such as TAPS, could equally be analysed in terms of duty, especially within a Hohfeldian framework.

120 *Gregg* (n 108) [99].

broader idea of blameworthiness. This broader idea is associated with not living up to a standard of conduct imposed by the law and which reflects 'external' norms of conduct, based in societal perceptions of when one person ought to be responsible for compensating another's loss.[121] It is important to record this shift as it shows the function of contemporary negligence law to be, in an important sense, a *social* function, which contrasts with the strong focus of TAPS on *individual* rights and interests. We find this change reflected in certain features of negligence. As we shall see, the question of whether a duty of care arises depends on consideration of public policy and societal expectations. The question of breach also involves a balancing calculus which entails weighing of costs of injury, and of prevention and wider social utility. We see this trend also in the objective nature of the standard for breach. As Cane observes, 'if the law's main aim was to reinforce some notion of personal fault, the law might pay more attention to the abilities of individual defendants',[122] and ask whether the care taken was reasonable given their capabilities, for example. Yet in general the standard is unresponsive to defendants' qualities, abilities, strengths or weaknesses. As Cane observes, this reflects the law's prioritisation of the compensatory goal and its social dimension.[123] For example, courts explicitly justify application of the same standard to learner and experienced drivers alike on the basis that third party insurance for road traffic accidents is compulsory. Application of the objective standard may be harsh on the learner driver. However, it is in society's interest that the claimant not be left to bear the loss, but that it should be spread among many through insurance.[124] This is not to say fault is not central to negligence, but that the concept has been increasingly stretched given the trajectory of legal development.

iii. Causation

Concepts of factual causation and remoteness are core features of negligence as they are inextricably connected to the question of whether the defendant ought to be held *responsible* for a particular *loss*: only if the defendant in fact caused the claimant's *loss*, and that *loss* was reasonably foreseeable will the defendant be liable. That questions of causation are fundamental to negligence reflects Lord Hoffmann's observation that, '[q]uestions of causation often arise for the purpose of attributing *responsibility* to someone, for

[121] Ibbetson (n 29) ch 10; DJ Ibbetson, 'The Tort of Negligence in England' in N Jansen (ed), *The Development and Making of Legal Doctrine, Vol 6* (CUP, 2010).
[122] P Cane, *Atiyah's Accidents, Compensation and the Law* 8th edn (CUP, 2013) 46.
[123] ibid.
[124] *Nettleship v Weston* [1971] 2 QB 691, 699–700, 703.

example, so as to *blame* him for something which has happened or to make him guilty of an offence or liable in damages'.[125]

The centrality of causation within negligence and the nature of that inquiry reflects the law's distinctive function; the limited role causal questions play in vindicatory torts and the different nature of the inquiry reflects the functional differences between the torts. A defendant may be liable for false imprisonment even if it was inevitable that if the defendant had not detained the claimant unlawfully, they would invariably have been detained lawfully in exactly the same way and for the same period.[126] As Lord Dyson said in *Lumba*, because harm is not an element of the action, 'there is no place for a causation test here',[127] by which he meant a causation test of the sort found in negligence and entailing 'but for' counterfactual analysis. If there is a causal question it is simply, did the defendant through his acts invade the claimant's protected interests?[128] In contrast, in negligence, 'but for' causation is central to determining liability, and its centrality reflects the law's focus on determining responsibility for losses.[129] If it was inevitable that the defendant's boat would have crashed into and damaged the claimant's boat even if the defendant had not acted negligently, the defendant shall not be liable because his negligence was not a necessary condition of or material to the claimant's suffering of harm.[130] The defendant through his careless act interfered with the claimant's proprietary interests but in a sense this is beside the point within negligence, given the tort's predominant concerns: there is no liability unless the defendant can be said to be responsible for losses suffered, and factual causation is one means of determining whether it is justifiable to hold the defendant responsible. Remoteness is also a core element of the negligence action, and is directly connected to the tort's principal functions, being a tool for delineating the scope of the defendant's responsibility for loss, and which implicates wider policy questions such as those over social utility of the defendant's activities, again reflecting the social dimension of the compensatory function;[131] as is discussed further below, this doctrine has no part to play in the TAPS.[132]

[125] *Environment Agency v Empress Car Co (Abertillery) Ltd* [1999] 2 AC 22, 29 (emphasis added).

[126] *Lumba* (n 2).

[127] ibid [64]–[65].

[128] The only real question that may arise is whether anything intervened between the act and the invasion: Weir 2006 (n 1) 17–18; *cf* Stevens (n 3) 133–37.

[129] There may be policy-based exceptions on occasion (as we shall see) but this is the general requirement: *Fairchild v Glenhaven Funeral Services Ltd* [2003] 1 AC 32, [8]–[9].

[130] See, eg, *The Empire Jamaica* [1957] AC 386; *McWilliams v Sir William Arrol* [1962] 1 All ER 623; *Barnett v Chelsea and Kensington Hospital Management Committee* [1969] 1 QB 428; *Wright* (n 114) [103].

[131] eg *Overseas Tankship (UK) Ltd v Miller Steamship Co Pty Ltd* [1967] 1 AC 167; *Jolley v Sutton LBC* [2000] 3 All ER 409.

[132] See further text to n 356 below.

For completeness, the courts have exceptionally countenanced departures from ordinary causation requirements, so as to afford protection to basic interests. As is discussed further below, such departures are best explained as 'vindicatory impulses'; that is, instances where courts consciously undermine the coherence of negligence for the purposes of not leaving a claimant, whose basic interests have been infringed, without remedy. For example *Chester* concerned a doctor's failure to warn a patient of the risks of surgery, in breach of their duty to do so.[133] The House of Lords considered that, on orthodox causation principles, damages could not be awarded for the claimant's losses, suffered through the resultant surgery, as the claimant would have gone ahead with the same surgery at a later date even if properly warned, so that the failure to warn did not cause the claimant to be subject to any greater risk of injury than if properly informed—they would have been exposed to the same risk anyhow.[134] However, the majority were unwilling to leave the claimant without remedy, as the basic interest in autonomy had been infringed by the doctor's negligence: '[the patient's] right of autonomy and dignity can and ought to be vindicated by a narrow and modest departure from traditional causation principles'.[135] The minority refused to endorse such 'a substantial and unjustified departure from sound and established principle'.[136] This difference reflected deeper disagreement as to how negligence ought to be conceptualised in this context. The majority reached their view by working out from the basic interest in autonomy: 'I start with the proposition that the law which imposed the duty to warn on the doctor has at its heart *the right of the patient* to make an informed choice'.[137] On the other hand, the minority adopted an orthodox loss-based starting-point:[138]

> It is trite law that damage is the gist of the action in the tort of negligence ... a claimant is not entitled to be compensated, and a defendant is not bound to compensate the claimant, for damage not caused by the negligence complained of.

That the majority characterised their approach as a *deviation* or *exception* proves the general rule that causation of loss is central to negligence. The *Chester* case also shows how very different negligence would be if founded upon a vindicatory rationale; rather than causation of loss being a prerequisite to a claim, all one would need to show to establish a prima facie case of liability is breach of an enumerated right, so that breach of rights rather

133 *Chester* (n 2).
134 Although the House of Lords took this view it is arguable that the claimant could have recovered on orthodox principles on the facts: Weir 2006 (n 1) 89–90; J Stapleton, 'Occam's Razor Reveals an Orthodox Basis for *Chester v Afshar*' (2006) 122 LQR 426; *cf* Stevens (n 3) 164–66.
135 *Chester* (n 2) [24].
136 ibid [9].
137 ibid [86] (emphasis added), [17], [22], [92], [101].
138 ibid [9], [28]–[36].

than material loss would be the gist of the action. In turn, that this is not the general approach illustrates that the tort is not based in a vindicatory, protective rationale. The law's focus on loss, which in turn implicates 'but for' causation and an inquiry into remoteness of loss, makes it difficult to conceptualise negligence as concerned principally with vindication and protection of basic interests in themselves, given it is a consequence of the tort's concern for material losses that negligent interferences with basic interests may well go without legal protection.

iv. Duty of Care

In a field constituted to determine when one person is responsible to compensate another for harms suffered we require a mechanism for determining when such responsibility may arise; negligence would be unwieldy if liability arose whenever one person negligently caused another some loss.[139] The duty of care concept serves this purpose, defining and delimiting the circumstances in which a person may be legally responsible for the harm they negligently cause another, and for what types of harms.

The question of when a duty ought to arise cannot be reduced to a single principle but implicates a rough and ready pragmatic, all-things-considered inquiry: there is no 'universal formula or yardstick', 'single general principle', 'blueprint',[140] 'common denominator',[141] or 'comprehensive touchstone'.[142] The relevant considerations are commonly said to fall into two categories,[143] but even the following 'tests' are not definitive and only intended as guides,[144] 'a set of fairly blunt tools'.[145]

First, there are considerations pertaining to the parties.[146] Importantly this aspect of the inquiry is defendant-orientated, focused on whether it is justifiable to impose a duty on the defendant, as opposed to focusing on protection of the claimant's interests or 'rights'. One consideration is whether the type of harm suffered was reasonably foreseeable. If it was not then the defendant could not have been expected to take steps to avoid it. Another consideration is proximity, that is the nature and closeness of the relationship between the parties. Essentially this test seeks to identify which

[139] The duty concept keeps 'the law of negligence within the bounds of common sense and practicality' (*Caparo v Dickman Industries Plc* [1990] 2 AC 605, 633).

[140] *Michael v Chief Constable of South Wales* [2015] 2 WLR 343, [103], [106].

[141] *Caparo* (n 139) 633.

[142] *An Informer v A Chief Constable* [2013] QB 579, [58].

[143] See generally *Caparo* (n 139); A Roberston, 'Justice, Community Welfare and the Duty of Care' (2011) 127 *LQR* 370.

[144] *Caparo* (n 139) 617–18; *Michael* (n 140) [103], [106].

[145] *Customs and Excise Commissioners v Barclays Bank Plc* [2007] 1 AC 181, [71].

[146] Although these considerations are generally focussed on the parties it would be an error to think that they do not also implicate wider policy concerns. See for example the approach to reasonable foreseeability in: *Annetts v Australian Stations Pty Ltd* (2002) 211 CLR 317.

person(s) were 'most appropriately placed to take care in the avoidance of damage'.[147]

Second, the courts ask whether recognising a duty is 'fair, just and reasonable', which 'means little more than the court should only impose a duty of care if it considers it right to do so'.[148] Within this inquiry courts take into account factors that go beyond the parties, 'often' including 'a mixture of policy considerations'.[149] That courts take into account such factors reflects that the decision whether to recognise a legal obligation is one concerning allocation of primary legal entitlements, such distributive questions naturally and legitimately implicating wider concerns which transcend a single case. This feature also reflects the tort's compensatory function:

> On a loss-based model … a judge has no option but to weigh the policy factors which militate in favour of and against liability. No legal system allows all loss which is caused by fault of another to be recoverable.[150]

In contrast, if the tort were organised around protection of a defined set of basic interests or rights, those interests or rights would delineate the tort's scope. The concern for public policy also reflects the trend towards conceptualising negligence as not so much grounded in individualist moral norms, such as rights, but in social perceptions of where losses should fall;[151] on what is 'socially justifiable'.[152] Partly because judges are not particularly well placed to make distributive decisions or design loss-allocation systems, and in order to keep liability within bounds, the courts have disciplined their approach to novel duty situations through an incrementalist method, only allowing modest expansions of the situations in which duties arise according to analogies with 'situation[s] in which liability has been established in the past'.[153]

v. Onus and Defences

In contrast to the position within TAPS, where it is for the defendant to show why they ought not to be held liable for an interference, within negligence the onus is on the claimant to prove that the defendant ought to be held responsible for the claimant's losses.[154] This again reflects the different functions of each field. The onus in TAPS is calibrated so as to afford

[147] C Witting, 'The Three-stage Test Abandoned in Australia—or Not?' 2002 118 *LQR* 214, 219.
[148] *Informer* (n 142) [58].
[149] *Michael* (n 140) [102]; see J Stapleton, 'Duty of Care Factors: A Selection from the Judicial Menus' in P Cane and J Stapleton (eds), *The Law of Obligations: Essays in Celebration of John Fleming* (Clarendon Press, 1998); Robertson (n 143); A Robertson, 'Policy-Based Reasoning in Duty of Care Cases' (2013) 33 *Legal Studies* 119.
[150] Stevens (n 3) 307.
[151] Text to n 121 above.
[152] *Michael* (n 140) [102].
[153] *Caparo* (n 139) 635, 617–18; ibid.
[154] *Donoghue v Stevenson* [1932] AC 562, 622; *Wright* (n 114) [75]; *Fairchild* (n 129) [8].

maximal protection to the claimant's basic interests, and reflects the importance placed on the claimant's interests.

Within negligence defences go to establishing responsibility for losses, specifically whether the claimant ought to bear the burden of all or part of their losses. Defences thus address whether the claimant contributed to the damage through his own negligence, and whether he voluntarily assumed a risk of injury. It is worth observing that the courts have held the partial defence of contributory negligence not to be available within battery.[155] This position is consonant with the view that where the law's concern is vindication of basic interests, rather than determining who is to blame for a given loss, questions of (relative) responsibility do not arise.

Thus, fundamental doctrinal features of negligence indicate that its primary function is to determine responsibility for compensating material loss, whereas the radically different features of TAPS indicate that the primary function of such torts is to afford strong protection from outside interference to and vindicate the importance of basic interests. It is because of these significant structural differences that it is commonly observed that '[t]he tort of trespass vindicates rights',[156] 'the law of negligence offers damages as compensation for harm'.[157]

vi. Rights-Based, Vindicatory Theories of Negligence

Some commentators, such as Stevens and Beever, have propounded what might be described as vindicatory accounts of negligence (and torts more generally).[158] On this view the primary function of negligence is to protect basic individual rights from negligent interference. So, for example, Stevens argues that the 'right to bodily safety' is protected against different types of interference by both battery and negligence; 'two torts but only one right'.[159] The nature of these rights is not altogether clear, but they are probably not Hohfeldian.[160] These theories are rich and stimulating, and important contributions. However, so far as they purport to offer explanations of the law, they are problematic.[161] For present purposes several brief observations shall suffice.

155 *Pritchard* (n 70) [62].

156 In the sense of legally protected interests.

157 Weir 2006 (n 1) 148.

158 Stevens (n 3); A Beever, *Rediscovering the Law of Negligence* (Hart Publishing, 2007).

159 ibid 293; Beever, ibid ch 6(II).

160 See McBride (n 10); Cane (n 10). Stevens (n 3) ch 2 claims allegiance to Hohfeld but it is difficult to see how the rights he describes could be Hohfeldian. For example, on Stevens' view rather than there being one duty which correlates with the right to bodily integrity, which is of identical content to the right, instead one right is associated with multiple duties of different content: a duty not to negligently interfere with the right and a duty not to intentionally interfere with the right.

161 Description and prescription are not always easily separated within these accounts.

First, that loss is the gist of the action tells against a rights-based conception. It indicates a focus on compensating claimants who are left materially worse off by the defendant's carelessness. Indeed, the loss-criterion could only be an impediment to protecting rights from negligent interference, as it presents a significant hurdle to a claimant seeking access to court to protect their rights. One response is to argue that actionable loss is a marker of or equivalent to rights-breach: 'Is what is meant the violation of a right, or the causation of loss?'[162] The answer is clear. It would seem odd for a field to revolve around rights but for judges never to refer to or reason by reference to those rights in determining whether a claim is actionable, unwaveringly speaking of loss. Perhaps more importantly, courts expressly equate actionable loss with being materially worse off, or incurring negative effects or consequences. A further response is to reject the legal definition of loss as erroneous.[163] At this point the argument must be a normative one as it is clearly inconsistent with the most important House of Lords decision on actionable loss.[164] Rejection of this definition suggests rights-theories are at variance with the law.

Second, the generalised nature of liability criteria—duty, loss, causation, breach—tells against the law's starting-point being protection of a bundle of individual rights. If this were the case there would be no unitary tort of negligence. Rather the law would consist of a number of distinct actions for negligent interference with particular rights, in the person, in property etc, each action being defined by reference to, and afforded its coherence by, the right to which it attaches. Further, if negligence were the field that protected rights from negligent interference, it is difficult to explain why a number of nominate torts, such as trespass to land and goods, conversion and defamation, protect rights from all types of interference whether negligent or not, through strict liability. How can we explain why certain very basic interests, such as liberty, are not protected by negligence?

Stevens, I think, accepts these points. He considers a single negligence tort to be the 'cuckoo in the nest', that the tort 'cuts across [a] rights-based classification', that the unitary tort is 'incoherent both internally as a category and as part of the law of torts in general' (if one adopts a vindicatory theory of tort). He therefore seeks to develop ways in which negligence might be 'accommodated' within a vindicatory-type framework.[165] But in doing so a stark reality is revealed: that negligence, as it exists, cannot be explained convincingly by Stevens' rights-based theory. Other concessions reinforce this:

> The first, and probably dominant, conception [of the law of torts] is that the defendant should be liable where he is at fault for causing the claimant loss

[162] Stevens (n 3) 292; D Nolan, 'Deconstructing the Duty of Care' (2013) 129 *LQR* 559.
[163] Stevens (n 2) 121.
[164] See text to n 115 above.
[165] Stevens (n 3) 295.

> unless there is a good reason why not. *This model dominates liability for negligence.*[166]

Third, such theories are difficult to reconcile with the centrality of causation within negligence, and the way that inquiry proceeds. That this would invariably be so follows from the causation inquiry being intimately connected to actionable loss, a concept rights-theorists wish to transubstantiate or expunge. For Stevens the factual causation inquiry within a vindicatory framework is: 'has the [defendant] by his action infringed the claimant's right?'[167] On this view it is irrelevant that the defendant would have interfered with the claimant's interests even if they had acted with due care; the fact of careless interference is sufficient for liability. Yet this approach does not characterise negligence: factual 'but for' causation is a fundamental element of the tort, the causative inquiry is directed to the causing of actionable loss, and pivots upon the defendant's conduct, ie would the loss have been suffered but for the defendant's carelessness?

Fourth, those who maintain a vindicatory conception of negligence generally oppose judges taking into account policy or social concerns at the duty-stage and more generally, not least because this challenges the view of torts as concerned with vindicating individual rights and moral wrongdoing and could therefore only undermine the law's coherence within a rights-framework.[168] But, that the rights-theorists' arguments are *against* a significant feature of negligence reveals that their account is at variance with the law. For example, Stevens says

> [o]nly if the duty of care is not a real duty, enabling real persons to determine ex ante what they are free to do, but rather a control device to be applied ex post in settling where losses fall, could it be thought acceptable to incorporate such policy concerns.[169]

Given judges at the highest level routinely and without question *do* incorporate policy concerns, Stevens' own analysis suggests that the later conception is more accurate. As discussed above, in the early twentieth century and prior a right-based account of negligence (or at least that fragmentary field that would coalesce into the unitary tort),[170] based principally in ideas of moral wrongdoing, may have been plausible. But given the turn to social norms and concerns since at least the middle of the twentieth century such conception fails to explain fundamental features of the law as we find it.[171]

166 ibid 1 (emphasis added).
167 ibid 136.
168 ibid particularly chs 14–15, 348–50; Beever (n 158) eg 3ff, 512ff.
169 ibid 340.
170 Ibbetson (n 29) chs 9–10.
171 ibid.

Fifth, if negligence is a vindicatory tort then the approach to damages ought to follow that in TAPS.[172] However, as we shall see, this is not the case. Damages in negligence are generally limited to compensating material loss. The approach within TAPS is markedly different.

Lastly, it does not necessarily follow that if we reject the vindicatory account and favour a compensatory account, that rights have no place in our analysis of negligence. For Stevens the law works *forwards* from general and in some sense 'prior' (non-Hohfeldian) rights which are formulated by reference to interests, such as the right to bodily integrity or property, towards legal duties in the law of negligence. But the more plausible view is that the law works *backwards* from determinations as to how responsibility for compensating loss ought to be allocated to recognising legal rights and duties which 'implement' the desired allocation, these rights and duties being different in kind to those described by Stevens and others. On this view 'legal norms [such as rights are] a valuable *by-product* of the common law's remedial business', rather than its starting point.[173] These legal rights are not defined by reference to specific interests. Rather their content incorporates the doctrinal elements of the tort, so that the legal right is one that the defendant take care, not cause the claimant loss, or compensate the claimant for fault-based loss (precisely how the right should be formulated is a matter for debate).[174] The duty owed by the defendant is correlative to this right, and mirrors the content of the right. Thus it is not uncommon to find judicial statements which suggest that any primary rights/duties in negligence are defined by reference to the law's primary 'remedial' function of allocating responsibility for compensating actual harm: '[t]he obligation which the law imposes in appropriate circumstances ... and which a claimant may enforce by legal proceedings, is an obligation to compensate the claimant against loss which was a reasonably foreseeable consequence of his carelessness'.[175]

Whether rights have a role in explaining negligence or not, the key point, which is of far more consequence for understanding negligence, is that the fundamental doctrinal features of the tort evince a primary focus on compensating for fault-based harm, and the tort's focus on loss and the defendant's responsibility make it difficult to characterise negligence as vindicatory in nature. If rights characterise negligence, they are rights which give effect to and reflect the tort's primary compensatory function. Vindicatory, rights-based theories are best viewed as a contemporary critical response to the

[172] See Stevens (n 3) ch 4.

[173] A Robertson, 'On the Function of the Law of Negligence' (2013) 33 *Oxford Journal of Legal Studies* 31, 54 (emphasis added).

[174] See, eg, NJ McBride, 'Duties of Care—Do They Really Exist?' (2004) 24 *Oxford Journal of Legal Studies* 417.

[175] *T & N Ltd* (n 111) [25].

gradual 'socialisation' of negligence, rather than accurate descriptions of what the law in fact is.

C. Torts Which Combine Vindication and Compensation: Private Nuisance

For completeness it is important to record that certain torts are chameleonic, at times performing a predominantly vindicatory function, and at other times performing a predominantly compensatory function. Private nuisance is the paradigm example.[176] Courts have long recognised a fundamental divide between two different types of private nuisance.[177] In 'nuisance by interference with enjoyment'[178] cases—the 'typical'[179] or 'classic nuisance action'[180]—where smells or noises affect enjoyment of land, the action performs a vindicatory function. In contrast, in 'nuisance by encroachment or damage'[181] cases the action is principally concerned to compensate fault-based factual losses.

In nuisance by interference cases the law's principal concern is not with factual losses which may be caused by excessive smells, noises or vibrations but with interference with the 'the plaintiff's interest in the possession and enjoyment of land';[182] 'the action is not for causing discomfort'.[183] Thus liability may be established and one may recover substantial damages for the interference with one's interest in possession and enjoyment of land in itself and regardless of whether the interference leaves one factually worse off; for example, regardless of whether the smells or noises cause pecuniary loss such as a fall in the capital value of the property,[184] or cause non-pecuniary losses such as distress or illness. Damages for the interference in itself are for an 'intangible[]'[185] damage but they are *not* for actual distress or other harm suffered by those on the property by reason of the smells etc; damages are *not* to be 'fixed by analogy with damages for loss of amenity in an action for personal injury',[186] and courts have stressed that claims in respect of physical

[176] Weir 2006 (n 1) ch 10.

[177] *St Helens Smelting Co v Tipping* (1865) 11 HL Cas 642, 650; *Coventry v Lawrence* [2014] 1 AC 822, [1], [175].

[178] *Coventry*, ibid [175] quoting MA Jones and AM Dugdale, *Clerk and Lindsell on Torts* 20th edn (Sweet and Maxwell, 2010) [20-07], [20-09].

[179] *Hunter v Canary Wharf Ltd* [1997] AC 655, 692.

[180] C Gearty, 'The Place of Private Nuisance in a Modern Law of Torts' (1989) *CLJ* 214, 217.

[181] *Coventry* (n 177) [175] quoting Jones and Dugdale (n 177) [20-07], [20-09].

[182] *Hunter* (n 179) 723, 688.

[183] ibid 706, 696, 725.

[184] ibid 706–07, 696–97.

[185] ibid 706, 696.

[186] ibid 706; *cf Coventry* (n 177) [172].

injury should be brought via negligence.[187] That liability may be established and substantial damages recovered notwithstanding that the claimant is not left factually worse off affords strong protection to and vindicates the importance of one's interest in quiet enjoyment of land in and of itself. Damage is said to be an element of the action for nuisance, however in the nuisance by interference with enjoyment cases damage is typically presumed in practice.

In contrast to the smells and noises cases, where a nuisance claim concerns physical damage to land, for example because the defendant failed to take reasonable steps to prevent a fire spreading to, or a tree from crashing onto the claimant's land, the tort performs a function akin to negligence: determining responsibility for fault-based material loss. Damages here are 'for causing damage to the land'.[188] The concern is, as in negligence, solely with 'material'[189] or 'actual'[190] loss, such as the cost of repairing damaged property or diminution in the property's capital value, and damages cannot be recovered in the absence of such loss. Further, in noise and smell cases the focus is on the claimant's interests: to establish liability the court considers whether there has been an unreasonable interference with peaceful enjoyment of land. In property damage cases the focus tends to be on the defendant's blameworthiness, the courts in effect asking whether the defendant took reasonable care to avoid causing the loss. Thus, commentators argue that property damage cases 'properly belong in the law of negligence', and that in such cases '[n]uisance may be the theoretical basis of liability, but negligence is its driving force'.[191]

Until the courts take the logical next step and shift claims for property damage into negligence, nuisance shall remain a tort which performs predominantly a compensatory function or a vindicatory function, depending on the nature of the claim.

III. VINDICATION AND DAMAGES

The overarching function of a tort, evinced by its significant doctrinal features, fundamentally shapes the approach to damages. Thus the vindicatory and protective functions of the TAPS carry through to the approach to damages within these torts, just as the compensatory function of negligence underpins the approach to damages for that tort. As Lord Reed observed in *AIB*, 'the loss resulting from a breach of duty has to be measured according

[187] ibid 687–88, 692, 696, 707; FH Newark, 'The Boundaries of Nuisance' (1949) 65 *LQR* 480.
[188] ibid 705–06, 695.
[189] *Tipping* (n 177) 650–51.
[190] *Coventry* (n 177) [1].
[191] Gearty (n 180) 217.

to legal rules, and different rules apply to the breach of different obligations' which reflect the distinctive 'nature' of the obligations breached.[192]

For compensatory torts damages are generally limited to compensatory damages for factual losses, that is the negative pecuniary, psychological, emotional or physical effects suffered by the claimant as a result of the defendant's tortious conduct. In contrast and importantly, a distinctive feature of vindicatory torts is that in addition to damages for factual loss, one may also recover substantial compensatory damages for the wrongful interference with one's protected interest in and of itself. In other words, the wrong will sound in damages, regardless of whether the claimant has suffered factual harm in consequence. Such damages are assessed objectively and redress a damage that is 'normative' in nature, recognition of this head of damage giving effect to the underlying vindicatory and protective functions of the law. In this context even though 'there may be no actual loss' 'the law takes the view as a matter of policy that the claimants if they prove their claims are entitled to substantial compensation for the mere invasion of their rights'.[193]

In addition to the distinctive approach to compensatory damages, within vindicatory torts a wider range of damages, including nominal and exemplary damages, is available compared to other torts, so as to ensure strong protection of basic interests and which vindicate the importance of those interests.

That there is internal coherence as between substantive law and remedies is consonant with Birks' insight that the full explanation for why certain consequences follow wrongs 'has to be completed in every case from the policies and values underlying the recognition of the primary duty'.[194]

A. Range of Damages

In negligence only one form of damages has been available traditionally: compensatory damages. This reflects the tort's primary function. As a result of the House of Lords' decision in *Kuddus* exemplary damages are now available in theory for any action, whereas their availability had previously been restricted to certain actions, that set not including compensatory torts such as negligence.[195] Despite this decision such damages have never been awarded for negligence and there are voices opposing their award.[196]

[192] *AIB Group Plc v Mark Redler & Co Solicitors* [2014] 3 WLR 1367, [92].

[193] *Devenish Nutrition Ltd v Sanofi-Aventis SA* [2009] Ch 390, [36].

[194] P Birks, 'The Concept of a Civil Wrong' in DG Owen (ed), *Philosophical Foundations of Tort Law* (Clarendon Press, 1995) 51.

[195] *Kuddus v Chief Constable Leicestershire Constabulary* [2001] 2 WLR 1789.

[196] ibid [122].

Similarly, while such damages are now theoretically available for misfeasance in public office, which is properly categorised as a compensatory tort, it will be rare for a court to make an award given dicta in *Watkins* that the tort's function is compensation not punishment, and that exemplary awards should be 'confine[d] ... very closely indeed'.[197]

In contrast a range of damages have been available traditionally and are awarded regularly for vindicatory torts. In addition to compensatory damages (considered below), non-compensatory damages are available to remedy wrongful interferences with basic interests, such as nominal damages and exemplary damages.

Nominal damages are peculiar to TAPS. Their availability to mark even a fleeting and miniscule interference, coupled with the fact they are unique to the TAPS, attests to the relative importance of the protected interests.

The 'micro' goal of exemplary damages is punishment, such damages responding to and sanctioning outrageous conduct by the defendant in perpetrating a tort. However, on a 'macro' level such damages serve protective and vindicatory functions. First, that significant awards may be made against defendants who interfere with protected interests in an outrageous manner, serves to afford those interests significant protection against such interference. Second, that the civil law takes the exceptional step of punishing a defendant for the manner of their interference with the claimant's interests, thus expressing 'vigorous disapproval'[198] of the defendant's conduct, signals the importance of the protected interests and reinforces that they ought to be afforded the utmost respect. Third, that such damages have traditionally not been available and/or their availability is tightly circumscribed for some torts whereas they have long been available and are freely awarded for the TAPS reinforces the importance of the interests protected by the TAPS. Exemplary damages have a long tradition within TAPS, being 'well established in the torts of defamation, false imprisonment and trespass to property'.[199] Where awarded for trespassory torts in particular such awards have long played a fundamental role in checking public power,[200] as evidenced by the first category of *Rookes* which recognises unconstitutional, arbitrary or oppressive conduct by public officials as one category of case in which exemplary damages may be awarded.[201] Exemplary damages

[197] *Watkins* (n 7) [26], [32], [81]. It is difficult to find modern misfeasance in public office cases where exemplary damages have been awarded: M Aronson, 'Misfeasance in Public Office: A Very Peculiar Tort' (2011) 35 *Melbourne University Law Review* 1, 13.

[198] *Rowlands v Chief Constable of Merseyside Police* [2007] 1 WLR 1065, [42].

[199] H McGregor, *McGregor on Damages* 19th edn (Sweet and Maxwell, 2014) [13-011].

[200] C Harlow, 'A Punitive Role for Tort Law?' in L Pearson et al (eds), *Administrative Law in a Changing State* (Hart Publishing, 2008).

[201] *Rookes v Barnard* [1964] AC 1129, 1226–28.

continue to play an important role within these torts and in claims against public defendants, being awarded on a not infrequent basis.

Although formally compensatory in nature, aggravated damages are not available for the compensatory tort of negligence[202] but are available for the TAPS.[203] As is discussed further below (section III.C.vi), their availability in TAPS reflects the special affront one may justifiably feel at a high-handed interference with one's most basic interests.

It had been mooted that a novel head of 'vindicatory' damages, awarded in a series of Privy Council appeals from the Caribbean for breaches of constitutional rights,[204] may be available for some TAPS.[205] However, in the wake of the Supreme Court decision in *Lumba* it seems such awards are unlikely to be recognised, at least in the near future, albeit a minority of the Court favoured recognising such awards.[206] This head of damages is discussed in detail in chapter 3, where it is argued that the Supreme Court was right to reject the availability of such awards.[207] Nonetheless, that such damages have been mooted specifically in the context of torts such as battery, assault and false imprisonment,[208] is indicative of the distinctive nature and concerns of these torts.

Lastly, with the rise of the restitution 'movement' it has increasingly been suggested—principally by restitution scholars—that gain-based damages are available for torts.[209] As discussed below, the claims are, at least in some respects, highly controversial and unconvincing. However, significantly, the actions for which such damages are generally said to be available are all vindicatory in nature, such as trespass to land and goods, conversion and private nuisance.[210] If the claims made by restitution scholars were correct this would reinforce the claim made here that where the law is performing a vindicatory and protective role, a range of remedies are available to a claimant to ensure their basic interests are strongly protected and vindicated at the remedial stage.

202 *Kralj v McGrath* [1986] 1 All ER 54, 60–61; *AB v South West Water Services Ltd* [1993] QB 507, 528; *cf Ashley* (n 2) [102].

203 See text to n 362 below.

204 See *Ramanoop* (n 4) [18]–[19]; *Merson* (n 8) [17]–[18].

205 *Ashley* (n 2) [22], [28]–[29].

206 *Lumba* (n 2).

207 See ch 3.II.A.iv.

208 *Ashley* (n 2) (battery and assault); *Lumba* (n 2) (false imprisonment).

209 eg A Burrows, *Remedies for Torts and Breach of Contract* 3rd edn (OUP, 2004) 375–95; J Edelman, *Gain-Based Damages* (Hart Publishing, 2002) ch 4; G Virgo, *Principles of the Law of Restitution* 2nd edn (OUP, 2006) ch 16.

210 That all of these torts protect proprietary interests suggests that if gain-based awards are available, they respond to the distinctive qualities of such interests. However, this does not detract from the claim that their availability reflects a vindicatory rationale, only that the means by which such interests are vindicated is distinctive, given the nature of those interests.

B. Compensatory Damages and Vindication

Compensation and vindication are conceptually distinct functions. Compensation offers 'a monetary equivalent of what has been lost as a result of a breach of duty',[211] whereas vindication entails reinforcing the importance of particular interests. Nonetheless the two functions can intertwine, and we see important differences between the nature of compensatory awards within negligence, where the focus is generally upon compensating factual harms, and within the TAPS. We might put it thus: while on a 'micro' level compensatory damages perform a compensatory function within the TAPS, the 'macro' vindicatory function of the law explains the distinctive heads of damage that are recoverable, the approach to recoverability, and to quantification. In an iconic article Fuller and Purdue said: 'it is impossible to separate the law of contract damages from the larger body of motives and policies which constitutes the general law of contracts'.[212] So too for torts.

An important feature of the approach to damages within the TAPS is that a claimant can recover damages for the 'injury' to his protected interest in and of itself, whether it be the interest in liberty, reputation, corporeal integrity or exclusive possession of land, regardless of the emotional, psychological, physical or financial effects the particular claimant suffers in consequence of the wrong. That an interference with the protected interest is in itself recognised as a form of damage is explicable by reference to the vindicatory and protective aims of the law: in 'constructing' this form of damage the law is seeking an end, to protect basic interests and to attest to and reinforce their importance and inherent worth. The status within the legal order and inherent value of the interests are reinforced by recognising an invasion of those interests as a harm in itself and providing for monetary redress wherever those interests are wrongfully interfered with regardless of whether the interference has any negative effects on the claimant, such as loss of earnings or mental suffering, and notwithstanding whether the claimant can be said to have suffered any 'material', 'special', or 'actionable' damage or loss. Affording monetary redress wherever protected interests are wrongfully interfered with affords those interests strong legal protection. The degree to which these damages are imbued with the law's vindicatory function has even led some judges to proclaim that they are purely vindicatory, though it is clear from authority that such damages are consistently categorised as compensatory.[213] Because recognition of such damage gives

[211] *AIB* (n 192) [136].

[212] LL Fuller and WR Purdue, 'The Reliance Interest in Contract Damages' (1936) 46 *Yale Law Journal* 52, 53.

[213] eg *Ruddock* (n 90) [141]; *Lumba* (n 2) [217]; see also the ambiguous dicta in *Ashley* (n 2) [22].

direct effect to the primary functions of the TAPS, and in order to mark the conceptual distinction between such damage, which exists solely on the legal plane, and other forms of damage which correspond with real-world effects, we might describe such damage as 'normative' in nature.[214] Others characterise such damages differently.[215] However, what is significant is that however such damages are characterised it is clear that within TAPS damages in the absence of actual loss are available and regularly awarded for the wrongful interference in itself.

In contrast, compensatory damages other than for factual effects are not available in negligence in principle. Indeed, it would make little sense if they were available given fundamental features of negligence tell against a vindicatory focus, including that factual loss is a prerequisite to founding an action in the first place.[216] Compensatory damages within this context are focused on factual losses, ie the specific and negative effects suffered by the claimant, physically, psychologically or financially, in consequence of the defendant's careless conduct. These might include non-pecuniary effects such as pain, suffering, mental distress and anxiety (but in general only if linked to some form of physical injury), or financial effects such as medical expenses, lost earnings, diminution in the value of property, or the cost of repairing property damage. Whereas in battery a claimant may recover substantial damages for the interference with physical integrity in itself despite suffering no loss of amenity, distress, psychological harm or pecuniary loss, within negligence only damages for those consequential factual effects of the interference with the person are recoverable. The position is captured by the following judicial statement of principle:

> [T]he general approach to damages in [negligence] is to compensate the plaintiff for the loss that she has *actually* suffered, so far as it is possible to do so, by the award of monetary compensation and *not* to treat those damages as being a matter which reflects the degree of negligence or breach of duty of the defendant ... What I am saying is no more than that what the court has to do is to judge the *effect* on the particular plaintiff of what happened to her. If the situation is one where the *consequences* are such that she feels able to make light of what has happened, then her loss is less than it will be where the situation is one where the *impact* of what has happened is accentuated because of the additional stress which the mother is undergoing at that time.[217]

[214] This idea is not to be equated with the idea of normative loss within corrective justice theories: Weinrib (n 38) ch 5.

[215] See, eg, Stevens (n 3) ch 4 (damages are 'substitutive' for rights); Weir 2004 (n 1) 7, 18 (such damages are a 'sanction'). For discussion of why the normative damage thesis should be preferred see: JNE Varuhas, 'The Concept of "Vindication" in the Law of Torts: Rights, Interests and Damages' (2014) 34 *Oxford Journal of Legal Studies* 253, 270–75.

[216] *Sephton* (n 110) [37] ('Until [the claimant] has suffered damage he cannot sue for damages').

[217] *Kralj* (n 202) 61 (emphasis added).

There are occasionally cases in which the law expressly sanctions departures from orthodoxy in negligence. But that these are exceptions and exceptional only goes to prove the general rule. Some of these ad hoc deviations are explicable as 'vindicatory impulses': situations where the law is anxious to ensure that an interference with a basic interest does not go without remedy.[218] For example, in *Rees* the Law Lords held, by a four to three majority, that where a sterilisation procedure is carried out negligently, with the result that a child is born, the parents are barred on policy grounds from recovering the cost of raising the unexpected child, but can recover: (1) damages for pain and suffering associated with pregnancy and birth, and medical expenses; and (2) a conventional sum of £15,000 for the 'injury' to their autonomy suffered as a result of not being able to live their lives as they had planned, the majority judges reasoning that such award ought to be available to mark the 'legal wrong'.[219] It is difficult to explain the conventional award as compensating for factual loss,[220] particularly as it does not vary with the particular claimant. One explanation is that it compensates for the interference with one's autonomy interest, quantum being held constant on the basis that normative damage is assessed objectively (that is, it does not vary with the circumstances of the claimant or how much they subjectively value their autonomy) and the nature and degree of the interference is roughly analogous in each case of failed sterilisation resulting in unexpected birth. Further their Lordships emphasised the basic nature of the interest in autonomy; for example Lord Millett, justifying the *sui generis* award, emphasised that autonomy is 'an aspect of human dignity, which is increasingly being regarded as an important human right which should be protected by the law'.[221] Thus we *may* have an example of normative damage in negligence. *But* both majority and minority Judges stated expressly that this approach deviated from the orthodox approach to damages in negligence[222]—the approach being described as 'radical', 'heterodox',[223] and 'contrary to principle'[224]—as well as observing that the decision was highly controversial, concerning an extraordinarily difficult issue which raises complex questions of policy and morality, upon which courts in different jurisdictions have reached different conclusions.[225] The decision does

[218] As discussed above, the law has also sanctioned departures from orthodoxy in respect of elements of the action itself, such as causation: eg *Chester* (n 2). Note that one Law Lord in *Chester* also considered making an award for the interference with the autonomy interest in itself: [34].

[219] *Rees v Darlington Memorial Hospital NHS Trust* [2004] 1 AC 309.

[220] Lord Bingham expressly stated that the award was not compensatory (ibid [8]), although Lord Millett took a different view: ibid [123]–[125], and see [148].

[221] ibid [123].

[222] ibid [4], [12], [45], [73], [87], [98], [104], [133]–[134], [138].

[223] ibid [43], [45].

[224] ibid [73].

[225] ibid [2]–[7], [11], [14]–[16], [29], [32]–[33], [39], [68], [103], [105].

not represent the general approach to damages in negligence; it represents a judicially acknowledged deviation from that approach in a hard case.

Some, principally those who favour a vindicatory account of negligence, have claimed that damages akin to normative damages are available more generally within negligence.[226] It is beyond the scope of this book to analyse such claims in depth. I have analysed them elsewhere, finding them to suffer from the 'capital mistake' Sherlock Holmes warned against—theories getting ahead of data.[227] To establish these claims commentators often end up overreaching in their analysis and conflating losses that can readily be explained as factual losses with normative damage. Or these theorists latch on to idiosyncratic lines of authority, such as the failed sterilisation cases. No doubt there are some pockets of negligence in which compensatory orthodoxy is challenged. For present purposes it suffices to observe that such phenomena do not represent the mainstream, and it is a grave error to extrapolate general propositions from examples which are marginal, specific to peculiar factual matrices, highly controversial, and which the courts acknowledge are heterodox. Even Stevens, a proponent of a rights-based or vindicatory conception of negligence, appears to acknowledge this (seemingly contradicting other claims he makes regarding damages in negligence): 'by far and away the most common remedial response [in negligence] is compensation for loss'.[228]

In any case, if damages for negligence are vindicatory in nature, or the tort generally can—contrary to orthodox understandings—be shown to perform a primarily vindicatory function (I do not accept this), it does not undermine this book's central argument, which rests on an analogy between obligations in human rights law and the TAPS, and indeed it may enhance my argument. Those who propound a vindicatory conception of negligence do not refute that the TAPS are vindicatory torts. Rather they wish to extend the vindicatory account across the law of torts.

C. Compensatory Damages within Torts Actionable Per Se

Thus, the golden thread which unites the approach to compensatory damages across the TAPS is that damages for normative damage are in general recoverable. That substantial damages are awarded routinely for the interference with the protected interest in itself and in the absence of factual loss serves to afford those interests strong protection and reinforces their relative importance and inherent value, such that there is internal coherence as

[226] Stevens (n 3) 72–78.
[227] Varuhas (n 215) 271–75.
[228] Stevens (n 3) 301. Contrast ch 4 of the same work.

between the vindicatory nature of the substantive obligations and remedies. Of course relevant factual damage suffered in consequence of a wrongful interference, including non-pecuniary losses such as mental distress or humiliation, and pecuniary losses such as lost earnings or medical expenses, is also recoverable, so that the claimant is placed in a position as if the wrong had not occurred and is left no worse off as a result of the wrong.

i. Overview

Thus, in false imprisonment a claimant can recover compensatory damages for 'loss of liberty' in and of itself.[229] On top of damages for the interference with liberty the claimant may recover pecuniary losses such as lost wages for the period of the wrongful imprisonment. Other non-pecuniary losses are recoverable such as humiliation and distress but are conceptually separate from normative damage; they are not inherent in the wrongful interference but consequential losses which '*result from* the loss of liberty',[230] with recovery dependent on the actual emotional effects experienced by the claimant. Thus the normative head of 'deprivation of liberty' 'is not an "impairment of a person's physical or mental condition"', and a damages claim in respect of such deprivation 'is not a "claim for personal injury damages"'.[231] As Giliker says of the approach in false imprisonment:

> [d]istress is not a necessary ingredient: the primary element is the loss of personal liberty. A person may therefore be compensated without being aware of the fact of his or her imprisonment, for example if drunk, asleep or mentally incapable. This again highlights the dependant nature of [damages for mental distress].[232]

Such remedial approach is consonant with the principal concern of the substantive obligations with the deprivation of liberty itself, rather than the claimant's levels of 'comfort or discomfort':[233] 'The gist of the action of false imprisonment is the mere imprisonment'.[234]

[229] eg *R v Governor of Brockhill Prison, ex p Evans (No 2)* [1999] QB 1043, 1060; McGregor (n 199) [40-012].

[230] *Evans* ibid (emphasis added).

[231] *NSW v Williamson* (2012) 248 CLR 417, [34]; *Kerman v City of New York* 374 F 3d 93 (2004).

[232] P Giliker, 'A "New" Head of Damages: Damages for Mental Distress in the English Law of Torts' (2000) 20 *Legal Studies* 19, 27 (regarding battery see: Trindade (n 70) 227). Some suggest only nominal damages are available where the claimant was unaware of their confinement: *Murray* (n 51) 529; *R v Bournewood Community and Mental Health NHS Trust, ex p L* [1998] 2 WLR 764, 778. Given loss of liberty in itself is an established head, and the gist of the action is interference with liberty in itself, the better view is damages should be more than nominal albeit 'damages might be diminished if the plaintiff was unconscious' as no negative emotional effects will have been suffered: *Weldon* (n 71) 469; *Meering* (n 78) 53–54.

[233] *Hague* (n 71) 178.

[234] *Carnegie v State of Victoria* (14 September 1989) unreported; SC Vic no 998 of 1976, 4.

In defamation the claimant can recover damages for damage to his interest in reputation in itself.[235] Consequential losses are also recoverable such as 'distress, hurt and humiliation which the defamatory publication has caused',[236] these emotional effects varying from one person to the next,[237] and proven pecuniary losses. Thus on the one hand damages respond to the 'seriousness of the [defamatory] allegation' (normative damage) and on the other 'its direct impact on [the claimant]' (consequential damage).[238] Peculiar to defamation, there is an extra 'vindicatory' element to damages: awards may be increased to vindicate the claimant's 'good name'.[239] This element can be rationalised within the normative damage hypothesis:[240] for damages to fully redress damage to the claimant's reputational interest, quantum must be sufficient to convince a reasonable bystander that the statements made about him were baseless.[241]

Although within battery it is difficult to identify a standalone head of damage which corresponds with normative injury, more than nominal damages (although often low in quantum, but sometimes sizeable)[242] have been awarded where a claimant is subject to unwanted touching and thereby suffers an interference with his physical integrity, even though he suffers no pain, suffering, loss of amenity or pecuniary loss.[243] In *Watkins* Lord Walker observed that the 'most trifling and transient physical assault' would give a claimant an action 'sounding in damages (and if appropriate aggravated or exemplary damages)'.[244]

Substantial damages are recoverable in trespass to land for mere wrongful interference with an individual's interest in exclusive possession; 'the damages represent the intrinsic value of [the] right [to exclusive possession]',[245] while the remedial approach reflects the 'policy of the law' which 'is to

[235] See text to n 267 onwards.

[236] *John v MGN Ltd* [1997] QB 586, 607–08.

[237] *McCarey v Associated Newspapers Ltd (No 2)* [1965] 2 QB 86, 108.

[238] *Cairns* (n 34) [41].

[239] *John* (n 236) 607; *Jameel v The Wall Street Journal Europe Sprl* [2004] 2 All ER 92, [7]; *McCarey* (n 237) 105, 107.

[240] Witzleb and Carroll (n 2) 33–35 argue in most tort contexts vindication is concerned with affirming the claimant's rights, but has a different meaning in defamation: to clear the individual's name in the eyes of others. This is confusing. Where the right is in respect of reputation—which is fundamentally about the way one is perceived by others—clearing the claimant's name entails affirmation of the right.

[241] *Broome* (n 34) 1071; *Rantzen v MGN Ltd* [1994] QB 670, 695–96.

[242] *Hurst v Picture Theatres Ltd* [1915] 1 KB 1. £150 (a substantial award at the time) for a non-violent battery causing no injury. The award was for the battery in itself—'for the assault which was committed upon him'—and also for the indignity of the battery to the claimant 'as a gentleman'.

[243] It is uncommon to find battery cases litigated absent physical injury or consequential losses. However, there are examples where substantial damages have been awarded: *Hurst*, ibid; *Pelling v Johnson* [2004] EWHC 492; *Shah v Gale* [2005] EWHC 1087, [52]; *Forde* (n 74); *Loudon v Ryder* [1953] QB 202; *B v NHS Hospital Trust* [2002] 2 All ER 449, [99].

[244] *Watkins* (n 7) [68].

[245] Pearce and Halson (n 2) 88–91.

protect the possession of property and the privacy and security of the occupier'.[246] The Privy Council has observed that damages are 'readily awarded at common law for the invasion of rights to tangible moveable or immoveable property', and acknowledged the availability of 'compensatory damages which exceed the actual financial loss caused to the claimant by an actionable breach of duty'.[247] In trespass 'loss' has a wider meaning than simply being left materially worse off:[248]

> It is an established principle ... that a person who has wrongfully used another's property without causing the latter any pecuniary loss may still be liable ... for more than nominal damages. In general, he is liable to pay, as damages, a reasonable sum for the wrongful use he has made of the other's property. The law has reached this conclusion by giving to the concept of loss or damage ... a wider meaning than merely financial loss calculated by comparing the property owner's financial position after the wrongdoing with what it would have been had the wrongdoing never occurred. Furthermore, in such a case it is no answer for the wrongdoer to show that the property owner would probably not have used the property himself had the wrongdoer not done so. In *The Mediana* [1900] AC 113, 117, Earl of Halsbury LC made the famous observation that a defendant who had deprived the plaintiff of one of the chairs in his room for 12 months could not diminish the damages by showing that the plaintiff did not usually sit upon that chair or that there were plenty of other chairs in the room.

Such damages have a venerable history. Holt CJ in the 1703 decision in *Ashby*, after observing that 'a damage is not merely pecuniary, but an injury imports a damage, when a man is thereby hindred of his right' said, 'a man shall have an action against another for riding over his ground, though it do him no damage; for it is an invasion of his property, and the other has no right to come there'.[249] Tellingly, his other examples of where 'injury imports a damage, though it does not cost the party one farthing' included interference with reputation and physical integrity.[250] In the 1814 decision in *Merest v Harvey* Gibbs CJ observed that substantial *compensation* is available for a brief, well-behaved trespass absent any real damage:

> Suppose a gentleman has a paved walk ... before his window, and that a man intrudes and walks up and down before the window of his house, and looks in while the owner is at dinner, is the trespasser to be permitted to say, 'here is a halfpenny for you, which is the full extent of all the mischief I have done?' Would that be a compensation? I cannot say that it would be.[251]

[246] *Plenty v Dillon* (1991) 171 CLR 635, 647.
[247] *Pell Frischmann Engineering Ltd v Bow Valley Iran Ltd* [2011] 1 WLR 2370, [46], [48].
[248] *Stoke-on-Trent City Council v W & J Wass Ltd* [1988] 1 WLR 1406, 1416.
[249] *Ashby v White* (1703) 2 Lord Raymond 938, 955.
[250] ibid.
[251] (1814) 5 Taunt 442, 443 (In *Merest* itself the defendant trod on the claimant's grass, and could therefore be said to have caused minor factual damage). See also *Loudon* (n 243): £1,500 for trespass to land (not being 'user' damages), the only factual damage being shattering of a small window.

Following on from the line of 'wayleave'[252] cases decided through the nineteenth century, in 1896 it was held that 'if one man runs trucks on rails over another man's land it does not do any harm whatever, and there is no pecuniary damage' but the claimant may still recover substantial damages for the reason that the defendant has made use of his land;[253] '[t]he principle is that a trespasser shall not be allowed to make use of another person's land without in some way compensating that other person for that user'.[254] Forty years on it was held that 'the trespass or interference with the right imports damage so long as it is something which the law can fix upon as being sufficiently substantial [ie not *de minimus*] to constitute an interference'.[255] The tradition continues today:

> True it is that the entry itself caused no damage to the appellant's land. But the purpose of an action for trespass to land is not merely to compensate the plaintiff for damage to the land. That action also serves the purpose of vindicating the plaintiff's right to the exclusive use and occupation of his or her land ... The appellant is entitled to have his right of property vindicated by a substantial award of damages.[256]

It should be noted that despite damages for trespass to land being classified as compensatory for nearly their entire history, under the influence of restitution theorists some courts have, in recent times, classified user damages as restitutionary,[257] having elements of both restitution and compensation,[258] or simply *sui generis*.[259] Elsewhere I have considered and rejected this restitutionary analysis, and those interested in such matters are directed to that work.[260] For present purposes it suffices to say that the catalyst for the search for alternative, gain-based explanations was that such damages are difficult to conceptualise as compensatory for actual loss. However, there is no need for recourse to explanations that deviate from longstanding compensatory orthodoxy in tort once it is recognised that 'loss' has a wider meaning than factual loss within vindicatory actions.

[252] eg *Martin v Porter* (1839) 5 M & W 351; *Phillips v Homfray (No 1)* (1870–71) LR 6 Ch App 770.

[253] *Whitwham v Westminster Brymbo Coal and Coke Company* [1896] 2 Ch 538, 542.

[254] ibid 543.

[255] *Ely Beet* (n 45) 353.

[256] *Plenty* (n 246) 654–55. See also *Swordheath Properties Ltd v Tabet* [1979] 1 WLR 285; *Enfield LBC v Outdoor Plus Ltd* [2012] EWCA Civ 608; *Strand Electric and Engineering Co Ltd v Brisford Entertainments Ltd* [1952] QB 246; *Penarth Dock Company v Pounds* [1963] 1 Lloyd's Rep 359; *Shi v Jiangsu Native Produce Import and Export Corp* [2009] EWCA Civ 1582; *Inverugie Investments Ltd v Hackett* [1995] 1 WLR 713.

[257] eg *MOD v Ashman* (1993) 25 HLR 513.

[258] eg *Inverugie* (n 256) 718.

[259] See the ambiguous dicta in *A-G v Blake* [2001] 1 AC 268, 279.

[260] Varuhas (n 215) 284–89.

ii. Normative Damage Inherent in the Interference

Normative damage can never be too remote, being inherent in the wrong.[261] It necessarily follows that if someone is falsely imprisoned, they suffer damage to their liberty interest: the loss of liberty is 'inseparable from the detention itself'.[262] Courts have expressed this idea by holding that damages are de jure 'presumed', or de facto assuming that the interference entails damage. Indeed substantial damages for the interference with underlying interests are known as 'presumed general damages' in the United States.[263] In the leading English authority of *Ratcliffe* the Court observed that the law 'implies' general damage 'in every breach of contract and every infringement of an absolute right'; 'In all such cases the law presumes that some damage will flow in the ordinary course of things from the mere invasion of the plaintiff's rights'.[264] This contrasts with the position within torts actionable only upon proof of factual loss: in this context 'it is the damage done that is the wrong; and the expression "special damage," when used of this damage, denotes the actual and temporal loss which has, in fact, occurred'.[265] Similarly, in *Forster* Stephenson LJ observed, the other Judges concurring, that '[w]hereas damage is presumed in trespass and libel, it is not presumed in negligence and has to be proved'.[266]

Thus, damage is presumed in defamation.[267] This is generally formulated as a formal rebuttable presumption. Although, it is slightly misleading to speak of a 'presumption' given a libellous statement is by definition one that damages an individual's interest in his reputation. It is important to be precise: what is damaged is not one's 'real-world' reputation,[268] for example what the greengrocer in the Market Square actually thinks of you, but one's *interest in* one's reputation. This is reflected in the legal position that the claimant does not have to prove that members of civil society have in fact read the publication and now think less of him. All he need establish is that the publication would *tend* to lead *right-thinking people* to think less of him.[269] The inquiry is objective; in theory one may prove defamation and recover substantial damages despite the reality that few people read the publication, and those that did in fact thought more highly of the claimant in consequence. Thus, when it comes to damages it may be misleading to

[261] See similarly Stevens (n 3) 60.

[262] *Kerman* (n 231) 130.

[263] JC Love, 'Presumed General Compensatory Damages in Constitutional Tort Litigation' (1992) 49 *Washington & Lee Law Review* 67.

[264] *Ratcliffe v Evans* [1892] 2 QB 524, 528; *Ely Beet* (n 45) 350–51.

[265] ibid.

[266] *Forster v Outred & Co* [1982] 1 WLR 86, 94.

[267] *Tripp v Thomas* (1824) 3 B & C 427; *Ley v Hamilton* (1935) 153 LT 384.

[268] Whether an individual has '*a* reputation' is questionable in itself given how we are perceived varies from one person to the next.

[269] *Sim v Stretch* [1936] 2 All ER 1237, 1240.

say damages compensate for 'damage to reputation';[270] more accurate is Windeyer J's oft-cited statement, that the claimant 'gets damages because he was *injured in his reputation*, that is simply because he was publically defamed'.[271] Or as the English courts have put it, '[d]efamation constitutes an injury to reputation' and such injury 'will always sound in damages'.[272]

For trespass to land 'compensation' is awarded 'for the bare possession wrongfully taken and held of the land itself';[273] 'once a plaintiff obtains a verdict in an action for damages, he or she is entitled to an award of damages'.[274] Thus, if X makes 'use' of Y's land without permission and thereby commits a trespass, X may recover substantial damages from Y—referred to as 'user damages'—traditionally assessed according to the objective measure of what would have been a reasonable fee for use.[275] Such damages are recoverable regardless of whether the claimant could or would have otherwise been able to lease or use the land in the absence of the trespasser, so that damages are awarded even where the trespass does not leave the claimant out of pocket relative to the position they would have been in but for the wrong.[276] Because of this the claimant, in order to recover, need not adduce evidence that he could or would have otherwise put the land to use.[277] These features of damages in trespass are the clearest indication possible that such damages do not compensate for actual damage. In determining a claim for user damages it is not relevant to consider what the claimant's actual position might have been but for the wrong, because any wrongful interference with one's interest in exclusive possession of land entails normative damage to that interest, which the law compensates as of course:

> the courts have awarded damages (commonly called 'user damages') by reference to the fair value of a right of which the defendant has wrongly deprived the claimant, and these awards have been made even if the claimant would not himself have sought to use that right and so incurred no loss.[278]

Just as one's reputational interest is by definition injured by a libel, and one's interest in exclusive possession is by definition injured by a trespass, so a wrongful imprisonment will ipso facto injure one's liberty interest.[279]

[270] eg *John* (n 236) 60.
[271] *Uren v John Fairfax & Sons Pty Ltd* (1966) 117 CLR 118, 150 (emphasis added).
[272] *Jameel* (n 44) [93], [119]; *Broome* (n 34) 1071.
[273] *Phillips v Homfray (No 2)* (1883) LR 24 ChD 439, 455.
[274] *Plenty* (n 246) 645, 654–55.
[275] See *Wass* (n 248) and those cases cited in n 256 above.
[276] *Swordheath* (n 256) 288; *Inverugie* (n 256) 717; *Wass* (n 248) 1416.
[277] *Swordheath* (n 256); *Inverugie* (n 256).
[278] *Devenish* (n 193) [68].
[279] See, eg, the following cases, which demonstrate the practice that damages follow wrongful imprisonment as of course: *Thompson v Commissioner of the Metropolis* [1998] QB 498 (for an orthodox application of the guidance therein see, eg: *R (Shaw) v SOSHD* [2013] EWHC 42, [43]); *Evans* (n 229) 1060.

Thus courts have held that they will 'normally grant compensation' for false imprisonment,[280] 'for false imprisonment there should *always* be an award of damages based on normal compensatory principles',[281] that one shall be 'entitled' 'to mandatory compensation'[282] for false imprisonment, that loss of liberty is 'inherent in the detention', and that false imprisonment 'accordingly, and without more' will 'entitl[e] [the claimant] to damages for the period of their unlawful detention'.[283] Courts have also emphasised that it is important that 'sufficient damages' should follow a wrongful imprisonment 'in order to give reality to the protection afforded by the law' to personal freedom,[284] and that 'the law should be able to vindicate in some way' the right not to be confined 'irrespective of whether compensatable harm has been suffered or the conduct of the authorities has been so egregious as to merit exemplary damages'.[285] At the highest appellate level judges have considered an entitlement to substantial damages to follow from unjustifiable imprisonment as a matter of course.[286]

This follows from earlier practice. In the past, where false imprisonment was proven, it was for a jury to assess damages, with damages said to be 'at large', there being little question that in every case of proven false imprisonment or battery there was an injury to be compensated, and juries would as a matter of course make substantial (more than nominal) awards for false imprisonment,[287] as for battery. When higher courts scrutinised jury awards they would typically consider a number of concerns which bore on quantum, including the simple 'fact of the plaintiff's being put into confinement'.[288] Dicey, writing at the end of the nineteenth century records prevailing practice:

> if … *X* interferes unlawfully to however slight a degree with the personal liberty of *A*, the offender exposes himself to proceedings in a court of law, and the sufferer, if he can enlist the sympathies of a jury, may recover heavy damages for the injury which he has or is supposed to have suffered. The law of England protects the right to personal liberty, as also every other legal right, against every kind of infringement, and gives the same kind of redress (I do not mean, of course, inflicts the same degree of punishment or penalty) for the pettiest as for the gravest invasions of personal freedom. This seems to us so much a matter of course as hardly to call for observation …[289]

280 *Lumba* (n 2) [197].

281 *Iqbal* (n 72) [83] (emphasis added); *Karagozlu v Commissioner of the Metropolis* [2007] 1 WLR 1881, [25].

282 *ID* (n 75) [109], [120]–[121].

283 *R (Lumba) v SOSHD* [2008] EWHC 3166, [130].

284 *Dumbell v Roberts* [1944] 1 All ER 326, 329.

285 *Lumba* (n 2) [217].

286 eg *Christie* (n 94) 603, and see discussion of *Lumba* below.

287 A good example is *Edgell v Francis* (1840) 1 Man & G 222 (£200—a very substantial award for 1840—awarded for one night in prison as 'fair compensation').

288 ibid 226–27.

289 AV Dicey, *Lectures Introductory to the Law of the Constitution* (MacMillan, 1885) 224–25. The same passage appears in the 10th edition: Dicey (n 46) 211–12.

Dicey observed that the principle, which judges adhered to strictly, that one could mount an action and recover substantial damages for a wrongful interference with liberty, whether that interference was serious or 'trifling', was one of

> two maxims or principles which underlie the whole law of the constitution, and the maintenance of which has gone a great way both to ensure the supremacy of the law of the land and ultimately to curb the arbitrariness of the Crown.[290]

Blackstone described similar practice, saying that for assault a person '*shall* recover damages as a compensation for the injury' 'though no actual suffering is proved', for battery 'the jury *will* give adequate damages',[291] and for the 'injury of false imprisonment' one '*shall* recover damages'.[292] Damages follow as of course from the finding of wrong.

iii. The Supreme Court Decision in Lumba*: Deviation from Orthodoxy*

Unfortunately the recent Supreme Court case of *Lumba* has muddied waters which have long been clear, by deviating from the venerable orthodoxy that substantial damages follow false imprisonment as of course. A majority held that compensatory damages should not be awarded where an individual whose liberty had been interfered with without lawful excuse would nonetheless have inevitably been subject to the same imprisonment had the defendant's statutory powers to detain been exercised lawfully. Regrettably the majority of the judgments are notable for the absence of any serious engagement with the traditional approach to damages. The decision is problematic in that it undermines the vindicatory function of false imprisonment at the remedial stage. Because the decision poses a challenge to orthodoxy it is important to consider why the decision is problematic, and what caused the Court to go off-track, not least so that this deviation may be corrected in future.

To understand this error one must begin by recognising that the tort is concerned to reinforce the importance of liberty and to afford that interest strong protection from outside interference. In the light of these goals the law starts from the premise that individuals ought to be free;[293] that is, a position in which one's interest in liberty is pristine and inviolate. This is reflected in the proposition that: 'in English law every imprisonment is prima facie unlawful and … it is for a person directing imprisonment to

[290] ibid 223 (1st edn); 210 (10th edn).

[291] W Blackstone, *Commentaries on the Laws of England* (Clarendon, 1765–1769) Book III, 120–21 (emphasis added).

[292] ibid Book III, 138 (emphasis added).

[293] eg *Christie* (n 94) 585, 587, 588; O'Sullivan (n 19) 27 ('The reasonable man of the law is naturally also a freeman. Freedom in the conception of the Common Law is a thing native to man as man').

justify his act'.[294] A strict approach is taken to justification, given the goals of the law. '[I]t is of the essence of the tort'[295] that the imprisonment must actually be justified: it is not enough that the encumbrance could be theoretically or potentially justified.[296] Where such defence fails the common law takes the claimant to have suffered an interference which they ought not to have suffered; in the absence of a justified interference the claimant 'was in principle entitled to his liberty'.[297] It is on this basis that a substantial award is justified. One recovers damages because the interference places the claimant in a normatively worse position than the law considers that the claimant is entitled to be in. Damages address the normative imbalance between the position the claimant is entitled to be in—one in which their interests are in pristine form—and their position given the wrongful interference, where their interests are subject to an encumbrance which they ought not to have been subject to. Within this remedial paradigm speculations as to what would have happened had the defendant acted lawfully are irrelevant.

Even if we accept the heterodoxy that damages for 'loss of liberty' depend on 'but for' counterfactual analysis, the same result may be reached. In such analysis one compares the claimant's position given the wrong with their position in a hypothetical in which the wrong never occurred. But what is the wrong here? There are two viable positions.[298] The difference between the two is whether one includes justifications, such as lawful excuse, within the definition of the wrong or not. On one view the wrong is breach of a duty not to imprison another *without justification*. If this is the wrong in false imprisonment then the conclusion in *Lumba* might be supportable: but for the unjustified imprisonment, the claimant would have been subject to a justified imprisonment, so they have suffered no loss.[299] The second view is that the wrong is breach of a duty not to confine another; on this view justification does not go to the nature of the wrong but is a defence to the wrong. On this view damages should have been awarded for loss of liberty in *Lumba*. On this account our counterfactual question is: what would the claimant's position have been if the defendant had not imprisoned the claimant? If the claimant were not detained by the defendant, he would have been free (unless, for example, there is evidence that someone else would have detained him), so substantial damages should follow as the claimant is in a worse position than he would have been in but for the imprisonment.

[294] *Liversidge v Anderson* [1942] AC 206, 245.
[295] *Evans* (n 76) 32.
[296] *Lumba* (n 2) [62]; *Christie* (n 94).
[297] *Roberts v Chief Constable Cheshire Constabulary* [1999] 1 WLR 662, 667.
[298] See further J Gardner, *Offences and Defences* (OUP, 2007) ch 4; J Goudkamp, *Tort Law Defences* (Hart Publishing, 2013) 76–80.
[299] eg *Lumba* (n 2) [95], [176].

There are at least two reasons why we should favour the second conception of the wrong. First, by characterising every interference with liberty as wrongful, notwithstanding whether the defendant ultimately avoids liability by proving justification, the law signals that liberty is an interest of such importance that normative significance ought to be attached to every interference with it, consonant with the vindicatory nature of the action. The law signals that it is not ambivalent as between non-interference and justified interference, maintaining a normative preference for preservation of liberty in pristine form. Second, features of the case law support the second conception. For example, justifications have been analogised with apologies. Lord Abinger CB in *Warwick* said: '[a] justification of a false imprisonment ... is in the nature of an apology for the defendant's conduct'.[300] If imprisonment were not wrongful in itself, why should the defendant apologise?

A principal problem with *Lumba* is that a majority of Justices did not recognise the common law tradition that damages follow protective, vindicatory torts, nor that they were deviating from that tradition. No authority was invoked in support of the majority's approach to damages, and the view that the claimant had not suffered any loss was arrived at through cursory reasoning. If *Lumba* represented orthodoxy there would have been far fewer cases across English legal history in which substantial damages were awarded. This is because many such cases concern detention pursuant to statutory or common law powers, for example in the criminal, vagrancy and mental health contexts. In many of these cases it would have been open to courts to deny awards on the basis that the defendant would have otherwise exercised their powers lawfully. Yet courts never engaged in or even contemplated counterfactual reasoning in such cases, including where such cases reached the higher courts.[301]

For example in the House of Lords decision in *Christie* the claimant was falsely imprisoned in circumstances where the arresting officer failed to give the claimant notice of the charge on which he was being arrested, such that the arrest was unlawful.[302] This scenario is not materially different from *Lumba*: the officer could have otherwise arrested the claimant lawfully, by giving him the requisite notice, and there was nothing on the facts to suggest that the officer would have done anything other than arrest the claimant, given he held a reasonable suspicion that an offence had been committed. In *Lumba* Lords Rodger and Brown, in dissent, said: 'Search as one may in the judgments both of the Court of Appeal and of the House of Lords in *Christie* ... there is no hint of a suggestion that the false imprisonment which followed upon the unlawful arrest in that case might properly attract only

[300] *Warwick v Foulkes* (1844) 12 Meeson and Welsby 507, 509; *Evans* (n 76) 42 ('Imprisonment involves the infringement of a legally protected right and therefore must be justified').

[301] eg *Christie* (n 94); *Roberts* (n 297); *ID* (n 75).

[302] *Christie* ibid.

a nominal award of damages'.[303] One can go further. Lord du Parcq, in the most comprehensive of the speeches in *Christie*, and with whom three other Law Lords concurred, said: 'the arrest of the respondent and his detention down to the time when he was first brought before a magistrate were unlawful, and ... he is entitled to recover damages for false imprisonment in respect of them'.[304] There is no contemplation of counterfactual analysis; damages are the reflex of a finding of false imprisonment. This reflects the common understanding of the remedial approach in this field: it is so basic a proposition that an entitlement to substantial damages follows a finding of false imprisonment that it does not even require elaboration. It is simply the case that for trespassory torts, of which false imprisonment is one, 'once a plaintiff obtains a verdict ... he or she is entitled to an award of damages'.[305] Members of the majority in *Lumba* did refer to *Christie*, but they did not consider the implications of the decision specifically in respect of damages.

Also indicating error in the Court's approach is that it creates incongruity across TAPS. Whereas in other torts protective of basic interests, such as defamation or trespass to land, normative damages do not depend on 'but for' analysis, the effect of *Lumba* is that such a limitation will now be applied in false imprisonment. It is not clear why this should be the case: why should liberty be less strongly protected than interests in land or in the person? Is liberty any less basic? The judiciary does not seem to think so given judgments are replete with stirring statements of the supreme importance of liberty.[306]

There is no principle in battery that damages are denied for a successful claim where the claimant would have otherwise consented to the touching. As we have seen, in defamation one receives damages simply because one was defamed; damages (other than those for consequential loss) are not dependent on what would actually have happened but for the wrong. In trespass, too, it is irrelevant to recovery of user damages that the claimant could not and would not have used the land but for the trespasser's use, such that the claimant is not materially worse off;[307] 'there may be no *actual* loss' however 'the law takes the view as a matter of policy that the claimants ... are entitled to *substantial compensation* for the mere invasion of their rights'.[308] As such in vindicatory contexts 'damages do not necessarily depend upon precisely what would have occurred but for the wrong'.[309] Thus, in conversion a claimant may recover damages for

303 (n 2) [345].
304 *Christie* (n 94) 603.
305 *Plenty* (n 246) 654 and 645.
306 *Christie* (n 94) 588; *Murray* (n 51) 529; *R v SOSHD, ex p Khawaja* [1984] AC 74, 111.
307 See text to n 276.
308 *Devenish* (n 193) [36] (emphasis added).
309 *Experience Hendrix LLC v PPX Enterprises Inc* [2003] EMLR 25, [26].

wrongful interference with their possessory interests regardless of whether, on ordinary 'but for' analysis, the wrong leaves them factually worse off. It is irrelevant to recovery of damages for the wrong in itself that but for X's conversion of Y's goods, another party would inevitably have converted the goods. Similarly it would be irrelevant if a third party in fact converted the goods before X converted them such that but for X's conversion Y would not have had his goods anyway.[310] In these scenarios courts assess damages by reference to 'the owner's position had he retained his goods'—that is the position the law considers the owner *ought* to have been in—as opposed to the position he *actually* would have been in but for the wrong.[311] As Lord Hoffmann said in *Kuwait*, there is 'no uniform causal requirement for liability in tort. Instead, there are varying causal requirements, depending upon the basis and purpose of liability', and in conversion the ordinary 'but for' approach found in negligence[312] does not apply except to consequential factual loss, given the tort's strictly protective and vindicatory functions: 'causal requirements follow from the nature of the tort'.[313] So too in false imprisonment, but for *Lumba*.

Lastly, it should not be overlooked that other jurisdictions maintain orthodoxy where application of *Lumba* would likely lead to denial of damages[314] and, post-*Lumba*, the English Divisional Court considered damages to follow as a matter of course even though the claimant may otherwise have been detained lawfully; orthodoxy is not easily shaken off.[315] Indeed, even in *Lumba* itself, although the claimant only received nominal damages, out of a panel of nine Justices three (Lords Hope and Walker, Lady Hale) who found false imprisonment would have awarded more than nominal damages, while Lords Brown and Rodger, who would have dismissed the false imprisonment claim, maintained that substantial damages ought to follow wrongful imprisonment as of course; to hold otherwise would 'devalue the whole concept of false imprisonment'.[316] As Lord Walker said, 'the common law has always recognised that an award of more than nominal damages should be made to vindicate an assault on an individual's person or reputation, even if the claimant can prove no special damage'.[317] These dicta are

310 *Kuwait Airways Corp v Iraqi Airways Co* [2002] 2 AC 883, [82], [129] (considered by one Justice in *Lumba*, but not engaged with seriously: [94]).

311 *Kuwait* ibid [80]–[83].

312 eg *Wright* (n 114) [103].

313 *Kuwait* (n 310) [127]–[129]; see also *Empress* (n 125) 31; *Chester* (n 2) [8], [85].

314 eg *NSW v TD* [2013] NSWCA 32 (AUS$80,000 awarded for detention in prison whereas there was only lawful authority to detain in hospital); *NSW v Abed* [2014] NSWCA 419 (AUS$20,000 for trespass to the person and false imprisonment for procedurally defective arrest and imprisonment on facts analogous to *Christie*). There are, however, warning signs that Australian courts may follow *Lumba*: *Fernando v Commonwealth (No 5)* [2013] FCA 901; [2014] FCAFC 181; *CPCF v Minister for Immigration* [2015] HCA 1.

315 *Sessay* (n 76) [54], [59].

316 *Lumba* (n 2) [343].

317 ibid [195]. And see [181].

consonant with vindicatory instincts of generations of common law judges (and juries and jurists). It is to be hoped that when the waters clear orthodoxy emerges, given the importance of the traditional remedial approach in giving effect to the law's vindicatory and protective functions.

a. *Lumba*: Possible Explanations for the Embrace of Heterodoxy

What explains the heterodox decision in *Lumba*? There are at least two possible explanations. Each reinforces that the Court fell into error.

One explanation is that *the public law dimensions of the case 'eclipsed' the private law dimensions*, which in turn distorted the remedial approach. Although the claim was in false imprisonment, and therefore one of private rights and interests, the whole case revolved around the defendant's defence of lawful excuse, and therefore the legality of the defendant's actions, according to common law judicial review norms, such as *Wednesbury* unreasonableness and procedural fairness. Seemingly because of this focus, the Court made a number of key analytical or conceptual errors. In particular the wrong was seemingly conceptualised as 'public law' illegality: Lord Collins said that 'breach of principles of public law can found an action at common law for damages for false imprisonment'.[318] But it is not breach of public duties in common law review that founds an action but breach of a personal, individual right. Similarly Lord Dyson said the claimants 'suffered no loss or damage as a result of the unlawful exercise of the power to detain'.[319] Again, the question is not whether the claimants suffered loss in consequence of unlawful administrative action, but what damage they suffered through breach of their individual right not to be confined.[320] By treating public law illegality as the wrong the Supreme Court effectively treated loss of liberty as a type of *material or factual harm consequential* upon the wrong, which may or may not be suffered in false imprisonment, as opposed to normative damage inherent in wrongful deprivation of liberty and compensable as of course.

A second possible explanation is the *imperialism of negligence-type thinking*. The dominance of negligence in, and its tendency to shape thinking across tort has long been recognised, and this phenomenon goes a long way towards explaining *Lumba*.

318 ibid [221].

319 ibid [95].

320 Contrast the correct reasoning in *Roberts* (n 297) 668: where the defendant failed to carry out statutorily-required review of claimant's detention, '[t]he plaintiff's claim was not for damages for breach of duty to carry out a review ... but for false imprisonment ... the reason why the continued detention was unlawful was that no review was carried out. The wrong was not, however, the failure to carry out the review but the continued detention'. Similarly in *ID* (n 75) [56], [76] the Court rightly characterised the tort as involving the defendant 'unlawfully infring[ing] [the claimant's] private rights', rejecting the view that false imprisonment entailed 'strict liability at common law for ... a "simple public law error"'.

Lumba introduces negligence-type thinking into false imprisonment in two interconnected ways. First, by conceptualising recoverable damage and loss as solely material in nature. Recall Woolf J's important statement of principle, in *Kralj*, where he said that negligence is concerned with loss the claimant 'actually' suffered or the 'effect' or 'impact' of the negligence on the claimant.[321] The language used to describe recoverable losses in *Lumba* was similar. Lord Dyson spoke of the claimant suffering no 'real loss';[322] Lord Hope of the claimant's inability to 'point to any quantifiable loss or damage';[323] Lord Kerr of the 'actual impact' of imprisonment;[324] while Lady Hale spoke of 'harm' and said the claimant should not be compensated for something he could never have 'enjoyed'.[325] These quotes suggest that the Justices adopted a narrow conception of loss as factual losses.

The second way negligence reasoning is introduced—which is a by-product of conceptualising losses as solely material in nature—is by making 'but for' causation central to the action. This diminishes the action's traditional focus on ensuring protection and vindication of the claimant's rights and interests and shifts the focus onto whether the defendant ought to be held responsible for the claimant's material losses. As Ibbetson observes, 'analysis of liability in terms of the culpability of the defendant's conduct inevitably cut[s] across ... analysis in terms of the interest of the plaintiff that has been invaded'.[326]

In turn a focus on material loss and the defendant's responsibility for that loss undermine the traditional vindicatory and protective nature of false imprisonment. As Weir observed, 'awareness of the difference' in function between vindicatory torts and negligence 'is vital if negligence is not to take over completely, with unfortunate effects on the rights of the citizen'.[327] Where the action is 'in trespass not in case ... the plaintiff is entitled to some damages in vindication of his right'.[328]

iv. Recovery and Assessment of Damages for Normative Damage

So much for *Lumba*. Let us return to our account of orthodoxy. Neither recovery nor quantum of normative damages depend on the specific emotional, psychological, physiological or economic effects of the wrong on the individual claimant. An individual may be treated very civilly and fed with beef-steaks and beer while detained such that they suffer no distress.[329]

[321] Above n 217.
[322] *Lumba* (n 2) [93].
[323] ibid [176].
[324] ibid [253].
[325] ibid [212]–[213].
[326] Ibbetson (n 29) 200.
[327] Weir 2006 (n 1) 134.
[328] *Plenty* (n 246) 645.
[329] *Huckle v Money* (1763) 2 Wils KB 205.

An individual may be of such dispassionate disposition that publication of untrue statements about his personal life in national newspapers causes him no distress or humiliation. An individual may have such physical fortitude that being hit on the back with a crowbar causes him no pain, suffering, loss of amenity or medical expenses. A trespasser may camp on a person's land for weeks on end, causing no damage to the property and no distress or inconvenience to the owner, in circumstances where the land-owner had no intention whatsoever of using the land himself or renting it out. Indeed, the imprisonment may be rather pleasant; the printing of untrue statements may lead to pecuniary gains for the claimant as they raise his profile; some might derive a peculiar thrill from being hit with a crowbar; while the land-owner may rejoice at the fact that someone made use of their land whereas it would not have been enjoyed otherwise. There is no consequential factual loss in these scenarios. However, the individuals' basic interests in liberty, reputation, physical integrity and exclusive possession of land, which are the object of the law's protection, have been interfered with and the law provides compensation to redress the normative damage.

Normative damage is assessed objectively in the sense that quantum depends on the relative importance of the interest (the more important, the greater quantum) and the extent or seriousness of the interference with the interest (the more serious, the greater quantum), and not on the specific factual effects on particular claimants which flow from the interference. It is important to make clear that compensation is awarded only for the *extent* of the interference with the interest, not for the entire value of the interest; put another way, damages are 'proportionate'[330] to the extent of the interference. In assessing the seriousness or extent of the interference courts typically consider a set of factors. For example, in assessing damage to reputational interests 'the most important factor is the gravity of the libel', 'the more closely it touches the claimant's personal integrity, professional reputation, honour, courage, loyalty and the core attributes of his personality, the more serious it is likely to be', while other factors are also relevant such as the extent of publication, 'a libel published to millions has a greater potential to cause damage than a libel published to a handful of people'.[331] In false imprisonment seriousness depends on, inter alia: (1) duration of imprisonment, the longer the period, the greater the interference;[332] and (2) degree of confinement, the interference with liberty being far greater where imprisonment is within a small cubicle compared to imprisonment in a large warehouse.[333] The seriousness of the interference is conceptually

330 *Rantzen* (n 241) 696; *Cairns* (n 34) [41].
331 *John* (n 236) 607; *Cairns* (n 34) [24]; Tettenborn and Wilby (n 106) [18.17]ff.
332 See the timescale-based guidance in *Thompson* (n 279) 515.
333 eg *Iqbal* (n 72) [46], [48]–[49].

separate from the manner in which the tort was perpetrated, which is the province of aggravated damages (see section III.C.vi below).

Unlike interests in physical integrity or liberty, interests in property are commonly valued by the market in monetary terms, and such valuations serve as a benchmark for quantification of the objective value of normative damage. In user cases the courts typically assess these damages according to the market rate for use,[334] which—given it is an objective measure—will not necessarily coincide with the rate in, for example, a pre-existing rental agreement between the parties.[335] As with other vindicatory torts, damages are only awarded for the extent of the interference, assessed according to a number of factors, including the duration of wrongful use and the amount of land used. If X wrongfully occupies a small vale within Y's highland estate, he will only be liable to pay a reasonable fee in respect of use of that small pocket of land for the period of use.[336]

In terms of the importance of the interests, we should not expect quantum to vary a great deal on this basis among the TAPS, given each action protects interests of great importance, while it may be difficult to compare awards which respond to discrete facts, and especially difficult to compare awards for interests susceptible to market valuation (for example interests in land) and those that are not (for example liberty, reputation, physical integrity). However, differences are observable at the margins. For example, as we have seen, in most cases of false imprisonment (and arguably battery), including brief or transitory interferences, the courts have made clear that a more than nominal sum will generally be awarded (even if relatively modest); 'any detention even for a very short period, is not insignificant and deserves something more than mere nominal damages for a technical false imprisonment'.[337] In contrast, in cases of transitory trespass to land, such as where an individual fleetingly walks over a narrow strip of land, we would expect a nominal sum. Weir has argued that this variation demonstrates the relatively greater importance the law attaches to liberty over proprietary interests,[338] while courts too consistently stress the primacy of liberty.[339]

[334] *Wass* (n 248) and those cases cited in n 256 above.

[335] eg *Ashman* (n 257) 522.

[336] eg *Whitwham v Westminster Brymbo Coal and Coke Company* [1896] 1 Ch 894, 899.

[337] *Petticrew v Chief Constable Royal Ulster Constabulary* [1988] NI 192, 204 (£300 for 35 minutes wrongful detention); *Nellins v Chief Constable Royal Ulster Constabulary* (20 February 1998) unreported; High Court QBD (NI) (£45 for five minutes); *Abed* (n 314) (AUS$10,000 for three hours); *Watson v Marshall* (1971) 124 CLR 621, 632 ('An interference with personal liberty even for a short period is not a trivial wrong').

[338] Weir 2006 (n 1) 138. Although, liability is stricter for trespass to land; the law is seldom tidy.

[339] Above n 306.

v. Consequential Losses

Consequential non-pecuniary losses, such as distress, humiliation, anxiety or frustration, are not inherent in the rights-violation, and may or may not be suffered in consequence of a wrong. Damages here respond to the actual effects of the tort on the specific claimant: such loss is not assessed objectively, but by examining the 'degree of distress suffered by the claimant'.[340] The court may have before it direct evidence of the claimant's distress, such as a medical report or witness statements. More typical, however, is that the court does not have such a 'solid evidential foundation' upon which to base assessment, as it would for financial loss.[341] The courts will therefore engage seriously with the factual matrix in order to identify any features from which it could reasonably be *inferred* that greater or lesser distress was suffered. For example in *Lunt*, a case of false imprisonment by the police, the Court of Appeal said that 'humiliation, distress, degradation and a sense of anxiety' were 'inseparable' from what Mr Lunt had been through.[342] Mr Lunt was not in the best health and had always been a law-abiding citizen who had never before experienced custody, such that the Court was understandably willing to infer reasonably significant distress. In contrast where a seasoned prisoner is kept in jail past his release date, the courts may not infer distress or only award a small sum for distress as the prisoner is accustomed to imprisonment and did not know they were being treated wrongfully (normative damages for loss of liberty will however be awarded).[343]

Much may depend on the individual claimant. As Diplock LJ observed in a defamation case:

> having seen the plaintiff (as we have not), the jury were in a position to form their own view of his personality and to assess the grief and annoyance which the libel would cause him *as the sort of person they thought him to be*.[344]

If a claimant gives evidence that they were not distressed at all by the publication, there would be no basis for an award for distress. However, this would be unusual and the judge or jury will typically consider some distress to flow from the defamation, such that it is common for the courts to speak of '*natural* grief which [the claimant] would feel at this libel being published about him'.[345]

[340] Burrows (n 209) 30.

[341] *Vento v Chief Constable of West Yorkshire* [2003] ICR 318, [51].

[342] *Lunt v Liverpool City Justices* (5 March 1991) unreported; Court of Appeal Civil Division, transcript no 158/91.

[343] *Evans* (n 229) 1060.

[344] *McCarey* (n 237) 108 (emphasis added); *Gulati* (n 56) [229](viii) ('A thinner-skinned individual may be caused more upset, and therefore receive more compensation, than a thicker-skinned individual').

[345] ibid 105 (emphasis added).

There is likely to be some overlap with factors relevant to normative damage. For example the greater the attack on the claimant's reputation, the more likely it is to cause her distress; the greater the distribution of the defamatory publication, the more upset it is likely to cause the claimant. However, this is not necessarily so. It may be that on a particular set of facts the degree of normative damage is relatively minor, but the defamation may cause the claimant immense distress, given their particular sensitivities.[346]

As is the case with consequential non-pecuniary loss, recovery of pecuniary losses consequent upon a wrongful invasion of protected interests, such as loss of earnings, the cost of repairing damaged property, or medical expenses, are dependent on the loss actually suffered.[347] Unlike non-pecuniary losses, such losses must be specifically pleaded and concrete evidence of loss will generally be required.

Unlike normative damage, which is inherent in the wrong and recoverable as of course, recovery of factual loss is dependent on ordinary 'but for' analysis. So if you were distressed during a period of wrongful imprisonment because you learned that one of your friends had lost your Game of Thrones DVD collection, then you cannot recover for that distress because you would have suffered it notwithstanding the wrongful imprisonment. Similarly, you may not recover for lost wages in a claim for false imprisonment, where you cannot prove that you would have been in work if you had been free.

Lastly, it is clearly established that difficulty in putting a monetary value on damage or loss is not a sound basis for refusing damages.[348] Damages for torts such as defamation and false imprisonment are said to be 'at large', meaning they 'cannot be arrived at by any purely objective computation':[349] 'They are therefore in a large measure indeterminate'.[350] Damages place a figure on damage that is intangible, but '[t]he law of damages is sufficiently flexible to be able to do justice in such a case'.[351] While placing monetary value on such loss is somewhat crude and artificial—cash and liberty are incommensurable—arbitrariness is avoided through following an established and consistent method of assessment. In particular, by applying an established set of factors that increase or decrease awards, setting of tariffs and scales of awards, and checking awards against those made in previous cases. As Lord Bingham MR said in the defamation context:

> There could never be any precise, arithmetical formula to govern the assessment of general damages in defamation, but if such cases were routinely tried by judges

[346] *Cairns* (n 34) [22].
[347] See further ch 3.II.B.iii.
[348] *The Mediana* [1900] AC 113, 116; *Gulati* (n 56) [111], [132]; Burrows (n 209) 63.
[349] *Broome* (n 34) 1070–71.
[350] Tettenborn and Wilby (n 106) [18.11].
[351] *Hunter* (n 179) 696, 706.

> sitting alone there would no doubt emerge a more or less coherent framework of awards which would, while recognising the particular features of particular cases, ensure that broadly comparable cases led to broadly comparable awards.[352]

vi. Other Features of Damages within Torts Actionable Per Se

While recovery of factual non-pecuniary losses, such as distress, is tightly circumscribed within negligence—such losses may only typically be recovered where linked to physical damage[353]—such losses are recovered routinely within the TAPS, without the need to link loss to physical injury, interference with a protected interest being sufficient to 'unlock' liability. It has been argued that this permissive approach is linked to the functions of TAPS, the policy goal of protection of fundamental interests being powerful enough to overcome a general judicial reluctance, based on policy concerns such as floodgates, to compensate for non-pecuniary losses.[354]

In negligence recovery is limited to losses that were reasonably foreseeable.[355] In contrast, it is strongly arguable that within the TAPS there is no such limitation and a claimant may recover for any factual losses that are the direct and natural consequence of the wrong. It has been suggested at the highest level that a remoteness test does not apply where the wrong is committed dishonestly or is intentional in nature.[356] Courts are unwilling to apply remoteness to torts for which 'foreseeability of damages [is not] the gist of the tort'—and where such requirement is not required by the 'policy objectives' underlying the action.[357] On this basis a remoteness test is not applied within the tort of harassment,[358] nor for anti-discrimination torts—and it has been assumed that the test does not apply in assault or battery.[359] It is very unlikely that the courts would take a different approach within other TAPS. It is difficult to see how the strongly protective nature of TAPS would necessitate such requirement; indeed the nature of such torts strongly tells against imposition of such requirement, the absence of a remoteness criterion affording the plaintiff greater protection against harms suffered through wrongful interference with their most basic interests.

352 *John* (n 236) 608.

353 *Hunter* (n 179) 707. There are exceptions, as in a confined class of psychiatric injury negligence cases.

354 See Giliker (n 232).

355 *Overseas Tankship* (n 113); *Page v Smith* [1996] AC 155, 197.

356 *Kuwait* (n 310) [99]–[104].

357 *Jones v Ruth* [2012] 1 WLR 1495, [32]; *Essa v Laing* [2004] ICR 746, [48]; *Kuwait* [71].

358 *Jones* ibid.

359 *Essa* (n 357) (on assault and battery see: [38]–[39]); see also *Massey v UNIFI* [2008] ICR 62.

In contrast to negligence,[360] aggravated damages are available for TAPS.[361] Such damages are a form of mental distress damages,[362] and compensate for the injury to the claimant's proper feelings of dignity and pride, where the tort is committed with malice, arrogance, malevolence, insolence or spite.[363] Although they are dependent on the nature of the defendant's conduct such damages are not punitive but compensatory. The defendant's conduct is an indicator of the claimant's loss: account is taken of 'the motives and conduct of the defendant where they aggravate *the injury* done to the plaintiff. There may be malevolence or spite or the manner of committing the wrong may be such as to *injure* the plaintiff's proper feelings of dignity and pride';[364] the '*injury* ... is made worse for the plaintiff because it is more difficult to excuse' when the defendant acts despicably.[365] That these damages are compensatory for actual loss is also illustrated by their unavailability where the claimant does not know of the maliciousness of the defendant's conduct.[366] It is right that such damages are available within a vindicatory body of law: such damages recognise that a deplorable and disrespectful interference with one's fundamental interests is so serious an affront that it will naturally damage one's feelings of dignity and pride.

IV. CONCLUSIONS

In *Watkins* Lord Bingham said 'the primary role of the law of torts is to provide monetary compensation for those who have suffered material damage rather than to vindicate the rights of those who have not'.[367] In *Fairchild* he said, '[t]he overall object of tort law is to define cases in which the law may justly hold one party liable to compensate another'.[368] While true of misfeasance in public office and negligence, which these cases concerned respectively, these observations clearly do not capture the nature of TAPS, where an action can be founded even though no material harm has been suffered, compensation is regularly awarded for non-material damage (normative damage), and nominal and punitive damages are available, which do not compensate for harm at all. Thus, 'that the sole purpose of the law of tort generally ... should be to compensate the victims of civil wrongs ... is far too narrow a view'.[369]

360 *Kralj* (n 202); *AB* (n 202).
361 *Aggravated, Exemplary and Restitutionary Damages*, Law Com 246 (1997) [1.10].
362 *Rookes* (n 201) 1221, 1229; *Broome* (n 34) 1124; *Commissioner of the Metropolis v Shaw* [2012] ICR 464.
363 *Rookes* ibid.
364 ibid (emphasis added).
365 *Thompson* (n 279) 512 (emphasis added).
366 Law Commission (n 361) [1.9].
367 *Watkins* (n 7) [6].
368 *Fairchild* (n 129) [9].
369 *Smith New Court Securities Ltd v Citibank* [1997] AC 254, 279.

This vindicatory strain in tort may be forgotten in an age where we continue to witness the 'staggering march of negligence' and associated modes of thinking in tort,[370] and in which there is little scholarly focus on torts other than negligence. This danger is well illustrated by cases such as *Lumba*, and judicial statements such as the following from McLachlin CJ in a significant human rights damages case: 'When we move from compensation to the objectives of vindication and deterrence, tort law is less useful'.[371] Similarly, as Stevens says,[372] Lord Bingham's view in *Greenfield* that the Human Rights Act 1998 is 'not a tort statute'[373] as its objects go beyond ensuring compensation for loss, is based on a mistaken conception of tort—evident also in his Lordship's statements in *Watkins* and *Fairchild*—as only being concerned with affording compensation for actual loss. As Steele observes, damages decisions under the Act, such as *Greenfield*, have tended to adopt 'an artificially narrow understanding of the functions both of tort, and of the HRA itself'.[374] This has not been so in other jurisdictions, the Irish Supreme Court, for example, observing in a constitutional remedies case:

> [t]here is ... authority both judicial and academic for the proposition that the law of tort is, at least in certain circumstances, an important tool for the vindication of constitutional rights, and no authority whatever for the proposition that it is concerned exclusively for the allocation of damages and with nothing else whatsoever.[375]

Likewise there is sometimes a tendency among courts to wrongly view compensation, and vindication and/or protection as mutually exclusive.[376] True it is that these are conceptually distinct functions. But as we have seen, compensation, as well as other forms of monetary relief, have long played a significant role in protecting and vindicating fundamental rights and interests. As Lord Scott observed in *Ashley*, '[a]lthough the principal aim of an award of compensatory damages is to compensate the claimant for loss suffered, there is no reason in principle why an award of compensatory damages should not also fulfil a vindicatory purpose'.[377]

In contrast to those who present tort as a monolith I have argued that the law of torts is a complex human and social institution that cannot be reduced to one principle or function. In this chapter I have elaborated a

[370] T Weir, 'The Staggering March of Negligence' in Cane and Stapleton (n 149); MA Millner, *Negligence in the Modern Law* (Butterworths, 1967).
[371] *Ward* (n 5) [51].
[372] Stevens (n 3) 288–89.
[373] *R (Greenfield) v SOSHD* [2005] 1 WLR 673, [19].
[374] J Steele, 'Damages in Tort and Under the Human Rights Act: Remedial or Functional Separation' (2008) 67 *CLJ* 606, 634.
[375] *Grant v Roche Products (Ireland) Ltd* (2008) 104 BMLR 1, 19.
[376] eg *Greenfield* (n 373) [9], [19]; *Michael* (n 140) [127].
[377] *Ashley* (n 2) [22]; *Lumba* (n 2) [236].

dichotomy between those torts that are concerned principally with vindication and those concerned principally with compensation for material harm. In so doing I have sought to be rigorously bottom-up, and this has entailed acknowledging that some torts, such as nuisance, perform compensatory and vindicatory functions in more equal measure, while yet other torts may not fit comfortably within either category. Further, some anomalies stand out, such as the theoretical availability of exemplary damages for negligence, and the award of conventional sums in some negligence cases. Nonetheless, the foregoing analysis demonstrates that significant doctrinal features of TAPS strongly evidence an underlying policy of protection of fundamental interests, with the courts cast as vindicators of those interests. By contrast, the structure of negligence evidences a policy of compensation for actual harm. In each context the primary function of the tort shapes fundamentally the approach to damages.

Now that this framework has been elaborated, we have the tools to determine whether a tort-based approach should be taken to human rights damages, and if so, which tort-based approach.

3

A Tort-Based Approach to Human Rights Damages

THIS CHAPTER CONSIDERS the approach that ought to be taken to human rights damages in the light of the framework developed in chapter 2. The chapter's central argument is that the approach to human rights damages ought to follow that within vindicatory torts. Section I argues a vindicatory, tort-based approach is sound as a matter of principle given both torts actionable per se (TAPS) and human rights law perform common functions of protection and vindication of fundamental interests, and there are important benefits associated with a tort-based approach. Section II sets out the tort-based approach. It addresses the kinds of damages that ought to be available for rights-violations, when damages ought to be awarded, and how courts should assess damages. Section III elaborates the relationship between human rights damages and other remedies, such as damages awards for concurrent actions and specific relief, under a tort-based approach. Section IV examines whether a tort-based approach is compatible with the terms of the Human Rights Act 1998 (HRA). Section V considers flawed tort-based approaches, focusing on the United States, where the approach to damages for constitutional torts has been modelled on the approach within loss-based torts, such as negligence.

I. A TORT-BASED APPROACH AS A MATTER OF PRINCIPLE

Despite doctrinal categorisation of the TAPS as a field of private law and human rights law as a public law field,[1] there are strong similarities between the two areas which make a common approach to damages sound as a matter of principle. Specifically, human rights law and TAPS serve similar protective and vindicatory functions and protect common fundamental interests.

[1] On the relevance of the public law–private law division to human rights damages see ch 4.

A. Common Aims of Protection and Vindication: Background

In *Qazi* Lord Bingham said that the Convention 'was an attempt to identify the rights and freedoms most central to the enjoyment of human life in civil society and to give those rights and freedoms an appropriate measure of protection',[2] while the European Court of Human Rights (ECtHR) has said that the Convention's purpose is 'effective protection of individual human rights'.[3] This is clear when one considers the post-World War II context within which the Convention was drafted:

> The master builders of the Convention were determined, in the aftermath of a second terrible war in half a century, never again to permit state sovereignty to shield from international liability the perpetrators of crimes against humanity; never again to allow governments to shelter behind the argument that what a state does to its own citizens or to the stateless is within its exclusive jurisdiction and beyond the reach of the international community. So they resolved to create a binding international code of human rights, with safeguards against abuses of power and effective remedies for victims of violations by contracting states.[4]

Thus, Convention rights are underpinned by a strong policy of 'protection of individual human beings' through 'safeguards' that are 'practical and effective'.[5]

Turning to the aims of the HRA itself, the rhetoric of 'bringing rights home', which surrounded passage of the legislation through Parliament, and has permeated the jurisprudence since, including the approach to damages,[6] can obscure the reason *why* rights were brought home. The Lord Chancellor who led the legislation through Parliament said the Government's aim was 'to provide as much protection as possible for the rights of individuals against the misuse of power by the state within the framework of a Bill which preserves parliamentary sovereignty'.[7] Thus the Act brought rights home—this is obvious from the fact that Convention rights now have force in domestic law—but the *reason* for bringing those rights home was to ensure basic interests were afforded strong protection against incursion.

Similarly, as we saw in chapter 2, it has also long been the principal function of TAPS to afford strong protection to those interests fundamental to English civil society. Significantly, these torts have long been of central

[2] *Harrow London Borough Council v Qazi* [2004] 1 AC 983, [8].

[3] *Saadi v UK* (2008) 47 EHRR 17, [62].

[4] A Lester, 'The European Court of Human Rights After 50 Years' [2009] *European Human Rights Law Review* 461, 463; see further AWB Simpson, *Human Rights and the End of Empire* (OUP, 2004).

[5] *Soering v UK* (1989) 11 EHRR 439, [87].

[6] See ch 5.

[7] HL Deb vol 583 col 808 (24 November 1997); HL Deb vol 582 col 1228–29 (3 November 1997) ('[The design of the Bill] maximises the protection of human rights without trespassing on parliamentary sovereignty').

constitutional importance, serving a similar function to bills of rights in affording strong protection to basic interests in the face of public power, and through their operation serving wider constitutional functions, such as maintenance of the rule of law and offering a vehicle for elaboration of constitutional principle.

For example, Blackstone classified certain rights as 'absolute rights', which were those rights man had in the state of nature and is entitled to enjoy whether out of society or within; they were divine rights of man of which human rights might be viewed as the secular successor.[8] He considered protection of these rights to be the principal aim of society and of laws; these included rights in physical security, personal liberty and private property.[9] Blackstone explained that these rights were protected by *the constitution*: 'in vain would these rights be declared, ascertained, and protected by the dead letter of the laws, if the constitution had provided no other method to secure their actual enjoyment'.[10] One of the ways the 'constitution' kept these rights secure was through the liberty 'of applying to the courts of justice *for redress of injuries*';[11] in this way actions in tort, which protected these basic rights, were constitutional in nature.

Similarly tort was at the very heart of Dicey's account of the constitution. He elevated the principle of equal application of ordinary law to citizen and official alike to the status of a fundamental principle of the rule of law.[12] In particular, Dicey placed heavy emphasis on the importance of equal application of claims in tort for damages for breach of fundamental rights. It was with pride that Dicey recorded,

> [t]he Reports abound with cases in which officials have been brought before the courts, and made, in their personal capacity, liable to punishment, or to the payment of damages, for acts done in their official character but in excess of their lawful authority.[13]

This constitutional tradition continues today, the judiciary maintaining that there is 'nothing in the slightest bit peculiar about an individual bringing a private law claim for damages against an executive official who has unlawfully infringed his private rights',[14] while actions continue to be brought against officials including those at the apex of Government.[15]

[8] W Blackstone, *Commentaries on the Laws of England* (Clarendon, 1765–1769) Book I, 123.

[9] ibid Book I, 123, 129, 141.

[10] ibid Book I, 140.

[11] ibid Book I, 141 (emphasis added). It is for breach of these 'absolute rights' that courts award presumed damages absent proven material loss: *Ratcliffe v Evans* [1892] 2 QB 524, 528; *Nicholls v Ely Beet Sugar Factory Ltd* [1936] 1 Ch 343, 350–51.

[12] AV Dicey, *Introduction to the Study of the Law of the Constitution* 10th edn (MacMillan, 1960) 193–94, 202–03.

[13] ibid 193.

[14] *ID v Home Office* [2006] 1 WLR 1003, [57].

[15] *Belhaj v Straw* [2015] 2 WLR 1105.

Damages actions against public actors for breach of basic rights have, through their operation, served and continue to serve other wider constitutional functions. Awarding significant sums against officials where they have interfered with basic interests without lawful justification symbolically reinforces the normative force of legal constraints on government, and in Dicey's words 'ensure[s] the supremacy of the law of the land', thus carrying forward the first principle of the rule of law: government under law.[16] Dicey also considered it important that imposition of damages liability served to 'curb the arbitrariness of the Crown'.[17] It is difficult to know precisely what consequential effects have followed from imposition of liability. But it is difficult to dispute the more modest claim already made: that is, tort has served, through its operation, to reinforce symbolically the normative force of legal constraints on government, while also providing a concrete remedy for those who suffer wrongful interferences with basic interests through unlawful executive action.

More generally, because of equal application of tort to officials, and absent a written constitution, bill of rights or separate field of public law, in English law it was the 'principles of private law' that determined 'the position of the Crown and its servants'[18] and their constitutional relationship with the governed. So it could be said, 'the constitution is the result of the ordinary law of the land' and the law of the constitution was 'the consequence of the rights of individuals, as defined and enforced by the courts'.[19] For this reason much of Dicey's famous constitutional treatise reads as a treatise on the law of civil wrongs; the book offers detailed accounts of the law of torts such as false imprisonment and defamation because it is these actions which have long protected rights considered constitutional. As ECS Wade, in his introduction to the tenth edition of Dicey's treatise, said:

> Foreign constitutions contain statements of guaranteed rights. Such rights with us proceed from the enforcement of private rights by the courts which are able to punish all illegalities. Therefore the constitution, so far as it is concerned with the protection of private rights, comes from the common law.[20]

Given this background it is not at all odd, but commonplace to find statements in tort cases that 'the case raises important questions affecting the rule of law',[21] and for judges to describe aspects of tort doctrine as 'fundamental principles of constitutional law',[22] and torts cases as having 'constitutional

[16] Dicey (n 12) 210.
[17] ibid.
[18] ibid 203.
[19] ibid.
[20] ibid cviii.
[21] *Ledwith v Roberts* [1937] 1 KB 232, 260.
[22] *Bici v MOD* [2004] EWHC 786, [85].

and public interest aspects',[23] vindicatory torts as 'important constitutional safeguards',[24] and rights protected by vindicatory torts as 'fundamental rights'[25] or 'of fundamental constitutional importance'.[26] Courts observe that damages in tort play a fundamental role in 'restraining the arbitrary use of executive power and buttressing civil liberties'[27] and 'vindicat[ing] the rule of law',[28] while damages claims continue to provide an important vehicle for testing the legality of exercises of public power.[29] Commentators observe that '[d]ecisions such as those involving the tort of trespass against public officials like the police are actually defining what, in a subjective rights structure, would be constitutional rights'.[30] For Harlow the traditional English

> conception of the law of torts as a system of protected interests can be of the greatest importance in *public law* … It creates a presumption that interference with certain interests is wrongful and casts the burden upon the defendant to show that this is not the case. The clearest examples of this process in operation are to be found in trespass cases where liberty of the person or simple property rights are in question.[31]

Despite the dominance of negligence within the law of torts, emergence of human rights legislation, expansion of judicial review, establishment of alternative paths to compensation (such as compensation schemes and Ombudsmen), and advances in political accountability mechanisms, the TAPS continue to play a vital role in protecting and vindicating basic interests and upholding fundamental principles of the English constitutional order. *Muuse* is a prime example.[32] The Court awarded heavy damages for a long period of wrongful imprisonment, during which Muuse was subject to poor treatment, and which was the result of officials' 'manifest incompetence', while the overarching system which allowed these events to transpire, for which the Minister and senior officials were responsible, was also flawed. However, despite these serious failings there was no internal nor parliamentary inquiry, no Minister or senior official held accountable, and a 'paucity of measures' taken to prevent recurrence: '[t]he *only* way in

[23] *Ashley v Chief Constable of Sussex Police* [2008] 1 AC 962, [115].

[24] *R v Governor of Brockhill Prison, ex p Evans (No 2)* [2001] 2 AC 19, 43 [*Evans* HL].

[25] ibid; *R (Lumba) v SOSHD* [2012] 1 AC 245, [53]; *Morris v Beardmore* [1981] AC 446, 463–65; *SOSHD v GG* [2010] QB 585.

[26] *Lumba*, ibid [217].

[27] *Muuse v SOSHD* [2010] EWCA Civ 453, [77]; *Rookes v Barnard* [1964] AC 1129, 1223; *Ashby v White* (1703) 2 Lord Raymond 938, 956.

[28] *Kuddus v Chief Constable Leicestershire Constabulary* [2001] 2 WLR 1789, [79].

[29] *Lumba* (n 25); *Holgate-Mohammed v Duke* [1984] AC 437.

[30] G Samuel, 'Governmental Liability in Tort and the Public and Private Law Division' (1988) 8 *Legal Studies* 277, 288.

[31] C Harlow, *Compensation and Government Torts* (Sweet and Maxwell, 1982) 40–41 (emphasis added).

[32] *Muuse* (n 27).

which the misconduct of the Home Office has been exposed to public view and [Muuse's] rights vindicated is by the action in the High Court'.[33] The case also demonstrates the potential for actions to play wider extrinsic functions; through the litigation the Minister was held to account in a public forum for systemic failures and a lack of subsequent action, while the Court took the opportunity to entreat that this episode required urgent investigation by the Minister.

Indeed, despite proliferation of alternative redress and accountability mechanisms, it is no exaggeration to observe that vindicatory torts have undergone resurgence in recent times as public authorities have gradually gained greater and more varied powers to interfere with basic interests, creating greater potential for misuse or abuse; indeed as Weir observed, tort's role in vindicating constitutional rights 'has rarely been more important than now'.[34] False imprisonment remains a staple in the prison[35] and mental health contexts.[36] It is increasingly relevant in novel contexts, such as where protesters are confined within a police cordon,[37] women have been trafficked for sexual exploitation,[38] and applicants for release suffer excessive delays before the Parole Board due to under-resourcing,[39] while immigration has been a real growth area, given contemporary trends towards 'administrative' detention of asylum seekers, refugees and those awaiting deportation.[40] Assault and battery claims continue to play their traditional role in protecting and vindicating physical and mental integrity in the face of overzealous police action,[41] but also in other diverse contexts such as in the medical field,[42] in historical claims of state-sanctioned torture,[43] in the military context,[44] and in claims by those subject to extraordinary rendition.[45] The law's vindicatory function has even been enhanced within recent years. For example, the House of Lords, in *Ashley*, held that assault and battery claims against a police officer who had shot

[33] ibid [75]–[77] (emphasis added).

[34] T Weir, *A Casebook on Tort* 10th edn (Sweet and Maxwell, 2004) 322.

[35] *Evans* HL (n 24); *Iqbal v POA* [2010] QB 732.

[36] *R (Sessay) v South London and Maudsley NHS Trust* [2012] QB 760; *R (M) v Hackney LBC* [2011] 1 WLR 2873.

[37] *Austin v Commissioner of the Metropolis* [2007] EWCA Civ 989 (no appeal on the false imprisonment issue: [2009] 1 AC 564, [11]).

[38] *AT v Dulghieru* [2009] EWHC 225.

[39] *R (Faulkner) v SOSJ* [2013] 2 AC 254.

[40] *Lumba* (n 25); *R (Kambadzi) v SOSHD* [2011] WLR 1299; *ID* (n 14); *Muuse* (n 27); *R (AA) v SOSHD* [2013] 1 WLR 2224.

[41] *Rowlands v Chief Constable Merseyside Police* [2007] 1 WLR 1065; *Ashley* (n 23).

[42] *B v NHS Hospital Trust* [2002] 2 All ER 449; *In re F* [1990] 2 AC 1.

[43] *Mutua v FCO* [2012] EWHC 2678.

[44] *Bici* (n 22).

[45] *Belhaj* (n 15).

dead an unarmed man in the course of a police raid could proceed to trial despite full compensation already having been paid, because of the importance of vindicating the victim's legal rights.[46] Outside the courtroom it remains the case that, for example, each year the police pay out not insignificant compensation in out-of-court settlements for assault, battery and false imprisonment.[47]

Against this background the not uncommon assertion that '[d]amages and compensatory remedies have not traditionally played a major role in British public law' is misleading if stated without elaboration or caveat.[48] Damages actions have long protected and vindicated basic interests in the face of executive interference; indeed, '[h]istorically, damages have been regarded as the ordinary remedy for an invasion of personal interests in liberty'.[49] Through operation of such claims tort has served wider, extrinsic constitutional functions. Thus, within the English tradition damages for breaches of fundamental rights are not a novelty, and damages claims for breaches of the HRA may be viewed as a continuation and extension of this long tradition. Importantly, that the common law has developed an elaborate approach to damages for wrongful invasions of fundamental interests means we need not reinvent the wheel when it comes to developing the approach to human rights damages.

B. Common Aims of Protection and Vindication: Significant Doctrinal Features

Thus, human rights law and TAPS have a great deal in common, sharing common functions of protecting and vindicating fundamental interests, while both fields are of constitutional significance. This commonality is conclusively evidenced by detailed doctrinal analysis, which shows that the two fields share near-identical significant doctrinal features. In turn these similarities strongly support a common approach to damages.

[46] *Ashley* (n 23). This development is consonant with Trindade's observation that development of alternative paths to compensation may reduce the importance of vindicatory torts in compensating material harms, but their function in protecting constitutional rights would continue to be of 'considerable importance': 'Intentional Torts: Some Thoughts on Assault and Battery' (1982) 2 *Oxford Journal of Legal Studies* 211, 237.

[47] R Clayton and H Tomlinson, *Civil Actions Against the Police* 3rd edn (Sweet and Maxwell, 2004) 14–15, 18, Table 2 (and *First Supplement* (2005) 2–3).

[48] C Turpin and A Tomkins, *British Government and the Constitution* 6th edn (CUP, 2007) 276, 340; 7th edn (CUP, 2011) 361.

[49] *Bivens v Six Unknown Named Agents of Federal Bureau of Narcotics* 403 US 388, 395 (1971).

i. Standing

In general only the individual rights-holder may bring a claim under the HRA.[50] Likewise, in the law of torts standing is limited to the rights-holder.[51] Human rights claims are non-transferable: the victim may not assign claims to others.[52] Again, the position is the same in tort: actions considered 'essentially personal', such as defamation or false imprisonment, are not assignable.[53] These features suggest the norms in both fields are constituted to afford protection to interests personal to individuals.[54]

ii. Actionable Per Se

In common with the TAPS, in human rights law the claimant generally need not demonstrate that the alleged interference has left them worse off in order to bring a claim. All they need show is a prima facie interference with their protected interests: 'the status of "victim" may exist even where there is no damage'.[55] Thus, a claimant whose right to religious freedom has been interfered with need not show that they are physically, emotionally, psychologically or economically worse off as a result of the interference in order to bring a claim; the fact of interference shall suffice. This feature facilitates the law's primary function of protecting basic interests *in themselves*, regardless of the chance element of whether interference happens to result in material losses. It also reinforces the high intrinsic value placed on those interests and that they ought to be inviolate, reflecting the field's vindicatory function: an interference may well leave a victim materially better off, but it remains the case that their basic interests ought not, given their importance, to have been interfered with. Because material or factual loss is not the gist of human rights claims, and because the law's focus is protection of basic interests rather than determining the defendant's culpability for harm, 'but for' causation is not an element of most human rights claims, nor a prerequisite to establishing a violation.

iii. Strict Liability

In common with TAPS, liability in human rights law is generally strict, not fault-based: 'When constitutional rights are in issue what matters is

[50] HRA, s 7. There are some exceptions: see, eg, text to n 178 below.

[51] eg *Morris* (n 25) 454E; *Hunter v Canary Wharf Ltd* [1997] AC 655, 692, 724; *MCC Proceeds Inc v Lehman Bros* [1998] 4 All ER 675, 685–86.

[52] *Nassau Verzekering Maatschappij NV v Netherlands* (4 October 2011) App no 57602/09 (ECtHR Third Section).

[53] *Glegg v Bromley* [1912] 3 KB 474, 488; *24 Seven Utility Services Ltd v Rosekey Ltd* [2003] EWHC 3415, [25].

[54] I elaborate on this claim, and the rights-based nature of human rights law, in ch 4.

[55] *Cullen v Chief Constable Royal Ulster Constabulary* [2003] 1 WLR 1763, [81].

whether they have been infringed, not whether the defendant can really be blamed for infringing them'.[56] Thus, whether an authority acted reasonably, in good faith, without fault or blame, or with benevolence is not generally relevant to liability (although these factors may go to defences and remedies). The court's inquiry is focused firmly on whether the claimant's interests were interfered with, rather than the defendant's conduct, mental state or motivations:[57] human rights law is geared towards protecting individuals from rights-violations 'however motivated or caused'.[58] Such approach affords the underlying interests strong protection, and vindicates their fundamental importance.

Thus, in *MS* the ECtHR found a violation of Article 3 despite the public authority having no intention to treat MS incompatibly with Article 3.[59] MS was treated with real concern in a place of relative safety and kept under observation but a violation was found nonetheless: 'The issue is whether the authorities fulfilled their obligation to protect the applicant from treatment contrary to article 3'.[60] Similarly in *ZH* the Court of Appeal found a violation of Article 3, notwithstanding that police officers had acted in what they considered to be the claimant's best interests and not intended to humiliate or debase him.[61] In *P* the Supreme Court found a violation of Article 5 where detention was in caring conditions and genuinely motivated by the claimant's best interests; what matters is the fact of interference with protected interests, not whether the interference has beneficial or negative consequential effects for the claimant, or was motivated by admirable concerns.[62] As Lady Hale said, '[t]he fact that my living arrangements are comfortable, and indeed make my life as enjoyable as it could possibly be, should make no difference. A gilded cage is still a cage'.[63] In similar vein, Lord Clarke in *A*, a case on the right to education, said, '[t]he question is not ... whether the local authority were *at fault* but whether the limitations on A's education impaired the very essence of his right to education and deprived his right of effectiveness'.[64] The focus is on the rights-holder's interests, not the defendant's blameworthiness.

It should be noted that where an authority takes its human rights responsibilities seriously, reasoning its actions by reference to those responsibilities,

[56] Weir (n 34) 322.

[57] As is often said of property rights, what is mine is no less mine because the defendant did not know it was mine or acted reasonably: P Cane, *The Anatomy of Tort Law* (Hart Publishing, 1997) 139.

[58] *Keegan v UK* (2007) 44 EHRR 33, [34].

[59] *MS v UK* (2012) 55 EHRR 23.

[60] ibid [39].

[61] *ZH v Commissioner for the Metropolis* [2013] 1 WLR 3021.

[62] *P v Cheshire West and Chester Council* [2014] 1 AC 896.

[63] ibid [46].

[64] *A v Essex CC* [2011] 1 AC 280, [51] (emphasis added).

a court will afford the authority's view of the justifiability of an interference weight in the court's own determination as to whether the interference is justified.[65] But the authority's efforts at compliance do not affect the question of whether the claimant's interests were interfered with in the first place. Further, where courts give an authority's view weight in an inquiry into justifications courts are not rewarding the authority for its efforts (even if this may be the effect) but rather responding to the convincingness of the authority's reasons, in light of its comparative institutional expertise and knowledge. If the court is not *itself* convinced, giving due weight to the authority's view, it will find for the claimant no matter how admirable the authority's attempts at compliance.

iv. Defences

Just as countervailing interests are protected in tort via defences and immunities, in human rights law such interests are protected through defences, prescribed in clauses juxtaposed with the statement of right,[66] and derogation clauses, which detail under what conditions authorities may be freed from compliance with human rights norms.[67]

However, while there must be scope for countervailing concerns, as in TAPS, the law only takes cognisance of those countervailing concerns of the utmost importance, such as 'national security, public safety or the economic well-being of the country, for the prevention of disorder or crime, for the protection of health or morals, or for the protection of the rights and freedoms of others'.[68] Something weighty is required to justify interference with basic interests. Also in common with vindicatory torts, the scope of protection afforded to the claimant's interests is generous while justifications for interference are interpreted narrowly and subject to strict criteria. For example the ECtHR has said

> [t]he circumstances in which deprivation of life may be justified must ... be strictly construed ... In the light of the importance of the protection afforded by Article 2, the Court must subject deprivations of life to the most careful scrutiny.[69]

And while it is rather easy for the claimant to establish prima facie liability—only having to show an interference with their protected interests—once interference is established the justificatory burden, which may be heavy, is

[65] *R (Begum) v Governors of Denbigh High School* [2007] 1 AC 100; *Belfast CC v Miss Behavin' Ltd* [2007] 1 WLR 1420; *R (Quila) v SOSHD* [2012] 1 AC 621.

[66] eg ECHR, arts 2(2), 5(1)(a)–(f), 10(2).

[67] ECHR, art 15.

[68] ECHR, art 8(2).

[69] *Kallis and Androulla Panayi v Turkey* (27 October 2009) App no 45388/99, [52] (ECtHR Fourth Section).

placed on the defendant.[70] As in TAPS, this approach attests to the importance placed on the claimant's basic interests.

There are various defences to a human rights claim, some of which are peculiar to the right in issue.

Article 3 'does not allow for any exceptions or justifying factors or balancing of interests', such that conduct proscribed by Article 3 cannot be legally justified even if undertaken to save the life of another.[71] For the most important rights, such as that against torture, there is no provision for derogation, even in national emergencies.[72] The only possible defence under the HRA, consistent with parliamentary sovereignty, is where statute authorises a violation; this defence of statutory authorisation is applicable to all rights in principle.[73] However, any purported statutory authorisation would, to be effective, need to be express. Even then it may be read down.[74] As is the case within TAPS, courts take a strict approach to purported statutory authorisations of wrongful conduct, given the importance of the interests at stake.

Other Articles enumerate specific grounds of justification.[75] These are construed narrowly and justifications are necessarily limited to the enumerated grounds. Burdens of justification may be added to those in the text. For example, to justify interference with liberty it is necessary but insufficient for a defendant to prove a specified ground in Article 5(1)(a)–(f); the ECtHR has added the requirement that the defendant must not have acted arbitrarily.[76] There could be no clearer indication of the primacy placed on ensuring strong protection of the claimant's basic interests.

Another defence, specific to certain rights, is proportionality. The criteria of the proportionality defence are strict: (1) the authority's objective must be sufficiently important to justify limiting fundamental rights; (2) the measures put in place to achieve that aim must be rationally connected to it; (3) the means used to impair the right must be no more than necessary to achieve the aim; and (4) the measures must strike a 'fair balance' between the individual right and countervailing interests.[77] The justificatory burden is not light: 'particularly convincing and weighty reasons' must exist 'by way of justification'.[78] In particular, proving less restrictive means were unavailable may cast a heavy onus. The government may be required to produce concrete evidence to substantiate factual premises upon which its purported

[70] *Marcic v Thames Water Utilities Ltd* [2004] 2 AC 42, [37]; *Quila* (n 65) [44].
[71] *Gäfgen v Germany* (2011) 52 EHRR 1, [101]–[108].
[72] ECtHR, art 15(2).
[73] HRA, s 6(2); *Tovey v MOJ* [2011] EWHC 271 (s 6(2) relied on to deny HRA damages claim).
[74] HRA, s 3; *R (GC) v Commissioner of the Metropolis* [2011] 1 WLR 1230; *M* (n 36) [66].
[75] eg ECHR, art 5(1).
[76] *Saadi* (n 3); *James v UK* (2013) 56 EHRR 12.
[77] *R (Daly) v SOSHD* [2001] 2 AC 532, [27]; *Bank Mellat v HM Treasury (No 2)* [2013] 3 WLR 179, [20] (substantive appeal).
[78] *Smith and Grady v UK* (2000) 29 EHRR 493, [94]; *Daly* [27].

justification is founded, which the courts will examine thoroughly;[79] proportionality analysis 'depends on an exacting analysis of the factual case advanced in defence of the measure'.[80]

Thus defences exist. But the rules governing defences are stacked heavily in the claimant's favour, given the law's policy of affording strong protection to the claimant's most basic interests; in turn this again vindicates the importance of these interests.

v. Substantive Questions for the Judiciary

As discussed in detail in chapter 4,[81] in contrast to the position in common law judicial review, in human rights law substantive questions, including whether an interference is justified, are for the judiciary: it is for courts to exercise primary, determinative and objective judgment over whether interference is justified by public interest concerns. In turn this reveals something of the nature of human rights law. First, that the judiciary, the independent branch of state, has the final say over how the balance should be struck between competing interests serves to ensure effective protection of basic interests, and that they are not left vulnerable to being dispensed with where the executive finds such course convenient. Second, this feature indicates human rights claims are, like the TAPS, claims of *individual right*. Determination of claims of individual legal right, on the merits and objectively, is quintessentially a judicial function within the separation of powers and according to the rule of law.

vi. Remedies

Significant features of the courts' remedial jurisdiction also illustrate the law's protective and vindicatory functions. The UK is under a duty in international law, pursuant to Article 13 of the Convention, to afford every victim of a rights-violation an effective remedy. Article 13 is unqualified, and the ECtHR has said 'the place of art 13 in the scheme of human rights protection set up by the Convention would argue in favour of implied restrictions of art 13 being kept to a minimum'.[82] Article 13 was not incorporated directly by the HRA. Instead it was given effect via section 8(1),[83] which bestows courts with wide remedial jurisdiction, which, as discussed below, is designed to afford courts the requisite flexibility to ensure effective protection given the

[79] *R v Shayler* [2003] 1 AC 247, [61]; *Smith and Grady*, ibid [99]–[100]; *Quila* (n 65) [44]–[59], [74]–[77]. This may extend to consideration of statistical or empirical evidence: eg *Van Colle v UK* (2013) 56 EHRR 23, [96].

[80] *Bank Mellat* (n 77) [20].

[81] See ch 4.2.II.B.

[82] *Kudla v Poland* (2002) 35 EHRR 11, [152].

[83] See s IV below, and chs 5.1, 6.1.I–II.

demands of the case. The courts have held that the object of sections 7 and 8 of the HRA is to secure the remedy which Article 13 declares is the entitlement of every victim.[84] Thus there is scope for courts to tailor remedies to ensure effective protection of rights on the facts, and there is also very limited scope to refuse relief given the remedial jurisdiction must be exercised in the light of the demands of Article 13. In turn these features reflect the protective functions of the law—violations of basic rights must be met with effective redress.

The other significant feature of the remedial jurisdiction is the subject of this book: the Act expressly provides for damages.[85] In turn this further indicates the law's concern is, in common with TAPS, with protection of individual interests; damages claims are 'paradigms of personal claims', as they redress losses *personal and specific to* particular individuals.[86] Damages awards also afford a further, important layer of protection to rights at the remedial stage, ensuring a victim is not left to bear the losses caused through the wrong.

The fundamental principle of *ubi ius, ibi remedium*—where there is a right there ought to be a remedy—has similarly long characterised the approach to remedies for breaches of basic rights at common law, and particularly where legally recognised injury is suffered through a wrong.[87]

vii. Procedure

The procedural character of human rights claims further reflects the underlying protective and vindicatory concerns of the law, and commonalities with other rights-based fields. As discussed further in chapter 4,[88] whereas 'public law' claims generally must be streamed via judicial review procedure, which is characterised by procedural safeguards for public defendants and which severely restrict claimant access to court, it is increasingly clear HRA claims may be initiated via ordinary procedure, and that where initiated via review, procedural restrictions will be loosened. In other words human rights claims often have the same procedural character as claims in tort. Further, these procedural features reflect that restrictions on access to court (such as the permission stage or short limitation period within review procedure) or upon the court's ability to rigorously determine claims

[84] *Re S (Minors)* [2002] 2 AC 291, [61].
[85] HRA, s 8(2)–(5).
[86] J Beatson, '"Public" and "Private" in English Administrative Law' (1987) 103 *LQR* 34, 45. See further ch 4.2.
[87] See ch 6.1.III.A. Certain differences between common law and the HRA, which may appear material, such as that damages are not available as of right under the HRA, are discussed below in s IV.A.
[88] See ch 4.2.II.C.

(such as restrictions on discovery and oral evidence typical of review procedure) are inapt in claims of fundamental right, as they may impede robust judicial protection of those important rights.

viii. Miscellaneous

A miscellany of other features demonstrates human rights law's primary function of affording strong protection to fundamental interests. Just as there is a presumption that Parliament does not intend to override fundamental rights at common law, such as those protected by the TAPS,[89] there is an even stronger interpretive obligation on courts to construe legislation compatibly with human rights as far as possible.[90] Courts may examine primary legislation for compatibility with human rights; these rights are so fundamental that even statute should be examined for consistency with them.[91] Convention rights have also been interpreted as casting not only negative duties of non-interference, but also positive duties to protect, adding a further layer of protection to basic interests and vindicating the value which the law places upon them.[92]

Thus, there are striking similarities between the significant features of vindicatory torts and human rights law. The degree of similarity is not mere coincidence: the law has a common purpose in both fields, to protect and vindicate fundamental individual rights and interests, and it is from this common premise that the near identical legal structures flow.

C. Common Functions, the Implications for Damages, and the Prevailing Approach to Human Rights Damages

Given TAPS and human rights law perform similar functions, as evinced by their near-identical doctrinal features, there is a powerful argument of principle that the approach to damages ought to be analogous across the two fields. Importantly, a vindicatory approach to human rights damages, modelled on the remedial approach within vindicatory torts, would ensure internal coherence as between the policy of protection and vindication upon which the primary rights are founded and the approach to relief for interference with those rights. Such approach would carry forward and give practical effect to the goals of the law at the remedial stage.

[89] See ch 2.II.A.iv.

[90] HRA, s 3; *Ghaidan v Godin-Mendoza* [2004] 2 AC 557.

[91] HRA, s 4.

[92] eg *Osman v UK* (2000) 29 EHRR 245 (life); *Storck v Germany* (2006) 43 EHRR 6, [102] (liberty); *Z v UK* (2002) 34 EHRR 3 (torture, inhuman treatment); *Von Hannover v Germany* (2005) 40 EHRR 1 (privacy). See further s I.D below.

The implication of this argument is that in addition to other remedies, such as declaratory and specific relief, a wide range of damages ought to be available to ensure full and effective protection of basic interests. Compensatory damages ought to compensate not only for consequential factual losses, but also for normative damage to the protected interest imparted by a wrongful interference. Such approach affords strong protection to the interest in itself and vindicates its normative importance within the legal order, signalling such interests ought to be treated with the utmost respect and maintained inviolate.

Despite the logic of the proposition that a protective, vindicatory approach to remedies ought to characterise a field constituted to protect and vindicate fundamental interests, English courts have adopted a very restrictive approach to HRA damages which creates a marked disjuncture between the principal concerns of human rights law and remedies.

Since the House of Lords' decision in *Greenfield*, affirmed in the subsequent Supreme Court decision in *Faulkner*, English courts have, according to the 'mirror' approach, more or less followed the ECtHR's approach to monetary awards under Article 41 of the Convention in determining damages claims under the HRA.[93] There is no recognition in the ECtHR jurisprudence that a rights-violation imports normative damage which ought to be compensated regardless of the factual effects of the wrong,[94] and awards under the HRA have generally been 'confined to cases of actual damage'.[95] In terms of non-pecuniary loss the focus is on consequential factual losses, such as distress or injured feelings, so no award will be contemplated if 'the applicant would have been no better off' absent the violation.[96] As such, the great majority of awards under the Act have been very modest awards for distress. Thus, as Lord Millett observed in *Cullen*, '[i]t follows' from ECtHR practice that 'an award cannot be justified by a supposed need … to vindicate a Convention right'.[97]

Such approach ignores the normative dimensions of the wrong itself, the interests that are the law's principal concern, and the primary functions of

[93] *R (Greenfield) v SOSHD* [2005] 1 WLR 673; *Faulkner* (n 39); see ch 5.

[94] O Ichim, *Just Satisfaction under the European Convention on Human Rights* (CUP, 2015) 141–45. All heads of loss recognised by the ECtHR denote consequential factual loss: *Varnava v Turkey* (18 September 2009) App No 16064/90, [224] (GC); *Nikolova v Bulgaria* (2001) 31 EHRR 3, [O-III4]. Damages are limited to 'actual harmful consequences': *ECtHR Practice Direction: Just Satisfaction Claims* (2007) [9] (www.echr.coe.int/Documents/PD_satisfaction_claims_ENG.pdf); *Savriddin Dzhurayev v Russia* (25 April 2013) App no 71386/10, [252] (ECtHR First Section); *Scozzari v Italy* (2002) 35 EHRR 12, [250].

[95] J Steele, 'Damages in Tort and Under the Human Rights Act: Remedial or Functional Separation' (2008) 67 *CLJ* 606, 608, 630–31. One possible exception might be the Supreme Court's recognition of 'loss of liberty' as a recoverable head in *Faulkner* (n 39), though the nature of this head is unclear: see ch 5.2.II.C.i.

[96] *R (Wilkinson) v IRC* [2005] 1 WLR 1718, [24]–[28]; *A v UK* (2009) 49 EHRR 29, [252]; *Abdi v UK* (2013) 57 EHRR 16, [91]; *Shahid v Scottish Ministers* [2015] 3 WLR 1003, [89].

[97] (n 55) [82]; *cf Ashley* (n 23) [22].

human rights law. It makes little sense for the law to afford compensation for consequential losses, which are 'parasitic' on a rights-violation, but not for damage to the interest that is the very object of legal protection. The current approach would be at home within a field, such as negligence, that is concerned to apportion responsibility for material harms, but is not suited to a field concerned to afford strong protection to and vindicate the importance of basic interests in their own right. For example, the right to freedom of expression primarily exists to protect the individual's interest in speaking freely, voicing their opinions etc, not to protect against losses which may flow from interferences, such as loss of earnings. If it were otherwise the relevant right would be a right not to suffer pecuniary loss as a result of an unjustified interference with one's freedom of expression; it would be the suffering of the factual loss that would trigger a violation rather than interference with the interest in freedom of expression, which would simply be a condition-precedent to establishing liability for losses. As has been said of the action for misuse of private information,

> [t]he tort is not a right to be prevented from upset in a particular way. It is a right to have one's privacy respected. Misappropriating (misusing) private information without causing 'upset' is still a wrong. I fail to see why it should not, of itself, attract damages. Otherwise the right becomes empty.[98]

In this light, it is normative damage to protected interests, inherent in any violation of a fundamental right, which should be the first head of damage recognised by the law; it is this head which gives direct expression and effect to the law's primary concerns. It is damages for consequential loss that are less easily justified, being one step removed from the interest that is the object of the law's protection.[99] Nonetheless, availability of compensation for consequential losses, such as distress or lost earnings, is justified by reference to the basic compensatory principle that a victim of a rights-violation should not be left to bear the negative consequences of a wrong. But, as one Judge has observed in respect of damages for wrongful interference with liberty, '[a]n award for distress must of its nature be of less consequence than an award for the actual deprivation of liberty'.[100] It is also strange to find such a narrow focus on material losses, analogous to compensatory torts, given courts have themselves stressed protection and vindication are

[98] *Gulati v MGN Ltd* [2015] EWHC 1482, [143]. And see by analogy: *Hunter* (n 51) 706 (Lord Hoffmann dismissing the idea that nuisance claims are claims for consequential non-pecuniary losses on the basis that this would suggest 'the plaintiff's interest in the land'—the very object of the law's protection—is 'no more than a qualifying condition ... entitl[ing] him to sue for injury').

[99] For discussion see: B Chapman, 'Wrongdoing, Welfare, and Damages' in D Owen (ed), *Philosophical Foundations of Tort Law* (Clarendon Press, 1995).

[100] *R (Biggin) v SOSJ* [2009] EWHC 1704, [36].

central functions of human rights law and that the HRA's aims are wider than compensating material harms.[101]

Within vindicatory torts damages are awarded as of course for damage and loss suffered—both normative damage, and proven factual losses. In contrast, under the HRA courts have rendered damages peripheral, emphasising traditional judicial review remedies, such as quashing orders and declarations, and holding damages to be a remedy of secondary, if any importance, and a remedy of last resort.[102] In consequence damages awards have been rare. A few select areas have witnessed some liberalisation of approach relative to the generally very restrictive approach.[103] But it nonetheless remains the case that HRA awards are very uncommon and damages are a marginal remedy, especially relative to traditional review remedies and damages in tort.

Consistent with the view that damages are of secondary if any remedial importance, courts emphasise that they have a very broad discretion to refuse damages; the making of awards depends on whether the 'court considers that to be the right result'.[104] It is standard for courts to hold a finding of violation sufficient remedy, including in cases where consequential damage or loss may have been suffered and of serious violation, so that denial of awards is the result in very many cases; for example where a prisoner, in violation of his Article 8 rights, was subjected to continuous solitary confinement for an exceptionally long period of 58 months the Supreme Court, in its discretion, resolved that this was not a case entailing suffering of the sort that warranted any award of compensation, and concluding that a finding of violation and award of costs constituted 'just satisfaction'.[105] It is not uncommon to find statements in domestic cases such as: 'There is a factual basis for an award of damage, but that does not mean that an award must follow'.[106] Indeed, courts have emphasised that awards for non-pecuniary loss will be rare.[107] This follows the ECtHR's 'routine treatment of a finding of violation as, in itself, just satisfaction for the violation'[108] and its practice

[101] *Greenfield* (n 93) [9], [19]; *Michael v Chief Constable South Wales* [2015] 2 WLR 343, [127].

[102] *Anufrijeva v Southwark LBC* [2004] QB 1124, [52]–[56]; *Greenfield* (n 93) [9], [19]; *Dobson v Thames Valley Utilities Ltd* [2009] 3 All ER 319, [42] [*Dobson* CA]; *DSD v Commissioner of the Metropolis* [2015] EWCA Civ 646, [66] [*DSD* CA].

[103] Liberalisation has occurred in three main areas: Article 2: *Rabone v Pennine Care NHS Foundation Trust* [2012] 2 AC 72; *Van Colle v Chief Constable Hertfordshire Police* [2007] 1 WLR 1821; Article 3: *DSD v Commissioner for Police* [2015] 1 WLR 1833 [*DSD* HC]; *OOO v Commissioner for the Metropolis* [2011] HRLR 29; Article 5(4): *Faulkner* (n 39).

[104] *YA v A Local Authority* [2011] 1 WLR 1505, [35].

[105] *Shahid* (n 96) [87]–[90], and see for example *Greenfield* (n 93); *Osborn v Parole Board* [2014] AC 1115, [115]; see further ch 7.I.

[106] *R (Guntrip) v SOSJ* [2010] EWHC 3188, [53]; *R (Shaw) v SOSHD* [2013] EWHC 42, [45].

[107] *Greenfield* (n 93) [9], [29]–[30]; *Osborn* (n 105) [2](xiii).

[108] *Greenfield* (n 93) [9].

of only making awards for factual non-pecuniary loss where it considers loss 'sufficiently serious'.[109] In contrast, at common law it is clearly established that declaratory relief is insufficient remedy even for a brief wrongful interference with basic interests; damages are a reflex of the wrong.

Damages have been denied in the courts' discretion on all manner of grounds for which awards could not be denied in other fields of liability, while they have also been denied summarily with little explanation. Public policy concerns, such as floodgates arguments and protection of public funds, have been invoked by English courts to deny awards, while the importance of compensating the victim and vindicating the importance of the right is seldom mentioned nor at the forefront of a court's analysis of damages.[110] Although the ECtHR does not often expressly have recourse to wider policy concerns, it takes into account a range of factors including the parties' character and conduct 'to an extent which is hitherto unknown in English law',[111] for example denying awards according to the victim's moral worthiness, this practice alarmingly being replicated in domestic law.[112] More generally the ECtHR, whose practices English courts must follow according to the mirror approach, exercises a very broad, open-ended remedial discretion such that any number of factors can potentially be taken into account,[113] the Court emphasising its discretion turns on 'what is just, fair and reasonable in all the circumstances of the case'.[114] This formulation is striking in that it is identical—linguistically and in its open-endedness, at least—to the fair, just and reasonable incantation applied to duty of care analysis in negligence. But there are important differences. In negligence policy concerns are legitimately taken into account as they go to the all-encompassing distributive question of whether primary legal obligations ought to be recognised in the first place. In human rights law such wider concerns arise to—far more controversially—leave a victim without remedy for breach of established legal obligations. In neither vindicatory torts nor compensatory torts are damages so contingent.

No clear approach to pecuniary loss has emerged, and if awards for non-pecuniary loss have been rare awards for pecuniary losses have been exceptionally rare. However, in some of the very few cases considering pecuniary losses courts have shown greater willingness to follow common law principles, ie awarding damages for proven losses causally connected to the

[109] *Faulkner* (n 39) [62]–[66]; *Anufrijeva* (n 102) [66]–[70]; see ch 7.I.

[110] See in particular the approach in *Anufrijeva*; see further ch 6.

[111] *Damages Under the Human Rights Act 1998*, Law Com 266/Scot Law Com 180 (2000) [4.96] [Law Commissions Report].

[112] See chs 5.2.II.C.ii, 6.2.V.B.

[113] The Court does not often reason its decisions as to compensation, so it is often impossible to know which factors have influenced it: see ch 5.

[114] *Al-Jedda v UK* (2011) 53 EHRR 23, [114].

wrong, the heads of damage and standards of proof and causation mirroring those in common law fields. For example, in *Infinis*, where a company suffered financial loss through the unlawful denial of a pecuniary benefit to which it was statutorily entitled, in breach of Article 1, Protocol 1, the Court had no hesitation in awarding damages.[115] Policy-type arguments—which have readily been deployed to deny awards for non-pecuniary loss—were summarily dismissed.[116] The case was a strong one as the company had been wrongfully denied a benefit to which it was otherwise lawfully entitled; but even so the readiness with which the Court made an award—damages were 'manifestly appropriate'[117]—stands in stark contrast to the generally reticent approach to non-pecuniary loss. In *Faulkner* too the Supreme Court was seemingly more open to compensating pecuniary losses although its dicta were explicitly limited to losses causally connected to deprivations of liberty.[118]

The approach to pecuniary loss is difficult to marry up with the courts' staunch rejection of common law principles and scales in respect of non-pecuniary loss and adherence to ECtHR practice;[119] indeed, in *Infinis* the Court of Appeal expressly differentiated the general approach for financial loss and that for non-pecuniary loss.[120] An observer may also find the courts' 'warmer' attitudes to damages for financial loss for breach of property rights in commercial contexts, compared to the 'frosty' approach to awards for non-pecuniary losses to natural persons for breaches of 'dignitarian' rights, somewhat perplexing in *human* rights law. No doubt a critical (or not-all-that-critical) legal scholar would have much to say on this, along with the fact that by far and away the highest award made under the HRA was to a company, in *Infinis*.[121]

Notwithstanding the foregoing, English courts have, in other cases (not concerned with corporate proprietary interests), elaborated principles more restrictive than at common law. For example in *Anufrijeva* the Court observed 'significant' pecuniary losses 'clearly caused' by the violation

[115] *R (Infinis Plc) v Gas and Electricity Markets Authority* [2011] EWHC 1873; upheld by the Court of Appeal: [2013] JPL 1037.

[116] ibid [104]–[107]. There was similar enthusiasm for awarding damages for pecuniary loss to a company in *Breyer Group Plc v Department of Energy and Climate Change* [2014] JPL 1346, [151]–[159] (upheld: [2015] EWCA Civ 408).

[117] *Infinis* (n 115) [26]–[27] (Court of Appeal).

[118] (n 39) [13](8).

[119] The ECtHR's approach to pecuniary loss is at variance with domestic approaches. It adopts an open-ended discretionary approach to the decision whether to make awards and assessment of quantum, albeit its approach is relatively more predictable than its approach to non-pecuniary loss: Ichim (n 94) ch 4.

[120] (n 115) [27].

[121] £94,393.62. This award could be dwarfed if Bank Mallet's claim, for £4 billion for breach of Article 1, Protocol 1, is successful. The litigation is ongoing: *Bank Mellat v HM Treasury* [2015] EWHC 1258 (this judgment again evinces warm attitudes to damages claims by companies for pecuniary loss).

would 'usually' be assessed and an award made.[122] The corollary appears to be that if losses are less than 'significant' damages will likely be denied, and even if significant may still be denied. It is unclear whether the 'clearly caused' test is more stringent than typical causation requirements for factual loss. In *Greenfield* it was suggested that for breaches of Article 6, courts would be slow to award damages for pecuniary loss.[123] Such discretionary approach matches the ECtHR's approach.

For vindicatory torts courts presume normative damage and are willing to infer consequential non-pecuniary losses, such as mental distress or frustration, from the facts. Under the HRA no clear approach has emerged regarding proof of non-pecuniary losses. In one context—delay cases under Article 5(4)—courts presume loss where the delay exceeds three months, and presume no loss otherwise.[124] Outside this specific context English courts have sometimes—practice is inconsistent, mirroring the ECtHR's own inconsistent practice—required direct proof of non-pecuniary harm, such as mental distress, before they will consider an award, being unwilling to infer such losses, while some courts have been reluctant to countenance claims other than for 'concrete loss'[125] and, in common with negligence, sceptical about compensating 'free-standing' non-pecuniary losses absent 'severe or permanent injury to ... health'.[126]

A defining feature of the prevailing approach is that English courts tie quantum of awards for non-pecuniary loss to Strasbourg levels of awards, which are far lower than domestic scales for equivalent losses, and repeat as mantra that damages must be maintained at depressed levels even for serious violations and no comparison should be made with domestic scales.[127] Therefore, awards under the HRA 'are generally quite small'[128] and exceptionally modest by domestic standards,[129] while it is important to note

122 *Anufrijeva* (n 102) [59]. This was applied by the Court of Appeal in *Infinis* (n 115) [27].

123 (n 93) [11].

124 *Faulkner* (n 39) [13](12)–(13), (15).

125 *R (Sturnham) v SOSJ* [2012] 3 WLR 476, [16].

126 Ibid [21]–[22] and *Shahid* (n 96) [89]. See also *R (MA) v Independent Adjudicator* [2014] EWHC 3886, [61]; *Amis v Metropolitan Police Commissioner* [2004] EWHC 683, [50]; *R (KB) v South London and South and West Region MHRT* [2004] QB 936, [71]–[73]; *R (Bernard) v SOSHD* [2005] EWHC 452, [54]–[62]; *R (Baiai) v SOSHD* [2006] EWHC 1035, [34]ff; *R (Degainis) v SOSJ* [2010] EWHC 137, [18]; *R (B) v Camden LBC* [2005] EWHC 1366, [98]. It may be that a liberalisation of approach follows from adoption of the mirror approach given there is some precedent in the Strasbourg case law for the Court inferring consequential non-pecuniary losses; as well as the discussion of *Faulkner* in the text see: *Greenfield* (n 93) [16]; *DSD* HC (n 103); *Re Jordan's Application* [2014] NIQB 71, [26]ff; *R (Pennington) v Parole Board* [2010] EWHC 78, [24]–[25]; Law Commissions Report (n 111) [3.26]. Note, however, the Strasbourg Court's approach to proof is far from consistent: D Shelton, *Remedies in International Human Rights Law* 2nd edn (OUP, 2005) 320.

127 *Greenfield* (n 93) [17]–[19]; *Watkins v SOSHD* [2006] 2 AC 395, [73]; *Faulkner* (n 39) [13], [14], [27], [68], [96]; *Pennington* (n 126) [13](i), [20], [22]; *DSD* HC (n 103) [41].

128 *YA* (n 104) [35].

129 See s I.E below and ch 5.

that domestic scales themselves are not particularly high; as the Jackson Report observes, 'the level of general damages in England and Wales is not high at the moment'.[130] Whereas courts, in the light of the Jackson Report, have recently uplifted scales for general damages across tort by 10 per cent to ensure awards remain adequate and that there are sufficient incentives for litigation so as to enable access to justice,[131] a very different mind-set informs the approach under the HRA with courts continuing to depress awards: human rights should not be 'goldplat[ed]'.[132] Furthermore, not only are awards very low in general, but English courts have indicated awards may be further reduced if public interest concerns call for discounting.[133] The overall result is that on those occasions where damages are awarded, human rights claimants are radically undercompensated.

Thus, as far as compensatory damages under the Act go: (1) awards are not made for damage to protected interests; (2) courts may be unwilling to infer consequential non-pecuniary loss; (3) even where factual non-pecuniary losses have been or may have been suffered it is not uncommon for courts to refuse awards, whereas courts appear more willing to make awards for financial losses in particular contexts, although there are restrictive dicta in respect of pecuniary losses too and such awards have been extremely rare; and (4) where awards for factual non-pecuniary loss have been made they have been exceptionally low. Overall, damages are 'sparingly awarded and modest in amount'.[134]

In TAPS the law's primary function is reflected not only in the approach to compensatory damages, but also the range of available damages. The panoply of available damages includes nominal, compensatory, aggravated and exemplary damages (and maybe gain-based and vindicatory damages). In contrast only compensatory (and possibly, in an 'exceptional case', aggravated)[135] damages have been recognised under the HRA, while the Court of Appeal[136] has explicitly ruled out exemplary damages (although the Law Lords[137] have left this open), and nominal awards have been ruled

[130] R Jackson, *Review of Civil Litigation Costs: Final Report* (Stationery Office, 2009) ch 10 [5.6].

[131] ibid ch 10 [5.3]–[5.6], ch 32 [3.3]; *Simmons v Castle* [2013] 1 WLR 1239.

[132] *Michael* (n 101) [125].

[133] *Anufrijeva* (n 102) [75]–[76]; see further ch 6.

[134] *R (Calland) v Financial Services Ombudsman Ltd* [2013] EWHC 1327, [37].

[135] On the possible availability of aggravated damages see: *KB* (n 126) [50]; *DSD* HC (n 103) [40] (defendant's conduct possibly relevant to quantum); Law Commissions Report (n 111) [4.70] fn 132. Higher courts have not formally recognised such damages in human rights law, and it seems unlikely that they will as long as the mirror approach is maintained.

[136] *Anufrijeva* (n 102) [55]; *cf Faulkner v SOSJ* [2011] EWCA Civ 349, [12] (exemplary damages not ruled out in principle) [*Faulkner* CA]; *DSD* HC (n 103) [28], [40], [125]–[127], [138] (ruling out exemplary damages but perplexingly indicating awards could be increased to promote non-compensatory goals typically associated with exemplary awards).

[137] *Kuddus* (n 28) [46], [92]. But see: *Watkins* (n 127) [32], [64].

out.[138] Similarly, the ECtHR only makes compensatory awards; it does not award nominal,[139] aggravated[140] or exemplary[141] damages, and has not, given its compensatory focus, made gain-based awards, stripping the defendant of profits earned through wrongdoing.[142]

Overall, the current approach to HRA damages has very little in common with that for vindicatory torts, and more in common with the approach for compensatory torts, the principal feature of which is that only compensatory damages for actual loss are available. While a 'compensatory' approach makes sense in negligence, given that tort's central aims, it makes little sense in human rights law, where the law's principal aim is protection and vindication of fundamental interests. Further, the prevailing approach has, in general, been a very restrictive one with damages having been rarely awarded and exceptionally modest. Adoption of a restrictive compensatory approach results in a fundamental mismatch between the policy that underpins primary rights and that which characterises the remedial response to breach, and is difficult to justify in the context of the most basic of rights, especially given far less restrictive approaches are taken to award of damages for lesser interests in other fields.

D. Are Positive Obligations Distinguishable?

The HRA, and most human rights instruments in common law jurisdictions, protect only civil and political rights.[143] Such rights generally only impose negative obligations, requiring public authorities to refrain from interfering with citizens' basic interests. Thus, Article 2 imposes obligations on authorities not to kill and Article 10 casts obligations on authorities not to inhibit individuals from freely expressing themselves. These negative obligations are very similar to those within vindicatory torts: in trespass to land the defendant's duty is one not to enter the claimant's land, while in false imprisonment the defendant is under a duty not to confine the claimant.

While civil and political rights traditionally impose only negative obligations, they are increasingly interpreted as casting some limited positive

[138] *Cullen* (n 55) [81]–[82].

[139] *Marckx v Belgium* (1979–80) 2 EHRR 330, [68]; *Lehideux and Isorni v France* (2000) 30 EHRR 665, [60]–[63]; *cf Engel v Netherlands* (1979–80) 1 EHRR 706, [10].

[140] eg *Selcuk v Turkey* (1998) 26 EHRR 477, [116]–[119]; *BB v UK* (2004) 39 EHRR 30, [36]; *Greens v UK* (2011) 53 EHRR 21, [97].

[141] See those references ibid and *Varnava v Turkey* (2010) 50 EHRR 21, [156]. Some argue the ECtHR sometimes awards a 'disguised form of punitive damages' (D Fairgrieve, 'The Human Rights Act 1998, Damages and English Tort Law' in D Fairgrieve et al (eds), *Tort Liability of Public Authorities in Comparative Perspective* (BIICL, 2002) 92–94; Ichim (n 94) 164–70; *KB* (n 126) [50])).

[142] Law Commissions Report (n 111) [4.77].

[143] The South African Constitution being a notable exception.

obligations.[144] Positive obligations, as their name suggests, require authorities to take positive steps to safeguard the claimant's interests. Thus, an authority will breach the obligation by failing to act; in contrast, negative obligations require authorities not to interfere. In certain respects doctrinal features of positive obligations differ from those of negative obligations. In a claim of breach of a negative obligation the court considers whether the defendant interfered with the claimant's interests, and whether any interference was justifiable. In contrast, in adjudicating positive obligations, such as that under Article 2 to protect an individual's life from third-party threats (the *Osman* duty),[145] the court begins by examining whether the conditions-precedent for the positive duty to arise are fulfilled; in an *Osman* claim it must be shown that the authority knew or ought to have known of a real and immediate risk to the claimant's life from a third party. If so, the court examines whether the authority took the required action: in an *Osman* claim the authority's duty is one to take reasonable steps to prevent the risk from eventuating. While there are several types of positive obligation in human rights law, I shall focus on *Osman*-style duties here.

On the face of it there are similarities between positive human rights obligations and the tort of negligence. For example, in common with an *Osman* claim, in negligence the court will first consider whether a duty arises, and then examine breach. Given these structural similarities it may be tempting to argue that if a tort-based approach is taken to damages, the approach for breach of positive human rights obligations should follow that in negligence, an action for breach of a positive obligation being properly conceptualised as 'compensatory', rather than 'vindicatory'.

But care is needed here. Negligence and positive human rights obligations share some common features, and both have structures which are different from the legal structures of TAPS or negative obligations, because, for example, the law's structure must necessarily differ where an obligation is one to take precautions rather than not interfere. However, it does not follow that common policies underlie negligence and positive human rights obligations. While the legal structure of positive human rights obligations necessarily differs from that of negative obligations, both sets of obligations are underpinned by a policy of protection and vindication of basic interests. The reason the law imposes positive obligations, such as the *Osman* duty and similar obligations under Article 3, *on top of* negative obligations is to ensure the strongest possible protection of the most important interests that human rights law protects, such as life and corporeal integrity. The law not only requires authorities not to interfere with basic interests but also that

[144] See A Mowbray, *The Development of Positive Obligations under the European Convention on Human Rights by the European Court of Human Rights* (Hart Publishing, 2004).
[145] *Osman* (n 92).

they take positive steps to ensure those interests are adequately safeguarded against interference by others. That these interests are afforded such strong protection vindicates their importance within the legal order.

There are important differences between the significant doctrinal features of negligence and positive human rights obligations, which demonstrate the different nature of the two fields,[146] and that a compensatory approach to damages for breach of positive human rights duties would be inapt.

The House of Lords decision in *Smith*, recently affirmed by the Supreme Court in *Michael*, provides a good starting point.[147] The claimant argued that the defendant police authority owed a duty in negligence to take reasonable steps to protect an individual where there was a known, specific and imminent threat to that individual's life or personal safety from a third party; in other words they were arguing for a common-law carbon-copy of the *Osman* duty. The House of Lords held that no such duty arose and could only possibly arise at common law in exceptional circumstances. Lord Bingham, dissenting, would have recognised such duty. Whereas no duty arose in negligence, Lord Brown observed, 'the apparent strength of this case might well have brought it within the *Osman* principle so as to make a HRA claim here irresistible'.[148] Similarly, in *Michael* the Article 2 claim proceeded to trial whereas the negligence claim was struck out.

That a duty on authorities to take positive steps to protect life is recognised in human rights law but not negligence reflects that the principal goal of human rights law is to ensure strong protection and vindication of basic interests. The law works outwards from this starting-point to determine what legal obligations ought to be imposed to ensure attainment of this goal. This is not the starting-point within negligence. Negligence's principal concerns are not with protecting and vindicating basic interests but rather with allocating responsibility for material losses. It is therefore unsurprising that the two fields would reach different conclusions on recognition of a duty to protect.

We may see how these different starting points operate to produce different results if we consider how, in *Smith*, the majority—which adopted an orthodox compensatory conception of negligence—and the minority—which adopted a heterodox vindicatory conception of negligence—approached the duty question. Within an orthodox conception of negligence the duty question entails an inquiry into how to allocate responsibility for material loss within society.[149] This implicates a pragmatic, all-things-considered inquiry which goes beyond consideration of

[146] Note, others have also distinguished the fields, albeit on different grounds: F Du Bois, 'Human Rights and the Tort Liability of Public Authorities' (2011) 127 *LQR* 589; D Nolan, 'Negligence and Human Rights Law: the Case for Separate Development' (2013) 76 *MLR* 286.

[147] *Smith v Chief Constable Sussex Police* [2009] 1 AC 225; *Michael* (n 101).

[148] *Smith* ibid [135].

[149] See ch 2.II.B.iv.

the interests of the parties to the dispute; none of the factors taken into account in duty-of-care analysis are afforded a priori priority. If there is a starting-point it is pre-existing duty categories. Importantly the law does not take protection of basic interests as its starting-point, and work outwards to concrete legal obligations; indeed the majority in *Smith* warned against 'yielding to arguments based on civil liberties'[150] and sought to insulate negligence from human rights thinking, maintaining strict separation between the fields.[151] Also of some importance, and diluting any emphasis on individual rights and interests, is the now dominant conception of negligence as a *social* mechanism for allocating responsibility of loss, which in turn implicates a strong focus on which allocation would 'best serve[]' 'the wider public interest'.[152] Given all of this it is unexceptional for courts, as in *Smith*, to view denial of a duty as a necessary 'price to be paid by individuals' in securing 'the interests of the community as a whole'.[153] In reaching this conclusion the majority relied on public policy considerations which indicated imposition of a duty could undermine the public good; these included possible chilling effects on police decision-making and diversion of resources away from front-line services. The claimant's individual interests were given little attention, let alone weight, in the analysis. This reflects the fundamental functional differences between negligence and human rights law. Lord Brown, in rejecting the proposition that negligence should develop to reflect human rights norms, said: 'Convention claims have very different objectives from civil actions. Where civil actions'—specifically negligence—'are designed essentially to compensate claimants for their losses, Convention claims are intended rather to uphold minimum human rights standards and to vindicate those rights'.[154] He said this difference explains, inter alia, the shorter limitation period for HRA claims, which is comparable with the time limit for vindicatory torts such as defamation which is 'intended, analogously, to vindicate a claimant's reputation'.[155]

In contrast, Lord Bingham, adopting a heterodox vindicatory conception of negligence, inspired by human rights thinking, took as his starting

[150] *Smith* (n 147) [74]–[75]; *Elguzouli-Daf v Commissioner for the Metropolis* [1995] QB 335, 349.

[151] *Smith* ibid [81]–[82], [136]–[139]; *Michael* (n 101) [125]ff. A similar approach was taken to arguments that the compensatory tort of misfeasance in public office should be conceived of as a tort for protection of 'constitutional rights': *Watkins* (n 127).

[152] *Smith* ibid [139], [75]–[76], [78]–[79], [106]; *Elguzouli-Daf* (n 150) 349. And see those cases surveyed in *Michael* (n 101) [29]–[96].

[153] *Smith* ibid [139], [75], [106]; see similarly *Smith v MOD* [2014] AC 52, [169]–[170].

[154] *Smith* ibid [138]; *Michael* (n 101) [127]. But note that my view of the implications of this difference for the approach to HRA damages differs from their Lordships.

[155] *Smith* ibid.

point the fundamental importance of the 'right to life'.[156] Adopting this starting-point weights the duty analysis in favour of recognition of duties that would ensure effective protection of relevant interests. Further, within such a human rights framework public policy concerns are less likely to militate against recognition of such a duty. They are conceptualised as countervailing concerns which must be weighty and stand up to searching scrutiny if they are to trump the primary concern with protecting basic interests.[157]

While it is standard, certainly since the case of *Hill* and as illustrated by *Smith* and *Michael*,[158] for policy considerations to militate against imposition of positive duties on public authorities *in negligence*,[159] *in human rights law* the underlying policy of protection of fundamental interests has operated to counterbalance[160] such concerns (it was this approach, *drawn from human rights law*, which informed Lord Bingham's approach in *Smith*). In *Osman* countervailing policy concerns were considered in formulating the conditions-precedent for the Article 2 positive duty to arise and the standard for breach.[161] However, the importance of and normative pull of protecting the fundamental interest in life was such as to ensure that countervailing considerations did not completely negative recognition of a duty.[162] Furthermore, the importance of protecting life shaped the ECtHR's approach to standard for breach. It rejected the British Government's contention that the standard should be gross negligence or wilful disregard. Such standards would be

> incompatible with the requirements of Article 1 ... and the obligations of Contracting States under that Article to secure the practical and effective protection of the rights and freedoms laid down therein, including Article 2. For the Court, and *having regard to the nature of the right protected by Article 2, a right fundamental in the scheme of the Convention*, it is sufficient for an applicant to show that the authorities did not do all that could be reasonably expected of them to avoid a real and immediate risk to life of which they have or ought to have knowledge.[163]

[156] ibid [55]–[58]; *Michael* (n 101) [196] (Lady Hale, dissenting, would, like Lord Bingham, have recognised a positive protective duty at common law, 'leveraging' from human rights law). Tellingly, while novel duties asserted against authorities are often denied on policy grounds, where Lord Bingham's approach—emphasising protection of fundamental interests—has exerted influence positive duties have been found or not ruled out: *Smith v MOD* (n 153) [98].

[157] See similarly Lord Kerr's dissent in *Michael* (n 101) [182]–[186].

[158] *Hill v Chief Constable of West Yorkshire* [1989] AC 53.

[159] A useful survey is offered in *Michael* (n 101) [29]–[96].

[160] But note, recently some judges, albeit in minority, have sought to import negligence-style policy reasoning into the Article 2 context, so as to 'level down' positive obligations: eg *Smith v MOD* (n 153) [146].

[161] *Osman* (n 92) [116].

[162] *Osman* (n 92) [115]–[116]. Contrast the English courts' refusal to recognise a duty in the domestic litigation: *Osman v Ferguson* [1993] 4 All ER 344.

[163] *Osman* ibid [116] (emphasis added).

Significantly, proof of 'actionable loss' is not a prerequisite in human rights law.[164] Breach of a positive duty may be actionable where the only loss suffered is 'free-standing' non-pecuniary loss such as mental distress, or indeed, where no factual loss is suffered. In contrast in negligence loss is the gist of the action, and proof of actual physical or economic damage is a fundamental element of the action. Some might respond that this makes little practical difference given that for those Convention rights discussed here, such as the right to life and not to be tortured, breach of a positive duty to protect and infliction of physical harm will generally run together. However, inhuman or degrading treatment and psychological torture, which are proscribed by Article 3, stand out as instances where there may be no physical or economic harm.[165] The Court of Appeal has indicated in an Article 2 case that damages for mental suffering—not caused by physical injury—endured during the period in which the defendant authority was in breach of its duty may be recoverable.[166] While the focus here has been on Articles 2 and 3, positive obligations arise under other Articles. Whereas negligent deprivation of liberty would only generally be actionable in negligence if it caused physical injury, within human rights law a duty to protect, framed in identical terms to the *Osman* duty, is recognised in respect of third party threats to liberty, and the claimant's action is not dependant on her ability to prove physical harm.[167] Whether the failure to take reasonable steps leaves the claimant materially worse off or not is irrelevant to the question of violation. Similarly, a claimant need not demonstrate loss before bringing a claim for breach of positive duties under Articles 8 and 9,[168] to take but two examples. A damage requirement would only stymie the law's aim of ensuring protection and vindication of individual interests *in themselves*.

Because actionable loss is not a prerequisite to bringing a claim 'but for' causation is not an element either. If the defendant was under a positive duty but failed to take reasonable steps, then a wrong has been committed; the courts have recognised this by observing a 'looser approach to causation' in *Osman* claims compared to negligence claims.[169]

Various other significant differences between positive human rights duties and negligence further evidence the functional divide between them.

[164] But note that Articles 2 and 3 do not impose general, all-encompassing duties to protect life and guard against torture. Claims must allege a breach of a specific obligation owed to a specific individual: *R (Gentle) v Prime Minister* [2008] 1 AC 1356, [6]–[7].

[165] eg *Rahimi v Greece* (5 April 2011) App no 8687/08 (ECtHR First Section): the state breached its Article 3 positive duty to protect, with the result that the applicant 'must have experienced profound anxiety and concern'. There could be no negligence claim here as mere distress is not actionable. Article 3 was also breached by substandard conditions of detention. Again, there could be no negligence claim here as no physical damage was suffered: *R v Deputy Governor of Parkhurst Prison, ex p Hague* [1992] 1 AC 58.

[166] *Van Colle* (n 103) [119].

[167] *Storck* (n 92).

[168] See *Von Hannover* (n 92); *Eweida v UK* (2013) 57 EHRR 8.

[169] *Smith* (n 147) [138]; *Michael* (n 101) [127].

Negligence generally sets its face against imposing liability for omissions (especially where harm is due to third parties); the traditional concern is misfeasance not nonfeasance.[170] A common rationale is positive duties may make significant inroads into defendants' freedom of action, while defendants may not have control over the relevant risk of harm. However, as recognition of positive duties in human rights law attests to, such countervailing considerations may be more easily overcome where the law's policy is one of protection of fundamental interests.

Concepts governing liability in human rights law may be less restrictive than equivalent concepts in negligence. For example, in negligence before a duty of care may be recognised in 'assumption of responsibility' cases the claimant must demonstrate reliance;[171] however, in human rights law the idea of 'assumption of responsibility' has been invoked in a much looser sense, and reliance is not a formal requirement.[172] Further, whereas assumption of responsibility or linked concepts such as a relationship of dependence or the giving of an undertaking to assist may often be prerequisites to holding a defendant liable for omissions in negligence,[173] these are not necessarily prerequisites in human rights law; the tests applied by domestic courts to determine when positive duties arise are far more flexible,[174] while it is now strongly arguable that the *Osman* duty to protect is being generalised by the ECtHR so that in principle it may arise wherever an authority knows or ought to know of a real and immediate threat to life.

While standing under the HRA is generally limited to the right-holder, peculiar to the duty to protect under Article 2, where the right-holder has died relatives or others with a close relationship to the deceased may be afforded standing to bring a claim in respect of breach of the duty owed to the deceased. The deceased's estate may bring a claim in negligence,[175] but this is also true in human rights law.[176] The wider standing rule in human rights law allows a relative to bring a claim where the deceased's estate cannot or is unwilling.[177] The wider rule is justified by the policies underlying human rights law; the rule is explained by the 'nature of the violation

[170] *Stovin v Wise* [1996] AC 923, 943; *Michael* (n 101) [97]ff.

[171] eg *An Informer v A Chief Constable* [2013] QB 579.

[172] *Rabone* (n 103) [22].

[173] WE Peel and J Goudkamp, *Winfield and Jolowicz on Tort* 19th edn (Sweet and Maxwell, 2014) 100–14.

[174] *Rabone* (n 103) [15]ff.

[175] Law Reform (Miscellaneous Provisions) Act 1934.

[176] eg *Van Colle* (n 103) (HRA damages awarded to victim's estate). Overturned on liability: *Smith* (n 147).

[177] *Rabone* (n 103) [44]–[48]; *Nassau* (n 52) [18]–[19]. There is of course an action for dependants under the Fatal Accidents Act 1976, but this is a claim of a different nature, not brought in respect of violation of the primary rights-holder's rights, but a distinct statutory action purely for the benefit of the deceased's dependants. There is also provision for a claim for bereavement damages, but eligibility criteria are exceptionally restrictive.

alleged and considerations of the effective implementation of one of the most fundamental provisions in the Convention system'.[178] Life would not be protected effectively if a victim were killed in consequence of breach of the duty to protect, but no legal finding to that effect could ever be secured because the victim were not alive to sue.

Overall, positive human rights obligations, while they may bear passing resemblance to negligence, are underpinned by a policy of protection and vindication of basic interests, as opposed to compensation for harm. This different rationale is reflected in significant doctrinal differences. For example, where protection of fundamental interests is the primary concern countervailing considerations will be less likely to militate against recognition of positive duties, and there is no place for an actionable loss requirement. Thus, while significant features of positive human rights obligations necessarily differ from those of negative obligations and vindicatory torts, their function is still a protective, vindicatory one *and the approach to damages should follow suit.*[179]

E. Common Functions, Common Interests and Coherence

The argument that vindicatory torts and human rights law share common bonds and should share a common approach to damages, is strengthened by the fact that both fields, while not coextensive in their coverage, protect very similar interests. As Gault J observed, in the New Zealand context,

> [p]rior to the enactment of the [New Zealand Bill of Rights Act 1990] the recognition of the majority of the declared rights and the provision of remedies had evolved in the common law. The modern declarations of rights and freedoms can be seen as a progression in an evolutionary process rather than a departure from the common law.[180]

Thus, for example, false imprisonment and the right to liberty and security protect interests in liberty; battery and the right not to be tortured protect similar interests in corporeal integrity; trespass to land and goods, conversion and nuisance and the right to peaceful enjoyment of possessions all protect proprietary interests. Given the two fields perform near-identical functions *and* protect identical interests or interests similarly fundamental

[178] *Nassau* (n 52) [19].

[179] Even if one rejects this argument and maintains positive obligations are functionally analogous to negligence, the implication for damages would still be that a tort-based approach should be taken, albeit a compensatory approach analogous to that within negligence.

[180] *Simpson v Attorney-General [Baigent's Case]* [1994] 3 NZLR 667, 709. Note: from the perspective of international law both false imprisonment and the HRA claim for invasion of liberty, for example, are performing the same function, affording legal protection to interests in liberty as required by Article 5 ECHR: *Osborn* (n 105) [54]–[63].

in nature, the remedial approach should be analogous across the fields. It would undermine the coherence of English law if the approach to damages for wrongful interference with identical interests protected in identical fashion by actions with near-identical features varied according to whether a claim happens to be made in human rights law or tort. For example, why should liberty or physical integrity be afforded stronger protection at common law compared to human rights law, especially as the polity has, through its elected representatives, specifically designated the interests protected by human rights law as having fundamental status through enactment of a charter of rights. As we have seen, remedial responses not only afford protection to interests, but also play a vindicatory, signalling role, attesting to the importance of protected interests within the law's normative hierarchy. The law takes on a schizophrenic character if remedies in tort signal that an interest is of utmost importance, only for a limp remedial approach in human rights law to suggest those interests are not that important after all. 'One would expect the remedies to be concurrent'.[181]

The following examples illustrate the incoherence and injustice caused by parallel approaches.

Where the interest in privacy is protected horizontally by the action for misuse of private information compensatory damages are available as of course,[182] and precedent increasingly points towards a vindicatory approach, analogous to TAPS. For example *Cooper* seemed to confirm substantial damages (in *Cooper*, £30,000) were available for interference with privacy in itself regardless of consequential loss.[183] Earlier, in *Campbell* Lord Hoffmann endorsed a similar proposition: 'An infringement of privacy is an affront to the personality, which is damaged both by the violation and by the demonstration that the personal space is not inviolate'.[184] In other words, damages may be recovered for the wrong in itself. This approach has now been confirmed in *Gulati*, the Court holding damages may be awarded to 'reflect infringements of the right itself' regardless of consequential losses:[185] 'The absence of distress does not mean that there was any the less an invasion of privacy … If there was an invasion of a right then prima facie there ought to be a remedy'.[186] Aggravated damages are also available for such interferences.[187] In contrast, where a claimant successfully sues directly under the HRA for an identical interference with

[181] A Mason, 'Human Rights and the Law of Torts' in P Cane and J Stapleton (eds), *The Law of Obligations: Essays in Celebration of John Fleming* (Clarendon Press, 1998) 23.

[182] eg *Mosley v News Group Newspapers Ltd* [2008] EMLR 20, [212]–[231].

[183] *Cooper v Turrell* [2011] EWHC 3269.

[184] *Campbell v MGN Ltd* [2004] 2 AC 457, [75] citing *R v Broadcasting Standards Commission, ex p BBC* [2001] QB 885, 900.

[185] *Gulati* (n 98) [111].

[186] ibid [115].

[187] ibid [203].

privacy, damages would be unlikely to be awarded and could be denied on a discretionary basis on a range of grounds, including that the finding of violation is sufficient remedy. If awarded damages would be limited to consequential factual loss, if suffered, and awarded on a significantly lower scale than damages at common law, while aggravated damages are probably unavailable. Given each action protects the very same interest, is underpinned by the very same policy of protection and vindication—human rights law even having spurred the development of the tort—it is difficult to reconcile why such a limp approach is taken to HRA damages.

There is significant divergence between levels of awards for factual non-pecuniary losses, such as distress, awarded under the HRA, compared to scales applied in other fields for identical heads. For example, it is very common for damages for injured feelings to be awarded for statutory equality torts, which prohibit discrimination on various grounds, such as sex, race or union involvement.[188] In that context the following bands have been adopted to guide awards for injured feelings, distress and similar consequential non-pecuniary losses: £500–£6,600 for a less-serious case, such as a one-off or isolated incident of discrimination; £6,600–£19,800 for serious cases which do not merit an award in the top band; £19,800–£33,000 for discriminatory treatment over a lengthy period, with awards over £33,000 being exceptional.[189]

Compared to these scales awards under the HRA have been very low. For example, in *Guntrip* the Court made an award to a prisoner who suffered distress, frustration, stress and annoyance during a two year rights-violating delay, in breach of Article 5(4), in the holding of a Parole Board hearing to determine whether he would be freed or moved to open conditions; this was a 'long period of uncertainty'.[190] On top of the significant period over which distress was suffered there were other aggravating features, the most significant being that Guntrip suffered mental illness, which made it more difficult for him to cope. Despite these significant aggravating features only a modest sum of £1,200 was awarded. Of course it is difficult to compare the distress that one would naturally suffer because of discriminatory treatment, and in consequence of such delay, while much depends on the facts. Even so, it is difficult to justify damages for mental distress at whether one will regain one's liberty or remain in prison, suffered continuously over two years, exacerbated by mental health issues, being equivalent to an award for distress one may feel at an isolated incident of discrimination of the least

[188] In *Greenfield* the Law Lords expressly rejected a submission that HRA awards for distress should follow scales applied in discrimination law: (n 93) [18]–[19].

[189] *Vento v Chief Constable West Yorkshire* [2003] ICR 318 (the bands stated in the text take into account subsequent uplifts since *Vento: Da'Bell v NSPCC* [2009] UKEAT 0227_09_2809; *The Cadogan Hotel Partners Ltd v Ozog* [2014] UKEAT 0001_14_1505).

[190] *Guntrip* (n 106) [52].

serious kind. For example, in the discrimination field an award five times higher than that made in *Guntrip*—£6,000 (accounting for inflation)[191]—was made for distress suffered as a result of an offer of promotion being withdrawn on the basis of the claimant's union activities, where significant *mitigating* factors were present, in particular, the individual took a higher level job in the same organisation a few months later.[192] In another case £5,200 (inflation-adjusted) was awarded for a one-off racist comment.[193]

In *Sturnham* the Supreme Court awarded £300 under the HRA to a prisoner for distress suffered during a six month unlawful delay before the Parole Board.[194] This sum is below the minimum award that would be entertained in discrimination law. The reason that 'awards of less than £500 are to be avoided altogether' in discrimination law is 'they risk being regarded as so low as not to be a proper recognition of injury to feelings'; in other words an award so low would trivialise the claimant's mental suffering.[195] It is difficult to justify why, if an award of less than £500 is not considered proper recognition of injury to feelings in the most trivial case of discrimination, an award of £300 is considered proper recognition of distress, frustration and anxiety suffered over a six month period because of uncertainty over a matter as vital as whether one will regain one's liberty, all in the context of a moderately serious breach of basic rights.

So much for awards for distress alone. The contrast between awards for deprivation of liberty in human rights law and in other fields of English law is just as stark.

The logic that awards for loss of liberty should be equivalent was recognised in the early case law under the HRA. In *KB* Stanley Burnton J, in a statement the gist of which was later approved by the Court of Appeal, said:

> I see no justification for an award of damages being lower under the [HRA] than it would be for a comparable tort. For example, the tort of false imprisonment, if committed by a public authority, will normally, if not invariably, coincide with infringement of article 5(1). I see no reason why there should be any difference between the measure of damages for the wrongful detention of an individual under the two causes of action: in both cases, the object of the award is to compensate the individual for the same wrongful detention.[196]

[191] All adjustments for inflation herein have been calculated using the Bank of England's Inflation Calculator: www.bankofengland.co.uk/education/Pages/resources/inflationtools/calculator/index1.aspx.

[192] *London Borough of Hackney v Adams* [2003] IRLR 402 (award adjusted to 2010 levels, the year of the award in *Guntrip*).

[193] *MOD v Kemeh* [2014] ICR 625 (adjusted to 2010 levels).

[194] *Faulkner* (n 39). See the similarly miniscule awards of £500 and £600 for non-pecuniary loss consequent upon breach of Article 5 made in *R (Haney) v SOSJ* [2015] 2 WLR 76.

[195] *Vento* (n 189) [65].

[196] (n 126) [56]; *Anufrijeva* (n 102) [72]–[73]; *R (Bernard) v Enfield LBC* [2003] LGR 423, [59]–[60].

Significant sums have been awarded for deprivation of liberty in human rights law where common law guidance has been followed. For example in *Kingshott*, the Judge, following awards in false imprisonment, awarded £7,500 under the HRA for 10 days of wrongful imprisonment, where the imprisonment was in good faith and there were no aggravating features.[197] More generally it is perhaps unsurprising that relatively substantial—ie more than modest—awards for non-pecuniary loss, whether in the liberty context or outside it, have been made in cases where the judge has considered common law principles, scales or guidelines.[198] Further, where a tort analogy has been drawn courts have shown little hesitation in exercising their discretion in favour of making awards.[199]

However, the logic of aligned approaches has steadily been lost since the prescription in *Greenfield*, that awards under the HRA should follow Strasbourg levels, has become embedded in judicial practice. Post-*Greenfield* awards for deprivation of liberty have, in general, been modest, and often exceptionally modest, compared to awards for false imprisonment. This is evident if one analyses damages awards to prisoners kept in prison longer than they should have been.

The award in *Evans* serves as an authoritative benchmark for scales at common law, as it was upheld by the House of Lords.[200] In *Evans* a prisoner's release date was miscalculated resulting in her spending 59 more days in prison than she ought to have. Evans was awarded £5,000 for false imprisonment in 1998 (it is important to note the date for the purposes of comparison, given inflation). The imprisonment was in good faith; there were no aggravating features.

Let us compare the award in *Evans* with two awards under the HRA. In the 2010 case of *Pennington* the claimant sought damages for a rights-violating delay of roughly three months between the date the Parole Board should have made and communicated its decision that Pennington should be released from custody on license, and the date when it was in fact communicated.[201] The delay meant that the prisoner spent three more months in prison than he ought to have. As he was bound by *Greenfield* the Judge rejected the submission that damages should follow scales in false imprisonment. The Judge awarded £1,750. This award is nearly four times *less* than that made to Evans, in circumstances where Pennington was wrongly deprived of his liberty for one month *more* than Evans (in 2010

[197] *Kingshott v MOJ* [2009] EWHC 3666, [46]–[49].
[198] eg *DSD* HC (n 103) [130]; *Bernard* (n 196) [62]; *Faulkner* CA (n 136) [12], [18], [22].
[199] *MA* (n 126) [61]–[64]; *KB* (n 126); *Bernard* (n 196); *Kingshott* (n 197); *Faulkner* CA (n 136) [12], [18].
[200] *R v Governor of Brockhill Prison, ex p Evans (No 2)* [1999] QB 1043 [*Evans* CA], upheld: *Evans* HL (n 24).
[201] *Pennington* (n 126).

terms Evans' award was roughly £6,800).[202] Indeed, in *Evans* Lord Woolf MR had observed that a sum of £2,500 (in 2010 terms) would have been 'well below the appropriate figure for 59 extra days of imprisonment';[203] if that figure is 'well below' the appropriate amount for 59 days' imprisonment, it is difficult to see how an amount less than that could constitute appropriate compensation for over 90 days' wrongful imprisonment. An even more striking comparison might be drawn with *Shaw*, in which £2,000 (£1,780 in 2010 terms) was awarded for only 10 hours' false imprisonment, where there were no aggravating features cited.[204] Thus more is awarded for loss of liberty at common law to a person detained for 10 hours than to a human rights claimant wrongly detained for three months.

In its 2011 decision in *Faulkner* the Court of Appeal awarded £10,000 in compensatory damages to a prisoner kept in prison ten months longer than he ought to have been, due to a rights-violating delay before the Parole Board. The Court did not follow a common law approach but did 'place weight on the high value that the common law has always placed on personal liberty and on the courts' consequent disapproval of executive action which unlawfully restricts or interferes with it'.[205] However, on appeal, the Supreme Court, apparently applying Strasbourg levels,[206] reduced the award to £6,500. As in *Evans* there were no aggravating factors, the Court observing that Faulkner's longer stay in prison was down to human errors likely to be made in any administrative system.[207] In 2011 terms Evans was awarded approximately £7,200 for a little under two months' imprisonment, whereas Faulkner was awarded *less* for a period of imprisonment that was *five times longer* than that endured by Evans. A significant factor that reduced the award in *Faulkner* was that the prisoner would have been released on licence, so that he would not have enjoyed complete freedom. But this cannot distinguish *Evans*, given Evans too would have been released on licence. As a matter of principle it is difficult to rationalise why liberty is considered less valuable—*far* less valuable—in human rights law than at common law.

It is not only quantum that varies markedly as between tort and human rights law. Whereas damages follow as of course for vindicatory torts, they have not uncommonly been denied under the HRA for wrongful interference with interests identical to or of analogous importance to those protected by tort. Take for example *Austin*, which involved concurrent claims against

[202] Counsel for Pennington submitted £10,000 should be awarded based on scales in false imprisonment. This seems about right (the figure may be a little high) going by *Evans*.

[203] *Evans* CA (n 200) 1060.

[204] *Shaw* (n 106) [43].

[205] (n 136) [12].

[206] (n 39) [87].

[207] ibid [86].

the police for false imprisonment and breach of Article 5 in circumstances where the police had cordoned off a large protest, with many prevented from leaving for hours.[208] Both claims failed. However, in case he was wrong, the Judge assessed damages. For false imprisonment he would have made awards, albeit very low awards because the Judge did not consider the wrongful imprisonment to be particularly grave.[209] In deciding quantum the Judge considered the damages guideline judgment for false imprisonment.[210] In line with the orthodox common law method the Judge considered the conditions of confinement, the circumstances in which the deprivation of liberty occurred, and the gravity and length of the detention.[211] Turning to the human rights claim the Judge said: 'Damages under the HRA are awarded on different principles from those awarded at common law'.[212] If Article 5 had been breached he would have found that the finding of violation constituted sufficient remedy.[213] Very different factors influenced the Judge compared to those considered at common law. That a declaration of violation would be made told against awarding damages.[214] Seemingly following the Court of Appeal's direction in *Anufrijeva*, that expensive litigation under the HRA seeking small sums should be minimised,[215] the Judge said only the clarification of the point of law raised in the case could have justified the 'great expenditure of public resources on both sides in the conduct of this case'.[216] The Judge continued: 'The thoroughness with which the case has been conducted on both sides would not have been proportionate to any award of damage [sic] that I would regard as within the range of possible awards'.[217] More generally, it has been common for courts to rely on a range of wider concerns—which would be irrelevant to the award of damages at common law—to deny awards. These have included policy concerns such as floodgates arguments and a concern to preserve public funds, as well as other factors, such as the claimant's moral worthiness.[218]

Development of parallel approaches is highly questionable. Whether damages are claimed for deprivation of liberty at common law or under the HRA should make no difference: the tort of false imprisonment and

[208] *Austin v Commissioner of the Metropolis* [2005] EWHC 480 (affirmed: n 37).

[209] ibid [596]. Even in the false imprisonment claim, the Judge probably erred in making such low awards (£100 to one claimant, and nominal damages to another), but it is nonetheless significant that he would have made some award for false imprisonment but not for violation of the HRA.

[210] ibid [581]–[583].

[211] ibid [590]–[599].

[212] ibid [585].

[213] ibid [597].

[214] ibid.

[215] *Anufrijeva* (n 102) [80]–[81].

[216] *Austin* (n 208) [597]; see similarly *B* (n 126) [104]; *R (MD) v SOSHD* [2011] EWCA Civ 453.

[217] *Austin* ibid.

[218] See ch 6.

Article 5 protect the same underlying interest, and victims of rights-violations in each context suffer the same types of damage and loss. Why should these interests be less well protected, damages for mental suffering be awarded on an exceptionally modest scale, and recovery be subject to questionable considerations of efficiency or moral status, simply because the claim is under the HRA? Such approach disrupts the internal coherence of English law and devalues fundamental interests that the common law has long served to protect and vindicate. As Stevens has said of the approach to damages under the HRA: 'Rights at common law are usually treated more seriously'.[219]

Development of parallel approaches is not inevitable. Some jurisdictions take tort-based approaches to constitutional or human rights damages, albeit not necessarily *vindicatory* tort-based approaches, or at least utilise principles derived from tort. For example, Rishworth and Huscroft, in a comparative survey of human rights damages, stated as one of their main conclusions that their research 'tends to indicate that … the courts draw on tort principles when considering whether there has been a breach of the right and when calculating damages'.[220]

To take one jurisdiction as an example, in the New Zealand case of *Dunlea* the Court of Appeal opined that there were 'strong reasons' for not adopting an approach to damages under the New Zealand Bill of Rights Act 1990 (NZBORA) that deviated from tort.[221] This followed on from statements in the seminal case of *Baigent*, which first established the damages remedy, that whether a claim is made in human rights law for 'deprivation of liberty or invasion of privacy', or in 'false imprisonment or trespass', '[t]he same damages may be recoverable by either route'.[222] In *Dunlea* the claimant proved false imprisonment and trespass to land and concurrent breaches of the right to be free from unreasonable search and seizure (NZBORA, section 21) and the right against arbitrary detention (section 22). Keith J, for the majority, reasoned that similar approaches should be taken to damages given

> essentially the same facts lie behind the twin rulings … that the State through its officers has acted in breach of the rights of the plaintiffs, rights long protected by tortious remedies and now affirmed, along with other human rights and fundamental freedoms, in the Bill of Rights.[223]

[219] R Stevens, *Torts and Rights* (OUP, 2007) 91.

[220] *Crown Liability and Judicial Immunity: A Response to* Baigent's Case *and* Harvey v Derrick, NZLC R37 (1997) App B.

[221] *Dunlea v Attorney-General* [2000] 3 NZLR 136, [38]. Note, however, that the New Zealand courts have begun to move away from such approach, towards a wrongheaded 'public interest' conception of damages: *Taunoa v Attorney-General* [2008] 1 NZLR 429; see ch 4.2.I.B, 4.2.IV.

[222] *Baigent* (n 180) 718.

[223] *Dunlea* (n 221) [38].

A further reason against divergent approaches related to the long-standing constitutional function of tort. Keith J said, drawing on seminal tort cases such as *Entick v Carrington*,[224] that '[t]he common law courts have long affirmed that breaches of important rights by officers of the State are to be marked by appropriate awards of damages'.[225] Consistent with the vindicatory approach propounded herein, Keith J observed that in assessing damages it was important to take into account the 'value of the right infringed, both generally and to the individual',[226] later judgments also endorsing the proposition that damages may be awarded for interference with the right in itself, absent factual loss.[227] Thomas J, writing separately, took a different route to reach a similar conclusion. He concluded that damages should vindicate the 'intrinsic value to the plaintiff' of the right, so that damages ought to be awarded for the invasion of the right in itself notwithstanding whether consequential losses were suffered.[228] Thomas J thought damages should not be 'miserly' lest they 'depreciate' the value which the community through Parliament has placed on these rights; he would have gone so far as to set scales *above* tort.[229] As Tipping J said in a later case:[230]

> it must generally be appropriate to compensate for demonstrable harm suffered as a result of a breach of a right of sufficient importance to be affirmed in a Bill of Rights Act. The law would be in a strange state if relatively innocuous common law breaches were compensated as of right whereas breaches of a statutorily affirmed human right of an important kind were deemed less worthy of compensatory redress.

It is also worth noting that comparative jurisprudence shows that even if the decision whether to award damages is a discretionary one, it need not follow necessarily that human rights claimants should be undercompensated relative to tort claimants. In Canada, where damages are subject to judicial discretion, tort is nonetheless considered a useful guide in quantifying damages.[231] Similarly damages under the Trinidadian Constitution are discretionary however '[t]he comparable common law measure of damages will often be a useful guide in assessing the amount'.[232] In Ireland damages under the European Convention on Human Rights Act 2003, while not

[224] (1765) 19 State Trials 1030.
[225] *Dunlea* (n 221) [41].
[226] ibid [42].
[227] *Wilding v Attorney-General* [2003] 3 NZLR 787, [13], [16] (recovery of factual losses barred by accident compensation legislation, however damages for the breach in itself may still be recovered).
[228] *Dunlea* (n 221) [66]–[67].
[229] ibid [83].
[230] *Taunoa* (n 221) [318].
[231] *City of Vancouver v Ward* [2010] 2 SCR 28, [46]ff (albeit the award made in *Ward* itself seems on the low side by tort standards).
[232] *Attorney-General of Trinidad and Tobago v Ramanoop* [2006] 1 AC 328, [18].

available as of right, where awarded have been set at scales above the modest Strasbourg levels of awards, and tort principles are relevant in quantifying awards,[233] not least because a tort-based approach is taken to damages for breaches of the Irish Constitution, according to which substantial sums have been awarded.[234] Thus, as Steele observes, 'the distinction from tort remedies is more glaring in respect of the HRA than it is in respect of constitutional damages claims in many other jurisdictions'.[235]

Overall, the vindicatory approach to damages developed within TAPS offers an appropriate model for adoption in human rights law. This approach has been developed in a field which has the same underlying function as human rights law, and long protected individuals from unjustified interferences by public actors with their basic rights. Adoption of this model would ensure the approach to damages in human rights law was consonant with and gave effect to the policy of protection of fundamental interests that underlies the primary obligations. It would also ensure coherence across English damages law, and fairness among claimants: those who suffer wrongful interferences with their basic interests should not receive wildly different remedies depending on whether they happen to claim in tort or human rights law.

F. What Tort Can Offer

Thus, as a matter of principle, the approach to damages for human rights violations should follow that within vindicatory torts. On top of this an approach informed by tort offers significant benefits.

Tort offers a reasoned and generally coherent, consistent and principled body of existing precedent which can guide the award of damages and assessment of quantum in human rights law, as well as an analytical approach and robust methodology characteristic of the common law method.[236] It offers an established and elaborate set of principles concerning, inter alia, recoverable heads of loss, proof, pleading, contribution, remoteness, causation and assessment, as well as reasoned guidance as to scales of awards. As we

[233] *Pullen v Dublin CC* [2009] IEHC 452.

[234] *Conway v Irish National Teachers Organisation* [1991] 2 IR 305. See, eg, the significant awards made in *Shortt v The Commissioner of an Garda Síochána* [2007] 4 IR 587 (€4,623,871 awarded on a constitutional tort measure for miscarriage of justice); *Sinnott v Minister for Education* [2001] 2 IR 505 (IR£222,500 for non-pecuniary and pecuniary losses pursuant to breach of right to education).

[235] Steele (n 95) 608.

[236] This is not to say that the approach in tort is 'perfect', only that it has many benefits over other approaches, such as one based in Strasbourg practice. Realistically it is probably impossible to devise a perfectly robust or principled approach to damages, especially for non-pecuniary loss.

shall see in chapter 5, the near-inverse is true of Strasbourg jurisprudence on 'just satisfaction', which in large part accounts for the troubled nature of the HRA damages jurisprudence under the mirror approach. These common law principles have been developed over centuries. In particular, much has been achieved in the last 100 to 150 years to place damages within a principled normative framework in the context of which specific and elaborate rules and principles have been and may be developed, as damages increasingly became the province of judges rather than juries, and appellate courts increasingly set down guidance. The resultant rules and principles represent the best efforts of generations of common law judges to mould a law of damages that is fair, coherent and rational, and is consonant with domestic values, conditions and legal traditions. The common law is an authoritative source of principle in this area. It would be folly to disregard it, only to start over again.

The availability of a reasonably coherent, and reasoned corpus of precedent is particularly important when it comes to non-pecuniary loss. Because there is no objective method for calculating such damages, a principled normative framework, consistency and predictability are fundamental to ensuring the legitimacy of awards. Damages for normative damage to basic interests as well as damages for consequential, factual loss have long been awarded within TAPS, meaning there exists a developed set of English principles and reasoned precedents to guide courts adjudicating claims in the human rights context, in terms of what heads of loss ought to be recognised, method of assessment and scales of damages. Further, consistency and certainty have in recent times been improved markedly through provision of tariff-style guidance from courts[237] and the Judicial Studies Board (JSB, now Judicial College).[238]

Some may ask how a court would approach a case concerning wrongful interference with an interest which has not traditionally been directly protected by tort, such as freedom of expression? Courts would take the same approach as where they have been required to assess damages for new heads of liability. For example, in formulating guidance for awards for injury to feelings in anti-discrimination law the Court of Appeal considered previous awards made for discrimination, guidance provided in case law and by the JSB, and had regard to the scales applied in personal injury, malicious prosecution and defamation cases.[239] In *KD* the Court was faced with

[237] See *Thompson v Commissioner for the Metropolis* [1998] QB 498 (false imprisonment); *Heil v Rankin* [2001] QB 272 (personal injury); *Vento* (n 189) (discrimination); *Simmons* (n 131) (general damages across tort). Although they do not set scales, *John v MGN Ltd* [1997] QB 586 and *Cairns v Modi* [2013] 1 WLR 1015 combine to provide detailed guidance on damages in defamation. *Gulati* (n 98) does the same for misuse of private information, and sets a tariff for phone hacking cases (at [230]).

[238] *Guidelines for the Assessment of General Damages in Personal Injury Cases* 12th edn (OUP, 2013).

[239] *Vento* (n 189) [45]–[64].

the novel task of assessing damages under the Protection from Harassment Act 1997.[240] In assessing damages for injury to feelings and anxiety caused by harassment the Court drew on the JSB guidelines on personal injury awards, and the Court of Appeal's guideline judgments for false imprisonment, and discrimination. For the fledgling action of misuse of private information courts have variously considered practice in the fields of defamation, personal injury and anti-discrimination law, as well as those awards made by other courts for the privacy action itself.[241] Of course, as the Court in *Gulati*, the most important decision on privacy damages, observed, as well as surveying the general liability landscape courts must also take seriously the distinctive nature of the privacy action in articulating guidance peculiar to that context; while guidance from other fields is important and helpful, it cannot be transposed automatically or directly.[242] Similarly, Elias CJ, in the New Zealand context, has said, 'when considering redress for breach of [human rights] analogies with awards of damages for other wrongs need to be viewed with care. They may, however, be broadly illustrative for comparative purposes'.[243]

Importantly, in each area discussed here the respective courts did not have to engage afresh with basic questions of principle; while there is legitimate and natural variation in the approach taken in each field, each court was able to elaborate their approach and guidance with reference to established normative frameworks derived from tort and drawing on established methods of assessment.[244] In contrast, the general experience under the mirror approach has been that considerable party and judicial time, effort and resources have been expended trying to divine helpful guidance from Strasbourg jurisprudence with even answers to very basic questions of principle proving illusive, while guidance as to scales is non-existent. Altogether the experience has been rather tortured.[245]

It has become judicial practice to look to awards in other contexts even in established fields of liability.[246] For example, courts now look to (or instruct juries to take notice of) the levels of awards in personal injury cases

[240] *KD v Chief Constable of Hampshire* [2005] EWHC 2550, [184]–[193].

[241] eg *Mosley* (n 182) [212]–[231]; *Cooper* (n 183) [102]–[107]; *WXY v Gewanter* [2013] EWHC 589, [25]ff.

[242] (n 98) [108]ff. For example, scales of damages for anti-discrimination torts could not be drawn upon directly as damages in that context are limited to damages for injured feelings, and there is no recognised head of normative damage, as there is in privacy: at [185]ff.

[243] *Taunoa* (n 221) [10], [323].

[244] As has been the case where courts have drawn on tort in developing the approach to human rights damages elsewhere: eg *Conway* (n 234); *Dunlea* (n 221); *Carey v Piphus* 435 US 247 (1978).

[245] See ch 5.

[246] Though, for a long time, this was not the case: eg *Broome v Cassell & Co Ltd* [1972] AC 1027, 1071–72; *Sutcliffe v Pressdram Ltd* [1991] 1 QB 153, 176, 189–90; *Rantzen v MGN Ltd* [1994] QB 670, 693–96 (all defamation cases).

in assessing general damages for defamation[247] and false imprisonment.[248] This is a welcome development in that such cross-checking facilitates coherence and consistency across the law. As Lord Bingham MR said in *John*:

> It is in our view offensive to public opinion, and rightly so, that a defamation plaintiff should recover damages for injury to reputation greater, perhaps by a significant factor, than if that same plaintiff had been rendered a helpless cripple or an insensate vegetable.[249]

We know that money and physical integrity or reputation are incommensurable, but we also know that physical integrity is, relatively speaking, more important than what others think of us and that, generally, the consequences of interference with one's person can be more drastic and life-changing than the consequences of being libelled.

Overall, the experience in comparatively new fields of liability such as discrimination or privacy demonstrates rules and principles governing damages within torts as well as common law methods for quantifying awards can successfully be adapted to new fields, avoiding the need to reinvent the wheel, and maintaining coherence across English damages law. Similarly, scales applied in established fields have been relied on as a helpful guide for gauging quantum in new fields, this in turn facilitating consistency and fairness across fields of liability, while courts have also been alive to the distinctiveness of each field and adapted scales accordingly. It is thus difficult to disagree with the conclusion reached by the English and Scottish Law Commissions, in their report into human rights damages:

> [W]e consider that in the majority of cases under the HRA the courts in England and Wales will find it possible and appropriate to apply the rules by which damages in tort are usually assessed to claims under the HRA. Indeed, they may find it appropriate to treat those rules as the prima facie measure to be applied ...[250]

II. THE TORT-BASED APPROACH: CORE FEATURES

A. Non-Compensatory Damages

Thus, the approach to damages for breaches of human rights ought to follow that within vindicatory torts, or at the least this model should be the starting point for developing an approach to human rights damages. A core

[247] *John* (n 237) 612–16; *Cairns* (n 237) [25].
[248] *Thompson* (n 237) 512, 515.
[249] *John* (n 237) 614.
[250] Law Commissions Report (n 111) [4.26]. The Commissions added the caveat that results should be checked against the broad principles applied by the Strasbourg Court, in the light of s 8(4) HRA.

feature of this vindicatory approach is that a range of damages ought to be available to remedy rights-violations. These include non-compensatory damages such as nominal, gain-based, punitive and possibly vindicatory damages, discussed herein. Compensatory and aggravated damages are discussed in the next section.

i. Nominal Damages

Nominal damages ought to be available to remedy transitory wrongs in human rights law.[251] As in TAPS such damages would perform a symbolic function, marking out a wrongful interference, that protected interests ought not to have been interfered with, and highlighting the importance of those interests: they are so important that even the most fleeting interference should be marked by an award.[252] Their award also provides a peg upon which to hang costs,[253] which is significant given litigation costs are exorbitant and legal aid increasingly scarce.[254] It is true that commentators increasingly argue nominal damages are otiose, given declarations serve similar functions. But critics often pass over the legal position that declarations are discretionary whereas nominal damages issue as of course.

While nominal awards should be available one would expect such meagre damages to be rare in human rights law, following the practice in false imprisonment and battery, where substantial (that is, more than nominal) damages are generally awarded even for relatively minor infringements, on the basis that a nominal award is insufficient to vindicate the importance of and afford adequate protection to the claimant's basic interests.[255] Further, interferences with basic dignitary interests, even if relatively minor, will often be accompanied by consequential non-pecuniary losses, rendering nominal damages inapt. Transitory interferences with proprietary interests are one class of wrong for which nominal damages may play a larger role, given such interferences seem less likely to cause consequential non-pecuniary losses.

ii. User and Gain-Based Measures

Restitution theorists seek to conceptualise user damages—basic damages for wrongful use of land or a chattel—as restitutionary damages; that is,

[251] Such damages are available to remedy constitutional violations in other jurisdictions: eg *Kearney v MOJ* [1986] IR 116 (Ireland); *Carey* (n 244) 248, 266–67 (US).

[252] *The Mediana* [1900] AC 113, 116; AM Tettenborn and D Wilby, *The Law of Damages* 2nd edn (LexisNexis, 2010) [1.45]–[1.46], [2.05]–[2.08].

[253] But see *Anglo-Cyrian Trade Agencies v Paphos Wine Industries Ltd* [1951] 1 All ER 873; *Barnett v Chief Constable West Yorkshire* [1998] CLY 1451.

[254] See ch 6.2.IV.

[255] Tettenborn and Wilby (n 252) [2.13], [16.04], [16.11]–[16.12].

damages that reverse a gain made by the defendant through their wrong. However, as observed in chapter 2 (section III.C.i), such damages are better classified as compensatory for the normative damage inherent in wrongful interference with proprietary interests. But notwithstanding how one classifies such damages they have natural application in Article 1, Protocol 1 cases in particular. Take the example where a public authority occupies one's land for several years without lawful authority. Such actions violate the right to peaceful enjoyment of property under Article 1, and constitute trespass. It is therefore unsurprising that Article 1 and trespass claims have been made concurrently.[256] In both contexts the wrong entails interference with interests in exclusive possession and use of land, and in both contexts the law's concern is protection of such basic interests and vindication of their importance. English law has an established approach to damages for wrongs of this nature: user damages are awarded as of right, for damage to the claimant's interests inherent in the wrong, assessed according to what would have been a reasonable fee for use.

Unlike user damages, which are best explained as compensatory for normative damage, an 'account of profits' is clearly a *gain-based* remedy, requiring the defendant to disgorge profits made through her wrongful conduct. The remedy is generally confined to equity. For example such awards are made for breaches of fiduciary duty and confidence. They are also available for intellectual property torts, originally via equitable jurisdiction. More recently the House of Lords held such remedy may be awarded exceptionally for breach of contract.[257]

Despite the limited availability of such awards outside equity, some commentators[258] argue profit-based awards should be available more widely and for tortious interferences with non-proprietary interests, such as physical integrity or liberty. If this argument were convincing, it *may* similarly ground a case for recognition of such awards in human rights law according to a tort-based approach. If such awards were available, according to the basic rules that apply to profit-based awards, and which guard against double recovery, the claimant would have the power to elect between compensatory damages and a gain-based award as their basic award, but could not recover both;[259] profit-based awards would be an alternative to

[256] *Bocardo SA v Star Energy UK Onshore Ltd* [2011] 1 AC 380. Similarly, Article 1 claims have been pleaded concurrently with other property-based torts such as conversion: *R (Atapattu) v SOSHD* [2011] EWHC 1388.

[257] *Attorney-General v Blake* [2001] 1 AC 268.

[258] See A Burrows, *Remedies for Torts and Breach of Contract* 3rd edn (OUP, 2004) 384ff; H McGregor, *McGregor on Damages* 19th edn (Sweet and Maxwell, 2014) [14-019]–[14-020]; J Edelman, *Gain-Based Damages* (Hart Publishing, 2002) 145; C Rotherham, 'Gain-based Relief in Tort After *Attorney-General v Blake*' (2010) 126 *LQR* 102.

[259] *Neilson v Betts* (1871–72) LR 5 HL 1; *Island Records Ltd v Tring International Plc* [1996] 1 WLR 1256.

compensation. Just as one may reason—as Lord Nicholls did in *Blake*—that 'it is not easy to see why, as between the parties to a contract, a violation of a party's contractual rights should attract a lesser degree of remedy than a violation of his property rights', one may query why such remedy should not be available to protect those basic interests protected by human rights law.[260]

But one should always be wary of 'no reason why not' arguments, not least because they often ignore the distinctiveness of the doctrinal context in which the argument is being made.

There are strong arguments that the equitable context, from which the remedy originates, is meaningfully distinct from the tort context, which in turn likely explains why different remedies emerged in each field. For example, courts observe the reason a 'fiduciary must disgorge any profits obtained from use of his position' is that he 'ought to be acting for his beneficiary and therefore the beneficiary is to be put in the same position as if the fiduciary had done so'.[261] Such concerns are peculiar to equity. In contrast, awards calculated according to the defendant's profit depart from the basic remedial principle for tortious wrongs: compensation.[262] Where a profit-based measure would exceed a compensatory measure—exactly the type of case in which a claimant would elect the profit measure—quantum would be greater than required to make the claimant whole. In turn this implicates the sorts of objections made to exemplary damages, such as that they constitute a windfall to the claimant. Further, the law's concern in vindicatory torts and human rights law is ensuring protection and vindication of the claimant's interests, and it is consonant with this concern that basic awards should respond directly to damage to those interests.

The common premise of arguments for recognition of account as an alternative to compensatory damages is that the latter may be inadequate on certain facts, say because no loss is suffered, leaving the claimant with no remedy for what may be a serious wrong.[263] But on a vindicatory approach, compensatory damages would be awarded as a matter of course, including in the absence of factual loss, and respond to the seriousness of the interference. Thus, within a vindicatory paradigm it would be a rare situation in which the premise for availability of alternative measures of basic damages would be fulfilled.[264]

260 *Blake* (n 257) 283–84.
261 *Forsyth-Grant v Allen* [2008] EWCA Civ 505, [41].
262 ibid [38].
263 *Blake* (n 257) 285–86.
264 Making a similar point in the contract context, see: ibid.

All of the foregoing suggests that if profit-based awards were recognised as an alternative to compensatory damages within human rights law, their availability ought to be tightly circumscribed.[265] And, indeed, where courts have contemplated the possibility of profit-based awards within tort, they have emphasised such awards would only be awarded 'exceptionally'.[266] Similarly, in contract the remedy is exceptional.[267] However, little judicial guidance has been given as to what constitutes an exceptional case. This 'reflects a lack of clarity as to the objectives served by' such relief.[268]

Various objectives have been articulated. The rationale propounded most commonly is deterrence. But this rationale is not without problems.[269] There is little evidence as to whether profit-based awards in fact deter. Courts are not well placed to assess when such awards are needed to strengthen incentives for compliance. If the rationale is one based in positive consequential effects we would need to know the benefits of such effects outweigh any negative consequential effects that may flow from such awards. Also, rationales for profit-based awards are typically elaborated by proponents of gain-based relief without much sensitivity to the different doctrinal contexts in which they make their arguments; for example deterrence is offered as a general justification across torts, equity and contract.

Thus, if gain-based relief is to be recognised in human rights law (and vindicatory torts), we need to locate a rationale that connects with the law's underlying purposes, and avoids rationales based in speculative behavioural effects. A possible rationale is that such awards could afford *added* protection to basic interests and serve to *strongly* vindicate the importance of those interests and that they ought to be respected *in exceptional circumstances where such added protection and vindication is warranted, and the factual circumstances make stripping profits a rational way of achieving these objectives*.

On this rationale an 'exceptional' circumstance, which would justify a profit-based award, might be one in which fundamental interests are particularly vulnerable to wrongful interference because there are acute financial incentives to commit the wrong, the claimant is a member of a class that is particularly vulnerable to exploitation, and the defendant acted on those incentives, earning a profit through the violation.[270] In such circumstances

[265] The Law Commissions speculated that such damages might be appropriate under the HRA where no other remedy was adequate: Law Commissions Report (n 111) [4.75]–[4.77].

[266] *Forsyth-Grant* (n 261) [31], [33]; *Devenish Nutrition Ltd v Sanofi-Aventis SA* [2009] Ch 390, [88]; *Coventry v Lawrence* [2014] 1 AC 822, [131], [248].

[267] *Blake* (n 257) 285.

[268] C Rotherham, 'Deterrence as a Justification for Awarding Accounts of Profits' (2012) 32 *Oxford Journal of Legal Studies* 537, 537.

[269] ibid.

[270] Drawing on factors propounded by Rotherham ibid.

availability of an award stripping the defendant's profit would afford added protection to the interest, in circumstances where the interest is particularly vulnerable to incursion, and powerfully vindicate the interest in the face of a profit-driven violation, sending a strong signal that the interest is one of fundamental importance, to be treated with utmost respect. The availability of such award may be of particular relevance where the defendant is a private, profit-driven business performing public functions, as is commonplace in the current era of contracting-out and privatisation.[271] Indeed, government itself is increasingly guided by market considerations, while some branches of government operate for profit or are required to break even.[272]

One obvious context in which provision for such awards might be appropriate, and which serves to usefully illustrate the potential role of profit-based awards, is Article 4, which prohibits slavery and forced labour. The Article has recently risen to prominence because of its relevance to human trafficking and work-for-benefits schemes. Consider the following scenario: W is enslaved by Y and Y sells W's labour to Z for a profit (but does not remunerate W in any way). If gain-based awards were available, and the court considered the case exceptional, say because Y deliberately enslaved W to earn a profit, W was in a class particularly vulnerable to exploitation, and Article 4 is among the most important of all human rights, W would have a choice of measures of basic damages. Either (1) an account of profits calculated according to the profits made by Y in selling W's labour to Z; or (2) compensatory damages for losses suffered as a result of enslavement. Obviously, it would be in the claimant's pecuniary interest (and consonant with the law's vindicatory goals) for her to elect the measure which resulted in highest quantum.

Another example might be where a public news agency breaches the claimant's right to privacy by photographing him engaged in intimate acts, intending to publish the photographs to increase circulation of their print media, boost advertising revenue derived from their website, or on-sell the photos for profit.[273] Assuming a court was convinced the circumstances were exceptional, the claimant could elect (i) compensatory damages for normative damage to their privacy interests and consequential losses, or (ii) a profit-based award.

Another example where profit-based awards could have a significant role is where a private business, in its capacity as a public functionary, has possession of individuals' private information, and on-sells that information to a marketing firm for significant profit, in breach of Article 8. Or, consider a

[271] HRA, s 6(3), (5). See ch 4.1.

[272] See ch 4.1.

[273] See further, N Witzleb, 'Justifying Gain-Based Remedies for Invasions of Privacy' (2009) 29 *Oxford Journal of Legal Studies* 325.

situation where a private entity, carrying out public functions in the NHS, skimps on patient care and medical treatment so as to reduce costs and thereby increase revenues, resulting in breaches of Article 3, as patients suffer in degrading conditions through neglect. A similar type of scenario may arise in respect of care of prisoners within private prisons.

As an aside, it is worth observing that the user measure, discussed above,[274] could be adapted to the forced labour and privacy contexts, in order to assess compensatory damages for normative damage to protected interests. For example, where an individual is forced to work without remuneration, in addition to damages for consequential losses such as mental suffering or the economic costs of counselling to cope with trauma, we might consider calculating the award for normative damage according to what would have been a reasonable wage for work performed. Similarly we might assess normative damage in the above privacy scenarios according to what would have been a reasonable fee for sale of the photographs or personal information.

However, that user damages may have natural application in these scenarios is not conclusive of whether normative damages ought to be assessed according to this measure. The reasonable fee measure is typically confined to calculating normative damage to interests in property, ie interests typically valued in market terms. Where damage is to interests such as liberty or physical integrity, not typically valued in market terms, a reasonable price measure is not applied. Similarly, as courts recognise,[275] it would be inappropriate to assess damage inherent in being enslaved or having intimate pictures taken of oneself according to market value, given it entails treating basic dignitarian interests as interests in tradable commodities.[276]

iii. Exemplary Damages

On a vindicatory approach exemplary damages should be available for human rights violations.[277] Because they are a contentious remedy,[278] which go beyond compensation and entail punishment, a function ordinarily reserved for criminal law, they are an exceptional remedy, reserved for

[274] Text to n 256.

[275] *Douglas v Hello! Ltd (No 3)* [2006] QB 125, [246]. The same issues do not arise in relation to account of profits as such remedy does not value the interest, nor serve a compensatory end: [249].

[276] An exception where the reasonable fee measure might be appropriate is where the breach of privacy entails misuse of commercial information.

[277] Note: human rights law imposes at least one restriction. The non-compensatory award cannot be so high as to disproportionately infringe another Convention right: *Tolstoy Miloslavsky v UK* (1995) 20 EHRR 442; *Steel and Morris v UK* (2005) 41 EHRR 22.

[278] Courts acknowledge such damages are anomalous (*Broome* (n 246) 1091; *Kuddus* (n 28) [75]) but ultimately maintain exemplary awards perform a valuable set of functions.

egregious wrongdoing.[279] In *Rookes* Lord Devlin delimited the categories of case in which exemplary damages may be awarded.[280]

One such category is where the defendant cynically commits a tort to make a profit:

> Where a defendant with a cynical disregard for a plaintiff's rights has calculated that money to be made out of his wrongdoing will probably exceed the damages at risk, it is necessary for the law to show that it cannot be broken with impunity.[281]

Thus, even if gain-based damages were unavailable in human rights law, exemplary damages could be awarded against a defendant—whether public authority or public functionary—which committed the wrong driven by potential gains.

It has been suggested that if an account-of-profits-type award was available more widely, this category of *Rookes* could be abolished.[282] The argument should be rejected. Let us start from the premise, posited above, that in certain exceptional situations, where a defendant deliberately breaches a fundamental right, driven by gain, a remedy that goes beyond compensation may be warranted to effectively protect and vindicate basic interests.

First, an account would be ineffective in achieving this added protection and vindication where the cynical wrongdoer, though intending to profit through his wrong, does not realise a profit, say because he incompetently executes his profit-making plan, or ends up making a profit lower than the amount of compensatory damages that could be awarded for the wrong. Exemplary damages may be awarded against the cynical, profit-seeking wrongdoer even if they fail to realise a gain; what matters is that they *intended* to profit from their wrongdoing. Further, exemplary damages are not assessed according to a defendant's profits (although these may be taken into account in assessment), but rather what sum is required to punish the defendant's deplorable conduct, so that it does not follow from an absence of profits that damages should be set at zero.

[279] Many other arguments can be made against availability of exemplary damages, including that they constitute an unjustified windfall for the claimant (see, eg, *Aggravated, Exemplary and Restitutionary Damages*, Law Com 246 (1997) Pts IV–V). The issue can be and has been debated endlessly. However, these sorts of arguments explain why the remedy is an exceptional one, while such damages are a fundamental feature of the English damages tradition, specifically where public entities are defendants, and are consonant with the vindicatory, protective function of TAPS; if such damages are a justifiable response to egregious violations of basic rights by public entities within other vindicatory fields, it is difficult to see why they should not also be available in human rights law. Nonetheless some courts have been reluctant to award exemplary damages for human rights violations: *Ward* (n 231) [56]; *Taunoa* (n 221) [319]–[321]; *Fose v Minister of Safety and Security* [1997] 3 SA 786. But see: *Smith v Wade* 461 US 30, 56 (1983); *Conway* (n 234); *Shortt* (n 234).

[280] *Rookes* (n 27).

[281] ibid 1226–27.

[282] See, eg, the discussion in *Borders v Commissioner for the Metropolis* [2005] EWCA Civ 197, the Court drawing heavily on academic commentary.

Second, an account will only afford effective protection and vindication if the gain sought and realised is financial; other sorts of gain may be difficult to measure and value. However, if our concern is to ensure added protection of basic interests where they are peculiarly vulnerable and interfered with for gain, it is unclear why the law should only address situations where incentives and gains are financial. For example, other types of gains, such as the prospect of political gains or administrative expeditiousness, may operate as strong incentives on authorities to breach legal obligations. Whereas an account cannot afford added protection here—given any gain would not be financial, nor calculable in financial terms—exemplary damages *can*: the conception of 'gain' in the second category of *Rookes* has been interpreted to be wider than financial profits.[283]

Thus even if an account-type remedy were available in human rights law the second category of *Rookes* should be retained. In taking the exceptional and serious step of punishing the defendant for cynically seeking to profit through wrongdoing, exemplary damages serve the 'macro' function of human rights law. These damages afford added *protection* to the claimant's interests where they are particularly vulnerable given gain-based incentives, and strongly *vindicate* the fundamental importance of the interests and that they should be respected, in the face of a deplorable attempt to profit from wrongful interference.

Another category of case in which exemplary damages are available is where public servants have acted oppressively, arbitrarily or unconstitutionally, and compensatory damages are inadequate to punish the outrageous behaviour.[284] This is a longstanding feature of the law of damages, and defining feature of English constitutional tradition. It is difficult to think of a better example to fit this category than a flagrant or wanton breach of a citizen's fundamental rights. Indeed, it would be anomalous if exemplary damages were available in this category for interferences with basic interests at common law, but the very same conduct did not lead to an exemplary award within a field specifically addressed to public defendants where exactly the same or equally fundamental interests were interfered with. A flagrant or wanton wrongful interference with fundamental interests ought to be met with strong affirmation of the importance of those interests, that they ought to be respected, and that 'the law will not tolerate such behaviour';[285] where the law exceptionally punishes a defendant, this 'macro' vindicatory purpose is served: 'the rights of the citizen are vindicated'.[286] It is worth noting that the means of individual officers are

[283] *Rookes* (n 27) 1227 ('This category is not confined to moneymaking in the strict sense'); Burrows (n 258) 414.
[284] *Rookes* (n 27) 1226–28.
[285] *Kuddus* (n 28) [63], [79].
[286] *McIntyre v Lewis* [1991] 1 IR 121, 134.

relevant in determining quantum. However, where awards have been made against the vicariously liable employer, such as the Home Office or Chief Officer of Police, the means of the individual officers is not relevant and damages are unlikely to be reduced according to this factor.[287] Given the defendant in HRA litigation is a public authority rather than official/s, by analogy this factor should not generally affect quantum.

In terms of precedent there was some doubt as to whether exemplary damages could be awarded for breaches of rights under the HRA as the Court of Appeal had, in *AB*, held such damages could only be awarded for an action for which they had been awarded prior to 1964 (the year of the decision in *Rookes*).[288] However, in *Kuddus* the House of Lords overturned this rule and expressly left open the question of whether exemplary damages were available under the HRA.[289]

iv. Vindicatory Damages

'Vindicatory damages' are a novel type of damages. They have been awarded by the Privy Council in a series of Caribbean appeals for violations of constitutional rights,[290] and been recognised or contemplated in other jurisdictions for breaches of human rights.[291] So far no English case has squarely addressed the availability of vindicatory damages under the HRA although, as we shall see, the courts have considered whether such awards should be available for vindicatory torts.

Vindicatory damages are conceptually distinct from damages for normative damage. The former are *super-compensatory* in nature, whereas the latter, while strongly informed by the law's vindicatory purpose, are *compensatory* for damage to the claimant's protected interests. The principles governing vindicatory damages 'are not greatly developed'.[292] However, some principles are discernible. Vindicatory damages are only generally awarded where compensatory damages are insufficient to 'vindicate' the right, and an additional award is considered necessary to mark the sense of public outrage at the violation, the importance of the right and gravity of the violation, and deter future violations.[293] In terms of assessment it has been suggested that awards are 'conventional', '[a]llowance must be made for the importance of the right and the gravity of the breach', account taken of possible deterrence effects of the award,[294] and quantum no more than

[287] *Muuse* (n 27) [84]; *Thompson* (n 237) 517.
[288] *AB v South West Water Services Ltd* [1993] QB 507.
[289] *Kuddus* (n 28) [46], [92] and see the references in nn 136–37 above.
[290] eg *Ramanoop* (n 232); *Merson v Cartwright* [2005] All ER (D) 144.
[291] For example there are elements of such approach in *Taunoa* (n 221).
[292] *Lumba* (n 25) [177].
[293] *Ramanoop* (n 232) [19].
[294] *Lumba* (n 25) [178]–[180].

necessary to recognise the wrong but not derisory.[295] It is not entirely clear how these different, apparently conflicting goals, are to be reconciled in setting awards.

One might consider that, going by their name, such damages ought to form an element of a vindicatory approach to remedies. More specifically one may argue, if such damages are available for constitutional violations they ought to be available for violations of human rights, and for vindicatory torts, which have traditionally protected rights considered 'constitutional'. Thus, in *Ashley* Lord Scott seemed to suggest that vindicatory damages might be available for vindicatory torts such as assault and battery, and breaches of the HRA given human rights, such as the right to life, were at least as important as those protected by Caribbean constitutions.[296]

However, within a vindicatory approach this novel head would be otiose. This was recognised in the post-*Ashley* case of *Lumba*, in which the Supreme Court held, in a false imprisonment claim, such damages are not available in tort, albeit members of the minority[297] would have made a vindicatory award. With one important caveat, the majority was right to reject their availability for vindicatory torts, and the reasoning applies with equal force within a vindicatory approach to human rights damages. Two interrelated reasons given by the majority for rejecting such awards are particularly convincing: the purpose of vindication is met by existing remedies,[298] and vindicatory damages perform similar functions to exemplary damages.[299] Put simply, there is no remedial gap which needs to be filled.

Two of the three main aims of vindicatory awards are to express public outrage at the manner of the interference, and to deter, in circumstances where compensatory damages inadequately perform these functions. However, given exemplary damages are available in tort and would be available in human rights law on a vindicatory approach, and such damages respond to and express outrage at the manner of the violation by punishing the defendant, reinforce the normative force of legal constraints on public officials, and at least in theory deter future interferences, vindicatory damages are not required.[300] The degree of overlap is recognised in the Caribbean cases. Vindicatory and exemplary awards cannot be recovered concurrently; where a vindicatory award is made, 'the purpose of exemplary damages

[295] ibid [180].
[296] *Ashley* (n 23) [22].
[297] (n 25) [176]–[180] (Lord Hope), [195] (Lord Walker), [212]–[217] (Lady Hale).
[298] ibid [101], [236], [237].
[299] ibid [100], [233], [255].
[300] See similarly A Burrows, 'Damages and Rights' in D Nolan and A Robertson (eds), *Rights and Private Law* (Hart Publishing, 2012). One might argue vindicatory damages would be more freely available than exemplary damages, which are limited by the *Rookes* categories. However, vindicatory damages have been developed within constitutional claims against public actors. This category of case roughly maps onto the category of unconstitutional conduct recognised in *Rookes*.

has largely been achieved' given the element of deterrence '[t]hat a substantial award carries'.[301] The overlap was also evident in *Lumba*, where those aspects of the case that convinced the minority a vindicatory award was warranted were the same features that came close to convincing other Justices to make an exemplary award.[302]

The degree of overlap is patent if one considers the sorts of cases in which the Privy Council has made vindicatory awards. If these cases arose in English law it is clear exemplary damages would be awarded as each involves outrageous official conduct. For example, in *Takitota* an individual unlawfully detained for eight years in appalling conditions pursuant to 'flagrant misuse/abuse of power' was awarded $100,000 vindicatory damages in addition to $400,000 compensatory damages.[303] In *Ramanoop* liability for vindicatory damages was established where a police officer, with no justification whatsoever, detained a civilian, severely beat him, subjected him to inhumane treatment and forced him to initial a written document.[304] In *Merson* an award of $100,000 vindicatory damages was upheld where the claimant was subjected to 'outrageous treatment ... with no shadow of justification' by police and prosecutors, including unlawful detention, fabrication of criminal charges, malicious prosecution, and humiliating and degrading treatment.[305]

The third aim of vindicatory awards is to respond to the seriousness/extent of the interference (a consideration distinct from the *manner* of the interference, which concerns the defendant's conduct). But according to a vindicatory, tort-based approach compensatory damages for damage to protected interests would be awarded as of course upon proof of the wrong. Such damages are proportionate to the extent of the interference with the claimant's interests, and take account of and reinforce the normative importance of the interest. There is therefore no need for an extra category of award which responds to seriousness of the interference.

However, an important caveat ought to be entered. If, as in *Lumba* itself,[306] courts, over time, deviate from orthodoxy such that the common law's tradition of making normative awards is lost or weakened, then it may be worth considering the novel remedy of vindicatory damages. Nonetheless, one hopes this does not transpire, given it would be nonsensical to depart from orthodoxy only to have to depart from orthodoxy again to correct for the original departure. Further, as we shall see, vindicatory

[301] *Takitota v Attorney General of The Bahamas* [2009] UKPC 11, [15]; *Webster v Attorney General of Trinidad and Tobago* [2011] UKPC 22, [16]; *Lumba* (n 25) [233]; *Ramanoop* (n 232) [19].

[302] Compare: *Lumba* (n 25) [176], [194] with [165]–[168].

[303] (n 301).

[304] (n 232).

[305] (n 290).

[306] See ch 2.III.C.iii.

damages are far from a perfect substitute for normative damages. Similarly, if English courts persist in limiting compensatory damages under the HRA to factual losses, then there may be an argument for recognition of vindicatory damages, so that, at least in some cases, the normative dimensions of the wrong—ie the extent of the interference with protected interests—are given some recognition at the remedial stage, and victims are not left without remedy according to the happenstance that they did not suffer consequential loss. But this could only ever be a second-best alternative to routine compensatory awards for normative damage.

In this regard, it is important to stress that it would be an error of the first order to view vindicatory damages as a substitute for or analogous to damages for normative damage.

First, vindicatory damages are, as conceptualised in constitutional cases, an exceptional remedy, reserved for serious cases, where other remedies are insufficient. In contrast, normative damages are a standard remedy for violation of basic rights, awarded as of course.

Second, as we have seen, in most cases where vindicatory awards have been made they serve as a surrogate form of exemplary damages. They do not play the same role as normative damages, which specifically respond to and redress damage to the claimant's basic interests: 'Damages awarded to reflect the infringement [of the right in itself] are not vindicatory in the sense of *Lumba*. They are truly compensatory'.[307]

Third, vindicatory damages have been contemplated in cases outside those concerning egregious wrongdoing (ie outside of exemplary-damages-type cases), for example where no compensatory damages were available—on a factual loss analysis—but it was considered important to make an award to mark the wrong. Are vindicatory damages here a substitute for normative damages? The answer is 'no'. First, even if vindicatory damages were awarded in some such cases they would not be awarded as of course, as they are a discretionary, exceptional remedy. Second, quantum of vindicatory damages in these cases is exceptionally modest. For example in *Lumba* the minority Justices would have awarded vindicatory damages of between £500 and £1000 to mark a reasonably serious two year false imprisonment.[308] As argued in chapter 2, the Court in *Lumba* fell into serious error in not making a compensatory award, wrongly conceptualising damages in false imprisonment as concerned solely with factual loss.[309] If the common law tradition had been adhered to, so that damages were

[307] *Gulati* (n 98) [132].

[308] See the references in n 297 above. These figures seem to be plucked out of thin air, it being unclear how they were calculated. Unlike normative damages, for which there is an established analytical framework for setting quantum, awards corresponding with extent of the interference with underlying interests, there is no such framework for vindicatory damages.

[309] See ch 2.III.C.iii.

awarded for normative damage to liberty inherent in the false imprisonment, one would have expected a compensatory award for normative damage, suffered over a two year period, excluding consequential losses, to have been in the tens of thousands of pounds. An award of £500 or £1000 is no substitute.

If vindicatory damages in cases of outrageous violation, such as *Merson* and *Ramanoop*, serve as surrogate exemplary damages, vindicatory damages as mooted by the minority in *Lumba* are equivalent to nominal awards,[310] uplifted a little to reflect that the wrong was serious, or a type of enhanced declaration.[311] In the sense in which vindication is used in this book—to affirm and reinforce the importance of basic interests—an award of £500 for a serious, two year wrongful imprisonment does not vindicate the liberty interest. It achieves the inverse. Such award trivialises an interest of fundamental importance, long afforded strong protection by the common law through routine imposition of substantial damages liability. In this respect there is glaring inconsonance between Lord Hope's remarks in *Lumba* that the defendant's breach was 'deplorable', 'the right is a valuable one', vindicatory awards should recognise the 'gravity of the breach of the fundamental right', any award should not be 'nominal' or 'derisory', and his conclusion that any award of vindicatory damages on the facts should be 'modest', and 'substantially lower' than £1,000.[312] Further, it is worth noting that it is tenuous to suggest, as certain of the minority Justices did in *Lumba*, that such paltry awards would 'encourage all concerned to avoid anything like it happening again';[313] if anything were to alter the Home Office's incentives structure, it is unlikely to be an award that is utterly insignificant relative to the Home Office's Budget, especially in circumstances such as those in *Lumba* where there were powerful political incentives to commit the wrong (which were seemingly acted upon by public officials, with full appreciation of liability risks).[314]

B. Compensatory Damages

Compensatory damages are by far the most important type of damages under a vindicatory, tort-based approach. Other damages, such as nominal or exemplary damages, represent important aspects of a vindicatory approach, but their award would be relatively rare compared to the frequency with

310 For example Lady Hale said vindicatory damages were designed to 'mark the law's recognition that a wrong has been done': *Lumba* (n 25) [213].

311 *Taunoa* (n 221) [255].

312 *Lumba* (n 25) [176], [178], [180].

313 ibid [217].

314 See ibid [154]–[164] for discussion of the officials' conduct.

which compensatory damages would be awarded under such approach. The major implications of a vindicatory approach to compensatory damages for human rights breaches are: (1) such damages should be available *as of course* for recognised damage or loss inherent in or caused by the wrong; and (2) compensatory damages for normative damage to protected interests, inherent in the wrong, ought to be available and awarded regardless of what factual consequences flow from the wrong.

i. Non-Pecuniary Damage and Loss

According to a vindicatory approach all losses inherent in or caused by the rights-violation, both pecuniary and non-pecuniary, should be compensated. Further, where the only loss suffered is non-pecuniary this should be fully compensated regardless of whether it stems from physical damage to person or property. Such 'free-standing' non-pecuniary losses are routinely recovered for vindicatory torts. This contrasts with the position in negligence where non-pecuniary losses such as mental distress are generally only recoverable if linked to physical damage.

In assessing damages for non-pecuniary damage and loss it is important to identify specific heads. Our starting point, given the functional similarities between human rights law and vindicatory torts, is those heads for which damages are awarded routinely within vindicatory torts. As we saw in chapter 2, those heads fall into two categories: (1) injury to the claimant's underlying interests, whether in liberty, physical integrity or reputation etc ('normative' damage), and (2) non-pecuniary, factual losses consequential upon the wrong such as mental distress, humiliation, anxiety, frustration etc. This general framework may readily be read across to human rights law. For example, for violation of freedom of expression the recoverable heads of non-pecuniary loss would include: (1) damage to the claimant's interest in free expression, inherent in the wrong; and (2) non-pecuniary, factual losses consequential upon wrongful interference with free expression, including mental distress, humiliation, frustration etc. The ease with which the framework can be applied should not be surprising given human rights law and the vindicatory torts are close in nature, performing similar functions and protecting similar types of interests.

In common with TAPS, general damages would be 'at large' given damage to interests such as free expression or privacy and consequential non-pecuniary losses such as distress are not susceptible to objective calculation, having no market value. (For interests typically valued in market terms, such as proprietary interests, more concrete measures may be applied to calculate normative damage, such as the reasonable fee measure applied to user damages.)[315]

[315] See text to n 256 above; ch 2.III.C.

Let us first turn to normative damages. Following the vindicatory approach in tort, it necessarily follows that if someone suffers violation of their right to freedom of expression, they suffer damage to their underlying interest in freely expressing themselves, so that damages for normative damage ought to follow as of course. As in vindicatory torts, normative injury ought to be compensated notwithstanding actual effects of the violation. For example, a pacifist campaigner may be completely at peace with an administrative decision prohibiting him from protesting in a public place in violation of his right to free speech, so that he suffers no distress or anxiety in consequence. But he should still receive damages for damage to his interest in freely expressing himself, inherent in violation of his right. Because of his training a secret agent may be immune to methods of non-physical torture, but he should still receive compensation for the very serious violation of his Article 3 rights. An individual, banned from voting in breach of her right to vote, may actually be relieved at not having to choose between political parties for which she has equal contempt, and may well not have voted because of her disillusionment with politics. But she ought to receive damages for being denied the most fundamental of democratic rights. An individual forced into labour in breach of Article 4 may have gained a lot from the experience, and been treated very well, so that he suffers no mental distress or physical suffering; still he ought to be compensated for damage to his fundamental interests in freedom and dignity, that goes with forced labour. This approach gives effect to the underlying policy of the law. It reinforces the normative importance of the underlying interests in and of themselves, as well as affording them strong protection.

When quantifying damages for *normative damage* in tort the courts refer to relevant precedents, including guideline judgments, and also use a factor-based approach to gauge the degree of damage suffered. The most important factors are seriousness of the interference and relative normative importance of the protected interest. In terms of normative importance, *ceteris paribus*, one would expect damages for normative damage inherent in breach of the right to life to be on a higher scale than damages for normative damage inherent in breach of privacy, given the former is arguably the most important of all human rights. In this way damages affirm and reinforce the law's normative hierarchy of protected interests. However, even for those human rights which are, *relatively speaking*, not among the most important, such as life and the prohibition on torture, they nonetheless protect interests considered basic and scales should not be so low as to trivialise the interest.

The seriousness of the interference is the most significant factor in calculating normative damages.[316] It is conceptually separate from the manner

316 Under the HRA the seriousness of the wrong has sometimes been factored into assessment of consequential factual harm (eg *DSD* HC (n 103) [118]ff). However, there is no necessary connection between seriousness of a wrong and degree of actual consequential harm suffered

of infringement, which is the province of aggravated damages (see below in this section). Importantly, a claimant is only compensated for the *extent* of the interference, not for the entire value of the interest: the more serious the interference, the greater the damage to protected interests, the higher the award.

The seriousness or extent of the interference is gauged according to a range of factors. Relevant factors will vary from one right to the next. Just as factors relevant to assessing damage to reputation in defamation, such as how closely the libel touched the claimant's personal integrity or honour, have no relevance in assessing damage to liberty in false imprisonment, and vice versa, factors relevant to gauging seriousness in freedom of expression cases may have no applicability in cases of torture. In developing a tort-based approach courts would need to elaborate the factors relevant to assessing seriousness for different rights. This should be straightforward. For example, for violation of privacy, the sorts of factors which go to whether there is a reasonable expectation of privacy and the nature of that expectation, are likely to be relevant to gauging the seriousness of the interference.[317] Where the violation entails the taking of information, the nature of that information will be material: *ceteris paribus* damages should be higher where the violation entails unauthorised taking of intimate pictures versus unauthorised accessing of the claimant's order history on the Star Wars online store. Extent of publication will be relevant: if the defendant publishes the information in a national newspaper, the interference shall be far more serious than if they publish it to no one. Location may be pertinent: installing a camera in the claimant's family home, and recording them, is likely to entail a far more serious interference with privacy, than recording someone on a public street. Duration shall also bear on quantum: *ceteris paribus*, damages should be higher where the defendant bugs my house for four months relative to where they bug my house for two weeks. The more times a violation is repeated—for example if there have been multiple instances of wrongful accessing of private information—the greater the award should be.

Turning to *consequential non-pecuniary losses*, such as distress, such losses ought to be assessed in light of available evidence, and ought only to be awarded if they would not have been suffered but for the wrong.

(see ch 2.III.C.v); a wrong may be serious but cause no distress whatsoever. Because only consequential harms are currently recoverable under the HRA judges who—understandably—consider that seriousness of the wrong should be reflected in quantum are forced to artificially manipulate awards for distress. However, it is far more preferable to recognise 'compensation for an infringement of the values protected by the right' in itself as recoverable, there being a logical connection between seriousness of the wrong and damages for the wrong in itself. Such approach is 'much more satisfactory, and intellectually justifiable' and 'avoids the undesirable consequences of using distress as some sort of measure of the seriousness of the wrong, for which purpose it is highly imperfect': *Gulati* (n 98) [135].

[317] See further the factors enumerated in *Gulati* (n 98) [229].

However, often there will be no hard evidence to verify whether such losses were indeed suffered, and causally connected to the wrong. In these situations, as at common law, a 'common sense' approach ought to be taken with the court drawing reasonable inferences from the facts. For example, it would be natural for an individual to suffer significant distress at being deported and thereby separated from their family in breach in Article 8. If there is evidence that the claimant has a very close relationship to their family and is also highly sensitive, and thus likely to have suffered greater distress than the ordinary person, then the award is likely to be uplifted; equally if they are a person of exceptional phlegm it may be reasonable to infer that any distress would be less intense. Similarly, we may reasonably infer that a prisoner, imprisoned for many years, would be unlikely to suffer any distress in consequence of being kept in prison several days past his release date, given (i) he is so accustomed to his conditions, and (ii) he may have had no knowledge of the wrong, so that he would have had no reason to be more distressed than he otherwise would have been.

On a vindicatory approach aggravated damages would be awarded where the manner in which the wrong was committed was 'such as to injure the plaintiff's proper feelings of dignity and pride', for example where committed with malice, arrogance, malevolence, insolence or spite.[318] Although triggered by the manner of the defendant's behaviour, such damages are not a punishment.[319] Rather the court gains 'epistemological access to the claimant's injury ... through examination of the defendant's actions';[320] if a claimant knows that the defendant acted spitefully in interfering with their basic interests it is reasonable to infer that this will add to their distress. Thus the same conduct may, and not uncommonly does, warrant both aggravated and punitive damages. However, in principle each serves a different function. Although, it is worth observing that as a matter of practice availability of aggravated damages tends to ensure that the defendant's 'fault' (broadly defined) finds some reflection in quantum: damages for consequential non-pecuniary loss where the defendant acted with good faith will, generally speaking, be substantially lower than damages where the wrong was malicious.

It is pertinent that aggravated damages have traditionally played an important role in claims against public defendants, particularly for battery and false imprisonment. For example, such damages are awarded where the police wrongly arrest or imprison someone in humiliating circumstances or in a 'high handed, insulting, malicious or oppressive manner'.[321] It would

[318] *Rookes* (n 27) 1221, 1229.

[319] See ch 2.III.C.vi.

[320] A Beever, 'The Structure of Aggravated and Exemplary Damages' (2003) 23 *Oxford Journal of Legal Studies* 87, 92–93. But note Beever does not agree with the mental distress conception of aggravated damages.

[321] *Thompson* (n 237) 516.

therefore be a natural extension for such damages to be made available where public officials infringe citizens' fundamental human rights in a similar manner; indeed it would be incongruous if the law were not so extended. For example, it would be difficult to justify why a claimant in false imprisonment ought to receive aggravated damages for high-handed police conduct but not a protestor who is arrested, in violation of his rights to free expression and public assembly, and who, although he is willing to peacefully submit to arrest, is manhandled and subjected to racist remarks by arresting officers. Similarly one would expect aggravated damages to follow strip search of a prisoner by prison guards carried out in a degrading and insulting manner, with no lawful justification in violation of Articles 3 and 8, or a Prison Governor's decision, motivated by personal animus, to intercept and destroy letters between a prisoner and his loved ones in violation of Article 8.

ii. Flexibility in Methodology

The methodology for calculating awards outlined in the previous section is a model approach. As with all models it can be moulded to fit particular contexts.

Take the example of someone deprived of liberty in breach of Article 5. In such cases the courts could follow the approach in false imprisonment, given the similarity of the underlying interests and proscribed conduct. The Court of Appeal has set down scale-based guidelines.[322] Holding all other factors constant, the guidelines indicate that damages be increased according to time detained, on a reducing scale, based on the rationale that gravity of loss/damage will generally correlate with time detained, but at a decreasing rate. As a guideline the Court suggested an award of £500 for the first hour of detention, and roughly £3,000 for 24 hours in custody.[323] For subsequent days the per diem sum would be calculated on a reducing scale.

One reason for adoption of such methodology is that it fits well with the nature of the particular interests. There is an obvious nexus between time imprisoned and resulting injury to liberty, and consequential non-pecuniary losses such as distress. Second, in providing judges with greater guidance, adoption of such approach should facilitate greater consistency.

This scale-based approach remains faithful to the overall framework detailed above. The figures represent the combined sum for injury to liberty and consequential non-pecuniary losses. Further, the court will still use a factor-based approach in deciding whether to increase or decrease quantum, and consider any relevant evidence that goes to factual loss.

[322] ibid 514–18. By way of contrast see the tariff-based approach in *Gulati* (n 98) [230] for breach of privacy by phone hacking.

[323] ibid 514–15 (these figures would be higher now, accounting for inflation).

iii. Pecuniary Loss[324]

While the only damage suffered in many human rights cases will be non-pecuniary, some violations invariably cause consequential financial losses.

One head of pecuniary loss likely to arise is 'loss of earnings'. Where a violation causes personal injury, as in a case of physical torture, the victim's ability to work may be impaired for any period between a short time following the injury, up to the rest of her working life. In such cases the claimant can recover for diminution in her future earning capacity; that is, the difference between the future wages she could have earned and those which she can earn with her diminished capacity. The common law has developed reasonably sophisticated methods for assessing such future losses, involving application of multipliers which incorporate discount rates based in actuarial evidence, with other variables also bearing on final quantum, such as reductions to account for the vicissitudes of life.[325] Another head likely to arise in human rights law is property damage. For example in the course of a rights-violating raid on one's factory the police may cause damage to the building in the course of forcing their way in, while use of smoke or stun grenades may cause damage to delicate factory equipment. Such damage would either be assessed according to the cost of replacement or repair (while one may also recover for the cost of hiring replacement equipment while the damaged equipment is out of action and/or profits lost through loss of use of the equipment).[326] Some rights-violations, such as those involving noise pollution or leakage of sewage, may diminish the capital value of one's land.[327] Such losses can be calculated via the orthodox common law method of subtracting the value of the blighted property from the hypothetical value of the property absent the rights-violating conduct, the court typically assessing these values with the aid of expert testimony.

McGregor identifies a further three categories of pecuniary loss.[328] All have potential application in human rights law. The first is gains prevented by the wrong. For example, a claimant unlawfully deprived of his liberty could claim for lost business profits suffered as a result of his time imprisoned (and the damage this causes his business reputation).[329] The second category includes expenses caused by the wrong. For example, a victim of physical torture could claim medical expenses incurred to treat his injuries

[324] Herein I draw on McGregor's useful categorisations of pecuniary loss: (n 258) [4-049]ff.

[325] See *Wells v Wells* [1999] 1 AC 345; Government Actuary's Department, *Actuarial Tables for Use in Personal Injury and Fatal Accident Cases* 7th edn (Stationery Office, 2011); Burrows (n 258) 281ff.

[326] See Burrows (n 258) 232ff.

[327] eg *Dennis v MOD* [2003] Env LR 34; *Marcic v Thames Water Utilities Ltd (No 2)* [2002] QB 1003 (overturned on liability: [2004] 2 AC 42). See also *Dobson v Thames Water Utilities Ltd* [2011] EWHC 3253 [*Dobson* HC].

[328] McGregor (n 258) [4-053]–[4-061].

[329] *Childs v Lewis* (1924) 40 TLR 870.

and any ongoing and future expenses, such as the cost of medicines, rehabilitative therapy etc.[330] Where the authorities ban release of an author's books in breach of his right of freedom of expression, causing him to hire out a facility to store the books in the meantime, the author could recover the cost of storage. The last category is that of expenses rendered futile. For example the author, whose books were banned, may have paid for the hire of a market stall to sell his books. He may try and mitigate his loss, but if he cannot, the expenses incurred in hiring the stall would be recoverable.

Claimants must specifically plead all pecuniary losses and prove such losses are causally connected to the wrong, while unlike the approach to non-pecuniary losses courts generally require concrete evidence of loss. In respect of some vindicatory torts such as defamation it is rare for pecuniary losses to be claimed and recovered because concrete evidence of such losses is seldom available. Similar difficulties could be expected in some human rights cases, for example where the claimed stigma and damage to reputation caused by an unlawful search of someone's business premises is alleged to have caused a fall in custom.[331] Similarly, where a rights-violating delay before the Parole Board results in the prisoner being kept in prison longer than she should have been, she may find it difficult to recover loss of earnings. It is unlikely she will be able to produce concrete evidence to convince a court on the balance of probabilities that she would have secured a job and been earning a particular wage had she been released when she ought to have been. Such claims are likely to be considered speculative.

iv. Recoverable Heads Not Limited to those Recognised at Common Law

Under the proposed approach human rights damages would not be denied on the basis that a specific head of damage, such as normative damage to one's interest in free expression, is not currently recognised in tort.[332] This point may well seem obvious: the argument is for adoption of a tort-based, vindicatory *framework*, within which the specifics of the human rights approach should be worked out; 'to take the view that breach of Convention

[330] See *DSD* HC (n 103) [123], [136].

[331] As claimed in *Link Technology 2000 Ltd v Attorney-General* [2006] 1 NZLR 1, [22], [88]–[89].

[332] In support of this view see, eg, *Carey* (n 244) 258; *Taunoa* (n 221) [323]; Law Commissions Report (n 111) [4.25]. Within Irish constitutional tort jurisprudence it has been said that 'a right guaranteed by the Constitution or granted by the Constitution can be protected by action or enforced by action even though such action may not fit into any of the ordinary forms of action in either common law or equity and that the constitutional right carries within it its own right to a remedy or for the enforcement of it', while courts specifically envision a claimant will not be confined to pre-existing actions if those are 'ineffective to protect his constitutional right' (*Sinnott* (n 234) 586–87, drawing on a number of earlier judgments).

rights was only actionable in tort if the activity in question is already tortious at common law' 'would be arbitrary'.[333] However, the point requires to be made in the light of views such as those of Laws LJ in *Sturnham*, that damages should not be awarded for a human rights violation except where it has an 'outcome' or 'consequence' 'for the claimant which constitutes or is akin to' a pre-existing private wrong.[334] Laws LJ's examples of where this would be so include deprivation of liberty or diagnosable illness. Also, as a matter of practice English courts have been relatively more willing to countenance damages claims in pockets of human rights law where the claim closely resembles existing torts, as in the context of deprivation of liberty or where physical harm is suffered.[335] This contrasts with great reluctance to award damages for infringements of interests not traditionally protected by damages liability in English law.[336]

One might readily accept that availability of damages for certain consequences in tort may be an indication that such consequences, when they flow from a human rights violation, ought to be compensated. But it does not follow from this that heads of damage in human rights law should be *limited* to those recognised in tort law. Recoverable heads of damage at common law such as loss of liberty, damage to reputation and damages for use of land simply reflect the set of interests that currently benefit from direct legal protection through imposition of liability at common law. Although Laws LJ describes these as 'outcomes' or 'consequences' they are rather heads of normative damage which directly correspond with the interests protected by each action, and are inherent in wrongs rather than consequential upon them. Likewise, losses accurately described as consequential and currently recoverable in tort such as diagnosable illness, mentioned by Laws LJ, or mental distress, reflect the types of negative consequence which are likely to result where interests currently protected by tort are wrongfully interfered with.

Through the HRA Parliament has quite deliberately updated and expanded the range of interests to be afforded legal protection through imposition of liability, beyond interests in person and property protected traditionally by tort. To restrict damages liability to circumstances where

[333] D Oliver, 'The Human Rights Act and Public Law/Private Law Divides' [2000] *European Human Rights Law Review* 343, 350.

[334] *Sturnham* (n 125) [15]. See also, eg, *Shahid* (n 96) [89] (Supreme Court refusing to make award for breach of Article 8 partly on the basis that the violation did not result in 'severe or permanent injury to ... health').

[335] See n 103 above and note property cases at nn 115–16.

[336] eg *Greenfield* (n 93) (procedural rights); *Anufrijeva* (n 102) (duty to protect family life); *Osborn* (n 105) (procedural rights); *V (A Child)* [2004] EWCA Civ 1575 (procedural rights in care context); *Baiai* (n 126) (right to marry); *Shaw* (n 106) (family life); *Shahid* (n 96) (deprivation of private life, social interaction). Contrast the US Supreme Court's (early) approach to constitutional torts, rejecting 'a two-tiered system of constitutional rights': *Memphis Community School District v Stachura* 477 US 299, 309 (1985).

liability arose prior to the HRA is to frustrate the policy underlying the Act: to afford strong protection to and vindicate the importance of enumerated rights. If damages were only to be awarded where the facts could give rise to a successful claim in tort or where there is a direct analogy with an existing tort there would have been little point in providing for damages under the HRA, given damages could in most circumstances (though perhaps not all) have been recovered via existing actions for already recognised heads of damage. By analogy, where new types of damages claim have been created, such as the action for misuse of private information or the statutory anti-discrimination actions, courts have not limited liability to circumstances where the consequences or outcomes of breach would attract liability in pre-existing tort law. To have done so would have been to frustrate the very reasons why new actions were thought necessary.

But to understand fully why Laws LJ's approach is flawed, one must dig a little deeper. Underlying his approach is the idea that wrongs in human rights law are, in general, analogous to 'public wrongs' such as breach of duties of reasonableness, legality and procedural propriety in common law judicial review.[337] As Laws LJ observes, damages are not recoverable for breach of such duties alone, so the implication of an analogy between the fields is that damages ought to be marginalised in human rights law. However, Laws LJ considers an exception should apply and damages should be available where the human rights 'violation amounts to a private law wrong', for which damages would be available in tort; for Laws LJ a human rights violation amounts to a 'private law wrong' where the 'consequence' or 'outcome' of the violation is the sort of consequence for which damages would be awarded in tort.[338] With respect, this argument is unconvincing and ought to be rejected.

If we are to classify the nature of wrongs and their remedial implications according to *consequences*, on Laws LJ's own analysis many breaches of public duties of reasonableness or procedural propriety should be classified as private wrongs and damages ought to be recoverable. Take the example of the Parole Board, with bias and in breach of their common law duty of procedural propriety, deciding not to release a prisoner on licence when, but for the bias, the prisoner would have been released earlier. Because the consequence for the claimant is analogous to the 'consequence' of false imprisonment—deprivation of liberty—the wrong ought, following through Laws LJ's reasoning, to be classified as a private wrong and damages ought to be available for the breach of procedural fairness in itself, that is, in the absence of any tort claim. Yet this is not the law; such breaches will never generate damages liability in themselves regardless of the consequences

337 *Sturnham* (n 125) [15].
338 ibid [15]ff.

that flow from them. Injury to feelings is the most common consequence of assault and of anti-discrimination torts, and often forms the only basis of an award in both contexts. If we are to follow Laws LJ's analysis through, this would suggest that every *Wednesbury* unreasonable or ultra vires decision which causes injury to feelings ought to be classified as a private law wrong, with damages an available remedy. Yet damages are not an available remedy for breach of duties of reasonableness or legality. Indeed, this is not a position one suspects Laws LJ would support, yet it is the position that follows from his reasoning in *Sturnham*.

If we wish to know why damages follow some wrongs but not others we need to look beyond analysis in terms of consequences/outcomes. As is discussed in detail in chapter 4, public wrongs such as breach of the duties in common law review are fundamentally different in nature from wrongs in vindicatory torts or human rights law. Duties such as reasonableness or procedural propriety are duties imposed on public bodies in the interests of the public as a whole, to ensure public power is exercised properly, and which are owed to the public as a collectivity. In stark contrast rights under the HRA, like rights within vindicatory torts, are individual, personal rights, bestowed to protect individual, personal interests. It is therefore a critical error to draw any sort of analogy between common law review and the HRA; they are fundamentally distinct fields. Damages for individuated, personal loss are out of place in common law review because the law's focus is generally not preservation of individual, personal interests but upon the community interest. In contrast damages for personal damage are appropriate for vindicatory torts and across human rights law given each field's concern is protection and vindication of personal, individual interests.

Thus we should reject emphatically the argument that human rights violations are generally analogous to public wrongs, and its implication that damages should generally not be available for human rights violations, except where the wrong has a consequence for which compensation would be awarded in tort. In turn recoverable heads in human rights law should not 'be so limited or confined' to those recognised in pre-existing actions.[339] If human rights law is to fulfil its distinctive purpose, of affording strong protection to and vindicating those interests protected by the HRA, then new heads must be recognised.

Examples of new heads of normative damage that would need to be recognised include damage to one's interest in freedom of expression (Article 10), privacy (Article 8), religious freedom (Article 9) and fair treatment (Article 6). It may also be necessary to recognise new heads of consequential loss or adapt existing heads, given novel circumstances in which damages liability might arise in human rights law. Examples might include

[339] *Taunoa* (n 221) [323].

loss of a relationship with a child in the Article 8 context[340] and loss of real opportunities where procedural rights are breached.[341] Notably the common law has the resources to accommodate even these apparently novel heads: the former is analogous to mental distress while the common law has begun to develop principles to govern damages for loss of a chance.[342]

III. THE RELATIONSHIP BETWEEN HUMAN RIGHTS DAMAGES AND OTHER JUDICIAL REMEDIES

In some cases grant of judicial remedies other than human rights damages, such as declaratory or specific relief, or damages for another wrong, may constitute sufficient remedy, rendering human rights damages unnecessary. In other cases human rights damages ought to be granted in addition to other relief in order to ensure proper protection and vindication of protected interests. That judicial grant of other remedies may affect the decision whether to award human rights damages is reflected in section 8(3) HRA: in deciding whether an award is 'necessary' a court must consider 'any other relief or remedy' granted by a court in respect of the impugned act.

Just as the common law offers a model for human rights damages, so too does it provide the resources for deciding when particular remedies, out of a range of available remedies, ought to be granted. The availability of a range of remedial tools is not novel in English law: 'As a jellyfish trails its tentacles in the warm sea, so from many civil wrongs dangle a plurality of remedial strings'.[343]

This section considers (i) the relationship between human rights damages and monetary remedies for other wrongs, and (ii) the relationship between human rights damages and specific relief.

A. Monetary Remedies

i. General

Applying the ordinary common law rules on concurrent liability a monetary award in tort may suffice to fully remedy a human rights violation. For example, if concurrent claims in false imprisonment and for violation of

[340] See *W v UK* (1991) 13 EHRR 453; Law Commissions Report (n 111) [3.27], [6.160].

[341] See *Tinnelly & Sons Ltd v UK* (1999) 27 EHRR 249, [93]; *Goddi v Italy* (1984) 6 EHRR 457, [35]–[36]; *Lechner and Hess v Austria* (1987) 9 EHRR 490, [64].

[342] Burrows (n 258) ch 4; S Steel, 'Rationalising Loss of a Chance in Tort' in SGA Pitel et al (eds), *Tort Law: Challenging Orthodoxy* (Hart Publishing, 2014). Note: in one context HRA damages for loss of a chance have been explicitly ruled out: *Faulkner* (n 39) [13](10). But see: *Greenfield* (n 93) [12]–[13].

[343] P Birks, 'Rights, Wrongs, and Remedies' (2000) 20 *Oxford Journal of Legal Studies* 1, 7.

Article 5(1) are upheld, then the award for the tort would compensate for all relevant damage and loss suffered, rendering a separate award under the HRA unnecessary; to make two awards for the same damage would constitute double recovery and an unjustified windfall for the claimant.[344] The award for false imprisonment includes compensation for normative injury to liberty as well as for consequential non-pecuniary or economic effects. That an award for a concurrent action may fully remedy a human rights violation and thus render human rights damages unnecessary does not render human rights damages a 'residual' remedy or remedy of 'last resort', as is sometimes claimed;[345] such examples simply illustrate that, as is the case in any liability context, '[t]he measure of any compensatory damages may overlap in some cases but may not be the same at all in others'.[346]

Thus there may be overlaps between human rights law and other liability fields. However, human rights damages will play a particularly important remedial role where no other damages action protects those interests protected by human rights law.[347] Obvious examples include freedom of expression, freedom of assembly and freedom of religion; such interests have not traditionally been protected directly by positive legal rights and imposition of damages liability in English law.[348] Individual interests in being treated fairly, including accessing court, have been afforded legal protection through, inter alia, the duty of procedural fairness in common law judicial review, contempt of court in criminal law and maxims of statutory construction.[349] But those interests have not previously been protected by positive legal rights based in a rationale of individual protection and vindication nor have they been protected through imposition of damages liability, outside limited circumstances.

Certain interests protected by rights under the HRA may be afforded some protection through parallel actions, but the scope of protection may be narrower than under the HRA. For example, false imprisonment protects against interferences with liberty which cannot be lawfully justified. However, if the Parole Board fails to make a speedy determination as to whether a prisoner should be released on licence, with the result that the prisoner is kept in prison longer than he would have been otherwise, there

[344] See, eg, *Manga v Attorney-General* [2000] 2 NZLR 65; *Fose* (n 279) (in respect of assaults); *ZH v Commissioner for the Metropolis* [2012] EWHC 604 (upheld: *ZH* (n 61)) (awards in tort rendered separate awards for breaches of Articles 3, 5 and 8 unnecessary); *Ogieriakhi v Minister for Justice and Equality (No 2)* [2014] IEHC 582 (overlapping liability in EU law, constitutional tort law, and tort law); *cf Stellato v MOJ* [2010] EWCA Civ 1435, [34].

[345] *Anufrijeva* (n 102) [56].

[346] *Taunoa* (n 221) [108].

[347] As was the case in the seminal cases of *Baigent* (n 180); *Bivens* (n 49); *Ward* (n 231).

[348] JNE Varuhas, 'The Reformation of English Administrative Law? "Rights", Rhetoric and Reality' (2013) 72 *CLJ* 369, 403–04.

[349] ibid 404–05.

shall be no false imprisonment because there was still statutory authority to detain the prisoner for the relevant period.[350] But under the HRA the prisoner's liberty interests are afforded stronger procedural protection, in that the prisoner has a right against the Parole Board to a speedy determination in situations where his liberty is at stake, so that there would be a human rights violation in the scenario just described.[351] Similarly, false imprisonment is not an action concerned with conditions of detention, while negligence only protects against physical harm or illness suffered in custody in some circumstances. In contrast Article 3 specifically protects against conditions that are degrading or inhuman, whether or not they result in physical harm.[352] There is generally no duty on authorities in tort equivalent to the *Osman* duty,[353] nor is there a duty in tort to investigate deaths in custody, as there is under Article 2, or allegations of torture, as under Article 3. Beyond informational privacy interests protected by the fledgling action for misuse of private information, there continues to be no direct and comprehensive protection of privacy interests more generally by a damages action other than that under the HRA.[354]

Thus, sometimes damages awarded for other actions may serve to effectively remedy human rights violations. In other cases HRA damages will be the only relief available to redress damage incurred through a violation.

ii. Disciplining the Current Approach to Concurrent Liability Under the HRA: Case Study on Nuisance and Article 8

The common law rules governing concurrent liability are clear and straightforward, and based upon the axiomatic idea that a claimant should not enjoy a windfall by recovering twice for the same loss.[355] In contrast the approach to concurrent liability in human rights cases has at times been perplexing, and difficult to justify on any principled basis. Indeed concurrent liability is one of the most problematic features of HRA damages jurisprudence.

Let us consider the illustrative example of a household comprised of Bilbo, who is sole owner of the property, Frodo, who is Bilbo's nephew, and Samwise, a friend of Bilbo's and Frodo's, who lives with them as a member of the family. Over the past year their home lives have been seriously affected by odours and smells emanating from a sewage treatment plant situated on the nearby Brandywine River operated by Saruman Industries Ltd, a public functionary. The smells and odours are such as to constitute

350 *Faulkner* (n 39) [16].
351 ECHR, art 5(4); ibid.
352 See text to n 165.
353 See s I.D above.
354 *Wainwright v Home Office* [2004] 2 AC 406; NA Moreham, 'Beyond Information: Physical Privacy in English Law' (2014) 73 *CLJ* 350.
355 For an example of straightforward application of this principle see *Cooper* (n 183) [107].

private nuisance *and* violation of each of Bilbo, Frodo and Samwise's Article 8 rights. The odours and smells have a serious impact on their daily lives, with each suffering distress. Let us assume there is no consequential pecuniary loss, such as diminution in the capital value of the land.

In *Dobson* the High Court[356] held, following Court of Appeal guidance,[357] that in such a situation, Bilbo, having the proprietary interest in the home, would recover damages in nuisance for loss of amenity, as of right. He would receive no damages for the Article 8 violation because the award in nuisance constituted 'just satisfaction'.[358] According to the orthodox position in nuisance neither Frodo nor Samwise can recover because neither has a proprietary interest in the land.[359] Following *Dobson* neither would recover under the HRA either on the basis that damages are not necessary to afford just satisfaction because (i) Bilbo received damages in nuisance, (ii) the Court would declare that Frodo and Samwise's Article 8 rights had been breached, and (iii) because they could pursue other 'remedies' such as abatement notices under dedicated legislation or make a complaint to the water industry regulator, which could fine Saruman Industries. More generally the Court, again following appellate-level guidance, observed that a broad discretionary approach is taken to HRA damages; damages are a last resort; that a balance had to be drawn between interests of the victim and the public; and the Court should have recourse to Strasbourg jurisprudence on compensation—though, as is common, the Court could discern no clear guidance from the ECtHR.

The result would differ on a vindicatory, tort-based approach. Application of such approach to the hypothetical serves to illustrate the lack of a principled basis for the outcomes dictated by *Dobson*. On the approach propounded in this chapter, Bilbo, Frodo and Samwise have all suffered loss through breach of their Article 8 rights: each has suffered normative damage to the protected interest in family and home life and each has suffered significant distress for a year. Is this damage and loss redressed by the other remedies invoked by the Court in *Dobson* to justify denying human rights damages?

The Court in *Dobson* was right to hold that a person in Bilbo's position should receive damages in nuisance for 'loss of amenity'. As we saw in chapter 2 this is not a head of consequential non-pecuniary or pecuniary loss but rather a head of normative damage, for damage to the protected interest in use of land.[360] Is there an overlap between this head of damage and the normative damage to Bilbo's interest in family and home life inherent in

356 *Dobson* HC (n 327) [1017]–[1101].
357 *Dobson* CA (n 102). And see *DSD* HC (n 103) [10]–[14].
358 See similarly *Dennis* (n 327) [91].
359 This is not a prerequisite under Article 8.
360 See ch 2.II.C.

the violation of Article 8? There is some overlap, but not complete overlap. Nuisance protects the amenity interest in land, or the inherent usefulness or utility of one's land; if land is blighted by smells or noises then the land's usefulness is diminished. Protection of one's interest in use of land in turn facilitates the landowner's ability to foster family and home life; this is one use to which the landowner may put his land. But the nature of the protected interest in nuisance is proprietary—the tort is a tort 'against land',[361] a 'property-based tort'[362]—whereas the interests protected by Article 8 are non-proprietary in nature. Article 8 recognises and protects the intrinsic value in fostering and enjoying home life, by oneself and/or through relationships with others. Given the different nature of each interest, and that there is not a complete overlap between the two interests, a substantial (ie more than nominal) award of damages for normative damage under the HRA should be made to Bilbo in addition to the award in nuisance, to reflect that the award in nuisance cannot offer complete compensation for the interference with the interest protected by Article 8, and which also serves to vindicate the importance of that discrete interest. However, the normative award under Article 8 should be a reduced award, in order to account for the degree of overlap between the interests protected by Article 8 and nuisance, and thus to ensure Bilbo is not over-compensated at the defendant's expense.

Turning to Bilbo's consequential non-pecuniary losses, such as distress, it is now fairly clear from precedent that damages for distress cannot be recovered in nuisance, given its proprietary nature.[363] Thus the damages awarded to Bilbo in nuisance do not address his distress, and should not therefore bar Bilbo recovering HRA damages for mental distress suffered in consequence of the odours and smells. Without an award under the HRA Bilbo's consequential non-pecuniary losses, suffered through breach of his dignitarian, non-proprietary rights, would go uncompensated.

Let us turn to the three bases in *Dobson* on which Frodo and Samwise would be denied HRA damages. The first was that Bilbo would be awarded damages in nuisance. It is difficult to follow why this should bear on the decision whether to make Frodo or Samwise an award.[364] It is clear that in

[361] *Hunter* (n 51) 702, 705, 707.

[362] *Coventry* (n 266) [52].

[363] *Hunter* (n 51) 706. In *Dobson* awards for distress were not made, rather 'damages awarded for nuisance, where there has been personal discomfort, are assessed on the basis of compensation for diminution of the amenity value of the land rather than damages for that personal discomfort': (n 327) [1029](1).

[364] Despite the problematic nature of this reasoning, it is pervasive in human rights law. For example in *Rabone v Pennine Care NHS Foundation Trust* [2011] QB 1019 the Court of Appeal determined two damages claims for breach of the *Osman* duty: (i) a claim by the now-deceased victim's estate for damage suffered by the victim in the lead up to her death, and (ii) a claim by the right-holder's relatives for their bereavement. The Court ([94]–[107]) held

nuisance the person who has the right to sue (here, Bilbo) is not 'recovering damages on behalf of other occupiers of the property';[365] rather, he is recovering for the damage to *his own personal*, *individual* interests. The award to Bilbo does not afford a remedy to Frodo or Samwise for the normative damage to their *personal* interests in family and home life, inherent in the violation of Article 8. Further, there can be no argument whatsoever that Bilbo's award compensates Frodo and Samwise for their consequential non-pecuniary loss, such as distress, given damages for such losses are not even available in nuisance.

The second ground for refusing an award was that the court would declare a violation of Article 8. This remedy does not redress loss. If the violation was transitory or minor then a declaration (or nominal damages), on its own, might constitute sufficient remedy. But this was, as in *Dobson*, a reasonably serious violation that lasted for a significant period of time, and caused not insubstantial loss. It is therefore difficult to see how the declaration could constitute adequate remedy.

The third ground was the availability of statutory procedures for application for enforcement or abatement notices, and fines against the company.[366] These are means of enforcing statutory duties or licence conditions owed by Saruman Industries or punishing non-compliance with such duties. An abatement or enforcement notice is analogous in effect to specific relief; it may require the company to cease the conduct which is causing the odours, or reduce its smell pollution, with the possible effect of bringing the rights-violation to an end.[367] But such notice is prospective and does not redress losses already suffered through the rights-violation. A fine is in the nature of a sanction, rather than compensatory for loss, and the proceeds would not, in any case, go to Frodo or Samwise. Thus neither remedy redresses loss suffered in the past through the rights-violation. The availability of these sorts of statutory procedures could not be relied upon to deny damages for loss suffered in nuisance; it is therefore unclear why it is permissible to rely on them to deny damages for loss suffered in consequence of a human rights breach.

damages awarded to the estate can afford just satisfaction for distress suffered by the relatives. But how can damages for distress suffered by person X in the lead up to their death, awarded to that person's estate, constitute redress for distress suffered by a relative of person X, in consequence of person X's death? Contrast the approach of the Supreme Court in *Rabone* (n 103) [62]. Also contrast the more defensible approach in *Van Colle* (n 103) [111] ('We dare say that if any award had been made to the son's estate as such it would have gone to the parents in practice, but it seems better in principle to make separate awards to different victims').

[365] *Dobson* CA (n 102) [36].

[366] eg Water Industry Act 1991, ch II [WIA]; Environmental Protection Act 1990, s 80.

[367] Under legislation compensation may be awarded where an enforcement notice is breached causing loss, but this, again, does not address past loss, and is dependent on such order being in place: WIA, s 22.

Thus, patently, none of the three 'remedies' invoked by the Judge in *Dobson* to deny damages would address or even partially address any of the losses suffered by Frodo or Samwise, and it is therefore difficult to see the rationale for concluding HRA damages are unnecessary on such facts.

English courts have endorsed a 'broad-brush' approach to determination of human rights damages claims.[368] As one might expect of any approach described as 'broad-brush' this has resulted in less than robust, conceptually confused reasoning, and victims being denied awards where they have suffered not insignificant losses, on the basis of reasoning that does not hold water. In contrast a tort-based approach offers a rigorous analytical framework for determining damages claims in cases of concurrent liability; in particular, it offers the tools for identification of different heads of damage suffered by different actors within possibly complex factual matrices, and therefore enables courts to avoid the 'twin evils' of under-compensation and double-counting.

B. Specific Relief

i. Situations where Specific Relief shall be Sufficient Remedy

In some cases specific-type relief—be it a prohibitory or mandatory injunction, or a quashing or prohibiting order—may effectively remedy a violation.[369] Thus, where an administrative decision-maker violates an individual's procedural rights under Article 6 by denying them an oral hearing where they ought to have provided one, an order quashing the administrative decision coupled with a referral back to the original decision-maker will ensure the victim enjoys their primary entitlement. The referral back might be supplemented by a mandatory order, to ensure the oral hearing proceeds in accordance with Article 6. Similarly, where the defendant fails to fulfil its investigatory duties in respect of a death in custody under Article 2, a mandatory order or injunction compelling an investigation would ensure actual fulfilment of those duties. If an authority refuses to allow an eligible voter to vote in breach of the right to vote, a court may issue a mandatory order or injunction requiring the authority to allow the individual to vote. Where an individual is convicted absent due process, a retrial would secure their primary entitlement to a fair trial.

In these scenarios specific relief in fact places the claimant in the position he is entitled to be in, that is one in which his right is respected (or, put another way, the duty owed to him is properly performed). Compared with

[368] *Anufrijeva* (n 102) [65].

[369] Note: quashing, prohibiting and mandatory orders may only be sought via judicial review procedure: Senior Courts Act 1981, s 31.

ensuring actual performance through specific relief, damages can only ever be a 'second-best' and imperfect remedy; as the courts observe of personal injury claims: 'the overwhelming majority of claimants would prefer to forgo any damages in exchange for their pre-accident health and fitness'.[370] As the examples above show, specific-type relief will often have an important role to play in remedying breaches of positive duties, that is duties on authorities to take certain steps, rather than to merely refrain from some action. Specific relief can ensure the authority takes the actual steps it ought to have taken in the first place. In contrast, where the duty is a negative one not to interfere and there has been an interference, that interference cannot possibly be undone by specific relief (albeit an ongoing interference may be halted by specific relief).

ii. Situations where Specific Relief is Granted to Prevent a Wrong

Grant of specific relief may render damages unnecessary by preventing a potential violation ex ante, for which an award would otherwise be required to ensure effective relief, ex post. For example, if, given the delay already suffered, the claimant is virtually certain to suffer violation of their Article 5(4) right if they are not afforded a hearing before the Parole Board within the near future, and there is no indication the Board intends to hear the case soon, the court might consider granting a *quia timet* injunction[371] expediting the claimant's hearing before the Board. As the ECtHR observes, grant of such specific relief is preferable as it ensures the claimant enjoys her primary entitlement rather than the second-best alternative of suffering a violation and receiving damages ex post.[372] Similarly, injunctive relief might be sought where the Home Office intends imminently to deport an individual in clear breach of Article 3; in such a case the failure to prevent the violation may lead to irreparable harm which is unlikely ever to be redressed through damages or other relief.[373]

Interim injunctions can play an important role in preserving the claimant's interests in the face of the defendant's proposed conduct, prior to the wrongfulness of that conduct being conclusively determined at full trial.[374] Such injunctions have, for example, played an important role in actions for

[370] *Cairns* (n 237) [23].

[371] Burrows (n 258) 543–45.

[372] *McFarlane v Ireland* (2011) 52 EHRR 20, [108]; *Nagovitsyn v Russia* (23 September 2010) App no 27451/09, [33] (ECtHR First Section). Specific relief, such as injunctions and mandatory orders, being discretionary, there may be any number of grounds for denying such relief, including futility: see, eg, *R (Betteridge) v Parole Board* [2009] EWHC 1638, [31].

[373] Though there are examples of successful claims for specific relief ordering the return of those unlawfully deported and damages for losses suffered through the wrong: *R (M) v SOSHD* [2011] EWHC 3667.

[374] *American Cyanamid Co v Ethicon Ltd* [1975] AC 396.

misuse of private information, restraining publication of newspaper stories which may entail wrongful invasion of privacy, ahead of full trial.[375] Interim relief could play a similar role in proceedings concerning Article 8.[376] At the supranational level interim measures have featured prominently in the deportation context.[377]

iii. Situations where Specific Relief and Damages are Both Required

In some cases both specific relief and damages may be required to effectively remedy rights-violations. For example, specific relief may issue to bring a continuing violation to an end, with damages also awarded for damage already incurred.[378] It is thus in tort: if a cricket ground is opened next to my house and cricket balls continually strike my house

> in such a way as to be an actionable nuisance, I have two remedies: first, a remedy of damages, which is a response to the wrong which has been committed and, secondly, an injunction to prevent any future infringement of my primary right to my land.[379]

Specific and monetary relief have different roles: specific relief requires the defendant to perform her legal duty now and into the future, while damages make good damage suffered by the claimant through the defendant's breach of duty: 'they cover the past only and not the future'.[380]

One example where both remedies may be relevant is where prison guards interfere with a prisoner's confidential correspondence with his lawyer, in violation of Articles 6 and 8.[381] If the practice had not yet ceased, or to be sure that it does not occur again, a court may grant a prohibitory injunction or prohibiting order, so as to bring the ongoing infringement to an end or prevent repetition. But what of the damage already suffered? The violation caused normative damage to the prisoner's interests in communicating with his lawyer and privacy, and may have caused him mental distress,

[375] eg *CTB v NGN Ltd* [2011] EWHC 1232.

[376] Where a claimant seeks to restrain publication to protect their privacy, s 12 HRA appears to set down a higher threshold for grant of interim relief compared to the ordinary rules (though the common law too has traditionally applied a higher threshold where free speech may be compromised). However, the courts hold there is no one rigid standard for grant of such relief; all depends on the circumstances: *Cream Holdings Ltd v Banerjee* [2005] 1 AC 253.

[377] eg *Abdollahi v Turkey* (3 November 2009) App no 23980/08 (ECtHR Second Section); *FH v Sweden* (20 January 2009) App no 32621/06 (ECtHR Third Section). And see: *M v Home Office* [1994] 1 AC 377.

[378] Even if one puts aside orthodox common law principle, the ECtHR maintains that where a violation is found the state must 'put an end to the violation … *and* … redress so far as possible the effects' (*Scozzari* (n 94) [249] (emphasis added)).

[379] Stevens (n 219) 57; *Coventry* (n 266) [101].

[380] *Jaggard v Sawyer* [1995] 1 WLR 269, 284; *A* (n 64) [116].

[381] Drawing on the facts of *Watkins* (n 127).

frustration and anxiety. Such damage and loss are not remedied by specific relief, while a damages claim could not be made in tort for misfeasance in public office unless, for example, special damage had been suffered, which is unlikely (and, in any case, damages for normative injury are not recoverable in misfeasance, for which damages only address factual loss).[382] Only an award of human rights damages could, in combination with specific relief, ensure full and effective redress.

Another example where both forms of relief may be granted is where a claimant suffers *mala fides* and serious denial of fair process guarantees. In such circumstances the order of a retrial which complies with the requirements of a fair trial would, in effect, 'undo' the normative damage by placing the claimant in the position he was entitled to be in: one in which his protected interests are respected. However, the order, by itself, does not afford complete remedy. For example it does not compensate for consequential non-pecuniary losses such as mental distress caused by the violation, that go beyond and are independent of the ordinary stresses of litigation. Further, aggravated and exemplary damages may be justified given the presence of bad faith.

The foregoing examples are particularly interesting as they illustrate situations where damages may not have been available prior to the HRA. For example there is no general tort of interference with fair trial rights.[383] Thus, deciding how specific relief should interact with damages is a novel enterprise. However, as we have seen, basic, long-standing principles of English law governing the relationship between specific and monetary relief, and which help to identify relevant heads of damage and loss, offer guidance for resolving such matters. It is worth noting that, in contrast, as Lord Woolf observed in *Anufrijeva*, 'Strasbourg fails to give a consistent or coherent answer'[384] to the question of the interrelationship between monetary and specific relief, given that Court generally lacks jurisdiction to grant specific relief.[385]

iv. Situations where Specific Relief is of No Relevance

So far we have considered situations where specific relief may constitute adequate redress, and situations where damages and specific relief are both relevant. Of course there will also be instances where specific relief has no role. For example, where the wrong and associated losses have been suffered in the past, and are not ongoing, such as where prisoners, since transferred to rights-compliant conditions or released, were subjected to degrading and

382 See ibid.
383 Albeit torts such as malicious prosecution and misfeasance in public office may be actionable in certain, narrowly confined circumstances where such interests are interfered with, and special damage suffered.
384 (n 102) [60].
385 See ch 5.

inhuman conditions,[386] or where an individual has been injured or killed, or committed suicide, in circumstances where a public authority failed to properly safeguard their life or bodily integrity.[387] In such cases damages are of prime importance.

v. Situations where Damages may be Awarded in Lieu of Injunctive Relief

Let us turn to situations where it may be appropriate for damages to be awarded *in place of* an injunction. Where rights, such as those protected by tort, are subject to ongoing breach, and the case for grant of an injunction has been made out, a court may, in its discretion, nonetheless refuse such relief and award damages in lieu.[388] It is, however, a long-standing principle that 'very exceptional circumstances'[389] will be required—generally where grant of the injunction would be 'oppressive' to the defendant[390]—before a court will refuse an injunction in the face of a continuing wrong, awarding damages instead.[391] As Lord Kingsdown said in *Imperial Gas Light*,

> if a plaintiff applies for an injunction to restrain a violation of a common law right, if either the existence of the right or the fact of its violation be disputed, he must establish that right ... but when he has established his right at law, I apprehend that unless there be something special in the case, he is entitled *as of course* to an injunction to prevent the recurrence of that violation...[392]

'[T]he Court has always protested against the notion that it ought to allow a wrong to continue simply because the wrongdoer is able and willing to pay for the injury he may inflict'.[393] The principle applies equally to public bodies:

> Neither has the circumstance that the wrongdoer is in some sense a public benefactor (eg, a gas or water company or a sewer authority) ever been considered a

[386] eg *Napier v Scottish Ministers* [2005] 1 SC 229 (upheld: [2005] 1 SC 307); *Taunoa* (n 221).

[387] eg *Rabone* (n 103).

[388] *Shelfer v City of London Electric Lighting Co* [1895] 1 Ch 287; *Coventry* (n 266). There is debate over how to assess such awards. In my view they should be assessed according to a hypothetical bargain between claimant and defendant over a price for releasing the defendant from its legal duty. Damages thus reflect the 'value of the [claimant's] rights' (*Jaggard* (n 380) 288); such damages go beyond compensation for a one-off interference, and entail 'appropriation' of the right's entire value, or much of its value.

[389] *Shelfer* ibid 316. At least in nuisance the Supreme Court has recently endorsed a less strict approach, but nonetheless maintained: 'the *prima facie* position is that an injunction should be granted' (*Coventry* (n 266) [101], [121]). See also *Jaggard* (n 380) 282–83 (test should not collapse into a general balancing calculus).

[390] *Jaggard* (n 380) 287.

[391] See generally the judgments in *Shelfer* (n 388), particularly AL Smith LJ's working rule: 322–23.

[392] *Imperial Gas Light and Coke Company v Broadbent* (1859) 7 HL Cas 600, 612 (emphasis added).

[393] *Shelfer* (n 388) 315–16, 322; *cf Coventry* (n 266) [160].

> sufficient reason for refusing to protect by injunction an individual whose rights are being persistently infringed.[394]

However, it may be that, whether the defendant is a private person or public authority, one ground for denying the injunction and awarding damages in lieu is grant of specific relief would be seriously prejudicial to public interests or third parties.[395]

If such strict approach is taken to awarding damages in lieu of specific relief generally, courts ought to be even more reluctant to allow an ongoing infringement of fundamental human rights to continue, awarding damages in place of specific relief. This argument has special force where interests outside of those typically valued in market terms, such as proprietary interests, are at stake, because damages will offer even less adequate compensation for ongoing wrongful infringement.[396] As Lord Mance observed in *Coventry*, counselling against courts too readily granting damages in lieu for continuing nuisance: 'the right to enjoy one's home without disturbance is one which I would believe that many, indeed most, people value for reasons largely if not entirely independent of money'.[397] Thus one would hope a court would never refuse specific relief where the case for it has otherwise been made, awarding damages in its place, for ongoing inhuman treatment, wrongful imprisonment or denial of free speech, just as it is unthinkable that a court would award damages in lieu of injunctive relief for an ongoing battery or false imprisonment.

That such strict approach ought to be taken where fundamental interests are at stake finds reflection in the 'great writ' of habeas corpus, which is analogous to specific relief in its effects. Where lawful justification cannot be shown for imprisonment habeas corpus issues *as of right* to free the prisoner.[398] As Dicey observed,

> The right of a person who has been wrongfully imprisoned on regaining his freedom to put his oppressor to trial as a criminal, or by means of an action to obtain pecuniary compensation ... affords a most insufficient security for personal freedom ... [l]iberty is not secure unless the law, in addition to punishing every kind of interference with a man's lawful freedom, provides adequate security that everyone who without legal justification is placed in confinement shall be able to get free.[399]

394 *Shelfer* ibid 316.

395 *Coventry* (n 266); *Dennis* (n 327). The majority in *Coventry* rejected the proposition that injunctions should usually be denied for continuing nuisance where public interests are engaged: this would put 'the significance of ... public benefit too high' (at [168]).

396 Adequacy of damages to remedy the wrong is one factor in determining whether damages should be substituted for an injunction: *Coventry* [121], [159].

397 ibid [168] and see [127], [247].

398 eg *Rahmatullah v SOSD* [2012] 3 WLR 1087, [74].

399 Dicey (n 12) 212–13.

Having said all of this, if a human rights violation is, very exceptionally, to be permitted to continue where the case for specific relief has otherwise been made out, 'it should at least be permitted on a basis that affords compensation'.[400]

vi. Specific Relief of Primary Importance in Human Rights Law?

Situations discussed in this section, where specific relief does not fully remedy a rights-violation or has no role, illustrate that on a vindicatory approach damages would play an important role in remedying human rights violations, ensuring strong protection of basic interests and vindicating the importance of those interests, *despite* the in principle availability of specific relief. I highlight this aspect of a tort-based approach because it stands in stark contrast to consistent statements in English decisions that the concern in human rights (or 'public law') cases will usually be to bring the rights-infringement to an end, with compensation of secondary, if any importance.[401]

As has been discussed above[402] and is discussed in more detail in chapter 4, this ordering of remedial priority has been read across from common law judicial review, on the basis that both judicial review and human rights law are fields of public law and should thus share a common remedial approach. Within common law review damages have never been an available remedy and the focus has been on orders based on the prerogative writs, injunctive relief and declarations. A result of reading across this remedial framework to human rights law is damages are viewed as alien and thus marginalised. But the problem with this move is that while common law review and human rights law may have some superficial similarities and are both categorised doctrinally as public law fields, they are fundamentally different in nature. Common law review, at least traditionally, is not concerned with individual rights and interests but with questions of *vires*, and remedies have therefore focused on regulating the exercise of public power so that it is in fact carried out for the public purposes for which it has been conferred. In contrast the gist of human rights law is protection and vindication of individual rights and interests. The approach to remedies for human rights violations ought to follow from the distinctive concerns of human rights law, not those of common law review. By analogy, the law of torts and the law of equity are both fields of private law, but fundamentally different remedial approaches are taken in each field, which reflect distinct concerns. With the coming into force of the HRA the nature of English public law changed, as did the

[400] *Coventry* (n 266) [165].

[401] *Anufrijeva* (n 102) [53]–[56]; *Greenfield* (n 93) [9]; *Dobson* CA (n 102) [42]; *Rabone* (n 103) [82]; *DSD* CA (n 102) [65]–[66].

[402] Text to n 332ff.

range of available relief, and courts must adjust to this new reality, rather than subordinate novel, distinctive fields to pre-existing habits of public law thinking.

For now it suffices to observe that such a generalised setting of remedial priority makes no sense on a vindicatory, tort-based approach. What relief is relevant and/or appropriate in any given case depends on the facts, and further, what relief is claimed by the claimant. As we have seen, in many cases specific relief will have no relevance whatsoever, say, because the claim relates to a past violation. In such situation it cannot be said that damages are of secondary importance, because there is no other remedy in respect of which an order of remedial priority could be set. In other cases, say, of continuing violation, specific relief would be of importance but so too would damages, if damage and loss had been incurred. The idea of remedial priority makes little sense in such situations because different remedies perform different roles. It is probably for these reasons that one does not find an ordering of remedial priority within tort. All depends on the facts, and the remedies sought by the right-holder.

IV. THE TORT-BASED APPROACH AND THE PROVISIONS OF THE HRA

Notwithstanding the normative strength of an argument for a vindicatory, tort-based approach, can such approach be supported on the terms of the HRA? Some important aspects of the Act which bear on this are considered in greater detail in later chapters. In particular, chapter 5 discusses section 8(4), which requires English courts, in deciding whether to make an award and quantum, to 'take into account' the 'principles' applied by the ECtHR in its approach to 'just satisfaction' under Article 41. I argue that this provision does not mandate the mirror approach adopted under the Act nor exclude an approach to HRA damages which takes common law principles and scales as its starting point. Sections 8(1) and (3) are addressed herein, and also analysed in chapter 6.

A. Decision to Award Damages

At common law damages are available as of right: upon proof of the tort there is a general rule that damages issue for recognised heads of damage inherent in or consequential upon the wrong. The HRA does not state an equivalent rule. Does it follow that damages should not, in general, be awarded in circumstances where they would be awarded for common law actions which are functionally analogous to human rights actions?

Section 8(1) provides that a court may grant such remedies as are 'just and appropriate'. Formally, damages are made pursuant to this section as it is the section which empowers courts to grant remedies. Because of this damages are not available as of right: the phrase 'just and appropriate' denotes discretion. However, it does not follow that Parliament intended damages should be freely denied where loss is suffered or a restrictive approach more generally.[403] The wide grant of decision-making power in section 8(1) is explicable according to other considerations.

Pragmatically a wide grant of power is explicable on the basis that it enables courts to draw on a range of remedial tools without legislation having to specify each and every possible tool, and also given the range of interests protected by human rights and the myriad situations in which a violation may occur: 'The width of the discretion thus granted to the court is to be expected. The circumstances where section 6(1) [of the HRA] is in point will vary greatly'.[404] Indeed, it would be impractical and likely impossible to prescribe an exhaustive code setting out all rules and principles governing each type of possible relief, including injunctive relief, declaratory relief, orders based on the old prerogative writs, damages etc. Furthermore, it would be undesirable; a prescriptive set of rules could very well impede the courts' ability to ensure full and effective redress on the facts and develop remedies as required to ensure proper protection and vindication of basic interests. Hansard reveals Government ensured section 8(1) was 'of the widest amplitude'[405] so as to give courts flexibility to respond to violations in such a way as to ensure compliance with Article 13 of the Convention (right to an effective remedy)[406] and 'to do full justice in the cases that come before them'.[407] The courts have similarly held the object of sections 7 and 8 is to secure the effective remedy which Article 13 declares is the entitlement of every victim.[408]

Such wide grant also enables courts to pick up and develop existing principles and rules built-up around particular remedies, so that they do not have to reinvent the wheel in light of fresh statutory language. As well as common law rules on damages, the courts have developed detailed rules

[403] In contrast the Court in *Anufrijeva* (n 102) [56] said: 'Damages [under the HRA] are not an automatic entitlement but ... a remedy of "last resort"'. However, it does not necessarily follow from damages not being available as of right that they are a remedy of last resort, or that a restrictive approach should be taken.

[404] *Re Attorney General's Reference (No 2 of 2001)* [2004] 2 AC 72, [33].

[405] HL Deb vol 584 col 1266 (19 January 1998) Lord Irvine of Lairg.

[406] Note one reason for not incorporating Article 13, other than it was unnecessary because ss 7 and 8 fulfil its requirements, was that it may have led courts to recognise novel remedies which were unintended: HL Deb vol 583 col 475 (18 November 1997) Lord Irvine of Lairg. Of course, damages are well-known to English law, and express provision is made for them.

[407] HL Deb vol 585 col 385 (29 January 1998) Lord Irvine of Lairg; HC Deb vol 312 col 979 (20 May 1998) Mr Jack Straw ('clause 8(1) gives the courts considerable scope for doing justice when unlawful acts have been committed. Indeed, no one has been able to suggest any respect in which the Bill is deficient in providing effective remedies').

[408] *Re S* [2002] 2 AC 291, [61].

and principles governing grant of injunctive relief, orders based on the prerogative writs, and declarations. Parliamentary debates reveal Government intended courts would draw on established principle;[409] the Lord Chancellor said, '[o]ur courts are rich in remedies and have every freedom under Clause 8'.[410] The terms of section 8(1) reinforce this. It states that the court may grant such relief '*within its powers* as it considers just and appropriate'.[411] In light of this language Lord Wilson has observed, 'the subsection *does not confer powers*. It refers to *existing* powers and *confirms their applicability* to unlawful acts of public authorities'.[412] Thus the provision directs courts to *pre-existing* remedial tools, which of course are governed by pre-existing rules and principles of English law.

Thus the broad terms of section 8(1) are not conclusive as to the specific approach that ought to be taken to damages; it is left to the courts to determine the circumstances in which it shall be just and appropriate to make awards. However, there are indicia as to how the power should be exercised. The most obvious starting point for determining how broadly-framed remedial power should be exercised is the law's purpose; relief should be granted so as to ensure strong protection of and vindication of basic interests. It is also clear that courts ought to exercise their power under section 8(1) compatibly with Article 13, so that effective remedies follow violations as of course—it was the framers' plain intention that section 8 would give effect to that Article, and it is axiomatic that a statutory provision should be read to ensure compliance with the international norm it implements.[413] More generally the framers wished courts to have adequate flexibility and powers to ensure full and effective redress to victims in the different contexts in which violations could occur—consistent with the law's protective and vindicatory functions—while there is no indication in section 8(1) that Parliament endorsed a more restrictive remedial approach than at common law. Indeed, Hansard and the terms of section 8(1) indicate a clear expectation that courts would draw upon, indeed be led by, English remedies law.

Moving from the general to the particular, section 8(3) specifically addresses when courts ought to award damages; it is the 'key' damages provision. It provides that damages should only be awarded where necessary to afford just satisfaction to the victim. As the Law Lords held in *Greenfield*, if a court determines it is necessary to grant an award, it is difficult to see how making an award could be other than just and appropriate under section 8(1).[414] In turn this begs the question as to when damages are

409 See ch 5.1.
410 HL Deb vol 584 col 1266 (19 January 1998).
411 Emphasis added.
412 *R (T) v SOSHD* [2015] AC 49, [63] (emphasis added).
413 On the requirements of this Article see ch 6.1.II.
414 *Greenfield* (n 93) [6].

necessary. Given damages have long been available within vindicatory torts and vindicatory torts perform similar functions to and protect similar interests to human rights law, there is a powerful argument that courts ought to decide when damages are 'necessary' by reference to when damages are considered necessary for such torts. Such approach would ensure that the approach to award of damages is consonant with the purpose of the Act, and the policy underlying creation of the primary rights, that is, awards will be made so as to afford strong protection to and vindicate basic interests. Not only is this protective purpose recorded in Hansard,[415] but it is, as we saw above, apparent in fundamental features of the human rights action and scheme of the Act. An approach which ensures strong protection of victims' interests and reinforces their significance in the face of wrongful interference is also consonant with the focus of section 8(3), which is specifically upon the *victim's* interests, as opposed to other concerns, such as, for example, those in protection of the public interest.[416] A vindicatory, tort-based approach would ensure victims receive effective redress wherever they suffer damage as a result of a violation, thus ensuring compliance with Article 13.[417]

There are further features of the Act which lend support to such approach. The term for the monetary award under the Act is 'damages', a term which has a recognised meaning at common law. It is a maxim of interpretation that where Parliament adopts an element of the general law in statute, the element is taken to be adopted with its ordinary incidents, except so far as the statute displaces them.[418] The direction that damages be awarded where just and appropriate does not necessarily indicate an intention to deviate from ordinary principle, given the framing of section 8(1) is, as we have seen, explicable by reference to other concerns. Similarly, a requirement that it is necessary to award damages does not in itself indicate an intention to deviate from common law, not least because it is perfectly possible to read that direction as consonant with the common law approach to damages: the common law has a set of principles governing whether damages are a necessary remedy or not. As Lord Millett observed in *Cullen*, '[t]he most obvious case where an award of damages is not necessary is where there is no damage to compensate'.[419] Two other cases are expressly contemplated in section 8(3), each of which is consonant with an approach based in established principle. One is where other judicial relief is granted which renders an award otiose;[420] an obvious example is where all relevant losses are addressed by an award made for another action, or where all relevant

[415] See n 7 above.
[416] For fuller analysis see ch 6.1.I.
[417] See chs 5.2.I.F, 6.1.II.
[418] *Capewell v Revenue and Customs Comrs* [2007] 1 WLR 386, [18], [21], [23]–[25]; *Mansfield v DPP* (2006) 226 CLR 486.
[419] (n 55) [84].
[420] HRA, s 8(3)(a).

damage can be 'undone' by grant of specific relief.[421] The other is where some consequence of a judgment renders a judicial award unnecessary;[422] for example, the parties may agree a settlement, following a judicial finding of violation but before a damages hearing, rendering court-ordered relief unnecessary.[423]

Section 8(2) provides that damages may only be awarded by a court that has power to award damages or a compensation order in civil proceedings. Section 8(5)(b) makes a defendant subject to the Civil Liability (Contribution) Act 1978, so that they may recover contribution from any other person liable in respect of the same damage (and vice versa), as would be the case where civil liability is established at common law. Both of these features suggest Parliament considered human rights damages liability to be analogous in nature to ordinary civil liability.

So, the Act does not expressly state a tort-based approach ought to be taken, but nor do the relevant provisions necessarily tell against such an approach, just as they do not tell against an ordinary approach to injunctions or declarations. Indeed, the remedial provisions are capable of supporting a tort-based approach, and the terms of the Act, the object and purpose of the Act, and Hansard, provide some positive support.

Although it is discussed in detail elsewhere in this book, it is worth noting briefly that section 8(4) requires English courts to 'take into account' the 'principles' applied by the ECtHR in its determinations as to monetary awards under Article 41, in deciding damages claims under the Act. As chapter 5 argues, this provision does not undermine the claim that the starting point under the HRA ought to be the established domestic approach to damages; it simply means domestic courts need take account of any relevant Strasbourg principles in application of the domestic approach. As we shall see, those principles are few and far between and exceptionally broad in nature so the Strasbourg material cannot provide a worked-out law of human rights damages in any case, while those broad principles which are discernible are roughly consonant with those underlying basic damages in English law.

B. Quantum and Range of Damages

We have seen that the statutory term for the monetary remedy under the Act is 'damages'. 'Damages' is quintessentially a *common law* term of art. This,

[421] *Re Jordan* (n 126) [29] (previous award to claimant taken into account in assessing quantum); s III.B above.

[422] HRA, s 8(3)(b).

[423] For example in *DSD* HC (n 103) the Judge, in determining HRA damages, took into account awards made to the claimants under the Criminal Injuries Compensation Scheme. Settlements may also be taken into account but a prior settlement will not necessarily exclude a further award: *Rabone* (n 103); *Ashley* (n 23).

in itself, is a strong indicator that it is legitimate for courts to look to heads of damage recognised at common law and common law scales in assessing quantum. A term other than damages, such as 'money award', 'compensation' or 'solatium', could have been used to describe the remedy and distinguish it from damages at common law, but was not. As discussed above, it is difficult to identify a principled justification for scales for losses such as distress or loss of liberty being lower (or higher) under the HRA than those applied at common law for the very same heads; why should distress or loss of liberty be worth less (or more) in human rights law than common law? A loss is a loss.

In terms of the kinds of damages available, no provision of the Act states specific types of awards, such as exemplary damages, are unavailable, or that damages are limited to compensation. Of course, at common law the most common form of 'damages' is compensatory. However, clearly 'damages' has a wider meaning in English law: 'it would be a mistake to imagine that damages and compensation are synonymous. This is because some awards of damages are non-compensatory'.[424] Indeed, use of the term 'damages', rather than a narrower, more specific term such as 'compensation', is in itself indicative of the absence of a legislative intention to necessarily limit monetary awards to compensation. The object and purpose of the Act—affording strong protection to and vindicating human rights—supports a broader rather than narrower interpretation. Lending further force to this argument, the HRA juxtaposes the terms 'compensation' and 'damages'; this reinforces that the two are conceptually distinct.[425] Whereas section 9(3) expressly limits damages for judicial acts performed in good faith to compensatory damages (specifically for breach of Article 5(5)), there is no such limitation in section 8 for all other classes of rights-violation. It is true that the ECtHR, within its own remedial jurisdiction, does not make nominal or exemplary awards. But one must recall that domestic courts are only under an obligation to take Strasbourg principles into account—not necessarily to follow them—while, according to the ECtHR's own jurisprudence, it is open to Member States to organise remedies consonantly with domestic legal traditions.[426] Furthermore, as we shall see in chapter 5, the ECtHR's reluctance to make exemplary awards is attributable to its role as a supranational court, so its practice in this respect is not a good guide for domestic institutions. Also, domestic courts are only required to take into account the principles applied by the ECtHR in respect of its award of 'com-

[424] Burrows (n 258) 29; *Blake* (n 257) 285; *Smith New Court Securities Ltd v Citibank* [1997] AC 254, 279–80.

[425] See HRA, ss 8(2), (4), 9(3).

[426] See ch 5.

pensation'; one possible inference is any principles applied by the ECtHR are only relevant to the award and quantum of compensatory damages.[427]

Overall, the terms of the Act considered here do not tell against a vindicatory, tort-based approach. Rather, they are capable of supporting such an approach and provide some positive support for it; when added to the powerful argument of principle for a vindicatory approach, the case for adoption of such approach is very powerful indeed.

By way of comparison, in Ireland damages for breaches of human rights under the ECHR Act 2003[428] are governed by a statutory framework with features not dissimilar to the framework under the HRA. In that context, albeit the approach taken under the Act is not without its shortcomings, the courts have held with little hesitation that damages should issue to compensate all of the negative effects causally connected to a wrong even though damages are not formally available as of right; adopted an ordinary meaning approach to interpretation of the statutory term 'damages', taking into account the purpose of the Act as an Act guaranteeing fundamental rights; held that while the few, broad principles discernible from Strasbourg Article 41 jurisprudence must be taken into account, those broad principles are not so different from basic principles applied in common law fields and domestic courts should have regard to common law approaches to calculating damages; held the damages provisions must be interpreted consistently with Article 13; readily inferred non-pecuniary losses; and awarded substantial damages for non-pecuniary losses, above the miserly levels applied under the HRA, and somewhat closer to common-law levels.[429]

V. FLAWED TORT-BASED APPROACHES: THE UNITED STATES CONSTITUTIONAL TORT JURISPRUDENCE

This chapter has propounded a vindicatory tort-based approach, founded on an analogy with vindicatory torts. A defining feature of this approach is that compensatory damages ought to be awarded for wrongful interference with protected interests notwithstanding whether factual losses are suffered in consequence of the wrong.

However, some jurisdictions have adopted what might be described as a 'compensatory' tort-based approach. Such approach is founded on the erroneous assumption that the law of torts is monolithic and this beast is

[427] Others may argue for a different inference, that only ECtHR principles applied to compensation are relevant because damages under the Act are limited to compensation. However, the implication I have argued for is the more plausible one, in the light of the other arguments made herein.

[428] See in particular ss 3 and 4.

[429] *Pullen* (n 233) particularly [5.2], [5.7]–[5.10], [6.2]–[6.3], [6.6].

concerned principally or solely with provision of compensation for factual losses. Such approach should be rejected.

A paradigm example is the US Supreme Court's approach to damages actions for violations of constitutional rights, known as 'constitutional torts'.[430] These actions can be brought against state and federal officials. The basis for claims against state officials is statutory: 42 USC § 1983. The federal action is a judicial creation: in *Bivens* the action was inferred from the terms of the Constitution.[431] In general the actions are governed by similar principles, according to a principle of 'parallelism'.[432]

Such actions constitute a 'species of tort liability', with 'the level of damages ... ordinarily determined according to principles derived from the common law of torts'.[433] However, this tort-based approach differs from that propounded herein. In *Stachura* the Supreme Court held that for a constitutional tort the claimant could recover compensatory damages for actual, provable loss, such as the economic, physical and psychological effects of the violation, but ruled out damages for the rights-violation in itself.[434] The Court's approach was based on the following chain of reasoning:

1. '[D]amages in tort ... provide "*compensation* for the injury caused to plaintiff by defendant's breach of duty"';[435] and:
2. The approach in constitutional torts is based on the common law system of recovery; therefore:
3. Compensatory damages for constitutional torts can only be awarded for actual losses occasioned by the violation: the basic purpose of damages actions is 'to *compensate injuries* caused by the [constitutional] deprivation'.[436] Damages for the violation in itself 'are wholly divorced from any compensatory purpose'.[437]

This reasoning is flawed. For example, some damages in tort are non-compensatory. Indeed, there is incongruity between the Court's repeated assertion in *Stachura* that the purpose of § 1983 is compensation for loss,[438] and the legal position that for constitutional torts nominal damages (to mark 'the importance to organized society that ... rights be scrupulously observed'),[439] and punitive damages (to punish and deter conduct motivated

[430] See further ch 7.III.
[431] *Bivens* (n 49).
[432] *Correctional Services Corp v Malesko* 534 US 61, 82 (2001); *Ashcroft v Iqbal* 129 S Ct 1937, 1948 (2009).
[433] See *Stachura* (n 336) 305–06; *Carey* (n 244) 253.
[434] *Stachura* ibid; *Farrar v Hobby* 506 US 103, 112 (1992).
[435] *Stachura* ibid 306, quoting FV Harper et al, *The Law of Torts* 2nd edn (Little Brown, 1986) 490.
[436] ibid 309, drawing on *Carey* (n 244) 265.
[437] *Stachura* ibid 311.
[438] ibid 307, quoting *Carey* (n 244) 254, 257.
[439] *Carey* (n 244) 266.

by evil intent, or which is recklessly or callously indifferent to constitutional rights)[440] are available.

But the main error is that the Court refers to 'tort' as though that field were monolithic and 'damages in tort' as though there were a unitary approach to damages across torts.[441] As we have seen, the law of torts is a diverse field, comprised of disparate actions which have different functions. Consistent with this functional variation, different approaches to damages have emerged. The result of the Court's reductionism was it conflated damages in tort with the approach to damages in one tort, negligence—a not uncommon mistake given the dominance of negligence.[442] This error was not lost on American commentators. Of one of the precursor cases to *Stachura*, *Carey*,[443] which adopted a similar approach (albeit in respect of a different right), Love wrote:

> In its examination of analogous common law remedies, the Court cited the following principle from ... Harper and James' torts treatise [the same passage being relied upon by the Court in *Stachura*]:[444] 'The cardinal principle of damages in Anglo-American law is that of *compensation* for the injury caused to the plaintiff by defendant's breach of duty'. Negligence actions are indeed brought primarily to compensate, and therefore proven compensatory damages are the only remedy allowed in such actions. But section 1983 actions for deprivations of due process are not analogous to negligence actions. Instead, the intangible constitutional interests protected by the procedural due process clause more closely resemble the dignitary interests protected by such tort actions as defamation, false imprisonment and invasion of privacy. These actions are discussed by Harper and James in ... their treatise,[445] where the authors state that deterrence and the vindication of the personal interests are as important as compensation in dignitary tort actions, and that these three objectives are accomplished through an award of presumed general damages.[446]

As Love observes, it was, amongst other things, the Court's failure to consult 'the proper body of common law doctrine' that led it into error.[447]

On top of its flawed common law analogy, the Supreme Court marshalled a number of arguments against awarding normative damages.

[440] *Smith* (n 279) 56.

[441] At one point the Court acknowledges variations in the elements of different torts, but does not connect these to variations in the rules governing damages, instead reiterating a unitary conception of damages: *Stachura* (n 336) 309.

[442] We find similar errors in England (*Greenfield* (n 93) [19]) and elsewhere: eg *Ward* (n 231) [51]; *Dunlea* (n 221) [66], [68]; *Attorney-General v Chapman* [2012] 1 NZLR 462, [30]. See further ch 2.IV.

[443] (n 244).

[444] FV Harper and F James, *The Law of Torts* (Little Brown, 1956) 1299. Cited in *Carey* (n 244) 254–55; *Stachura* (n 336) 306 (citing 2nd edition: (n 435) 490).

[445] Harper and James ibid §§ 3.6–3.9, 4.7, 5.30, 9.6–9.7.

[446] JC Love, 'Damages: A Remedy for the Violation of Constitutional Rights' (1979) 67 *California Law Review* 1242, 1261.

[447] (n 444) 1264.

The Court said such damages are unnecessary to 'vindicate' those constitutional rights protected by constitutional torts: § 1983 'presupposes that damages that compensate for actual harm ordinarily suffice to deter constitutional violations'.[448] This reasoning is problematic in that it conflates distinct functions of vindication and deterrence, and assumes that the only possible justification for damages absent actual loss could be deterrence; in turn this may stem from an assumption, erroneous yet not uncommon, that if damages are not for actual loss, they cannot be compensatory.[449] However, as we saw in chapter 2, in those fields of liability where damages are awarded absent actual loss their rationale is not deterrence. Rather such damages compensate for damage to protected interests inherent in the wrong, and in so doing give effect to the law's wider functions of protecting and affirming the importance of those basic interests. As Harlan J said in *Bivens*, '[d]amages as a traditional form of compensation for invasion of a legally protected interest may be entirely appropriate even if no substantial deterrent effects on future official lawfulness might be thought to result'.[450]

The Court also reasoned that if damages for the wrong in itself

> were ... available, juries would be free to award arbitrary amounts without any evidential basis, or to use their unbounded discretion to punish unpopular defendants ... Such damages would be too uncertain to be of any great value to plaintiffs, and would inject caprice into determinations of damages in § 1983 cases.[451]

First, problems associated with juries need not concern us as judges assess HRA damages. Second, clearly there is some artificiality in valuing a setback to an intangible interest in money terms. But there is also artificiality in placing monetary value on intangible consequential losses such as pain and suffering, mental distress, humiliation etc, for which damages are regularly awarded in tort (absent direct evidence). Further, artificiality need not equate with caprice or arbitrariness. As we have seen, within vindicatory torts there is a reasonably coherent and principled framework for assessment of normative damage, with courts differentiating more or less serious interferences according to relevant factors. Further, courts reason quantum by reference to awards in analogous cases and guideline judgments, and may cross-check figures against scales in other fields, thus ensuring reasonable consistency from one judge to another in specific fields and across fields.

[448] *Stachura* (n 336) 310.
[449] As discussed in ch 7.III.A.iv the focus on deterrence in American tort thinking also reflects the influence of Law and Economics.
[450] (n 49) 408.
[451] *Stachura* (n 336) 310.

Ultimately, if, as the Court in *Stachura* maintained, the aim of constitutional guarantees is 'to protect persons from injuries to particular interests',[452] or as Harlan J said in *Bivens*, 'vindication of constitutional interests',[453] then surely the first injury the law should redress is damage to the interest that is the subject of constitutional protection.

Lastly, we should note Marshall J's concurring opinion in *Stachura*, in which three other Justices joined. He observed that aspects of the Court's opinion 'can be read to suggest that damages in § 1983 cases are necessarily limited to "out-of-pocket loss," "other monetary harms," and "such injuries as 'impairment of reputation ... personal humiliation, and mental anguish and suffering'"';[454] basically, factual loss. However, Marshall J said he did not understand 'the Court to so hold', explaining that he chose to write separately 'to emphasize that the violation of a constitutional right, in proper cases, may itself constitute a compensable injury'.[455] With respect, Marshall J's interpretation of the Court's opinion seems a stretch, and his opinion is probably best interpreted as a strategic attempt to preserve the possibility at least of such damages being recognised in future.[456] The implications of the Court's opinion are rather clear: it held damages were only recoverable for 'proved actual injury caused by the denial of the constitutional right', '*no* compensatory damages could be awarded for violation of that right absent proof of actual injury', and 'the abstract value of a constitutional right may not form the basis for § 1983 damages', while it rejected an approach which involved a jury 'determining how much was necessary to "compensate [respondent] for the deprivation" of his constitutional rights' and placing 'a money value on the "rights" themselves'.[457] Further, later cases interpret *Stachura* as standing for the proposition that 'no compensatory damages may be awarded in a § 1983 suit absent proof of actual injury'.[458]

Nonetheless Marshall J's opinion is significant because it entails judicial endorsement of a vindicatory alternative. In contrast to the unitary conception of damages that pervades the Court's opinion Marshall J emphasised the field's plurality: 'common-law rules of damages themselves were defined by the interests protected in various branches of tort law'.[459] He relied on

[452] ibid 308, quoting *Carey* (n 244) 254.
[453] *Bivens* (n 49) 407.
[454] *Stachura* (n 336) 313.
[455] ibid.
[456] But note some commentators also hold out hope that normative damages may be recognised (JC Love, 'Presumed General Compensatory Damages in Constitutional Tort Litigation' (1992) 49 *Washington & Lee Law Review* 67), while lower courts have divided as to the *ratio* of *Stachura*: eg *Kerman v City of New York* 374 F 3d 93 (2004).
[457] *Stachura* (n 336) 307–08.
[458] *Farrar* (n 434) 112.
[459] *Stachura* (n 336) 314 quoting *Carey* (n 244) 257.

examples of compensatory damages being awarded in tort in the absence of loss: 'substantial damages' have been awarded 'simply upon a showing that a plaintiff was wrongly deprived the right to vote, without requiring any further demonstration of damages'.[460] By analogy he argued:

> [w]hen a plaintiff is deprived, for example, of the opportunity to engage in a demonstration to express his political views '[i]t is facile to suggest that no damage is done' ... Loss of such an opportunity constitutes loss of First Amendment rights 'in their most pristine and classic form' ... There is no reason why such an injury should not be compensable.[461]

In other words the claimant suffers damage because the violation places them in a position other than that in which they are constitutionally entitled to be in: one in which their protected interests are unencumbered and maintained in 'pristine' form. Consistent with the approach within vindicatory torts, Marshall J said damages for the wrong in itself should not equate to the entire value of the right, but rather should 'be proportional'.[462]

[460] ibid 314.
[461] ibid 315.
[462] ibid.

Part 2

Human Rights Damages and the Public Law–Private Law Distinction

4

The Public Law–Private Law Distinction

SOME MAY CONTEST a vindicatory, tort-based approach to human rights damages on the basis that it is inappropriate to apply damages principles developed in *private law* in a *public law* context. It might be argued that there is something special or unique about public law which justifies or requires distinctive solutions to legal questions. The belief that there is a meaningful, determinate and coherent distinction between public law and private law and this distinction ought to be treated as normative and—in the extreme—dispositive of questions concerning legal development, while relatively recent within the English legal tradition, has become increasingly common, particularly since the late 1970s.[1] At that time a procedural innovation was introduced which was interpreted as meaning that 'public law' and 'private law' claims should be streamed down distinct procedural paths.[2] This procedural cleaving of public law claims from other claims gave public law a distinct space, separate from private law. In turn, this allowed principles of public law to develop along their own trajectory in relative isolation from private law, and an idea of public law substantively distinct from private law to gain increased momentum and influence.

The idea that there is a fundamental divide between the nature of private law and public law, and that this distinction ought to influence legal development, is pervasive in the human rights damages jurisprudence. In the important early case of *Anufrijeva* Lord Woolf MR, for the Court, asserted that 'damages or compensation should play a different role in relation to

[1] Although, note the important early contribution: JDB Mitchell, 'The Causes and Effects of the Absence of a System of Public Law in the United Kingdom' [1965] *PL* 95. On emergence of the use of the public law–private law distinction as an analytical tool in contemporary English law see: JNE Varuhas, 'The Public Interest Conception of Public Law: Its Procedural Origins and Substantive Implications' in J Bell et al (eds), *Public Law Adjudication in Common Law Systems: Process and Substance* (Hart Publishing, forthcoming 2016) [Varuhas 2016].

[2] Rules of the Supreme Court (Amendment No 3) SI 1977 No 1955, r 5; Rules of the Supreme Court (Amendment No 4) SI 1980 No 2000, rr 2–7; Supreme Court Act 1981, ss 29–31 (as enacted); *O'Reilly v Mackman* [1983] 2 AC 237; *Cocks v Thanet DC* [1983] 2 AC 286. See now Senior Courts Act 1981, ss 29–31A; Civil Procedure Rules SI 1998 No 3132, Pt 54 [CPR].

claims in respect of *public law* rights from that which it plays in *private law* proceedings'.[3] He said this proposition is not confined to damages under the Human Rights Act 1998 (HRA) but also holds true for damages claims in other areas of public law, such as EU law, and damages for human rights breaches in other jurisdictions. A central plank of this distinctive 'public law' remedial approach is that primary importance is placed upon bringing the public authority's unlawful conduct to an end, with compensation of secondary, if any, importance.[4] Damages thus play a 'less prominent role' for human rights violations compared to their role in remedying 'breaches of private law obligations'.[5] Contrary to the position in 'private law', damages are a remedy of 'last resort', subject to 'wide discretion', and awards may be denied, despite the suffering of loss, or reduced below full compensation in the 'interests of the wider public'.[6] Thus, in public law damages are a marginal remedy, and even if there is a factual basis for an award, damages may well be denied in the court's discretion if the balance of interests favours denial. This 'new approach' stands in stark contrast to 'the approach at common law where a claimant is invariably entitled, so far as money can achieve this, to be restored in the position he would have been in if he had not suffered the injury'.[7]

This chapter argues that the approach elaborated in *Anufrijeva* is based in a particular conception of public law, which has its roots in common law judicial review. Indeed, Lord Woolf explicitly analogised his approach to human rights damages with the remedial approach within domestic administrative law.[8] That conception of public law holds that its principal function is to ensure public power is exercised properly in the interests of the public. From this premise it follows that the remedial focus ought to be upon ensuring power is in fact exercised as it ought to be in the interests of all, through declaratory and specific relief, rather than upon compensating personal losses. This has long been the remedial approach in common law review, the dominant field of 'public law' before introduction of the HRA. In marginalising damages *Anufrijeva* maintains, as far as possible, what Lord Woolf saw as the pre-HRA remedial division between public and private law:

> there is a basic distinction between a claim under the HRA for compensation in respect of the consequences of maladministration and a claim by a member of the public against a public officer for damages for breach of a duty owed in tort. In the former case the claimant is seeking a remedy that would not be available in this jurisdiction for misfeasance prior to the HRA.[9]

[3] *Anufrijeva v Southwark LBC* [2004] QB 1124, [54] (emphasis added).
[4] ibid [53].
[5] ibid [52].
[6] ibid [56].
[7] ibid [55]–[56].
[8] ibid [56] and see [53], [81].
[9] ibid [49].

Thus, the remedial approach in human rights law is subsumed into pre-existing habits of thinking about public law remedies. As is discussed herein, the fundamental problem with this approach is it suppresses the distinctive nature of human rights law, and stymies that field's distinctive goals.

The 'mirror' approach, first adopted in *Greenfield*, which ties domestic HRA damages practice to the Strasbourg Court's practice of making compensatory awards, is now the prevailing approach to HRA damages.[10] This approach has been justified principally by reference to section 8(4) of the HRA. That provision requires domestic courts, in making awards under the Act, to take into account the principles applied by the European Court of Human Rights (ECtHR) in exercise of its remedial jurisdiction. Notwithstanding the formal legal basis for such approach, alignment of damages under the HRA with the ECtHR's jurisprudence has the *effect* of producing a domestic approach to human rights damages which is to a significant degree consonant with the approach favoured in *Anufrijeva*, and therefore the conception of public law which has characterised domestic administrative law. The ECtHR treats monetary relief as marginal and subject to broad discretion, while awards are low. One might hypothesise that, even though section 8(4) does not mandate a mirror approach (as discussed in chapter 5), this approach was a natural one for domestic courts to adopt because it is consonant with a pre-existing conception of public law, embedded in domestic public law, and maintains a pre-existing remedial divide between public and private law.

So, for example, in *Greenfield*, Lord Bingham affirmed Lord Woolf's views in *Anufrijeva*, that damages play a less prominent role under the HRA than in private law, the principal remedial concern being to bring infringements to an end, with damages of limited importance.[11] Lord Bingham reinforced these propositions by reference to 'the focus of the Convention' which 'is on the protection of human rights and not the award of compensation', the ECtHR's practice being to often hold that a finding of violation constitutes sufficient remedy in itself, including where loss has been suffered.[12] In the subsequent case of *Dobson* the Court of Appeal explicitly melded the mirror approach mandated by *Greenfield* and the 'public law' approach in *Anufrijeva*:

> The Convention serves principally public law aims; the principal objective is to declare any infringement and to put a stop to it. Compensation is ancillary and discretionary. The interests of the individual are part of the equation, but so are those of the wider public.[13]

[10] *R (Greenfield) v SOSHD* [2005] 1 WLR 673; *R (Faulkner) v SOSJ* [2013] 2 AC 254. See ch 5.

[11] ibid [9].

[12] ibid.

[13] *Dobson v Thames Valley Utilities Ltd* [2009] 3 All ER 319, [42].

In *Sturnham* Laws LJ considered the 'territory of section 8 [HRA] is often a closer neighbour to our public law than our private law', and in public law 'damages are not generally recoverable for administrative tort'.[14] He considered this view 'is reflected' in Strasbourg cases;[15] 'the focus is on the State's compliance, not the claimant's loss', 'compensation for loss' being a 'private law purpose'.[16]

Now, clearly, it is implausible to maintain—though this has not stopped some courts—that the remedial practice of a supranational court reflects a *sui generis* remedial divide in English law between private wrongs and public wrongs or gives effect to 'public law aims' as English courts have conceptualised those aims in domestic administrative law.[17] But what *Dobson* and *Sturnham* render explicit is the degree of synergy between an approach to HRA damages based in the ECtHR's practice—ie an approach that holds compensation to be a marginal, discretionary remedy—and a view that there is a significant normative difference between private law and public law, reflected in domestic law, which ought to result in distinct remedial approaches.

Specific elements of HRA jurisprudence, such as the interest-balancing approach proposed in *Anufrijeva*, and the mirror approach, are discussed in other chapters. This chapter examines the general proposition that the approach to human rights damages should not follow that in tort because there is an important distinction between the nature of public law and that of private law.

Section 1 considers, at a general level, the problems with using the public law–private law distinction as a tool to guide legal development. The distinction lacks an anchor in English law, is bound up in interminable theoretical disagreement, and wrongly suggests public law is a unitary field reducible to a single set of ideas; rather the field is pluralistic, comprised of different sub-fields, each characterised by distinct concerns.

Section 2 examines how the public law–private law distinction has informed the approach to HRA damages, and critically analyses judicial reliance on the distinction to guide doctrinal development. A central problem is that use of the divide has suppressed the distinctive nature of human rights law and undermined its functions at the remedial stage.

Ultimately, the distinction does not offer a sound foundation upon which to build a law of human rights damages.

[14] *R (Sturnham) v SOSJ* [2012] 3 WLR 476, [15].
[15] ibid [18]ff.
[16] *DSD v Commissioner for the Metropolis* [2015] EWCA Civ 646, [65]–[66] (Laws LJ) [*DSD* CA].
[17] As discussed in ch 5, the ECtHR's approach is explicable by reference to completely different concerns.

SECTION 1. THE PUBLIC LAW–PRIVATE LAW DISTINCTION AS A TOOL FOR LEGAL DEVELOPMENT

The idea of a fundamental divide between public and private law has intuitive appeal and has been influential in modern judicial decision-making, and pervades much commentary. However, there are significant problems in drawing the distinction and discerning its implications, which make it an unsafe tool to guide legal development.

I. LACK OF AN ANCHOR

Many arguments for 'public' entities to be governed by a legal framework distinct from that applicable to 'private' entities rely, expressly or implicitly, on the idea of 'the state' as a unique entity.[18] However, that concept is foreign to English law:

> In Britain there is no legal entity called 'the state' in which powers are vested or to which allegiance or other duties are owed. The non-admission of the idea of the state helps to explain the tardy and partial development, in Britain, of a system of public law.[19]

While in continental jurisdictions legal development proceeded according to the nature of juridical relationships (person–person, person–thing, person–state),[20] in England the law developed on the basis of disparate forms (then, causes) of action,[21] which paid little attention to the relationship between claimant and defendant.[22] The key concern was whether a case fitted the 'procedural pigeonhole' or 'receptacle'[23] required for issuance of a particular remedy, the law 'develop[ing] from a maze of individual sets of circumstances',[24] substantive law being 'gradually secreted in the interstices of procedure'.[25] Thus Lord Wilberforce observed famously:

> [t]he expressions 'private law' and 'public law' have recently been imported into the law of England from countries which, unlike our own, have separate systems

[18] See C Harlow and R Rawlings, *Law and Administration* 3rd edn (CUP, 2009) 19–20.

[19] C Turpin and A Tomkins, *British Government and the Constitution* 7th edn (CUP, 2011) 10–11; *cf* J McLean, *Searching for the State in British Legal Thought* (CUP, 2012) (propounding that absence of a developed concept of state and field of public law, and the consequences of this, evidence a distinctive state tradition).

[20] These divisions are in turn rooted in Roman law: HF Jolowicz, *Roman Foundations of Modern Law* (Clarendon, 1957) ch VI, VIII.

[21] See FW Maitland, *Equity; also, The Forms of Action at Common Law* (CUP, 1910) 294ff.

[22] JWF Allison, *A Continental Distinction in the Common Law* (OUP, 1996) ch 6 [Allison 1996]; G Samuel, 'Public and Private Law: A Private Lawyer's Response' (1983) 46 *MLR* 558, 558–64.

[23] Maitland (n 21) 298.

[24] *R v Lord President of the Privy Council, ex p Page* [1993] AC 682, 700.

[25] Maitland (n 21) 295, quoting HS Maine, *Dissertations on Early Law and Custom* (J Murray, 1891) 389.

> concerning public law and private law. No doubt they are convenient expressions for descriptive purposes. In this country they must be used with caution, for, typically, English law fastens, not upon principles but upon remedies.[26]

Further impeding development of a distinctive public law regime was the normative force of the equality principle: it is a fundamental principle of the rule of law in England that public actors are subject to the ordinary, private law that applies to all other persons.[27] In this way private law *was*, in a meaningful and important sense, public law and vice versa, while equal application of tort to public official and private individual alike operated to prevent development of a distinctive 'public law' of tort.[28] Linked to the equality principle is the 'traditional preoccupation [in English law] with official persons to the exclusion of a concept of the state'.[29] In common with Dicey, Barker, Hale, Blackstone and Austin all 'dealt with what we might call public-law issues under the law of persons', viewing public power as exercised by individual officials or aggregations of officials who had no superior legal status to other citizens, rather than a distinct legal entity such as 'the state'. 'Through the emphasis on persons, the state administration remained obscure'.[30]

The growth of the modern administrative state in the post-War period and concomitant expansion of administrative law caused judges and academics to think more seriously about the idea of the state, the administration and the relationship between public entities and individuals. This led to a great irony.[31] Just as lawyers began to explore discrete public law rules, the 'brave new world'[32] of privatisation, deregulation, corporatisation, contracting-out, QUANGOs, public–private partnerships, bestowal of

[26] *Davy v Spelthorne BC* [1984] AC 262, 276.

[27] AV Dicey, *Introduction to the Study of the Law of the Constitution* 10th edn (MacMillan, 1960) 193–94, 202–03.

[28] *cf* T Cornford, *Towards a Public Law of Tort* (Ashgate, 2008).

[29] Allison 1996 (n 22) 77–79; McLean (n 19) 1, ch 2 (English law focused on 'real people vested with real powers' rather than abstractions).

[30] Allison 1996 ibid. There are many other reasons for absence of a concept of state, including the traditional insularity of the English legal profession from wider political thought and pragmatic, anti-theoretical ethos of English law (JWF Allison, 'Theoretical and Institutional Underpinnings of a Separate Administrative Law' in M Taggart (ed), *The Province of Administrative Law* (Hart Publishing, 1997) 77 [Allison 1997]; ibid 127). Unlike in post-revolutionary France the constitutional settlement that emerged during the Glorious Revolution did not 'express a theory of popular sovereignty conducive to administrative centralization' (Allison 1996, 72). In England, Acts of Parliament and their enforcement in ordinary courts, as opposed to official ordinances, became the mechanism for regulating administrative power (M Loughlin, 'Why the History of English Administrative Law is Not Written' in D Dyzenhaus et al (eds), *A Simple Common Lawyer* (Hart Publishing, 2009) 158). The English 'tradition of local government', centred on historic local communities, stymied development of a strong central administration around which to construct legal norms (Loughlin ibid). See generally Allison 1996, chs 5–6.

[31] Allison 1996 (n 22) 107–08.

[32] M Taggart, 'Reinvented Government, Traffic Lights and the Convergence of Public and Private Law' [1999] *PL* 124, 125.

public power upon non-governmental entities, Next Steps agencies etc had begun.[33] The era of 'mixed administration'[34] had arrived with responsibility for regulation, service delivery and policy design and implementation shared between public and private actors or, sometimes, completely outsourced;[35] today around a third of taxpayer money spent on public services goes to non-public-sector entities,[36] while expenditure on contracting-out accounts for approximately half of the £187 billion spent by the public sector on goods and services per annum.[37] Further, the public service itself is increasingly organised around private sector organisational models, and inculcated with market-based mantras of efficiency, economy, effectiveness, value for money and individual choice.[38] In this way the public sphere was increasingly rendered indistinct, undermining attempts to identify an anchor for a distinctive idea of public law.

On the other hand, ideas such as fairness, equality, ethics, checked power, participation, accountability, public interest etc, often associated with the public side of the putative divide, inform the work of charitable and voluntary organisations, and increasingly inform conduct of business and commercial enterprise and find expression in the law regulating non-governmental activity. In turn, these developments reflect evolving understandings of the nature and role of non-governmental entities in society, and illustrate the difficulties in distinguishing public and private spheres.

Numerous examples can be given. There is increasing official recognition that corporations have human rights and other wider social obligations,[39]

[33] See, eg, R Rhodes, 'The Hollowing Out of the State: the Changing Nature of Public Services in Britain' (1994) 65 *Political Quarterly* 138; Harlow and Rawlings (n 18) ch 2, 6–9; M Taggart (ed), *The Province of Administrative Law* (Hart Publishing, 1997) [Taggart 1997]; 'The Nature and Functions of the State' in P Cane and M Tushnet (eds), *The Oxford Handbook of Legal Studies* (OUP, 2003) [Taggart 2003]; McLean (n 19) ch 8; G Drewry, 'The Executive: Towards Accountable Government and Effective Governance?' in J Jowell and D Oliver (eds), *The Changing Constitution* 6th edn (OUP, 2007); I Harden, *The Contracting State* (Open UP, 1992); P Vincent-Jones, *The New Public Contracting* (OUP, 2006); C Graham and T Prosser, *Privatising Public Enterprises* (Clarendon, 1991).

[34] J Freeman, 'The Private Role in Public Governance' (2000) 75 *New York University Law Review* 543; M Aronson, 'A Public Lawyer's Responses to Privatisation and Outsourcing' in Taggart 1997, ibid.

[35] Although in many areas where government has apparently retreated, formally ceding power to regulators, private entities and supranational institutions, it has maintained a degree of control through various mechanisms: C Harlow, 'The "Hidden Paw" of the State and the Publicisation of Private Law' in D Dyzenhaus et al (n 30).

[36] National Audit Office, *Deciding Prices in Public Services Markets: Principles for Value for Money* (NAO, 2013) 4.

[37] *The Role of Major Contractors in the Delivery of Public Services*, HC 810 (2013) 10.

[38] P Dunleavy and C Hood, 'From Old Public Administration to New Public Management' (1994) 14 *Public Money and Management* 9; C Hood and R Dixon, *A Government that Worked Better and Cost Less?* (OUP, 2015); *Open Public Services White Paper*, Cm 8145 (2011).

[39] OECD, *Guidelines for Multinational Enterprises* (2011); UNHRC, *Guiding Principles on Business and Human Rights* (2011); *Any of Our Business? Human Rights and the UK Private Sector*, HC 64-I/HL 5-I (2009).

while corporate entities may voluntarily commit to human rights and social norms.[40] Quoted companies must report on the environmental impact of their operations, as well as 'social, community and human rights issues', and gender distribution within the company.[41] Legislation provides for 'community interest' companies,[42] prospective charities must fulfil a 'public benefit requirement',[43] and Ministers may intervene in mergers implicating the 'public interest'.[44] In the wake of the financial crisis various regulatory reforms were implemented to 'secure a more level playing field between firms and consumers', and safeguard the public interest in financial stability.[45] The Leveson Inquiry concluded that press regulation must impose 'ethical standards', and that '[a]ll standards for good practice in journalism should be driven by the public interest'.[46]

It is axiomatic that '[p]ower has never been the monopoly of the state or its institutions'[47] and commentators have long observed 'growing acceptance of a philosophy that *all* those who wield power should be accountable and should be subject to general principles of good administration'; 'the citizen is concerned that *all* power, public or private, should be conformable with liberty, fair dealing and good administration'.[48] Reflecting such philosophy, which betrays strict cleaving of public and private spheres, sex equality clauses are read into the terms of private sector employment;[49] private sector discrimination on prohibited grounds is unlawful;[50] there are legal protections for tenants vis-à-vis landlords and employees vis-à-vis employers; consumers are protected against exploitation by dedicated legislative regimes;[51] broad contractual discretions are subject to implied limits to prevent abuse;[52] natural justice requirements may be implied into

[40] UN Global Compact www.unglobalcompact.org/AboutTheGC/index.html.
[41] Companies Act 2006, s 414C(7)–(8).
[42] Companies (Audit, Investigations and Community Enterprise) Act 2004, Pt 2.
[43] Charities Act 2011, s 4.
[44] Enterprise Act 2002, Pt 3, ch 2, particularly s 58.
[45] *A New Approach to Financial Regulation*, Cm 8268 (2012).
[46] *An Inquiry into the Culture, Practices and Ethics of the Press: Report*, HC 780-I (2012).
[47] Harlow and Rawlings (n 18) 21.
[48] G Borrie, 'The Regulation of Public and Private Power' [1989] *PL* 552, 558–59; D Oliver, 'Common Values in Public and Private Law and the Public/Private Divide' [1997] *PL* 630; P Finn, 'Controlling the Exercise of Power' (1996) 7 *Public Law Review* 86.
[49] Equality Act 2010, Pt 5, ch 3.
[50] Equality Act 2010.
[51] eg Consumer Protection Act 1987; Trade Descriptions Act 1968; Consumer Credit Act 1974; Unfair Contract Terms Act 1977; Unfair Terms in Consumer Contracts Regulations SI 1999 No 2083.
[52] eg *Braganza v BP Shipping Ltd* [2015] UKSC 17. The device used for implying such terms has been the reasonable expectations of the parties, but implication of such terms is 'consistent with a judicial concern for the fairness of the contract concluded by the parties', specifically that the more powerful party does not exploit the less powerful party (E McKendrick, 'Judicial Control of Contractual Discretion' in M Freedland and JB Auby (eds), *The Public-Private Divide—Une Entente Assez Cordiale*? (Editions Panthéon-Assas, 2004) 203).

contracts or simply imposed upon private associations;[53] equitable doctrines of undue influence[54] and unconscionable dealings[55] protect against exploitation;[56] fiduciary duties guard against abuse of power;[57] minority shareholders enjoy protections vis-à-vis majority shareholders;[58] and 'competition law and policy ... has always concerned itself with controlling and constraining the exercise of private power'.[59]

Further complicating matters, phenomena such as devolution and ceding of sovereignty to supranational and international organisations through twin processes of Europeanisation and globalisation have led to a world of fragmented governmental structures meaning that there are multiple 'nodes' of public power, while the interconnections between these nodes are complex and opaque.[60] Within this postnational legal order the search for a home-grown, unitary idea of the state seems anachronistic and likely illusory, while such idea would form an incomplete basis for a distinctive public law. Furthermore, at the supranational level one may observe many of the same phenomena which have rendered public and private spheres increasingly indistinct domestically.

Adding another layer of difficulty to any search for a durable concept of state is the political reality that 'what is or is not a governmental function is socially constructed and hence society-specific, and can (and does) change over time';[61] the scope of governmental activity has a tidal quality, receding and advancing over time. The traditional 'economic neutrality' of the British constitution, which entrenched no particular economic paradigm, left governments relatively free to redefine public and private realms at will.[62]

[53] P Murray, 'Natural Justice at the Boundaries of Public Law' (University of Cambridge Legal Studies Research Paper No 3/2014) (papers.ssrn.com/sol3/papers.cfm?abstract_id=2360010); J Morgan, 'A Mare's Nest? The Jockey Club and Judicial Review of Sports Governing Bodies' (2012) 12 *Legal Information Management* 102.

[54] *RBS Plc v Etridge (No 2)* [2002] 2 AC 773, [18]. While the speeches in *Etridge* suggest a protective rationale, at least for some classes of undue influence case, the law's theoretical foundations are contested: R Bigwood, 'Undue Influence: "Impaired Consent" or "Wicked Exploitation"?' (1996) 16 *Oxford Journal of Legal Studies* 503.

[55] *Commercial Bank of Australia v Amadio* (1983) 151 CLR 447, 474.

[56] Bigwood (n 54) 514.

[57] *Re Hospital Products Ltd v United States Surgical Corp* (1984) 4 IPR 291, 329; *cf* M Conaglen, 'Public-Private Intersection: Comparing Fiduciary Conflict Doctrine and Bias' [2008] *PL* 58.

[58] eg Companies Act 2006, Pt 30; Insolvency Act 1986, s 125.

[59] K Yeung, 'Competition Law and the Public/Private Divide' in Freedland and Auby (n 52).

[60] eg M Loughlin, *Sword and Scales* (Hart Publishing, 2000) ch 10; N Walker, *Questioning Sovereignty* (OUP, 2002); N Krisch, *Beyond Constitutionalism* (OUP, 2010).

[61] Taggart 2003 (n 33) 105.

[62] T Daintith and M Sah, 'Privatisation and the Economic Neutrality of the Constitution' [1993] *PL* 465. Note that influx of EU norms, among other developments, has arguably undermined this relative neutrality by embedding neo-liberal economic precepts into the legal system: D Nicol, *The Constitutional Protection of Capitalism* (Hart Publishing, 2010).

While the idea of the state is the most obvious anchor for a distinctive public law, alternatives have been propounded. Each is problematic. First, some argue the distinctiveness of public power lies in an idea of monopoly: public law norms ought to regulate performance of a function where only one entity performs that function.[63] The idea has significant shortcomings.[64] Most importantly, it is not an account of *public* power, but entails repudiation of any distinction between public and private, recognising all monopoly power, whether exercised by a private equity group or the Home Office, is liable to abuse and ought to be regulated. Second, it may be tempting to use the Crown as a proxy for the state. But this anachronistic concept is bound up in long-standing theoretical disagreement. Further, such approach entails classifying entities as 'public' according to status rather than the functions they perform; something must be awry where an account of public power excludes local government and statutory bodies. Third, some rely on the idea of 'power'. But, as Allison, observes, '[b]y changing a conception of the state for one of power ... English lawyers ... would be moving from the unknown to the more unknown, from one area of difficult political theory to another, even more difficult'.[65] As Allison concludes, for all the possible anchors propounded, it is difficult to escape the significance of the state and the work that concept would do in delineating public from private,[66] yet that idea remains elusive.

Public and private spheres 'have become inextricably interwoven in a process better analogised to the scrambling of an egg than to the weaving of a two-stranded rope' so that seeking to delineate public and private seems increasingly anachronistic and impossible.[67] In a world in which '[n]o activity is typically governmental in character nor wholly without parallels in private law'[68]—private firms run prisons and perform military and foreign affairs functions,[69] private persons are seconded into the service of government,[70] corporations exercise statutory powers,[71] charities provide welfare, government owns commercial banks, Cabinet Office policy units

[63] C Campbell, 'Monopoly Power as Public Power for the Purposes of Judicial Review' (2009) 125 *LQR* 491.
[64] Very few functions are performed exclusively by one entity (unless one defines functions semantically narrowly). Further, it is unclear why, if our concern is preventing abuse of power, we would limit legal regulation to monopolists given entities which are not monopolists but dominate their sphere of activity may also exercise immense power that could be abused.
[65] Allison 1997 (n 30) 88–90.
[66] ibid 88–89.
[67] P Cane, "Accountability and the Public/Private Distinction" in N Bamforth and P Leyland (eds), *Public Law in a Multi-Layered Constitution* (Hart Publishing, 2003) 248 [Cane 2003].
[68] C Harlow, '"Public" and "Private" Law: Definition without Distinction' (1980) 43 *MLR* 241, 257.
[69] PW Singer, *Corporate Warriors* (Cornell, 2007); LA Dickinson, *Outsourcing War and Peace* (Yale, 2011).
[70] Immigration Act 2014, ss 22–28, 40.
[71] eg Financial Services and Markets Act 2000, Pt 1A; Lloyd's Act 1982.

turn joint venture,[72] private entities pay for police services[73]—a conception of the state as unique remains as elusive as ever and cannot perform the theoretical anchoring role for a distinctive idea or system of public law.

Cane criticises such 'descriptive attacks' on the basis that the distinction is in an important respect not descriptive but normative: to say a body or activity is public or private is to say 'that, according to some norm or set of norms, the term "public" or "private" is appropriately applied to that body'.[74] But by the same token the terms are not simply normative.[75] One may develop normative criteria for delineating public and private entities, but if 'the "public/private" classification ... is wholly irrelevant to the organisation of modern society',[76] it is difficult to see the relevance of such criteria, how they could sensibly be applied and what work they could do. Such neat normative schemes are likely to strike a host of difficulties when attempts are made to apply them to the messy reality of modern social, economic and political organisation,[77] and could end up distorting our thinking. Another way to put this is that normative theories must incorporate some understanding of actual social organisation, and of legal and political context,[78] if they are to be comprehensible and practically workable, for example in judicial decision-making: 'facts and causal mechanisms may limit the opportunity set (or choice set or feasible set) of constitutional rules or policies'.[79]

Further, there are simply better and more transparent ways to make normative arguments than by reference to public and private; where those terms are invoked they are usually, as Cane more or less acknowledges, code for a host of different ideas, such as public interest or protection of weak from strong, across a range of contexts. Why not simply make those arguments, rather than viewing them through the blurring, distorting lens of the public–private divide? Such lenses are liable to cause headaches.

[72] '"Nudge unit" Sold Off to Charity and Employees' at www.bbc.com/news/uk-politics-26030205.

[73] Police Act 1996, ss 25, 93; *R v Zinga* [2014] 1 WLR 2228; 'Private Firms Give UK Police Forces Millions of Pounds to Investigate Crimes' at www.telegraph.co.uk/news/uknews/law-and-order/9061383/Private-firms-give-UK-police-forces-millions-of-pounds-to-investigate-crimes.html.

[74] P Cane, 'Public Law and Private Law: A Study of the Analysis and Use of a Legal Concept' in J Eekalaar and J Bell (eds), *Oxford Essays in Jurisprudence, 3rd series* (Clarendon, 1987) 64–66 [Cane 1987].

[75] Allison 1997 (n 30) 86.

[76] Harlow (n 68) 256.

[77] As Aronson argues, the era of 'mixed administration' and 'mixed economy' 'makes it difficult to choose sensibly within a dichotomous legal structure which is not reflected in political reality', which in turn makes it 'difficult to predict which sorts of power will be adjudged public, and which private' ((n 34) 47).

[78] The very point of Allison's magisterial study: above (n 22).

[79] A Vermeule, 'Connecting Positive and Normative Legal Theory' (2008) 10 *Journal of Constitutional Law* 387, 395.

Cane accepts the attack that '[i]f the distinction is going to be of any dispositive legal use it needs to be refined, sharped, and focused so that its use will yield results which are reasonably consistent and predictable', and he sees the key task for protagonists of the divide as developing a set of concepts 'which are useful in decided cases and guiding action'.[80] This quest is unfulfilled and the good money is on it proving illusory; in the meantime, as we shall see, courts, in certain contexts, rest legal development on concepts of 'publicness' which are caught in a 'theoretical twilight zone'.[81] Part of the reason for these difficulties, apart from the distinction's inconsonance with contemporary society and English legal tradition, is that, as Cane says, within a legal paradigm how we define public and private depends in part on what we consider the normative implications of doing so to be—but those normative implications are bound up in interminable disagreement (as we shall see in the next section).

Reflecting these problems, when mobilised the distinction has proven deeply problematic—to the point of being outright unworkable.

The most prominent example is the much maligned House of Lords decisions in *O'Reilly* and *Cocks*, ruling that cases concerning 'public law rights' must be streamed through judicial review procedure, while cases concerning 'private law rights' must not be.[82] Through the 1980s and 1990s there was much litigation on the meaning of 'public law rights' that typically required determination by appellate courts.[83] Courts were unable to articulate clearly 'what characteristics make a right private rather than public'.[84] Cases turned on fine, often arbitrary and unpredictable distinctions, leading commentators to conclude: 'the conceptual distinction ... is not sufficiently clear or predictable to justify allowing choice of procedure to depend on it';[85] '[s]eparate public and private law principles are hard to apply in the post-modern world of fragmented governmental structures; the outcome is the sterile jurisdictional disputes in which lawyers specialise'.[86]

Over time the higher courts rowed back, moving to a more flexible approach.[87] In the Supreme Court case of *Ruddy*, Lord Hope, for the Court, charted the development of the case law towards a less prescriptive approach, and observed, with Sedley LJ in *Clark*,[88] that 'the ground has

[80] Cane 1987 (n 74) 70.
[81] To borrow Allison's phrase: 1997 (n 30) 87.
[82] Above n 2.
[83] GS Morris and S Fredman, 'The Costs of Exclusivity: Public and Private Re-Examined' [1994] *PL* 69.
[84] GS Morris and S Fredman, 'A Snake or a Ladder? *O'Reilly v Mackman* Reconsidered' (1992) 108 *LQR* 353, 356.
[85] ibid 353–54.
[86] Harlow and Rawlings (n 18) 21.
[87] *Davy* (n 26) 276G; *Wandsworth LBC v Winder* [1985] AC 461; *Roy v Kensington and Chelsea and Westminster FPC* [1992] 1 AC 624; *Clark v University of Lincolnshire and Humberside* [2000] 1 WLR 1988; *cf Trim v North Dorset DC* [2010] EWCA Civ 1446.
[88] *Clark* ibid [16] ('The ground has shifted considerably since [*O'Reilly*]').

shifted considerably since *Cocks* ... was decided'.[89] This is a polite way of saying the *O'Reilly* prescriptions no longer hold much sway, and many claimants enjoy a genuine choice of procedure.

Identical difficulties are observable in other contexts. For example, in determining whether an authority's contracting decisions pursuant to statutory enabling powers are reviewable courts require a 'sufficient public law element'.[90] Courts have failed to give clear guidance as to the meaning of this test, drawing 'arbitrary and unconvincing' distinctions, resulting in 'a waste of litigation time and cost analogous in kind although not extent to waste generated by *O'Reilly*'.[91] Similarly courts have found 'no single test of universal application'[92] to determine what constitutes a public function under section 6, HRA, cases turning on the balancing of an open-ended[93] list of factors. Inconsistent decision-making seems inevitable, not least because different judges have demonstrated different background understandings of 'publicness'.[94] For example in *YL* their Lordships split 3–2 on whether a care home which provided accommodation and care services pursuant to an arrangement with a local authority was performing a public function, only for Parliament to reverse.[95]

As one commentator observes, having reviewed the various tests applied to delineate public and private, the 'difficulties inhering in those tests' 'are serious and entrenched'.[96] They cannot be resolved satisfactorily. It is therefore unsurprising to find commentators observing 'deep erosion of [the distinction] both at the level of practical and positive law and, more particularly, at the theoretical or doctrinal level',[97] while those who remain wedded to the distinction increasingly acknowledge the need to recast it as 'multidimensional', 'flexible' and 'porous'.[98]

II. CHOPPY SEAS: THE IMPLICATIONS OF 'PUBLICNESS'

Even if we could identify a basis upon which to found a distinctive idea or system of public law, such as a concept of the state, the legal implications

[89] *Ruddy v Chief Constable Strathclyde Police* [2012] UKSC 57, [17].

[90] SH Bailey, 'Judicial Review of Contracting Decisions' [2007] *PL* 444.

[91] ibid 451, 462–63.

[92] *Aston Cantlow PPC v Wallbank* [2004] 1 AC 546, [12].

[93] *YL v Birmingham* CC [2008] 1 AC 95, [13].

[94] S Palmer, 'Public, Private and the Human Rights Act 1998: An Ideological Divide' (2007) 66 *CLJ* 559.

[95] Health and Social Care Act 2008, s 145; Care Act 2014, s 73.

[96] C Campbell, 'The Nature of Power as Public in English Judicial Review' (2009) 68 *CLJ* 90, 91; J Beatson, '"Public" and "Private" in English Administrative Law' (1987) 103 *LQR* 34.

[97] M Freedland, 'The Evolving Approach to the Public/Private Distinction in English Law' in Freedland and Auby (n 52) 115.

[98] ibid; Cane 2003 (n 67).

of 'publicness' are unclear. This is partly because the implications would depend on the anchor to which public law is hitched. But also, there is entrenched disagreement as to what should follow from a matter being classified as one of public law. For example 'conservative normativists'[99] or 'red light'[100] theorists, traditionally informed by libertarian political philosophy, emphasise the role of courts and ordinary common law in protecting individuals against abuse of power and controlling power. 'Functionalists' or 'green light' theorists, traditionally informed by welfarist political philosophy, argue public law ought to enable and facilitate proper exercise of government power for the benefit of the collectivity. 'Liberal normativists' or 'amber light' theorists, traditionally informed by liberal political philosophy, emphasise the importance of law in protecting individual human rights, possibly through a bill of rights, and are generally more accepting than conservative normativists of a role for government beyond 'night-watchman' functions.

These are necessarily stylised summaries of mainstream conceptions of public law. However, they are sufficient to demonstrate the variety of view as to the nature of public law. Given the idea of public law is bound up in longstanding and deep-seated disagreement it is difficult to see how it could be invoked as a useful, non-contentious normative tool, particularly in judicial decision-making. Indeed, invocation of the distinction may well draw courts into politically contested waters or mask politically-motivated judgments beneath a formalist veneer: generic appeals to 'public law' are incredibly opaque and can obscure the true basis of a decision given 'public law' is 'shorthand for a whole collection of ideas'.[101] This flags another problem, there is simply not enough discipline around use of the term to make it a useful analytical tool.

Furthermore, these conceptions of public law are very general in nature, and disagreement is inevitable in application. Indeed, each could arguably support a vindicatory approach to human rights damages (equally arguments could be made within each tradition against such approach), albeit it seems likely application of each would alter the precise detail of the approach to damages. Amber lighters might favour such approach given the strong protection it affords individual rights. Red lighters might oppose a bill of rights given their traditional faith in the common law. However, they would likely have sympathy with an approach to human rights damages, founded on ordinary common law principles, that afforded strong protection to individual, negative rights vis-à-vis authorities. One might consider a

[99] On conservative and liberal normativism, and functionalism see: M Loughlin, *Public Law and Political Theory* (OUP, 1992).

[100] The traffic-light metaphor was devised by Harlow and Rawlings: *Law and Administration* (Weidenfeld and Nicolson, 1984) chs 1–2; 2nd edn (Butterworths, 1997) chs 2–4; (n 18) ch 1.

[101] D Oliver, *Common Values and the Public-Private Divide* (Butterworths, 1999) 14.

vindicatory approach would not mesh with green light theories on the basis that such approach arguably prioritises individual interests ahead of those of the community and may, for example, stymie implementation of progressive government policy. But many green lighters accept that the most basic of individual interests ought to be afforded strong legal protection. Indeed, human rights are afforded strong protection because they benefit individuals *as well as* the public as a whole. Some rights, such as freedom of association and expression, privacy and religion, have strong social or group dimensions, while the Convention's scheme ensures the public interest is afforded due weight through limitation and derogation clauses. After all, it is only where an interference cannot be justified in the public interest that liability arises. Further, provision of compensation for citizens who suffer particularised negative impacts through exercises of public power undertaken for the common good is arguably supportable on a collectivist principle of social solidarity (indeed, on this view limiting compensation to those who suffer rights-violations may be too restrictive).[102] Victims of rights-violations are as much members of the political community as those who benefit from governmental intervention, and where government errs in pursuit of collective goals, in a manner which cannot be justified according to those goals, it ought to make good damage caused to members of the community.

Various other attempts have been made to pin down the idea of public law. One recent and prominent account is proffered by Loughlin, who has developed what he describes as a 'pure' theory of public law, seeking to provide an account of public law shorn of political ideology, and distinct from private law.[103] Among the fundamental features of this theory are that public law relates to the activity of governing the state, which it conditions, sustains and regulates; the concept of representation is the foundation of public law; sovereignty is the most basic concept of public law; and prudential reasoning is public law's method. Central to Loughlin's thesis is the claim that public law is not an exercise in moral reasoning but a form of political reasoning driven by prudential concerns.

While no doubt an interesting, thought-provoking contribution, as Loughlin himself acknowledges, his account is only one 'contribution' to the 'British debate' as to the nature of the idea of public law.[104] In turn this reinforces that the idea is bound up in strong disagreement, with no set meaning in English legal discourse.

Indeed, consideration of Loughlin's theoretical account, in the light of the realities of contemporary English law, shows how far English law is

[102] See, eg, the approach to administrative liability in French law, which is informed by a principle of social solidarity: NL Brown and JS Bell, *French Administrative Law* 5th edn (OUP, 1998) ch 8; D Fairgrieve, *State Liability in Tort* (OUP, 2003).

[103] M Loughlin, *The Idea of Public Law* (OUP, 2003); *Foundations of Public Law* (OUP, 2010).

[104] Loughlin 2010, ibid 6.

from a system in which public and private law are fundamentally distinct. This should not come as a surprise because Loughlin's task—though not always clear—seems to be to develop an idealised conception of public law as distinct from private law, drawing on Western European political and philosophical thinking over several centuries. It is an exercise in 'imagining public law',[105] and this imagined idea, while based in European thought and history, exists outside of a specific time or jurisdiction. For this reason one is hard pressed to find any reference to court decisions in Loughlin's writing. Importantly, it is a conception nearly wholly removed from English or British contexts. Apart from considering some early British sources, Loughlin's study focuses on continental sources. This selectivity is explained by Loughlin's belief that 'the concept of public law has remained suppressed in British legal practice for much of the last 250 years',[106] and that this suppression is regrettable. His view is rightly described as a 'radical', 'reformist' one:[107] that we ought now to 're-connect with the mainstream of the European tradition of public law'.[108] As Allison observes, Loughlin is looking outside English law for ideas to reform it.[109]

Loughlin himself acknowledges that his account, which conceptualises public law as a special form of 'fundamental' law, is at variance with traditional English understandings of public law as 'ordinary law';[110] and indeed his conception varies a great deal from contemporary English law. The state is central to Loughlin's thesis, yet English law has no conception of the state and it seems wholly unlikely such conception will emerge. Loughlin's idea of an 'autonomous political sphere', and strict separation of power based in collective action and power based in material wealth, seems wholly out of step in a society within which public and private spheres are inexorably intermingled. Significant bodies of private law such as tort, contract, equity and restitution, which as conceptualised by Loughlin are the exclusive province of morality and moral reason rather than politics and prudential reasoning, nonetheless are significant bodies of law that regulate the activity of governing. Indeed, tort has long been the *principal* means of individual protection in the face of public power. Further, private law, as it exists in the world, is not solely the province of moral reason; for example, negligence analysis is replete with public policy concerns. As Loughlin himself observes, the influx of 'rights' discourse into public law brings with it the 'moralization'

[105] P Cane, 'Imagining Public Law' (2006) 31 *Australian Journal of Legal Philosophy* 153.

[106] Whether such concept ever characterised British legal practice is far from clear: M Walters, 'Is Public Law Ordinary?' (2012) 75 *MLR* 894.

[107] JWF Allison, 'History to Understand, and History to Reform, English Public Law' (2013) 72 *CLJ* 526, 538.

[108] Loughlin 2010 (n 103) 6.

[109] Allison (n 107) 538–39.

[110] Loughlin 2010 (n 103) 2–6.

of law;[111] it becomes difficult therefore to maintain a clear divide between politics and morality (while even as a matter of pure theory Loughlin's strict separation of political and moral seems difficult to sustain).[112] Ultimately, as Barber says, responding to Loughlin, when it comes to contemporary English law, '[t]he objectives of public and private law overlap; no deep division can be detected'.[113] Loughlin's work helps us to reach this conclusion given the incongruity between contemporary English law and his account.

Others seek to capture the distinctiveness of public law other than via grand monistic theory. A common method is identification of 'public law values'.[114] However, values-based approaches are unlikely to clarify the implications of 'publicness'. There is likely to be significant disagreement over what those values are—various laundry lists have been produced[115]—their interpretation, the relative weight or focus given to particular values, how conflicts between values should be resolved, and linked to this, whether these values are part of a normative hierarchy, and if so, where particular values fall within that hierarchy. Such disagreements will likely lead one back into the realm of contested theory. Further, these values are typically elaborated at such a level of abstraction that they cannot aid resolution of concrete legal controversies; as Cane, a protagonist of values-based approaches, acknowledges,

> the abstractness of values and theory also limits their explanatory power as well as their normative force. For instance, it is unlikely that any value or normative theory would indicate a choice between unreasonableness and proportionality as standards of judicial review.[116]

Similarly, knowing 'protection of the individual' and 'promotion of the public interest'[117] are public law values does not take one very far in choosing between a vindicatory tort-based approach to human rights damages or a public interest conception (see section 2 below). These problems are not limited to values-based accounts which seek to present public law as distinctive.

[111] Loughlin 2003 (n 103) ch 7.

[112] See NW Barber, 'Professor Loughlin's Idea of Public Law' (2005) 25 *Oxford Journal of Legal Studies* 157, 158ff; P Craig, 'Theory, "Pure Theory" and Values in Public Law' [2005] *PL* 440, 443–44. Private law implicates politics as much as any other field: eg R Abel, 'A Critique of Torts' (1990) 37 *UCLA Law Review* 785.

[113] Barber, ibid 166.

[114] Originally in response to the spectacular rise of neo-liberal economic thinking and its influence on government during the 1980s: Taggart 2003 (n 33) 102–03, 106–07; 'The Province of Administrative Law Determined' in Taggart 1997 (n 33) 3; P McAuslan, 'Public Law and Public Choice' (1988) 51 *MLR* 681.

[115] Harlow and Rawlings (n 18) 46; P Cane, 'Theories and Values in Public Law' in P Craig and R Rawlings (eds), *Law and Administration in Europe* (OUP, 2003) 14–16; Taggart 2003 (n 33) 103; Oliver (n 101); P Daly, 'A Values-Based Approach to Administrative Law' in Bell et al (n 1).

[116] Cane, ibid 20.

[117] ibid 15–16.

For example, Oliver has challenged the public law–private law divide on the basis that public law and private law are underpinned by common values such as dignity, security and autonomy.[118] But such values are so abstract that they could be imputed to pretty much any legal field. Not only does this not much enhance our understanding of the law, but it also surely passes over significant and meaningful differences not only between fields of private law and fields of public law, but also amongst different fields of private law, and different fields of public law.

III. OCEANS OR SEAS OF DOCTRINE? THE PLURALISTIC NATURE OF PUBLIC LAW DOCTRINE

A premise underlying invocation of 'public law' to guide legal development is that public law has some sort of inherent unity. The idea seems to be that public law is unified around a set of core ideas, functions, methods, principles or values, these ideas etc being fundamentally different from those that characterise and unify private law. These ideas, functions etc might then be resorted to in order to determine answers to specific questions across public law, such as the approach to human rights damages. So, for example, Lord Woolf in *Anufrijeva* reasoned by reference to *a* set of 'public law aims', and *a* 'public law' approach to remedies, these unitary ideas in turn shaping legal development. The nature of such unitary ideas is not always clear. In particular it is often ambiguous whether they are intended to capture the law as we find it, or are normative. The answer is likely that they fall in between, being interpretive in nature: '[t]here is considerable diversity of opinion concerning the nature and purpose of administrative law. Description and prescription are not easily separated'.[119]

On the one hand such unitary accounts may be set at a very high level of abstraction, so as to comprehend the array of doctrine which comprises public law, and in consequence have little use when it comes to explaining particular doctrines or helping to answer specific legal questions. On the other hand, a core problem with unitary accounts other than those elaborated from a birds-eye perspective is that they are likely to be fundamentally at odds with the nature of contemporary public law, which is a varied, pluralistic field, not reducible to one set of functions of ideas. Reliance on an account of public law fundamentally at odds with core structural features of public law as we find it is very likely to give rise to a host of problems. These include suppressing and stymieing distinctively valuable functions which particular sub-fields are specifically constituted to perform, and introducing incoherence into sub-fields not sensibly analysed according to the given unitary account.

[118] Oliver (n 101).

[119] P Craig, *Administrative Law* 7th edn (Sweet and Maxwell, 2012) 1.

Contemporary public law includes a plurality of meaningfully distinct bodies, sub-bodies, and sub-sub-bodies of doctrine, which have their own distinctive functions, internal structures and philosophical foundations.[120] There may be overlaps, interrelationships and spill-overs between areas, but meaningfully distinct fields exist, which occupy their own terrain on the public law landscape.[121] As De Smith observed in 1952 in respect of one category of public law,

> [a]dministrative law is not a homogenous body of jurisprudence, but is rather an agglomeration of diverse and complex branches of law ... and judicial review in each individual branch of administrative law has tended to develop in a distinctive manner.[122]

Today administrative law and public law more generally are even more diverse. Take the law streamed via judicial review procedure as a sample. Modern judicial review is a 'multi-streamed' jurisdiction, likened to 'Spaghetti Junction' because of its complexity and the plurality of doctrine it encompasses.[123] A variety of types of claims may be streamed via review, including those under the HRA, in EU law, and those based in common law grounds of review, while authors have observed an emergent international law dimension.[124] (It is also worth observing that private law claims, for example in tort, often originate via review).

There are fundamental differences between these parts of public law. For example, the most common review doctrines applied in EU challenges, such as direct effect and indirect effect, rest on an integrationist rationale, being designed to ensure EU norms are embedded in and effective in the domestic legal system. And while EU law is itself an increasingly pluralistic order, with non-economic ideas such as human rights, anti-discrimination or environmental protection exerting increasing influence, 'the EU's dominant focus remains economic',[125] reflecting its foundational goals. Thus, many

[120] Doctrinal categorisation of private law has attracted much interest in recent times, in large part due to the work of Peter Birks (eg 'Equity in the Modern Law: An Exercise in Taxonomy' (1996) 26 *University of Western Australia Law Review* 1; 'Introduction' in P Birks (ed), *English Private Law* (OUP, 2000)). In contrast little fine-grained work in doctrinal categorisation has been undertaken in public law. The resulting lack of doctrinal clarity and understanding can breed confusion in academic debate and more importantly incoherence and irrationality in doctrine; as Birks observed, information that cannot be sorted is not knowledge ('Introduction' li). One explanation for the lack of research on this topic may be the comparatively recent development of major fields of English public law, such as human rights law. Contract, equity and torts have longer histories. Further, the focus on private law in modern scholarly taxonomies is unsurprising as they are rooted in the work of Roman lawyers, who also focused on private law: B Nicholas, *An Introduction to Roman Law* (Clarendon, 1975) 2.

[121] SA De Smith, *The Lawyers and the Constitution* (Bell and Sons, 1960) 16.

[122] SA De Smith, 'Wrongs and Remedies in Administrative Law' (1952) 15 *MLR* 189, 189.

[123] R Rawlings, "Modelling Judicial Review" (2008) 61 *Current Legal Problems* 95, 114ff.

[124] ibid.

[125] P Craig and G De Búrca, *EU Law* 5th edn (OUP, 2011) 364.

norms in EU law, applied in review proceedings, are underpinned by the instrumentalist goal of facilitating wealth maximisation by promoting market integration, or protect individuals' economic interests. Within the EU legal order, economic freedoms such as freedom of trade and competition have the same normative status—as principles of fundamental rights—as human rights, and where economic freedoms have clashed with fundamental, non-economic freedoms, economic freedoms have been afforded primacy.[126] The theoretical foundations of such economic norms, and the integrationalist rationale of doctrines such as direct effect, are altogether different from the rationale for human rights law, which is to afford strong protection to inherently valuable and basic human interests, or common law judicial review, fundamental features of which suggest a dominant concern with ensuring public power is exercised properly for the common good (see further section 2 below).

Further casting doubt on any meaningful, inherent unity is the reality that each of these fields has a different source and is influenced by a different legal order. For example EU law and HRA law are to different degrees directly influenced by different supranational legal orders, whereas the common law is in general not; as a result each field has its own 'genetic imprint'.[127] Human rights law is sourced in one statute, whereas developments at common law are principally the result of judicial creation in the shadow of myriad parent statutes. Such significant institutional variations further suggest unity is unlikely.

So far we have focused only on a few fields of public law. There are different accounts of public law, but on most accounts it would encompass much more. For example public law could be said to include the law of public finance, the prerogative, public procurement, public employment, planning, tribunals, inquiries, freedom of information, devolution, the Parliamentary and Local Government Ombudsmen, public sector equality duties, local government law, as well as 'non-legal' phenomena, such as constitutional conventions, parliamentary standing orders, administrative codes of practice, policy guidance, in-house, departmental mechanisms for dispute resolution, the practice of governmental ex gratia payments etc. All leading 'administrative law' textbooks include chapters on public authority liability in 'private law' fields, while the major treatise on English public law includes criminal law within its scope.[128]

Once the pluralistic nature of public law is recognised, it becomes clear that unitary accounts are wholly out of step with public law's basic structure. When commentators observe, the 'functional separation between negligence

[126] *International Transport Workers' Federation v Viking Line ABP* [2008] 1 CMLR 51; *Laval un Partneri Ltd v Svenska Byggnadsarbetareforbundet* [2008] 2 CMLR 9.

[127] Rawlings (n 123) 121.

[128] D Feldman (ed), *English Public Law* 2nd edn (OUP, 2009).

law and human rights law reflects the more general functional separation between private law and public law',[129] one is left wondering what exactly that 'general functional separation' is. It is a fundamental structural feature of contemporary public law that different fields of public law perform fundamentally distinct functions from other bodies of public law doctrine, just as contract performs distinct functions from torts or equity or the law of maritime insurance. Over-simplifications should be repudiated as they run counter to this basic feature, are likely to distort our understanding of the law and warp legal development.

IV. PULLING INTO PORT: CONCLUSION

This section has highlighted fundamental problems with allowing the public law–private law distinction to lead legal development. A more enlightened approach is proposed by Harlow and Rawlings: 'Specific situations call for thoughtful specific answers and not the mechanical application of the totemic word "public"'.[130] Or, as Aronson argues, valuable responses to specific issues, whether characterised as involving 'public' or 'private' activities, or entities, however defined, might be derived from within public law or private law or combine a mix of insights from both.[131] His further observation is also insightful:

> It often assists analysis to set up opposing models as ideal types, even if we know that their differences may be only a matter of degree, and that not everything fits comfortably within this construct. The real difficulties occur when too little fits within the construct, or when it starts to limit one's vision.[132]

It may be that an issue arising within a citizen–public authority relationship requires an approach and/or solution that differs from that within other relationships, and one ought to be open to this. But simply stating the issue is one of public law is not likely to advance the analysis and can certainly obscure it, pre-empt conclusions, cut off legitimate debate, and is opaque, given the indeterminacy of public law as a guiding idea, and can hide and often does hide contentious political concerns. There are real problems with relying on the divide in legal decision-making: it is at odds with the organisation of modern society which betrays any neat compartmentalisation of public and private, it runs against the basic ordering of the English legal system, it may hide clear connections between fields of public

[129] D Nolan, 'Negligence and Human Rights Law: the Case for Separate Development' (2013) 76 *MLR* 286, 295.

[130] Harlow and Rawlings (n 18) 21.

[131] Aronson (n 34) 51ff.

[132] ibid 51.

and private law, it is bound up in interminable disagreement and is indeterminate, and the distinction encourages reductionist accounts of public law and private law, fundamentally at odds with the basic, pluralistic nature of each field.

It is simplistic and unduly constraining to determine legal issues according to whether they fall into one of two and only ever two paradigms, such as (take your pick of dichotomies) market individualism versus social co-operation. Why ought we to so narrow and limit our thinking, and why would we desire a legal system based in such binary thinking? It is far more preferable to consider all aspects of a legal issue, taking account of all relevant factors including the nature of the specific field of doctrine within which it arises, not just one (questionable, indeterminate) dichotomy: '[d]ynamic flexibility rather than formal separation is required'.[133] In particular we need to be aware of the intrinsic rationality and norms of the distinct subject-matter that is the focus of legal regulation, so that the legal regime 'fits' with rather than distorts or suppresses the internal rationality of the underlying phenomena.[134] This is not to say that theories of public law, some of which were discussed above, cannot provide useful insights; rather it is to argue that no one concept or dichotomy can be dispositive of specific questions arising across the vast, varied terrain of public law and private law.

Given this analysis the reasoning of the high appellate courts that the approach to damages for human rights violations ought to differ from that in tort because human rights law is part of public law and tort is part of private law is simplistic, unsafe, unconvincing and conceals more than it reveals. In this light it is difficult to disagree with the conclusion reached by Ackermann J, sitting in the South African Constitutional Court, having charted reliance on the idea of 'public law' in comparative human rights damages jurisprudence:

> It is both undesirable and unnecessary, for purposes of this case, to attempt to do that which has seemingly eluded scholars in the past and given rise to wide differences of opinion among them, namely, the drawing of a clear and permanent line between the domains of private law and public law and the utility of any such efforts … Suffice it to say that it could be dangerous to attach consequences to or infer solutions from concepts such as 'public law' and 'private law' when the validity of such concepts and the distinctions which they imply are being seriously questioned.[135]

[133] C Harlow, 'Review' (2008) 14 *European Public Law* 433, 439. Even prominent supporters of the distinction acknowledge its weakness in being unable to respond to very different contexts and situations, and advocate a more nuanced approach: Cane 1987 (n 74) 70; Cane 2003 (n 67) 269–75.

[134] G Teubner, 'After Privatization? The Many Autonomies of Private Law' (1998) 51 *Current Legal Problems* 393.

[135] *Fose v Minister of Safety and Security* [1997] 3 SA 786, [57].

SECTION 2. THE PUBLIC LAW–PRIVATE LAW DISTINCTION AND HUMAN RIGHTS DAMAGES

Given this background it should come as no surprise that judicial reliance on the public law–private law distinction within HRA damages jurisprudence has resulted in problematic reasoning and development of questionable approaches.

This section takes *Anufrijeva* as its starting point. Of the several major decisions on HRA damages, this case most starkly invokes 'public law' as a normative tool to guide the approach to damages. The Court of Appeal adopted a monolithic 'public interest' conception of public law which led it to an approach to damages that is deeply at odds with the nature of human rights law. While some areas of public law doctrine, such as common law judicial review, can be explained adequately by such conception, human rights law cannot. In turn, adoption of a remedial approach based in a public interest conception of public law within a field concerned with protection of fundamental individual interests serves to disrupt human rights law's coherence and stymies its distinctive functions. The section goes on to show, by reference to academic debates and New Zealand human rights damages jurisprudence, that even if one thought it wise to rest development of the damages remedy on a monolithic conception of 'public law', this need not necessarily lead to a public interest approach.

The section concludes that the public law–private law distinction should not be the starting point for deciding the approach to human rights damages. Rather we ought to start with the distinctive nature of obligations within human rights law, which are individual rights constituted to protect and vindicate basic interests. Analysis of the distinction's use and influence within human rights damages cases reinforces critiques that the distinction can distort legal development, suppress the internal rationality and functions of discrete bodies of doctrine, lead to drawing of artificial and reductionist distinctions, cut off legitimate debate, lead courts into ordinary politics, artificially shield authorities from liability, and blind or distract judges from obvious solutions based in established principle.

I. PROTECTION OF THE PUBLIC AND HUMAN RIGHTS DAMAGES: THE APPROACH IN *ANUFRIJEVA*

This section identifies the 'public interest' theory of public law, and explains how this theory shaped the approach to damages in *Anufrijeva*. The next section demonstrates this 'public interest' approach to remedies is deeply at odds with the nature of human rights law. In turn, the experience in this field illustrates the serious problems that can arise when one rests legal development on a unitary conception of public law.

A. The Public Interest Theory of Public Law[136]

Lord Woolf, who gave the Court's decision in *Anufrijeva*, is a leading proponent of the 'public interest' theory.[137] This theory rose to prominence and shaped development of judicial review doctrine in the formative period following the procedural reforms of the late 1970s. The theory is evident in judgments of other influential judges of that era, including Lord Diplock, who introduced the public law–private law division into English law, and Lord Donaldson.[138] The theory remains influential, while common law judicial review in particular continues to bear its hallmarks.

This theory holds that public law is principally concerned with enforcement of public duties and protection of the public interest. For example Lord Woolf defined public law as 'the system which enforces the proper performance by public bodies of the duties which they owe to the public'.[139] Although individuals enforce such duties, they are general duties owed to the public at large. Individuals do not possess enforceable rights in public law, even though securing enforcement of a public duty may incidentally protect a claimant's rights or interests; all a review applicant is entitled to do is insist that an authority perform its duties properly.[140] In contrast private law is 'the system which protects the private rights of private individuals or the private rights of public bodies'.[141] An individual who suffers a tort may bring proceedings to establish 'the infringement of his personal rights, in respect of which he is entitled to damages'.[142] Thus, for Lord Woolf, '[t]he critical distinction arises out of the fact that it is the public as a whole ... who are the beneficiaries of what is protected by public law and it is the individuals or bodies entitled to the rights who are the beneficiaries of the protection provided by private law'.[143] It follows that when courts intervene in public law they do so 'on behalf of the public'[144] or 'in defence of the citizenry'.[145]

Within this paradigm, whether an issue is one of public duty or private right makes a 'fundamental difference' to the courts' role and remedies.[146]

[136] On emergence of the public interest theory see: Varuhas 2016 (n 1).

[137] H Woolf, 'Public Law–Private Law: Why the Divide? A Personal View' [1986] *PL* 220; see also H Woolf, *Protection of the Public—A New Challenge* (Stevens, 1990); H Woolf, 'Droit Public—English Style' [1995] *PL* 57.

[138] Varuhas 2016 (n 1).

[139] Woolf 1986 (n 137) 221; Woolf 1995 (n 137) 64.

[140] Woolf 1986 ibid 221–23, 227, 237.

[141] ibid 221. This rights-based conception carries weight with many private lawyers. Birks said '[p]rivate law is above all concerned with the rights which, one against another, people are able to realise in courts'. He saw the notion of 'realizable rights' as providing the underlying unity for his taxonomy of private law: Birks 2000 (n 120) xxxvi.

[142] Woolf 1986 (n 137) 223.

[143] ibid 221.

[144] *R v Panel on Take-Overs and Mergers, ex p Guinness Plc* [1990] 1 QB 146, 193G.

[145] *R v Panel on Take-Overs and Mergers, ex p Datafin Plc* [1987] 1 QB 815, 839.

[146] Woolf 1986 (n 137) 225.

Where private rights are at stake courts have primary responsibility for finding facts, whereas in public law it is not typically the court's role to determine factual matters, but rather that of the administrative decision-maker.[147] In private law it is the court's responsibility to determine substantive matters; for example it is the court's view of what is 'reasonable', in adjudicating defences to torts actionable per se (TAPS) or in assessing breach within negligence, that is determinative. In contrast, it is inappropriate for courts to judge the substantive reasonableness of executive action: 'courts cannot usurp the duty of the public body to make the decision'.[148] Lord Woolf argues that these concerns also affect remedies.[149] If a court finds an executive decision unlawful it will, if it grants relief, generally quash the decision and refer it back to the responsible authority. The court does not take the decision itself.

Lord Woolf emphasises the procedural differences between public and private law.[150] He cites the principle of exclusivity established in *O'Reilly*, and argues, echoing the policy-rationale for that principle,[151] that the procedural peculiarities of review, such as the permission requirement, short three month limitation period and panoply of judicial discretions, are necessary because in public law cases it is not only the parties' interests at stake, but also those of 'the public'.[152] These procedural rules protect the public interest in seeing that litigation does not unduly or unnecessarily interfere with the functioning of government.[153] Without such safeguards 'the public would be unprotected'.[154] He also links the field's public interest ethos to liberal standing rules within common law review, which allow any party with 'sufficient interest' in proper performance of the public duty to apply for review.[155] He observes that limited provision for oral evidence in public law proceedings reflects that it is not for courts to conduct fact-finding,[156] but rather the executive decision-maker, and that discovery can cause increased costs, delay, and 'immense inconvenience' for public bodies, thus why it is seldom ordered in review proceedings.[157]

[147] See similarly *R v Hillingdon LBC, ex p Puhlhofer* [1986] AC 484, 517–18.

[148] Woolf 1986 (n 137) 225.

[149] ibid 225.

[150] ibid 227ff.

[151] ie litigants in public law should not be able to evade the public law procedure's safeguards, as this would undermine the public interest in protection of authorities from tardy or unmeritorious claims: *O'Reilly* (n 2) 282; *R v IRC, ex p National Federation of Self-Employed and Small Businesses Ltd* [1982] AC 617, 630, 643.

[152] Woolf 1986 (n 137) 229–30, 238; Woolf 1995 (n 137) 60ff.

[153] Woolf 1986, ibid 230.

[154] ibid 233.

[155] ibid 230–31; Woolf 1995 (n 137) 62; Senior Courts Act, s 31(3).

[156] Of course this argument is weakened by development of error of fact as a review ground: *E v SOSHD* [2004] QB 1044.

[157] Woolf 1986 (n 137) 231. These concerns are echoed in the case law: *O'Reilly* (n 2) 257, 282, 284.

Importantly for present purposes, Lord Woolf emphasises the remedial discretion within judicial review, which he believes affords a court 'considerable power' to determine whether to interfere with administrative decisions, is an important safeguard for public bodies.[158] And indeed, the remedial discretion within common law review is steeped in public interest concerns. For example Lord Donaldson, in *Datafin*, saw the remedial discretion as intimately connected to the public interest dimensions of public law: the court has

> an ultimate discretion whether to set [decisions] aside and may refuse to do so in the public interest ... such decisions affect a very wide public which will not be parties to the dispute and ... their interests have to be taken into account as much as those of the immediate disputants.[159]

In *Argyll* he enumerated grounds on which review remedies, such as quashing orders, could be denied, most of which evinced a concern with ensuring minimal disruption to administrative process: remedies may be denied where their grant would undermine administrative interests in speediness, certainty and/or finality.[160] Lord Donaldson emphasised a focus on declaratory relief in public law, grant of which would ensure authorities did not repeat errors, but also ensured administrative processes which had already run their course were not disturbed. This 'educative' function for public law—guiding authorities into the future so they do 'not ... repeat any error'[161]—was at one with Lord Donaldson's view, consonant with Lord Woolf's,[162] that courts and authorities are, within the province of public law, together engaged in 'a workable and valuable *partnership ... in the public interest*',[163] with 'a common aim, namely the maintenance of the highest standards of public administration'.[164]

I refer to this theory as the 'public interest' conception of public law. It is necessary to clarify what is meant by 'public interest' in this regard. Lord Woolf does not squarely address the concept. But from significant features of public interest theories, it seems that at the forefront of public interest theorists' thinking is the public interest Parliament has sought to pursue in passing empowering legislation; the courts' role is to regulate public power so as to facilitate attainment of those goals. Of course, what decision would best serve the public interests embedded in the terms of the parent statute is for the official bestowed with the statutory power of decision:

> Parliament has entrusted to the department or authority charged with the administration of the statute the exclusive right to determine the particular means

[158] Woolf 1995 (n 137) 61.
[159] *Datafin* (n 145) 840–41.
[160] *R v Monopolies and Mergers Commission, ex p Argyll* [1986] 1 WLR 763, 774–75.
[161] *Datafin* (n 145) 842.
[162] Consider Lord Woolf's sentiments in *M v Home Office* [1994] 1 AC 377, 425: 'the Crown's relationship with the courts does not depend on coercion'. See also *Greenfield* (n 10) [19].
[163] *Datafin* (n 145) 842 (emphasis added).
[164] *R v Lancashire CC, ex p Huddleston* [1986] 2 All ER 941, 945.

within the limits laid down by the statute by which its [public] purpose can best be fulfilled.[165]

From this premise, the court's role is a supervisory one, simply to ensure decision-makers broadly keep on track and do not go 'off the rails',[166] genuinely pursuing those ends which Parliament has set for them; if this is done then the public interest, as determined by Parliament, will be preserved. It also follows from the proposition that protection of the public interest is the principal concern of public law, that it is incumbent on courts in administering public law to ensure officials are not unduly impeded in their pursuit of statutory public goals, which involves protecting administrative interests in timely, certain, efficient, effective and vigorous administration. Such concern is particularly evident in the public interest approach to remedies and public law procedure; wide discretions in respect of each allow courts to regulate interventions on a case-by-case basis so the administration is not unduly burdened.

Other commentators have reached similar conclusions. Cane argues that supporters of the public law–private law divide tend to interpret the public interest in terms of the administration doing what *it* perceives to be in the public interest as efficiently and quickly as possible.[167] As Beatson observes, the emphasis in judicial decisions during the 1980s—the time when public interest theories rose to prominence—was on 'judicial review as a discretionary and residual remedy which should only be given where alternative remedies are inadequate *and where to do so would not prejudice the requirements of good public administration*'.[168] Similarly, in 1990 Feldman, in a study of the values that had influenced the Law Lords in their public law decisions, observed they 'display a political and professional élitism which discourages interference with discretionary decisions of government and professional administrators. This encourages the House to facilitate, rather than restrict, social programmes and administrative processes'.[169]

B. The Public Interest Theory and Human Rights Damages

Now that the public interest theory has been identified and elaborated, it becomes clear that it is this conception of public law or a variant that informed the Court's approach to damages in *Anufrijeva*. Importantly, fundamental aspects of this approach were approved or not disturbed by the

[165] *Home Office v Dorset Yacht Co Ltd* [1970] AC 1004, 1067.
[166] *Datafin* (n 145) 827.
[167] Cane 1987 (n 74) 63–64 and see 75–77.
[168] Beatson (n 96) 41 (emphasis added).
[169] D Feldman, 'Public Law Values in the House of Lords' (1990) 106 *LQR* 246, 275–76.

Law Lords or Supreme Court in *Greenfield* and *Faulkner*, while the practical effect of the prevailing mirror approach is an approach to human rights damages which bears striking similarities to one based in a public interest conception.[170]

Anufrijeva 'shoehorns' human rights law into the public interest conception by adopting a remedial approach synonymous with a concern for proper performance of public duties in the public interest. This is reflected in the strong remedial emphasis in *Anufrijeva* on declaratory relief, quashing orders and specific-type relief, all of which are geared to ensuring public duties are in fact carried out as they ought to be.[171] On the other hand, damages, being a personal remedy for harm specific to an individual, is a conceptual outlier within the public interest theory, and is therefore marginalised.

Anufrijeva 'downplays damages as a remedy in HRA cases' in a number of ways.[172] The Court expressly stated that the individual interest in compensation for personal loss is of secondary, if any, importance in human rights law.[173] This idea forms a golden thread that runs through HRA damages jurisprudence, and has been reinforced by adoption of the mirror approach. For example in *Dobson* the Court of Appeal said, '[t]he Convention serves principally public law aims; the principal objective is to declare any infringement and to put a stop to it. Compensation is ancillary and discretionary. The interests of the individual are part of the equation, but so are those of the wider public';[174] 'The focus is on the State's compliance, not the claimant's loss'.[175] Further, the Court in *Anufrijeva* emphasised it had a 'wide discretion' to decide whether to award damages, analogising with the approach to remedies in common law review.[176] The Court, in emphasising remedial discretion, affords courts leeway and flexibility to deny relief where its grant would compromise administrative and public interests. Contrary to the position in tort, the Court indicated HRA damages will rarely be awarded, being a remedy of 'last resort' (language borrowed from common law review),[177] and if awarded are likely to be modest.[178] This approach is of a piece with Lord Woolf's extra-judicial view that in public law protection of the individual

> is incidental to the court's primary obligation, which is to stop the public body abusing its powers and the court does not so much establish the rights of the

[170] See the Introduction to Pt 3 of this book, ch 5, and text to n 10ff above.
[171] (n 3) [52]–[56].
[172] C Harlow, *State Liability* (OUP, 2004) 114.
[173] *Anufrijeva* (n 3) [53].
[174] *Dobson* (n 13) [42], and see: *Greenfield* (n 10) [9]; *Rabone v Pennine Care NHS Foundation Trust* [2012] 2 AC 72, [82]; *Sturnham* (n 14) [22].
[175] *DSD* CA (n 16) [65]–[66].
[176] *Anufrijeva* (n 3) [56].
[177] ibid. On review as a remedy of last resort see, eg, *R v Chief Constable of Merseyside, ex p Calveley* [1986] QB 424.
[178] ibid [75]–[76].

> individual but confines the public body to performing its obligations and not exceeding its authority.[179]

By contrast, where private rights are at stake protection of individual interests is afforded primacy, with damages issuing as of right to compensate personal loss.

Anufrijeva emphasises protection of the public interest over individual protection. The Court said that in deciding whether to award damages and quantum, 'there is a balance to be drawn between the interests of the victim and those of the public as a whole'.[180] While the Court drew attention to the negative effects that awards may have on public funds set aside to benefit the wider community and the administration's ability to perform its functions,[181] little, if anything, was said of the negative effects of denying an individual damages for harm suffered pursuant to wrongful government action.[182] The judgment strikes the balance firmly in favour of the public interest more generally, in holding that awards should be rare. In this way public interests in, for example, preservation of public funds and preventing administrative disruption through excessive damages litigation are prioritised well ahead of interests in individual redress. This order of priority matches the traditional approach within common law review. For example, we saw that in *Argyll* considerable emphasis was placed on the importance of protecting administrative and public interests at the remedies stage. Lord Donaldson said: 'Good public administration requires a proper consideration of the legitimate interests of individual citizens … But in judging the relevance of an interest, however legitimate, regard has to be had to the purpose of the administrative process concerned'.[183] In other words, individual interests, but only those deemed legitimate, may be relevant to the remedial inquiry as an aspect of good administration (rather than because they are inherently important), but their relevance and weight is contingent on the public purposes for which power is conferred. The public interest remains the overarching concern, the touchstone: if the individual interest is not consonant with 'the purpose of the administrative process' '[t]o that extent [the individual] interest is not therefore of any great, or possibly any, weight'.[184]

The Court in *Anufrijeva* also held human rights damages claims were to be treated as 'public law' claims for procedural purposes,[185] to be streamed

[179] Woolf 1986 (n 137) 227. This approach to public law remedies helps to explain a prominent tort lawyer's observation that '[p]ublic lawyers … sometimes seem to concentrate on the wrong of the governmental unit, and ignore, except as a question of standing … the harm suffered by the claimant' (T Weir, 'Governmental Torts' [1989] *PL* 40, 56).

[180] *Anufrijeva* (n 3) [56].

[181] ibid eg [56], [75].

[182] See further ch 6.

[183] *Argyll* (n 160) 774 (emphasis added).

[184] ibid.

[185] (n 3) [79]–[81].

via judicial review procedure where possible, with all of its concomitant safeguards for public authorities. Lord Woolf stressed that the Administrative Court was the appropriate court to hear such claims as it 'is well placed to take action expeditiously', again reflecting a concern that administrative interests in speed and efficiency should be prioritised.[186] Further, reflecting that damages are a last resort, where possible, human rights claims for loss incurred through maladministration should be streamed via alternative routes such as the Parliamentary Ombudsman.[187] This contrasts with claims for damages based in private law rights which are quintessentially the province of courts. At the forefront of the Court's thinking was the amount of money spent on the litigation in *Anufrijeva*, and what made the situation 'even more worrying' was that 'all the parties [were] funded out of *public* funds';[188] these concerns were reiterated by the Law Lords in *Greenfield*.[189]

Lastly, it is important to highlight observations sometimes made in HRA damages cases to the effect that damages should be awarded if there is 'a need to encourage compliance by individual officials or classes of official'[190] or 'so that lessons can be learned'[191].[192] Courts in other jurisdictions, influenced by HRA damages jurisprudence, have made similar statements. For example in the New Zealand human rights damages case of *Taunoa* Blanchard J effectively cut and paste the general approach from *Anufrijeva*, and said

> [i]n public law, making amends to a victim is generally a secondary or subsidiary function. It is usually less important than bringing the infringing conduct to an end *and ensuring future compliance with the law by governmental agencies and officials, which is the primary function of public law.* Thus the award of public law damages is normally more to mark *society's* disapproval of official conduct than it is to compensate for hurt to personal feelings.[193]

Consonant with the courts' role within a public interest conception of public law the court here 'acts on behalf of society'.[194] This suggests a distinctive conception of damages as a tool for ensuring public power is used as it ought to be into the future, in the interests of society as a whole rather

[186] ibid [53].
[187] ibid [79]–[81].
[188] ibid (emphasis added).
[189] *Greenfield* (n 10) [30].
[190] ibid [19].
[191] *A v Essex CC* [2011] 1 AC 280, [118].
[192] See also *DSD v Commissioner for Police* [2015] 1 WLR 1833, [40], [125]–[127], [138] [*DSD* HC].
[193] *Taunoa v Attorney-General* [2008] 1 NZLR 429, [259] (emphasis added); *Combined Beneficiaries Union Inc v Auckland City COGS Committee* [2009] 2 NZLR 56, [62] ('The primary purpose [of NZBORA damages] is to mark the breach and to deter repetition of the breach ... rather than redress').
[194] ibid [255].

than for any one individual, consonant with the traditional remedial concerns within common law review. This approach also reflects the educative conception of remedies, based in an idea of partnership between courts and administration in the service of good administration. The idea of partnership is patent in the judicial starting-point that damages will not typically be required as the executive can generally be trusted to act properly: '[d]amages need not ordinarily be awarded to encourage high standards of compliance'.[195]

On this view, damages are calculated according to individual losses, but they are only likely to be awarded where they would serve the public goal of ensuring public power is properly exercised into the future. There are fundamental problems with this conception of damages, principally that it is at war with itself: if the goal is to incentivise compliance, why calculate damages according to compensatory principles rather than choosing the amount that would produce optimal incentive effects? And why should damages awarded for the purpose of securing compliance rather than individual justice be paid to the claimant rather than anyone else? Notwithstanding these concerns, for present purposes the key point is that under such approach individual justice is nearly completely subordinated to a concern to ensure public power is exercised properly for the benefit of all.

In Canada we find a more balanced approach, which does not suggest damages will necessarily be rare or marginal, and which does not completely sideline guidance that could be derived from private law.[196] However, the Canadian Supreme Court, heavily influenced by comparative jurisprudence including *Anufrijeva* and *Taunoa*, has similarly conceptualised Charter damages as a 'unique public law remedy'.[197] From this premise it follows almost naturally that damages become a site of public interest calculations. In the important case of *Ward* the Supreme Court held damages may only be awarded if at least one of three objects is served: individual compensation, vindication *in the sense of* addressing harm to '*society as a whole*', and deterrence, in the sense of 'influencing government behaviour in order to secure state compliance with the Charter in the future', which would promote 'good governance'.[198] Compensation is a recognised goal but the Court observes that in most cases where awards are made all three objects will be present, except 'the fact that the claimant has not suffered personal loss does not preclude damages where the objectives of vindication or deterrence clearly call for an award'.[199] Thus, generally it must be the case that damages would serve a public purpose if they are to be awarded, while individual justice is not a prerequisite. Further, damages may, as in *Anufrijeva*,

[195] *Greenfield* (n 10) [19].
[196] *City of Vancouver v Ward* [2010] 2 SCR 28.
[197] ibid [31].
[198] ibid [28]–[29], [38] (emphasis added).
[199] ibid [30].

be denied in the public interest where an award would undermine 'good' or 'effective governance'.[200] Consonant with this relative emphasis on the public good, subsequent cases in which the Supreme Court has applied this framework have been shot through with public interest calculations, with individual interests lost sight of.[201]

Thus, the Court's remedial approach in *Anufrijeva*, in marginalising damages, prioritising traditional forms of relief geared towards regulation of public duties, emphasising protection of the public, requiring damages claims where possible to be streamed via procedure protective of public authorities, and maintaining that the approach to human rights damages is not to be compared with that in private law, as well as adoption of a distinctive conception of damages as a tool for facilitating compliance, engenders a strong remedial divide between public and private law. Such remedial dichotomy is a central tenet of Lord Woolf's more general theoretical distinction. Private law is concerned with individual rights and interests and the main remedy is naturally damages for individual losses, awarded to afford individual justice. Whereas public law's concern is with the common good and relief is geared towards regulating public power so that it is exercised properly and for the good of the public at large.

C. Understanding the Public Interest Theory as a Product of Its Time

The public interest theory is problematic. To understand the theory's main weakness—that it cannot explain the nature of the entire body of public law doctrine—one must recognise that it is a product of its time. In the early 1980s, when the theory was formulated and put into practice by dominant figures of the era such as Lord Diplock,[202] there was a 'shared view that a developmental theory of public law as largely autonomous of private law could be constructed around the vigorous growth of judicial review'.[203] Creation of a unified review procedure in the late 1970s, separate from ordinary procedure, and conceptualised by the judiciary as a 'public law procedure',[204] provided the golden opportunity for experimentation with the idea of a distinctive body of public law rules within a dedicated public law forum, in isolation from 'private law' claims;[205] it was in this post-reform

200 ibid [38]ff.
201 *Henry v British Columbia* [2015] SCC 24.
202 See Varuhas 2016 (n 1).
203 Freedland (n 97) 111.
204 eg *Cocks* (n 2) 293; *O'Reilly* (n 2). See references in n 2 above.
205 There were other contextual features which arguably gave the public interest view traction, such as anxieties over inculcation of public administration with market-based values during Margaret Thatcher's premiership. See further McAuslan (n 114); Taggart 2003 (n 33) 102–06.

era that a 'newly fledged' 'new-found' 'distinction between public and private law' emerged.[206] As is so common in English legal history, substantive law was secreted in the interstices of procedure. Because of these developments judicial review was at the very heart of analyses of public law, leading many to equate public law with the law streamed via review procedure. In the 1980s that procedure was dominated by applications brought on common law grounds of review. It is therefore unsurprising that all of Lord Woolf's analysis of the nature of public law, in his influential 1986 article on the public–private divide,[207] concerns review of statutory powers according to orthodox common law grounds. And herein lies the fundamental problem with the public interest theory.[208] It is a theory formulated by reference to a field that constitutes but one branch of contemporary public law. While the theory may provide a plausible, perhaps compelling explanation of common law review, it does not satisfactorily explain contemporary public law *as a whole*. For example, it is a theory formulated well before the advent of the HRA, and ignores review on EU grounds. It does not address other significant fields of public law, mentioned above.[209] It is not therefore a complete theory of public law, but a theory of one branch of public law: common law review.

II. INDIVIDUAL RIGHTS AND THE PUBLIC INTEREST THEORY OF PUBLIC LAW

Leaving aside criticisms of the public interest theory, it is submitted that if we accept and apply Lord Woolf's dichotomy between public law as concerned with regulation of public duties for the good of the collectivity, and private law as concerned with protection of private rights for the benefit of specific individuals, human rights law, on closer examination, more closely resembles Lord Woolf's conception of private law. So it turns out that even according to Lord Woolf's own theoretical dichotomy the remedial approach adopted in *Anufrijeva*, synonymous with a field concerned with regulation of public duties in the public interest, is flawed: it creates a mismatch between the nature of the primary obligations in human rights law, which resemble private rights, and the approach to remedies for breach. The result is serious distortion of the internal coherence of human rights law and stymieing of its primary function: to reinforce the importance of and afford strong protection to fundamental, individual rights and interests. Adherence

[206] *Gillick v West Norfolk and Wisbech AHA* [1986] AC 112, 178; *Datafin* (n 145) 845.
[207] (n 137).
[208] See further Varuhas 2016 (n 1).
[209] See s 1.III above.

to and application of Lord Woolf's dichotomy thus ironically leads us to the opposite conclusion to that reached in *Anufrijeva*: an approach to damages synonymous with private law fields should be adopted in human rights law.

The section proceeds by considering three fundamental features of human rights law which indicate that it sits comfortably within Lord Woolf's *private law* paradigm (and uncomfortably within his theory of *public law*): (i) nature of the legal norms and their rationale; (ii) role of the court; and (iii) procedural treatment of claims.

A. Individual Rights versus Public Duties, Individual Interests versus Public Interests

Fundamental to Lord Woolf's dichotomy is his claim that in public law *individuals* do not possess *rights*, only the ability to enforce *duties* owed to the *public*.

This is certainly an influential view of *common law review*, courts in this sphere drawing a sharp distinction between duties owed to the public at large, properly enforced via review, and those owed to specific individuals, correlative to individual rights.[210] For example statutory duties on authorities to prevent road traffic accidents are

> not owed to any individual. [Section 39 of the Road Traffic Act 1988] imposes a duty owed to the *public as a whole*. It forms part of the corpus of public law, not private law, and can only be enforced by the procedures and remedies available for enforcing public law duties.[211]

Similarly the duty of the police to maintain the Queen's peace 'is owed to members of the public at large'.[212] Courts consistently maintain that public powers regulated by common law review are conferred 'for the public good',[213] 'for the public benefit',[214] 'for public purposes',[215] 'protection of the public',[216] or to be carried out 'in the public interest',[217] 'in the interests of the public generally'[218] or 'in the interests of the community',[219] rather

[210] eg *Bourgoin SA v Ministry of Agriculture, Fisheries and Food* [1986] QB 716, 761B-C, 763G; *O'Reilly* (n 2) 255–56; *Anns v Merton LBC* [1978] AC 728, 754; *IRC v City of London* [1953] 1 WLR 652, 661–62; *Lord Leconfield v Thornely* [1926] AC 10, 17–18; *M* (n 162) 416A; *Swain v Law Society* [1983] 1 AC 598, 608; *Michael v Chief Constable South Wales* [2015] 2 WLR 343, [33], [35], [37], [120], [191].

[211] *Gorringe v Calderdale MBC* [2004] 1 WLR 1057, [70] (emphasis added).

[212] *Michael* (n 210) [120].

[213] *Stovin v Wise* [1996] AC 923, 935D, 951H.

[214] *Cutler v Wandsworth Stadium Ltd* [1949] AC 398, 408.

[215] *X v Bedfordshire CC* [1995] 2 AC 633, 737; *Swain* (n 210) 618.

[216] *Swain* (n 210) 607; *Michael* (n 210) [115].

[217] *R (Niazi) v SOSHD* [2008] EWCA Civ 755, [41]; *Cutler* (n 214) 409.

[218] *Financial Services Authority v Sinaloa Gold Plc* [2013] 2 AC 28, [31], [33].

[219] *Brooks v Commissioner for the Metropolis* [2005] 1 WLR 1495, [30].

than for the interests of any one individual. It has been made clear at the highest level that 'in a legal system based on the rule of law executive or administrative power "may be exercised only for the public good" and not for ulterior and improper purposes', and public officers 'must always act for the public good';[220] this follows from the premise that '[e]very public body exists for the service of the public'.[221]

In this light common law duties of legality, reasonableness and procedural fairness all exist to ensure public bodies stay 'on track', exercising their powers properly and in genuine pursuit of the public purposes for which they have been conferred. A decision that is wholly irrational, one taken for a purpose other than that for which the power was conferred, a decision based in extraneous concerns or affected by personal bias, or one taken in breach of statutory conditions for exercise of power cannot be said to have been genuinely exercised for the public purposes for which it was conferred.

While courts emphasise that the concern within review proceedings is ensuring enforcement of public duties in the public interest, they have equally emphasised that individual rights and interests do not form the basis of such proceedings.[222] In *O'Reilly*, Lord Diplock contrasted a challenge to an administrative decision 'on the ground that in one way or another the [authority] in reaching its decision had acted outwith the powers conferred upon it by the legislation under which it was acting', and which could be initiated by anyone with a 'sufficient interest', with one in 'private law' in which the basis of the claim is the 'right of the appellant'.[223] Similarly in the *Fleet Street Casuals* case Lords Diplock and Scarman emphasised that in 'private law' a claimant would need to show a 'legal right of his own was threatened or infringed'.[224] This approach was not appropriate within common law review, otherwise the remedy 'would lose its public law character, being no more than a remedy for a private wrong'.[225]

Wrongs within common law review are not individual wrongs, that is breaches of individual rights, but rather public wrongs, that is breaches of

[220] *Three Rivers DC v Bank of England (No 3)* [2003] 2 AC 1, 190, 196.

[221] *Kennedy v Charity Commission* [2015] AC 455, [107].

[222] This is not to say courts do not at times consider rights and interests of individuals affected by administrative action in determining questions of legality and the requirements of the public interest, only that those do not form the *basis* of the review application, as they would in a tort or contract claim. Further, while the language of 'rights' is sometimes used in common law review this does not necessarily denote the presence of genuine, Hohfeldian claim-rights: see JNE Varuhas, 'The Reformation of English Administrative Law? "Rights", Rhetoric and Reality' (2013) 72 *CLJ* 369 [Varuhas 2013].

[223] (n 2) 275.

[224] *IRC* (n 151) 639, 649.

[225] ibid 653. See similarly *Walton v Scottish Ministers* [2012] UKSC 44, [90]–[94]; *R v Somerset CC, ex p Dixon* [1998] Env LR 111, 121; *AXA General Insurance Ltd v HM Advocate* [2012] 1 AC 868, [169]–[170].

duties owed to the public as a whole.[226] For example, Sedley J, in a pre-HRA dictum, said, '[p]ublic law is not at base about rights, even though abuses of power may and often do invade private rights; it is about wrongs—that is to say misuses of public power'.[227] Oliver LJ, in the context of legality review, opined:

> a mere 'right' to have the provisions of the law observed, shared as it is by every member of the public whether or not he is likely to suffer by breach, is, it seems to me, the antithesis of an 'individual' right requiring protection.[228]

In the *Fleet Street Casuals* case Lord Scarman explained that the Inland Revenue Commissioners' statutory duties and powers were imposed and conferred not for the personal interests of specific taxpayers, but 'in the interest of good management', and the Commissioners' common law duty of fairness, owed in carrying out its statutory tasks, was 'a legal duty owed by the revenue to the general body of taxpayers' *as a collectivity*.[229] Breach of that duty is a 'public wrong'.[230] Indeed, pandering to personal interests would entail breach of a duty of a public character: there must be 'no favourites'.[231]

Thus, there are strong indications that within common law review

> the primary concern of the courts, analytically speaking, is to remedy breaches of a duty owed by public authorities either to society at large or to sections of society, and that protection of a particular litigant's interest is always contingent on this.[232]

Importantly this understanding of the primary obligations explains the rule against damages for breaches of duties within common law review.[233] Whereas in 'private law' the litigant may claim damages for loss suffered through breach of a 'duty owed specifically to him'—and imposed 'for the benefit of private individuals to whom loss and damage is caused by breach of that duty'[234]—in 'public law' only the 'remedy of judicial review is available to one who can establish a sufficient interest' and the concern is 'to have the law properly and fairly enforced and administered by a public authority

[226] See further Varuhas 2013 (n 222) 408–11; JNE Varuhas, 'Against Unification' in H Wilberg and M Elliott (eds), *The Scope and Intensity of Substantive Review* (Hart Publishing, 2015) 101–08.

[227] *Dixon* (n 225) 121.

[228] *Bourgoin* (n 210) 767, 761.

[229] *IRC* (n 151) 651–53.

[230] ibid 651, 648.

[231] ibid 651.

[232] N Bamforth, 'Hohfeldian Rights and Public Law' in MH Kramer (ed), *Rights, Wrongs and Responsibilities* (Palgrave, 2001) 15. See also McLean (n 19) 232–38.

[233] *cf* P Cane, 'Damages in Public Law' (1999) 9 *Otago Law Review* 489, 508–09 [Cane 1999].

[234] *Garden Cottage Foods Ltd v Milk Marketing Board* [1984] AC 130, 141.

in the performance of its *duties to the public at large*'.[235] The link between individual rights and availability of damages is so strong that courts have observed in judicial review, working backwards from remedy to substantive obligation: '[i]f the law gives [the litigant] no remedy for ... damage [suffered in consequence of breach of a duty] then he would not ordinarily be said to have any "individual right"'.[236]

The justifiability of broad remedial discretion within common law review is similarly dependant on the nature of the primary obligations; it is justifiable precisely because the obligations are not individual rights. First, the discretion to refuse relief, at first blush, might be criticised for abrogating the basic idea of *ubi ius, ibi remedium*. However, there is no such breach if the basic norms are not 'rights', as traditionally understood in English law as individual rights. Second, whereas in fields such as contract or tort it is for litigants to elect their remedy, the only question for the court being whether to grant the selected remedy, within common law review the court has 'complete discretion to select and grant the appropriate remedy'.[237] The difference follows from the distinct nature of the primary obligations in each field. In tort or contract party autonomy is accepted given litigation concerns the litigant's personal right. In contrast, within common law review the applicant is acting for the public good in seeking to ensure public power is exercised properly; and it may be that the public good requires grant of a different remedy to that sought or no remedy.

In contrast to the public nature of obligations in common law review, fundamental features of human rights law suggest the presence of *individual rights* and a central concern for protection of *individual interests*, consonant with Woolf's conception of *private law*. It may seem strange that one should need to substantiate this claim, given the relevant norms are referred to as 'rights', and the very gist of human rights law is generally understood to be individual protection. However, as we have seen, the analysis in *Anufrijeva*, which absorbs human rights law into pre-HRA habits of public law thought, poses a distinct challenge. Further, it is not only public interest theorists who consider 'rights' to be foreign to public law; others similarly distinguish private law from public law on the basis that the former is concerned with *individuals* and their *rights*, while the latter is concerned with *collective* goals.[238] Also, although there has been surprisingly little analysis of the nature of the rights under the HRA, some commentators clearly

[235] *Bourgoin* (n 210) 761 (emphasis added).

[236] ibid 761, 767.

[237] *IRC* (n 151) 647.

[238] NE Simmonds, 'Rights at the Cutting Edge' in MH Kramer et al, *A Debate Over Rights* (OUP, 1998) 141–42. At the opposite extreme are those who claim protection of rights is public law's principal function: eg Craig (n 119) ch 1; TRS Allan, *The Sovereignty of Law* (OUP, 2013).

consider these 'rights' to be generalised standards or principles of legality[239] or more amorphously, values,[240] as opposed to genuine individual rights (often analogising with common law grounds of review). Others sideline the rights themselves and consider that the main effect of the Act was to introduce proportionality as a ground of review.[241]

There is much loose talk about 'rights' in public law scholarship.[242] The following analysis is disciplined by Hohfeld's analytical scheme, the acknowledged strengths of which are conceptual clarity and precision.[243] The nature of such rights was explained in chapter 2[244] and I will not repeat that explanation, other than to recall such rights are characterised by correlativity between right and duty. Hohfeld's account is of acute significance because it is generally accepted that if his concept of 'claim-rights' captures the structure of legal norms in any field it is private law fields.

Where Convention rights form the basis for an action against a public authority under section 7, HRA—the context in which damages are available—individual claim-rights can be shown to be in play. It may not appear so at first as Convention rights, as they are drafted, are expressed as rights *to* something, such as a right *to* liberty or a right *to* freedom of expression, rather than Hohfeldian rights *that* another refrain from or perform some action. However, this does not exclude the presence of Hohfeldian rights because Convention rights, as formulated, are explicable as 'umbrella' or 'summary'[245] terms:[246] each Convention right is a marker of a set or bundle of norms united by their subject-matter (for example freedom of expression or privacy), including a multitude of norms which can be explained convincingly as claim-rights, being held by specific individuals against specific public authorities.[247]

I will first provide an example of how Convention rights may be analysed in Hohfeldian terms, then examine significant features of the Act and related jurisprudence which support such conceptualisation.

[239] eg D Feldman, 'Convention Rights and Substantive Ultra Vires' in C Forsyth (ed), *Judicial Review and the Constitution* (Hart Publishing, 2000); M Elliott, 'Beyond the European Convention: Human Rights and the Common Law' (2015) 68 *Current Legal Problems* 85.

[240] The Canadian Supreme Court in particular increasingly reconceptualises rights under the Canadian Charter as 'values'. For critical analysis of the Court's turn to this amorphous notion see: (2014) 67 *Supreme Court Law Review* Pt V; A Macklin, 'Charter Right or Charter-Lite? Administrative Discretion and the Charter' (2014) 67 *Supreme Court Law Review* 561.

[241] See the discussion in Varuhas 2013 (n 222) 387–90. As discussed in ch 3.I.B.iv proportionality is not a free-standing ground of review but a defence to a rights-breach, and only applies to some rights.

[242] For analysis and critique of such rights-talk see: Varuhas 2013 (n 222).

[243] WN Hohfeld, 'Some Fundamental Legal Conceptions as Applied in Judicial Reasoning' (1913) 23 *Yale Law Journal* 16; (1917) 26 *Yale Law Journal* 710.

[244] See ch 2.I.A.

[245] Simmonds (n 238) 158.

[246] See similarly R Alexy, *A Theory of Constitutional Rights* (OUP, 2010).

[247] I leave open the possibility, which cannot be explored here, that Convention rights also entail legal phenomena other than claim-rights, such as Hohfeldian immunities or liberties.

It is well-established that Article 2 imposes a number of 'distinct duties'[248] which relate to the interest in life: some are negative, requiring authorities not to interfere with an individual's interests, while others are positive, requiring authorities to take positive steps to safeguard an individual's interests. On a Hohfeldian analysis such duties do not exist 'in the air'; they are owed by specific authorities to specific individuals, such that there are literally millions of discrete duties owed by specific public authorities to specific individuals. Thus the Home Office, being a public authority, owes me a negative duty to refrain from taking my life and I have a right, which is unique to me, against the Home Office which correlates with that duty, and mirrors the content of that duty. Equally the Home Office owes you a duty of identical content, which is unique to you, and you have a negative right which correlates with that duty, which is again unique to you. The same analysis is applicable to 'positive duties'. For example by virtue of the decision in *Osman*,[249] X has a claim-right that the relevant authority take reasonable steps to protect X's life when the authority knows or ought to know of a real and immediate threat to X's life, while the authority owes a correlative duty to X of identical content. This is a right possessed by a specific individual—the person whose life is at risk—against a specific authority—that which knew or ought to have known of the risk. Thus in Hohfeldian terms the Article 2 'right to life' denotes a multiplicity of rights held by specific individuals against specific authorities in relation to their interest in life; just as a jellyfish trails its tentacles in the warm sea, so from each Convention right dangle a plurality of discrete rights (and corresponding duties).[250]

The HRA's procedural provisions are crucial to understanding the field's rights-based nature. On the Hohfeldian account a fundamental feature of these rights is they are personal to particular individuals, and correlative to duties owed by specific public authorities. Under section 7 only a 'victim' of a violation may bring a claim. If rights are personal to particular individuals it makes sense that only those who suffer a rights-violation are able to launch proceedings.[251] As Miles observes, '[a] narrow victim test supports the individualist view that rights are the property of their holders, and that only those persons should be entitled to move the court in relation to an alleged violation'.[252] Standing rules are identical in tort and contract.[253]

248 *Rabone* (n 174) [12].

249 *Osman v UK* (2000) 29 EHRR 245.

250 Paraphrasing Birks on an unrelated topic: 'Rights, Wrongs, and Remedies' (2000) 20 *Oxford Journal of Legal Studies* 1, 7.

251 The EHRC has power to initiate proceedings under the HRA, but importantly 'may act only if there is or would be one or more victims of the unlawful act', and cannot be awarded HRA damages: Equality Act 2006, s 30(3).

252 J Miles, 'Standing in a Multi-Layered Constitution' in N Bamforth and P Leyland (eds), *Public Law in a Multi-Layered Constitution* (Hart Publishing, 2003) 404.

253 eg *Morris v Beardmore* [1981] AC 446, 454E; *IRC* (n 151) 639; *Alfred McAlpine Construction Ltd v Panatown Ltd* [2001] 1 AC 518.

In contrast standing rules within common law review are exceptionally liberal, so those whose rights or interests are not directly affected by the challenged administrative action may nonetheless have standing; duties are owed to the public as a whole, therefore all members of the political community have a legitimate interest in their performance. Also strongly indicating that HRA rights are personal is that human rights claims are non-transferable; they may not be assigned,[254] mirroring the position in torts such as defamation and false imprisonment.[255]

Under section 7 proceedings are brought against 'the authority' which 'has acted (or proposes to act) in a way which is made unlawful by section 6(1)';[256] a HRA claim 'cannot be directed at "the state" at large, but rather at the organ or organs of the state, the public authorities, that are responsible for the breach'.[257] Again, it makes sense that if duties are owed by specific authorities to specific individuals, actions may only be initiated against that authority alleged to have breached its duty, correlative to the claimant's right. The position matches that in tort and contract: for X to have a claim against Y it must be the case that Y owed a legal duty to X specifically.[258]

On top of procedural features, in section 7 claims the House of Lords and Supreme Court consistently refer to rights in a manner which suggests they are personal to the claimant; these rights do not exist in the air but are 'rights of the applicants',[259] 'Convention rights of these particular young people',[260] 'his' or 'her' rights,[261] 'the company's article 10 rights',[262] 'individual's rights',[263] 'rights of designated persons',[264] 'personal rights of the individual'.[265] This explains Lord Wilson's dictum in *Quila* that 'decisions

[254] *Nassau Verzekering Maatschappij NV v Netherlands* (4 October 2011) App no 57602/09 (ECtHR Third Section).

[255] *Glegg v Bromley* [1912] 3 KB 474, 488; *24 Seven Utility Services Ltd v Rosekey Ltd* [2003] EWHC 3415, [25].

[256] Section 6 makes it unlawful for an authority to act incompatibly with enumerated rights and thereby gives rights legal force. We can make sense of 'incompatibility' as breach of a duty correlative to the claimant's right, which cannot be justified.

[257] *R (K) v Camden and Islington HA* [2002] QB 198, [73], applied in the HRA damages context in *R (A) v SOSHD* [2003] 1 WLR 330, [73]–[75]. Thus, where two authorities are legally responsible for particular losses, those losses are apportioned between them: *R (Guntrip) v SOSJ* [2010] EWHC 3188, [57].

[258] For an illustration of this see: *Iqbal v POA* [2010] QB 732, [22], [68].

[259] *R (Quila) v SOSHD* [2012] 1 AC 621, [44]; *Belfast CC v Miss Behavin' Ltd* [2007] 1 WLR 1420, [12]–[13], [15]–[16], [20].

[260] *Quila* ibid [61].

[261] *R (Begum) v Governors of Denbigh High School* [2007] 1 AC 100, [48], [59]; *Rabone* (n 174) [107]; *Tweed v Parades Commission* [2007] 1 AC 650, [5].

[262] *Miss Behavin'* (n 259) [90].

[263] *R (Wilkinson) v Broadmoor SHA* [2002] 1 WLR 419, [61]–[62].

[264] *Bank Mellat v Her Majesty's Treasury (No 2)* [2013] 3 WLR 179, [21] (substantive appeal).

[265] *Re Officer L* [2007] 1 WLR 2135, [21].

founded on human rights are essentially individual', in that a determination in a particular case that a claimant's rights have been breached is a determination of breach only in respect of that claimant's rights.[266]

It is worth recalling briefly that, as we saw in chapter 3, significant features of human rights law are nearly identical to significant features of TAPS, demonstrating a common function between the fields, and a common focus on the individual. These strong similarities reinforce that legal norms within human rights law are individual rights. This is because: (1) doctrinal features, along with the language used by official actors, are the only 'pointers' or 'clues' we have as to the existence of rights; and (2) it is generally accepted that if there is any field in which the basic norms are individual rights it is in private law fields such as tort, and particularly TAPS.

The foregoing has shown the *juridical structure* of legal relations within human rights law is consonant with the structure of Hohfeldian claim-rights. Brief consideration of the two major philosophical schools of thought on the *nature* or *role* of rights further supports the claim that the HRA creates genuine individual rights.

According to will-theories a right is 'a form of choice'.[267] An individual's claim only has the status of a right if the individual has exclusive control over certain important choices or decisions in respect of the putative right, such as the power to enforce the right (if actual) or waive enforcement;[268] in this way 'right-holders are small-scale sovereigns'[269] with each right 'a vehicle for some aspect of an individual's self-determination or initiative'.[270] As we have seen, under the HRA, in general, exclusive power of 'decisive control' over 'effectuation'[271] of rights lies with the individual victim.

According to interest-theories it is a necessary (though not necessarily sufficient) condition of X's holding of a right that 'the right, when actual, preserves one or more of X's interests'.[272] Raz, a leading interest-theorist, argues that one must discern whether a legal right exists by 'reference to the intentions of the law': 'a law creates a right if it is based on and expresses the view that someone has an interest which is sufficient ground for holding

[266] *Quila* (n 259) [59], [80].

[267] P Jones, *Rights* (Palgrave, 1994) 32.

[268] H Steiner, 'Working Rights' in Kramer et al (n 238) 239–47. For the *locus classicus* see: HLA Hart, 'Bentham on Legal Rights' in AWB Simpson (ed), *Oxford Essays in Jurisprudence, Second Series* (Clarendon, 1973).

[269] Steiner ibid 262.

[270] MH Kramer, 'Rights Without Trimmings' in Kramer et al (n 238) 62.

[271] ibid 63.

[272] ibid 62. Will-theorists do not consider a necessary precondition for X's holding of a right that the right preserves X's interests, however their theories do not necessarily preclude the possibility that rights may protect X's interests.

another subject to a duty'.[273] Similarly MacCormick, in an influential essay, says, 'the essential feature of rules which confer rights is that they have as their specific aim the protection or advancement of individual interests or goods'.[274] In human rights law legal norms do not only protect individuals' most basic interests but, as we have seen from parliamentary debates on the Human Rights Bill, fundamental features of the Act, the internal structure of human rights law, and judicial dicta as to the purpose of the obligations,[275] the preservation of those interests, in life, liberty etc, is the law's central, motivating concern, and forms the rationale for imposing legal obligations on authorities. Further, the Act and jurisprudence under it strongly express the view that these interests are among the most fundamental of human interests; if these interests were insufficient ground for imposing legal duties, it is difficult to think of interests that could be sufficient.

Before going on it is important to observe that the foregoing analysis demonstrates the fundamental flaw at the heart of Laws LJ's observations in *Sturnham*. He considers human rights claims are typically closer in nature to 'our public [law]', with the implication that damages should not generally be awarded for breach given compensation is unavailable for 'public law wrongs'.[276] This analysis ignores the possibility that there are fundamentally different types of wrong within public law, which may call for and justify different remedial responses. The general rule against monetary relief invoked by Laws LJ is a rule applicable to certain wrongs: those that prevail within common law review, and are traditionally conceptualised as breaches of duties owed to the public. As we have seen, the rule against compensation for individual harm makes sense in that context given duties are not owed to individuals, nor do they exist for their benefit. In contrast wrongs within human rights law are fundamentally different: the wrong is breach of an individual right, founded on the idea that basic individual interests should be afforded strong protection and vindicated. Thus, as far as the nature of the wrong goes, it is difficult to view human rights law as a close neighbour of traditional bodies of English public law, based in public duties; rather human rights law is a paradigm of individual rights, and damages fit comfortably within such a paradigm.

In similar vein to Laws LJ, Lord Woolf, in *Anufrijeva*, was reluctant to open up the human rights damages remedy given damages have not traditionally been available for 'maladministration' in public law. In this respect

[273] J Raz, *The Morality of Freedom* (OUP, 2003) 166; 'Legal Rights' (1984) 4 *Oxford Journal of Legal Studies* 1, 13–14. Note Raz's view of rights is non-Hohfeldian. He conceptualises a right as a ground for imposing duties on others, such that a single right may ground multiple different duties, rather than conceptualising each duty as correlative to a discrete right.

[274] N MacCormick, 'Rights in Legislation' in PMS Hacker and J Raz (eds), *Law, Morality and Society* (Clarendon, 1977) 192.

[275] See ch 3, especially s I.B.

[276] (n 14) [15]. See also ch 3.II.B.iv.

he distinguishes 'a claim under the HRA for compensation in respect of the consequences of maladministration and a claim by a member of the public against a public officer for damages for breach of a duty owed in tort'.[277] This analysis is confusing and confused. Maladministration might be the *cause* of a rights-violation *as a matter of fact*, in human rights law, or indeed tort or contract, but the *legal event* which opens up remedies in human rights law is the same as in the tort claim: breach of an individual right (or put another way, a duty owed to an individual), whether caused by 'maladministration', good administration or neither.

As Cane observes:

> Saying no more than damages is a remedy for common law wrongs [eg in tort or contract], not for ... public law wrongs, would provide no ... reason [to justify denial of damages where loss is suffered in public law] unless there were some difference between common law wrongs on the one hand and ... public law wrongs on the other on which the statement could be soundly based.[278]

While there is a good argument that there is an important difference in the nature of wrongs as between common law review and common law fields of liability such as tort, there is no such difference as between human rights law and fields such as tort: the wrong in both fields is breach of an individual, personal right. In this way human rights law resembles Lord Woolf's account of *private law*, suggesting an approach to damages analogous to that adopted in private law fields would not be out of place.

B. Rights versus Public Duties: The Role of the Court

Thus the nature of the norms in human rights law indicates that this field falls within Lord Woolf's category of private law. Further supporting this proposition is Woolf's distinction between the role of courts in private law and public law cases. Woolf argues that in the latter context a defining feature of the court's role is that it cannot judge the substantive quality of executive decisions, being limited to assessing the *Wednesbury* reasonableness of the decision, as well as the legality and procedural regularity of the decision. For example, even where courts apply the strictest, anxious scrutiny variant of *Wednesbury*, they maintain that they exercise a secondary, supervisory judgement, with the primary judgement as to the balance between competing interests for the primary decision-maker, while the final question for the court remains whether the decision was so untenable as to be absurd.[279] According to the public interest account this restrained, supervisory

[277] *Anufrijeva* (n 3) [49].
[278] Cane 1999 (n 233) 492.
[279] *R v SOSHD, ex p Brind* [1991] 1 AC 696, 748–49.

approach is premised on the view that balancing of interests, and determination of what lies in the public interest more generally, is first and foremost for the delegate assigned by Parliament to perform the public duty.[280] The courts thus limit themselves to intervening only at the outer limits of acceptability, where there has plainly been deviation from pursuit of the common good, for example where a decision has been made for improper purposes or with bias, where the empowering statute was breached, where the decision-maker was guided by extraneous concerns, failed to consider relevant concerns, or acted with utter irrationality. As Aronson observes, '[j]udicial deference to the views and actions of the primary decision maker is in one sense the *essence* of judicial review's technique'.[281]

Woolf contrasts this restrained, supervisory approach with the court's role in adjudicating private law claims, where the court exercises primary and determinative judgement over substantive questions such as whether a defendant took reasonable care, whether interference with quiet enjoyment of land was unreasonable, or whether force applied by the defendant in purported self-defence was proportionate. Although Woolf does not explore the matter, the primacy of the courts' role in determining such issues flows from such cases entailing adjudication of legal rights and liabilities: resolution of such claims is the quintessential judicial function.[282]

The judicial role in private law adjudication resembles that in human rights adjudication. Two illustrative examples shall suffice.

In an Article 2 claim that an authority has breached its positive operational duty to protect the claimant against a mortal threat, the court applies the criteria for establishing a violation in the same manner it would apply elements of a tort to given facts. The court forms its own view, given the evidence, on whether the risk to life was 'real and immediate', and whether the authority 'knew or ought to have known' of the relevant risk; these questions are 'objectively considered' and determined by the court.[283] If those criteria are satisfied the court examines whether the authority took all steps reasonably necessary to prevent the risk from materialising. It is the court's view of the steps that ought to have been taken that is determinative. In *Rabone* Lord Dyson rejected as 'misplaced' the submission that the court afford the defendant a 'margin of discretion' in determining what steps should have been taken: 'The standard demanded for the performance of the operational duty is one of reasonableness', and whether the authority

[280] eg *Gouriet v Union of Post Office Workers* [1978] AC 435, 482 (whereas judges 'are equipped to find legal rights', 'decisions to be made as to the public interest are not such as courts are fitted or equipped to make').

[281] Aronson (n 34) 48 (emphasis added).

[282] *Kable v DPP (NSW)* (1996) 189 CLR 51, 123; T Bingham, *The Rule of Law* (Allen Lane, 2010) ch 4.

[283] *Van Colle v UK* (2013) 56 EHRR 23, [95]; *Officer L* (n 265) [20].

met that standard is for the court to determine given various considerations, including 'the circumstances of the case, the ease or difficulty of taking precautions and the resources available'.[284] Given this approach it is unsurprising that Lady Hale observed, '[a] claim such as this ... is more in the nature of a claim in tort than for judicial review'.[285]

The courts' approach to adjudicating defences, such as the justificatory defence of proportionality, also matches Woolf's conception of the judicial role in private law; the contrast with the courts' traditional supervisory role on review is stark.[286] As Leigh and Lustgarten say, the court's focus in human rights litigation is upon '*outcome*, not on the decision-making process'.[287] The courts hold that in adjudicating proportionality they must 'make a value judgment, an evaluation' *for themselves*;[288] 'Proportionality must be judged objectively, by the court'.[289] Lord Hoffmann, in *Miss Behavin'*, captured the contrast between the anxious scrutiny approach to human rights cases in common law review and the approach under the HRA: 'the question is ... whether there has actually been a violation of the applicant's Convention rights and not whether the decision-maker properly considered the question of whether his rights would be violated or not'.[290] Similarly, Lord Carnwath in two recent cases captured the difference between the courts' supervisory role on review, and their role in human rights adjudication. His Lordship said that even in anxious scrutiny cases at common law, 'the role of the courts is often more about process than merits';[291] the concern is the proceduralist one that 'decisions ... show by their reasoning that every factor which might tell in favour of an applicant has been properly taken into account'.[292] In contrast, in HRA cases '[t]he court's function ... is to decide for itself whether the decision was in accordance with Convention rights; it is not a purely reviewing function'; 'Under the HRA ... the claimant would have a right to full merits review by the court, again on fact and law'.[293] Of

[284] (n 174) [43].

[285] ibid [108]; *Smith v MOD* [2014] AC 52, [142].

[286] But even within common law review there have been recent developments which arguably challenge the supervisory conception of the judicial role: eg *Kennedy* (n 221); *Pham v SOSHD* [2015] 1 WLR 1591; JNE Varuhas, 'Judicial Review at the Crossroads' (2015) 74 *CLJ* 215.

[287] ID Leigh and L Lustgarten, 'Making Rights Real: The Courts, Remedies, and the Human Rights Act' (1999) 58 *CLJ* 509, 518. Contrast Woolf's view that public law's concern is process: 1986 (n 137) 226–27.

[288] *Denbigh* (n 261) [30].

[289] ibid; *Tweed* (n 261) [55]; *R (Williamson) v SOS Education and Employment* [2005] 2 AC 246, [51].

[290] (n 259) [12]–[15], [31], [44] (Lady Hale made exactly the same point); *Denbigh* (n 261) [29]–[31]; *Huang v SOSHD* [2007] 2 AC 167. And see: *Quila* (n 259) [46], [61], [91]; *E v Chief Constable Royal Ulster Constabulary* [2009] 1 AC 536, [13], [52]ff.

[291] *Kennedy* (n 221) [245].

[292] *SOSHD v MN and KY* [2014] 1 WLR 2064, [31].

[293] *Kennedy* (n 221) [244].

course a court, adjudicating proportionality, may give 'weight' to a balance struck by an administrative decision-maker, just as any court would give weight to relevant opinions of those with expertise, who are responsible for given subject matters.[294] But the crucial point is that it is nonetheless the court's determination of proportionality that is determinative:[295] the judgment is 'for [the courts] and not others'.[296] This follows from the judicial role in the separation of powers: questions of legal right are the province of courts.

Amos observes that in the HRA's early days, when the majority of HRA claims were presented to the courts via the judicial review procedure, it was common for human rights to be seen as another ground of judicial review, alongside common law heads, and 'in many cases the role of the court was moulded accordingly' with judges 'anxious to appear sufficiently deferential to the decision of the primary decision-maker'.[297] However as the jurisprudence has matured human rights adjudication has been more clearly decoupled from the supervisory jurisdiction and 'given its own space, separate from judicial review'.[298]

C. Public Law and Private Law: The Procedural Dimension

The guidance in *Anufrijeva* that human rights damages claims should be treated as common law review claims for procedural purposes—specifically, that such damages claims should generally be streamed via the Administrative Court and judicial review procedure, with all of its safeguards for public authorities and the public interest—has been side-lined. The turn away from the *Anufrijeva* guidance reflects the inaptness of the review analogy that underpinned it, and that human rights law is a field based in individual rights, rights-based claims traditionally being streamed via ordinary procedure.

Courts have gone so far as to indicate HRA claims, or at least certain classes of human rights claim, ought to be brought via ordinary procedure; in doing so courts have emphasised commonalities between such claims and claims in tort.[299]

Where human rights claims are initiated via review standard procedural restrictions, for the benefit of authorities, have been loosened so that the procedure comes to resemble ordinary procedure in significant respects.

[294] *Huang* (n 290) [16]; *Bank Mellat* (n 264) [129] (substantive appeal).
[295] *Miss Behavin'* (n 259) [31], [37].
[296] *R v MOD, ex p Smith* [1996] QB 517, 541.
[297] M Amos, 'Separating Human Rights Adjudication from Judicial Review' [2007] *European Human Rights Law Review* 679, 696–97.
[298] ibid.
[299] *Ruddy* (n 89); *Wilkinson* (n 263) [61]; *ID v Home Office* [2006] 1 WLR 1003, [105].

For example, cross-examination and discovery have rarely been ordered in review proceedings because of the expense to the court and defendant authority,[300] and the traditional idea associated with common law review that it is not the court's role to determine disputed questions of fact in public law.[301] However, human rights adjudication is distinct in that it entails determination of claims of right, which implicates adjudication akin to merits review. Because of the nature of such claims courts are necessarily required to engage with factual questions in a manner they are not within common law review: within human rights law 'a closer factual analysis of the justification for restrictions imposed [on rights], is required than used to be undertaken on judicial review challenges'.[302] As courts have come to recognise this, there has been a concomitant procedural 'cleaving' of human rights claims from common law claims *within* review procedure, aligning the procedure more closely with ordinary procedure for human rights claims. First, the House of Lords held 'a more flexible and less prescriptive'[303] approach ought to be taken to applications for disclosure in HRA claims, so that discovery will be ordered more often. Second, restrictions on cross-examination have been loosened.[304] In *Wilkinson*, which involved a HRA challenge to a medical decision that the claimant be administered drugs, the Court of Appeal ordered that medical experts give oral evidence and be cross-examined within proceedings initiated via review procedure, citing the enhanced judicial role in human rights law.[305] It was also significant that the facts could equally have given rise to a battery claim, which would have proceeded via ordinary procedure.[306] Other judgments indicate that because 'contested actions involving a human rights element often require cross-examination' it may be preferable that they be streamed via ordinary procedure.[307]

Thus, unmodified judicial review procedure has been found unsuitable for proper disposal of HRA claims, or at least certain classes of HRA claim. In turn this reflects the distinctiveness of human rights law as a rights-based field; as the procedural jurisprudence has long recognised: '[w]hen individual rights are claimed, there should not be a need for leave or a special time

[300] eg *O'Reilly* (n 2) 257, 263, 282, 284; *Huddleston* (n 164) 947; *IRC* (n 151) 638, 654; *Tweed* (n 261) [2], [29]. More generally courts emphasise review procedure is inappropriate for determining factual questions: *Roy* (n 87) 650, 654; *R v East Berkshire HA, ex p Walsh* [1985] QB 152, 173.

[301] *O'Reilly* (n 2) 282. But note courts are increasingly willing to engage with factual questions within common law review: eg *E* (n 156).

[302] *Tweed* (n 261) [54].

[303] ibid [32].

[304] *R (A) v Chief Constable Kent Constabulary* [2013] EWCA Civ 1706, [58]; *R (Al-Sweady) v SOSD* [2010] HRLR 12, [29].

[305] *Wilkinson* (n 263) [25]–[26].

[306] ibid [24], [56]–[59], [62].

[307] *ID* (n 299) [105].

limit, nor should the relief be discretionary'.[308] In contrast, fields characterised by a public interest ethos, such as common law review, are naturally housed within procedures which reflect the substantive law's concern for protection of authorities and the public good.

Importantly, review procedure is even more inapt where the HRA claim is for *damages*. The courts have come to recognise this over time, with Lord Woolf's procedural prescriptions in *Anufrijeva* side-lined in practice and in principle.

In terms of practice, since *Anufrijeva* damages claims have been determined regularly in the County Court[309]—the Court of Appeal recently advising that at least certain classes of human rights damages claims should be initiated in the County Court[310]—and via ordinary procedure in the Queen's Bench Division, with no mention of the *Anufrijeva* guidance,[311] including in specialist courts such as the Technology and Construction Court.[312] Damages claims have also proceeded via the Family Court, Family Division of the High Court and Court of Protection: 'there is no statutory provision, rule or practice direction which requires [human rights] challenges to be brought in the Administrative Court'.[313] It is also worth recording that there are examples of the procedural guidance in *Anufrijeva* causing a great deal of confusion for judges and parties alike, with proceedings ping-ponging among different courts, wasting court time and party funds;[314] that is, causing the very problem the guidance was intended to prevent.

In terms of principle, Lord Woolf's procedural prescription—that wherever possible HRA damages claims ought to be brought via judicial review, if not via alternative routes such as the Ombudsman—received its quietus in the Supreme Court decision in *Ruddy*.[315] The Court held unanimously that

[308] *Roy* (n 87) 654; *Boddington v British Transport Police* [1999] 2 AC 143, 172; *ID* (n 299) [102]–[108].

[309] eg *ZH v Commissioner for the Metropolis* [2012] EWHC 604.

[310] *R (Parratt) v SOSJ* [2014] EWCA Civ 1478, [42]; *ID* (n 299) [107] (no reason why the County Court is not an appropriate forum for HRA damages claims).

[311] The following are HRA damages cases initiated via ordinary procedure in the Queen's Bench Division: *DSD* HC (n 192); *Rabone v Pennine Care NHS Trust* [2010] PIQR P2; *Savage v South Essex Partnership NHS Foundation Trust* [2010] EWHC 865; *R (Sessay) v South London and Maudsley NHS Trust* [2012] QB 760; *OOO v Commissioner for the Metropolis* [2011] HRLR 29; *Breyer Group Plc v Department of Energy and Climate Change* [2014] JPL 1346; *Dennis v MOD* [2003] Env LR 34; *Ahmad v Brent LBC* [2011] EWHC 80.

[312] *Dobson v Thames Water Utilities Ltd* [2011] EWHC 3253; *Marcic v Thames Water Utilities Ltd (No 2)* [2002] QB 1003.

[313] *R (P) v SOSHD* [2001] 1 WLR 2002, [120]. See, eg, *Northamptonshire CC v AS* [2015] EWHC 199 (Fam); *Re H (A Child: Breach of Convention Rights: Damages)* [2014] EWFC 38; *YA v A Local Authority* [2011] 1 WLR 1505 (Court of Protection).

[314] eg *Andrews v Reading BC* [2004] EWHC 970, [1]–[10].

[315] (n 89). This was a Scottish appeal, but Lord Hope, for the Court, expressly considered his pronouncements of principle were equally applicable south of the border: [18] and see [16]–[17].

it was positively inappropriate for a damages claim for breach of Article 3 to be brought as a review claim. In doing so it overturned the lower Court's determination that such claim must be brought as a review application, the lower Court reasoning such claim was 'distinct' 'from a claim based on common law assault ... involv[ing a challenge], in administrative law'.[316] Fundamental to the Supreme Court's rejection of this view was its recognition that review proceedings seeking exercise of the court's supervisory jurisdiction are fundamentally different in nature from rights-based claims for damages; this contrasts with Woolf's approach, which treats human rights claims *as* administrative law claims. Lord Hope, for the Court, could not have been clearer when he said:

> The fallacy which undermines the Extra Division's whole approach ... lies in its assumption that the appellant is seeking an exercise of the court's supervisory jurisdiction. That is not so. He is not asking for the review or setting aside of any decision ... He is not asking the court to control [the authority's] actions in that way at all ... The allegations are of completed acts or failures to act. He is not seeking to have them corrected in order to provide a foundation for his claim, nor does he need to do so. What he seeks is just satisfaction for the fact that, on his averments, his article 3 Convention rights have been breached. The essence of his claim is simply one of damages.[317]

Lord Hope endorsed Lord Hamilton's dictum in *Docherty*[318] that 'the process of judicial review would be quite inept for proceedings in which damages are claimed for an isolated act of physical violence which was in breach of the article 3 Convention right'.[319] In accepting that such 'public law' claims ought to be made via *ordinary procedure* Lord Hope gave the Supreme Court's blessing to a move away from the strictures of *O'Reilly*, towards a flexible approach to procedural treatment of public law claims.[320] In this way the increasingly pluralistic nature of public law, now boasting rights and damages dimensions, has been reflected in explicit rejection of a single procedural path—a one-size-fits-all approach—for public law claims.

The reason review procedure is 'quite inept' for determination of damages claims is that it was designed as a procedural route first and foremost for applications on common law grounds for orders based on the old prerogative writs; indeed, the Civil Procedure Rules provide that claims only seeking damages may not be brought via review procedure.[321] Damages claims are unlike claims for remedies for breaches of public duties. They are 'paradigms of personal claims with individuated losses suffered by those

316 ibid [9].
317 ibid [15].
318 *Docherty v Scottish Ministers* [2011] CSIH 58, [20].
319 *Ruddy* (n 89) [18].
320 ibid [16]–[18].
321 CPR, r 54.3(2).

affected':[322] damages, being an individuated remedy, vary from one claimant to the next depending on losses suffered. It is therefore of the very essence of such claims that their proper determination demands examination of the specific factual circumstances of the case, often requiring disclosure and/or oral evidence, not typically provided for on review. For example, in the HRA damages case of *Faulkner* Sedley LJ, for the Court of Appeal, said: '[w]e do not see how an award itself can be quantified without attention, sometimes detailed attention, to what has happened'.[323] In turn he eschewed the 'summary determination' method propounded in *Anufrijeva* which prescribed that facts should not be examined closely.[324]

The distinctive nature of human rights damages claims suggests many restrictions within review procedure, which protect authorities or the public interest generally, while apt for claims for quashing or mandatory orders based in breaches of public duties are inappropriate and unjustifiable for damages claims based in rights-violations.[325] For example, the short three-month-limit on review is justified on the basis that the

> *[t]he public interest in good administration* requires that public authorities and third parties should not be kept in suspense as to the legal validity of a decision the authority has reached ... for any longer period than is absolutely necessary in fairness to the person affected by the decision.[326]

While this may be a legitimate reason for requiring application for a quashing order to be brought promptly, particularly within a field concerned to safeguard administrative interests, such reasoning is inapplicable to a rights-based claim for damages. As Lady Hale said in *A v Essex County Council*:

> The judge ... placed at the forefront of his account ... that 'there is a significant public interest in public law claims against public bodies being brought expeditiously'. That is of course true in judicial review, when remedies are sought to quash administrative decisions which may affect large numbers of people or upon which other decisions have depended and action been taken. It is normally a prospective remedy, aiming not only to quash the past but also to put right the future. Expedition is less obviously necessary in a claim for a declaration in vindication of the claimant's human rights, upon which nothing else depends, or of a claim for damages. These are retrospective remedies, aimed at marking or compensating what has happened in the past ... This claim is more akin to a tort claim than to judicial review.[327]

[322] Beatson (n 96) 45.

[323] *R (Faulkner) v SOSJ* [2011] HRLR 23, [19]. On appeal the Supreme Court affirmed that '[c]ourts should resolve disputed issues of fact in the usual way': (n 10) [13](5), [39].

[324] ibid.

[325] Note ordinary procedure does not leave defendants unprotected, incorporating mechanisms for dealing with unmeritorious claims, such as strike-out and summary judgment.

[326] *O'Reilly* (n 2) 280–81 (emphasis added); *Cocks* (n 2) 294–95.

[327] (n 191) [116]. See also *Davy* (n 26) 274; *Wandsworth LBC v Winder* (1984) 15 HLR 1, 23; D Oliver, 'The Human Rights Act and Public Law/Private Law Divides' [2000] *European Human Rights Law Review* 343, 350–51.

It is thus not surprising that longer limitation periods apply to tort and human rights claims,[328] nor that courts take a relatively liberal approach to applications to extend the limitation period in HRA damages claims, where this is required to ensure vindication of the claimant's rights.[329] Indeed, on occasion courts have extended the limitation period so it is equivalent to that for claims in tort, on the basis that the two sets of claims are analogous and HRA claimants ought not to be disadvantaged.[330]

Lastly, the *Anufrijeva* guidance that permission should not be granted in review proceedings for a human rights damages claim unless explanation is given as to why the claim is not being made to the Ombudsman has now been departed from.[331] The reason is that neither the Parliamentary nor Local Ombudsman have jurisdiction over legal claims for which a judicial remedy is available,[332] while we might add the ECtHR has held Ombudsman processes—as well as other non-legal mechanisms—do not fulfil the requirements of an effective remedy for human rights violations.[333] The *Anufrijeva* Court's eagerness to keep human rights damages claims out of court, in order to protect public funds, led it into manifest legal error. But despite the Ombudsman guidance being eschewed there are still odd examples of courts giving expediency or availability of informal, alternative routes to redress as reasons to deny access to court and damages.[334] Thus, one must restate that which should not require restatement: claims of legal right are quintessentially the province of courts, and it is not open to courts to abrogate their constitutional duty to hear and determine such claims. '[V]indication of right in a society based on the rule of law must ultimately be able to be achieved by claim of right to the courts'.[335] As the courts have reiterated time and again, there is a 'principle not by any means to be whittled down that the subject's recourse to Her Majesty's courts for the

[328] The time period under the Act is one year, which matches defamation; limitation periods for other torts are longer. The three month time limit for judicial review only applies to HRA claims where brought via review procedure: HRA, s 7.

[329] *Rabone* (n 174) [108]; *cf Dunn v Parole Board* [2009] 1 WLR 728.

[330] *Dobson* (n 312) [1072]–[1074].

[331] *K v Cornwall CC* [2005] EWHC 1585, [11].

[332] ibid; Local Government Act 1974, s 26(6)(c); Parliamentary Commissioner Act 1967, s 5(2).

[333] The Ombudsman process is considered to lack sufficient independence from the political branches. More importantly Ombudsmen do not have jurisdiction to make binding legal determinations and compel redress. Other mechanisms such as inquests and internal agency investigations are unlikely to fulfil Article 13 for the same reasons. See *Klass v Germany* (1979–80) 2 EHRR 214, [55], [67]; *Peck v UK* (2003) 36 EHRR 41, [109]; *Silver v UK* (1983) 5 EHRR 347, [115]; *Campbell v UK* (1985) 7 EHRR 165, [126]; *Štrucl v Slovenia* (20 October 2011) App no 5903/10, [130]; *Reynolds v UK* (2012) 55 EHRR 35, [62]; *Bubbins v UK* (2005) 41 EHRR 24, [170].

[334] *R (MD) v SOSHD* [2011] EWCA Civ 453; *Anyasinti v SOSHD* [2010] EWHC 1676, [21].

[335] *Attorney-General v Chapman* [2012] 1 NZLR 462, [26].

determination of his rights is not to be excluded except by clear [statutory] words', and that if access to court to enforce one's rights is to be curtailed 'in the interests of good administration, *then this is for Parliament*';[336] 'to deny jurisdiction on the ground of expediency seems to me ... to be tantamount to abdicating a primary function of the judiciary'.[337] If this fundamental principle is ever to be departed from it should most certainly not be in the context of basic rights.

III. CONCLUSION: SLAYING CHIMAERA

When placed within Lord Woolf's public law–private law paradigm, human rights law is much closer to private law: the basic legal norms are individual legal rights, the courts' role is closely analogous to the courts' role in private law adjudication, and the procedures governing such claims are increasingly analogous to those governing private law claims. This illustrates the fundamental flaw in the Court's approach in *Anufrijeva*. The Court in effect adopted an approach to damages founded on a theory of public law which holds that public law is concerned with duties owed to the public and the 'protection of the public', in a field constituted to ensure the *protection and vindication of the most fundamental of individual rights and interests*. Fundamentally different fields have been conflated under the umbrella of 'public law' with the consequence that the general remedial approach within common law review was inaptly read across to human rights law.

While there is a good argument that a discretionary public interest approach to remedies, which emphasises quashing, declaratory and specific-type relief, is 'inherent' in a body of law concerned with proper performance of 'public law duties ... owed either to the public at large or a specific section of the public'[338] it is out of place in a field specifically constituted to ensure protection of individual rights and interests. As Feldman observes, the broad discretionary approach to HRA damages has been carried over from the traditional discretionary approach to remedies such as quashing orders at common law, such approach being premised on a concern with protecting the public interest.[339] But that remedial approach is a remnant of the 'obligation-dominated days of public law' before 'rights'—and damages—had a 'genuine place in English public law'.[340] Times have changed. 'Public law' has moved on, and so must the remedial approach.

[336] *Winder* (n 87) 510 (emphasis added); *ID* (n 299) [108].
[337] *R v Board of Visitors of Hull Prison, ex p St Germain* [1979] QB 425, 455.
[338] Bamforth (n 232) 11.
[339] D Feldman, 'Remedies for Violations of Convention Rights' in Feldman (n 128) [19.08].
[340] ibid.

The importance of the individualist, rights-based nature of human rights law for remedies is reflected in the fact that while there may be disagreements as to what approach ought to be taken to human rights damages there is nonetheless 'a widely held view that there are vertical rights against government which deserve the protection of the damages remedy' and that '[f]oremost amongst those rights are those classified as fundamental human rights'.[341] In stark contrast there is long-standing, deep-seated disagreement as to whether monetary relief should be available within common law review, a field not traditionally concerned with protection of individual rights. Courts maintain the rule against monetary relief for breach of public duties,[342] while creation of such a system of liability via statute is 'not on the cards in the United Kingdom'[343] following kyboshing of the Law Commission's project on public authority liability.[344] It is notable that a number of consultees opposed to creation of a damages remedy for common law unlawfulness cited the distinction between private law as concerned with individual rights, and common law review as concerned with enforcement of duties owed to the public at large, the nature of the obligations within review making damages inapt.[345] The Law Commission, although maintaining its view that damages ought to be available on a limited basis, appeared to accept the relevant 'wrong' within common law review, which opens up remedies, is not breach of individual rights, but 'public law illegality'.[346]

The foregoing analysis demonstrates the danger in placing heavy emphasis on any general distinction between public and private law. Treating vast areas of doctrine as unitary can obscure the true nature and nuances of sub-categories of doctrine which have their own distinctive internal coherence, functions and modes of reasoning. Distinct bodies of doctrine can be pushed together despite important differences between them. It also demonstrates the dangers of adopting purely top-down reasoning. Such approach can lead to the warping of doctrine, with courts 'reinventing' the nature of a field according to their unitary conception of public law, despite a complete mismatch between theory and fundamental doctrinal features. In this respect adoption of a public interest approach to damages muddies 'conceptual clarity' and coherence within human rights law: the 'gap between response and the normative ground of the causative event means that the remedy obscures the nature of the injustice being remedied'.[347] The result

[341] Cane 1999 (n 233) 502–03.

[342] eg *X* (n 215) 730–31; *Watkins v SOSHD* [2006] 2 AC 395, [26]; *R (Wells) v Parole Board* [2010] 1 AC 553, [5]; *Mohammed v Home Office* [2011] 1 WLR 2862.

[343] *Mohammed* ibid [24].

[344] *Administrative Redress: Public Bodies and the Citizen*, Law Com 322 (2010); see discussion of the project's fate in ibid [20]–[24].

[345] ibid [2.9]–[2.12].

[346] ibid [2.58]–[2.59].

[347] EJ Weinrib, 'Two Conceptions of Remedies' in CEF Rickett (ed), *Justifying Private Law Remedies* (Hart Publishing, 2008) 15–16.

of appending a public interest approach to remedies, based in the idea that public law is concerned with protection of the collective good, to human rights law, which has a radically different function of affording strong protection to basic, individual personal rights and interests, is the spawning of something akin to the mythical beast, Chimaera, described in Homer's *Illiad*: a monstrous, dangerous incongruity.

However, the fundamental mismatch between the public interest approach to damages and the nature of human rights law not only gives rise to a formal issue of doctrinal incoherence: the 'limp' approach to damages propounded in *Anufrijeva* positively undermines the distinctive goals of human rights law, which underpin creation of the primary rights. Such approach hardly resonates with a policy of strong protection of fundamental interests, particularly when compared with approaches to damages in other fields, which afford far greater protection to interests of equivalent or lesser importance. These are *human rights* damages, not public law damages, and the approach to such damages ought to be founded on an understanding of the distinctive nature of the norms within and functions of *that* field.[348]

In terms of procedure, if human rights damages claims were routinely streamed via review procedure, in unmodified form, this would only serve to impede individuals from vindicating their fundamental rights and courts from fairly determining such claims. It is therefore welcome that significant progress has been made towards matching procedure to the nature of claims.

IV. IS THE PUBLIC INTEREST APPROACH THE ONLY 'PUBLIC LAW' APPROACH?

If one subscribes to the view that the public law–private law distinction is a sound one that ought to guide legal development, and one assumes human rights fall on the public law side of that divide, it *still* does not necessarily follow that one will subscribe to the approach to damages adopted in *Anufrijeva*. This point may be illustrated by two examples. First, by considering an important debate between Harlow and Samuel, and specifically their discussion of the famous constitutional damages case, *Maharaj*, decided in the late 1970s.[349] Second, by considering the variation of approach to human rights damages within the New Zealand jurisprudence, which has been influenced by *Maharaj* from the outset.

In the Privy Council case of *Maharaj* the appellant sought damages under the Trinidadian Constitution for infringement of constitutional rights by the Trinidadian High Court. In creating such a right of action the Constitution deliberately abrogated common law judicial immunity. As with English

[348] See *Fose* (n 135) [57].
[349] *Maharaj v Attorney General of Trinidad and Tobago (No 2)* [1979] AC 385.

courts' approach to HRA damages, the reasoning of the Privy Council rested heavily on the public law–private law distinction. As Harlow[350] records, Lord Diplock—the originator of the public law–private law distinction in English law and a chief protagonist of the public interest conception of public law[351]—contrasted a 'private law' 'action in tort' for an 'award of damages', such as false imprisonment, with a 'public law' 'claim' for 'compensation' for deprivation of liberty, with comparatively fewer heads of loss being recoverable in the public law context, compensation not being at large, and exemplary damages apparently ruled out.[352]

Harlow, questioning judicial use of the distinction, argued that the terms 'public law' and 'private law' were treated as 'classificatory in character and condition[ed] substantive rights'.[353] 'The distinction is of great significance, for a "right" has been transmuted into a "claim" with a resultant reduction in the amount of money payable to the plaintiff'.[354] Harlow argues that there is no precedent for such distinction and asks: 'What is this but a new judge-made "special" exception which flies in the face of the Trinidadian legislature by refusing whole-heartedly to endorse their intended abrogation of the common law rule of judicial immunity?'[355]

Samuel, replying to Harlow, did not contest the Board's invocation of the distinction.[356] However, he did query the *use* made of it.[357] He argued that the Privy Council 'ought to have interpreted the interference with the plaintiff from quite a different angle' 'given the unique position of the state and unequal power relationship';[358] on his view the 'public law' relationship between citizen and state is distinct from other legal relationships, with a distinctive feature being substantial power imbalance between parties.[359] In this light he considered the Privy Council to have wrongly interpreted the claim 'along narrow compensatory lines' whereas in his view 'the remedy, being a public law one, went far beyond just compensation' being concerned with 'some very basic and very clearly defined rights'.[360] Significantly he argued that if the Privy Council 'wanted to draw an analogy with types of action in private law, then they might well have done better to look at remedies more specifically designed to define and protect rights'.[361] Such actions include property torts for which damages may be awarded absent

350 Harlow (n 68) 244.
351 See Varuhas 2016 (n 1).
352 *Maharaj* (n 349) particularly 397–99.
353 Harlow (n 68) 244.
354 ibid.
355 ibid.
356 Samuel (n 22) 558.
357 ibid 570–73.
358 ibid 572.
359 ibid eg at 572, 576.
360 ibid.
361 ibid 573.

consequential loss and liability is strict, and which aim to afford the claimant's interests strong protection from outside interference.[362] In other words Samuel analogises with vindicatory torts. Thus, although Samuel embraces the distinction he does not arrive at a public interest approach to damages but rather a vindicatory, tort-based approach.

We find similar variation of view as to the implications of the distinction in the damages jurisprudence under the New Zealand Bill of Rights Act 1990 (NZBORA). The remedy has been classed as a 'public law remedy' since its recognition in *Baigent*;[363] all indications are that the remedy was originally so classified so as to enable the Court to reason around a statutory provision that would bar the claim if it were classed as tortious.[364] Our inquiry comes full circle as the *Baigent* Court sourced the idea for so classifying the remedy from *Maharaj*.[365] Notwithstanding the original reasons for so classifying the remedy, the classification has cast a long shadow over the jurisprudence and resulted in a jurisprudence characterised by perpetual uncertainty and confusion; this ought to stand as a warning beacon to the courts of other jurisdictions tempted to rest development of damages on the divide. Twenty-five years after enactment of the NZBORA, and 21 years after *Baigent*, no settled, clear and coherent approach has emerged. Commentators observe, 'while a good many Judges have noted the public law origins of BORA compensation ... few have explored those origins and fewer still have built anything of significance out of them',[366] while the Chief Justice more recently commented that '[t]he principles upon which damages for breaches of rights are to be assessed are not greatly developed in New Zealand or in comparable jurisdictions'.[367]

One critical source of uncertainty has been the normative implications of classifying damages as a public law remedy. While in the 2000 case of *Dunlea* there was some prospect of emergence of a vindicatory, tort-based approach,[368] in the 2007 case of *Taunoa* some members of the Supreme Court, most prominently Blanchard J, sought to distance human rights damages from tort, utilising the public law–private law distinction to place human rights damages within a public interest paradigm, drawing heavily on *Anufrijeva*.[369] The Chief Justice took a different view, not thinking it 'appropriate to consider the usefulness of a dichotomy between "private law" and "public law" damages without further consideration how such a

[362] ibid 573, 576.

[363] *Simpson v Attorney-General [Baigent's case]* [1994] 3 NZLR 667.

[364] On this point and evolution of the damages jurisprudence more generally see: JNE Varuhas, 'The Development of the Damages Remedy under the New Zealand Bill of Rights Act 1990: From Torts to Administrative Law' [2016] *New Zealand Law Review* (forthcoming).

[365] *Baigent* (n 363) 678–79, 692, 700, 718.

[366] A Butler and G McLay, *Liability of Public Authorities* (NZLS, 2004) 128.

[367] *Taunoa* (n 193) [108].

[368] *Dunlea v Attorney-General* [2000] 3 NZLR 136 (discussed ch 3.I.E).

[369] Above n 193.

division fits within the New Zealand legal tradition',[370] a tradition which shares much with England.

Other judges have also rested their approach to damages on the supposed distinctiveness of public law but, significantly, have reached different conclusions from Blanchard J. For example, in *Dunlea*, Thomas J, dissenting from the majority's approach to human rights damages modelled on trespassory torts, emphasised the importance of 'vindication' in the human rights context, and the difference between *private* rights and *public* rights:

> Damages for a private wrong do not ordinarily extend to the vindication of the right which has been violated. In a tortious claim the plaintiff claims damages for the breach of a duty owed to the plaintiff. It is in the nature of a private right to remedy a private wrong. In a claim under the Bill of Rights the plaintiff seeks compensation for the breach of a right of a different character. It is a public right in the sense that it is a right against the state possessed by all citizens, but the breach occurs to the plaintiff and it is the intrinsic value of that right to the plaintiff which then falls to be compensated. The plaintiff is compensated, not just as the victim of a private law proceeding, but as a citizen possessing a thing of value in itself.[371]

Starting from the proposition that human rights are public law rights, and viewing this as a categorisation of normative significance, Thomas J does not come to a public interest conception of damages, analogous to that propounded in *Taunoa* and *Anufrijeva*. Rather, in common with Samuel, he comes to a position that mirrors the approach to damages in vindicatory fields, ie damages ought to reflect the inherent value of the infringed right. Of course, this is a little confusing given Thomas J was, in *Dunlea*, dissenting from a majority that held that the approach to damages ought to be aligned with that in trespassory torts. The reasoning is illustrative of the flaw in treating all of private law, and all of public law as unitary. It may be that vindication is not the primary function of many parts of private law, such that a 'loss-centred approach to damages'[372] is taken in some sub-fields. But we have seen that TAPS do have a primary function of vindication and protection of fundamental interests, and damages follow suit. Thomas J paints damages for the violation per se as a novel public law concept, but it is a concept that has long endured in tort.

We find similar examples elsewhere in the NZBORA jurisprudence. For example in *Manga* Hammond J heard concurrent damages claims for false imprisonment and arbitrary detention (NZBORA, section 22).[373] He awarded damages for the tort on orthodox principles and made no extra award for the human rights violation, because of the overlap between the claims. However, obiter, he considered the approach to human rights

[370] *Taunoa* (n 193) [108], and see [318].
[371] *Dunlea* (n 368) [66]ff.
[372] ibid [68]; *Chapman* (n 335) [30].
[373] *Manga v Attorney-General* [2000] 2 NZLR 65.

damages. He opined that damages in 'private law' and in 'public law' should not necessarily be placed on the same footing. After a lengthy analysis of the supposed differences between public law and private law he postulated that one ramification of recognising the 'distinct' nature of public law is that 'moral damages' might be available to recognise 'that a fundamental value had been infringed by government action, per se'.[374] This proposed head is remarkably similar in nature to normative injury, for which damages are recoverable in vindicatory torts;[375] public law is not so distinctive after all.

What ought we to take from the foregoing?

First, Samuel, Thomas J and Hammond J's analyses beg the question of what the public law–private law distinction adds as an analytical tool. Part 1 of this book reached the conclusion that a vindicatory approach ought to be taken without recourse to this amorphous distinction, and it did so via orthodox techniques of legal reasoning. Samuel's analysis even resulted in the explicit drawing together of private law and public law doctrine, thus undermining the idea of a fundamental distinction between the two with which he had started.

Thomas J's judgment in *Dunlea* and Hammond J's judgment in *Manga* illustrate the 'blinding' and 'obscuring' effects of the distinction: the distinction blinds judges to clear bonds between bodies of private law and public law doctrine which could, for example, help in formulating the detailed rules and principles governing human rights damages.[376] Further, reliance on the distinction leads to unconvincing reasoning, for example treating vast swathes of doctrine—private law and public law—as having some sort of inherent unity, which in turn leads judges to make grand over-generalisations. The distinction is reminiscent of the Sirens in Homer's *Odyssey*. It lures in jurists with its seductive appeal, only to leave their reasoning in a wreck.

Second, we find a plurality of differing views as to the implications of the putative distinction: Samuel, Thomas J and Hammond J concluded that classifying damages as a public law remedy led to a vindicatory approach, whereas Lord Woolf, in *Anufrijeva*, and Blanchard J, in *Taunoa*, concluded application of the divide led to a public interest approach. This, along with the perpetually uncertain nature of the New Zealand damages jurisprudence, confirms the argument made above: recourse to the divide, which is inherently contentious and suffers from lack of an accepted meaning, is more likely to lead into more intense disagreement than aid resolution of discrete questions over legal development, while use of the divide can hide the normative concerns which underpin its invocation and application, and which should be the true focus of debate. As Sir Robin Cooke observed

[374] ibid [137].

[375] Note the nature of these moral damages was not completely clear, and aspects of Hammond J's analysis indicate they may not be identical to damages for normative injury (although, as discussed in the text, there are similarities).

[376] See similarly Harlow (n 68) 245–50.

> [i]t can be convenient to speak of public law as an indication that the discussion is concerned with the activities of some emanation of central or local government. In itself, though, the characterization is no automatic determinant of the content or bounds of principle.[377]

The foregoing analysis also confirms another argument made above: the implications of the public law–private law divide are bound up in differences of opinion as to, inter alia, the nature of public power and the role of law in regulating the relationship between public institutions and individuals, leading one into the black hole of contested political theory. For example, if one subscribes to communitarian political philosophy, which emphasises the importance of decision-making in the community interest, then one may be more likely to view litigation aimed at protection of individual material interests as an illegitimate attempt to distort such decision-making.[378] By contrast if one subscribes to liberal political theory, which emphasises individual rights and protection of personal freedom, then one may be more likely to view litigation aimed at vindicating important individual interests in the face of public power as legitimate.[379] An approach to legal analysis which leads into such contested territory will—either overtly or more likely, obliquely (through boilerplate invocations of 'public law')—reopen open-ended debates that have been settled by the polity in the actual terms of the charter of rights, and the nature of the primary obligations enumerated therein. This leads on to an insight of great importance: *if one wishes to uncover the idea of the relationship between individuals and public institutions that underpins those rights in the HRA, the best place to look is the obligations themselves.*[380]

Where application of the divide leads to judicial assertion of legal rules at odds with the nature of those obligations, and favourable to government, it may invite the conclusion that 'the "public/private" classification ... is nothing more than an attempt by the judiciary to conceal political issues behind a formalist facade and to shield from public criticism some highly executive-minded decisions'.[381]

377 R Cooke, 'The Struggle for Simplicity in Administrative Law' in M Taggart (ed), *Judicial Review of Administrative Action in the 1980s* (OUP, 1986) 3.

378 D Feldman, 'Public Interest Litigation and Constitutional Theory in Comparative Perspective' (1992) 55 *MLR* 44, 47.

379 ibid.

380 In similar vein see: J McLean, 'Public Function Tests: Bringing Back the State' in D Dyzenhaus et al (n 30) 199, 207.

381 Harlow (n 68) 265. In other jurisdictions reliance on the divide has not necessarily led to more restrictive liability principles. For example, Allison (1996 (n 22) ch 8) records that in France the substantive distinction between public and private law enabled the *Conseil d'Etat* to extend principles of state liability over time, in particular developing a form of no-fault, risk-based liability. He cites Waline's observation that '[t]he result is that, if one were today to subject the liability of the State to the rules of the Civil Code, one would in certain cases run the risk of a regression. That is without doubt the best reason which is able today to legitimate the maintenance of an autonomous administrative law of liability: it works to the advantage of victims' (Allison 1996, 176 fn 42; M Waline, *Droit Administratif* 9th edn (Éditions Sirey, 1963) [15]).

Part 3

Alternative Approaches to Damages for Human Rights Breaches

INTRODUCTION

This Part examines approaches to human rights damages not based in tort. If such approaches have clear benefits, this may call for modification of the tort-based approach, or such approaches may be preferable to an approach based in tort.

Those approaches developed by the English courts under the Human Rights Act 1998 (HRA) are given priority in the analysis that follows given this book is concerned principally with English law, and those approaches adopted under the HRA are realistically the most relevant competitors to a tort-based approach. However, certain approaches considered here, particularly the interest-balancing approach and adoption of immunities for public defendants, characterise the human rights or constitutional damages jurisprudence of other common law jurisdictions. Also, like other aspects of human rights law the field of human rights damages has been characterised by 'transnational judicial conversations'[1] so that other common law jurisdictions have been or could be influenced by the English jurisprudence. Therefore, analysis of the English jurisprudence will be of relevance to courts outside of England, considering whether they ought to draw upon or follow the English jurisprudence (as the chapters make clear: they should not).

Chapter 5 considers the mirror approach which is now the dominant approach under the Act. Chapter 6 examines the interest-balancing approach propounded by the Court of Appeal in *Anufrijeva*,[2] which continues to exert influence on HRA damages practice, and variants of which have proven popular in other common law jurisdictions. Chapter 7 considers other possible techniques of limiting human rights damages, drawn from European Court of Human Rights (ECtHR), European Court of Justice (ECJ) and American constitutional practice. Note that some features of HRA jurisprudence which deviate from the tort-based approach have already been addressed in previous chapters, while some of the key reasons for such deviation were explored in chapter 4.

Common to all of the approaches discussed in Part 3 is that they are more restrictive than the vindicatory, tort-based approach developed in Part 1; they will result in fewer awards of damages and/or lower awards. As discussed in previous chapters, it is clear that entrenchment of the mirror approach combined with the continuing influence of *Anufrijeva* has had the effect of greatly restricting the number of awards made under the Act as well as depressing quantum; despite some liberalisation of approach in select areas damages are 'peripheral to the HRA'.[3] A Government review

[1] C McCrudden, 'Common Law of Human Rights?: Transnational Judicial Conversations on Constitutional Rights' (2000) 20 *Oxford Journal of Legal Studies* 499.

[2] *Anufrijeva v Southwark LBC* [2004] QB 1124.

[3] J Steele, 'Damages in Tort and Under the Human Rights Act: Remedial or Functional Separation' (2008) 67 *CLJ* 606, 608.

of the HRA found that courts had interpreted section 8 'so strictly ... that the general view of legal commentators is that it is now very difficult to obtain damages under the HRA'.[4] Government advises civil servants that '[t]he approach of the Court has so far been fairly cautious'.[5] Courts have gone so far as to say that damages should be reserved for exceptional cases, be very rare, are of secondary if any importance, and that the focus is on securing legal compliance not the claimant's loss.[6] In terms of quantum both the Government review[7] and Law Commission[8] have observed the modest level of awards under the Act. Indeed, awards have often been exceptionally modest relative to domestic standards, so that it is no exaggeration to say that human rights claimants have often been radically undercompensated.[9] The courts have even indicated that damages for non-pecuniary loss will be 'modest' in the case of *deliberate* wrongdoing.[10] Commentators describe the courts' overall approach as 'miserly', and certain decisions as 'unnecessarily restrictive'.[11] All in all damages are 'sparingly awarded and modest in amount'.[12] One may question immediately whether such restrictive approach is appropriate in the context of the most fundamental of rights.

Before continuing to analyse these approaches some preliminary matters require comment. In particular, it is important to clarify the current state of the HRA jurisprudence, and the relationship between the approach enunciated in *Anufrijeva* and the mirror approach endorsed in *Greenfield* and *Faulkner*.[13]

I. THE CASE LAW UNDER THE ACT

The appellate courts have on three occasions—in *Anufrijeva*, *Greenfield* and *Faulkner*—sought to set out guidance for lower courts as to when damages should be awarded and how they should be assessed. All three decisions

4 Department for Constitutional Affairs, *Review of the Implementation of the Human Rights Act* (2006) 18.

5 Treasury Solicitor's Department, *The Judge Over Your Shoulder* 4th edn (2006) [3.41].

6 eg *Anufrijeva* (n 2) [52]–[53]; *R (Greenfield) v SOSHD* [2005] 1 WLR 673, [9], [30]; *R (Sturnham) v SOSJ* [2012] 3 WLR 476, [22]; *Commissioner for the Metropolis v DSD* [2015] EWCA Civ 646, [66]; *R (Baiai) v SOSHD* [2006] EWHC 1035, [34]; *R (N) v SOSHD* [2003] EWHC 207, [198]; *V (A Child)* [2004] EWCA Civ 1575, [38]; *R (Guntrip) v SOSJ* [2010] EWHC 3188, [54].

7 DCA (n 4) 18.

8 *Administrative Redress: Public Bodies and the Citizen*, Law Com Consultation Paper 187 (2008) [3.183].

9 See ch 3.I.E.

10 *Watkins v SOSHD* [2006] 2 AC 395, [73].

11 R Moules, *Actions Against Public Officials: Legitimate Expectations, Misstatements and Misconduct* (Sweet and Maxwell, 2009) [1-037].

12 *R (Calland) v Financial Services Ombudsman Ltd* [2013] EWHC 1327, [37].

13 *Anufrijeva* (n 2); *Greenfield* (n 6); *R (Faulkner) v SOSJ* [2013] 2 AC 254.

are united in expressly distinguishing and distancing HRA damages from those at common law and adopting approaches more restrictive than at common law. Both the mirror and interest-balancing approach would not uncommonly lead to discretionary denial of awards and low quantum; each operates to marginalise damages. Further, some principles are common to both the approach articulated in *Anufrijeva* and the jurisprudence emerging under the mirror approach. However, despite these similarities the approaches are meaningfully distinct, and significant aspects of each are not compatible.

The mirror approach mandates that domestic courts mechanically replicate Strasbourg practice under Article 41 of the Convention in deciding when to award damages and quantum. *Anufrijeva*, on the other hand, while acknowledging the relevance of the Strasbourg jurisprudence, but also its lack of clarity, mandates that lower courts should conduct a balancing exercise in determining whether damages should be awarded, weighing individual and wider public interests. In terms of quantum the Court in *Anufrijeva* was open to courts seeking guidance from common law scales—at least where the claim was analogous to pre-existing common law actions—and awards recommended by the Ombudsman, but also considered wider public interests should be taken into account in setting quantum, that may justify depressing awards.

At a general level there are commonalities between the two approaches, as discussed in chapter 4. In particular, according to both approaches damages are subject to broad discretion, and the remedial focus is more on securing actual compliance with human rights duties through declaratory and specific-type relief than compensating loss suffered by the claimant. In *Anufrijeva* these features were, it has been suggested, derived from pre-existing remedial practices in English judicial review, and underpinned by a concern to ensure protection of public interests, foremost amongst these being public interests in effective and vigorous administration and preservation of public funds. In *Greenfield* and *Faulkner* these features were endorsed on the formal basis that they are consonant with the mirror approach and the ECtHR's own remedial practice as a supranational court more concerned with the system-goal of maintaining basic human rights standards than redressing individual grievances. Of course, it may be more than coincidence that adoption of the mirror approach operates to maintain a remedial approach consonant with domestic judicial review traditions and affords authorities strong protection from damages suits. Further, even within the rubric of the mirror approach it is not uncommon to see public interest factors bubbling to the surface.

However, there are important differences between the approaches. The most important is that the ECtHR, in its remedial practice, has not endorsed or applied an interest-balancing approach, and nor did Lord Bingham in *Greenfield* or Lord Reed in his lead judgment in *Faulkner* endorse this aspect of *Anufrijeva*. Indeed, the ECtHR has disapproved of domestic courts denying awards so as to preserve public funds, and it does not in general invoke such public policy concerns in its determinations under Article 41. The focus under the mirror approach is a narrow one on replicating Strasbourg practice, whatever that practice may be, whereas on an interest-balancing approach the decision whether to make an award depends on where the balance between private and public interests lies on the facts of the case. These different decision-criteria would very likely make a practical difference: it is entirely possible that application of an interest-balancing approach would lead to denial of damages in cases where awards would be made under the mirror approach, and awards of damages in cases where damages would be denied under the mirror approach, depending on the vagaries of ECtHR jurisprudence. Another difference is that in *Greenfield* Lord Bingham placed some emphasis on the direction in section 8(3) that awards should be awarded where necessary to afford just satisfaction to the victim, indicating a focus on the victim's needs. In contrast, in *Anufrijeva*, the focus was on section 8(1), with public interest considerations read into the overarching remedial discretion to grant such relief as is 'just and appropriate', the Court paying little attention to the needs of victims.

As a matter of precedent courts should follow the mirror approach, as it has been endorsed by the highest court on several occasions, and indeed the mirror approach has been the prevailing approach since *Greenfield*. However, lower court decisions on human rights damages are a mixed bag, which is unsurprising given higher courts have emphasised that damages are subject to open-ended discretion: the making of an award depends on whether the 'court considers that to be the right result'.[14] Thus, lower courts have, on occasion, continued to consider the guidance in *Anufrijeva*, in particular that a balance must be drawn between individual and public interests, sometimes in tandem with consideration of Strasbourg material.[15] Further, both lower and higher courts have, even if they have not relied explicitly on *Anufrijeva*, more generally had recourse to wider public interest concerns consonant with the approach in *Anufrijeva*.[16]

There may be several reasons for the continuing influence of *Anufrijeva*. First, it reflects, as discussed in chapter 4, pre-existing habits of thinking about remedies in public law, and endogenises common and intuitive concerns over public authority liability into the damages inquiry.

[14] *YA v A Local Authority* [2011] 1 WLR 1505, [35].

[15] eg *R (H) v Crown Court at Wood Green* [2006] EWHC 2683, [39]–[42]; *Dobson v Thames Valley Utilities Ltd* [2009] 3 All ER 319, [42]; *Dobson v Thames Water Utilities Ltd* [2011] EWHC 3253 [1085], [1096]; *R (AM) v Chief Constable West Midlands Police* [2010] EWHC 1228, [24]–[26], [44]; *YA* [35]; *R (Anyasinti) v SOSHD* [2010] EWHC 1676, [20]–[21]; *DSD v Commissioner for Police* [2015] 1 WLR 1833.

[16] eg *R (Wilkinson) v IRC* [2005] 1 WLR 1718, [48]ff.

Second, it is written as an authoritative guideline decision and was penned by a very strong panel of the Court of Appeal including the then Master of the Rolls and Lord Chief Justice, while in neither *Greenfield* nor *Faulkner* did the Law Lords specifically and expressly address whether significant features of *Anufrijeva*, such as taking into account wider public interest considerations, should be followed by lower courts; in this way the public interest dimension lingers on.

Third, as we shall see in chapter 5, courts have struggled to derive meaningful guidance from Strasbourg jurisprudence, while decisions of domestic higher courts do not offer a great deal of guidance either; higher courts advise lower courts to simply do the best they can given a dearth of guidance from Strasbourg. In this vacuum some lower court judges have reverted to balancing a range of factors in exercising their remedial discretion, at times with reference to *Anufrijeva* and other times not. This vacuum of principle is also a likely reason why some judges continue to have recourse to common law damages principles despite the clear prohibition on looking to domestic precedents under the mirror approach.

Fourth, open-ended and unelaborated statements by the ECtHR, such as that compensation should be awarded where 'fair, just and reasonable',[17] are an invitation to domestic courts to read something akin to interest-balancing into the mirror approach, so that courts take into account wider public interests as part of an inquiry into what is fair, just and reasonable—even though the ECtHR does not itself generally take into account wider public policy concerns, such as preservation of public funds.[18]

Thus, while there may be some commonalities and interactions between the mirror approach and that favoured in *Anufrijeva* the approaches do not add up to one coherent approach, but are meaningfully distinct. As such I do not analyse the case law as though one particular approach emerges from HRA damages jurisprudence, but instead analyse the approaches set out in *Anufrijeva* and *Greenfield/Faulkner* separately. One might say that I should only consider the mirror approach as that is the approach endorsed by the House of Lords and Supreme Court. However, *Anufrijeva* exerts continuing influence on damages jurisprudence. In any case, my inquiry is a normative one and *Anufrijeva* articulates an interesting approach which is meaningfully different from the mirror approach, and raises distinct issues which warrant examination. It is also an intuitively attractive approach because it directly addresses many public interest concerns that understandably arise in connection with human rights damages, including that damages awards may undermine public service provision, lead to a flood of claims or stymie vigorous public administration, thus why it continues to exert influence. If the mirror approach were to be abandoned,

[17] *Al-Jedda v UK* (2011) 53 EHRR 23, [114].
[18] *DSD* (n 15) [36], [125]–[127], [138]–[140].

say because a British Bill of Rights replaced the HRA and thereby broke the formal link between ECtHR practice and domestic human rights law[19] or because domestic courts decided to move away from the troubled mirror approach under the HRA, then the approach articulated in *Anufrijeva* would no doubt be a leading contender to replace the mirror approach. The significance and attractiveness of interest-balancing approaches is highlighted by the fact that such approaches characterise human rights or constitutional damages in several common law systems including Canada and New Zealand. Importantly, the public interest concerns made explicit by the interest-balancing approach warrant examination in themselves, because they are part of the wider context of human rights damages, which ought to be considered in any normative inquiry into such remedy.

II. CONTEXT: NO OTHER REMEDY

This Part principally focuses on the question of what approach ought to be taken to human rights damages in a situation where a rights-violation has been perpetrated and no other remedy apart from damages under the HRA is available to redress the wrong, such as specific relief or damages awarded in tort.[20] It is in such cases that debates about the approach to human rights damages will have real ramifications for victims, and where divergence among the vindicatory, tort-based approach, the mirror approach and the interest-balancing approach is most stark.

[19] For example by repealing ss 2 and 8(4) of the HRA.

[20] In many jurisdictions it is these types of case in which damages for breaches constitutional or human rights were first recognised: eg *Bivens v Six Unknown Named Agents of Federal Bureau of Narcotics* 403 US 388 (1971); *Simpson v Attorney-General [Baigent's Case]* [1994] 3 NZLR 667.

5

Human Rights Damages and 'Just Satisfaction': The 'Mirror' Approach

[H]eard assumptions are strong, but those unheard are stronger.

T Weir, 'Errare Humanum Est' in P Birks (ed), Frontiers of Liability, Vol 2 (OUP, 1994) 107.

IN THE LEADING case of *Greenfield* Lord Bingham, speaking for a unanimous House, rejected counsel's submissions that, inter alia, English courts are free to depart from scales of awards applied by the European Court of Human Rights (ECtHR) in its remedial jurisdiction under Article 41 and apply domestic scales in awarding damages under the Human Rights Act 1998 (HRA), and that in calculating awards for non-pecuniary loss English courts should use domestic damages awards as a comparator.[1] In addition to the assertion that the HRA is not a tort statute his Lordship gave two principal reasons. First, drawing on a passage in the HRA White Paper,[2] Lord Bingham said that the aim of incorporating the Convention 'was not to give victims better remedies at home than they could recover in Strasbourg but to give them the same remedies without the delay and expense of resort to Strasbourg'.[3] Second, and crucially, he opined that the requirement in section 8(4) of the HRA, that courts take into account those principles applied by the ECtHR in awarding 'just satisfaction' under Article 41, was the clearest indication possible 'that courts in this country should look to Strasbourg and not to domestic precedents' in deciding both whether to make an award and quantum.[4] The Law Lords' decision effectively disapproved previous guidance from the Court of Appeal that,

[1] *R (Greenfield) v SOSHD* [2005] 1 WLR 673, [18]–[19]. The mirror approach has subsequently been approved at House of Lords or Supreme Court level in: *R (Wilkinson) v IRC* [2005] 1 WLR 1718, [25]–[28]; *Watkins v SOSHD* [2006] 2 AC 395, [64]; *Rabone v Pennine Care NHS Foundation Trust* [2012] 2 AC 72, [80]–[88]; *R (Faulkner) v SOSJ* [2013] 2 AC 254; *Osborn v Parole Board* [2014] AC 1115, [114]–[115]; *R (Haney) v SOSJ* [2015] 2 WLR 76; *Shahid v Scottish Ministers* [2015] 3 WLR 1003, [87]–[90].

[2] *Rights Brought Home: The Human Rights Bill*, Cm 3782 (1997) [2.6] [White Paper].

[3] *Greenfield* (n 1) [19].

[4] ibid.

in assessing quantum, courts could seek guidance from the levels of awards made in tort and recommended by bodies such as the Ombudsman.[5]

The effect of *Greenfield* has been that English courts apply a 'mirror' approach to assessing HRA damages: English courts seek to ensure that domestic jurisprudence reflects Strasbourg practice in terms of how the discretion to award damages is exercised and levels of awards. The corollary has been that guidance that could be derived from common law has been side-lined, and that a parallel approach to remedies is developing under the Act.

For example in *Van Colle* the Court of Appeal, in assessing damages for fear and distress suffered by a victim in the lead up to his murder in the context of a breach of the positive obligation to protect life under Article 2, refused to consider scales applied in domestic personal injury cases.[6] Given *Greenfield*, 'the guide to quantum is to be found in Strasbourg cases rather than English decisions'.[7] Similarly, in assessing damages for grief suffered by the victim's relatives the Court refused to consider amounts awarded under the Fatal Accidents Act 1976.[8] The same approach was taken by the Supreme Court in the subsequent Article 2 case of *Rabone*.[9] In the important Supreme Court decision in *Faulkner*, the Court, in assessing damages for breach of Article 5(4) for deprivation of liberty and distress looked to Strasbourg only, having no recourse to domestic damages jurisprudence.[10] It construed the damages remedy under the HRA as 'an entirely novel remedy' drawn from the supranational plane, which is 'not tortious in nature'.[11] The Court of Appeal, which had drawn on false imprisonment, had been 'wrong to take as its starting point the treatment of wrongs under the common law'.[12]

Whether courts adopt a tort-based or mirror approach makes a difference. As discussed in chapter 3, there is no concept of normative damage at Strasbourg, so that only proven and causally connected material losses may possibly be recovered. The ECtHR also exercises an extremely broad discretion as to whether to make a monetary award, so that even where consequential losses are suffered awards may be denied. For example the

[5] *Anufrijeva v Southwark LBC* [2004] QB 1124, [74], [77]–[78]. See also *R (KB) v South London and South and West Region MHRT* [2004] QB 936, [50]–[54]; *R (Bernard) v Enfield LBC* [2003] LGR 423, [59]–[60].

[6] *Van Colle v Chief Constable Hertfordshire Police* [2007] 1 WLR 1821, [120] [*Van Colle* CA] (overturned on liability: [2009] 1 AC 225).

[7] *Van Colle* CA ibid [104].

[8] ibid [121].

[9] *Rabone* (n 1) [80]–[88]. In contrast the Court of Appeal had considered the amounts awarded under domestic legislation: *Rabone v Pennine Care NHS Foundation Trust* [2011] QB 1019, [112] [*Rabone* CA].

[10] *Faulkner* (n 1).

[11] ibid [29].

[12] ibid [96].

Court 'frequently holds that the finding of a violation is sufficient satisfaction without any further monetary award',[13] including where consequential loss is acknowledged to have been suffered;[14] as such the Court 'does not routinely award compensation to successful applicants',[15] albeit practice may vary according to the nature of the violation. English courts have followed ECtHR practice and denied awards in many cases.[16] As the courts acknowledge, and indeed emphasise,[17] Strasbourg scales are 'ungenerous'[18] by English tort standards. Awards for non-pecuniary loss in particular are modest 'even in the most serious cases'.[19] In *Faulkner* Lord Reed, giving the lead judgment, considered the effect of *Greenfield* had been that '[d]icta in earlier cases, suggesting that awards under section 8 should not be on the low side as compared with tortious awards and that English awards should provide the appropriate comparator, were implicitly disapproved'.[20] In consequence awards under the Act have been *very* low relative to English scales. On top of this, aggravated, punitive and nominal damages are unlikely to be available under a mirror approach given the ECtHR refuses to make such awards.[21]

Apart from the practical difference that claimants will recover awards under the HRA less often and far lower than in tort for wrongful interference with similarly basic interests, the mirror approach gives rise to other serious concerns. For example, it is leading to emergence of a domestic jurisprudence which mirrors many of the problematic features of the Strasbourg Court's Article 41 jurisprudence. These include inconsistency and incoherence, parsimonious and opaque reasoning, absence of detailed rules and principles and guidance as to scales, and decision-making influenced by highly subjective concerns and, possibly, unstated political or moral concerns. As we shall see, lower court judges have struggled with the mirror approach, routinely recording that they are unable to derive any meaningful guidance from Strasbourg.

This chapter argues that the mirror approach ought to be rejected. Section 1 contends that arguments adopted by the courts to justify the mirror approach are patently inconsistent with the terms of the Act, while the

13 *A v UK* (2009) 49 EHRR 29, [250].

14 See ch 7.I.

15 R Clayton and H Tomlinson, *The Law of Human Rights* 2nd edn (OUP, 2009) [21.60].

16 For discussion of this practice see ch 7.I.

17 *Greenfield* (n 1) [17]–[19]; *Watkins* (n 1) [73]; *Faulkner* (n 1) [13](14), [27], [68], [96]; *R (Pennington) v Parole Board* [2010] EWHC 78, [13](i), [20], [22]; *Dobson v Thames Valley Utilities Ltd* [2009] 3 All ER 319, [52]; *DSD v Commissioner for Police* [2015] 1 WLR 1833, [41]; *R (Parratt) v SOSJ* [2014] EWCA Civ 1478, [42]. And see the comparisons made in ch 3.I.E.

18 *Watkins* (n 1) [26].

19 J Beatson et al, *Human Rights: Judicial Protection in the United Kingdom* (Sweet and Maxwell, 2008) [7-103].

20 *Faulkner* (n 1) [27].

21 See ch 3.I.C.

Act clearly does not *mandate* such approach. With no clear mandate in the Act, the normative basis for such approach is obscure. Those arguments that might support application of a mirror approach to interpreting substantive rights pursuant to section 2(1) HRA have no application in the damages context.

Section 2 argues that the mirror approach should be abandoned for both reasons of principle and practice. First, there is no requirement in international law that domestic courts must follow the Strasbourg Court's remedial approach, nor does that Court intend domestic courts to follow its approach; indeed the ECtHR has encouraged domestic institutions to develop remedies according to their own legal traditions.

Second, the approach of the Strasbourg Court, a supranational, subsidiary and supervisory institution, to the award and assessment of 'just satisfaction' is not an appropriate model for domestic courts, which have primary responsibility for provision of an 'effective remedy'.

Third, the mirror approach should be rejected as it requires domestic courts to follow a European jurisprudence lacking principle, coherence and consistency, with the result that a problematic domestic jurisprudence is emerging. Further, the lack of guidance that may be discerned from Strasbourg jurisprudence has arguably led English courts to source rules and/or principles from outside that jurisprudence, calling into the question the credibility of the mirror approach and demonstrating the artificiality of seeking to develop human rights damages in isolation from common law damages.

Section 3 questions the robustness of the methodology employed by higher courts to give effect to the mirror approach, and argues that different courts have employed different methodologies—these differences affecting conclusions as to availability of damages—without recognising or offering reasons for such variations. Further, the mirror method imposes significant costs on courts and parties, which are not counterbalanced by any discernible benefits.

Section 4 considers the future of the mirror approach in the light of Delphic judicial pronouncements in the Supreme Court's *Faulkner* decision and Governmental proposals for a British Bill of Rights.

In light of the patent and serious problems with the mirror approach, and the lack of any sound normative justification for such approach, one may come to question whether the higher courts' adoption of and persistence with such flawed approach is based in unstated normative concerns, such as safeguarding government funds.

SECTION 1. THE TERMS OF THE HRA

Aspects of the analysis in *Greenfield* and its progeny are patently inconsistent with the terms of the HRA. In *Greenfield* Lord Bingham considered that there could be 'no clearer indication' than section 8(4) that 'courts in this country should look to Strasbourg and not to domestic precedents'.[22] While that section does direct domestic courts to consider principles applied by the ECtHR, there is nothing in its terms to suggest that this should be to the exclusion of considering English damages law. Section 8(4) requires only that domestic courts 'take into account' the Strasbourg 'principles' in deciding whether to make an award and quantum.[23] The provision makes Strasbourg principles a relevant consideration, not a sole determinative one. This is far from being the clearest indication possible that domestic courts ought solely to look to Strasbourg. As Laws LJ has said, '[t]he expression "take into account" simply does not mean "follow" or "treat as binding" (or something close to it)'—the plain words of the statute 'cannot surely bear such a weight'.[24]

In the subsequent case of *Faulkner* the Supreme Court interpreted Lord Bingham as having 'construed' sections 8(3) and (4) as

> introduc[ing] into our domestic law an entirely novel remedy ... which is described as damages but is not tortious in nature, inspired by article 41 ... Reflecting the international origins of the remedy and its lack of any native roots, the primary source of the principles which are to guide the courts in its application is said to be the practice of the international court that is its native habitat.[25]

This reasoning proceeds in two steps: (1) section 8 introduced an entirely novel remedy into domestic law, of international origin; (2) it is therefore to the international case law that courts must look.

The chain of reasoning breaks down from the off. The only basis for the claim in (1) is given by Lord Bingham in *Greenfield*: section 8(4) directs domestic courts to Strasbourg principles. But this provision in fact tells against the claim that the international remedy has been plucked from its 'native habitat' and transposed into domestic law. To require domestic courts to take principles into account is simultaneously to confer upon courts a liberty, not subject to any constraint in the terms of the Act, to depart from those principles. In other words the very fact that domestic courts are required to take into account Strasbourg principles makes clear that the enterprise of deciding damages claims under the HRA is distinct from the remedial enterprise in which the ECtHR is engaged. If the intent behind the damages provisions was that domestic courts should act as a surrogate

[22] *Greenfield* (n 1) [19].

[23] A point made in *Greenfield* (n 1) [6], but which was of little consequence in deciding the final approach to damages.

[24] J Laws, *The Common Law Constitution* (CUP, 2014) 80. Comments made in the context of discussion of s 2 HRA, but they are equally applicable to the terms of s 8. For judicial decisions endorsing this interpretation see, eg, *Re P* [2009] 1 AC 173, [34], *Doherty v Birmingham CC* [2009] AC 367, [126], and see further those cases cited in nn 77–83 below.

[25] *Faulkner* (n 1) [29].

for the ECtHR, effectively exercising the ECtHR's remedial jurisdiction on the domestic plane, Parliament would have imposed a more prescriptive obligation than to require merely that domestic courts have regard to the general principles applied by the ECtHR; for example, Parliament could have provided that domestic courts are mandated to follow the ECtHR's practice or jurisprudence more generally. With respect, to extrapolate from a provision directing courts to take into account principles applied under Article 41 that Article 41 has been imported into domestic law entails a feat of interpretation.

Neither Lord Bingham nor Lord Reed considered arguments against their construction. For example, if Parliament had intended that the monetary remedy under the HRA should be equivalent to that in international law one would have expected the legislature not to have described the remedy as 'damages', given that term has a specialised meaning in English law; 'compensation', 'monetary award' or simply 'just satisfaction' could have been used to conclusively distinguish the remedy. Other key aspects of the legislative scheme, discussed elsewhere in this book,[26] which support a tort-based approach were not discussed in either decision, including sub-sections (2) and (5). Article 13, which requires Member States to grant effective remedies to victims, and which section 8 was intended to give domestic effect to,[27] was not mentioned in either *Faulkner* or *Greenfield*. This is striking given the long-standing maxim that where a domestic provision is intended to give effect to an international obligation, it ought to be construed so as to ensure compliance with that obligation.

The terms of the statute are clear. The principles adopted by the ECtHR are merely a relevant consideration for a court determining HRA damages claims, and it is not the case that the mirror approach *follows from* or is *mandated* by section 8(4) as *Greenfield* and *Faulkner* suggest.

However, if one thought the Act ambiguous, parliamentary debates on the Human Rights Bill confirm that it was not Parliament's intention that Strasbourg practice be followed doggedly: the then Lord Chancellor posited that 'our courts must be free to try to give a lead to Europe as well as to be led';[28] 'British judges will be enabled to make a distinctively British contribution to the development of the jurisprudence of human rights across Europe'.[29] Indeed, key arguments for incorporation were that 'British judges are denied the opportunity of building a body of case law on the Convention

[26] See chs 3.IV, 6.1.I.

[27] See further s 2 below.

[28] HL Deb vol 583 cols 513–515 (18 November 1997); P Boateng and J Straw 'Bringing Rights Home: Labour's Plans to Incorporate the European Convention on Human Rights into UK Law' [1997] *European Human Rights Law Review* 71, 72.

[29] HC Deb vol 307 col 770 (16 February 1998) Mr Jack Straw; HL vol 582 col 1227 (3 November 1997) Lord Irvine of Lairg.

which is properly sensitive to *British legal and constitutional traditions*'[30] and the HRA would 'give power back to British courts'.[31] In deciding not to incorporate Article 13 the Government emphasised that English courts are 'rich in remedies'[32] and that English remedies law 'is one of the most sophisticated and developed systems in the world'.[33] This suggests that there was an expectation that courts would have at least some recourse to the long-established law of remedies in English law. More recently the two legislators who led the Bill through Parliament reiterated that the Act was never intended to bind domestic courts to Strasbourg practice.[34] Overall, as Burrows argues: '"To bring home" rights might be thought to require that rights are compensated in the way that home regards as appropriate'.[35]

I. PRINCIPLES OR PRACTICE?

It would be one thing for domestic courts to follow faithfully the Strasbourg 'principles'—the term used in section 8(4)—but they have gone much further, effectively treating the ECtHR's Article 41 *jurisprudence* as binding. As the Law Commissions observed, there is a clear conceptual distinction between 'principles' developed by a court and its 'practice' or 'jurisprudence': '"Principles" are normally understood to refer to the basic objectives of the system, as opposed to the application of those principles to assessing damages in individual cases'.[36] One may look to practice to discern an overarching principle which may then be taken into account in domestic decision-making, but this is a different enterprise to seeking to *replicate* a practice. It is the latter approach that characterises the HRA damages jurisprudence; as Lord Reed said in *Faulkner*, the focus is upon the 'ordinary practice'[37] of the ECtHR, his Lordship proceeding to trawl through one ECtHR case after another to discern that practice, so that it could be replicated.

The Supreme Court found a convenient remedy for the incongruity between such approach and the plain terms of section 8: the Court defined 'principles' 'in a broad sense' as 'ordinary practice'.[38] The main explanation

[30] Boateng and Straw (n 28) 72 (emphasis added).

[31] ibid 71. But see the ambivalent statements regarding damages: at 77.

[32] HL Deb vol 583 col 479 (18 November 1997); HL Deb vol 584 col 1266 (19 January 1998) Lord Irvine of Lairg.

[33] HL Deb vol 583 col 477 (18 November 1997) Lord Irvine of Lairg.

[34] Lord Irvine, 'A British Interpretation of Convention Rights' [2012] *PL* 237; J Straw, *Aspects of Law Reform* (CUP, 2013) ch 2.

[35] A Burrows, 'Damages and Rights' in D Nolan and A Robertson (eds), *Rights and Private Law* (Hart Publishing, 2012) 303.

[36] *Damages Under the Human Rights Act 1998*, Law Com 266/Scot Law Com 180 (2000) [4.6]–[4.11] [Law Commissions Report].

[37] (n 1) [36].

[38] ibid [31]–[36].

given was that the ECtHR does not often articulate principles and it may be unsafe to rely on any statements of principle without examining practice, as practice may be inconsistent with such statements; the focus ought therefore to be on 'how the [ECtHR] applies article 41'.[39]

First, in construing section 8(4) in this way Lord Reed gave no consideration to the differences between sections 8(4) and 2(1). While section 8(4) only refers to 'principles', section 2(1) requires domestic courts, in interpreting substantive rights, to 'take into account' any Strasbourg 'judgment, decision, declaration or advisory opinion' on point. If Parliament wished courts to take into account ECtHR *practice* under Article 41 it could have modelled section 8(4) on section 2(1), yet different terms were chosen.[40]

Second, the nature of the jurisprudence under Article 41, rather than supporting imposition of an unnatural meaning on the term 'principles', sheds light on why the legislature might have referred courts to principles rather than practice. A leading work on the European Convention on Human Rights (ECHR) summarises the Article 41 jurisprudence thus:

> The case law under Article 41 ... is characterized by the lack of a consistently applied law of damages at the level of detail which one would find in national systems and which permit specific calculations to be made on the basis of precedent ... The Court applies a series of general principles ... to the facts of each case.[41]

From this one can understand the drafting of section 8(4). Domestic courts are not directed to ECtHR practice because that practice is unsatisfactory, not being characterised by a consistently applied and worked-out law of damages. However, while the jurisprudence lacks the detail that characterises English damages law, a small set of general principles permeate the jurisprudence, such as *restitutio in integrum* and factual causation. It makes perfect sense that the legislature would not refer domestic courts to a troubled practice but rather to readily discernible and basic overarching principles. In *Faulkner*, Lord Carnwath, writing separately, linked these features of the Strasbourg jurisprudence to the difference in wording between sections 8(4) and 2(1), saying: '[t]he more specific wording of section 8(4) in my view reflects the reality that not all decisions of the Strasbourg court in relation to damages will be determinative, or even illustrative, of any principle of general application'.[42] This is because—as we shall see below—each such decision entails a discretionary, equitable response to the facts of the

[39] ibid [31].

[40] See *KB* (n 5) [22] (the difference in drafting may indicate that 'Parliament ... wanted the UK court to have somewhat greater freedom in relation to decisions of the European Court on the amount of damages awarded in particular cases, quantum normally being a matter for the forum').

[41] D Harris et al, *Law of the European Convention on Human Rights* 3rd edn (OUP, 2014) 155; see also *Anufrijeva* (n 5) [59]–[60].

[42] (n 1) [113].

case rather than application of a worked-out set of detailed rules.[43] Lord Carnwath's recognition of the nature of Strasbourg practice led him to a view—contrary to the majority—more faithful to the plain terms of section 8: domestic courts should be guided by general principles clearly enunciated by the ECtHR rather than seeking to mirror practice not based in a worked-out law of damages.[44]

More generally, if Strasbourg jurisprudence is characterised by certain oft-repeated, basic principles, such as causation, but particular cases deviate from such principle, it is not clear why a court should prioritise practice, when the statute directs them specifically to principles. Further, it is in the nature of a principle that it is not always followed; a principle is a guide not a prescriptive rule. Thus, deviation from a principle does not necessarily cast doubt on its existence.

Third, Lord Reed's analysis is based upon an erroneous premise. A key reason given for imposing an unnatural meaning upon 'principles' is that the ECtHR does not often articulate statements of principle. The concern appears to be that an approach that entailed solely looking to Strasbourg would be unworkable if courts were restricted to considering only *genuine* principles, because these are few. But lack of genuine principles is only concerning if one accepts the premise—erroneous for reasons given above—that courts may only look to Strasbourg.

Fourth, the great irony of treating 'practice' as 'principle' is that *genuine* Strasbourg principles are side-lined. For example in *Greenfield* Lord Bingham observed that the ECtHR seldom made awards for non-pecuniary loss for particular breaches of Article 6, as the Court is not often satisfied of a causative link between claimed loss and the rights-violation.[45] Going by the plain terms of section 8(4) one would expect domestic courts to take into account the basic principle of causation in deciding whether to make an award in similar cases. This was not Lord Bingham's approach. Rather, he signalled that domestic courts should follow the ECtHR's *ordinary practice*,[46] which his Lordship saw as being that awards should rarely be made, except where a case has some 'special feature … which warrants an award'.[47] Not only does this ignore the principle applied by the ECtHR, it enunciates a principle distinct and at variance from that applied by the ECtHR: while the ECtHR applies a principle of causation, domestic courts determine such claims according to the principle that awards should be rare. This illustrates the extent to which higher courts have distorted the plain meaning of the HRA damages provisions.

[43] ibid [105].
[44] ibid [113]–[114].
[45] (n 1) [11], [16].
[46] ibid [16], [26]. See also *Faulkner* (n 1) [36].
[47] ibid [29].

A. Quantum

Lord Bingham's dicta, in *Greenfield*, on quantum are worth considering in a little more detail. His Lordship rejected the appellant's argument that 'the levels of Strasbourg awards are not "principles" applied by the court' on the basis that it involved a 'legalistic distinction', and that it was 'contradicted by the White Paper and the language of section 8'.[48] As a result domestic courts, in setting quantum, must look to the ECtHR's 'practice in relation to the level of awards in different circumstances';[49] 'section 8(4) … merely means that courts should aim to pitch their awards at the general levels indicated by Strasbourg awards in comparable cases, so far as that can be estimated'.[50]

With respect, the distinction between 'scales' or 'levels', which represent the ECtHR's *practice* as to quantum, and 'principles' which frame how the court approaches determination of quantum, is conceptually sound and not pedantic. It is not apparent how statutory language undermines the appellant's argument. Section 8(4) expressly refers to 'principles' as opposed to 'practice', 'scales', 'quanta' or 'levels of awards'. And even if the Act did include one such formulation, Strasbourg levels would not be binding; they would only need to be taken into account. On the other hand the White Paper does provide some support for Lord Bingham's view. It says:

> The Bill provides that, in considering an award of damages on Convention grounds, the courts are to take into account the principles applied by the [ECtHR] in awarding compensation, *so that people will be able to receive compensation from a domestic court equivalent to what they would have received in Strasbourg*.[51]

However, the Law Commissions felt that this statement should not be taken 'too literally'.[52] Furthermore, when it comes to statutory interpretation, '[t]he text is the law, and it is the text that must be observed'.[53] The text of section 8(4) is unambiguous. If Parliament wished domestic courts to hitch domestic scales to those applied at Strasbourg it would have expressly prescribed this. It did not.

Another reason given by Lord Bingham for rejecting the applicant's argument that scales do not constitute principles, was that 'principle' has 'little application' 'in a decision on … quantum';[54] in other words, it would be

[48] ibid [19].
[49] *Faulkner* (n 1) [31].
[50] ibid [35].
[51] White Paper (n 2) [2.6] (emphasis added).
[52] Law Commissions Report (n 36) [4.4].
[53] A Scalia, *A Matter of Interpretation* (Princeton, 1997) 22. In the parliamentary debates on the remedial provisions of the Human Rights Bill Jack Straw, the then Home Secretary, expressed a similar view: 'I have always taken the view that what Parliament passes is not what Ministers say, but what is on the face of the Bill' (HC Deb vol 312 col 987 (20 May 1998)).
[54] *Greenfield* (n 1) [19].

difficult to see how section 8(4) regulates quantum if 'principles' is not interpreted to include scales. However, a cursory glance at the detailed rules and principles governing quantum in English damages law rebuts the idea that principle is irrelevant to quantum.[55] Indeed, statements in *Greenfield* itself reveal that principle is relevant. For example, Lord Bingham referred to the Strasbourg Court's acceptance of the 'principle' of *restitutio in integrum*,[56] and cited the ECtHR's dictum that it is 'well established' that *restitutio in integrum* is 'the *principle* underlying the provision of just satisfaction for a breach of article 6'.[57] This is a principle which plainly governs quantum: each award is a product of application of this principle, being the amount necessary to restore the victim to a position as if the wrong had not occurred.

As in the context of deciding whether to make awards, the courts' treatment of practice as principle has led to *genuine* Strasbourg principles, such as *restitutio in integrum*, being side-lined and abrogated. Thus in *Faulkner*, Lord Reed, having surveyed multiple Strasbourg cases, discerned that awards for distress in Article 5(4) cases have often been 'modest'. According to the interpretation of section 8(4) adopted by the Court this summary statement of practice is a principle.[58] But, of course, the relatively modest levels of awards are not principles in any ordinary sense of that word but rather the product of application of a general principle, namely *restitutio in integrum*, to those cases that happen to have come to the ECtHR; if the circumstances of the majority of those cases had been more traumatic, awards may very well have been higher in general, to reflect greater losses (even if still low relative to domestic levels). However, *restitutio in integrum* is never mentioned in *Faulkner* despite being the ECtHR's central principle. The result is likely to be under-compensation in more serious cases as lower courts concentrate on ensuring awards are small, and lose sight of the principle that quantum must be sufficient to make the victim whole, given the degree of loss suffered. As other judges have observed, prescriptions that awards should be low do not really assist, given the court's task is to calibrate quantum to the degree of injury in fact suffered so that the award is sufficient compensation.[59]

II. A SECTION 2(1) ANALOGY?

We have already observed the material difference in legislative drafting between sections 8(4) and 2(1). Despite this, Lord Reed, giving the lead

[55] See chs 2.III, 3.II, III.

[56] *Greenfield* (n 1) [10]; see also, eg, *Bernard* (n 5) [42]; *Breyer Group Plc v Department of Energy and Climate Change* [2014] JPL 1346, [152].

[57] *Kingsley v UK* (2002) 35 EHRR 10, [40] (emphasis added), cited in *Greenfield* (n 1) [10].

[58] *Faulkner* (n 1) [13](14), [68].

[59] *Taunoa v Attorney-General* [2008] 1 NZLR 429, [109].

judgment in *Faulkner*, aligned the general approach to Strasbourg jurisprudence under the two provisions. The starting point of this approach is that the domestic 'court should follow any clear and constant jurisprudence of the European court'.[60] Lord Reed did not address the differences in drafting between sections 2 and 8.

On top of the material drafting differences, there are further good reasons why it is inappropriate to read across to section 8 the approach applied under section 2.

The 'clear and consistent' test is not viable in the damages context. Where the ECtHR finds violation of a *substantive right* it typically recalls articulated rules and principles governing that right, as established in previous case law, and reasons according to those norms to a conclusion as to compliance.[61] It gives substantial reasons, in the knowledge that such determinations afford important guidance to Member States which are bound to comply with rights-guarantees, while determination of these substantive rights-issues is the Court's central function (see further section 2.I.B below). A search for clear and consistent jurisprudence is therefore likely to bear some fruit. The ECtHR's approach to *Article 41* is markedly different. It adopts a discretionary, case-by-case approach, determining whether to make awards and quantum according to what would be 'equitable' on the facts: 'most of the decisions are not intended to have precedential effect, and it is a mistake ... to treat them as if they were',[62] such decisions being 'little more than equitable assessments of the facts of the individual case'.[63] Few if any reasons are typically given by the Court for why awards are made or refused while there is seldom any reasoned justification of quantum.[64] Therefore, the search for clear and consistent jurisprudence is misplaced; indeed it is difficult to view a set of discretionary, case-by-case determinations as constituting a 'jurisprudence' as such.

Importantly, core justifications for adopting the 'clear and constant' test in adjudication of *substantive rights* have little or no relevance in the *damages* context.[65]

The main justification[66] for taking the ECtHR's interpretation of Convention rights as the default interpretation of rights under the HRA is the

[60] *Faulkner* (n 1) [36] following *R (Alconbury Developments Ltd) v SOS for the Environment, Transport and the Regions* [2003] 2 AC 295, [26].

[61] Even this description of the ECtHR's method in respect of substantive rights adjudication may be somewhat rose-tinted.

[62] *Faulkner* (n 1) [105].

[63] A Lester and D Pannick, *Human Rights Law and Practice* (LexisNexis, 1999) [2.8.4] fn 3, quoted in ibid [108].

[64] See s 2.II below.

[65] The discussion herein may also help to explain the different statutory language as between ss 2 and 8.

[66] The rationales discussed herein derive from the case law. See, eg, *R (Ullah) v Special Adjudicator* [2004] 2 AC 323, [20]; *Re P* (n 24) [35]–[36]; *SOSHD v AF (No 3)* [2010] 2 AC 269, [70]; *R (Al-Skeini) v SOSD* [2008] 1 AC 153, [105]–[106].

practical concern that if domestic courts fail to give effect to the ECtHR's rights-jurisprudence, the consequence will likely be a finding of violation at Strasbourg. This concern is reinforced by the principle that legislation based on an international treaty ought to be construed consistently with that treaty. Linked to the primary practical concern is a concern not to put litigants to the expense of travelling to Strasbourg unnecessarily. Amongst other reasons for faithfully following consistent Strasbourg jurisprudence are the importance of uniform interpretation of the Convention across Member States, and the principle that domestic courts ought to respect decisions of foreign courts decided on the same point.

Whether these concerns justify adoption of a mirror approach under section 2 has been a matter of protracted debate.[67] However, notwithstanding whether such approach is justifiable under section 2, none of these concerns justify domestic courts mirroring the ECtHR's Article 41 jurisprudence under section 8. Principally this is because Article 41 is not a provision addressed to Member States, with which they are required to adhere; the Article solely governs the ECtHR's *own* remedial practice. Article 41 does not appear in Section I of the Convention, entitled 'Rights and Freedoms', which sets out those rights which Member States must secure to everyone in their jurisdiction. Rather, it appears in Section II, entitled 'European Court of Human Rights', which establishes the ECtHR, its institutional structure and procedural machinery. Thus, while a domestic court's decision not to follow ECtHR jurisprudence under Articles 5 or 8 carries the risk that the UK may be found in violation of the Convention, a decision not to follow Article 41 jurisprudence does not carry such risk. The erroneous premise underpinning a mirror approach to damages is reflected in Lord Reed's observation in *Faulkner* that in respect of domestic damages practice it is necessary 'to ensure that our law does not fall short of Convention standards'; neither Article 41 nor the jurisprudence under it entail 'standards' intended to govern the conduct of Member States or which bind Member States.[68]

The argument for uniform treaty interpretation has little relevance given a domestic court's task under section 8 is not to *interpret* Article 41, but rather, in making its own determination as to damages, to *take into account* the principles the ECtHR has developed under Article 41; domestic courts take the Strasbourg principles as they find them. The task of domestic courts means there is no risk of divergent interpretation. For this reason also there may be no argument that by adopting a different approach to monetary relief than the ECtHR domestic courts are challenging the position of the Strasbourg Court as the 'authoritative expounder' of the meaning of the Convention text.[69] Further, uniform interpretation is presumably based

[67] There are too many articles and extra-judicial speeches on the topic to cite here.

[68] *Faulkner* (n 1) [29].

[69] *Ullah* (n 66) [20].

on the concern that human rights standards should not vary across Member States. Article 41 does not set human rights standards. It is far more parochial, addressed 'inwards' rather than 'outwards', to the ECtHR's own remedial practice.

In terms of the principle of respect for foreign judgments decided on the same points, one might argue that the ECtHR under Article 41, and domestic courts under section 8 are determining the same points: what monetary compensation ought to be awarded to a victim? However, they are doing so under distinct provisions framed in different terms; the ECtHR is acting directly pursuant to Article 41, whereas domestic courts are charged with taking into account the principles applied under Article 41 in exercising their own, *distinct* remedial jurisdiction under domestic statute. This contrasts with the position in respect of those Articles, enumerating substantive rights, scheduled to the HRA, which are in identical terms to those in the Convention. Further, as discussed in section 2 below, the ECtHR approaches its remedial task as a subsidiary, supervisory institution whereas domestic courts are charged with primary responsibility for relief, such that there is a convincing argument that the 'points' are not the 'same'.

If there is any jurisprudence which should guide interpretation of section 8 according to the interpretive principle of consistent construction it is that under Article 13.[70] Article 13 is the Article which governs the remedial obligations of Member States, requiring States to provide an effective remedy for rights-violations. Further, section 8 was specifically intended to give effect to *this* Article *not* Article 41. This was made clear in the parliamentary debates on the Human Rights Bill;[71] indeed, it was because section 8 gave full effect to Article 13 that it was not considered necessary to incorporate Article 13.[72] As Lord Nicholls said in *Re S*, '[t]he object of [sections 7 and 8 of the HRA] is to provide in English law the very remedy Art 13 declares is the entitlement of everyone whose rights are violated',[73] this view being oft-repeated by members of the House of Lords.[74] Specifically in respect of damages Lord Rodger in *Somerville* said, '[b]y giving the court power to grant the necessary damages, the law provides the effective remedy for the violation of the victim's Convention rights which article 13 ... requires'.[75] Surprisingly Article 13 was not mentioned in either *Greenfield* or *Faulkner*.

[70] See *Al-Skeini* (n 66) [56]–[57], [147]–[149] (Act should be read so as to give effect to Article 13).

[71] See the following statements by Lord Irvine: HL Deb vol 583 cols 475–81 (18 November 1997); HL Deb vol 584 cols 1265–68 (19 January 1998); HL Deb vol 585 cols 384–85 (29 January 1998).

[72] ibid. See also HL Deb vol 582 col 1308 (3 November 1997) Lord Williams of Mostyn.

[73] *Re S* [2002] 2 AC 291, [61].

[74] eg *R v Kansal (No 2)* [2002] 2 AC 69, [70]; *Brown v Stott* [2003] 1 AC 681, 715; *Re Attorney General's Reference (No 2 of 2001)* [2004] 2 AC 72, [175].

[75] *Somerville v Scottish Ministers* [2007] 1 WLR 2734, [131]

Whereas the main rationale for adoption of the mirror approach is to avoid running afoul of Convention requirements, as Feldman observes, '[t]oo great a concentration on Article 41 may make [it] impossible in some cases' for domestic courts to comply with Article 13.[76] As discussed further below, this is because the ECtHR's approach under Article 41 is that of a supranational, subsidiary, supervisory body, and does not represent a model for domestic courts to follow in fulfilling the UK's obligations under Article 13.

It is important to observe that even under section 2 HRA the courts have signalled a move away from strict adherence to Strasbourg jurisprudence, such that a stronger variant of the mirror approach is applied under section 8 than section 2, despite the case for a mirror approach being far weaker under section 8. For example, in *Re P* Lord Hoffmann, while noting that there are good reasons for following the ECtHR's interpretation of rights, said that the direction in section 2(1) that domestic courts 'take into account' Strasbourg decisions

> makes it clear that the United Kingdom courts are not bound by such decisions; their first duty is to give effect to the domestic statute according to what they consider to be its proper meaning, even if its provisions are in the same language as the international instrument which is interpreted in Strasbourg.[77]

In the same case Lord Hope observed that the 'Strasbourg jurisprudence is not to be treated as a straightjacket from which there is no escape'.[78] In *Rabone* Lord Mance said '[w]e are required to "take account of" the case-law of the European Court of Human Rights—no less but no more'.[79] Lord Brown, in the same case, indicated that domestic courts should not feel 'driven' by Strasbourg jurisprudence to 'unwillingly' decide a question a particular way unless the jurisprudence *compelled* such result, this high threshold indicating a wide margin for domestic courts to chart their own course.[80] In *Pinnock* Lord Neuberger said that the Supreme Court 'is not bound to follow every decision of the EurCtHR'.[81] His judgment also evinced a concern not to undermine basic features of English law, indicating that even clear and constant ECtHR jurisprudence could be departed from where it cut across substantive or procedural domestic law 'in some fundamental way'.[82] Given this specific concern, and the increased willingness of domestic courts to forge their own path under the Act, it is odd then that

[76] D Feldman, 'Remedies for Violations of Convention Rights' in D Feldman (ed), *English Public Law* 2nd edn (OUP, 2009) [19.42].

[77] (n 24) [34].

[78] ibid [50].

[79] *Rabone* (n 1) [123].

[80] ibid [112].

[81] *Manchester City Council v Pinnock* [2011] 2 AC 104, [48]–[49]. See also, eg, *R v Horncastle* [2010] 2 WLR 47; *R (Chester) v SOSJ* [2014] 1 AC 271; *R (Nicklinson) v MOJ* [2015] AC 657.

[82] *Pinnock* ibid [49]; see also *Horncastle* ibid [11]; *Chester* ibid [25]–[27], [120]–[124].

under section 8 the courts have departed radically from the long-standing English approach to award and quantification of money relief for wrongful interference with basic interests, and dogmatically sought to replicate Strasbourg remedial practice.

Lastly, given sections 8(4) and 2(1) both require courts to take Strasbourg material 'into account', and that the arguments for a mirror approach are far stronger in respect of section 2, it is rather difficult to reconcile (i) the propositions in *Faulkner* that section 8(4) effectively imports the international remedy and that domestic courts must mechanistically replicate Strasbourg remedial practice; with (ii) the prevailing judicial view that substantive rights under the Act are 'domestic and not international rights', and that pursuant to section 2 'UK judges' must 'ultimately ... form their own view as to whether or not there is an infringement of Convention right for domestic purposes'.[83] This variation of approach is perplexing.

III. THE 'ORDINARY' APPROACH

Section 8(4) does not mandate a mirror approach, while the provision has been given a tenuous interpretation which cannot sustain the mirror approach; the provision cannot bear the weight placed on it by the higher judiciary. Importantly that provision, given its natural meaning, does not bar adoption of a principally common-law-based approach to damages, as long as domestic courts have regard—as they are required to—to what broad principles can be divined from the Strasbourg jurisprudence.[84] The central principle at common law and at Strasbourg[85] is the same, at least in regard to compensatory damages: *restitutio in integrum*. Given the general lack of detailed rules in the Strasbourg material, the elaborate rules and principles developed at common law could be drawn on to fill the gap within the rubric of such overarching principles. The foregoing analysis also suggests that a domestic court has freedom to set awards at domestic tort levels given section 8(4) does not, on its plain meaning, address levels of awards, let alone bind domestic courts to Strasbourg levels. Indeed, not only does the Act not bar an approach to damages which takes common law principle and scales as its starting point, as we saw in chapter 3,[86] the terms of the Act provide some positive support for such approach. Further,

[83] *Nicklinson* (n 81) [71]ff.

[84] The Law Commissions came to a similar conclusion in their report on HRA damages: (n 36) [4.11].

[85] *Kingsley* (n 57) [40]; *Hobbs v UK* (2007) 44 EHRR 54, [67]; Law Commissions Report [3.19]–[3.21], [4.14]; LG Loucaides, 'Reparation for Violations of Human Rights under the European Convention and Restitutio in Integrum' [2008] *European Human Rights Law Review* 182.

[86] See ch 3.IV.

there is a strong normative argument for a tort-based approach, whereas the normative justification for the mirror approach is plunged into doubt once we recognise that such approach does not follow necessarily from the terms of the Act.

In *Faulkner* Lord Reed observed that the approach to damages under section 8

> differs from the ordinary approach to the relationship between domestic law and the Convention, according to which the courts endeavour to apply (and, if need be, develop) the common law, and interpret and apply statutory provisions, so as to arrive at a result which is in compliance with the UK's international obligations; the starting point being our own legal principles rather than the judgments of an international court.[87]

This 'ordinary' approach is consonant with that just outlined: the English law of damages would provide the starting point in determining damages claims, while courts would take account of those broad principles that could be divined from Article 41 jurisprudence (applying section 8(4)), and also Article 13. The ordinary approach is consonant with views expressed in early damages decisions: in *Cullen* Lord Millett, having noted the problematic nature of the Strasbourg jurisprudence, said: 'we may have to develop our own jurisprudence, while keeping an eye open on the case law of the Strasbourg court to ensure that we do not stray too far from the principles which that court may lay down'.[88] It is also analogous to the approach Irish courts have adopted under the European Convention on Human Rights Act 2003, which sets out a statutory framework governing damages not dissimilar to that under the HRA.[89]

If this is the 'ordinary' approach then one would expect good reasons for deviating from it. Justification cannot lie in section 8, given the ordinary approach is perfectly consonant with that provision. And, for reasons discussed, it cannot lie in an argument that the approach to Strasbourg jurisprudence ought to be consistent across sections 2 and 8. In any case, in the post-*Faulkner* decision in *Osborn* Lord Reed, consistent with the more general trend away from the mirror approach under section 2, signalled that the 'ordinary approach' was the correct approach to questions concerning *substantive rights*:

> [The HRA does not] supersede the protection of human rights under the common law or statute, *or create a discrete body of law based upon the judgments of the*

[87] *Faulkner* (n 1) [29]. See also, eg, *Osborn* (n 1) [54]ff; *Kennedy v Charity Commission* [2015] AC 455, [46] ('the natural starting point in any dispute is to start with domestic law, and it is certainly not to focus exclusively on the Convention rights, without surveying the wider common law scene').

[88] *Cullen v Chief Constable Royal Ulster Constabulary* [2003] 1 WLR 1763, [80].

[89] See particularly ss 3 and 4 of the Act and *Pullen v Dublin CC* [2009] IEHC 452; see further ch 3.IV.B.

> *European court*. Human rights continue to be protected by our domestic law, interpreted and developed in accordance with the Act *when appropriate*.[90]

He continued, '*the starting point [is] our own legal principles*'.[91] If the ordinary approach is that taken to adjudication of substantive rights, then it is not clear what the normative basis is for taking the inverse approach to damages.

SECTION 2. THE SUPRANATIONAL DIMENSION

I. SUPRANATIONAL VERSUS DOMESTIC CONTEXT

There is no requirement in international law that domestic courts follow the Article 41 jurisprudence. On a normative level, the Strasbourg Court's approach to relief under Article 41 does not provide an appropriate model for human rights damages in domestic law. In the absence of statutory terms mandating the mirror approach, such approach ought to be rejected as without normative basis.

A. No Strasbourg Imperative

There is no obligation on Member States to follow the ECtHR's Article 41 jurisprudence. This is because Article 41 governs *the ECtHR's* remedial jurisdiction, not the remedial responsibilities of Member States.

However, Member States are under remedial obligations pursuant to Article 13, and the ECtHR has developed a substantial jurisprudence under that provision, which is distinct from that under Article 41. The Article 13 jurisprudence does not entail prescriptions as to the precise scales states ought to apply or detailed rules which domestic courts must employ when assessing compensation. Rather, the jurisprudence articulates a framework of minimum standards, including that awards ought not to be so low as to undermine effective protection, that remedies must be effective in practice as well as in principle, and that both pecuniary and preventive remedies ought to be available.[92] Within that basic framework domestic courts have 'discretion'[93] to organise remedies consistently with their own traditions. This approach is not dissimilar to that taken within EU law: Member States may organise remedies for breaches of EU law according to their own

[90] *Osborn* (n 1) [57] (emphasis added).
[91] ibid [67] (emphasis added).
[92] See ch 6.1.II; Council of Europe Directorate-General (Human Rights and Rule of Law), *Guide to Good Practice in Respect of Domestic Remedies* (2013).
[93] *Cocchiarella v Italy* (26 March 2006) App no 64886/01, [79]–[80] (GC).

traditions, subject to basic requirements that the remedial approach ought not to render exercise of EU rights impossible or excessively difficult, and/or afford EU rights less protection than equivalent rights in domestic law.[94] The approach is also consonant with the position in private international law, that remedies are quintessentially for the forum.[95]

Under Article 13 the Grand Chamber has emphasised, specifically in regard to compensation, that it is open to a Member State 'to organise the remedy in a manner consistent with its own legal system and traditions and consonant with the standard of living in the country concerned' and stated that domestic approaches may legitimately deviate from the ECtHR's own remedial practice.[96] Indeed, the Court envisions that rather than following Article 41 practice it is open to and would be 'easier for the domestic courts to refer to the amounts awarded at domestic level for other types of damage', including 'personal injury, damage relating to a relative's death or damage in defamation cases'.[97] Similarly, where the Court has held, pursuant to Article 46, that it is incumbent on domestic institutions to take general and/or individual measures to effect *restitutio in integrum*, it has emphasised that as long as this general principle is adhered to and remedies are effective, domestic institutions are free to choose the manner in which they afford redress.[98] This has included situations where those measures are likely to include monetary relief; in such cases the Court has not sought to pre-empt how such awards are calculated or quantum.[99] Reflecting the degree to which organisation of remedies, and particularly assessment of monetary awards, is viewed as properly for domestic institutions, there have been high-level proposals (not so far implemented) that where the ECtHR finds a violation and determines compensation should be awarded, assessment ought as a 'general rule' to be remitted to domestic institutions.[100]

Given the absence of any prescription that Article 41 jurisprudence must be followed, it is rather odd that the Strasbourg Court has been the target of domestic judges' ire at feeling compelled to follow Strasbourg's remedial approach. For example, in *Rabone* Lord Mance was seemingly frustrated

[94] See generally A Arnull, 'The Principle of Effective Judicial Protection in EU Law: An Unruly Horse?' (2011) 36 *EL Rev* 51; M Dougan, 'The Vicissitudes of Life at the Coalface: Remedies and Procedures for Enforcing Union Law Before the National Courts' in P Craig and G de de Búrca (eds), *The Evolution of EU Law* 2nd edn (OUP, 2011).

[95] eg *Iraqi Civilians v MOD* [2014] EWHC 3686; *KB* (n 5) [22].

[96] *Scordino v Italy (No 1)* (2007) 45 EHRR 7, [188]–[189]; *Cocchiarella* (n 93) [79]–[80]; *Burdov v Russia (No 2)* (15 January 2009) App no 33509/04, [99] (ECtHR First Section).

[97] *Scordino* ibid.

[98] eg *Assanidze v Georgia* (2004) 39 EHRR 32, [198], [202].

[99] eg *Kuric v Slovenia* (2013) 56 EHRR 20, [406]–[415]; *Bittó v Slovenia* (28 January 2014) App no 30255/09, [135] (ECtHR Third Section).

[100] *Report of the Wise Persons to the Committee of Ministers*, CM(2006)203 (15 November 2006) [94]–[99]. See also Commission on a Bill of Rights, *A UK Bill of Rights? The Choice Before Us, Vol 1* (2012) [11.6], [11.13].

at what he perceived to be the Strasbourg Court's overzealous interference with the domestic order, saying:

> [The ECtHR] could have left it to national systems, in the event of any failure by state authorities to address such a risk [to life under Article 2], to recognise a range of victims *and to provide compensation consistent with their ordinary law of tort* ... But that is not how the Convention has been interpreted.[101]

This criticism, as it applies to compensation, is misdirected. It is the House of Lords, through *Greenfield*, sustained by Supreme Court decisions in *Faulkner* and *Rabone* itself, which have tied the domestic approach to Article 41 practice. The Strasbourg Court has *explicitly* left it open to domestic courts to adopt an approach to monetary relief consistent with domestic traditions; indeed, it has suggested that domestic scales applied in torts such as defamation would be an appropriate comparator.

B. The Subsidiary Role of the European Court of Human Rights

The mirror approach is not required by the Convention. In addition, the ECtHR's approach under Article 41 does not offer an appropriate remedial model for domestic law.

The ECtHR grants monetary compensation under Article 41 to afford 'just satisfaction', whereas states parties are charged with affording victims an 'effective remedy' under Article 13. When the ECtHR makes an award under Article 41 it does not purport to be granting the effective remedy which it is the obligation of the Member State to afford the applicant, but is rather exercising its own distinct remedial jurisdiction.

Importantly, the Strasbourg Court exercises that remedial jurisdiction according to the principle of subsidiarity, which holds that the protection of rights and provision of remedies is first and foremost the responsibility of domestic institutions and that the Court acts only in a secondary, supervisory role:[102] 'It is fundamental to the machinery of protection established by the Convention that the national systems themselves provide redress for breaches of its provisions, with the Court exercising a supervisory role *subject to* the principle of subsidiarity';[103] the Court emphasises that it 'cannot, and must not, usurp' the primary role of domestic institutions.[104]

[101] *Rabone* (n 1) [121] (emphasis added).

[102] ECHR, Protocol 15, art 1 (not yet in force); *McFarlane v Ireland* (2011) 52 EHRR 20, [112]; *Gross v Switzerland* (2014) 58 EHRR 7, [68]; *Papamichalopoulos v Greece* (1996) 21 EHRR 439, [34] ('If the nature of the breach allows of restitutio in integrum, it is for the respondent State to effect it, the Court having neither the power nor the practical possibility of doing so itself'); *Salah v Netherlands* (2007) 44 EHRR 55, [70]; *Scordino* (n 96) [179], [247]; *Handyside v UK* (1979–80) 1 EHRR 737, [48]–[50]; *Z v UK* (2002) 34 EHRR 3, [103].

[103] *A* (n 13) [174] (emphasis added).

[104] *Gough v UK* (2015) 61 EHRR 8, [137].

What constitutes just satisfaction at the supranational level, afforded by a supervisory and subsidiary institution, will naturally and legitimately differ from what constitutes effective redress provided by domestic institutions with principal responsibility for redress.[105] The Court has said that its role in provision of relief is not analogous to that of domestic courts: 'Article 41 ... does not provide a mechanism for compensation in a manner comparable to domestic court systems';[106] 'it is not [the Court's] role under art 41 to function akin to a domestic tort mechanism court [sic] in apportioning fault and compensatory damages between civil parties'.[107] The Grand Chamber says: '[i]t is primordial that the machinery of protection established by the Convention is subsidiary to the national systems safeguarding human rights' and the Court

> *cannot emphasise enough* that it is not a court of first instance; it does not have the capacity, nor is it appropriate to its function as an international court, to adjudicate on large numbers of cases which require the finding of basic facts or the calculation of monetary compensation—both of which should, as a matter of principle and effective practice, be the domain of domestic jurisdictions.[108]

As such, '[t]he [ECtHR] is not the usual forum for ordering compensation in respect of human rights violations; that is a question for national courts'.[109]

That the ECtHR's remedial function is subsidiary to and not comparable to that of domestic courts is made clear by Article 41 itself. It provides that the ECtHR may only make an award if domestic law 'allows only partial reparation to be made'. In this respect commentators observe that the reference to Article 41 in section 8(4) HRA is 'curious' given 'Article 41 is, in terms, directed to a situation in which domestic law fails to make adequate provision' for monetary relief.[110] It is also illustrative of the ECtHR's subsidiary position that it may only grant two remedies: a finding that rights have been violated and monetary compensation.[111] It has not traditionally possessed power to grant coercive relief[112]—a judgment of the Court 'cannot

[105] See Feldman (n 76) [19.42].

[106] *Varnava v Turkey* (2010) 50 EHRR 21, [156] [*Varnava* Third Section].

[107] *Al-Jedda v UK* (2011) 53 EHRR 23, [114]; *Varnava v Turkey* (18 September 2009) App no 16064/90, [224] (GC) [*Varnava* GC].

[108] *Demopoulos v Turkey* (1 March 2010) App no 46113/99, [69] (GC) (emphasis added).

[109] C Harlow, *State Liability* (OUP, 2004) 68.

[110] Clayton and Tomlinson (n 15) [21.58].

[111] See Law Commissions Report (n 36) [3.31], where a wealth of authorities are cited. This explains the absence of guidance in the Article 41 jurisprudence as to how monetary and specific remedies ought to interact: *Anufrijeva* (n 5) [60].

[112] But note that this is gradually changing: P Leach, 'No Longer Offering Fine Mantras to a Parched Child? The European Court's Developing Approach to Remedies' in A Føllesdal et al (eds), *Constituting Europe: The European Court of Human Rights in a National, European and Global Context* (CUP, 2013). For example the Court may, pursuant to Article 46, indicate specific and individual measures that it considers the Member State ought to implement at domestic level to, for example, remove the source of ongoing or systemic violations and/or redress the consequences of violations: eg *Stanev v Bulgaria* (2012) 55 EHRR 22, [254]–[258]; *Savriddin Dzhurayev v Russia* (25 April 2013) App no 71386/10, [242]–[264] (ECtHR First Section).

of itself annul or repeal' impugned domestic measures[113]—while it did not even make monetary awards before 1987. As commentators observe,[114] that the Court's role is supervisory partly explains why relief is not available as of right at the supranational level and subject to a wide discretion; satisfaction may not be required if remedial steps have been taken or may be taken by domestic institutions.[115] Contrast the position under Article 13, where it is the *entitlement* of every victim to be afforded an effective remedy by the Member State. This reinforces that the remedial roles of domestic courts and the supranational Court ought not to be conflated.

The Court does not see its task under Article 41 as being to stand in the shoes of a domestic court and grant the remedy that a domestic court would grant. For example, domestic courts may take a tort-based approach to damages for breaches of human rights. However, they may not have extended the damages remedy to a certain type of rights-violation. In turn, the unavailability of damages may constitute violation of Article 13. The ECtHR's response is not to provide the tort-based remedy that domestic courts would have awarded had they recognised that a compensatory award was required. Instead the ECtHR follows its own *sui generis* approach under Article 41.[116] In general the Court does *not* assess compensation 'by reference to the principles or scales of assessment used by domestic courts'.[117] This is not because it disapproves of domestic approaches. Rather, it sees its own role as distinct. This is further illustrated by those exceptional instances where the Court has by necessity been required to function as a court of first instance for repeat claims for compensation arising from some systemic defect in the domestic legal system and for which no effective remedy is available domestically. In such circumstances the ECtHR has expressly stated that it *uplifts* scales under Article 41 so as not to disadvantage applicants relative to awards they could be expected to have received domestically had damages been available.[118] Such practice makes it plain that the Court envisions that its *usual* remedial practice, including ordinary levels of its awards, will be at variance with that appropriate for domestic institutions.

That the Court does not perform a remedial function analogous to domestic courts, is explained by its central concerns, which reflect its position as a supranational court. Those concerns, as the Court increasingly stresses, are setting minimum human rights standards across Europe and monitoring implementation: 'The emphasis is not on providing a mechanism for

[113] *Marckx v Belgium* (1979–80) 2 EHRR 330, [58]; *Selcuk v Turkey* (1998) 26 EHRR 477, [125].

[114] Harris et al (n 41) 157.

[115] *Broniowski v Poland* (2004) 40 EHRR 495, [198].

[116] This example is based on *McFarlane* (n 102).

[117] *Osman v UK* (2000) 29 EHRR 245, [164]; *Beet v UK* (2005) 41 EHRR 441, [46]. The ECtHR may well take domestic scales into account—but they are not decisive: *Z* (n 102) [131].

[118] *Scordino* (n 96) [176].

enriching successful applicants but on [the Court's] role in making public and binding findings of applicable human rights standards'.[119] Whereas the 'trigger' for the Court's consideration of a case is an individual petition, 'the Court serves a purpose beyond the individual interest in the setting and applying of minimum human rights standards for the legal space of the Contracting States. The individual interest is subordinate to the latter';[120] 'The Court is concerned with the supervision of the implementation by Contracting States of their obligations under the Convention'.[121] That the Court has a very different role to domestic courts, focused on international standard-setting, helps to explain why the Court considers that 'the awarding of sums of money to applicants by way of just satisfaction is not one of [its] main duties'.[122]

The ECtHR's ordering of priorities is evident in various features of its practices. It may refuse to make compensatory awards or indeed consider individual cases where there is an ongoing violation and the state has indicated it is taking measures to resolve the violation;[123] the Court's principal concern is not to resolve individual grievances but ensuring implementation of treaty obligations and observance of minimum standards. Whereas an applicant would not normally be required to exhaust a remedy that was not in place at the time of lodging their application, the Court—'[g]iving weight ... to the subsidiary character of its role'—has been increasingly willing to declare applications inadmissible for non-exhaustion of domestic remedies on the basis that the state had introduced a domestic remedy since the application was lodged.[124] Again, this reflects a primary concern for state compliance, and a view that individual redress is first and foremost for domestic institutions. The ordering of priorities—specifically, subordination of individual interests to the wider aim of standard-setting—is also evident in (i) the Court's power to 'continue the examination of an application, even if the applicant no longer wishes to pursue his case' 'where respect for human rights so requires',[125] and (ii) its power to examine an application even though the applicant has not suffered 'significant disadvantage'—as is typically required for an application to be admissible—where 'respect for human rights as defined in the Convention ... requires an examination of

[119] K Reid, *A Practitioner's Guide to the ECHR* (Sweet and Maxwell, 1998) 398, cited by the Law Commissions (n 36) [3.9].

[120] *Varnava* Third Section (n 106) [156].

[121] *Demopoulos* (n 108) [69].

[122] *Salah* (n 102) [70]. Of course, dissenting views have been aired, reflecting different conceptions of the ECtHR's primary role: eg *Kingsley* (n 57) 196–97 (partly dissenting opinion of Judges Casadevall and Kovler) ('Applicants are entitled to something more than a mere moral victory or the satisfaction of having contributed to enriching the Court's case law').

[123] eg *Greens v UK* (2011) 53 EHRR 21, [98], [116]–[122].

[124] *Demopoulos* (n 108) [87]–[88].

[125] ECHR, art 37(1); *Varnava* Third Section (n 106) [156].

the application'.[126] Even where what is 'at stake' for the *individual* applicant is 'considerable', if they have not suffered significant disadvantage the application will be inadmissible if consideration of the application would not 'amplify or contribute to [the Court's relevant] case-law'.[127] Giving further expression to the prioritisation of standard-setting is the Court's long-standing view that its judgments 'are essentially declaratory' in nature, 'leav[ing] to the State the choice of the means to be utilised in its domestic legal system for performance of its [remedial] obligation[s]'.[128] Also, one may observe that the contexts in which the Court has more consistently been willing to make awards include those where there is a systemic failing in the domestic system which the respondent state has omitted to adequately address, the best examples being breaches of Article 6 caused by systemic delays in the court systems of Member States, or where the respondent state is persistently recalcitrant, as in the case of Russia. One reading of such remedial practices is that they are guided by the central priority of securing state compliance: money awards are made so as to incentivise the respondent state to take steps towards compliance or desist from persistent rights-violating behaviour.

Albeit that normative debates continue as to the Court's role,[129] it seems inevitable that the focus on standard-setting and compliance-control will only intensify at the expense of individual redress, as the Court and Member States seek to combat the overwhelming backlog of applications faced by Court;[130] in this respect recent measures, specifically Protocols 14–16, point in only one direction.[131]

C. The Conceptual Nature of Convention Rights: International Law versus Domestic Law

Linked to the different roles of the ECtHR and domestic courts, and just as important in understanding why remedial approaches legitimately vary, is that the basis of liability is arguably different between domestic and international contexts.

The basis of liability in domestic law is breach of individual personal rights.[132] In contrast it is far from clear that this is the basis of liability at

[126] ECHR, art 35(3)(b).

[127] *Heather Moor and Edgecomb Ltd (No 2) v UK* (26 June 2012) App no 30802/11, [25]–[26] (ECtHR Fourth Section).

[128] *Marckx* (n 113) [58].

[129] eg S Greer and L Wildhaber, 'Revisiting the Debate about "Constitutionalizing" the European Court of Human Rights' (2012) 12 *Human Rights Law Review* 655.

[130] See Harris et al (n 41) 38–40.

[131] For discussion of those measures see ibid 165–71.

[132] See ch 4.2.II.A.

the supranational level. That the bases of liability may be distinct further helps to explain the distinctiveness of the ECtHR's remedial approach, and the inaptness of transposing it to the domestic order.

Henkin observes that while human rights treaties 'deal' with and refer to individual rights, there are different perspectives as to whether these treaties *create* individual rights, that is legal rights *in international law* possessed by individuals and correlative to duties owed by states.[133] He outlines three possibilities: (1) the orthodox view that treaties only create rights and duties between states; (2) while creating obligations between states, these treaties may *also* bestow individuals with rights; and (3) states parties as legislators, have legislated human rights into international law as 'affirmative individual values';[134] Henkin says that while this third perspective is independent of the previous two, it might be compatible with either.

In terms of the present discussion, which is concerned with understanding ECtHR remedial practice, the relevant inquiry is not whether there is an intellectual argument that the Convention creates individual rights, but how *the ECtHR* conceptualises the basis of liability under the Convention.

In a canonical statement the ECtHR said: 'the Convention comprises more than mere reciprocal engagements between contracting States. It creates, over and above a network of mutual, bilateral undertakings, objective obligations which, in the words of the Preamble, benefit from a "collective enforcement"'.[135] The description of treaty obligations as 'objective' does not in itself suggest that they are obligations owed to individuals. Indeed, there is an obvious contrast with the idea of 'subjective rights', which are personal and individualistic. The idea of objective obligations would rather suggest a position consonant with Henkin's third perspective, that is, the Convention creates obligations between states parties while also 'enacting' free-standing objective obligations with which Member States must comply. This is similar to Simma's view that human rights treaties legislate into international law free-standing standards of international public policy, which serve the general interest.[136] This explains why, for example, a contracting party may 'require the observance of [Convention] obligations without having to justify an interest deriving, for example, from the fact that a measure they complain of has prejudiced one of their own nationals'.[137] The ECtHR and European Commission have similarly described the Convention as a 'law-making treaty'[138] which establishes a 'common public order of the free

[133] L Henkin, *The Age of Rights* (Columbia, 1990) 34.

[134] ibid 34–37.

[135] *Ireland v UK* (1979–80) 2 EHRR 25, [239].

[136] B Simma, 'From Bilateralism to Community Interest in International Law' (1994) 250 *Recueil des Cours de l'Académie de Droit International* 217, ch V.

[137] ibid 366–67.

[138] *Wemhoff v Germany* (1979–80) 1 EHRR 55, [8].

democracies of Europe'.[139] Such view is further reinforced by the excerpts cited above in which the Court characterises individual applications not as claims of individual right, but as 'triggers' for the Court's jurisdiction. That jurisdiction is not described as entailing adjudication of individuals' *rights*, but rather setting of minimum *standards*; this task transcending individual interests, albeit individuals naturally have an interest in seeing those standards observed.[140] This may be contrasted with the approach of other international human rights bodies, such as the Inter-American Court of Human Rights, which has explicitly spoken in terms of international law obligations owed directly to individuals.[141]

The central obligation on Member States under Article 1 is to 'secure to everyone within their jurisdiction the rights and freedoms defined in Section I of this Convention'. This obligation renders enumerated rights legally relevant.[142] It is clear that this obligation is owed by state parties to one another. It is less clear that the Convention imposes obligations on states owed directly to individuals in international law, correlative to individual rights. The ECtHR's statements on Article 1 suggest it conceptualises that Article as imposing a duty on states parties to implement in domestic law the protections envisioned by the Convention, rather than directly creating rights in international law. For example the Court repeatedly says the 'object and purpose of the Convention, as set out in art 1' is 'that rights and freedoms should be secured by the Contracting State within its jurisdiction',[143] rather than to create individual rights in international law. In similar vein it says that domestic incorporation is a particularly faithful reflection of the intention behind Article 1.[144] Also oft-repeated by the Court is that its role is to supervise 'implementation' of treaty obligations, rather than, say, direct enforcement of individual rights.

The trajectory of these statements is consonant with the plain wording of Article 1: a legal obligation on states to 'secure' rights to those in their jurisdiction suggests a duty of implementation. Such obligation is conceptually distinct from owing a legal obligation to each such person by virtue of their actual holding of rights.

[139] *Austria v Italy* (1961) 4 YBECHR 112 (EComHR); see similarly, *Loizidou v Turkey* (1995) 20 EHRR 99, [75], [93] ('constitutional instrument of European public order ("ordre public")').

[140] Above at nn 120ff.

[141] *The Effect of Reservations on the Entry into Force of the American Convention (Arts 74 and 75)* (24 September 1982) Advisory Opinion OC-2/82, IACHR Series A No 2, [29]; M Carven, 'Legal Differentiation and the Concept of the Human Rights Treaty in International Law' (2000) 11 *European Journal of International Law* 489, 513.

[142] Albeit, *in practice* the Article is not that prominent nor considered to be of great importance: *Ireland v UK* (n 135) [238].

[143] eg *Chagos Islanders v UK* (2013) 56 EHRR SE15, [81].

[144] *Ireland v UK* (n 135) [239].

From the foregoing it is at best unclear that the ECtHR considers the basis for exercise of its remedial jurisdiction to be breach of a duty owed to an individual rights-bearer. In turn this bears on remedies. If the obligation breached is not owed to an individual, then the normative basis and imperative for provision of individual redress is obviously weaker than where the obligation is owed directly to the individual; in these circumstances, where the Court awards monetary compensation to an individual it is *not* on the basis of a personal legal wrong. In turn this may help to explain the Court's cautious approach to money awards, and the Court's greater focus on compliance. These insights also help to explain the absence of an idea within the Article 41 jurisprudence of compensation for damage to the right itself (normative damage), given the obligation breached is not a personal right. Importantly this discussion casts further doubt on the mirror approach: it is difficult to see how the approach of a subsidiary, supervisory international court to provision of satisfaction to an individual harmed in consequence of a breach of a duty not owed to that individual is an apt model for a domestic court with primary responsibility for provision of redress to an individual who has suffered a personal wrong in domestic law.

To the foregoing we may add that Article 41 has its origin in clauses in classic-style arbitration treaties which provided for settlement of disputes *between states*.[145] Such clauses empowered an arbitral tribunal to award 'equitable satisfaction' where it found that a domestic measure enjoining one of the parties to the arbitration was wholly or partly contrary to international law but domestic law did not allow annulment of the consequences of the measure. It is difficult to envision how awards made under a clause with such lineage could provide a sound model for provision of awards by domestic courts for breaches of fundamental personal rights in municipal law.

D. The Supranational Context

There are wider contextual considerations, specific to the supranational plane, which further indicate that the ECtHR's remedial approach is inappropriate for transplantation into domestic law.

These wider considerations further help to explain the Strasbourg Court's cautious approach to awards and the modesty of awards. If the Court routinely ordered Member States to pay substantial compensation and/or awarded aggravated and/or punitive damages, it could compromise its political legitimacy and the goodwill of Member States on which the entire

[145] See, eg, *De Wilde v Belgium (No 2)* (1979–80) 1 EHRR 438; German Swiss Treaty on Arbitration and Conciliation 1921, art 10; Geneva General Act for the Pacific Settlement of International Disputes 1928, art 32.

supranational system depends, and which have been fostered carefully by the Court over the last half-century.[146] Even putting aside liabilities to pay money awards Member States have exposed themselves to significant 'burdens' within and ceded a fair degree of sovereign control to the European human rights system, especially compared to the lighter burdens typically associated with Treaty regimes;[147] states have accepted the jurisdiction of a supranational court which issues legally binding judgments, backed by strong enforcement machinery led by the Committee of Ministers, as well as accepting rights of individual and state petition. It is therefore unsurprising that the Court is reluctant to impose further burdens in the form of regular and substantial money awards and that the Court refused to make any monetary awards during its first few decades.

Against this backdrop, it is unsurprising that Shelton has observed 'a clear concern for the reaction of governments' in the Court's decisions on just satisfaction.[148] She quotes a former judge of the Court as saying, a 'parsimonious' approach is warranted because 'one mistake and the whole system collapses'.[149] Fear of Member States ignoring judgments or even withdrawing from the Convention looms large. Consider an issue such as prisoner voting.[150] The ECtHR's finding[151] that the UK ban on prisoner voting violated the Convention has caused a great deal of consternation among UK politicians, the Prime Minister sharing that he felt 'physically ill' at the idea of giving prisoners the vote, while there have been increasing calls for withdrawal from the Convention in the wake of this litigation (amongst other ECtHR rulings). If the ECtHR's ruling was coupled with substantial monetary awards to prisoners, the ire of domestic politicians would only have been raised even further. It is not surprising therefore that the ECtHR, in follow-up applications by UK prisoners, has consistently refused to make awards, despite the UK still not having implemented the original 2005 ruling.[152]

[146] LR Helfer and AM Slaughter, 'Toward a Theory of Effective Supranational Adjudication' (1997) 107 *Yale Law Journal* 273, 316–17, discussing how the ECtHR's awareness of political boundaries and incremental approach has been a key determinant of its success. In respect of the ECtHR's gradual expansion of its power to award compensation see, eg, Harlow (n 109) 68ff.

[147] For example, in *Golder v UK* (1979–80) 1 EHRR 524 Judge Fitzmaurice observed (at [38] of his separate opinion) that the Convention had 'broken entirely new ground internationally, making heavy inroads on some of the most cherished preserves of governments in the sphere of their domestic jurisdiction'.

[148] D Shelton, *Remedies in International Human Rights Law* 2nd edn (OUP, 2005) 259; Leach (n 112) 145.

[149] Shelton, ibid.

[150] For analysis of this saga see: E Bates, 'Analysing the Prisoner Voting Saga and the British Challenge to Strasbourg' (2014) 14 *Human Rights Law Review* 504.

[151] *Hirst v UK* (2006) 42 EHRR 41.

[152] *Greens* (n 123) [94]–[98]; *Firth v UK* (12 August 2014) App no 47784/09, [17]–[18] (ECtHR Fourth Section); *McHugh v UK* (10 February 2015) App no 51987/08, [12]–[17] (ECtHR Fourth Section).

In addition, there are significant wealth disparities between Member States. This makes it difficult for the Court to, for example, raise levels of awards across the board, or for it to impose liability for monetary awards with the regularity of a domestic court. In deciding upon quantum the Court has regard to the standard of living in the defendant state, such that awards against the UK may be higher than those against Turkey.[153] In *Faulkner* the Supreme Court held that in assessing quantum English courts should only have regard to awards made against the UK or states with similar costs of living.[154] However, if English courts wanted to calibrate awards to English conditions it is unclear why awards have not been calibrated to domestic scales.[155] Also, the Court in *Faulkner* neglected the wider contextual and other reasons which have been traversed above, which serve to explain why Strasbourg levels of awards are low *in general* compared to domestic law.

E. The English Courts' (Lack of) Consideration of the Distinctiveness of Supranational Context

In light of the foregoing Lord Bingham's observation in *Greenfield* that 'the focus of the Convention is on the protection of human rights and not the award of compensation' does not take one far in the domestic context.[156] Similarly, in *Faulkner* Lord Reed observed that the ECtHR 'has not regarded the award of just satisfaction as its principal concern'.[157] In both decisions their Lordships made these statements in the course of elaborating the nature of the approach that was being read across to domestic law. In neither case did their Lordships pause to consider that the ECtHR's ordering of priorities follows from the distinctive context within which it operates and its role as a supranational court, such that its remedial practice is neither apt for nor intended for importation. Nor did their Lordships refer to any statements made by the ECtHR explaining the differing remedial responsibilities of that Court and domestic institutions.

Other distinctive features of the ECtHR's approach have similarly been noted by English courts but not led to more general reflection upon the mirror approach. For example, Lord Reed in *Faulkner* observed that the ECtHR does not undertake detailed fact-finding. His response was that domestic

[153] *ECtHR Practice Direction: Justice Satisfaction Claims* (28 March 2007) [2]–[3] (http://www.echr.coe.int/Documents/PD_satisfaction_claims_ENG.pdf); Harris et al (n 41) 156.

[154] (n 1) [38]–[40].

[155] Rather unsurprisingly scales in English tort law are calibrated to domestic conditions: eg *Heil v Rankin* [2001] QB 272, [38].

[156] (n 1) [9]. In any case, is award of compensation not one means of protecting rights?

[157] (n 1) [34].

courts ought to resolve disputed questions of fact in the ordinary way even if the ECtHR would, in similar circumstances, not do so.[158] This is a welcome tweak to a flawed approach. However, Lord Reed did not pause to consider that this feature of the ECtHR's approach, like many others, reflects that the ECtHR does not function as a domestic court, which in turn casts doubt on the appropriateness of following its remedial practices in general.

For example, fundamental features of the ECtHR's practice are shaped by its lack of fact-finding capacity, yet these features have been mechanically read into domestic law. In *Greenfield* Lord Bingham observed that in Article 41 decisions on pecuniary loss suffered in consequence of breach of Article 6, '[i]t is enough to say that the court has looked for a causal connection, and has on the whole been slow to award such compensation';[159] under the mirror approach this is 'practice' that will guide domestic courts, such that domestic courts will be slow to make awards. However, there was no consideration of whether the rarity of awards might be due to causation being heavily fact-dependent such that it would be difficult for the ECtHR to find a 'clear causal link'[160] absent hearing and testing evidence, which that Court generally does not do. As the ECtHR has said itself, it 'is acutely aware of its own shortcomings as a first instance tribunal of fact';[161] it does not have the capacity to and nor would it be appropriate for it to routinely undertake detailed fact-finding in connection with claims of compensation as if it were a first-instance court;[162] and 'domestic authorities or courts are clearly in a better position than the Court to determine the existence and quantum of pecuniary damage'.[163]

Similarly, where the ECtHR awards compensation for non-pecuniary loss such as mental distress it does not typically have evidence of actual suffering, nor evidence as to the precise factual circumstances of the violation. That it cannot be sure whether loss has in fact been suffered and does not have a firm basis for making reliable factual inferences, may further help[164] to explain its cautious approach to compensation for mental distress, confining awards to cases of 'evident trauma',[165] and those entailing more serious violations, presumably on the basis that it is safer to assume loss for such violations. Again, domestic courts have not considered this in reading across the ECtHR's generally cautious approach.

[158] ibid [37], [39].
[159] (n 1) [11].
[160] Practice Direction (n 153) [7].
[161] *Denizci v Cyprus* (23 May 2001) App no 25316/94, [315] (ECtHR Fourth Section).
[162] *Demopoulos* (n 108) [69].
[163] *Dimitrov v Bulgaria* (10 May 2011) App no 48059/06, [125] (ECtHR Fourth Section).
[164] In addition to other factors mentioned above and below, including the Court's concern not to undermine its political legitimacy, its lack of an express power to award non-pecuniary loss, and its conception of itself as a standard-setting court rather than small-claims tribunal.
[165] *Varnava* GC (n 107) [224].

A major feature of domestic courts' practice under the mirror approach has been adoption of the ECtHR's practice of denying awards for non-pecuniary loss that is not 'sufficiently serious'.[166] The ECtHR has held that

> [i]n *many* cases where a law, procedure or practice has been found to fall short of Convention standards [a finding of violation] is enough to put matters right ... In some situations, however, the impact of the violation may be ... of a nature and degree as to have impinged *so significantly* on the moral well-being of the applicant as to require something further.[167]

In addition to the ECtHR's lack of fact-finding capacity, this approach is explicable by reference to the ECtHR's primary role being maintenance of basic standards; it is not constituted to be a small-claims tribunal. Its position as a subsidiary institution is also relevant: if the Court were to operate routinely as a redress mechanism wherever some consequential loss were suffered it would usurp domestic institutions' primary responsibility for provision of redress. Further, the ECtHR has specifically linked the 'sufficiently serious' criterion to the terms of Article 41 which make 'no express provision for non-pecuniary or moral damage'.[168] Against this backdrop the Court limits itself to awarding compensation where there is a particularly strong imperative for it to deviate from its default setting, ie where the impact of the violation is 'so significant' that it would be remiss even for a subsidiary institution not to afford some measure of redress.

Perhaps the most striking instance of English courts reading across ECtHR practice where that practice is significantly shaped by concerns irrelevant to the domestic context is in Article 5(4) cases. As is discussed below, the effect of the Supreme Court decisions in *Faulkner* and *Osborn* is that awards for distress will be made regularly for breaches of Article 5(4) caused by delay (i.e. a failure to conduct proceedings speedily)—as the ECtHR has often made awards for such breaches—but will generally not be made for breaches of Article 5(4) caused by a procedural fault other than delay, as Strasbourg practice as to awards has not been clear and consistent in this context. However, it seems that the main reason why awards have regularly been made in delay cases is because the ECtHR has had to deal with a deluge of repeat claims caused by systemic delays in domestic systems.[169] In this context the Court has effectively had to function as a first instance

[166] *Faulkner* (n 1) [62]–[66]; see further ch 7.I. Note this practice is not equivalent to a principle recognised at common law, that de minimus loss can be disregarded. More than de minimus loss, but which is not 'so significant', is routinely compensated within torts actionable per se, and where loss is de minimus nominal damages are awarded.

[167] *Varnava* GC (n 107) [224] (emphasis added).

[168] ibid.

[169] See, eg, *Scordino* (n 96); *Cocchiarella* (n 93). Those cases concerned violations caused by delay in the context of Article 6(1), however it was the remedial approach developed in these Article 6(1) delay cases that was then read across to Article 5(4) delay cases on the basis that a consistent approach should be taken to delay cases: *HL v UK* (2005) 40 EHRR 32, [149].

court given the lack of domestic remedies for such delays, and further, has arguably been more willing to exercise its remedial discretion in favour of awards so as to incentivise respondent states to address systemic defects and introduce effective domestic remedies. The ECtHR has not faced such issues in respect of other types of procedural breach under Article 5(4), such that it has not had reason to depart from its default, parsimonious approach. It makes no sense for legal propositions in English damages law to depend on the fact that several European states, at one time or another, suffered systemic delays in their respective court systems.

F. Compliance with Convention Requirements

While one of the core justifications for adoption of a mirror approach is to ensure compliance with Convention requirements, a focus on Article 41 could in fact cause the UK to fall foul of Article 13.[170]

The risk of non-compliance is not high in respect of quantum, given awards have needed to be meagre before the ECtHR will find violation of Article 13. However, this is not to say that the ECtHR has not found violations on this basis. One source of risk of breach of Article 13 is the oft-repeated direction from higher courts, that awards for non-pecuniary loss should be modest, higher courts going so far as to advise that damages will be "modest" even for deliberate wrongdoing.[171] If this direction were followed in a case of serious violation there would be a real risk of breach of Article 13. There are such examples under the HRA. For example an award of £1,200 was made to a prisoner for distress caused by a delay before the Parole Board, where the distress stretched over a very long period of two years, there being significant aggravating features in the case, in particular that the prisoner suffered mental health issues, which made the delay more difficult to cope with.[172]

There are greater risks associated with other features of a mirror approach, such as following the ECtHR's practice of holding a finding of breach to be sufficient relief in the presence of loss. If such practice became dominant in general or characterised the remedial approach for particular types of violation, there is a good chance it would lead to violation of Article 13. This is the case for breaches of Article 6: *Greenfield* holds that awards will generally not be made, despite the ECtHR itself having made awards for such breaches in a not insignificant number of cases.[173] In *Osborn* the Supreme Court held that awards would ordinarily not be recovered for breaches of

[170] On the requirements of Article 13 see ch 6.1.II.
[171] *Watkins* (n 1) [73].
[172] *R (Guntrip) v SOSJ* [2010] EWHC 3188; see further s 2.II.C.iii below.
[173] See n 396 below.

Article 5(4) (not involving delay) if such violations had not resulted in deprivation of liberty.[174] Yet, as the Supreme Court in *Osborn* and *Faulkner* observed, there are 'numerous cases' in which awards have been made for such violations by the ECtHR for distress alone.[175] Putting to the side that it is striking that the practice of domestic courts is even more restrictive than that of a subsidiary, supranational Court, such approach is likely to fall foul of Article 13. The ECtHR maintains that compensation ought to be available for rights-violations. An available remedy is one available not only *in theory*, but also *in practice*. The ECtHR has found breaches of Article 13 where, despite compensation being available in principle for a particular type of violation, there was no clear domestic practice of awards actually being made.[176] If there is no pattern of awards *plus* express statements from the highest courts maintaining that awards will generally not be made, as in *Greenfield* and *Osborn*, violations of Article 13 seem inevitable. Indeed, the unavailability in English law of awards for distress alone, consequential upon breaches of Article 5(4) (not involving delay), has previously been held to violate Article 5(5);[177] that provision provides that compensation ought to be available for Article 5 breaches, with similar principles being applied as those under Article 13. Neither Article 5(5) nor 13 was considered in *Osborn*.

In contrast, it is highly unlikely that a tort-based approach would run afoul of Article 13. As Lord Woolf has said: 'The domestic approach to the quantum of compensation would certainly meet the requirements of the [Convention]'.[178] The ECtHR has itself observed of claims in English tort law, 'the possibility of obtaining compensation in civil proceedings for the claims of the breach of the rights … will generally, and in normal circumstances, constitute adequate and sufficient remedy'.[179] In other cases it has specifically found awards in tort, including for vindicatory torts such as battery, to constitute effective redress.[180]

In any case, if there is any risk that quantum under a tort-based approach might contravene Article 13, it must be a far lower risk than that in respect of the mirror approach, given scales applied by the ECtHR are in general modest compared with domestic scales. Further, the ECtHR has shown greater tolerance for awards lower than what it would ordinarily consider adequate where scales are explicable according to domestic legal traditions

174 *Osborn* (n 1) [2](xiii).

175 ibid [114]; *Faulkner* (n 1) [61].

176 See ch 6.1.II.

177 *Waite v UK* (2003) 36 EHRR 54; *Kolanis v UK* (2006) 42 EHRR 12.

178 H Woolf, 'The Human Rights Act 1998 and Remedies' in M Andenas and D Fairgrieve (eds), *Judicial Review in International Perspective* (Kluwer, 2000) 431.

179 eg *Chagos* (n 143) [81]; see the tort claims for damages made in domestic proceedings: *Chagos Islanders v Attorney General* [2003] EWHC 2222, [102].

180 eg *Wainwright v UK* (2007) 44 EHRR 40, [55]; see also *Hay v UK* (2000) 30 EHRR CD188; *Caraher v UK* (2000) 29 EHRR CD119.

or living standards;[181] whereas such considerations might 'save' an unusually low award made according to a tort-based approach they could not save an equivalent award made pursuant to the mirror approach.

According to a tort-based approach damages would be awarded more frequently than under the mirror approach, generally wherever damage or loss is suffered. It would therefore be most unlikely that a domestic court would fail to make an award in a case in which Article 13 demanded an award, while there could be no argument that the damages remedy was not effective in practice, as a clear practice of making awards would naturally follow from a tort-based approach.

Indeed, in cases where the ECtHR has been more prescriptive as to the requirements of Article 13, especially where very important rights are at stake, it has enunciated an approach for domestic courts akin to the vindicatory, tort-based approach argued for in Part 1 of this book:

> [T]he Court is of the opinion that the domestic courts, as the custodians of individual rights and freedoms, should have felt it their duty to mark their disapproval of the State's wrongful conduct to the extent of awarding an adequate and sufficient quantum of damages to the applicant, taking into account the fundamental importance of the right of which they had found a breach in the present case, even if they considered that breach to have been an inadvertent rather than an intended consequence of the State's conduct. As a corollary this would have conveyed the message that the State may not set individual rights and freedoms at nought or circumvent them with impunity.[182]

As at least one English judge has observed, in evaluating the justifiability of a remedial approach to breach of basic rights focused solely upon consequential factual harm and which excludes damages for the wrong in itself: 'a regime in which damages were confined to damages for distress would render the rights (to a degree) "illusory" (to use the word used by the ECHR) and would, to a degree, fail to provide an effective remedy [as required by Article 13]'.[183]

II. PROBLEMATIC JURISPRUDENCES: SUPRANATIONAL AND MUNICIPAL

The mirror approach requires English courts to follow a deeply problematic jurisprudence: the Strasbourg jurisprudence lacks consistency, coherence and principle, offers little guidance as to when awards should be made and assessment of quantum, and is characterised by opaque, flawed and minimal reasoning. This section demonstrates that the result of tying domestic

[181] ibid [77]; *Cocchiarella* (n 93) [80]; *Scordino* (n 96) [206].

[182] *Shilbergs v Russia* (17 December 2009) App no 20075/03, [78] (ECtHR First Section).

[183] *Gulati v MGN Ltd* [2015] EWHC 1482, [113] (in the context of the action of misuse of private information).

practice to Strasbourg practice is emergence of a domestic damages jurisprudence which mirrors the most problematic features of the supranational jurisprudence. The section also argues that where domestic courts have elaborated more meaningful guidance, this guidance has not been sourced from Strasbourg. Rather, it resembles aspects of the common law of damages. In turn this calls into question the credibility and sustainability of the mirror approach, and illustrates the artificiality of seeking to maintain strict separation between HRA damages and ordinary law.

A. The Supranational Jurisprudence

The Strasbourg jurisprudence is riddled with problems. Commentators,[184] the Law Commissions[185] and judges[186] are united in the view that apart from some broad general principles, such as *restitutio in integrum*, the Strasbourg Court's approach to just satisfaction lacks consistency, coherence, predictability and principle.[187] The Law Commissions considered the 'lack of clear principles as to when damages should be awarded and how they should be measured' to be perhaps 'the most striking feature of the Strasbourg case-law'.[188] Members of the Court are quoted as saying that, when it comes to just satisfaction, they either have no principles or do, but do not apply them.[189] Commentators advise practitioners to avoid searching the case law for principles which do not exist,[190] and that 'there are cases where different results have occurred even though they appear to be indistinguishable on their facts'.[191] A book-length study of the ECtHR's Article 41 jurisprudence reaches the following conclusions: 'it is difficult to discern any

[184] eg Feldman (n 76) [19.42]; R Clayton, 'Damage Limitation: the Courts and the Human Rights Act Damages' [2005] *PL* 429, 431–33; Clayton and Tomlinson (n 15) [21.30]; M Amos, 'Damages for Breach of the Human Rights Act 1998' [1999] *European Human Rights Law Review* 178, 189; AR Mowbray, 'The European Court of Human Rights' Approach to Just Satisfaction' [1997] *PL* 647, 658–59; Beatson et al (n 19) [7-141]; K Starmer, *European Human Rights Law* (LAG, 1999) [2.44], [2.51]; Woolf (n 178) 432.

[185] Law Commissions Report (n 36) [3.4]–[3.15].

[186] See those quotes below from judges at lower court and Supreme Court level (at nn 216–33); *cf Greenfield* (n 1) [15], and see the discussion of *Faulkner* below at n 234.

[187] Note that the ECtHR has taken some steps to try and ameliorate the problem of inconsistency (Harris et al (n 41) 155–56) including establishment of an Article 41 Unit in the Court's Registrary (O Ichim, *Just Satisfaction under the European Convention on Human Rights* (CUP, 2015) 256–57, noting the Unit's exact role remains undisclosed). But given inconsistency remains a core feature of the jurisprudence these efforts do not seem to have proven particularly successful.

[188] Law Commissions Report (n 36) [3.4].

[189] Shelton (n 148) 2. Although, given the emergence of some general principles, Shelton is, relatively speaking, more optimistic about the development of the jurisprudence compared to the first edition of her book: *Remedies in International Human Rights Law* (OUP, 1999) 1.

[190] A Lester et al, *Human Rights Law and Practice* 3rd edn (LexisNexis, 2009) [2.8.4] n 3.

[191] H McGregor, *McGregor on Damages* 19th edn (Sweet and Maxwell, 2014) [48-025].

logic in the current practice of the Court';[192] 'the Strasbourg system of reparation lacks consistency and predictability'; 'broad discretion and lack of reasoning reverberate negatively on the coherence of the system. The result is a practice that may sometimes be characterised as being arbitrary';[193] and Article 41 determinations 'lack ... transparency' with the judges 'unwilling[] to give legal reasoning for their awards of reparation'.[194] The study also reveals shocking examples of inconsistency and incoherence, such as private companies being awarded more for non-pecuniary loss associated with violation of property rights than human victims of inhuman and degrading treatment.[195] The author rightly describes such practice as the 'perversion of human rights'.[196]

The state of the jurisprudence is unsurprising[197] when one considers that the Court adopts a broad discretionary approach, which emphasises a flexible case-by-case methodology,[198] and generally does not rationalise its decisions by reference to past awards,[199] nor in general explain the basis on which it decides whether to make an award or how it comes to quantum, only typically saying it has done so on an 'equitable basis'. Of one of the Court's significant remedial practices it has been observed that:

> [W]hether a finding of breach ... is sufficient to accord the applicant just satisfaction is a peculiarly subjective matter, and it is not therefore surprising to find the case law does not provide any coherent principles to apply in deciding whether or not this is the case.[200]

The discretionary approach even extends to pecuniary loss—losses that can be objectively quantified—with both the decision[201] whether to award damages for pecuniary loss and assessment[202] ultimately turning on what the ECtHR considers equitable and just on the facts, while even in respect of such objective loss the Court often does not offer reasoned justification

[192] Ichim (n 187) 258.
[193] ibid 271.
[194] ibid 235–38.
[195] ibid 157.
[196] ibid.
[197] Certain other factors have arguably contributed to the state of the jurisprudence including that the Court is divided into chambers, which hinders consistency; that the Court does not see compensation as its primary concern; and it is perhaps unsurprising that a Court comprised of members from different legal traditions should express conclusions on damages in general terms (although this does not prevent the Court giving more detailed reasons for its decisions as to rights-compliance).
[198] See *Varnava* GC (n 107) [224]; *Al-Jedda* (n 107) [114].
[199] There are notable exceptions: eg *MAK v UK* (2010) 51 EHRR 14, [91]–[99].
[200] McGregor (n 191) [48-025].
[201] *Varnava* Third Section (n 106) [155] (summary dismissal of claim for pecuniary loss).
[202] eg *Smith and Grady v UK* (2001) 31 EHRR 24, [19]; *Assanidze* (n 98) [200]–[201]; *Surek v Turkey (No 4)* (8 July 1999) App no 24762/94, [78] (GC); *O'Keeffe v Ireland* (28 January 2014) App no 35810/09, [201] (GC); Mowbray (n 184) 650–51; Clayton and Tomlinson (n 15) [21.68].

for sums awarded.[203] The Court has given its discretionary approach as a reason for not adopting defined scales in particular areas.[204] It has only explicitly adopted scales in few contexts where it has dealt with many repeat cases caused by systemic defects in domestic systems,[205] though it refuses to publish those scales, does not explicitly reason by reference to them, and awards still ultimately rest on the Court's absolute discretion.[206]

To give a flavour of the ECtHR's general approach, consider the extent of the reasoning given in support of awards in the following examples:

— 'The Court does not discern any causal link between the violation found and the pecuniary damage alleged; it therefore rejects this claim. On the other hand, it awards the applicant EUR 7,500 in respect of non-pecuniary damage'.[207]
— 'Having regard to previous cases and making an assessment on an equitable basis, the Court considers it reasonable to award each applicant EUR 1,000 in respect of non-pecuniary damage'.[208]
— 'The Court does not discern any causal link between the violations found and the pecuniary damage alleged; it therefore rejects this claim. On the other hand, taking into account the nature of the violations found and ruling on an equitable basis, it awards the applicant EUR 20,000 in respect of non-pecuniary damage'.[209]
— 'It considers that the applicant must have experienced certain distress which cannot be compensated for by the Court's findings of violations alone. Having regard to the nature of the violations found in the instant case, the Court considers it equitable to uphold the applicant's claim and awards him EUR 1,000 in respect of non-pecuniary damage'.[210]

[203] But note that the Court's remedial practice in respect of pecuniary loss is more predictable relative to its wildly unpredictable approach to non-pecuniary loss: Ichim (n 187) 98–117, 155–56.

[204] *Varanava* GC (n 107) [225].

[205] *Scordino* (n 96) [176].

[206] Ichim (n 187) 121ff, 156ff; Harris et al (n 41) 155–56. Rumour has it that the Court Registrary has produced tables to guide assessment more generally. But those tables remain unpublished, the Court does not explicitly refer to them, it is unclear what their legal status is or what legal principles they are based in—the Court has not generally articulated principles to guide quantification so it is unclear what principles the tables encapsulate—and in any case they do not seem to have greatly aided consistency. Until the Court disciplines its open-ended, unreasoned discretionary approach by articulating, adhering to and reasoning by reference to a set of worked-out rules and principles consistency will remain elusive. Yet commentators observe the Court has 'no intention of renouncing such wide power' (Ichim (n 187) 17).

[207] *Venskutė v Lithuania* (11 December 2012) App no 10645/08, [92] (ECtHR Second Section).

[208] *Goussev and Marenk v Finland* (17 January 2006) App no 35083/97, [64] (ECtHR Fourth Section).

[209] *Mosendz v Ukraine* (17 January 2013) App no 52013/08, [129] (ECtHR Fifth Section).

[210] *MSS v Belgium and Greece* (2011) 53 EHRR 2, [406].

— '43. The applicant claimed 5,000 euros (EUR) in respect of non-pecuniary damage.
  44. The Government considered this claim unsubstantiated.
  45. The Court considers that the finding of a violation, constitutes in itself sufficient just satisfaction for any non-pecuniary damage suffered by the applicant'.[211]
— 'The Court considers that the applicant must have sustained non-pecuniary damage. Ruling on an equitable basis, it awards him EUR 2,500 under this head'.[212]
— 'The Court agrees with the Government that the finding of a violation constitutes sufficient just satisfaction'.[213]

Of course there are some cases in which greater reasoning is proffered, particularly in claims for pecuniary loss, and the odd case where the Court articulates a few more detailed considerations or considers past cases, but these are rare and the foregoing represent the Court's standard approach: 'There is virtually never any real articulation as to why the Court has awarded a particular sum'.[214] The Court's practice of conjuring figures out of thin air has led to it being described as a 'calculating machine', with commentators—quite genuinely—speculating that the Court uses a computer programme to fix quantum.[215]

Not surprisingly domestic courts have struggled with the direction that they ought to look to Strasbourg. The following statements by lower court judges give some insight into the difficulties faced:

— 'it is far from simple to see the principles which the ECtHR applies'.[216]
— 'it is not at all clear from the reports how the ECtHR arrived at particular figures'.[217]
— 'there is little in the cases that I have been referred to that assist in the assessment process ... other than that they illustrate [that awards are modest]'.[218]
— 'Stanley Burton J [in a pre-*Greenfield* case] reviewed the European cases and demonstrated that there were no consistent principles applied by the European Court as to when to award damages ... That situation remains substantially the same now'.[219]
— 'I cannot reconcile ... those two European authorities'.[220]

[211] *Garnaga v Ukraine* (16 May 2013) App no 20390/07, [43]–[45] (ECtHR Fifth Section).
[212] *Jaanti v Finland* (24 February 2009) App no 39105/05, [35] (ECtHR Fourth Section).
[213] *Gillan v UK* (2010) 50 EHRR 45, [94].
[214] *DSD* (n 17) [68](iii).
[215] Ichim (n 187) 127.
[216] *Savage v South Essex Partnership NHS Foundation Trust* [2010] EWHC 865, [97].
[217] *Pennington* (n 17) [20].
[218] ibid [22].
[219] *R (Degainis) v SOSJ* [2010] EWHC 137, [18].
[220] *KB* (n 5) [57].

— 'Beyond [a few] basic principles, however, with some exceptions it is impossible to identify a relevant set of principles consistently applied by the European Court when considering awards ... The Court tends to award global sums on an 'equitable' basis, and its judgments do not analyse the basis of calculation ... or give a breakdown between different items of damages. They may even not distinguish between damages and the costs and the expenses of the proceedings ... These characteristics render it difficult to identify more than very general principles'.[221]

— 'This broad discretionary approach to the award of compensation is no doubt the reason for what has been identified by [the Law Commissions], as the "lack of clear principles [in the Strasbourg case law] as to when damages should be awarded and how they should be measured"'.[222]

— 'In general the "principles" applied by the European Court, which we are thus enjoined to "take into account", are not clear or coherent'.[223]

— 'This selection of authorities is typical of the proposition agreed between counsel that there are authorities from the European Court which go in either direction and ... it is hard to discern any hard and fast principles from those judgments'.[224]

— 'If the parties are agreed upon one thing in this case it is the difficulty of identifying any principles upon which the European Court of Human Rights decides whether it is necessary to afford just satisfaction under Article 41'.[225]

— 'whilst in this jurisdiction the principles governing awards of "general damages" are well established ... the same is not true of the Strasbourg jurisprudence'.[226]

— 'the assistance to be derived from [the Strasbourg] jurisprudence is limited'; 'The difficulty lies in identifying ... clear and coherent principles governing the award of damages'.[227]

— 'Although there is now a good deal of jurisprudence both here and in Strasbourg on the issue of compensation for breach of article 5.4, the ascertainment of clear principles governing the issue is with respect an elusive exercise'.[228]

— 'It is notoriously difficult to deduce clear principles in relation to "just satisfaction" from the Strasbourg jurisprudence'.[229]

221 ibid [24]–[25].
222 *Dobson* (n 17) [43].
223 *Re C* [2007] HRLR 14, [64].
224 *Downing v Parole Board* [2008] EWHC 3198, [20], see also [14].
225 *Bernard* (n 5) [35].
226 *Van Colle v Chief Constable Hertfordshire Police* [2006] EWHC 360, [111].
227 *Anufrijeva* (n 5) [52], [57].
228 *R (Sturnham) v SOSJ* [2012] 3 WLR 476, [13].
229 *R (Hooper) v SOS for Work and* Pensions [2003] WLR 2623, [147].

— 'the Strasbourg jurisprudence fails to give a consistent answer as to when the primary relief sought is by itself "just satisfaction"'.[230]
— 'it is well known, and is common ground before us, that there are no articulated principles, and no discernible tariff, by which [the ECtHR's] awards [under Article 41] are set ... the use in the statute of the definite article—"*the* principles"—may have been something of a legislative act of faith ... nothing approaching a tariff has yet emerged from the awards made under art 5(4) in Strasbourg'.[231]

It has not only been lower court judges who have found life tough. In *Rabone* Lord Mance observed that there are 'numerous [ECtHR] cases giving only limited guidance on the factors governing and the range of compensation appropriate under the Convention', while Lord Dyson observed that

> [n]o decision has been cited to us which purports to be a guideline case in which the range of compensation is specified and the relevant considerations are articulated. It is, therefore, necessary for our courts to do their best in the light of such guidance as can be gleaned from the Strasbourg decisions on the facts of individual cases.[232]

Lord Millett, in the pre-*Greenfield* case of *Cullen*, having observed the lack of principles in ECtHR jurisprudence, suggested: '[i]n this situation, we may have to develop our own jurisprudence' while keeping an eye on Strasbourg.[233]

In *Faulkner* Lord Reed noted academic commentary criticising the Strasbourg jurisprudence and advising of the futility of seeking to identify principle, as well as Crown counsel's submission that there was an 'air of unreality' in seeking to analyse an accumulation of ad hoc decisions of a Court that does not have the same regard for precedent as English courts.[234] Lord Reed considered such scepticism 'over-stated'.[235] This was not because he thought detailed rules and consistently applied scales do in fact characterise the Strasbourg material but because the term 'principles' in section 8(4) HRA is to be construed broadly as *practice*.[236] Lord Reed's view appears to be that English courts ought not to be concerned by the lack of a detailed law of damages within the Strasbourg jurisprudence because a domestic court's task, according to the mirror approach, is not to discern legal principle but to replicate ECtHR *practice*. This is a striking view. Most striking is that it evinces no alarm that the practice followed is the product of an approach

230 *R (AM) v Chief Constable West Midlands Police* [2010] EWHC 1228, [25].
231 *Faulkner v SOSJ* [2011] EWCA Civ 349, [6], [15] [*Faulkner* CA].
232 *Rabone* (n 1) [84], [122].
233 *Cullen* (n 88) [80].
234 *Faulkner* (n 1) [35].
235 ibid.
236 ibid.

devoid of specific rules and principles, which does not accord weight to values of consistency or coherence, and which is not characterised by reasoned judgment; the normative driver for following such jurisprudence is obscure. Making this state of affairs even more troubling has been the higher courts' seeming reluctance to evaluate critically any practices which they discern from Strasbourg, such that practices based in a troubled jurisprudence are imported without evaluation of their substantive merits. One would expect the higher courts to be a little more discerning.

Also striking is that in rejecting concerns over the Strasbourg jurisprudence Lord Reed did not consider that the lack of detailed rules and principles in that jurisprudence suggests it is unlikely that the ECtHR's practice will be 'clear and consistent', such that concrete guidance may be discerned from it according to the mirror method. These concerns are borne out by some of Lord Reed's own observations in *Faulkner*: the ECtHR 'has offered little explanation of its reasons for awarding particular amounts or for declining to make an award';[237] 'The cases are therefore of limited assistance in relation to the point now under consideration';[238] 'none of the awards which I have mentioned offers any clear guidance';[239] 'It is however impossible to derive any precise guidance from these awards'.[240]

B. Limited Guidance

Let us assume, contrary to all evidence to the contrary, that there are convincing reasons for deriving domestic norms from the ECtHR's remedial practice. Even making this generous assumption, the stark reality is that the mirror approach has borne limited guidance. In general it is difficult to identify clear and consistent practice, while where such practice is identifiable only limited assistance may be derived from it. This is unsurprising given the general features of the Strasbourg jurisprudence already discussed.

Let us consider the two major HRA damages decisions from the House of Lords and Supreme Court, given that if concrete guidance were to emerge one would expect it to come from the highest courts.

In *Greenfield* the only guidance elaborated by the Law Lords as to *quantum* for non-pecuniary loss consequent upon breach of Article 6 was that awards should be 'modest', with no indicative scale proffered.[241] The guidance as to *whether* awards for *distress* ought to be made specifically in cases of structural bias was that the ECtHR's ordinary practice is not to make an award. From this it is clear that awards should seldom be made but when

[237] ibid [34].
[238] ibid [63].
[239] ibid [74].
[240] ibid [75].
[241] (n 1) [17].

should they be made? There is little if any guidance on this. Lord Bingham observed that the ECtHR has, in some cases, made awards for distress on the basis that distress 'must have' been suffered.[242] However, no guidance is given in *Greenfield* nor by the ECtHR as to why loss was inferred and an award merited in those cases but not others with apparently similar facts and for similar violations.[243] The ECtHR has applied a causation principle, but it is not clear how this relates to Lord Bingham's prescription that awards should be made sparingly. The guidance derived in respect of awards for *loss of real opportunities* caused by defective procedure was that the ECtHR does not generally make such awards on the assumption of a lack of causal connection but 'has softened this response where it was persuaded that justice required it to do so'.[244] Appeals to amorphous notions of 'justice' do not provide a great deal of guidance. Lord Bingham rejected counsel's criticism of variations in the language used by the ECtHR to explain how probable it must be that an outcome would have been more favourable to the claimant if Article 6 had been complied with before an award for lost opportunities may be contemplated.[245] He said that the linguistic variations reflect different assessments by the ECtHR of the probability of a different outcome in each case. Even if we are charitable to the ECtHR and assume this is correct (it seems more likely to be the result of undisciplined use of language and/or lack of any clear principle), this still leaves open and unresolved what level of probability of a more favourable outcome is required before an award can be contemplated. The ECtHR follows no clear and consistent threshold or standard; as counsel in *Greenfield* pointed out, the ECtHR's jurisprudence is marked by varied linguistic formulations, while Lord Bingham himself observed that there are cases where one might have expected an award but none was made. No guidance is given in *Greenfield* other than the generic appeal to 'justice', while Lord Bingham even praised the ECtHR for not laying down any firm rules(!). One does not envy a lower court judge faced with such 'guidance'.

Faulkner was intended as a guideline judgment for damages in Article 5(4) delay cases. The Supreme Court's guidance as to quantum for distress caused by delay was that awards should be modest barring special circumstances; no guidance as to defined scales, or factors which might increase or decrease awards was given,[246] other than mental illness.[247] That such limited guidance was discernible is particularly striking given the ECtHR has had to consider just satisfaction in a plethora of delay cases caused by systemic delays in the court systems of Member States.

[242] ibid [16].
[243] ibid.
[244] ibid [14]–[15].
[245] ibid.
[246] *Faulkner* (n 1) [13](14), [67]–[68].
[247] ibid [66].

In terms of guidance for assessment of quantum for 'loss of liberty', Lord Reed concluded that it was impossible to derive any precise guidance from Strasbourg such that

> a judgment has to be made by domestic courts as to what is just and appropriate in the individual case, taking into account such guidance as is available from awards made by the European court, or by domestic courts under ... the [HRA] in comparable cases.[248]

The only general guidance given was that awards for loss of liberty would be more than awards for frustration alone, and that where the victim would have been on conditional release from prison but for the delay, the award would be lower compared to where their freedom would have been unconditional (as discussed in the next section, it is not clear that this guidance comes from Strasbourg). No guidance as to scales was elaborated. The only Strasbourg material which Lord Reed postulated might offer guidance as to quantum was a single case.[249] But it is questionable whether even this case was on point: the award was not for loss of liberty but a combined award for loss of an *opportunity* of release *and* distress.[250] Given the ECtHR does not disaggregate awards according to heads of loss it is impossible to know what proportion of the award related to liberty, while a *definite* loss of liberty and *loss of an opportunity* of liberty are conceptually distinct, such that it is difficult to see how levels of awards for each could be equated. So, lower courts are effectively left with no specific guidance as to quantum for actual loss of liberty.

This is very limited guidance indeed, *especially* in respect of scales. It stands in contrast to typical damages guideline judgments, in which higher courts see it as 'an important function'—indeed, a 'positive duty'[251]—to lay down guidelines 'as to the quantum of damages appropriate to compensate for various types of commonly occurring injuries' and keep them up to date.[252] For example such judgments may state a tariff and then enumerate considerations which justify an uplift or decrease.[253] Alternatively courts may set out bands, each associated with a scale of damages, say £500–£6,600, £6,600–£19,800, £19,800–£33,000,[254] offering general guidance as to the type of case that would fall into each. Once a case is

[248] ibid [75].
[249] ibid [74]; *Kolanis* (n 177).
[250] *Kolanis* ibid [92].
[251] *Simmons v Castle* [2013] 1 WLR 1239, [12].
[252] *Wright v British Railways Board* [1983] 2 AC 773, 784; *Simmons* ibid [8]–[12].
[253] eg *Gulati* (n 183) [229]–[231]; *Thompson v Commissioner for the Metropolis* [1998] QB 498.
[254] *Vento v Chief Constable West Yorkshire* [2003] ICR 318. These bands are for assessment of damages for injured feelings in the discrimination context. The bands stated in the text take into account two uplifts subsequent to *Vento*: *Da'Bell v NSPCC* [2009] UKEAT 0227_09_2809; *The Cadogan Hotel Partners Ltd v Ozog* [2014] UKEAT 0001_14_1505.

allocated to a band, further factors are relied on to place the case within the band. Such judgments provide a structured method for setting quantum based in a clear framework of principle, yet allow scope for judges to adjust awards according to the facts before them. In turn such guidance facilitates a rational, coherent and consistent body of jurisprudence, and a basis for settlement.[255] In formulating guidance courts have not been hamstrung by past awards; while past practice is relevant, the court setting the guidance will ultimately determine appropriate scales for itself. Thus, where a higher court finds that 'variations [in past awards] disclose no logical pattern'[256] the response has not been that no guidance can or ought to be given. Rather, the unsatisfactory nature of existing jurisprudence is what prompts the court to set its own guidance. It is difficult to see how consistent jurisprudence will emerge if higher courts do not grasp the nettle. That they have not in the human rights context is seemingly the product of reluctance to step outside Strasbourg materials, where that material offers a paucity of guidance and no discernible scales.

If the highest courts have struggled to divine concrete guidance, so too have lower courts.[257] Take the example of *Pennington*, which entails a serious attempt by a lower court judge to apply the mirror approach.[258] The case was an Article 5(4) delay case, where the rights-violating delay caused the claimant to remain in detention several months longer than he would have otherwise. The Judge identified several general principles from the Strasbourg jurisprudence, which broadly framed his approach, including *restitutio in integrum*, causation, and that in assessing quantum regard should be had to any conduct of the claimant which exacerbated loss. Needless to say, we need not have travelled to Strasbourg for such edification.

The Judge was unable to extract any more detailed guidance. No guidance was extracted as to when damages should be awarded other than it was clear damages had been awarded for delay in some cases; the Judge was therefore required to exercise his own judgement.[259] As to assessment, the Judge, having examined the Strasbourg decisions, concluded: 'there is little in the cases that I have been referred to that assist in the assessment process for this case other than that they illustrate [that the awards are modest]'.[260] The defendants submitted that a figure could be extrapolated from individual Strasbourg decisions. The Judge rejected this: (i) the Strasbourg Court emphasises that awards are case-specific; (ii) the cases suggested no conventional approach; and (iii) it was not clear how the ECtHR arrived at

[255] *Heil* (n 155) [25]; *Wright* (n 252) 784.
[256] *Thompson* (n 253) 514.
[257] In addition to the discussion here see the quotes from lower court judges above expressing the difficulties they have faced in interpreting the Strasbourg material: nn 216–31.
[258] *Pennington* (n 17).
[259] See ibid [23]–[25].
[260] ibid [22].

particular figures; of one case the Judge noted that apart from stating an amount and that it had been reached on an equitable basis, '[t]here was no other reasoning'.[261]

If domestic courts cling to the mirror approach there is a real risk that, with little guidance upon which to peg awards and a ban on looking to domestic principles, domestic courts will end up mirroring the ECtHR's own subjective case-by-case approach. Indeed in *Greenfield* Lord Bingham positively directed courts to follow this approach:

> The [ECtHR] routinely describes its awards as equitable, which I take to mean that they are not precisely calculated but are judged by the court to be fair in the individual case. Judges in England and Wales must also make a similar judgment in the case before them.[262]

In *Faulkner* we saw that Lord Reed similarly indicated that courts should simply decide what is just and appropriate on the facts, given little guidance from Strasbourg. In the later case of *Shahid* the Supreme Court, having derived very little assistance from Strasbourg cases, itself resorted to a broad discretionary approach in deciding whether to award damages to a prisoner kept in solitary confinement in breach of Article 8; given this was an exercise of discretion limited to the facts of the case, supported by very brief reasons, it offers no meaningful guidance for lower courts, and nor did the Supreme Court attempt to articulate any more general guidance, the damages determination taking up roughly one page of the judgment.[263] It is thus not surprising that 15 years on from the HRA coming into force lower court judges continue to observe that '[t]here is little guidance in the authorities on the approach to be taken when quantifying an award of damages … If one looks at the authorities for appropriate comparators, again there is relatively little assistance'; as such judges have no choice but to adopt a justice-on-the-case approach similar to that taken by the ECtHR.[264] In turn, the risk that domestic jurisprudence will come to be characterised by those problems that dog the Strasbourg jurisprudence is now materialising.

C. Emergence of a Problematic Domestic Jurisprudence

A number of problems have emerged in the domestic jurisprudence, mirroring those that mark the Strasbourg case law. These include a lack of reasoning to justify outcomes and guide future decisions, opaque reasoning, flawed reasoning, inconsistency, and decision-making based in highly

[261] ibid [16]–[22].
[262] (n 1) [19].
[263] *Shahid* (n 1) [87]–[90].
[264] *Re H* [2014] EWFC 38, [84]–[91].

subjective concerns. The following are a series of examples illustrative of the emergent problems. These developments are deeply concerning in themselves. But there is also a wider concern that as judges grow accustomed to such bad habits in judicial decision-making, these habits may spread beyond human rights law and affect judicial decision-making more generally.

i. Problems of Reasoning

In *Faulkner* Lord Reed upheld damages of £300 for non-pecuniary losses, such as distress, caused by delay in breach of Article 5(4) for Sturnham.[265] His legal analysis of whether to make an award and quantum in Sturnham's case occupied one paragraph.[266] He considered that the frustration caused by a six month delay was sufficiently serious that an award was warranted, this determination resting on the following reasoning: 'in my view'.[267] The extent of reasoning as to quantum was: 'In the light of the awards made in the Strasbourg cases, of which [*Betteridge*] is the most nearly in point, the award of £300 which was made by the judge was reasonable in the circumstances of this case'.[268] In contrast to reasoning one might find at common law, there was no attempt to reason how Sturnham's case compared to *Betteridge*. It was also, with respect, odd that Lord Reed relied on one case to gauge quantum given he had previously said that not much could be made of individual awards given they are equitable responses to particular facts.[269] There was no attempt to place the award within a specific scale, to set scales, to articulate factors which led the Court to £300, nor to articulate factors more generally to guide lower courts. In other cases reasoning as to quantum has been even more cursory; in *Haney* the reasoning offered by the Supreme Court in support of quantum for distress suffered through breach of Article 5(4) was: 'An appropriate award is £500'.[270]

The Court in *Faulkner* also determined Faulkner's claim who, unlike Sturnham, suffered loss of liberty which he would not have suffered if the Parole Board had processed his parole application speedily. When it came to quantum Lord Reed reduced the £10,000 award made by the Court of Appeal, conjuring the alternative figure of £6,500 out of thin air.[271] The only factor referred to explicitly was that the liberty lost would have been conditional as Faulkner, if released earlier, would have been on licence. There was no attempt, for example, to articulate timescale-based guidance or justify

265 *Faulkner* (n 1) [97].
266 ibid.
267 Strangely the Court did not have express recourse to the very guidance it had given earlier in the judgment, although the result seems consistent with that guidance.
268 *Faulkner* (n 1) [97].
269 ibid [68].
270 *Haney* (n 1) [50], [60].
271 *Faulkner* (n 1) [75], [87].

the award according to general principles. The crux of the reasoning was similar to that in Sturnham's appeal: 'it appears to me that an award in the region of £6,500 would adequately compensate Mr Faulkner'.[272] Lord Reed did say he was applying the approach articulated earlier in his judgment. But given that the paragraph he refers back to states that it is impossible to derive precise guidance from Strasbourg such that domestic courts must decide what is just and appropriate on the facts, the reference back to this 'approach' sheds no light on the *reasons* for lowering the award.[273] Further, there was no recognition that the lower Court's award was for 'loss of an opportunity of conditional liberty',[274] which is distinct from the Supreme Court's conceptualisation of the relevant head:[275] *actual* loss of conditional liberty. Given compensation for loss of an opportunity of freedom would logically be on a lower scale than compensation for actual loss of liberty, the disparity between the lower Court's award and the Supreme Court's reduced award is even more marked. This brings into even greater focus the need for *reasoned elaboration*—which was not forthcoming.

Importantly, it is not clear what the award in Faulkner's case was for. The Court did not address whether the award was for mental suffering in fact suffered by Faulkner as a result of remaining in jail longer than he would have otherwise, or for the loss of liberty in itself, or both.[276] On the one hand the ECtHR's approach, which the Supreme Court was purporting to follow, is to award compensation only for actual loss, such as distress. On the other hand Lord Reed referred to the award being for 'loss of liberty', which is the term associated with the head of normative damage for interference with liberty interests in false imprisonment. Classification matters: if the award is for distress then an individual wrongly deprived of liberty who suffers no distress should receive no award, whereas if the award is for the deprivation in itself a substantial award should nonetheless be made. Classification is also made relevant by Lord Reed's view that if the liberty lost was conditional, because the prisoner would have been on licence rather than completely free, the award should be substantially reduced. If the award is for *distress* suffered through wrongful imprisonment—the basis for ECtHR awards—it is unclear why it matters whether one would otherwise have been completely or conditionally free; what matters is the degree of distress actually suffered, which is a factual question. Alternatively if damages address loss of liberty in itself it is not clear that there is a great deal of difference

[272] ibid.
[273] ibid [87].
[274] *Faulkner* CA (n 231) [18].
[275] The Supreme Court did note ((n 1) [84]) that the Court of Appeal had not reduced the award according to the chance of release, but this does not address the fact that the Court of Appeal appeared to be compensating a different head from that being compensated by the Supreme Court.
[276] See ibid [69]–[75].

between complete freedom and conditional freedom, such that awards for loss of conditional liberty ought to be 'well below'[277] those for loss of unconditional liberty. Even where one is subject to licence one may be free to do almost anything that a completely free citizen could do. Lord Reed seemed to justify the reduction on the basis that conditional liberty is 'more precarious'[278] as there is a chance that one might be recalled to custody if a condition of licence is breached. But elsewhere in his judgment he rejected explicitly the idea of reducing awards 'on the basis of speculation'—and *specifically* speculation as to whether a prisoner, if they had been released when they ought to have been, would have nonetheless been recalled to prison.[279] The key point is that lack of reasoned explanation of the award and the more general lack of analytical rigour, symptomatic of broad discretionary approaches, leaves lower courts to assess damages without it being clear what damages are for; inconsistency, incoherence and confusion seem inevitable.

Osborn offers a paradigm example of minimal reasoning.[280] In that case Lord Reed, for the Supreme Court, considered a damages claim for distress consequent upon breach of a procedural requirement of Article 5(4) other than speediness, in this case failure to hold an oral hearing when one ought to have been held. The damages issue was addressed in under one page.[281] Lord Reed observed that there were conflicting Strasbourg decisions as to whether awards ought to be made for such breaches, and that no award had been made in circumstances comparable to the present case. Lord Reed disposed of the claim as follows:

> 115. It is not argued that the appellant Reilly has suffered any deprivation of liberty as a result of the breach of article 5(4): damages are sought in respect of feelings of frustration and distress which the court is invited to assume he experienced. In the circumstances, taking into account the principles applied by the European court as required by section 8(4) of the Human Rights Act, the finding of a violation constitutes sufficient just satisfaction.[282]

The cursory reasoning bears striking similarity to the ECtHR's own approach. Compare the ECtHR's explanation in *Nikolova* for denying an award for a similar breach: 'As to the alleged frustration suffered by her on account of the absence of adequate procedural guarantees during her

[277] ibid [75].
[278] ibid [74], [87].
[279] ibid [83]. Further, if such approach were to be applied rigorously one would need to assess the probability that the particular claimant would breach his licence conditions rather than adopting a blanket approach; why should a claimant with a previous unblemished record on licence suffer a greatly reduced award on the basis that he might do something which could lead to his recall to prison?
[280] *Osborn* (n 1).
[281] ibid [114]–[115].
[282] ibid [115].

detention, the Court finds that in the particular circumstances of the case the finding of a violation is sufficient'.[283]

Several matters pertinent to disposal of the claim were either not adequately reasoned or not reasoned at all. The question of whether distress could be inferred was not expressly resolved. One must therefore speculate that either (i) the Court considered the claimant had suffered distress but that damages should nonetheless not be awarded for unstated reasons; or (ii) the Court considered that distress could not be inferred for unstated reasons. One might have expected this matter to be clearly addressed given it goes to the existence of loss. All the more so in *Osborn* given Lord Reed had, in determining the substantive rights-claim, quoted research documenting distress experienced by those in the claimant's position; that research

> reveals the frustration, anger and despair felt by prisoners who perceive the [Parole Board's] procedures as unfair, and the impact of those feelings upon their motivation and respect for authority ... The potential implications for the prospects of rehabilitation ... are evident.[284]

His Lordship recalled Lord Philips' observations in a previous decision that negative feelings will naturally be suffered by parties subject to unfair proceedings.[285] Indeed, Lord Reed gave as one of the rationales for procedural rights that their observance avoids infliction of negative feelings upon those subject to procedures.[286] Given all of this, one might have expected an explanation of what it was in *Osborn* which meant distress could not be inferred, or alternatively if the Court considered distress had been suffered, an explanation for why no award was warranted.

The theme of cursory reasoning is evident in other aspects of the decision. One of the reasons, if not the key reason no award was made was that Lord Reed did not consider any case in which the ECtHR made an award was comparable with *Osborn*. Let us put to the side that this is a flawed decision-criterion.[287] Lord Reed mentions two cases which one might have considered broadly analogous to *Osborn*. In *Osborn* the claim was brought

[283] *Nikolova v Bulgaria* (2001) 31 EHRR 3, [76].

[284] *Osborn* (n 1) [70]. Similarly, in *Shahid* (n 1) the Supreme Court, in determining whether a prisoner kept in solitary confinement had suffered violation of Article 8, cited multiple sources documenting that it is common for prisoners in solitary confinement to suffer serious negative effects on their mental wellbeing even where the period of confinement is brief (at [77]–[79]). But when it came to damages no mention was made of this material and the Court evidently considered that no loss warranting compensation could be inferred given it concluded that a declaration constituted sufficient remedy—despite the claimant having being detained in solitary confinement for the extraordinary period of *five* years (at [89]–[90]). With respect, it is very difficult to rationalise this conclusion.

[285] ibid citing *AF* (n 66) [63].

[286] ibid [68]–[70].

[287] What Lord Reed is *not* saying is that the ECtHR has considered a comparable case and denied an award, but that there simply has not been a case comparable to *Osborn* in which an award has been made. But this may simply be because no case on all fours with *Osborn* happens to have come before the ECtHR.

by a prisoner on an indeterminate sentence for distress suffered in consequence of wrongfully being denied an oral hearing when the Parole Board considered whether he ought to be released. The facts of the cases cited by Lord Reed in which the ECtHR made awards were different in only one way.[288] The single difference was that procedural unfairness—the breach of Article 5(4)—arose not from lack of a hearing but because the review was not conducted by a judicial body. Based on this difference Lord Reed did not consider these cases were comparable. But there was no elaboration of why this difference was material: why, as a matter of principle, is it justifiable to make an award for distress suffered in consequence of not having one's case determined by a judicial body, but not where distress was due to lack of an oral hearing? Further, there are ECtHR cases in which prisoners have been awarded compensation for assumed distress where the violation was due to failure to hold oral hearings, but which were not mentioned in relation to damages in *Osborn*—despite being referenced elsewhere in the judgment, and in Lord Reed's judgment in *Faulkner*.[289] For example, in *Waite*[290] an individual was not afforded an oral hearing in a Parole Board review of whether he should be recalled to prison. The ECtHR inferred distress, awarding 2,500 Euros. The similarities between the judicial method in *Osborn* and the ECtHR's standard practice of not engaging seriously with past decisions and cursory reasoning is disconcerting, as are inconsistencies in result across cases which are materially similar.

The last point to observe about *Osborn*, which is the most striking, is that in Lord Reed's bullet-point-style summary of his conclusions at the very beginning of his judgment his Lordship states that breach of Article 5(4) procedural requirements (other than speediness) will not normally result in damages unless the breach leads to deprivation of liberty.[291] However, this general guidance is not articulated outside of this summary. The section of the judgment dedicated to damages only considers whether damages should be awarded on the facts and there is no attempt at articulating general guidance nor justifying the general proposition found in the summary. Such decision-making bears an uncanny resemblance to the ECtHR's own unreasoned, opaque and 'declaratory' approach.

Such unsatisfactory practice is evident in lower court decisions. For example, in *Savage*, in which damages were claimed for breach of Article 2, the Judge considered the damages issue within one paragraph, noting difficulties he experienced in discerning Strasbourg principles. The only reasoning

[288] *Curley v UK* (2000) 31 EHRR 401; *Von Bülow v UK* (2004) 39 EHRR 16.

[289] *Waite* is mentioned at [104] and [110] of *Osborn*, while cases of violation of Article 5(4) not involving delay in which the ECtHR awarded compensation—including *Waite*—were discussed in *Faulkner* (n 1) [61].

[290] (n 177).

[291] *Osborn* (n 1) [2](xiii).

offered for making an award was that 'it was right to grant damages'.[292] Turning to quantum the Judge observed that the range of awards made by the ECtHR for this type of breach varied widely between 5,000 to 60,000 Euros, noted awards made by the Court of Appeal in *Van Colle* (but did not analyse those awards),[293] and that the claimant had not brought the claim for financial reward. The Judge then proclaimed: 'I assess the figure for just satisfaction purposes at £10,000'.[294] This is unsatisfactory reasoning. But it is unsurprising given the Strasbourg material that judges must follow provides limited assistance.

In *OOO* damages were awarded for breach of investigative duties under Articles 3 and 4. In assessing quantum the Judge considered one ECtHR decision, but found it did not provide 'suitable guidance'.[295] There was therefore no range within which the Judge could place the case before him. The Judge noted that the distress occurred over a period of 12 to 15 months. He then said: 'In all the circumstances, I have reached the conclusion that the appropriate award of damages for each Claimant is £5,000'.[296] No further reasoning was proffered. Again, while this is plainly unsatisfactory the Judge faced serious difficulties: *Greenfield* required him to look to Strasbourg, where he found no guidance, and he was barred from looking to domestic law.

In the recent High Court decision of *DSD* we find greater reasoning as to assessment, but that reasoning is, with respect, flawed in significant respects.[297] For example the Judge repeatedly described the nature of awards under the HRA as 'compensatory', observed that the ECtHR has not shown an interest in 'awarding exemplary or punitive damages which might go beyond compensation' and that the Court in *Anufrijeva* ruled out exemplary awards under the HRA, while he would not have made exemplary awards on the facts in any case.[298] However, in assessing damages for breach of the investigative duty under Article 3 the Judge adjusted quantum of damages—damages which were apparently for consequential non-pecuniary losses such as distress and psychological injury and pecuniary losses such as treatment costs—by reference to factors such as whether the sum needed to be 'enhanced' 'to encourage compliance', or to reflect that the defendant's failings were not 'merely operational' but 'systematic and of a deep and abiding nature'.[299] With respect, this reasoning is confused.

[292] *Savage* (n 216) [97].
[293] *Van Colle* CA (n 6).
[294] *Savage* (n 216) [97]. This sort of 'reasoning' is not uncommon: eg *R (Mohammed) v Chief Constable West Midlands* [2010] EWHC 1228, [45] ('The sum I award is £500').
[295] *OOO v Commissioner for the Metropolis* [2011] HRLR 29, [189].
[296] ibid [190].
[297] *DSD* (n 17).
[298] ibid [28].
[299] ibid [118]ff.

Goals of encouraging compliance and admonishing systemic failings have nothing to do with assessing factual loss. It is thus difficult to square the Court uplifting awards on this basis with the idea that awards are compensatory for loss. Furthermore, goals such as deterrence are traditionally associated with punitive damages, so that it is difficult to reconcile the Judge uplifting awards according to such factors with the proposition that exemplary damages are unavailable in HRA law and were not relevant on the facts of *DSD*. The Court justified consideration of these wider normative concerns on the basis that the ECtHR has said that it takes into account the overall circumstances of a case. However, by this the ECtHR only generally means that it will consider the relevant facts of the case and does not mean to implicate the wider normative concerns that guided the Court in *DSD*; the ECtHR has no consistent practice of express reliance on the types of factors that influenced the Judge in *DSD*. Further, augmenting awards for the purpose of deterrence is inconsistent with the ECtHR's own practice of refusing to make aggravated or exemplary awards. However, given the ECtHR rarely reasons its decisions as to just satisfaction, and indeed has not provided an authoritative explanation of the nature of just satisfaction or its guiding norm of equity[300] it is perhaps not surprising that such misunderstandings can occur in interpreting its case law. More generally, it is somewhat unsurprising that a domestic approach to damages led by appeals to woolly, unelaborated and ambiguous notions such as 'equity' or 'just satisfaction', and reliant upon interpretation of an unreasoned Strasbourg jurisprudence, would lead to incoherence and confusion.

ii. Problems of Broad Discretion: Subjective Concerns and Inconsistency[301]

Typical problems associated with an unstructured discretionary approach are evident within the fledging domestic jurisprudence, notably decision-making based in highly subjective concerns and inconsistency. Some such concerns (such as the victim's moral character) reflect Strasbourg practice, but others (such as most public policy concerns invoked by lower courts) do not; either way, domestic courts' practice of subjective decision-making is a natural consequence of following the ECtHR's justice-on-the-case approach, coupled with a lack of guidance to discipline decision-making.

Consider damages claims decided by lower courts in Article 5(4) delay cases prior to the Supreme Court decision in *Faulkner*. There were a number of such claims, brought by prisoners due to systemic failings in the parole system, such that there is a critical mass of decisions to consider.

[300] Ichim (n 187) 43ff, 264ff.

[301] See further ch 6.2.V.B, VI.

In determining such claims some judges took into account the claimant's moral worthiness, specifically that the claimant was a prisoner serving a sentence for a serious crime.[302] One judge considered whether the claimant would use any award to compensate the victim of their previous criminal wrongdoing.[303] Another concluded that an award to a prisoner, who was now on the run, would not be 'fair', given consideration of 'public confidence in the administration of justice'.[304] In contrast other judges stated explicitly that such considerations were irrelevant, in particular that the prisoner had previously committed an offence.[305] In each case where the prisoner's character was considered, no award was made. Where it was not, awards were made in some cases.

There are other significant variations. Partly based on an interpretation of the Strasbourg material some judges held that awards should rarely be made for Article 5(4) violations, except where the claimant could demonstrate they would have been released from prison earlier in the absence of the Parole Board's delay.[306] In contrast others considered that even in cases which were not serious, and where the claimant would not have been released earlier, an award should be made for distress suffered in consequence of the delay, so as to ensure the right to liberty is 'upheld'.[307] Different judges took into account different policy factors such as the potential deterrence effects of awards,[308] the possibility of precipitating a flood of claims,[309] and the costs associated with damages claims,[310] whereas other judges made no mention of such factors despite determining similar claims. Some looked to Strasbourg for guidance,[311] others cited no or very little Strasbourg material,[312] others identified their own considerations which they considered to be relevant,[313] while yet others referred to common law material, including the common law's traditional approach to protection of liberty.[314]

In this way which judge was allocated to one's case could determine the success or failure of one's claim. The rule-of-law concerns with such a state of affairs are manifest.

302 Partly on the basis that the ECtHR has had regard to such concerns. See *Downing* (n 224) [29], [31]; *R (Biggin) v SOSJ* [2009] EWHC 1704, [35]; see further ch 6.2.V.B.

303 *R (Parratt) v SOSJ* [2013] EWHC 17, [57]. This is contrary to the common law position: courts take no account of what a claimant will spend their award on.

304 *R (Faulkner) v SOSJ* [2009] EWHC 1507, [39].

305 *Guntrip* (n 172) [35]; *Degainis* (n 219) [19]–[20]; *R (Faulkner) v SOSJ* [2011] HRLR 7, [80].

306 *Sturnham* (n 228); *Mason v MOJ* [2008] EWHC 1787, [40].

307 *R (Sturnham) v Parole Board* [2011] EWHC 938, [51] [*Sturnham* HC]; *Faulkner* CA (n 231) [12], [18].

308 *Faulkner* CA (n 231) [12].

309 *Sturnham* HC (n 307) [51]; *Guntrip* (n 172) [54].

310 *R (Betteridge) v Parole Board* [2009] EWHC 1638, [31].

311 *Sturnham* (n 228).

312 *Guntrip* (n 172); *Biggin* (n 302).

313 *Guntrip* (n 172) [53]–[57]; *Pennington* (n 17) [23]–[25].

314 *Faulkner* CA (n 231) [12], [18].

Of course, this case law precedes *Faulkner*. While the guidance proffered by the Supreme Court is minimal the decision does settle some of these differences; for example the view that damages ought not ordinarily to be awarded for distress caused by delay has received its coup de grâce. However, other questions such as the relevance of policy factors or the victim's character were not squarely addressed, such that lower courts may continue to rely upon these factors on an ad hoc (and inconsistent) basis as part of a broad discretionary approach.[315]

Also significant is that *Faulkner* only provides guidance—however limited that guidance may be—for damages for one type of violation of one sub-section of one Article, ie breaches of sub-section (4) of Article 5 caused by delay. That guidance cannot simply be read across to damages claims in respect of other Articles because the higher courts have emphasised that under the mirror approach courts are required to look to Strasbourg practice in respect of the specific class of violation before them.[316] As a result, awards made for one type of violation are not generally referred to in adjudicating damages claims for other types.[317] In respect of the vast majority of classes of violation of the vast majority of Articles there is no guidance whatsoever from higher courts. In each of these contexts there is therefore an obvious and serious risk that domestic damages jurisprudence will resemble the pre-*Faulkner* Article 5(4) jurisprudence, especially given the difficulties in distilling concrete guidance from the Strasbourg material.

iii. Quantum

There is evidence of inconsistency between awards under the HRA. Consider two decisions made within months of each other, both concerning damages for the same heads of loss—distress and frustration—caused by procedural violations. In *Guntrip*, decided in December 2010, the Judge awarded £1,200 to the claimant who had suffered a two year delay before the Parole Board, in breach of Article 5(4).[318] In May 2011 in *OOO* the Judge awarded £5,000 to each claimant for frustration and distress suffered over a 12 to 15 month period due to the authorities' failure to investigate claims of mistreatment in breach of Articles 3 and 4.[319]

Broadly speaking, in both cases damages were awarded for frustration caused by an authority's failure to comply with procedural obligations, during a period of delay which the claimants ought not to have endured.

[315] For example the victim's character has been invoked as a relevant consideration in post-*Faulkner* case law: *DSD* (n 17) [37]–[39].

[316] *Greenfield* (n 1) [7]; *Faulkner* (n 1) [109].

[317] eg *Pennington* (n 17) [12]. In contrast awards made for breaches of different rights were referred to in pre-*Greenfield* decisions: eg *KB* (n 5) [54].

[318] *Guntrip* (n 172).

[319] *OOO* (n 295).

Despite these similarities it is difficult to reconcile the awards. One rough means of comparison, given awards relate to frustration during a period of delay, is to break the awards down into per month rates. In *Guntrip* that rate was £50, whereas in *OOO* it was £370.[320] Thus the rate in *OOO* was 7.4 times higher than that in *Guntrip*. To provide some perspective, if the length of the delay in *OOO* had been the same as in *Guntrip* then the award to the claimants in *OOO*, applying the per month rate, would have been £8,880, whereas in *Guntrip* the award was only £1,200. The difference is marked, especially assuming HRA awards are on a modest and therefore compressed scale. Such disparity calls for explanation.

One justification might lie in the fact that damages in *OOO* were for breach of a procedural norm constituted to protect among the most important interests protected by the HRA. But liberty too is close to the apex of the normative hierarchy of interests protected by the HRA, such that this factor could not in itself explain such marked disparity. Furthermore, it is difficult to see the significance of normative hierarchy given courts are not assessing damages for normative injury but for actual distress.

A significant aggravating feature was present in *Guntrip*: the claimant suffered mental health issues which heightened his frustration and distress, whereas no special factor was present in *OOO*. Also, in *OOO* the Judge considered that frustration would naturally increase over time during a period of delay, which suggests that the award should increase at an exponential rate for every extra month of frustration suffered; the delay in *Guntrip* was nearly a year longer than that in *OOO*. Given these factors, it is even more difficult to explain the marked disparity between awards in *Guntrip* and *OOO*.

Such incoherence is likely to continue to characterise human rights damages while a case-by-case approach is adopted and while awards for one type of violation are considered in isolation from awards for other types. Further, such approach prevents formulation of general rules and principles which would facilitate consistency and coherence.

It is worth adding that in the first instance decision in *Sturnham*[321] the Judge broke the award in *Guntrip* down into a per month rate—£50 per month—and applied that rate to Sturnham's case, awarding £300 for distress and frustration suffered during a six month delay. In doing so the Judge recorded the aggravating features in *Guntrip*, such as Guntrip's mental health issues, which were *not* present in *Sturnham*. He nonetheless asserted: 'I see no reason to depart from an award of approximately that amount'.[322] It is difficult to see the logic of this reasoning, given it was clear

[320] Assuming a delay of 13.5 months in *OOO*: the mid-point of the 12–15 month range indicated by the Judge.
[321] Above (n 307).
[322] ibid [52].

that the special features in *Guntrip* led to an uplift. The Supreme Court upheld the £300 award in *Sturnham*.[323]

iv. Incoherence

Faulkner establishes that damages will ordinarily be awarded for sufficiently serious distress suffered in consequence of a delay in breach of Article 5(4), and that in certain circumstances such losses are presumed. In stark contrast, in *Osborn* Lord Reed effectively ruled out damages for distress suffered in consequence of a procedural violation of Article 5(4) *other than delay*. *Greenfield* had earlier more or less ruled out damages under Article 6(1), outside of special cases.

It is difficult to rationalise this patchwork of public authority liabilities on the one hand and near-immunities on the other, and there is no attempt by courts at rational justification of these variations. If X suffers feelings of helplessness and anxiety in consequence of unfair treatment in breach of Article 6(1), it is not apparent why X ought not to recover whereas if they had suffered the same type and intensity of feelings at a delay in breach of Article 5(4) they could recover. Equally it is not clear why courts should readily infer distress in Article 5(4) delay cases, whereas short shrift is given to claims that distress should be inferred for breaches of Article 5(4) not involving delay, such as the frustration one may legitimately feel at wrongful denial of the opportunity to put one's case in proceedings concerning one's liberty; indeed, more generally it is difficult to reconcile routine assumption of loss in procedural delay cases with judicial reluctance to infer even some compensable non-pecuniary loss in the context of relatively serious breaches of other rights, such as where prisoners are subject to extensive periods in solitary confinement in breach of Article 8.[324] Similarly it is difficult to reconcile the proposition in *Greenfield* that pecuniary losses will only rarely be recoverable for breaches of Article 6,[325] with warmer attitudes expressed in *Faulkner*.[326] *Greenfield* recognises the possibility of recovering for loss of real opportunities caused by denial of fair process under Article 6,[327] whereas *Faulkner* rules out such awards for denial of fair process under Article 5(4).[328]

The ECtHR has made several statements, though its pronouncements and practice are far from consistent,[329] that it does not consider a causal link

[323] *Faulkner* (n 1) [88]ff.

[324] See text to nn 280ff (on Article 5(4) cases not involving delay); *Shahid* (n 1) and n 284 above (on Article 8 prisoner claims).

[325] (n 1) [11].

[326] *Faulkner* (n 1) [13](8), [53].

[327] *Greenfield* (n 1) [12]–[15].

[328] *Faulkner* (n 1) [13](10), [82].

[329] See, eg, examples of awards for breach of Article 6 caused by structural bias (below in n 396). Contrast these cases with statements in *Kingsley* (n 57) [43] that awards are not made for such violations.

between procedural violations and non-pecuniary loss can be shown, *except* where the violation is caused by delay. For example in *HL* the Court said: 'despite the procedural nature of ... a violation [of Article 5(4)], it is accepted that there can be a causal link between the violation (delay) and the non-pecuniary damage claimed'.[330] It is hard to identify a principled basis for this distinction.[331] Whether there is a causal link between any violation and claimed non-pecuniary loss is a question for case-by-case determination. It is not possible to definitively rule out the possibility of a causal link between a particular type of violation and distress. It might well be that in general it is easier to prove such link between distress and delay than between distress and other types of procedural unfairness. But this does not logically lead to the proposition that causation can *never* be proven in the latter type of case. Indeed, empirical research cited in *Osborn* shows that unfair procedures can cause significant feelings of distress and despair outside delay cases.[332]

Such anomalies would be unlikely to emerge under a 'joined-up' approach characterised by a framework of general rules and principles, which would serve to ensure consistency in analysis of analogous matters as they arise across human rights law. The approach under the HRA is the exact opposite. The domestic courts' focus on replicating Strasbourg practice on a right-by-right basis (and emphasis on a broad discretionary approach) has prevented the fashioning of a general, coherent and normatively justifiable framework of rules and principles, while there is marked judicial reluctance to subject propositions derived from Strasbourg to normative evaluation. Given the ECtHR does not approach cases within a consistently applied framework of detailed rules and principles, it is unsurprising that following Strasbourg practice has resulted in a domestic jurisprudence characterised by incoherence.

Of course we should acknowledge that questions over damages can be difficult. For example there is no perfect, scientific approach to placing a monetary figure on intangible loss. These difficulties are no doubt why judges observe: 'Personally I have a dislike, which I have reason to believe is shared by other judges, to the task of assessing damage'.[333] But whatever these difficulties there is no excuse for returning damages to the nineteenth century, when the advice offered by a leading treatise on damages for torts

[330] *HL* (n 169) [149].

[331] This is because the basis for it likely lies outside of purely legal concerns. As was discussed above (text to n 169), the ECtHR has faced many repeat cases in respect of delays caused by systemic defects in domestic legal systems. As a result the ECtHR has, in delay claims, had to function more or less as a court of first instance, so that it has been more willing to make awards in this context than it would otherwise have been, while it also seems likely that the Court has been more willing to routinely make awards for delay so as to incentivise respondent states to address systemic delays and introduce domestic remedies for delay.

[332] See n 284 above.

[333] *The Greta Holme* [1897] AC 596, 604.

such as false imprisonment—which were largely assessed by juries—was: 'damages are always a mere matter of speculation. The talents of the counsel, the temper of the jury, and the view taken by the judge, have a greater influence upon their amount than any principles of law which can be laid down'.[334] Since 1877, when that observation was made, English damages law has made incredible progress, with articulation of elaborate rules and principles and scales of awards, which have served to facilitate consistency, coherence and rigour.[335] The current approach to human rights damages threatens to reverse that progress.

D. Supplementing Strasbourg

Thus limited guidance has been derived from Strasbourg. What guidance has been derived is in general not edifying, so general that it cannot provide meaningful guidance, and/or the substance of the guidance is difficult to justify in principle. One result of this state of affairs is that problems associated with Strasbourg practice are emerging domestically. Another result is that domestic courts have, on an ad hoc basis, supplemented the Strasbourg material, formulating rules, principles or methods not sourced from Strasbourg, aspects of which resemble features of the common law of damages. In turn, this calls into question the viability and credibility of the mirror approach and the 'ban' on recourse to common law material.

As discussed in chapter 3,[336] domestic courts have at times taken an approach akin to a pure common law approach—the 'usual approach'[337]—to award and assessment of damages for consequential pecuniary losses, specifically in claims by companies for interference with proprietary interests. In these claims courts have not sought to gauge Strasbourg practice by trawling the cases, and then replicate that practice. Rather they have applied the broad Strasbourg principles (ie genuine principles) such as *restitutio in integrum* and causation, awarding damages as of course where causation is proven and assessing pecuniary losses as a domestic court would in tort or contract.[338] This approach contrasts with the ECtHR's approach which is to take a broad equitable approach to the question of award and assessment, although the Court's practice in respect of pecuniary loss, and particularly

[334] JD Mayne and L Smith, *Mayne's Treatise on Damages* 3rd edn (Stevens and Haynes, 1877) 402.

[335] See ch 3.I.F.

[336] See ch 3.I.C.

[337] *R (Infinis Plc) v Gas and Electricity Markets Authority* [2013] JPL 1037, [27].

[338] *R (Infinis Plc) v Gas and Electricity Markets Authority* [2011] EWHC 1873 (upheld: ibid); *Breyer Group Plc v Department of Energy and Climate Change* [2014] JPL 1346 (upheld: [2015] EWCA Civ 408).

losses connected to property, is more predictable than the wildly unpredictable approach to non-pecuniary loss.[339] This divergent practice—domestic courts have explicitly distinguished the approach to pecuniary damages from that taken to non-pecuniary loss[340]—poses a serious challenge to the credibility of the mirror approach: how can the courts maintain a mirror approach to non-pecuniary loss, but take an approach to pecuniary loss indistinguishable from domestic tort law? Why do courts apply broad Strasbourg *principles*—which are consonant with the common law—in respect of pecuniary loss, but generally look to replicate *practice* in respect of non-pecuniary loss?

Even in respect of non-pecuniary losses lower courts have, on occasion, formulated decision-criteria not sourced from Strasbourg. For example, in Article 5(4) claims by prisoners in respect of Parole Board delays courts have taken into account the claimant's belief as to the strength of their case for release, the stronger the belief (as long as reasonably held) the greater the distress likely to have been suffered.[341] Courts have also considered whether the claimant suffered mental illness, which might have made it more difficult to cope with delay.[342] One of the best examples of a judge taking it upon himself to formulate factors is *Pennington.* In that case the Judge, having found no detailed guidance in the Strasbourg material, articulated factors *he* considered indicated a higher or lower award.[343] In respect of each of these examples the relevant factors were not sourced in clear and constant Strasbourg practice; rather the judges had to come up with their own factors because of a lack of guidance from Strasbourg or higher courts. Indeed, of the mental health factor one Judge noted that '[t]he [ECtHR] jurisprudence ... does not suggest that any special legal principles apply to mental health cases as distinguished from other cases in which the lawfulness of detention falls to be determined under Article 5'.[344] Nonetheless the Judge considered this factor bore on quantum.

Similarly, where higher courts have propounded more detailed guidance, this guidance has not been sourced from Strasbourg. However, there have been tenuous efforts to link such guidance to Strasbourg. One might

[339] Ichim (n 187) ch 4. It is true that the ECtHR does not always have the same firm factual foundation to adjudicate such claims that domestic courts do but this cannot completely explain the ECtHR's approach, as the Court may be guided by 'equitable' concerns even where it is has evidence before it. This reflects that the Court's general approach to money awards—in respect of *both* non-pecuniary and pecuniary loss—is discretionary and subject to the Court's open-ended idea of 'equity'.

[340] *Infinis* (n 337) [26]–[27].

[341] *Pennington* (n 17) [24].

[342] *Guntrip* (n 172); *KB* (n 5).

[343] *Pennington* (n 17) [23]–[25]. For another good example see *R (AM) v Chief Constable West Midlands Police* [2010] EWHC 1228, [44] (the Judge having noted that Strasbourg provided little guidance on whether non-monetary relief affords just satisfaction: [25]).

[344] *KB* (n 5) [70].

speculate that this effort at 'keeping up appearances' is the product of higher courts feeling duty-bound to provide some more detailed guidance to lower courts, while not wishing to undermine the integrity of the mirror approach, which they have bound lower courts to apply.

In *Rabone* the Supreme Court assessed damages for non-pecuniary loss suffered by relatives of an individual who had died in circumstances where authorities breached their Article 2 obligations to the deceased. Lord Dyson enumerated several factors bearing on quantum, including the closeness of the family link between the deceased and the claimants, the nature of the breach and the seriousness of the non-pecuniary damage suffered by the relatives.[345] He introduced these factors as those which '[o]ne would expect the [ECtHR] to have regard to'.[346] The only evidence provided that the ECtHR *does* have regard to these factors is that there had been 'passing reference to some of these considerations' in a single case;[347] this is hardly clear and consistent practice. Despite the attempt to link the factors to Strasbourg, the factors were in truth those that Lord Dyson *himself* considered ought to guide assessment. To introduce the factors as those the ECtHR would be expected to consider is a construct; indeed, why should we assume the ECtHR approaches assessment according to a consistent set of factors at all, given most decisions are unreasoned and inconsistency characterises the Court's practice? Lord Dyson himself had observed that the Court had not been directed to any ECtHR judgment which serves as a guideline judgment and enumerates those considerations relevant to assessment.[348] Interestingly, the approach of setting out factors, as well as the content of those factors, focused as they are on factual features of the case that may indicate greater or lesser loss, are close to what one would find in a guideline judgment at common law. Also of note is that the award made for bereavement in *Rabone* was identical to what would have been awarded under domestic legislation governing damages for bereavement.[349]

As we saw above[350] Lord Reed in *Faulkner* indicated that damages for loss of conditional liberty will be less than for loss of unconditional liberty. Putting to the side that it is not clear what these damages compensate for, Lord Reed cited no ECtHR case in which this factor had been explicitly relied on to reduce awards.[351] He considered Strasbourg cases in which

[345] *Rabone* (n 1) [85]. This list is a little confusing in that what is being assessed is non-pecuniary damage, such that making non-pecuniary damage a factor does not make a great deal of sense, while it is unclear how the nature of the breach relates to quantifying factual losses.

[346] ibid.

[347] ibid [86]; *Kallis v Turkey* (27 October 2009) App no 45388/99 (ECtHR Fourth Section).

[348] *Rabone*, ibid [84].

[349] *Rabone* CA (n 9) [112], upheld in the Supreme Court although note that the Supreme Court felt the award was a little low: (n 1) [88].

[350] Text to nn 271ff.

[351] *Faulkner* (n 1) [69]–[76].

awards were made for lost *unconditional* liberty. He also considered ECtHR cases in which awards were made for *loss of an opportunity* of release, in circumstances where release would have been on licence. But there was no case in which awards had been made for *actual* loss of *conditional* liberty. Referring to one loss of opportunity case, in which the liberty that was potentially lost was conditional, Lord Reed said:

> A higher award would no doubt have been appropriate if there had been a definite loss of liberty for 12 months; but a lower award would have been appropriate if, instead of a patient losing her liberty, the case had concerned a convicted prisoner who had lost an opportunity of earlier release on licence.[352]

This is not the reasoning of the ECtHR, nor a statement as to the practice of the ECtHR—it is Lord Reed's proposition. The only other Article 5(4) ECtHR case which Lord Reed specifically relied on to support his proposition was *Weeks*.[353] He said that the level of award made in that case relative to awards in Article 5(1) cases, where liberty lost was unconditional, supported the proposition that awards for loss of conditional liberty should be reduced. But, with respect, this is thoroughly unconvincing given that in *Weeks* the ECtHR explicitly held that the award was *not* for lost liberty at all, but only for *distress* associated with the state's failure to comply with procedural guarantees.[354]

So, as in *Rabone*, we have an example of a more detailed proposition formulated by a domestic court, not sourced from Strasbourg, coupled with an *attempt* to find support for that proposition in Strasbourg material. Also in common with *Rabone*, this sort of guidance bears a passing resemblance to reasoning one might find at common law;[355] at common law the degree of interference with liberty bares on quantum.[356]

Also in *Faulkner* the Supreme Court asserted a rebuttable presumption that damages ought to be awarded for distress in Article 5(4) delay cases where the delay was at least three months.[357] This was coupled with guidance that awards should not ordinarily be made where the delay was less than three months. To support this guidance Lord Reed cited five ECtHR cases in which delay was three months or less. In two of these cases awards

352 ibid [74].

353 ibid; *Weeks v UK* (1991) 13 EHRR 435.

354 *Weeks* ibid [12], [14] ('no compensation is payable in respect of the harmful consequences attributable to the contested deprivation of liberty as such; for the purposes of an award of just satisfaction ... the only prejudice that may be taken into account is that caused by the lack of a remedy satisfying the requirements of Article 5 para 4 ... the absence of a remedy satisfying the requirements of Article 5 para 4 ... must have caused Mr Weeks a feeling of frustration and helplessness').

355 Although, as discussed above (text to nn 271ff) there are problems with the way this reasoning has been applied in the HRA context.

356 See ch 2.III.C.iv.

357 *Faulkner* (n 1) [13](15), [66].

were made for delays *under* three months; however, Lord Reed distinguished these on the basis that they concerned delay incurred during remand, which placed the claimants in a particularly sensitive position, whereas *Faulkner* concerned delay in processing applications for release from imprisonment following conviction.[358] But there is no evidence that this factor influenced the ECtHR, the ECtHR in both cases adopting its usual sparing approach to reasoning.[359] In two other cases the ECtHR refused to make an award;[360] prima facie this supports Lord Reed's guidance. However, these cases were decided in the early 1990s whereas Lord Reed had indicated earlier in his judgment that cases decided by the ECtHR during this earlier period may not offer reliable guidance as to the ECtHR's contemporary practice.[361] Indeed, Lord Reed himself observed that the decisions were 'somewhat dated'.[362] In the final case of the five relied upon—a more recent decision—the ECtHR refused to make an award for claimed distress suffered over a very short 17 day period.[363]

Thus, there is no *express* basis in Strasbourg decisions for ordinarily declining to make awards where delay is less than three months—such as a guideline judgment—nor can it be said, based on the cases invoked by Lord Reed, that there is clear and consistent ECtHR practice of declining awards for such delays. Only a single case from the Court's contemporary case law was cited by Lord Reed where the ECtHR had refused to make an award for delay of less than three months, and in that case the delay was *significantly* less than three months: 17 days. The presumption is *in truth* the Supreme Court's own creation. Lord Carnwath was a little more candid in his separate judgment in *Faulkner*, opining that the threshold is the result of the 'national court['s] ... view' in the light of its consideration of 'interests of certainty and proportionality', as well as any 'Strasbourg principles'.[364]

Two points are pertinent. First, that what meaningful guidance can be derived from domestic case law is not the product of the mirror approach casts further doubt upon the viability of that approach, while that some of this guidance closely resembles common law rules, principles or modes of reasoning is illustrative of the artificiality of attempting strict separation of human rights damages and common law. If one is concerned to develop a rational and coherent law of human rights damages, it makes little sense to take a flawed jurisprudence as one's starting point, and then seek to imperfectly ameliorate the shortcomings of an approach based on such

[358] ibid [64].

[359] *Mooren v Germany* (2010) 50 EHRR 23, [130]; *GB v Switzerland* (2002) 34 EHRR 10, [42].

[360] *Koendjbiharie v Netherlands* (1991) 13 EHRR 820; *E v Norway* (1994) 17 EHRR 30.

[361] *Faulkner* (n 1) [50].

[362] ibid [65].

[363] *Rutten v Netherlands* (24 July 2001) App No 32605/96 (ECtHR First Section).

[364] *Faulkner* (n 1) [127].

jurisprudence by supplementing it on an ad hoc basis with common law-like rules, principles or reasoning. It makes far more sense to take the common law as one's starting point, in accordance with the 'ordinary approach'.[365]

Second, while it is positive that judges have at times sought to articulate greater guidance, they have been relieved of justifying the substance of that guidance by attributing it to Strasbourg, often where there is no basis for such attribution. The reasoning in the domestic cases is in general cursory and highly formalistic; typically judges assert propositions by reference to Strasbourg decisions, without serious engagement with Strasbourg material or any elaboration upon the normative justifications for such propositions; the Strasbourg material itself does not offer such normative justifications given Article 41 decisions are typically unreasoned. At times the treatment of Strasbourg material gives the impression that that material is marshalled and presented in such a way as to support normative positions arrived at independently of that material, with the reasons underlying those normative positions left unarticulated.

SECTION 3. THE METHODOLOGY OF THE MIRROR APPROACH

I. A PROBLEMATIC METHOD

Even where guidance has been derived from Strasbourg the robustness of the *method* of derivation is questionable.

In *Faulkner* the Supreme Court's method was to extract the ECtHR's 'general practice' by sifting through a plethora of Strasbourg decisions, and to read that practice across to domestic law. Lord Reed found that in the majority of cases where the ECtHR found a violation of Article 5(4) by reason of delay, the Court had awarded compensation for distress. This was taken to be the Court's 'general practice'.[366] That practice was then effectively transformed into a norm in domestic law, the Court holding that damages should ordinarily be awarded for sufficiently serious distress in delay cases. In *Greenfield* Lord Bingham, adopting a similar method, concluded that the ECtHR's 'routine'[367] practice had been to make no award for breach of Article 6, as the ECtHR had denied awards in the 'great majority'[368] of cases, so that under the HRA awards should only be made exceptionally. In *Greenfield* the House of Lords did not come close to considering every successful Article 6 claim in which just satisfaction had been claimed. In *Faulkner* a significant number of Article 5(4) cases were cited; it is unclear what proportion of all relevant ECtHR cases were considered.

[365] See s 1.III above.
[366] *Faulkner* (n 1) [53].
[367] *Greenfield* (n 1) [9].
[368] ibid [8].

It is difficult to see the basis for transmuting raw data (the regularity of the making of awards for a particular violation) into a legal norm—'general principles'[369]—where that data derives from the case-by-case exercise of broad remedial discretion, the ECtHR determining whether to make awards and quantum according to 'what is just, fair and reasonable in all the circumstances of the case'.[370] That awards have been made in a majority of cases for a particular type of violation tells us only that the ECtHR considered awards equitable in the circumstances of those cases.[371] Where awards have been denied this tells us only that the Court considered awards inappropriate in those cases. That awards were made in a majority of cases may simply reflect the types of cases which happened to reach the Court: it may have just so happened that there were a higher proportion of cases presented to the ECtHR which had features which the Court, in its subjective judgement, considered warranted an award than cases in which the Court subjectively considered that awards were not warranted. Are we to take statistics which may well depend on the vicissitudes of the ECtHR's docket as a basis for creating domestic norms?

Further, it is difficult to see how it follows from, say, awards being denied in the majority of Article 6 cases that it is the ECtHR's 'routine' practice to refuse awards. If we assume Lord Bingham in *Greenfield* was correct that the ECtHR declined awards in the majority of successful Article 6 cases but also, for the sake of argument, assume that those cases in which awards *were* made constituted a third of all successful Article 6 cases then it would be misleading to say that the ECtHR's routine practice was to decline awards. Assuming a proportion of one third, awards would have been made in a significant proportion of cases, and such cases could not be said to be rare.

Given the stated goal of the mirror approach—to replicate what the ECtHR would do in a particular case domestically—knowing that the ECtHR has made awards in 64 per cent of cases of violation X or 37 per cent of cases of violation Y is not particularly illuminating. In order to replicate what the ECtHR would decide in a given case we would need to know the considerations which lead the Court to make or decline awards. But in general the Court offers no substantive reasoning. For example, Lord Justice Waller observed in *Dobson* of ECtHR practice in Article 8 pollution cases that '[a]ll one can say with any certainty is that damages have been awarded for non-pecuniary loss, ie for inconvenience and distress, in pollution cases'.[372] What is *un*certain is *when* such losses ought to be compensated. Similarly in *Shahid* the Supreme Court recorded that there were cases where the Strasbourg Court 'declined to make an award' to prisoners

369 *Faulkner* (n 1) [76].
370 ibid [34], quoting *Al-Jedda* (n 107) [114].
371 *Faulkner*, ibid [105].
372 *Dobson* (n 17) [43].

subjected to segregation in breach of Article 8, and cases where 'modest awards have been made', but was unable to distill any guidance as to *when* awards ought or ought not to be made.[373] In consequence the Court resorted to a broad discretionary approach, considering factors not sourced from Strasbourg. Another example is the Strasbourg practice in respect of awards for distress consequent upon breach of Article 5(4) outside of delay cases. In both *Faulkner* and *Osborn* Lord Reed observed that despite express statements from the ECtHR that awards should not be made in such cases, awards had in fact been made in 'numerous cases'.[374] Thus it could not be concluded that the overall 'bulk' of decisions went one way or the other. Of course because such decisions are largely unreasoned and discretionary it would be difficult, if not impossible, to explain why awards had been made in some cases but not others. Such a situation, which will not be uncommon given the state of Strasbourg jurisprudence, poses a distinct challenge to the viability of the mirror method. The outcome was for Lord Reed, in *Osborn*, to avoid the issue of how to discern ECtHR practice and simply assert that awards would generally not be made, except where there is a loss of liberty (see section 2.II.C.i above). Ironically, the result is that domestic practice will now depart from ECtHR practice, given the Strasbourg Court does make awards for such violations in 'numerous cases'.

These issues do not arise in application of the mirror approach to questions of substantive rights pursuant to section 2 HRA. This is because domestic courts do not, in determining questions of right, seek to divine aggregate trends in outcomes of particular sets of claims. Rather courts are concerned to identify consistently applied *rules* and *principles*, and then apply those rules and principles in domestic law. This is feasible because unlike determinations under Article 41, ECtHR determinations as to rights-violations are reasoned. Further, while the Strasbourg Court does not follow a doctrine of precedent equivalent to that in English law, there is some system of precedent in operation.[375] Also, the Court's decisions in respect of violations are not made pursuant to discretion, so that one is able to identify consistently-applied rules and principles through a stream of jurisprudence, which offer relatively safe guidance as to how the ECtHR would approach a given case. In contrast, as Lord Carnwath observed in *Faulkner*, '[t]he great majority of … awards [under Article 41] are made on an "equitable" basis reflecting particular facts … most of the decisions are not intended to have any precedential effect, and it is a mistake in my view to treat them as if they were'; he saw force in the view that 'the [ECtHR's] decisions on just

[373] *Shahid* (n 1) [88]–[89].

[374] *Osborn* (n 1) [114]; *Faulkner* (n 1) [61].

[375] See, eg, AR Mowbray, 'An Examination of the European Court of Human Rights' Approach to Overruling its Previous Case Law' (2009) 9 *Human Rights Law Review* 179.

satisfaction [are] "little more than equitable assessments of the facts of the individual case"'.[376]

Where, as is typically the case, there is little reasoning from the ECtHR in a particular stream of Article 41 determinations by reference to which one could discern whether patterns of outcomes reflect some rational design, it may be tempting to impute such design; equally there may be a temptation to explain away decisions which are inconsistent with a desired narrative. But this involves a real risk of revisionism, and of enunciation of rules which have no true basis in the Strasbourg jurisprudence. For example in *Faulkner* Lord Reed sought to explain one ECtHR Article 5(4) delay case in which an award had been *refused* on the basis that the delay in that case occurred not in proceedings addressed to whether detention continued to be justified, in which context awards had been made, but in the context of proceedings concerning whether the applicant's confinement ought to be extended.[377] But there was no reference to this factor in the ECtHR's reasoning, the Court adopting its usual style of reasoning, noting that some distress may well have been suffered but that '[t]he finding of a violation of Article 5 § 4 of the Convention constitutes in itself sufficient just satisfaction'.[378] How are we to know which factors bore on the Court's determination and what weight they were given? Further, if one is looking for a rational basis for refusal of an award Lord Reed's explanation does not offer one. Why should it make a difference, in terms of recovery, if the individual suffers serious anxiety as a result of delay in the context of proceedings concerning continued justification of their detention or in the context of proceedings concerning whether their confinement should be extended? In each case serious distress is suffered in consequence of a rights-violation, and in proceedings brought to determine whether the victim will regain their freedom. If anything, the variations in the ECtHR decisions demonstrate a *lack* of rational order.

A further issue with the mirror method, not addressed by courts, is the specificity or generality at which a court's inquiry into Strasbourg practice should be pitched. For example in *Faulkner* the Court considered practice in respect of particular types of violation: Lord Reed considered practice in respect of (1) Article 5(4) violations caused by delay, and (2) practice in respect of Article 5(4) violations caused by procedural breach other than delay, such as bias or failure to conduct an oral hearing.[379] In respect of (2), framing the inquiry according to procedural violations *as a general class* left open the possibility that awards would be available for such violations in domestic law; pitched at that level of generality one could possibly conclude that the ECtHR had a practice of making awards.[380] In contrast in *Osborn*,

[376] *Faulkner* (n 1) [105], [108], quoting Lester and Pannick (n 63) [2.8.4] fn 3.
[377] ibid [51].
[378] *Rutten* (n 363) [59].
[379] *Faulkner* (n 1) [41]–[61].
[380] ibid [61].

Lord Reed, in determining the damages claim, considered ECtHR practice at a far greater level of specificity, examining ECtHR practice for *specific* types of procedural violation *and* within the specific factual matrix at issue in *Osborn*.[381] So narrowly confined, the inquiry led to the conclusion that there were no Strasbourg cases comparable to *Osborn* in which awards had been made, the damages claim being summarily dismissed.

II. QUANTUM

As it relates to quantum the mirror approach requires English courts to aim not to be more or less generous than the ECtHR would be in a similar case.[382] In turn this implicates an inquiry into what award the Strasbourg Court would make. One cannot work this out by reference to ECtHR guidance as to scales and factors which increase or decrease quantum given the Court has not articulated such general, consistently-applied guidance.

One might search for an ECtHR case with facts similar to that under consideration and follow the award in that case. But this is problematic because, as Lord Bingham observed in *Greenfield*, each award is wholly dependent on what the ECtHR, in its discretion, considered 'fair' in the circumstances of that particular case, such that it would be wrong to treat the decision as setting a precedent.[383] In *Faulkner* too Lord Reed considered individual awards could not provide a reliable basis for decision-making, while Lord Carnwath observed, 'most [Article 41] decisions are not intended to have any precedential effect'.[384] This is consistent with the view of discretion in English law: no one exercise of discretion is

> binding authority on how the discretion should be exercised. The most that any of them can demonstrate is that in similar circumstances it would not be wrong to exercise the discretion in the same way. But it does not follow that it would be wrong to exercise the discretion differently.[385]

A core difference, of course, is that in English law judges generally reason why they exercise discretion one way or another, so that later judges may at least follow the considerations which guided previous exercises.

In any case, one would need to know *which* facts the ECtHR considered material to setting quantum in order to work out whether a domestic case is analogous. But the ECtHR does not typically analyse the facts in deciding compensation, usually offering no analysis whatsoever. Further, facts are not the only relevant consideration: the Court has been known to take

381 *Osborn* (n 1) [114].
382 *Greenfield* (n 1) [19]; *Faulkner* (n 1) [35].
383 *Greenfield* (n 1) [19].
384 *Faulkner* (n 1) [68], [105].
385 *Jaggard v Sawyer* [1995] 1 WLR 269, 288.

into account *normative* considerations on an ad hoc basis, such as the victim's moral status, some public interest concerns (albeit rarely), and other 'equitable' considerations.[386] Obviously where no reasoning is proffered it is impossible to know whether such concerns influenced the Court. Commentators observe that the ECtHR may well take into account certain concerns, such as moral status, even if they are not expressly mentioned.[387]

Another way one might implement the mirror approach is to determine awards in individual cases by reference to 'general' levels of awards at Strasbourg for particular classes of violation. However, there are problems with implementing this approach too. Take awards for indirect victims, such as relatives, for non-pecuniary losses suffered in consequence of Article 2 violations. In both *Savage* and *Rabone* each Court noted that the range of awards made by the ECtHR is 5,000 to 60,000 Euros.[388] There is no 'general' level of awards here—for example a clustering around a particular level—such that a domestic court could set an award within the 'ballpark' of that cluster. Rather, there is 'a considerable range'.[389] This leads on to an obvious problem; to determine quantum judges not only require a guideline range but a set of factors to guide them in placing the case before them *within* that range. As already discussed these factors cannot be derived from Strasbourg. And even if we had factors we would need to know whether the scale is weighted a particular way, if we are to take seriously the goal of ensuring broad consistency with Strasbourg. For example is 30,000 Euros a 'par' award or is the 30,000–60,000 Euros range reserved for exceptional cases?

Treating the highest and lowest awards made by the ECtHR as the polarities of a range within which awards should be set suggests that these are start- and end- points of a defined, clear and consistent scale of awards, with domestic courts' task being to determine where the ECtHR would place the case on that scale. Yet we do not know if the ECtHR applies such a scale, or if it does, what that scale is. The awards of 5,000 and 60,000 Euros are merely the lowest and highest awards the Court has made among those cases that have come before it; if the Court had dealt with a different set of cases the range might be 15,000 to 150,000 Euros. The 'range' is thus rather artificial.

One recent case entails a heroic attempt by a lower court judge to forge the Strasbourg case law on just satisfaction for procedural breaches of Article 3 into something akin to a guideline judgment.[390] He articulates

[386] As the Law Commissions observed ((n 36) [4.96]), the ECHR has been known to take into account 'a range of factors including the character and conduct of the parties, to an extent which is hitherto unknown in English law'.

[387] Shelton (n 148) 260–65; see ch 6.2.V.B.

[388] *Rabone* (n 1) [85]; *Savage* (n 216) [97].

[389] *Rabone* ibid; *Savage* ibid (range is 'wide').

[390] *DSD* (n 17).

bands and factors to guide assessment. This is, with respect, a commendable effort and the judgment offers far more guidance as to quantum than any higher court judgment. However, it is highly doubtful whether the guidance reflects the Strasbourg Court's own approach. Rather the guidance entails a 'reconstruction' of the Strasbourg material. For example bands are articulated by the Judge imposing his own order on the range of awards made by the Strasbourg Court. But there is no way of knowing whether these bands correlate with the Strasbourg Court's own method, if it has one, while as with *Rabone* and *Savage*, there are problems with treating the Strasbourg awards as setting a range. The factors which the Judge articulates to guide assessment are derived by going through one Strasbourg case after another and speculating as to the reasons why the Strasbourg Court awarded higher or lower figures in particular cases, unrealistically assuming these equitable case-by-case determinations must form a rational ordering, despite the general absence of any substantive reasoning from the ECtHR as to why it reached particular figures on particular facts.

It is a very odd thing that our law of human rights damages is the product of English judges reading Strasbourg tea leaves.

III. INCONSISTENT METHOD AND THE RISK OF SKEWED INTERPRETATION

There have been inconsistencies in the way different courts have 'interpreted' the Strasbourg material, which have affected conclusions as to the availability of damages. On one view this is a likely outcome where differently constituted courts interpret a troubled jurisprudence. On another view such inconsistencies raise the spectre of decision-making guided by unstated concerns.

Let us compare Lord Reed's analysis in *Faulkner* of ECtHR practice as to awards for distress in Article 5(4) cases concerning procedural unfairness other than delay, and Lord Bingham's analysis in *Greenfield* of ECtHR practice as to awards for distress in Article 6 structural bias cases (structural bias being a form of procedural unfairness).

Lord Bingham recorded that awards for distress had been made in some cases of breach of Article 6 but that the ECtHR had been 'very sparing' in making such awards, citing four ECtHR cases in which awards were declined.[391] Turning to cases of structural bias in particular, he concluded that the ECtHR's ordinary practice was not to make awards. This conclusion was based on a single statement from the ECtHR that it was 'normal practice' to refuse to make awards in such cases; he had also previously

[391] *Greenfield* (n 1) [16].

cited two structural bias cases in which awards were declined.[392] No serious attempt was made to check the ECtHR's statement as to its practice against actual practice by, for example, conducting a survey of relevant decisions.

In *Faulkner* Lord Reed recorded that the Strasbourg Court, including the Grand Chamber, had, in *Nikolova* and *HL*, made general statements that awards would not ordinarily be made for breaches of Article 5(4) (or 5(3)) caused by procedural failures other than delay and which did not result in loss of liberty.[393] However, Lord Reed thought these statements could not be said to lay down a strict rule because the ECtHR adopts a discretionary approach. Further, he observed that awards had been made in 'numerous cases' subsequent to the first of these statements. He did not reach a concluded view as to whether such awards ought to be available in principle in domestic law. However, his analysis tended to support availability of damages. In addition to his interpretation of *Nikolova* and *HL* as not setting down a rule against recovery, he placed emphasis on a statement of the ECtHR in *Abdi* in which the Court cited *HL* and *Nikolova* as supporting the proposition that awards would be made where causation was established.[394] Lord Reed's invocation of and reliance upon this single statement is rather difficult to marry up with his treatment of those statements in *HL* and *Nikolova* that awards ought not to be made, which he considered confined to their facts and not capable of offering general guidance. Lord Reed's willingness to leave open the making of awards for distress caused by procedural breaches of Article 5(4) contrasted with Lord Carnwath's view: his Lordship favoured following the ECtHR's express statements, and would have ruled out recovery of awards based on *Nikolova* and *HL*.[395]

Thus in *Faulkner* Lord Reed was willing to look past repeated, express statements from the ECtHR against awards to the ECtHR's practice. On this basis he did not rule out awards, and seemingly favoured availability of awards where causation was proven. In contrast Lord Bingham in *Greenfield* relied almost exclusively on a single statement from the ECtHR to conclude that awards ought not to be made in cases of structural bias. Unlike Lord Reed, Lord Bingham did not seriously consider Strasbourg practice. In fact a review of the ECtHR jurisprudence reveals that the ECtHR has made awards in a significant number of Article 6 structural bias cases.[396]

[392] ibid; *Kingsley* (n 57) [43].

[393] *Faulkner* (n 1) [55]–[61]; *Nikolova* (n 283) [76]; *HL* (n 169) [148]–[149].

[394] *Faulkner* ibid [61]; *Abdi v UK* (2013) 57 EHRR 16, [91]. Although, it is not clear that the statement from *Abdi* was made in respect of compensation for *distress*, which was the head of loss Lord Reed was concerned with; it seems rather to have been concerned with *loss of liberty*, which would be consistent with the views of the ECtHR in *HL* and *Nikolova*.

[395] *Faulkner* (n 1) [115]ff. This had also been the approach of the lower courts: [116].

[396] eg *De Cubber v Belgium* (1991) 13 EHRR 422, [24]; *Kadubec v Slovakia* (2001) 33 EHRR 41, [68]; *Lauko v Slovakia* (2001) 33 EHRR 40, [72]; *Sadak v Turkey (No 1)* (2003) 36 EHRR 26, [77]; *Tsfayo v UK* (2009) 48 EHRR 18, [56]; *Golubović v Croatia* (27 November 2012) App no 43947/10, [66] (ECtHR First Section); *Harabin v Slovakia*

Against this background Lord Reed's approach, in the post-*Faulkner* decision in *Osborn*, when he revisited the issue of whether damages could be recovered for distress consequent upon procedural breaches of Article 5(4), is striking. While in *Faulkner* his analysis suggested damages would be available if causation were established, in *Osborn* he asserted that procedural breach of Article 5(4) would not normally sound in damages (unless the breach resulted in loss of liberty). This general proposition was not the subject of reasoned justification.[397] What is pertinent for present purposes is that the rule in *Osborn* is identical to that articulated in *Nikolova* and *HL*. It is difficult to see this as mere coincidence. It seems Lord Reed has adopted, or at least been heavily influenced by an express statement of the ECtHR despite that statement not reflecting practice—as observed in *Faulkner* there is a practice of making awards for procedural breaches—and despite his own view, previously expressed in *Faulkner*, that such statements were unreliable. Indeed it was the very fact that express statements were unreliable *because* they conflicted with practice which led Lord Reed to interpret 'principles' in section 8 HRA as 'practice'.[398] Other unexplained variations between *Faulkner* and *Osborn* have already been canvassed such as variation in the generality or specificity of the inquiry into practice.[399] While there are other curious features of *Osborn* such as the glaring absence of any analysis of cases, such as *Waite*,[400] which were invoked in *Faulkner* in support of damages for procedural breaches outside delay cases.[401]

On the one hand these variations may be explicable on the basis that courts are engaging with a difficult, flawed jurisprudence, characterised by conflicting practices, and judicial pronouncements which conflict with practice. In light of such difficulties it may be inevitable that the courts' approach varies from one case to another. But while one might understand the cause of such inconsistency this does not mean it is defensible, especially given such variations are not explained even where it is the same judge adjudicating the same matter in two cases—*Faulkner* and *Osborn*—months apart. If such inconsistencies are a natural consequence of the mirror approach this is another reason for its abandonment. A victim's claim for damages should not depend on the idiosyncrasies of the judicial approach to interpreting the Strasbourg material in their particular case: if the focus in

(20 November 2012) App no 58688/11, [176] (ECtHR Third Section); *Ozerov v Russia* (18 May 2010) App no 64962/01, [62] (ECtHR Third Section); *Gajewski v Poland* (21 December 2010) App no 27225/05, [53] (ECtHR Fourth Section).

397 *Osborn* (n 1) [2](xiii). Text to n 291 above.

398 *Faulkner* (n 1) [31]; see s 1.I above.

399 Text to n 379 above.

400 Text to n 289 above.

401 *Faulkner* (n 1) [61].

Greenfield had been on ECtHR practice rather than dicta the claimant may well have obtained an award. Similarly, if Osborn's case had been joined in the *Faulkner* litigation an award may well have been made.

On the other hand stark inconsistencies of approach raise the spectre of judges interpreting Strasbourg material guided by unstated concerns. Lord Reed in *Faulkner* was willing to reason around ECtHR statements that told against liability, and yet rely on similar statements which supported liability, as well as highlighting practice favouring liability. This was all within a judgment notable, exceptionally so in the HRA damages context, for its willingness to open up liability. In stark contrast Lord Bingham in *Greenfield* accepted uncritically and at face value a statement of the ECtHR indicating compensation ought not to be awarded ordinarily, and did not explore Strasbourg practice in detail. This was all within a decision the general tenor of which was that damages ought not to be part of the ordinary response to rights-violations. It is not difficult to see how an observer might suspect that different normative concerns underpinned each Judge's 'interpretation' of Strasbourg materials. But it is more difficult to explain how the same judge, Lord Reed, took such different approaches to the same issue from *Faulkner* to *Osborn*, decisions made within months of one another. One may only speculate, given the lack of reasoning in *Osborn*. But one wonders whether Lord Carnwath's strong separate judgment in *Faulkner*, emphasising his experience as an ad hoc judge of the ECtHR and calling for a focus on express statements by the ECtHR, may have made an impact between innings. Further, as we shall see, Lord Reed's frustration at having to dedicate much time and effort to reading myriad Strasbourg decisions in order to discern clear and consistent practice was manifest in *Faulkner*, and one wonders whether the Court in *Osborn* was simply not willing to incur the same burden, in terms of time and effort, finding it more convenient to simply rule out awards.

Whatever the explanation, the foregoing highlights the *potential* at least for inconsistent approaches to Strasbourg material based in unstated concerns. The ECtHR jurisprudence is particularly open to 'massaging' in line with one's own normative concerns. Unreasoned decisions can be reconstructed to support particular propositions or distinguished based on fine distinctions; general statements can be selectively disposed of or relied upon depending on the desired narrative; practice can be analysed at a greater or lesser level of generality; while where there are conflicting streams of decisions one may selectively emphasise one over the other, or inconvenient cases may be ignored. Putting to the side that such approach entails a lack of transparency, inconsistency and possible reliance on subjective concerns which may not stand up to scrutiny if made explicit, a state of affairs in which different courts massage a flawed jurisprudence one way or the other on an ad hoc basis seems unlikely to produce a satisfactory law of damages.

IV. '[O]NE DAMN THING AFTER ANOTHER'[402]

The mirror approach imposes significant time and cost burdens on parties and the judiciary. This is because ECtHR 'practice' can only be discerned by trawling potentially vast numbers of decisions. For example in *Faulkner* large tracts of Lord Reed's judgment were occupied by summary descriptions of one Strasbourg case after another.[403] As Lord Reed observed, around 75 Strasbourg cases were cited to the Court. He explained that it had been time-consuming for counsel to take the Court through these cases, the appeal taking up over three days of hearing time. Seeking to extract 'principles' from a 'blizzard of authorities' had required 'painstaking effort'.[404] Indeed, one of Lord Carnwath's reasons for favouring express statements of principle made by the ECtHR ahead of practice was that it would be 'less laborious';[405] 'The court should not be subjected to a "blizzard of authorities" (as Lord Reed describes it)'.[406] In *Anufrijeva* Lord Woolf similarly observed that the Court had 'been deluged with extensive written and oral arguments and citation from numerous lever arch files crammed to overflowing with authorities', and that the Court had sought to save the parties costs 'by engaging in an intensive reading programme out of court'.[407] It was this experience that led Lord Woolf to prescribe that only three authorities should ordinarily be cited to the court;[408] this guidance has had virtually no effect in practice. In a recent case the High Court dedicated 39 paragraphs, spanning 20 pages of the Law Reports, to considering Strasbourg cases one by one in accordance with the mirror method articulated in *Faulkner*.[409] Avoiding costs associated with trawling endless Strasbourg decisions and seeking to reconcile them has been one reason why the courts have begun to favour the 'ordinary approach'[410] of looking to domestic law ahead of Convention jurisprudence in adjudication of substantive rights matters.[411]

[402] *Faulkner* (n 1) [103].
[403] eg ibid [41]–[54]. See also, eg, *Van Colle* CA (n 6) [106]–[110]; *DSD* (n 17) [69]–[108].
[404] *Faulkner* ibid [103].
[405] ibid [104].
[406] ibid [114]. Perhaps the experience in *Faulkner*, of painstaking effort, was one further explanation for why, in the follow-up case of *Osborn* a few months later, Lord Reed simply asserted that awards would not be made for procedural breaches of Article 5(4) with no real analysis of why this should be so, and nowhere near the level of engagement with Strasbourg practice that had gone into *Faulkner*. There is surely a limit to how much judicial time and effort can sensibly be spent trawling through Strasbourg cases, and it seems the time and effort that went into *Faulkner* may well have exhausted that quota during the time period in which *Faulkner* and *Osborn* were decided. See also the similarly cursory approach to consideration of Strasbourg cases in the Supreme Court's post-*Faulkner* decision in *Shahid* (n 1) [88], the analysis of Strasbourg cases taking up a solitary paragraph.
[407] *Anufrijeva* (n 5) [79], [81](vi).
[408] ibid [81](v).
[409] *DSD* (n 17) [69]–[108].
[410] See s 1.III above.
[411] *Kennedy* (n 87) [46].

Perhaps this expense of time, effort and cost could be justified if it led to distillation of helpful guidance or a satisfactory law of damages. Yet it is typical that little or no guidance is derived from Strasbourg, while a problematic domestic jurisprudence has emerged. As we saw above, in *Faulkner* itself despite Lord Reed's efforts, very little guidance was distilled, while the more detailed guidance articulated was not based in Strasbourg material. Thus, the concern is not merely one of cost but *wasted cost.*

One might consider that in important appellate cases in which courts attempt to articulate general guidance such as *Anufrijeva* and *Faulkner* the burden, in terms of time and effort, will naturally be greater than in other cases. Yet, wherever a first instance court is confronted with a HRA damages claim, the mirror approach, according to the methodology elaborated in *Faulkner*, binds them to investigate Strasbourg practice, which in turn requires the judge to trawl Strasbourg cases. Of course, some lower court judges have simply ignored Strasbourg material, perhaps because they do not have the same resources available to them as appellate judges, to undertake the time-intensive task of surveying a potentially vast jurisprudence, and also, perhaps, because quick examination of Strasbourg material indicates that little of significance may be gleaned from it. However, in the wake of *Faulkner* lower court judges may be rather anxious to ensure they analyse Strasbourg material exhaustively given the Court of Appeal's decision in *Sturnham* was overturned on the basis that the Court of Appeal had 'erred in its interpretation of the Strasbourg case law' and had not considered a key Strasbourg case which bore on the matter before them, apparently because the case had not been cited to the Court.[412] And indeed this has been the result. In the recent case of *DSD*, which involved damages claims for breach of procedural obligations under Article 3, the High Court followed the approach laid down in *Faulkner*; the result was that on top of a liability judgment spanning 315 paragraphs, the Judge issued a separate damages judgment spanning 145 paragraphs and 58 pages of the Law Reports.[413]

One may argue that as guideline appellate decisions are given, lower courts will no longer be required to trawl Strasbourg material, because the task will have been undertaken at appellate level. This is a not untenable argument. However, we are a very long way off such a state of affairs.

[412] *Faulkner* (n 1) [96]. Missing relevant Strasbourg cases is likely to be a not uncommon occurrence given that for any given type of rights-violation there are likely to be myriad ECtHR cases in which violations have been found and Article 41 considered. There is no other way to ensure one has not missed a relevant case other than by literally going through every case of violation one by one. Keyword searches on electronic databases such as the ECtHR's HUDOC database (www.hudoc.echr.coe.int/sites/eng/) are of very little help in narrowing the field of cases in this respect, not least because there is little judicial reasoning in respect of Article 41 to search. To make matters worse, there is also limited commentary on Article 41 jurisprudence.

[413] *DSD* (n 17). Liability judgment: [2014] EWHC 436.

One must bear in mind that for all the time, cost and effort that went into *Faulkner*, the Court only determined the approach to damages in respect of one type of breach (delay) of one sub-section of one Article, while the judgment left many issues unresolved even in this narrow context.[414] The 58 pages dedicated to the damages judgment in *DSD* only resolved the approach to one type of violation of Article 3 (and that is a type of violation for which domestic courts have considered damages in the past, so that there was prior authority to draw on). Given the higher courts reiterate that the approach to damages for one type of breach of a particular right cannot necessarily be read across to other types of breach, there is a great deal more trawling of Strasbourg material ahead. Further, guidance offered by higher courts not uncommonly offers little detailed guidance and/or refers lower courts back to Strasbourg; for example, in *Faulkner* the guidance as to quantum of damages for loss of liberty was that judges should determine what is just and appropriate on the facts, in the light of any guidance from Strasbourg.

In *Faulkner* Lord Reed laid out guidance aimed at ameliorating the burden posed by the mirror approach, including requiring counsel to produce a table summarising key information about Strasbourg cases and a chronological list of cases, while in their submissions counsel are instructed to explain the principles they consider derive from Strasbourg decisions and how the cases support those principles.[415] Perhaps this guidance will ameliorate the burdens of the mirror approach, or perhaps it will fare the same fate as Lord Woolf's procedural guidance in *Anufrijeva*. Even if the guidance is strictly adhered to, a judge would still need to be taken through the Strasbourg cases by counsel, read for himself all relevant cases cited, and come to his own conclusion on what, if anything, can be discerned from the material; the mirror approach will therefore still require painstaking effort, while the guidance does not prevent counsel from releasing a deluge of cases upon the court. Indeed, the mirror approach positively encourages this, given the focus on practice which requires analysis of aggregate trends in ECtHR decision-making. Notably Lord Reed did not criticise the volume of cases cited to the Court in *Faulkner*. Further, while Lord Reed's procedural guidance may reduce the burden on judges and perhaps save parties some costs by shortening the length of the hearing, the guidance may also increase time spent by counsel preparing the case, imposing costs on parties. A not unlikely outcome of a state of affairs in which proceedings are costly and potential awards modest is that claims are not made.

[414] Including the nature of the loss of liberty head, the scale on which awards for that head should be awarded, factors going to assessment of damages for distress, and whether it is permissible for courts to take into account the victim's moral character in deciding damages (all discussed above).

[415] *Faulkner* (n 1) [99]–[103].

SECTION 4. THE FUTURE OF THE MIRROR APPROACH POST-*FAULKNER*

I. DELPHIC DICTA

In *Faulkner* Lord Reed made a number of remarks concerning the development and future of the damages remedy. He said: '*At the present stage of the development of the remedy* … courts should be guided, following *Greenfield*, primarily by any clear and consistent practice of the European court';

> over time, and as the practice of the European court comes increasingly to be absorbed into our own case law through judgments such as this, *the remedy should become naturalised*. While it will remain necessary to ensure that our law does not fall short of Convention standards, we should have confidence in our own case law under section 8 once it has developed sufficiently, and not be perpetually looking to the case law of an international court as our primary source.[416]

The implications of Lord Reed's observations are not clear. Some, who favour adoption of a tort-based approach such as that propounded in this book, argue that Lord Reed (1) 'saw the position as being what one might term an evolutionary one, offering the prospect of a shift away from the current approach once the remedy has become "naturalised"'; (2) that Lord Reed's observations 'suggest[] that over time the approach to HRA damages may shift away from predominance of Strasbourg authority. As part of that "naturalisation" process, domestic principles may be applied to the extent that they are not inconsistent with Strasbourg practice'; and that (3) 'Lord Reed's judgment in *Faulkner* … holds out a prospect for further developments as the HRA damages remedy gradually becomes "naturalised", approximating the higher level of damages in English tort law'.[417] The strongest support for this reading is tucked away at the end of Lord Reed's judgment where, in determining Sturnham's appeal, Lord Reed juxtaposes rejection of a common law starting-point with an observation that Strasbourg practice is the proper starting-point '*at this stage* in the development of the remedy'.[418] This might be read as rejection of a common law approach *for the time-being*. And recall that neither party in *Faulkner* had argued for *Greenfield* to be overruled,[419] such that complete abandonment of the mirror approach was not open.

On the other hand, putting to the side one's normative preferences for how the jurisprudence should develop, there are reasons to be cautious about whether Lord Reed's dicta contemplate an eventual shift in general approach, especially when those observations are placed in the context of

416 ibid [29], [39] (emphasis added).
417 M Andenas et al, 'A Fair Price for Violations of Human Rights?' (2014) 130 *LQR* 48.
418 *Faulkner* (n 1) [96] (emphasis added).
419 ibid [29].

his judgment as a whole. In particular it is difficult to foresee alignment of quantum of HRA awards with those at common law, at least in the short-run.

What Lord Reed seemed to be emphasising, particularly in his discussion of 'naturalization' of the remedy, was that once a critical mass of damages decisions are made under the HRA there will be less reason to continually look to Strasbourg. But this does not in itself suggest a future change in the *general approach* to damages, away from a domestic jurisprudence which seeks to replicate Strasbourg practice, only that *the sources* that domestic courts draw upon may change.[420] For example, where a domestic court relies on the Supreme Court decision in *Faulkner* or the House of Lords decision in *Greenfield*, it will be relying on domestic sources, but those sources enunciate an approach designed to ensure that domestic damages practice matches Strasbourg practice. If there were some novel issue to determine, Strasbourg practice would continue to be the first port of call.

A strong clue as to the reason for Lord Reed's emphasis on a gradual shift in sources lies in the final paragraphs of his judgment, in which—as we have seen—he observed the painstaking effort involved in traversing myriad Strasbourg decisions (strongly echoed by Lord Carnwath). It was within this discussion that he stated that it would no longer be necessary for counsel to cite numerous Strasbourg cases in Article 5(4) damages claims, given *Faulkner* would now be the 'starting point'.[421] This suggests that rather than necessarily being a prelude to abandonment of the mirror approach, Lord Reed's observations as to naturalisation of the remedy may be motivated by pragmatic concerns over the amount of resources consumed by analysing myriad Strasbourg decisions wherever a damages claim arises.

One must also recall Lord Reed's views in *Faulkner*, expressed in no uncertain terms, that HRA damages are 'an entirely novel remedy', 'not tortious in nature', of 'international origin' and lacking in 'native roots', whose 'native habitat' is the international plane.[422] Read alongside these statements, it is more difficult to conclude that Lord Reed's observations that the remedy is at an intermediary stage of development contemplate that the end-point of that development is a tort-based approach.

It is entirely possible that a future Supreme Court, (rightly) concerned by the manifest problems with the mirror approach, may rely on Lord Reed's observations to justify a shift in general approach, reasoning away the

[420] Thus in the subsequent High Court decision in *DSD* ((n 17) [32]) the Judge said, following Lord Reed's dicta in *Faulkner*, '[o]ver time the domestic courts (applying Strasbourg guidance) will evolve their own corpus of jurisprudence in relation to HRA damages claims and hence the trend to look west towards Strasbourg for guidance will diminish'. The words in brackets are important—the domestic corpus of jurisprudence will flow from applying Strasbourg guidance.

[421] *Faulkner* (n 1) [100].

[422] ibid [29].

mirror approach as an intermediate step in the remedy's development. It is to be hoped that this transpires. However it is not obvious that Lord Reed's judgment, taken as a whole, envisions such course.

There are more specific reasons to be sceptical about the prospect that quantum in particular will come to be aligned with domestic scales. In *Greenfield* and *Faulkner especial* emphasis was placed on a core feature of the mirror approach being that quantum should follow Strasbourg levels; for example Lord Reed in *Faulkner* on a number of occasions followed up a general pronouncement as to the nature of the mirror approach with statements such as the following: '*In particular*, the quantum of awards … should broadly reflect the levels of awards made by the European court'.[423] In *Greenfield* Lord Bingham explicitly rejected a submission that awards should follow domestic scales, elaborating some of his core justificatory reasoning for adoption of the mirror approach by reference to the issue of levels of awards.[424] Lord Reed repeated all of that reasoning in *Faulkner*, reiterating that *Greenfield* had rejected the proposition that HRA damages should not be on the low side relative to awards in tort.[425] In the more recent decision in *Michael* the Supreme Court described the idea of awarding damages for human rights breaches on a common law basis as 'gold plating the claimant's Convention rights';[426] this does not suggest enthusiasm for increased awards.

Further, there was a perfect opportunity in *Faulkner* to align levels of awards under the HRA and in tort in a context where the argument for alignment is plain—that is, in respect of damages for loss of liberty, given the obvious analogy with false imprisonment. As we saw above,[427] there was a complete dearth of guidance as to levels of awards for such loss in the Strasbourg material. As Lord Reed indicated in *Faulkner*, absent such guidance it is for domestic courts to determine what is just and appropriate.[428] Given this leeway Lord Reed could have set levels so that they broadly aligned with common law levels, following the Court of Appeal's approach in *Faulkner* where, in making a higher award, the Court emphasised that awards should not be insubstantial where something of 'real value' is at stake, recalling the English tradition of affording strong protection to liberty.[429] Yet the Supreme Court did not take this path. Rather it reduced the Court of Appeal's award, which had been closer to common law levels for loss of liberty, to a level well below common law scales. Perhaps the

[423] ibid [13](4) (emphasis added).
[424] *Greenfield* (n 1) [18]–[19].
[425] *Faulkner* (n 1) [27].
[426] *Michael v Chief Constable South Wales* [2015] 2 WLR 343, [125].
[427] Text to n 248 above.
[428] *Faulkner* (n 1) [36], [75].
[429] *Faulkner* CA (n 231) [12], [18].

higher courts' emphasis on aligning quantum to Strasbourg levels is unsurprising given maintaining awards at a low level addresses anxieties that often arise in relation to public authority liability, such as concerns not to deplete public funds.

What seems more likely than the uplifting of awards or a sudden move away from replicating Strasbourg practice is that in implementing a general approach based in Strasbourg practice domestic damages rules, principles or methods will, to some extent, influence development of rules, principles or methods within HRA damages jurisprudence. This influence may be conscious or not; for example, it may be difficult for domestic judges who routinely try common law damages claims, to shake off engrained habits of common law thinking. As we have seen, there is already some evidence of common law reasoning infiltrating domestic damages jurisprudence.[430] Further examples include Lord Reed's prescriptions that loss must be proved 'according to the normal domestic principle' that the claimant bears the burden of proving loss on the balance of probabilities, and that courts should determine questions of fact 'in the usual way'.[431] One key reason courts are likely to have ad hoc recourse to domestic rules etc is the lack of detail in the Strasbourg material. Also, whereas typical policy concerns may support limiting frequency of awards and maintaining awards at low levels, such concerns have less relevance to more 'technical' aspects of damages law such as the burden of proving consequential losses or method for fact-finding.

II. BEGINNINGS OF A LIBERALISATION OF APPROACH?

Another important matter is whether *Faulkner* represents a break from the exceptionally restrictive approach established by *Anufrijeva* and *Greenfield*, and a first step towards a less restrictive law of human rights damages, given the decision should result in awards more regularly being made in Article 5(4) delay cases.

In respect of the particular type of violation in *Faulkner*, the law as to *availability* of damages is now less restrictive. The general practice in pre-*Faulkner* cases on Article 5(4) had been for courts to routinely deny damages, especially where the claim was for distress alone. Now damages should routinely be awarded for distress where the rights-violating delay was over three months, and for any loss of liberty. However, this was only one aspect of the Supreme Court decision. Damages will continue to be very low; the final award to Faulkner for loss of liberty was substantially below common law scales, while awards for distress will be *exceptionally* modest,

[430] s 2.II.D above.
[431] *Faulkner* (n 1) [82].

as evidenced by the £300 award to Sturnham for six months of distress.[432] Various other restrictions on recovery were imposed, such as the presumption that awards will not be made for distress where the rights-violating delay was less than three months. Further, claimants may face difficulties in practice; for example it may be difficult to establish loss of liberty given the tricky task of proving that the Parole Board would have ordered the prisoner's release earlier but for the delay. Other 'liberalising' aspects of the decision will have little impact. For example Lord Reed accepted that pecuniary losses suffered by a prisoner as a result of being detained for longer than they ought to have been are recoverable. However it will be nearly impossible for a prisoner to prove specific losses; for example claims for lost wages the prisoner could have been earning if free will be rejected absent specific evidence of, say, a job offer, which a prisoner is most unlikely to possess, especially given they will have been waiting for the delayed Parole Board hearing to determine whether they would in fact be freed. *Faulkner* does not mention non-compensatory awards such as exemplary damages.

So, relative to the *exceptionally* restrictive approach in previous Article 5(4) cases, *Faulkner* does mark a liberalisation of approach as far as availability of damages goes. Nonetheless the decision is consonant with previous decisions insofar as awards shall remain very low, control devices such as the 'sufficiently serious' criterion were endorsed, and it seemingly remains the case that only compensation is available.

The more important matter is whether *Faulkner* signals a more *general* liberalisation of approach. Clearly it does not in respect of quantum. But does it suggest courts will generally be more willing to make awards than before *Faulkner*? Only time will tell. The following observations may aid the reader who wishes to make an informed prediction.

The decision does seemingly challenge certain oft-repeated propositions in the damages jurisprudence, such as the proposition formulated in *Anufrijeva* and endorsed in *Greenfield* that damages play a limited, secondary role in human rights claims, in that at least for Article 5(4) delay cases awards will not be an uncommon remedy. But nonetheless in *Faulkner* Lord Carnwath, at least, invoked the proposition from *Anufrijeva*.[433]

Another feature of the decision which stands out is that where an individual suffers unlawful delay of three months or more they are assumed to suffer compensable distress. This is significant insofar as lower courts have, in human rights damages cases, often required direct proof of distress before making awards, and generally been unwilling to infer distress. However, several points are relevant to provide perspective.

[432] On how scales of awards under the HRA compare to common law scales see further ch 3.I.E.

[433] *Faulkner* (n 1) [110].

First, this rule is specific to Article 5(4) delay cases involving 'a convicted prisoner awaiting review of his case by the Board'.[434] The Court in *Faulkner* signalled that the general rule is that the claimant must prove loss on the balance of probabilities. This leaves open the possibility that outside the specific context considered in *Faulkner*, courts may still insist on direct evidence and be unwilling to infer loss.[435] One might argue that *Faulkner* sends a signal that claims of inferred distress are to be taken seriously and that evidence of distress is not a prerequisite, but the obvious counter is that the Supreme Court in *Osborn* did not even engage with the claimant's submission that distress should be inferred, flatly denying the claim.

Second, it may be tempting to associate adoption of a presumption of loss with presumptions of loss within vindicatory approaches to damages.[436] However, common law presumptions relate to normative damage, whereas such a head of damage is not recognised in the Strasbourg Article 41 case law. Also, the motivations for adoption of the presumption are other than to give effect to human rights law's vindicatory function. As Lord Carnwath expressly indicated, the three month rule and associated presumptions are motivated by a desire to ensure legal certainty.[437] From the wider context of the *Faulkner* litigation one may infer that such certainty was desirable so as to facilitate out-of-court settlements and avoid repeat litigation: *Faulkner* and many other Article 5(4) cases were the product of systemic delays in the parole system, caused by chronic underfunding, such that the class of potential claimants is sizeable. This contextual feature also hints at why the Court erected a presumption against recovery for rights-violating delays under three months; note that there are no such presumptions within vindicatory torts, the law only recognising presumptions that damage *has* been suffered. The presumption against loss might be viewed as a control mechanism, to avoid a hypothetical flood of small claims. This explanation is consonant with Lord Carnwath's explanation of the three month threshold as not only being justified by the value of certainty but also 'proportionality';[438] the reference to 'proportionality' is reminiscent of Lord Woolf's call in *Anufrijeva* for proportionality between litigation costs and awards, and that small claims should be discouraged.[439] Thus, features of *Faulkner* which at first glance might appear vindicatory, are more likely based in *public interest concerns*.

Third, delay cases are the single context in which the Strasbourg Court has explicitly held that a rebuttable presumption that non-pecuniary loss has been suffered arises, which further explains the Supreme Court's approach

[434] ibid [66].
[435] eg *R (MA) v Independent Adjudicator* [2014] EWHC 3886, [61].
[436] See ch 2.III.C.ii.
[437] *Faulkner* (n 1) [127].
[438] ibid.
[439] *Anufrijeva* (n 5) [79]–[81].

in *Faulkner*, albeit the Court did not place especial weight on these statements of principle, placing more weight on practice.[440] This unique phenomenon is not the result of some consideration of principle but rather the result of the ECtHR facing a flood of claims concerning rights-violating delays, due to systemic delays in the court systems of several European states.[441] As a result the Court, in this context, has had to function as a de facto court of first instance for many clone cases caused by systemic violations at the domestic level; the Court has arguably assumed loss and more readily made awards so as to incentivise respondent states to put in place effective national remedies; and it has laid down more detailed guidance so as to facilitate provision of effective redress at the domestic level, so that more clone cases do not further clog up the Court's docket. Given these contextual features one cannot draw more general conclusions from the ECtHR's (or Supreme Court's) approach in the field of delay.

There are further reasons to be cautious about resting general claims about trends in the jurisprudence on one decision. One reason is that in the sequel to *Faulkner*, *Osborn*, Lord Reed, who only a few months earlier penned the lead judgment in *Faulkner*, summarily proscribed awards for distress consequential upon breach of Article 5(4) outside delay cases. In another post-*Faulkner* decision Lord Reed, again giving the judgment of the Supreme Court, in *Shahid*, having found that the defendant had breached a prisoner's Article 8 rights by keeping him in solitary confinement continuously for an extraordinarily long period of five years, gave short shrift to the prisoner's claim for damages, considering a declaration constituted 'just satisfaction'.[442] This hardly suggests a trend towards liberalisation; rather this is one of the most restrictive damages determinations made under the Act.

Another reason is that there is a strong emphasis in HRA jurisprudence on a violation-by-violation approach, such that a less restrictive approach for one type of violation cannot be taken to suggest a less restrictive approach more generally; *Osborn* and *Shahid* again prove this point. Furthermore, we have seen that the mirror approach affords courts wide scope to extend or limit availability of awards depending on how they interpret Strasbourg materials. In this light it may be that, as in the field of public authority liability in negligence, the jurisprudence proceeds in fits and starts, with some

[440] *Scordino* (n 96) [204]; *Faulkner* (n 1) [53].

[441] See, eg, Directorate-General (n 92) 38ff; Council of Europe Directorate-General (Human Rights and Rule of Law), *Applying and Supervising the ECHR: The Improvement of Domestic Remedies with Particular Emphasis on Cases of Unreasonable Length of Proceedings* (2006); *Committee of Ministers Recommendation to Member States on Effective Remedies for Excessive Length of Proceedings*, CM/Rec(2010)3 (2010); *Round Table on 'Effective Remedies Against Non-Execution or Delayed Execution of Domestic Court Decisions'*, Ministers' Deputies, CM/Inf/DH(2010)15 (2010).

[442] *Shahid* (n 1) [87]–[90].

decisions, such as *Greenfield*, *Osborn* and *Shahid* taking a more restrictive approach, and others, such as *Faulkner*, taking a less restrictive approach, the result being an incoherent and unsatisfactory jurisprudence.

One must also recall that there is limited guidance from higher courts and Strasbourg. Because of this lower court cases will be settled according to case-by-case exercises of judicial discretion. If the pre-*Faulkner* Article 5(4) jurisprudence is anything to go by,[443] whether damages are awarded will depend on the factors the individual judge, in her subjective judgement, happens to think relevant. Given the general statements, repeated in *Anufrijeva*, *Greenfield* and *Faulkner*, that damages are of secondary, if any, importance in human rights adjudication, and given the general trend at first instance has been for courts to deny damages, it would be a brave punter who staked the house on across-the-board liberalisation of approach, at least in the short-run. It also seems likely that concerns which tell against making awards such as the victim's moral character[444] and floodgates are likely to continue to influence decision-making given that *Faulkner* did not specifically address their invocation by lower courts, nor address the status of the *Anufrijeva* guidance that public interest concerns are relevant.

Also significant in considering whether *Faulkner* indicates a broader trend is that there were an unusual number of factors that came together in the case which made it difficult for the Court to adopt the sort of restrictive approach which has characterised HRA damages.

As already discussed, and most significantly, the delay context is a unique one in which the ECtHR has given express and specific guidance that where individuals suffer rights-violating delays before adjudicative tribunals and specific relief is not available to expedite their case, Article 13 requires compensation to be available for non-pecuniary losses. Lord Reed may not have given especial weight to such statements in *Faulkner*, focusing on practice as per the mirror method, but it must have been clear that failure to observe these statements risked the ECtHR finding the UK in breach of Article 13.

This leads on to another factor: because the ECtHR happens to have dealt with so many delay claims there is a critical mass of Article 41 decisions made in similar factual matrices to that in *Faulkner*. Further this is an area where many awards have been made, for reasons already discussed. It will not often be the case that there will be such a body of jurisprudence addressing a particular factual matrix and in which awards have been made with regularity; the presence of such a significant body of decisions in turn makes it difficult for domestic courts, operating under the mirror approach with its focus on ECtHR practice, to rule out awards. Furthermore, the ECtHR had, just prior to *Faulkner*, handed down a decision against the UK,

[443] s 2.II.C.ii above.

[444] Courts continue to rely on this factor: *DSD* (n 17) [37]–[39].

Betteridge, in which it made an award in very similar factual circumstances to *Faulkner*.[445]

Also significant is Article 5(5), which prescribes an enforceable right to compensation where Article 5 is breached. This Article, like Article 13, was not mentioned in *Faulkner*. However, it is unlikely that the Court was unaware that the ECtHR has previously found violations of Article 5(5) against the UK, specifically for not making awards for distress in Article 5(4) cases;[446] indeed several such cases were cited in *Faulkner*.

It is not insignificant that *Faulkner* concerned violations of rights geared towards protection of liberty, an interest long protected at common law. Though Lord Reed rejected Laws LJ's view in *Sturnham* that if 'the violation involves an outcome for the claimant in the nature of a trespass to the person, just satisfaction was likely to require an award of damages'[447]—on the basis that it was inconsistent with the mirror approach[448]—it will be much more difficult for a court to justify refusing awards where awards are available in domestic law for interferences with identical interests:

> It is clearly an embarrassment for judges to have to say of a right with constitutional status that it merits a lesser remedy than those in traditional tort actions. When the right invoked overlaps with or mirrors a standard tort action, the embarrassment will be all the greater.[449]

Equally courts will naturally be less hesitant to make awards for interferences with interests they are accustomed to awarding compensation for, and which the common law has long protected.[450] This observation harks back to the hypothesis in chapter 4, that domestic courts tend to absorb new developments into pre-existing habits of thought. This helps to explain why, notwithstanding the approach to awards for distress alone, a violation of Article 5(3) or (4) which results in a claimant being imprisoned where they would not have been otherwise (ie a loss of liberty) will generally result in damages. Similarly the other areas where courts have shown relatively warmer attitudes to damages have been breaches of Articles 2 and 3,[451] and Article 1, Protocol 1,[452] which protect interests traditionally protected through damages liability in domestic law.

Overall, it is unlikely that this array of features, which in combination strongly favour the making of awards or at least make it difficult for domestic courts to rule out awards, will come together too often. Given the pattern

445 *Betteridge v UK* (2013) 57 EHRR 7.

446 Above n 177.

447 *Sturnham* (n 228) [22].

448 *Faulkner* (n 1) [96].

449 Harlow (n 109) 79–80.

450 See further ch 3.II.B.iv.

451 *Rabone* (n 1); *DSD* (n 17); *OOO* (n 295); *Savage* (n 216); *Van Colle* CA (n 6); *Re Jordan's Application* [2014] NIQB 71.

452 See text to nn 336ff above.

of jurisprudence so far it seems that at appellate level the HRA damages jurisprudence is likely to proceed in fits and starts, with some decisions being more restrictive, others less so, but with the overall approach to HRA damages remaining one far more restrictive than approaches to damages across the law of torts. At lower court level, excluding very early decisions under the Act, damages claims have often been denied outside of Article 2 and 3 cases, while claims for pecuniary loss have generally only succeeded where a corporate claimant suffers violation of Article 1, Protocol 1. It is telling that notwithstanding the features just mentioned that told strongly in favour of making awards in *Faulkner*, lower courts had, prior to the Supreme Court decision, adopted an *exceptionally* restrictive approach to awards in Article 5(4) delay cases, more or less ruling them out altogether. One thing is abundantly clear: whether courts make awards more or less frequently, damages will remain depressed at exceptionally low levels relative to common law scales, such that human rights victims will continue to be radically undercompensated relative to domestic standards.

III. A BRITISH BILL OF RIGHTS?

It has become an almost constant feature of British politics over the last few years that Governments wish to explore the idea of replacing the HRA with a 'British Bill of Rights'. The Labour Government, which originally passed the HRA, floated the idea of such a change just seven years after the HRA entered force,[453] while the 2010–2015 Conservative-Liberal Democrat coalition set up a Commission to examine the idea.[454] So far the idea of replacing the HRA with such a Bill has remained just that; the Commission's report, for example, was described by one commentator as 'a damp squib in the long grass', its proposals going nowhere.[455] However, the Conservative Party, before winning the 2015 general election, produced a policy document on changing Britain's human rights laws,[456] their party manifesto included a pledge to 'scrap the [HRA] and introduce a British Bill of Rights'[457] and, having won the election, the first Queen's Speech of the new Government included a commitment to 'bring forward proposals for a British Bill of Rights'.[458]

[453] *The Governance of Britain*, Cm 7170 (2007) [204]–[210].

[454] Commission on a BOR (n 100).

[455] M Elliott, 'A Damp Squib in the Long Grass: the Report of the Commission on a Bill of Rights' [2013] *European Human Rights Law Review* 137.

[456] Conservative Party, *Protecting Human Rights in the UK* (2014) [Policy Document].

[457] Conservative Party, *The Conservative Party Manifesto 2015* (2015) 60 [Manifesto].

[458] *Her Majesty's Most Gracious Speech to Both Houses of Parliament at the State Opening of Parliament 2015* (27 May 2015) (www.gov.uk/government/speeches/queens-speech-2015).

At the time of writing it is not clear what those final proposals will be, the proposals in the policy document and the manifesto are rather vague, it is widely reported that the proposals have been through many iterations, while there is to be a consultation on any proposals before they are made final. It is further unclear whether such proposals would ever find their way into law, not least because the Conservative Government has a slim majority in the House of Commons, for the first time a Conservative Government does not enjoy a majority in the House of Lords, and repeal of the HRA would be highly contentious. Like other proposals for major constitutional reform, such as perennial proposals for a written constitution or reform of the House of Lords, there may be some agreement that reform is required but real difficulties in formulating detailed proposals of what should replace the status quo capable of garnering widespread support.

Notwithstanding these points a number of common themes emerge from the Conservative Party's various documents and pronouncements which bear directly on the future of the mirror approach, and therefore warrant consideration briefly.

In particular both the policy document and manifesto stress[459] that any proposals brought forward would break the formal link between British courts and the ECtHR so that British courts would no longer be required to take into account Strasbourg decisions.[460] It is thus highly likely that any new British Bill of Rights (or amended HRA) would not include equivalents of sections 2(1) and 8(4). This should mark the end of the mirror approach to damages, given English courts' justification for adopting such approach has rested nearly entirely on section 8(4), and as we have seen there are no convincing normative arguments for following the mirror approach—and plenty against. This would be a welcome development, putting the mirror approach out of its misery, and offering a prime opportunity for the law of human rights damages to be 'reset' and placed on a principled footing. The arguments for a tort-based approach to human rights damages are strong. They would be irresistible in the context of a British Bill of Rights, given such approach reflects the home-grown, longstanding and orthodox approach to protecting basic, constitutional rights in British law. In this respect it is worth noting that the Conservative policy document explicitly recalls the British tradition of protecting human rights 'over the centuries through our Common Law tradition'.[461] Further, in observing that 'the UK's protection of human rights has always been grounded in real circumstance, rather than simply being a matter of abstract principle'[462] the document

[459] Policy Document (n 456) 4–6; Manifesto (n 457) 60. See also HC Deb vol 598 col 311 (8 July 2015) Prime Minister.
[460] Policy Document, ibid 8.
[461] ibid 2.
[462] ibid.

echoes Dicey's[463] preference for the common law tradition of starting with concrete remedies which respond to specific factual matrices rather than abstract statements of right, which may appear grand but ring hollow.

SECTION 5. OVERVIEW

The mirror approach ought to be repudiated. Ideally, sections 8(3) and (4) of the Act should be repealed. Replacement of the HRA with a British Bill of Rights would provide an opportunity for such repeal, and for human rights damages to be set on a principled course consonant with longstanding domestic traditions. 'Our own jurisprudence and legal culture require a more analytical approach'.[464]

Aspects of the analysis in *Greenfield* and *Faulkner* are patently inconsistent with the plain terms of the Act. The Act does not mandate a mirror approach. Absent such requirement, the normative basis for the mirror approach is unclear. Those arguments that might support adoption of a mirror approach in adjudication of substantive rights have no application to damages, while courts are moving away from the mirror approach even in adjudication of substantive rights.

There is no requirement under the Convention or within ECtHR jurisprudence that domestic courts must follow Strasbourg practice under Article 41. Indeed, the ECtHR emphasises that domestic courts are free to develop remedies in line with domestic traditions as long as the basic requirements of Article 13 are met. Article 13 governs the remedial obligations of Member States, rather than Article 41, which solely governs the ECtHR's own remedial jurisdiction.

On a normative level the ECtHR's remedial approach is fundamentally shaped by the supranational context within which it operates, which makes its approach inappropriate for importation into the very different context of domestic law. The ECtHR is a supranational, supervisory and subsidiary court. Remedying individual injustice is not its primary function, whereas domestic courts have primary responsibility for redressing individual violations. There is a strong argument that the normative basis of liability on the supranational plane—breach of obligations owed to other states or free-standing standards—is distinct from that in domestic law—breach of individual, personal rights. Additionally, there is a significant risk that the mirror approach will lead to the UK falling afoul of Article 13.

The mirror approach requires domestic courts to follow a deeply problematic supranational jurisprudence, characterised by unreasoned

[463] AV Dicey, *Introduction to the Study of the Law of the Constitution* 10th edn (MacMillan, 1960) 198–99.

[464] *KB* (n 5) [25].

decision-making, lack of coherence, consistency and principle, and a discretionary approach which encourages decision-making freed from the rigours of ordinary legal reasoning and based in highly subjective concerns. Unsurprisingly little meaningful guidance can be derived from such jurisprudence, while the result of following such jurisprudence has been that the domestic law of damages is coming to mirror many of the most problematic aspects of the supranational jurisprudence. Where domestic courts have elaborated more detailed guidance, it has not been sourced in Strasbourg material, but resembles common law rules, principles and modes of reasoning. In turn this casts doubt on the credibility of the mirror approach, and demonstrates the artificiality of seeking to insulate human rights damages from the ordinary law of damages.

The general methodology of the mirror approach is unsafe, courts have employed different methods without explanation, interpretation of the Strasbourg material is open to manipulation and arguably has been manipulated by domestic courts according to unstated normative concerns, while the mirror method imposes significant costs which are not counterbalanced by discernible benefits.

Assuming sections 8(3) and (4) remain in place the preferable approach is the 'ordinary approach' which the Supreme Court has recently endorsed in adjudication of substantive rights, and which was favoured by the Law Commissions in their report on human rights damages: domestic courts ought to apply those English damages principles and scales of awards applied in tort, while seeking to ensure broad consistency with general principles applied by the Strasbourg Court. This should not be difficult as far as compensatory damages go, given the principle of *restitutio in integrum* is common to the English law of damages and Strasbourg jurisprudence. Under the tort-based approach the exact manner in which the principle is applied domestically may vary from the way in which it is applied at Strasbourg. But, as we have seen, there are good reasons why the domestic approach to damages should be different from that applied by a supranational institution, and such variation is entirely consistent with the Act and has been endorsed by the ECtHR.

English courts should also feel free to depart from Strasbourg principles where they consider such a course justified. For example, while the ECtHR does not award exemplary or aggravated damages, consistent with the traditions of the English legal system a domestic court may consider that such award is warranted for a very serious rights-violation. As Starmer argues, the Strasbourg Court's reluctance to award exemplary damages 'is in keeping with its role as an international supervisory body'—'[d]omestic courts have a different role'.[465] In respect of aggravated damages the ECtHR, within its Article 13 jurisprudence, 'accepts that, applying the compensatory

[465] Starmer (n 184) [2.46]–[2.47].

principle, national courts might make an award taking into account the motives and conduct of the defendant'.[466]

Overall, it is difficult to see why English courts have adopted the mirror approach as opposed to a tort-based approach given neither section 8 of the HRA nor the Convention require English courts to follow Strasbourg practice, or bar an approach informed by domestic law. In turn one wonders whether unstated concerns underlie the mirror approach. One possible explanation is judicial anxiety over imposing liability on public bodies. Indeed this concern is conspicuous by the lack of any express reference to it in decisions such as *Greenfield* and *Faulkner*; *Anufrijeva* is a notable exception. Tying the approach under the HRA to Strasbourg practice has the effect of limiting the financial impact of human rights liability on government coffers, as awards will be uncommon and modest. As we have seen, even on the odd occasion where courts have opened up the availability of awards, they have continued to emphasise strongly that awards should be kept at Strasbourg levels, which are low—often exceptionally low—relative to domestic scales. If this is the unspoken reason for adoption of the mirror approach, it is a bad one. It is for the Chancellor to worry about the government books, not courts.

[466] *Shilbergs* (n 182) [78].

6

Interest-Balancing Approaches

IN *ANUFRIJEVA* THE Court of Appeal held that '[i]n considering whether to award compensation and, if so, how much, there is a balance to be drawn between the interests of the victim and those of the public as a whole'.[1] The Court read this 'interest-balancing' approach into section 8(1) of the Human Rights Act 1998 (HRA), which provides that a court may grant such relief as it considers 'just and appropriate'.[2] The approach, as propounded in *Anufrijeva*, would affect both the decision to award damages, and assessment: damages could be denied or reduced according to public interest concerns.

Despite espousing a 'balancing' approach the Court in *Anufrijeva* only really considered those public interest factors that told against making awards or in favour of reduced awards, consonant with the public interest conception of public law discussed in chapter 4. In terms of factors against granting damages, the Court placed heavy emphasis on public interests 'in the continued funding of a public service' and preservation of public funds more generally.[3] English courts have also considered, inter alia, the victim's moral status, pragmatic political concerns and floodgates arguments. Within an interest-balancing approach it is also highly likely that other 'usual suspects' will be taken into account including concerns over chilling effects, administrative disruption and propagation of litigation culture.

Wider considerations also affected the Court's approach to quantum. It held there were 'good reasons' for awards to be 'modest' where the violation results from 'maladministration'.[4] The specific obligation at issue in *Anufrijeva* was that under Article 8, that the state provide support to asylum seekers in certain circumstances. The 'good reasons' for keeping awards modest included that '[r]esources are limited and payments of substantial damages will deplete the resources available for other needs of the public including primary care', and it could bring the HRA into disrepute if the impression were created, genuine or not, that asylum seekers were profiting

1 *Anufrijeva v Southwark LBC* [2004] QB 1124, [56].
2 ibid.
3 ibid [56], and see [76] (and [47]).
4 ibid [75].

from their status.[5] In other jurisdictions too courts have asserted awards should be lower than those in tort and/or expressly stated that awards may be augmented according to public interest factors.[6]

Thus, the interest-balancing approach could lead to: (1) denial of damages where only a monetary award could remedy effectively the violation; or (2) reduction of quantum below ordinary compensatory levels, so that damages do not make the claimant whole. Under such approach there is no entitlement to damages where damage is suffered. Indeed, according to the approach in *Anufrijeva* denial of damages would not be at all uncommon where damage and loss are suffered.

Interest-balancing has proven a popular approach to human rights damages, with types of balancing approach being adopted in, for example, New Zealand, where *Anufrijeva* has been influential,[7] and Canada.[8] In the US the Supreme Court, in deciding whether to extend the damages action against Federal actors for breach of constitutional rights to a new constitutional right or new class of defendant considers, inter alia, whether there are any 'special factors' counselling hesitation.[9] This implicates an open-ended balancing inquiry, the Court weighing 'reasons for and against the creation of a new cause of action',[10] in the context of which the Court considers a wide range of public policy considerations.[11] Applying this method the Court has 'consistently refused to extend [damages] liability to any new context or category of defendant' since the early 1980s.[12] These approaches fit within a more general strain of thought that holds that within the domain of constitutional or human rights adjudication, 'determination of appropriate relief ... calls for the balancing of the various interests that might be affected by the remedy'.[13]

While an interest-balancing approach would entail denial or reduction of awards in cases where only full compensatory damages are capable of effectively remedying a rights-violation, one may understand the concerns underpinning such approaches. For example, there is a clear public interest in ensuring that authorities have sufficient resources to perform primary

[5] ibid.

[6] eg *Taunoa v Attorney-General* [2008] 1 NZLR 429, [258], [265], [318]–[319]; *City of Vancouver v Ward* [2010] 2 SCR 28, [53].

[7] *Taunoa* ibid particularly [253]ff.

[8] *Ward* (n 6). Note: as is discussed in *Ward*, the Canadian approach is heavily influenced by the functionalist approach to general damages which prevails in Canadian tort law. On such approaches see: AI Ogus, 'Damages for Lost Amenities: For a Foot, a Feeling or a Function?' (1973) 35 *MLR* 1.

[9] *Bush v Lucas* 462 US 367, 378 (1983); *Schweiker v Chilicky* 487 US 412, 423 (1988); *Wilkie v Robbins* 551 US 537, 550 (2007).

[10] *Wilkie* ibid 554.

[11] *Bush* (n 9) 388–90; *Schweiker* (n 9) 423–29; *FDIC v Meyer* 510 US 471, 484–86 (1994).

[12] *Correctional Services Corp v Malesko* 534 US 61, 68 (2001); see ch 7.III.

[13] *Hoffmann v South African Airways* (2001) (1) SA 1, [45].

functions, which benefit large sections of the community. It is an oft-expressed concern that administrators may respond to the threat of liability by adopting overly-cautious practices. More generally there are concerns about development of a 'compensation culture', and a growing tendency to view government as insurer of last resort where things run awry. By moderating frequency of awards and quantum interest-balancing might guard against negative effects and protect important community interests.

This chapter critically analyses the interest-balancing approach, and is divided into three sections. Section 1 considers doctrinal issues raised by such approach. Specifically, whether an interest-balancing approach is compatible with the terms of the HRA, Article 13 of the Convention, and fundamental principles of English law.

Section 2 considers whether the interest-balancing approach is normatively justifiable. It concludes that notwithstanding the importance of those interests that may be protected by such approach, the approach suffers not insignificant drawbacks, and should be rejected. If an interest-balancing approach is nonetheless to be adopted, the approach propounded in *Anufrijeva* should not be the model; this section proposes an alternative model.

Section 3 concludes.

Before continuing it is important to note that aspects of the analysis herein are relevant beyond assessing the interest-balancing approach, being pertinent to consideration of what approach ought to be taken to human rights damages more generally. For example, compatibility with Article 13 of the Convention, fundamental principles of English law, and the rule of law are concerns relevant to evaluating the viability of any potential approach to human rights damages, and especially those approaches which would entail discretionary denial of damages, including the mirror approach. Importantly, the public interest factors analysed herein generally play a role, either overtly or obliquely, in justifying any approach which would impose controls on and limit availability or quantum of human rights damages in cases where damage or loss is suffered through rights-violations.

SECTION 1: DOCTRINAL ANALYSIS OF THE INTEREST-BALANCING APPROACH

I. THE INTEREST-BALANCING APPROACH AND THE TERMS OF THE HRA

Whatever the merits of the interest-balancing approach, it is difficult to support on the terms of the HRA.

No provision *mandates* such approach. In *Anufrijeva* public interest considerations were read into the overall discretion in section 8(1) to grant such remedies as are 'just and appropriate'.[14] However, that provision does not mandate such approach: as explained in chapter 3, section 8(1) is a broad enabling clause, granting courts a general jurisdiction to grant remedies for rights-violations.[15] If anything the terms of section 8(1) point to established principle, rather than a radical break from such principle. By empowering a court to grant such relief '*within its powers* as it considers just and appropriate', the provision directs courts to *pre-existing* remedial tools.[16] Parliamentary debates on the provision similarly suggest that Parliament intended courts to draw on the ordinary, pre-existing English law of remedies.[17] The use in the statute of the term 'damages', a term of art with an established meaning in English law, similarly tells against any intention to effect radical departure from orthodoxy.

In *Greenfield* Lord Bingham held that 'if satisfied that it is necessary to [award damages] it is hard to see how the court could consider it other than just and appropriate to do so'.[18] Lord Bingham's reference to what is 'necessary' is to section 8(3), which specifically addresses damages. There is a basic logic to Lord Bingham's statement, which is difficult to resist. Furthermore, his approach is consonant with the most convincing interpretation of section 8(1) as a broad empowering clause, so that not much should be made to rest on it. As a matter of statutory interpretation too a court should, in considering damages, be guided principally by the specific clauses addressing that remedy, rather than general provisions.

As Lord Bingham's analysis indicates, section 8(3) is the pivotal section governing damages. Textual analysis shows that Parliament intended courts principally to exercise their power to award damages according to the demands of individual justice rather than the needs of the public purse.

Section 8(3) states that damages shall only be awarded if, 'taking account of all the circumstances of the case', an award is 'necessary to afford just satisfaction to the person in whose favour it is made'. The latter quote indicates that the touchstone for the award of damages is whether they are necessary to redress a violation; as the Law Commissions observed, '[t]hese words direct attention to the needs of the victim'.[19] The requirement that the court consider 'all the circumstances of the case' might be thought to implicate wider policy concerns. However, this would cut against the nature of the overarching inquiry, which is into whether damages are necessary *for the victim*. Further, the two circumstances expressly mentioned in the

[14] (n 1) [56].
[15] Ch 3.IV.A.
[16] See further ibid. All emphasis in quotations from statutes within this section is added.
[17] See chs 3.IV, 5.1.I.
[18] *R (Greenfield) v SOSHD* [2005] 1 WLR 673, [6].
[19] *Damages Under the Human Rights Act 1998*, Law Com 266/Scot Law Com 180 (2000) [4.41] [Law Commissions Report].

Act, which the courts must consider, point away from such conclusion and toward an exclusive focus on individual redress.

First, the court must consider 'any other relief or remedy' granted for the violation.[20] This reflects that other relief may effectively remedy the violation, rendering damages unnecessary. The focus is again on the victim's remedial needs.

Second, the court must take into account 'the consequences of any decision (of that or any other court) in respect of [the rights-violation]'.[21] Some suggest that the reference to 'the consequences of any decision' implicates wider policy concerns.[22] However, as the Law Commissions, citing the victim-orientation of section 8(3), concluded, this subsection most probably 'refers to the Strasbourg jurisprudence under which the court may hold that some non-judicial act by the state in light of the court's decision may constitute just satisfaction'.[23]

The references in section 8(3) to the 'circumstances of *the case*', other relief granted 'in relation to *the act in question*', and the consequences of any decision 'in respect of *that act*', similarly indicate a narrow focus on the claimant's case rather than wider concerns.

Against this backdrop, it would be a stretch to argue that the terms of the Act lend support to a balancing approach. The statute expressly provides that the touchstone for granting damages is the victim's interests, while considerations enumerated within section 8(3) reinforce this. This interpretation is consonant with the policy of protection and vindication that underlies the primary rights;[24] as Elias CJ, in the New Zealand context, has observed: 'it would be contrary to the *scheme and purpose* of the New Zealand Bill of Rights Act if those deprived of rights ... are denied the opportunity to obtain damages from the State, where an award of damages is necessary to provide effective remedies'.[25] As Clayton says, the *Anufrijeva* Court put a 'gloss'[26] on section 8, and adopted principles that 'are more restrictive than the terms of the Act itself would mandate'.[27] If Parliament intended courts to consider broader public interest considerations, such as the financial implications of awards, the statute would have stated this expressly, particularly as

[20] HRA, s 8(3)(a).

[21] HRA, s 8(3)(b).

[22] eg M Amos, 'Damages for Breach of the Human Rights Act 1998' [1999] *European Human Rights Law Review* 178, 186–87.

[23] Law Commissions Report (n 19) [4.42]. See also R Clayton and H Tomlinson, *The Law of Human Rights* 2nd edn (OUP, 2009) [21.26]; J Beatson et al, *Human Rights: Judicial Protection in the United Kingdom* (Sweet and Maxwell, 2008) [7-151].

[24] See ch 3.I.

[25] *Attorney-General v Chapman* [2012] 1 NZLR 462, [8] (emphasis added).

[26] R Clayton, 'Damage Limitation: the Courts and the Human Rights Act Damages' [2005] *PL* 429, 435.

[27] ibid 430.

there is no precedent for such approach to damages in English law and such practice would contravene fundamental principle (discussed in section 1.III below). Further, it is worth recording that the Government considered carefully the financial implications of damages awards, for itself, in formulating section 8;[28] courts should not reopen the balance of interests struck in the plain terms of the Act.

There is no mention in the remedial provisions of *quantum* being subject to public interest considerations. The use of the distinctly common law term 'damages' points to orthodoxy.[29] One could argue that quantum may be reduced where this is 'just and appropriate' pursuant to section 8(1). But given there is no precedent in English law for reducing quantum below ordinary compensatory levels on a case-by-case basis according to factors such as fiscal impact, it is difficult to maintain that Parliament intended to effect radical departure from orthodoxy by a side-wind, without express words and through a broadly-worded provision, especially as damages are addressed by more specific provisions.

The Act directs that domestic courts, in determining quantum, consider the principles applied by the Strasbourg Court under Article 41.[30] The central principle of the Strasbourg jurisprudence is *restitutio in integrum*. However, the implication of interest-balancing is that damages may be reduced below a level consonant with full reparation. It is also significant that beyond taking into account the cost of living in defendant states 'there is no evidence to suggest that', as a matter of legal principle, '[the ECtHR] has taken account of the State's financial situation or the impact on public funds in determining the level of ... compensation'.[31] Indeed, the European Court of Human Rights (ECtHR) has awarded substantial sums despite state pleas of financial hardship.[32] More generally, there is no clear and constant principle in Strasbourg Article 41 jurisprudence that supports the interest-balancing approach.[33]

Ultimately, as Stanley Burnton J has observed of Parliament's decision to create the damages jurisdiction, the state 'must be taken to have provided the resources to meet [damages] awards'.[34]

28 HC Deb vol 312 cols 979–80 (20 May 1998) Mr Jack Straw.

29 See further ch 3.IV.B.

30 HRA, s 8(4).

31 Beatson et al (n 23) [7-102], [7-151].

32 *Assanidze v Georgia* (2004) 39 EHRR 32, [197]ff.

33 Clayton (n 26) 435. Note however that there is support in the Strasbourg jurisprudence under Article 41 for denying an award based on the moral status of the victim (see s 2.V.B below and ch 5.2.II.C.ii). As discussed in the Introduction to Part 3 of this book, there may be a temptation for those who favour the interest-balancing approach to interpret open-ended statements which characterise the Article 41 jurisprudence as supporting such approach.

34 *R (KB) v South London and South and West Region MHRT* [2004] QB 936, [50].

II. THE INTEREST-BALANCING APPROACH AND CONVENTION REQUIREMENTS

Another consideration counselling against adoption of an interest-balancing approach is that it is likely to result in violations of Article 13, which requires Member States to provide effective remedies for violations of Convention rights.

Not only is Article 13 relevant because the UK is bound to comply with it, but section 8 HRA was specifically intended to fulfil the requirements of Article 13.[35] It is axiomatic that 'when legislation is based upon an international treaty, the courts will try to construe the legislation in a way which does not put the United Kingdom in breach of its international obligations'.[36] Despite this English courts have largely ignored Article 13 in their analysis of HRA damages.[37] If the maxim is applied, as it ought to be, the emphasis in Article 13 jurisprudence on awarding full compensation, and ensuring remedies are practically effective, reinforces the interpretation of section 8 argued for above: English courts' primary concern should be affording the victim effective redress.

It is important to record that the ECtHR has begun to strongly emphasise its role in policing domestic remedies, observing that

> less than full expression of the guarantees of art 13 would undermine the operation of the subsidiary character of the Court in the Convention system and, more generally, weaken the effective functioning, on both the national and international level, of the scheme of human rights protection set up by the Convention. Accordingly, less than full supervision of the existence and operation of domestic remedies would undermine and render illusory these guarantees.[38]

A key reason for the Court signalling an increasingly aggressive approach to policing Article 13 is that the Court faces a huge backlog of cases so that there is every incentive for it to ensure violations are adequately redressed domestically, so that cases need not be raised to the supranational level.[39] The ECtHR's renewed emphasis upon Article 13 provides even more reason for English courts to take that Article seriously in fashioning remedies domestically.

[35] See chs 3.IV, 5.1.

[36] *Re P (A Child)* [2009] 1 AC 173, [35]; *R (Al Skeini) v SOS for Defence* [2008] 1 AC 153, [57] (procedural and remedial provisions of HRA should be interpreted compatibility with Article 13).

[37] Contrast the approach of Irish courts under the ECHR Act 2003: *Pullen v Dublic CC* [2009] IEHC 452, [5.7].

[38] *McFarlane v Ireland* (2011) 52 EHRR 20, [112].

[39] This issue has dominated the Declarations of the successive High Level Conferences on the Future of the ECtHR at Interlaken in 2010, Izmir in 2011, Brighton in 2012 and Brussels in 2015 (all available here: www.echr.coe.int/Pages/home.aspx?p=court/reform&c).

A. Requirements of Article 13 (and Articles 34 and 35(1))

Let us move to test the interest-balancing approach against the requirements of Article 13. In considering these requirements I also draw upon ECtHR jurisprudence under Articles 34 and 35(1), which prescribe respectively the standing and admissibility rules governing individual petitions to the ECtHR, and under which the ECtHR may consider effectiveness of domestic remedies. There is a high degree of convergence in the principles governing effective redress in each context; as the ECtHR has observed, these Articles have a 'close affinity'.[40]

It is axiomatic that for the most important Convention rights, the rights to life and not to be subjected to torture, Article 13 *requires* compensation to be available.[41] Compensation means 'compensation for the damage suffered',[42] and 'compensation for the non-pecuniary damage flowing from the breach should in principle be part of the range of available remedies'.[43] Monetary redress that does not fully compensate damage suffered will not do. The position is the same under Article 34.[44]

More recently the ECtHR has stated the following as a *general* proposition: 'in appropriate cases, compensation for the pecuniary and non-pecuniary damage flowing from the breach should in principle be available as part of the range of redress'.[45] For Article 8 violations the Court has held that Article 13 requires that victims should have 'available to them a means of claiming that the [relevant public authority] was responsible for any damage which they suffered and obtaining compensation for that damage';[46] this includes non-pecuniary and pecuniary damage.[47] Similarly, under Article 34 the Court has held that for rights such as Article 6[48] and 11,[49] compensation for both pecuniary and non-pecuniary losses may be required to ensure effective redress. In *Burden v UK*, the Court contemplated cases where 'an effective remedy *necessitated* the award of damages in respect of past loss

[40] *McFarlane* (n 38) [107]–[108], [112].

[41] *Z v UK* (2002) 34 EHRR 3, [109]; *E v UK* (2003) 36 EHRR 31, [110]. Note that compensation is the least remedy required, and the state will likely also have positive remedial duties: Z at [109]. The Court's practice in this respect is consonant with the principle under Article 13 that 'the nature of the right that is alleged to have been infringed has implications on the extent of the obligations under Article 13': *Yasa v Turkey* (1999) 28 EHRR 408, [114].

[42] Z ibid [111].

[43] ibid [109]; *Keenan v UK* (2001) 33 EHRR 38, [129]; *Reynolds v UK* (2012) 55 EHRR 35, [67].

[44] *Gäfgen v Germany* (2011) 52 EHRR 1, [116].

[45] *Anguelova v Bulgaria* (2004) 38 EHRR 31, [161]. The case concerned Articles 2 and 3. However, the remedial principle was stated as a general one, without qualification.

[46] *RK and AK v UK* (2009) 48 EHRR 29, [45].

[47] *TP and KM v UK* (2002) 34 EHRR 2, [107].

[48] *Normann v Denmark* (14 June 2001) App no 44704/98 (ECtHR First Section); *Scordino v Italy (No 1)* (2007) 45 EHRR 7, [178]–[192], [195]–[207].

[49] *Jensen and Rasmussen v Denmark* (20 March 2003) App no 52620/99 (ECtHR First Section).

or damage caused by the alleged violation'.[50] The Court also recalled a line of cases where a declaration of incompatibility under section 4 HRA was found to be an ineffective remedy 'where the applicant claims to have suffered loss or damage as a result of the breach of his Convention rights' because 'a declaration of incompatibility ... is not binding on the parties to the proceedings in which it is made and cannot form the basis of an award of monetary compensation'.[51]

In respect of quantum the Court has indicated that it may constitute a violation of Article 13 if compensation were 'so derisory as to raise issues of the effectiveness of the redress';[52] monetary redress must 'provide an adequate level of compensation'.[53] More generally where a violation is found this imposes 'on the respondent State a legal obligation to make reparation for its consequences in such a way as to restore as far as possible the situation existing before the breach'.[54] These dicta suggest that, at least in certain classes of case, failure to afford full reparation seriously risks running afoul of Article 13.

Specific factors which figure prominently in the interest-balancing calculus endorsed in *Anufrijeva* have been disapproved explicitly by the ECtHR. In *Shilbergs* the Court, in assessing a low award made by a domestic court for violation of Article 3, and partly justified on the basis of protecting public funds, said:

> The Court finds it anomalous for the domestic courts to decrease the amount of compensation to be paid to the applicant for a wrong committed by the State by referring to the latter's lack of funds. It considers that in circumstances such as those under consideration the means available to the State should not be accepted as mitigating its conduct, and are thus irrelevant in assessing damages under the compensatory criterion.[55]

Rather, domestic courts were under a 'duty to mark their disapproval of the State's wrongful conduct to the extent of awarding an adequate and sufficient quantum of damages'.[56]

Given this legal framework, it seems inevitable that an interest-balancing approach which leads to awards being denied where loss is suffered or awards being reduced below compensatory levels would lead to violations

[50] (2008) 47 EHRR 38, [43] (emphasis added).

[51] ibid [40], citing *Dodds v UK* (8 April 2003) App no 59314/00; *Walker v UK* (16 March 2004) App no 37212/02; *Pearson v UK* (27 April 2004) App no 8374/03; *Hobbs v UK* (18 June 2002) App no 63684/00 (all ECtHR Fourth Section).

[52] *Wainwright v UK* (2007) 44 EHRR 40, [55].

[53] *McFarlane* (n 38) [108]. Similar principles apply under Article 34: *Gäfgen* (n 44) [118]; *Scordino* (n 48) [202].

[54] *Smith and Grady v UK* (2001) 31 EHRR 24, [18]; *Wessels-Bergervoet v Netherlands* (2004) 38 EHRR 37, [63]; *Dacia SRL v Moldova* (2009) 48 EHRR SE17, [37].

[55] *Shilbergs v Russia* (17 December 2009) App no 20075/03, [78] (ECtHR First Section).

[56] ibid.

of Article 13. By contrast ordinary remedies in private law have generally been found to comply with Article 13.[57]

The Grand Chamber's decision in *McFarlane*[58] is of acute significance in predicting how an interest-balancing approach would fare at Strasbourg. In that case, and also in the Grand Chamber decision in *Stanev*,[59] the Court emphasised that for a remedy to be effective it must be available not only in theory but also *in practice*. In assessing effectiveness the Court looks beyond the in-principle availability of damages, to judicial practice. In *McFarlane* it was clearly established that in Ireland damages are available for constitutional wrongs. However, this was insufficient to convince the ECtHR that such damages constituted effective redress for breach of Article 5(4) caused by excessive delay, given no award had ever been made for such violation. The Court considered that the 'significant uncertainty as to the availability of the proposed constitutional remedy' put in doubt the remedy's effectiveness: 'the development and availability of a remedy said to exist, including its scope and application, must be clearly set out and confirmed or complemented by practice or case law'.[60] Similarly in *Stanev* the Court said that 'effective enjoyment of the right to compensation guaranteed by Article 5 § 5 must be ensured with a sufficient degree of certainty',[61] finding a violation of Article 5(5) partly on the basis that the Government could not point to any domestic practice of awards being made to individuals in the applicant's position.[62] It found a violation of Article 13 in conjunction with Article 3 on similar grounds.[63]

First, on the basis of this guidance an interest-balancing approach could come a cropper if, in practice, it systematically led to denials of relief in general, for a class of violation or for similarly placed individuals, such that it could not be said that relief was realistically available. In the Strasbourg Court's parlance, there will be a violation if there is no reasonable prospect of successfully securing the remedy. The onus is on the government to prove that a remedy is effective in practice.[64] Second, the emphasis on certainty in *McFarlane* poses a distinct challenge to a case-by-case, all-things-considered balancing approach. A clear statement of when damages will be awarded would be impossible under such approach, the very rationale for which is to give judges flexibility to respond to the facts before them.

[57] A Lester et al, *Human Rights Law and Practice* 3rd edn (LexisNexis, 2009) [4.13.11]; *Chagos Islanders v UK* (2013) 56 EHRR SE15, [81]; *Wainwright* (n 52) [55].

[58] (n 38).

[59] *Stanev v Bulgaria* (2012) 55 EHRR 22.

[60] *McFarlane* (n 38) [117], [120].

[61] *Stanev* (n 59) [182].

[62] ibid [187].

[63] ibid [219].

[64] ibid [187]; *McFarlane* (n 38) [128].

These conclusions are reinforced by consideration of the ECtHR's application of the effectiveness criteria to damages practice under the HRA. In *Betteridge v UK* the effectiveness criteria were applied under Article 35, to test whether the HRA damages remedy was an effective remedy which the applicant ought to have exhausted before bringing his application to the ECtHR.[65]

The High Court's decision in *Betteridge*[66] was one of a line of pre-*Faulkner*[67] cases brought by prisoners for breach of Article 5(4) in respect of delays by the Parole Board in determining whether they should be released. Judges had taken an exceptionally restrictive approach, systematically denying awards, drawing on wider considerations such as the moral status of the claimant and public interest concerns.[68] In this vein the Judge in *Betteridge*, having found a violation of Article 5(4), held that there could be 'no conceivable claim for damages'[69] where the inevitable result of the delayed Parole Board hearing would have been that the prisoner would not be released; in such circumstances the court would not consider making awards for distress suffered in consequence of the delay suffered. Consonant with the sort of pragmatic, public interest reasoning in *Anufrijeva*,[70] the Judge indicated that similar claims ought to be discouraged given the Board's ongoing resourcing problems, which made delays inevitable: such claims 'are not likely to achieve any sensible redress and merely add to costs'.[71]

Unsurprisingly Betteridge complained to the ECtHR. The Government claimed Betteridge's application was inadmissible as he had not exhausted domestic remedies. However, the Court did not consider HRA damages to be an adequate or effective remedy, given the High Court decision made it 'highly unlikely that damages would have been awarded', while the Government could not draw 'the Court's attention to any similar case where damages were awarded'.[72] It was not therefore 'unreasonable for the applicant not to have sought an award of damages under the [HRA]'.[73]

B. Substantive Rights and Remedies

Restrictions on recovery may violate substantive rights. The Strasbourg Court has held that severe legislative limitations on judges' capacity to redress damage suffered by the victim of a privacy breach may violate

[65] (2013) 57 EHRR 7.
[66] *R (Betteridge) v Parole Board* [2009] EWHC 1638 [*Betteridge* HC].
[67] *R (Faulkner) v SOSJ* [2013] 2 AC 254.
[68] See ch 5.2.II.C.ii.
[69] *Betteridge* HC (n 66) [28].
[70] (n 1) [79]–[81].
[71] *Betteridge* HC (n 66) [31].
[72] *Betteridge* (n 65) [51].
[73] ibid.

the positive obligation under Article 8 to ensure respect for private life.[74] Domestic limits on levels of compensation 'must not be such as to deprive the individual of his or her privacy and thereby empty the right of its effective content'.[75] Although legislative limits were the subject of the challenge in that case, a judicial practice which led to no or very modest compensation for rights-breaches, could equally be expected to run afoul of Convention requirements. One must recall that the ECtHR is concerned to uphold the Convention's core intention: 'to guarantee not theoretical or illusory rights, but rights that are practical and effective'.[76] It is difficult to maintain that rights have practical force if they may be violated with no real consequence.

C. Absolute Nature of Article 13

Article 13 is an absolute right, there being no express limits on the right in the Convention text. The ECtHR has emphasised that 'the place of art 13 in the scheme of human rights protection set up by the Convention would argue in favour of implied restrictions of art 13 being kept to a minimum'.[77] This indicates very little scope for restrictions based in public interest considerations.[78] Further, the wording of Article 13 tells against adoption of a remedial approach that affords authorities special protection: everyone who suffers a rights-violation 'shall have an effective remedy before a national authority *notwithstanding that the violation has been committed by persons acting in an official capacity*'.[79] The ECtHR has said: Article 13 prohibits 'creation of immunities for public officials and any such immunity must be regarded as contrary to the object and purpose of the Convention'.[80] Thus, if damages are the only remedy that can effectively remedy a rights-violation

[74] *Armonienė v Lithuania* (25 November 2008) App no 36919/02, [47] (ECtHR Second Section); *Biriuk v Lithuania* (25 November 2008) App no 23373/03, [46] (ECtHR Second Section).

[75] *Armonienė* ibid [46]; *Biriuk* ibid [45].

[76] *Scordino* (n 48) [192].

[77] *Kudla v Poland* (2002) 35 EHRR 11, [152].

[78] Lester et al observe that 'even in cases at which national security issues are at the heart, such as expulsions on national security grounds, the ECtHR has emphasised the minimum content of an effective remedy' ((n 57) [4.13.10]).

[79] See also International Covenant on Civil and Political Rights, article 2(3)(a), which is in similar terms. The *travaux préparatoires* for this provision of the ICCPR, which are annexed to the *travaux* for Article 13 ECHR, record: 'Although an opinion was expressed that the strict application of paragraph 3(a) in cases when officials had acted in good faith might seriously hamper the course of justice and administration as a whole, it was argued that it should be made clear that no one could avoid responsibility for violating a person's freedom, especially by claiming that he was acting on higher authority' (European Commission of Human Rights, *Preparatory Work on Article 13 of the European Convention on Human Rights*, DH(57)5 (1957) 17).

[80] *Z* (n 41) [106].

it would arguably constitute a breach of Article 13 not to award damages or make sub-compensatory awards because of reasons inextricably linked to the official nature of the defendant—for example, because damages would deplete public funds. It should be noted that the Lord Chancellor, in the debates on the Human Rights Bill, made clear that the 'very ample definition of public authority' in what became section 6 of the HRA, 'makes it plain that there is no intention to protect persons acting in an official capacity'.[81] Further, the ECtHR has held that the existence of *personal immunities* for officials, such as judges, within domestic law does not relieve *the state* of its obligations under Article 13 to compensate rights-violations attributable in whole or part to acts of immunised officials.[82]

D. Proportionality

The ECtHR has often said that 'inherent in the whole of the Convention is a search for a fair balance between the demands of the general interest of the community and the requirements of the protection of the individual's fundamental rights'.[83] It may be tempting to invoke this idea to support a balancing approach, or restraint more generally.[84] However, fair balance is an idea that characterises adjudication of substantive rights, epitomised by the proportionality doctrine. As we have seen, the Strasbourg Court has stated clearly that implied limits on Article 13 ought to be kept to a minimum.

Indeed, the fact that important countervailing interests are accounted for by defences, such as proportionality, tells against countervailing interests resurfacing at the remedial stage. In *Anufrijeva* the Court said: 'The factors that weigh against recognising administrative delay as engaging article 8 militate equally in favour of either no award or modest awards where article 8 is engaged'.[85] However, this approach gives the state two bites at the same cherry: 'competing interests are afforded a second veto at the remedy stage'.[86] By analogy, in vindicatory torts a 'balancing'[87] of interests occurs when the court considers defences but where liability is established full damages issue as of right.

[81] HL Deb vol 583 col 475 (18 November 1997) Lord Irvine of Lairg.

[82] *McFarlane* (n 38) [121].

[83] *Soering v UK* (1989) 11 EHRR 439, [89].

[84] eg *R (Wilkinson) v IRC* [2005] 1 WLR 1718, [48], and see *Faulkner* (n 67) [127]; *Walton v Scottish Ministers* [2012] UKSC 44, [138] (in regard to specific-type relief).

[85] (n 1) [76].

[86] P Gewirtz, 'Remedies and Resistance' (1983) 92 *Yale Law Journal* 585, 602.

[87] C Harlow, *Compensation and Government Torts* (Sweet and Maxwell, 1982) 40–41; T Weir, *A Casebook on Tort* 10th edn (Sweet and Maxwell, 2004) 324.

III. THE INTEREST-BALANCING APPROACH AND FUNDAMENTAL PRINCIPLES OF ENGLISH LAW

Another concern with interest-balancing is that it is difficult to reconcile with important and long-standing principles of English law, specifically *ubi ius, ibi remedium* and the principle of equality. One would expect that, according to ordinary maxims of interpretation,[88] courts would interpret a broadly framed power to award damages consistently with such fundamental principles, especially as they are accepted precepts of the rule of law in England. One would certainly not expect courts to adopt interpretations which positively frustrate fundamental principle.

A. *Ubi Ius, Ibi Remedium*

It is a long-standing principle of English law that where there is a right, there ought to be a remedy. The principle is of some pedigree. For example, in 1703 Holt CJ in *Ashby* said famously:

> If the plaintiff has a right, he must of necessity have a means to vindicate and maintain it, and a remedy if he is injured in the exercise or enjoyment of it; and indeed it is a vain thing to imagine a right without a remedy; for want of right and want of remedy are reciprocal.[89]

The principle's centrality within the legal order has led to it being recognised as a 'fundamental principle',[90] the 'rule of public policy which has first claim on the loyalty of the law',[91] 'a cornerstone of our system of justice',[92] and a principle of the rule of law.[93] Turpin and Tomkins argue that '[a] state can only ... claim to uphold the rule of law if it provides effective means for the prevention and redress of illegal action by those who wield public powers',[94] while Feldman observes that the principle is of such importance that it is an aspect of the rule of law, underpins 'the legitimacy of judicial action' and where respected in public law, 'enhances the legitimacy of executive and legislative action'.[95]

[88] *R v SOSHD, ex p Pierson* [1998] AC 539, 575, 591; *R (Evans) v Attorney-General* [2015] 2 WLR 813, [51]–[59].
[89] *Ashby v White* (1703) 2 Lord Raymond 938, 953.
[90] *Chapman* (n 25) [65].
[91] *X (Minors) v Bedfordshire CC* [1995] 2 AC 633, 663, and often repeated since.
[92] *Jones v Kaney* [2011] 2 AC 398, [113].
[93] *Chapman* (n 25) [26], [58]
[94] C Turpin and A Tomkins, *British Government and the Constitution* 7th edn (CUP, 2011) 109 (emphasis added).
[95] D Feldman, 'The Human Rights Act 1998 and Constitutional Principles' (1999) 19 *Legal Studies* 165, 195; 'Remedies for Violations of Convention Rights' in D Feldman (ed), *English Public Law* 2nd edn (OUP, 2009) [19.06].

Stated as a generalised principle the right/remedy principle does not necessarily entitle a rights-holder to any particular remedy where their right is violated. However, if damages are the only remedy that could sensibly remedy the wrong—because it entails injury—then to deny such remedy would contravene the principle. Or, at least, this has been the longstanding view taken in English law. To see this, one must consider how the principle has been 'concretised' in practice. Significantly, the paradigm case of unerring adherence to the principle is where injury is suffered as a result of breach of basic rights.

Thus Holt CJ in *Ashby*, having enunciated the right/remedy principle, and held that invasion of basic rights in reputation, land or physical integrity entails injury in itself, then brought these two propositions together: 'every man that is injured ought to have his recompence'.[96]

As we saw in chapter 3,[97] Blackstone considered protection of absolute rights to be the principal aim of society and of laws; these included rights in physical security, personal liberty and private property, that is, those interests protected by vindicatory torts.[98] Blackstone considered that specifically in respect of these absolute rights, 'in vain would these rights be declared, ascertained, and protected by the dead letter of the laws, if the constitution had provided no other method to secure their actual enjoyment'.[99] One of the ways these were kept secure was through the liberty 'of applying to the courts of justice *for redress of injuries*', Blackstone citing Coke for the proposition that, 'every subject, for injury done to him *in bonis* [goods], *in terris* [lands], *vel persona* [person], by any other subject, be he ecclesiastical or temporal, *without any exception*, may take his remedy by the court of the law, and have justice and right *for the injury done to him*, freely without sale, fully without any denial, and speedily without delay'.[100] That a remedy follows invasion of a right is a 'general and indisputable rule',[101] 'a settled and invariable principle in the laws of England'.[102]

Dicey similarly observed 'strict adherence' by judges to the maxim 'which underlie[s] the whole law of the constitution',

> that the courts give a remedy for the infringement of a right whether the injury done be great or small ... The law of England protects the right to personal liberty,

[96] *Ashby* (n 89) 955.

[97] Ch 3.I.A.

[98] W Blackstone, *Commentaries on the Laws of England* (Clarendon, 1765–69) Book 1, 123.

[99] ibid Book 1, 140.

[100] ibid Book 1, 141 (emphasis added). It is specifically for breach of these 'absolute rights' that courts award presumed damages absent proven material loss: *Ratcliffe v Evans* [1892] 2 QB 524, 528; *Nicholls v Ely Beet Sugar Factory Ltd* [1936] 1 Ch 343, 350–51.

[101] ibid Book 3, 23.

[102] ibid Book 3, 109.

> as also every other legal right, against every kind of infringement, and gives the same kind of redress [ie damages] for the pettiest as for the gravest violations of person freedom.[103]

Thus, if there is any context in which *ubi ius, ibi remedium* is unwaveringly adhered to, it is where injury is suffered through breach of basic rights. The principle continues to characterise the modern approach to remedies for breaches of basic rights in tort. Where a tort is proven compensatory damages issue as of right. This is the case whether the defendant is an authority or not, whether the action is vindicatory or compensatory, and whether the tort protects dignitary or lesser interests. If this principle is axiomatic in fields which protect basic rights in English law, and is abided even where lesser interests are protected through imposition of liability, it is difficult to see why it should be abrogated where fundamental human rights are violated. That the principle should hold in human rights law is reflected in Article 13. As Sedley LJ observes, that Article 'reflects the longstanding principle of our law that where there is a right there should be a remedy'[104] and makes it a central principle of European law.[105]

For completeness it is important to observe that the principle, as practised in English law, does not require a remedy for every legal wrong. For example, some remedies are discretionary, such as injunctions and orders based on the prerogative writs within common law review, so that litigants may well be left without remedy. However, such examples do not undermine the argument that the right/remedy principle requires provision of damages where injury is suffered through breach of basic rights. Indeed the counter-examples reinforce that if there is one context in which the principle has special significance and must hold it is where basic rights are breached causing injury. Injunctions raise different concerns to damages,[106] while such remedies derive from equity, which is characterised historically by concerns removed from those which characterise common law actions. In any case, despite their discretionary nature it is unthinkable that injunctive relief would be denied where basic rights in the person are at stake.[107] As regards common law review, there are good reasons why the right/remedy principle does not apply: review is concerned with public wrongs rather than breaches of individual personal rights, the latter being the 'driver' of the right/remedy principle.[108]

103 AV Dicey, *Introduction to the Study of the Law of the Constitution* 10th edn (MacMillan, 1960) 211–12.

104 *R (K) v Camden and Islington Health Authority* [2002] QB 198, [54].

105 See Feldman 2009 (n 95) [19.01].

106 See s 2.V.A.iii, VI.

107 See ch 3.III.B.v.

108 See ch 4.2.II.A.

B. The Principle of Equality

In chapter 3 we saw that the principle of equality is a fundamental feature of the rule of law and legal doctrine in England.[109] Commentators observe that 'Dicey's equality doctrine reflects an attitude to government that forms an important part of our political culture';[110] 'Dicey captured, articulated and reinforced a fundamental attitude towards government which, at least in common law jurisdictions, is widespread both in the legal profession and in the community at large'; and that the principle of equality 'conforms to a widely held political ideal'.[111] The concern underlying this principle is that deviations from it will lead to special exceptions for the benefit of authorities. Public officials and institutions ought not to be above ordinary law because, inter alia, this would undermine the basic principle of government under law; where law ends, there is greater scope for abuse of power and freedom may be imperilled; and because of the basic idea that citizens should not be expected to comply with norms with which those that administer the law would not be prepared to abide. As with the right/remedy principle the concern that officials not benefit from special exemptions is reflected in Article 13.

On one view the equality principle has no bearing on human rights damages: human rights law imposes obligations specifically on public authorities, so that whatever the remedial approach for breach of such obligations, it cannot entail deviation from ordinary law.

However, much depends on how the matter is framed. For example it is an ordinary incident of English law that for those personal rights for breach of which damages are an available remedy, damages issue as of course. As we have seen, the proposition holds especially for breach of basic rights. It holds even where rights are held against a limited, specific class of persons or entities as, for example, for anti-discrimination rights or rights to a safe workplace held against employers, rights against occupiers that they keep

[109] Ch 3.I.A; Dicey (n 103) 193–95. There is much authority, ancient and modern: eg *Ashby* (n 89) per Holt CJ; *Wilkes v Wood* (1763) Lofft 1; *Entick v Carrington* (1765) 19 State Trials 1030; *Christie v Leachinsky* [1947] AC 57; *Southam v Smout* [1964] 1 QB 308, 320; *Ministry of Housing and Local Government v Sharp* [1970] 2 QB 223, 266; *Davy v Spelthorne BC* [1984] AC 262, 276; *Stovin v Wise* [1996] AC 923, 946G; *R v Governor of Brockhill Prison, ex p Evans (No 2)* [2001] 2 AC 19; *R (Wilkinson) v Broadmoor SHA* [2002] 1 WLR 419, [56]; *ID v Home Office* [2006] 1 WLR 1003, [57]. That this principle still holds sway is reflected in the consultation responses to the Law Commission's (now abandoned) proposals for a special scheme of public authority liability: *Administrative Redress: Public Bodies and the Citizen*, Law Com 322 (2010) [1.30], [3.14]–[3.15] [Administrative Redress Report].

[110] C Harlow, 'Rationalising Administrative Compensation' [2010] *PL* 321, 322–23.

[111] P Hogg, 'Compensation for Damage Caused by Government' (1995) 6 *National Journal of Constitutional Law* 7, 18–19. See also P Hogg et al, *Liability of the Crown* 4th edn (Carswell, 2011) 2–3. As the authors note, while there are examples of deviation from equality, it is 'the dominant characteristic of the law governing the liability of the Crown' (at 4).

their premises safe, or where private rights sounding in liability are implied within a particular statutory context and are held against a defined class. In this light the interest-balancing approach amounts to a special exception from ordinary damages law and the ordinary principle that where there is a right there ought to be a remedy, for the benefit of authorities.[112] To draw out the point, consider those contexts where Convention rights are protected horizontally through common law. Where a successful claim is brought against a private individual for misuse of private information, damages are available as of course and assessed on a vindicatory basis.[113] However, if a privacy claim were made against an authority under the HRA for an identical interference with privacy, damages may be denied or reduced below full compensation.[114]

To the foregoing one may add that bills of rights are designed, in part, to give further effect to the equality principle, or at least respond to the concerns underpinning that principle. Bills of rights reflect 'the general principle that, except to the extent of legal authority, no one (whether Crown or citizen) may lawfully interfere with another's interests of personal integrity and civil rights'.[115] ECS Wade, in the Introduction to the tenth edition of Dicey's treatise on the Constitution, wrote, '[t]he progress which has been made towards the recognition of the human rights of individual citizens within their own States approaches more closely to Dicey's conception of equality before the law'.[116] One might think such a statement curious given Dicey's well-known preference for common law protections over declarations of rights. However, it is not so if one recognises that one 'purpose of subjecting officials to the ordinary courts, applying primarily the rules of private law, was to make government subservient to principles of justice that protected fundamental interests in personal liberty and security'.[117] In this vein Neo-Diceyans had, before the HRA, argued that adoption of a rights-instrument may be necessary to plug gaps in common law protections. For example in the wake of the infamous *Malone*[118] case, finding it lawful for police to tap telephone calls despite having no statutory authority to do so, Harlow argued,

> [a] Bill of Rights which creates rights may be necessary if tort law is to do an effective job in vindicating civil liberties, particularly when these come in the form of

[112] See *Chapman* (n 25) [77].

[113] *Gulati v MGN Ltd* [2015] EWHC 1482.

[114] Oliver, when the HRA came into force, argued that as Convention rights are applied horizontally, public/private distinctions under the HRA would come to be viewed as special immunities and disintegrate: 'The Human Rights Act and Public Law/Private Law Divides' [2000] *European Human Rights Law Review* 343.

[115] *Crown Liability and Judicial Immunity: A Response to* Baigent's Case *and* Harvey v Derrick, NZLC R37 (1997) [17] [Crown Liability].

[116] Dicey (n 103) xcvii.

[117] TRS Allan, *Constitutional Justice* (OUP, 2003) 19.

[118] *Malone v Metropolitan Police Commissioner* [1979] Ch 344.

intangible values which do not fit neatly inside the person and property categories of the traditional tort law.[119]

It is difficult to reconcile giving greater effect to the equality principle by enacting legal rights against authorities, while departing from ordinary damages principles where authorities breach those rights, for the benefit of authorities.

We might also recall that where the law countenances formal departures from the equality principle within English damages law such departures have been consonant with the normative concerns underlying the principle: departures have been for the benefit of individuals given, inter alia, the importance of vindicating the principle of government under law, and protecting basic interests. Thus, the Law Lords in *Rookes* held, following longstanding practice,[120] that unconstitutional, arbitrary or oppressive action by public servants is one of a limited class of cases in which exemplary damages can be awarded;[121] such award can serve 'a valuable purpose in restraining the arbitrary and outrageous use of executive power'.[122] It is odd that within the English tradition damages have been so varied where defendants are public, but that in a field specifically dedicated to protecting basic interests in the face of public power, we find moves to marginalise rather than enhance the damages remedy. If these moves reach their logical end-point then we will have come far from the proposition that '[o]ur English law does not allow a public officer to shelter behind a droit administratif'.[123]

SECTION 2: NORMATIVE ANALYSIS OF THE INTEREST-BALANCING APPROACH

So much for doctrinal analysis of the interest-balancing approach. This section explores whether such approach is normatively justifiable.

Part 1 of this book advanced a strong normative argument of legal principle that the approach to human rights damages ought to follow the orthodox approach to damages for breaches of basic rights in English law. Some special justification would be required to overcome this powerful argument from orthodoxy. As discussed in chapter 4, that we are operating in a 'public law' context cannot *in itself* justify deviation from private

[119] C Harlow, *Understanding Tort Law* (Sweet and Maxwell, 1987) 128; see also Harlow (n 87) 43–46.

[120] eg *Ashby* (n 89) 956 ('[i]f publick officers will infringe mens rights, they ought to pay greater damages than other men, to deter and hinder other officers from the like offences'); *Wilkes* (n 109).

[121] *Rookes v Barnard* [1964] AC 1129, 1226.

[122] ibid 1223, 1226; *Kuddus v Chief Constable Leicestershire Constabulary* [2002] 2 AC 122, [75]ff.

[123] *Sharp* (n 109) 266.

law damages principles. Any approach must be justified on its merits. The interest-balancing approach, which entails radical departure from the pre-existing English law of damages, is premised on an understandable concern that awards against authorities may undermine important public interests. However, the argument for this approach is not straightforward and the approach suffers significant drawbacks.

Section I outlines concerns that may justify an interest-balancing approach, by way of introduction. Section II discusses an important drawback of such approach: that it would operate to deny victims effective redress. Section III considers whether those concerns which underpin the interest-balancing approach are peculiar to human rights law, such that a *sui generis* remedial approach is justified. Section IV analyses whether adoption of interest-balancing is necessary to protect important public interests, given many such interests are already afforded protection via aspects of substantive law, ordinary damages principles, and civil procedure, and non-legal phenomena. Section V undertakes detailed examination of public interest factors taken into account by courts under the HRA, or which may potentially be taken into account, to deny or reduce awards. The section considers whether such factors are appropriate for judicial consideration and, if so, how courts should factor them into their decision-making. Section VI discusses formal rule-of-law concerns associated with interest-balancing. Lastly, section VII considers how the interest-balancing approach propounded in *Anufrijeva* might be refined.

I. CONCERNS THAT MAY JUSTIFY AN INTEREST-BALANCING APPROACH

The legitimacy of courts considering public interest factors, and issues particular to individual factors, will be discussed below. This section sets out, by way of introduction, the sorts of concerns that might underpin adoption of an interest-balancing approach.

It is important that authorities have sufficient funds to perform their primary functions. Public authorities generally perform functions which are crucial to the welfare of the general population such as provision of health care and social security, and defence of the realm. They are typically required to perform such functions by statute, and if authorities were not to provide particular services, it *may* be that they are not provided at all. It seems unlikely that the odd damages judgment against a public authority with a large budget would undermine the authority's ability to function. On the other hand a spate of large awards against an authority with a small budget, in conjunction with sizeable litigation costs, might come to affect negatively the authority's ability to perform its primary tasks. Damages actions, whether successful or not, may, on top of imposing economic costs, divert time and energy away from primary tasks. One must also remember that damages liability in human rights law adds to existing sources of liability, including tort, contract, restitution, equity and EU law. Indeed some argue that tort is 'abounding', and that state liability in particular is expanding, fuelled by supranational forces, an increasingly consumerist and risk-averse society, as well as the increasing tendency of individuals to resort to tort law to secure accountability for misconduct, often because of the inadequacy of other means, and to view the state as 'guarantor'.[124] In addition to compensating legal wrongs, government makes *ex gratia* payments for loss occasioned by simple maladministration, as in response to recommendations made by the Parliamentary Ombudsman.[125] As the occupational pensions[126] and Equitable Life[127] sagas have shown, such payments may be massive,[128] and accompanied by protracted litigation.[129]

Administrators ought to feel free to engage in vigorous decision-making, making decisions which best serve the common good. Imposition of liability *may* have the negative effect of encouraging defensive behaviours, whereby administrators become unduly focused on avoiding legal liability at the expense of professional judgement and the public goals they are specifically charged with serving; for example, fear of liability may lead authorities to abandon policies that could benefit large sections of society.

There are growing concerns over development of a 'litigation' or 'compensation culture'. This issue has formed the subject of several official reports in recent years,[130] led Parliament to pass legislation[131] and prompted judicial comment.[132] Many negative effects can result from persons too easily resorting to litigation. Litigation typically entails significant expenditure, while the perceived threat of litigation can have a freezing effect on beneficial activity. If individuals too easily blame others for their misfortunes, or selfishly assert their interests without regard for others, this may undermine

[124] eg C Harlow, *State Liability* (OUP, 2004).

[125] Harlow (n 110).

[126] *Trusting in the Pensions Promise*, HC 984 (2006).

[127] *Equitable Life: A Decade of Regulatory Failure*, HC 815-I (2008).

[128] The Government initially allocated approximately £1.5 billion to compensate Equitable Life policyholders ('Equitable Life—Important Next Steps' at www.hm-treasury.gov.uk/fin_equitable_life.htm), and over £1 billion has so far been paid out ('Equitable Life Payment Scheme' at www.gov.uk/equitable-life-payment-scheme). In response to the Ombudsman's report on occupational pensions, the Government initially made available £8 billion in cumulative cash terms to compensate those who had lost all or part of their final salary occupational pensions: HC Deb vol 458 col 114WS (28 March 2007) Mr John Hutton.

[129] *R (Bradley) v SOS for Work and Pensions* [2008] EWCA Civ 36; *R (Equitable Members Action Group) v HM Treasury* [2009] EWHC 2495.

[130] See Better Regulation Taskforce, *Better Routes to Redress* (2004); *Compensation Culture*, HC 754-I (2006) [Compensation Culture]; Lord Young, *Common Sense, Common Safety* (Cabinet Office 2010).

[131] eg Compensation Act 2006; Social Action, Responsibility and Heroism Act 2015.

[132] eg *Gorringe v Calderdale* [2004] 1 WLR 1057, [2]. On prevailing judicial attitudes see, eg, JJ Spigelman, 'Tort Law Reform: An Overview' (2006) 14 *Tort Law Review* 5.

personal responsibility and social cohesion. Specific to public authorities, some argue that there is a growing tendency to view government as insurer of last resort; in other words if there is no one else to sue one might turn to government, particularly as it is perceived to have 'deep pockets'. Expansion of governmental functions over time, and the contemporary trend of government moving beyond direct provision of essential services to regulation and governance of vast areas of activity, has rendered government more susceptible to legal challenges, particularly where it may not be directly responsible for harm.

By tempering frequency and quantum of awards an interest-balancing approach might serve to protect important public interests, and guard against these undesirable phenomena.

II. THE IMPORTANCE OF REMEDYING RIGHTS-VIOLATIONS

On the other hand interest-balancing would result in denial of damages (or sub-compensatory awards) in cases where only damages could effectively remedy the wrong. This is a major drawback as there are powerful reasons for ensuring human rights violations are fully remedied.

As discussed in Part 1 of this book, the primary goals of human rights law are to protect basic interests from outside interference, to maintain those interests inviolate, and affirm and reinforce their importance and that they ought to be held in the utmost respect. A vindicatory approach to damages gives direct effect to these goals. Obviously the law's preference is that duties are actually complied with so that claimants' protected interests are in fact maintained inviolate. Wherever those interests are threatened with wrongful interference or subject to ongoing wrongful interference specific relief should generally be granted to secure actual compliance by the defendant and enjoyment of the right by the claimant. However, where a wrong has been committed in the past performance is now impossible; there is no way the wrong can literally be undone and the right actually enjoyed as it ought to have been. Nonetheless, the law can require a next-best alternative to actual performance in the form of damages, substituting one level of entitlement with another that is equivalent, thus restoring—notionally, at least—the entitlement that was wrongfully denied. Damages thus place the claimant, as far as a monetary award can, in the position in which their interests had not been wrongfully interfered with, the position in which they were legally entitled to be in: one in which their interests were maintained inviolate. Damages, under a vindicatory approach, achieve this through an award which redresses the wrongful incursion upon protected interests in itself, and also by reversing negative consequential effects caused by the interference. By placing the claimant in a position equivalent to one in which their interests were maintained in pristine form damages afford strong protection to these interests and affirm and reinforce that these interests are, in themselves, of the utmost importance and that they ought to be maintained inviolate and respected. In this way, despite the wrong, the law's goals are ultimately fulfilled or satisfied by the monetary award, and basic interests are afforded strong protection and vindicated.

In contrast, if the courts' routine response to past violations were that nothing should be done, it would be no exaggeration to say that the very goals which human rights law is constituted to perform will have been rendered hollow and the rights themselves emasculated, having little practical force as entitlements. It is remedies that give rights practical effect where threatened and interfered with; remedies '"'realise" a legal norm ... make it a "living truth"'.[133] If the remedial response to violations is that nothing should be done in practice protected interests will be afforded the same protection as interests not subject to legal protection. There is little point in enacting policies into law if the law's commitment to those policies is abandoned where the law is breached; indeed, cases of violation are the very circumstances in which the law's protective and vindicatory policies require positive reassertion. These points are captured in intuitive judicial statements, such as Cooke P's that it would be 'legislative window-dressing, of no practical consequence' to pass an Act 'which is aimed at protecting and promoting' human rights but no provision was made for 'appropriate remedies for those whose rights and freedoms have been violated';[134] McKay J's, that if courts allow a right to be infringed with no consequence '[s]uch right would exist only in name ... it would be a misnomer to call it a right, as it would be without substance';[135] Mann J's view that if damages are not given for the wrong in itself 'the right becomes empty';[136] Lord Ackner's view that 'rights are valueless unless there exists the means to enforce or protect them';[137] and those repeated dicta of the ECtHR that 'the Convention is intended to guarantee not rights that are theoretical or illusory but rights that are practical and effective';[138] 'the State may not set individual rights and freedoms at nought or circumvent them with impunity'.[139] If a court's response to a wrong is that nothing should be done in no sense can the fundamental importance of the right be said to have been affirmed or reinforced nor a signal sent that such rights should be maintained in pristine form and respected; indeed, the law, through its acquiescence, sends the opposite signal.

[133] Gewirtz (n 86) 587, drawing on *Cooper v Aaron* 358 US 1, 20 (1958).
[134] *Simpson v Attorney-General [Baigent's Case]* [1994] 3 NZLR 667, 691.
[135] ibid 717.
[136] *Gulati* (n 113) [143].
[137] HL Deb vol 582 col 1284 (3 November 1997) (debating the Human Rights Bill).
[138] *Artico v Italy* (1981) 3 EHRR 1, [33]; *Kudla* (n 77) [157].
[139] *Shilbergs* (n 55) [78].

It is important to emphasise that human rights are personal entitlements which authorities are lawfully required to satisfy, like rights in tort or contract. We are not here dealing with questions over whether liability should be imposed for a governmental failure to disperse a discretionary benefit, as under social security or housing legislation, or with cases where members of the public are simply left worse off by governmental policy decisions but there is no legal wrong. Imposition of liability in those contexts is controversial because it would entail courts ordering government to pay compensation where individuals have not been denied any legal entitlement; in turn this might be thought to illegitimately involve courts in bare allocative, redistributive decisions. In contrast where damages are awarded for breaches of human rights the courts are redressing denial of legal entitlements which Parliament, in the name of the polity, has determined each individual ought to enjoy, but which have been unlawfully denied. To draw on an article by Cohen and Smith,

> [t]hese are claims which assume a decision as to the provision of a public benefit and its allocation as already made by the legislative and bureaucratic arenas, and constitute demands that that which has been allocated must actually be given, or if it is too late for it to be given, compensation should be given instead [as an equivalent].[140]

Damages for rights-violations compensate for the denial of 'benefits which we as a society have determined [individuals] "ought to receive"'.[141]

Some might argue that awarding damages may in fact undermine rights-protection as government can 'buy off' violations. The argument has little force given: (1) specific relief is available to stop violations or prohibit rights-infringing conduct; and (2) damages may be the only relief that can effectively remedy the violation, meaning that the alternative would be to leave the victim without remedy. A stronger argument is that if damages are generally available the judiciary may interpret primary rights narrowly to limit state liability.[142] Whether this occurs is an empirical question, and difficult to predict. However, views may vary as to whether this would be a welcome development or not. For example routine availability of damages could have a 'disciplining' effect on judicial delineation of the scope of rights, which may, if not taken too far, be no bad thing. There is a plausible argument that certain rights, such as privacy, have been given such broad interpretations that they have come to protect interests which are, in truth, less than fundamental. The core doctrinal features of human rights law,

[140] D Cohen and JC Smith, 'Entitlement and the Body Politic: Rethinking Negligence in Public Law' (1986) 64 *Canadian Bar Review* 1, 19.

[141] ibid 26.

[142] See JC Jeffries, 'The Right-Remedy Gap in Constitutional Law' (1999) 109 *Yale Law Journal* 87.

which afford strong protection to underlying interests, are justified on the basis that human rights law protects basic interests. If the law turns out to protect interests which are far less than fundamental this could plunge the field into both an identity and legitimacy crisis.

Even leaving to the side arguments stemming from the nature of human rights law, there is the very basic principle that one should make full reparation for the losses one occasions through one's wrongs on the ground that one is responsible for one's wrongs.[143] Such a reparative duty is typically said to be grounded in, or more specifically a manifestation of, the Aristotelian norm of corrective justice. This norm has been described as a foundation stone of our moral order,[144] while full compensation, or *restitutio in integrum*, is a principle which finds almost universal recognition in legal fields in which money remedies are available, albeit that the details of its operation differ amongst contexts given the different nature of the fields in which it applies. This principle is considered axiomatic, fair and just across all of tort and in contract, and where compensatory remedies are available in equity,[145] and is applied where the defendant is a public authority. Indeed, it is the principle adopted by the Local Government[146] and Parliamentary Ombudsmen[147] in their guidance on remedies for non-legal wrongs; the principle applied by the ECtHR in calculating just satisfaction;[148] and the principle applied in the international law of state responsibility;[149] while the principle also characterises damages in EU law.[150] The UN has affirmed *restitutio in integrum* as a remedial principle for gross violations of international human rights law and serious violations of international humanitarian law,[151] while this basic compensatory principle is applied by the International Court of Justice in assessing money

[143] See, eg, J Gardner, 'What is Tort Law For? Part 1: The Place of Corrective Justice' (2010) 30 *Law & Philosophy* 1.

[144] P Schuck, *Suing Government: Citizen Remedies for Official Wrongs* (Yale, 1982) 112.

[145] *AIB Group (UK) Plc v Mark Redler & Co* [2014] 3 WLR 1367.

[146] Local Government Ombudsman, *Guidance on Good Practice: Remedies* (2015) 3, 5.

[147] Parliamentary and Health Service Ombudsman, *Principles for Remedy* (2009) 3, 10. As the document notes (at 3), the remedial principles adopted by the Ombudsman accord with and are reproduced in the HM Treasury's guidelines on remedy in *Managing Public Money* (2013) Annex 4.14 (the compensatory principle is adopted at [A4.14.4]), and are cited as best practice in the Department of Health's *NHS Finance Manual* (www.info.doh.gov.uk/doh/finman.nsf).

[148] See ch 5.

[149] ILC Draft Articles on State Responsibility for Internationally Wrongful Acts 2001 (with commentaries), article 31, and see: *The Factory at Chorzów (Merits)* (13 September 1928) PCIJ, Series A, No 17, 47.

[150] A Biondi and M Farley, *The Right to Damages in European Law* (Wolters Kluwer, 2009) 77–79 (state liability), 158–59 (Union liability).

[151] *Basic Principles and Guidelines on the Right to a Remedy and Reparation for Victims of Gross Violations of International Human Rights Law and Serious Violations of International Humanitarian Law*, UN General Assembly Resolution 60/147 (2005) arts 19, 20.

awards for breaches of international human rights law.[152] To depart from this near-universal principle specifically where fundamental rights are violated, with damages possibly reduced below ordinary compensatory levels or denied altogether, so that the claimant must bear all or a portion of wrongfully inflicted losses, would be incongruous. Furthermore, if awards of full compensation are made as of course for interference with equivalent or lesser interests, and even for non-legal wrongs, but not for human rights violations, this would 'depreciate'[153] the importance of the interests protected by human rights law.

Some, such as Levinson, would accept that corrective justice provides a sound justification for a duty to compensate in private law but doubt whether it can perform the same work in public law. For example, he questions whether it is right for the financial burden of a rights-violation perpetrated by government to fall on taxpayers, given taxpayers cannot be said to be morally responsible for the violation.[154] This argument is flawed. First, it ignores the fact that public authorities have a legal personality and identity of their own, including under the HRA; it is the public authority which pays damages for its own wrong.[155] Second, putting the first point aside, government is broadly working to fulfil the public's goals: the public elect the governing party into power on the basis of its manifesto, the government is accountable to the public through Parliament, while government's role is to implement legislative goals, which have been set by the polity's representatives. Once one accepts that government is constituted to act on behalf of and in the interests of the public it is difficult to resist the argument that '[w]hen the collectivity seeks to fulfil benign aspirations but errs and injures, as it often will, it must—like anyone else—repair its damage and compensate its victims'.[156] By analogy, in private law we do not accept the argument that a publically-listed company that violates an individual's rights should be excused from repairing the resulting loss on the basis that this would

[152] *Ahmadou Sadio Diallo (Republic of Guinea v Democratic Republic of the Congo), Compensation Judgment* [2012] ICJ Rep 324.

[153] *Dunlea v Attorney-General* [2000] 3 NZLR 136, [83].

[154] DJ Levinson, 'Making Government Pay: Markets, Politics, and the Allocation of Constitutional Costs' (2000) 67 *University of Chicago Law Review* 345, 408–09. Levinson more generally queries whether a collective entity can qualify as a moral agent for the purposes of corrective justice. This is a huge question which cannot be addressed here; Levinson himself leaves it unresolved. However, there are strong arguments that some groups do warrant the name agent and ought to be capable of bearing responsibility: P Pettit, 'Responsibility Incorporated' (2007) 117 *Ethics* 171; P Pettit, 'The Reality of Group Agents' in C Mantzavinos (ed), *Philosophy of the Social Sciences* (CUP, 2009).

[155] *Administrative Redress: Public Bodies and the Citizen*, Law Com Consultation Paper 187 (2008) [A.15] [Administrative Redress Consultation Paper]. See further: ibid.

[156] Schuck (n 144) 111–12; Harlow (n 124) 39. In a similar vein Hogg, in respect of government health programmes, argues: 'Like the cost of vaccine, needles, clinics, nurses, publicity and the like, the cost of compensation should be distributed to the community at large which benefits from the program' ((n 111) 13).

diminish the value of a shareholders' stake in the company or deplete the dividends payable to shareholders, who cannot be said to be directly responsible for the loss.

Levinson also argues that unlike in private law constitutional violations do not entail denial of anything analogous to an individual entitlement.[157] This is a common claim that I have shown to be wrong, at least in the HRA context, in chapter 4. Levinson further claims that for many constitutional violations, particularly 'systemic' violations, it may be difficult to identify the victim to be compensated.[158] But under the HRA the courts must identify the victim in every human rights case for the purposes of standing; the general approach has been that the claimant must show that their legally protected interests have been directly affected by the challenged act, and this test has caused no serious problems. One will not run into problems if one takes the correct analytical starting-point—individual rights. Take, for example, a situation where central government systematically underfunds the Parole Board, which in turn leads to delays in the hearing of prisoner applications for release.[159] Levinson might say this is simply a case of governmental mismanagement leading to the breakdown of an administrative system and it is difficult to say that any one individual is a victim. However, the legally salient question in human rights law is: has specific prisoner X suffered a violation of their right to a speedy determination under Article 5(4)? Approached in this way it is rather simple to identify victims: those who have an arguable case that they personally suffered unreasonable delay before the Board. Of course there may be many victims in such a scenario, but this has nothing to do with Levinson's objection.

A further objection to reparative duties in public law is that losses will often be dignitary or emotional in nature, money is incommensurable with such losses and cannot really replace what has been lost.[160] Given such damages are routinely awarded for torts, and many torts cases only involve claims for such losses, it is unclear why this is an argument against reparative duties specifically in public law. Another concern that Levinson has is that consequential losses in particular cases may have no correlation with the seriousness of the constitutional or human rights violation; one person may recover significant damages for a relatively minor violation because they happened to suffer financial loss, whereas for a significant violation another person may suffer no financial losses and receive very little. As far as consequential damages go, there is nothing objectionable about this. Damages for consequential losses will differ on different facts because such losses vary. The person who receives significant damages for significant financial losses

[157] Levinson (n 154) 409.
[158] ibid.
[159] These were the background facts of *Faulkner* (n 67).
[160] Levinson (n 154) 410–11.

does so because they are out of pocket; the person who is refused damages for factual loss receives nothing because they have suffered no financial losses. Levinson's concern seems to be that such damages fail to recognise the 'intrinsic wrongfulness of the constitutional harm'.[161] He says this could be addressed by 'scaling compensation to the intrinsic wrongfulness of the constitutional harm' but dismisses this as impossible.[162] However, as we saw in Part 1 of this book, this is quite possible: damages for normative damage have long performed this role within vindicatory torts. Levinson also raises complex issues concerning the interrelationship between distributive and corrective justice, including that corrective justice may operate to maintain a status quo that entails an unjust distribution. These issues cannot be done justice here and could be debated endlessly; Levinson reaches no firm conclusion. However, it is worth recording that the distribution of entitlements in the HRA, which reparative duties would operate to maintain, is one sanctioned by Parliament, the ultimate arbiter of distributive questions in the polity, as lying in the common good.

Lastly, there are wider reasons, which may be described as 'constitutional', for supporting damages for rights-violations.

Awarding damages against authorities where they violate legal rights reinforces the normative force of the rule of law principle of government under law. As we have seen, awarding substantial sums against public officers who interfere with basic interests is a hallmark of English legal tradition. Thus, Dicey said that the fact that one could recover substantial damages for the pettiest of interferences was one of the 'principles which underlie the whole law of the constitution, and the maintenance of which has gone a great way both to ensure the supremacy of the law of the land and ultimately to curb the arbitrariness of the Crown'.[163] On the other hand, as the President of the UK Supreme Court observes, where citizens are unable to 'render their legal rights a true reality rather than words on paper' 'then the possibility exists for society to become exploitative, as some elements take advantage of the fact that they can ignore law with relative impunity'.[164] Arguments based in deterrence are controversial because empirical research suggests such effects are variable.[165] But law can be important because of the signals it sends regardless of actual consequential effects, and the routine awarding of substantial damages against public defendants for unlawful interferences with basic interests strongly reinforces the normative force of legal constraints on

[161] ibid 411.
[162] ibid.
[163] Dicey (n 103) 210.
[164] Lord Neuberger, 'From Barretry, Maintenance and Champerty to Litigation Funding' (Harbour Litigation Funding First Annual Lecture, 8 May 2013) [47] (available at www.supremecourt.uk/docs/speech-130508.pdf) (albeit, speaking in the different context of access to justice).
[165] See s 2.VII.A below.

government, the fundamental principle of government under law, and that the law will not tolerate exploitative conduct. On the other hand it sends a troubling, perverse signal—'warping' the rule of law[166]—where citizens cannot seek and obtain appropriate redress where the government unlawfully trespasses upon their basic rights causing injury. Of course general compensatory damages are not awarded specifically to enhance rule of law principles. But if the law serves a constitutional function through its *practical operation* then that is something which we ought to bear in mind in settling the approach to damages.

It may breed a sense of unfairness and even resentment among victims, and ultimately undermine the legitimacy of government and the judiciary if public authorities may interfere with citizens' fundamental rights, causing injury, without compensating for such injury. As Gaudron and McHugh JJ said in *Plenty*:

> If the courts of common law do not uphold the rights of individuals by granting effective remedies, they invite anarchy, for nothing breeds social disorder as quickly as the sense of injustice which is apt to be generated by unlawful invasion of a person's rights, particularly where the invader is a government official.[167]

To deny relief is to treat members of the polity as subjects upon whom the government can inflict injury in breach of legal rights without consequence. It is also to afford public authorities a privileged position: whereas citizens are expected to remedy their violations of the personal rights of others, including rights of public authorities,[168] authorities are relieved of this obligation where the most basic interests of citizens are at stake; this is acutely troubling in a field, such as a human rights law, specifically constituted to protect basic interests in the face of public power. Further, this sends conflicting signals to citizens: judges maintain, through high-sounding statements in their judgments, that the protection of human rights is of fundamental importance, which would in the mind of a reasonable person create an expectation that any interference would be treated with utmost seriousness. It would then be a rude awakening if a court refused to award damages for damage suffered as a result of a proven rights-violation because it could undermine certain interests of the wrongdoer (especially where a court would, for example, grant such remedy for breach of lesser rights, or private rights of authorities). Such conflicting signals are a source of incoherence in the law and can, particularly within an unequal power relationship between ordinary citizen and authority, undermine trust and confidence in the political branches, who inflict injury through breach of

[166] J Caldwell, 'Judicial Review: the Fading of Remedial Discretion?' (2009) 23 *New Zealand Universities Law Review* 489, 490; see similarly *R (C (A Minor)) v SOSJ* [2009] QB 657, [49], [54]–[55], [85].

[167] *Plenty v Dillon* (1991) 171 CLR 635, 655.

[168] See, eg, *Customs and Excise Commissioners v Total Network SL* [2008] 1 AC 1174.

basic rights without offering remedy, and the judiciary, who lend the cloak of legal legitimacy to this. As Deane J said, speaking of false imprisonment, such 'basic matters' should not be 'the stuff of empty rhetoric. They are the very fabric of freedom under the law'.[169]

There are further public interest reasons why damages ought to follow injury. These are discussed below and will not be repeated here.[170] However, it is worth recording that the interest-balancing approach, as espoused by Lord Woolf in *Anufrijeva*, presents the balancing exercise as a contest between the rights-holder's interests and those of the public. Yet, the award of damages for breaches of human rights serves wider public interests; if we are to take into account wider interests in determining the approach to human rights damages we should not limit ourselves to considering only those that might by undermined by awards.

III. PREJUDICE TO THE PUBLIC INTEREST: ONLY IN PUBLIC LAW?

Underlying arguments for an interest-balancing approach must be a belief that the sorts of concerns addressed by such approach are of peculiar relevance in human rights law compared to other fields of liability, so as to justify radical divergence of approach. However, things are not so clear-cut.

For the Court in *Anufrijeva* the most important factor counselling against making awards was their potential impact on resources available to fund public services. The Law Commission, in its consultation paper on administrative redress, espoused a similar rationale for distinguishing damages actions against authorities from those against private persons, observing that where authorities are ordered to pay damages, money is diverted from the public interest to the claimant's private benefit, whereas where a private person must pay, money is diverted from one person's private interests to another's.[171]

Such arguments raise myriad issues. The issue I wish to focus on in this section is whether the stark contrast—that claims against authorities prejudice spending in the public interest, whereas claims against private persons only prejudice private interests—is sustainable, and a sound basis for an exceptional approach to human right damages? With a moment's reflection it is obvious that this stark distinction does not map onto reality. In turn normative arguments premised upon such stylised distinctions are questionable.

Of course many authorities are specifically funded to provide public services. But there is a naivety and gross oversimplification in the stark distinction drawn above. As we saw in chapter 4, the current era is one of mixed

[169] *Re Bolton, ex p Beane* (1987) 162 CLR 514, 528–29.

[170] See s 2.VII.A below.

[171] Administrative Redress Consultation Paper (n 155) [A.21].

administration, 'marketised' public services, privatised and contracted-out public services, interpenetration of public and private capital, and governmental engagement in commercial enterprise; as some observe, '[t]he economic paradigm is dominant nowadays, and it is bent upon transforming the public interest into something not far removed from commercial interests'.[172] Association of public interest with public entities and private interest with private entities passes over the complexities of contemporary society.

It would be erroneous to claim that expenditure of scarce resources by non-governmental entities does not also serve important public interests which may be compromised where such entities are required to compensate those who they wrong, or that wrongs between private individuals only raise issues of private benefit. Private enterprise may have significant community benefits, and it has long been thought that the state has a role in creating conditions conducive to economic activity for this reason. The recent economic crisis illustrates the fundamental importance of private institutions, such as financial service providers, to the national economy, with government investing heavily to keep these institutions afloat given the threat that collapse posed to the national interest. At a general level benefits of private enterprise include wealth creation (which increases tax revenue, which can fund public services) and employment (which leads to taxable income). Of course, these phenomena have wider indirect benefits. For example, people in work are generally less likely to engage in criminal or anti-social activities, while the fewer people on social security the more resources government has to pursue other public ends. Specific businesses may engage in activities or invest in activities which are quintessentially in the wider public interest such as the promulgation of green technology, or research into pharmaceuticals which can improve or save many lives. The private sector invests not insignificant funds in sponsorship of projects and activities which serve wider public interests, including charitable causes, education, research and the arts, and which may not be viable without support. And this is to say nothing of voluntary organisations and charities which are independent of government and specifically constituted to serve the public interest, contributing significantly to important causes such as cancer research, support for the vulnerable, environmental protection and promotion of human rights. On top of this, as we saw in chapter 4, many institutions and projects which serve the wider public are funded jointly by public and private money, while there are increasing expectations that private organisations should be guided by values beyond wealth maximisation.

[172] M Aronson, 'A Public Lawyer's Responses to Privatisation and Outsourcing' in M Taggart (ed), *The Province of Administrative Law* (Hart Publishing, 1997) 69.

Thus, when 'private' entities pay damages awards because they have committed wrongs in tort, anti-discrimination law, employment law etc, this may deplete funds that might otherwise be used to directly or indirectly benefit the wider community. Many non-governmental institutions are not specifically constituted to serve the public interest, in the way that public authorities must perform their statutory duties for the common good. However, this difference is of little practical significance when one considers that private entities do *in fact* produce significant public benefits. Just as authorities have no monopoly on power, nor do they have a monopoly on beneficent activity. Money is spent on the public good in all sorts of ways—through government payments to private firms which perform public services, through payments by private and public funds to voluntary organisations, through expenditure of private funds directly on the public good etc. Thus it is debatable whether human rights damages ought to be singled out for special treatment: if one favours a balancing approach where public interests could be compromised by damages awards, then one's argument should not be limited to public law. Indeed, we ought to note that the funding streams of some private entities that serve the common good, such as charities or NGOs, are far more precarious than government funding, while their budgets may be far smaller; in other words they have far less capacity to absorb damages awards.

We have focussed here on arguments concerning scarce funds, but similarly, other concerns which might justify interest-balancing, such as the possible chilling effects of damages liability, are not peculiar to public law. Private firms and individuals—such as doctors, for example—may also be deterred from beneficial activity because of liability fears.

Overall, because it is by no means clear that those concerns which underpin the interest-balancing approach are peculiar to human rights law, such concerns cannot in themselves justify singling out the approach to human rights damages. Furthermore, where authorities are held liable in tort, the law does not provide for an interest-balancing test, even though the very same public interests that may be undermined by human rights damages could be undermined by damages for tortious wrongs. The reason for this, of course, is that if one is serious about protecting individual rights then one must give effective redress where they are violated.

IV. IS THE INTEREST-BALANCING APPROACH NECESSARY?

We might accept that there are certain public interests which may potentially be compromised by human rights damages claims. However, is adoption of interest-balancing necessary to safeguard those interests? The substantive law of human rights, the ordinary law of damages (if it were applied in human rights law), and procedural rules already afford protection to a range of public interests, as well as defendant and third party interests, either through dedicated rules and principles, or through the law's operation. Non-legal factors, such as litigation costs and scarcity of legal aid, also militate against damages claims unduly prejudicing public interests.

The most important countervailing interests, including rights of others, public order, health and morals, and national security, are protected through defences in human rights law such as proportionality. It is only where an interference cannot be justified in the public interest that damages liability may arise. Countervailing interests may also be taken into account in delineating the scope of rights.[173] Further, interference with a right will not be unlawful if primary legislation required the relevant action.[174] On top of this, various doctrines or practices, such as the judicial practice of according an official's decision weight in assessing defences, will, through their operation, afford administrators leeway in their decision-making, and thus afford a layer of insulation from liability. In turn, such protection from liability may help to prevent negative consequences such as overly-cautious administration.

Positive duties in particular can impose significant burdens on authorities by requiring positive action, which generally entails expenditure of resources, while breach may expose authorities to widespread and significant liabilities where the authority is not the primary cause of the harm.[175] But such obligations are typically tempered by countervailing considerations. As the ECtHR has said, '[i]n both the negative *and positive contexts*, regard must be had to the fair balance which has to be struck between the competing interests of the individual and the community, including other concerned third parties'.[176] Thus, in framing the *Osman* duty the ECtHR took into account the difficulties of policing modern societies and allocating scarce police resources: 'such an obligation must be interpreted in a way which does not impose an impossible or disproportionate burden on the authorities',[177] while domestic courts observe that the threshold for the obligation to arise is 'high', and 'not readily satisfied'.[178] Similarly, in the context of a failure to provide state support the Court in *Anufrijeva* held that '[b]efore inaction can amount to a lack of respect for private and family life, there must be some ground for criticising the failure to act. There must be

[173] eg *Austin v Commissioner of the Metropolis* [2009] 1 AC 564.

[174] HRA, s 6(2); *R (Baiai) v SOSHD* [2006] EWHC 1035, [48] (HRA damages not recoverable as Minister acting pursuant to statute); *Tovey v MOJ* [2011] EWHC 271.

[175] See Harlow (n 124) 75ff; C Harlow, 'Damages and Human Rights' [2004] *New Zealand Law Review* 429, 444–45.

[176] *Glaser v UK* (2000) 33 EHRR 1, [63] (emphasis added); *Eweida v UK* (2013) 57 EHRR 8, [84]; *Smith v MOD* [2014] AC 52, [61].

[177] *Osman v UK* (2000) 29 EHRR 245, [116]; *Re Officer L* [2007] 1 WLR 2135, [21]; *Van Colle v UK* (2000) 56 EHRR 23 [88]; *Smith* ibid [76], [81].

[178] *Re Officer L* [20].

an element of culpability'.[179] Breach of domestic law requiring state support could provide the necessary element of culpability, 'provided that the impact on private or family life is sufficiently serious and was foreseeable'.[180] Also, the Court held that delays in administration of state support could violate Article 8, but imposed preconditions on liability:[181] '[t]he demands on resources would be significantly increased if states were to be faced with claims for breaches of article 8 simply on the ground of administrative delays'.[182]

Aspects of the common law of damages would guard against damages imposing undue burdens on public finances. Defendants are only liable for damage inherent in or caused by the violation; consequential losses that are not causally connected to the wrong are not recoverable. Further, the claimant must prove all pecuniary loss through provision of concrete evidence,[183] while damages for consequential non-pecuniary loss will only be awarded if loss can be inferred from the facts or there is evidence of loss. Difficulties in proving causation and loss should not be underestimated. The claimant must take reasonable steps to mitigate their loss, while it may be that deductions are made from damages for consequential loss for any advantages enjoyed by the claimant in consequence of the wrong.[184]

In terms of quantum courts 'have often stressed that awards should be kept at a moderate level',[185] so that awards do not constitute a windfall, or impose undue burdens on the defendant. As Sullivan J observed in a HRA damages case, moderation also ensures damages do 'not unduly deplet[e] the funds available to the defendant [public authority] for the benefit of others'.[186] Ensuring awards are not excessive may also reduce risks of defensive behaviour given administrators need not fear their actions will result in crippling liability for their employer. Where concurrent damages claims are made in tort and in human rights law double recovery would not be permitted.[187] If compensatory and gain-based damages are both available the claimant must choose: she cannot recover both.[188] Where alternative redress, such as specific relief, effectively vindicates the right, damages will be otiose.[189] A restrained approach is taken to exemplary damages.[190] Such

[179] *Anufrijeva* (n 1) [45]; *R (SG) v SOS for Work and Pensions* [2014] EWCA Civ 156, [94]–[98].
[180] *Anufrijeva* ibid.
[181] ibid [46]–[47].
[182] ibid.
[183] As discussed in ch 3.II.B.iii, this may be a difficult task.
[184] See A Burrows, *Remedies for Torts and Breach of Contract* 3rd edn (OUP, 2004) ch 7.
[185] ibid 342–43. A moderate approach is also taken to aggravated damages: *W v Meah* [1986] 1 All ER 935, 942.
[186] *R (Bernard) v Enfield LBC* [2003] LGR 423, [59].
[187] ch 3.III.
[188] ch 3.II.A.ii.
[189] ch 3.III.
[190] *Rookes* (n 121) 1227–28.

damages are reserved for the most outrageous violations where compensation is considered inadequate, and awards 'are rarely extravagant'.[191] Other restrictions apply; for example where a class of persons have been wronged by the same defendant, and not all of that class are before the court, exemplary awards may not be awarded, even if the conduct was outrageous.[192]

Procedural rules also operate to protect public interests. In particular such rules may aid preservation of public funds by protecting against excessive litigation costs and dissuading litigation more generally; this is significant because litigation costs were one factor that prompted Lord Woolf to limit recovery under the HRA.[193] Recall that human rights damages claims may be brought via ordinary procedure or judicial review.[194] Following the Woolf[195] and Jackson[196] reforms,

> [t]he bed-rock assumptions of the modern civil system of justice are: avoidance of litigation; encouragement of pre-trial settlement; or disposal of a case by summary judgment before trial; or abandonment of the case by claimants who realise that their claims are unsustainable.[197]

For better or worse,[198] these assumptions are embedded in the Civil Procedure Rules, which grant judges significant case-management powers to 'manag[e] and facilitat[e] trial avoidance'.[199] Thus, '[m]ost cases settle, or [are] terminated by summary procedures before trial, or the claims are abandoned',[200] while cases may never be set on the path of litigation: for example, costs sanctions provide strong incentives to mediate. This new procedural justice—in which a concern for 'money dominates'[201] and full trials are an endangered species[202]—means that much cost is saved through litigation avoidance.

We see similar trends in judicial review.[203] The Bowman[204] reforms introduced measures to facilitate early settlement, which added to pre-existing measures designed to weed out unmeritorious cases at an early stage, such

[191] *Kuddus* (n 122) [75].
[192] *R (Lumba) v SOSHD* [2012] 1 AC 245, [167].
[193] *Anufrijeva* (n 1) [79]–[81].
[194] Ch 4.2.II.C.
[195] H Woolf, *Access to Justice: Final Report* (Stationery Office, 1996).
[196] R Jackson, *Review of Civil Litigation Costs: Final Report* (Stationery Office, 2009).
[197] N Andrews, 'Money and Other Fundamentals: English Perspectives on Court Proceedings, Mediation, and Arbitration', University of Cambridge Legal Studies Research Paper No 38/2013, 6 (papers.ssrn.com/sol3/papers.cfm?abstract_id=2330317).
[198] N Andrews, 'Accessible, Affordable, and Accurate Civil Justice—Challenges Facing the English and Other Modern Systems', University of Cambridge Legal Studies Research Paper No 35/2013 (papers.ssrn.com/sol3/papers.cfm?abstract_id=2330309).
[199] ibid 15.
[200] Andrews (n 197) 33.
[201] ibid 1.
[202] See s 2.V.E below.
[203] See recently: Criminal Justice and Courts Act 2015, Pt 4.
[204] J Bowman, *Review of the Crown Office List* (Lord Chancellor's Department, 2000).

as the permission requirement. The result is that most review claims settle, settlement rates are increasing, and settlements have been occurring earlier and earlier.[205]

These trends in ordinary and review procedures towards trial avoidance and early settlement, in the context of claims against authorities, operate to protect public interests in preservation of public funds—money is saved through litigation avoidance—and effective administration, given administrative process is not disrupted by unmeritorious claims or long delays and lingering uncertainty as litigation plays out.

To all of this we may add other procedural features. The one year limitation period under the HRA is short compared to that for some torts, while where the claim is made via review the limitation period is very short indeed: three months.[206] These limitation periods provide strong protection against delay and administrative uncertainty, which can undermine good administration, but will also invariably exclude a number of otherwise meritorious damages claims, reducing the financial burden associated with liability. The HRA's narrow standing requirement means claims may only be made by those who have personally suffered a rights-violation.[207] This protects authorities against excessive litigation by strictly limiting the class of potential claimants.

Further militating against undue interference with frontline services or excessive litigation are factors exogenous to the legal system. Court fees are always rising.[208] Even before recent cuts to legal aid, it had been observed that legal aid was 'severely restricted' for public law,[209] one senior practitioner observing that since *Anufrijeva*, '[l]egal aid is ... routinely refused where HRA damages are sought'.[210] Funding litigation is only liable to become more difficult given recent reforms[211] which further restrict access to legal aid, and have significantly cut the legal aid budget. For a HRA damages claimant there are various hurdles to accessing legal aid. The alleged violation must be 'significant'; this test 'is intended to focus legal aid on the most serious cases'.[212] Thus, legal aid will only possibly be available in a limited class of case. There are further requirements, including that all other routes to remedy have been exhausted, that likely benefits of proceedings justify likely costs, that the case has a certain likelihood of success (which will be difficult to assess where outcome depends on

205 V Bondy and M Sunkin, *The Dynamics of Judicial Review Litigation* (PLP, 2009).
206 HRA, s 7(5).
207 HRA, s 7(1).
208 Civil Proceedings Fees (Amendment) Order SI 2014 No 874.
209 C Harlow and R Rawlings, *Law and Administration* 3rd edn (CUP, 2009) 715.
210 Clayton (n 26) 436.
211 Legal Aid, Sentencing and Punishment of Offenders Act 2012 [LASPO].
212 *Lord Chancellor's Guidance under Section 4 of the Legal Aid, Sentencing and Punishment of Offenders Act 2012* (June 2014) [11.1]; LASPO, Sch 1, Pt 1, para 22.

judicial balancing), and that the case is unsuitable for a conditional fee arrangement.[213] Outside these criteria there is provision for exceptional funding but applications for such funds almost always fail. There is also stringent means-testing. The percentage of the population with a means-tested entitlement to legal aid has declined drastically over time: in 2008 below a third of the population were so entitled, and that figure is now lower.[214] Thus, it may be exceptionally difficult to access legal aid to fund human rights damages claims.

It is not only those of modest means who face significant financial hurdles to vindicating their rights. For all outside the most well-off retaining legal services entails the risk of crippling expenditure. This operates as a very powerful disincentive to seeking redress. As Lord Neuberger observes, '[l]egal advice and legal proceedings are beyond the means of most people';[215] costs are *the* 'main barrier' to accessing legal services.[216] Various reforms have been implemented to reduce costs, however, as Lord Neuberger observes, they have largely failed.[217] Measures that exist to help mitigate costs such as protective costs orders and cost-capping are exceptional, while other measures such as qualified cost-shifting only apply to some classes of case.[218] Conditional fee arrangements or damages-based arrangements are 'fine where there is a reasonably sizeable claim or where there are lots of little claims. But they cannot do the business where the claim is small';[219] further, whatever one's own cost arrangements one still risks being lumped with the defendant's costs if one loses.

There are thus very significant pecuniary barriers to accessing legal services generally, let alone initiating Rolls-Royce litigation in the High Court. As a result many with arguable claims for human rights damages, will find it impossible to realise their claims, even on a tort-based approach. Such realities bring necessary perspective to bald assertions that awarding human rights damages would invite a flood of litigation that could cripple public services. The concern of recent costs reforms has been the inverse: to ensure those who are wronged have incentives to bring claims despite significant cost barriers. Thus, rather than recommending depressing levels of awards the Jackson report recommended a 10 per cent increase in general damages

[213] Civil Legal Aid (Merits Criteria) Regulations SI 2013 No 104, r 58.

[214] Neuberger (n 164) [38].

[215] Lord Neuberger, 'Judges and Policy: A Delicate Balance' (Speech at Institute of Government, 18 June 2013) [23].

[216] Andrews (n 198) 22.

[217] Lord Neuberger, 'Docketing: Completing Case Management's Unfinished Revolution' (Speech at Solicitors' Costs Conference, 9 February 2012) [3] (available at www.judiciary.gov.uk/wp-content/uploads/JCO/Documents/Speeches/mor-speech-solicitors-cost-conference-lecture-feb2012.pdf); *Coventry v Lawrence (No 2)* [2015] 1 AC 106, [32]ff.

[218] See generally Andrews (n 197) and (n 198).

[219] Neuberger (n 164) [55].

across tort to ensure victims are in a position to pay success fees, thereby facilitating access to justice.[220]

There are many other reasons individuals may not initiate damages claims, even where they have a good claim.[221] Some may not pursue claims given the time, stress and effort that is inseparable from legal process. Others may never realise they have suffered a violation. For others monetary redress may be unimportant, and they may bring a claim solely seeking a declaration, simply desiring 'closure' or official recognition that they have been wronged. Those with little experience of the legal system may be intimidated by the prospect of dealing with lawyers and initiating formal proceedings. Others may simply lack faith in the legal system's capacity to deliver 'justice'. Others still may choose to pursue other routes to redress, such as the ombudsman, statutory compensation schemes, mediation or departmental complaints procedures.[222] In this respect it is worth noting that authorities are increasingly encouraged to deal with complaints in-house, early-on and promptly.[223]

In light of this wider perspective, one may query whether the interest-balancing approach is necessary to ensure public and other interests are afforded due protection. An array of public, third party and defendant interests are given weight in the substance of human rights law, the common law of damages, and procedural law. Such interests are also preserved through *operation* of law and procedure. Non-legal phenomena, such as costs and restrictions on legal aid, serve as significant barriers to bringing claims. If one takes account of all possible hurdles, legal and non-legal, that a human rights damages claimant must overcome, to add the further hurdle of an interest-balancing approach at the remedies stage would begin to strike the overall balance away from protection of fundamental interests, which is the very aim of human rights law, and in favour of other interests, public and governmental.

V. PUBLIC INTEREST FACTORS: A CRITICAL ANALYSIS

This section analyses in detail those public interest factors that English courts have relied on to deny or reduce human rights damages, as well as other factors that courts are likely to consider under an interest-balancing

[220] Jackson (n 196) 463 (Recommendation 10); *Simmons v Castle* [2012] EWCA Civ 1039. Note that this uplift does not apply to HRA damages.

[221] See H Genn, *Paths to Justice* (Hart Publishing, 1999).

[222] See Administrative Redress Consultation Paper (n 155) Pt 3; R Moules, *Actions Against Public Officials* (Sweet and Maxwell, 2009) Pt IV; Harlow and Rawlings (n 209) ch 10; V Bondy and A Le Sueur, *Designing Redress* (PLP, 2012).

[223] Treasury (n 147) Annex 4.14; Parliamentary and Health Service Ombudsman, *Principles of Good Complaint Handling* (2009).

approach. It is important that we consider these factors in depth, because they are too often, in both judgments and commentary, either dismissed or invoked without detailed consideration.

These factors may reflect understandable concerns or anxieties associated with liability. However, that concerns may be understandable is insufficient to justify courts relying on them to deny or reduce awards. Such factors must be appropriate for judicial consideration and, if appropriate, courts must be satisfied that concerns are well-founded before denying awards based on them.

It is questionable whether certain factors are appropriate for judicial consideration *at all*. For example, there are significant constitutional and practical issues raised by judges taking into account the impact of awards on the public purse. It is doubtful whether courts are institutionally equipped to reliably predict whether imposition of liability will precipitate defensive administration. There are serious rule-of-law concerns with courts determining damages claims according to expectations of public or media reaction.

If it is legitimate—which is questionable—for courts to rely on such factors to justify the serious step of denying redress for violation of fundamental rights then a rigorous approach must be taken to evaluating these factors. Principally, courts must be sure that public interest concerns are well-founded. For example, a court should not accept at face value a defendant's assertion that an award would undermine its ability to perform primary functions, but rather seek to establish whether this would *in fact* be the likely effect, possibly requiring evidence in support of the defendant's submission. Similarly, if a court is to deny awards on the basis that imposing liability would undermine vigorous administration, it should not do so according to intuition but assess whether such consequence is *in fact* likely to result by reference to available evidence. The detailed examination of public interest concerns in the sections that follow shows some to be unfounded, and others questionable.

The section's general conclusion is that wider policy concerns raised by human rights damages are best left to the political branches. These branches possess the constitutional legitimacy to make difficult political, economic and moral value-judgements, such as whether too much public money is being spent on redressing wrongs, and are institutionally well-placed to gauge whether concerns are well-founded, and to formulate appropriate responses, if necessary. In this respect, the last subsection considers whether it is realistic to expect the political branches to respond to public interest concerns raised by human rights damages. Consideration of a series of case studies demonstrates that this expectation is realistic. Thus, judges ought to concentrate on developing a rational and coherent law of human rights damages according to legal principle and orthodox techniques of legal reasoning, and leave politics and public policy calculations to the political branches.

A. Depletion of Resources Available to Benefit the Wider Community

In *Anufrijeva* the Court held that damages may be denied or reduced to preserve public resources. The Court was specifically concerned that compensating individual losses may deplete resources available to authorities to perform their primary tasks, which benefit the wider community.[224]

It is perhaps unsurprising that the Court fixated on this factor. In certain tort contexts commentators observe, '[t]he question of resources is ... emerging as an issue of particular difficulty and unease for the judiciary, especially when the liability of the state is in issue',[225] and that 'current trends, it could be said, sacrifice justice so completely to the altar of financial good management'.[226]

However, it is important to recognise that the foregoing observations generally refer to the English courts' approach to public authority liability *in negligence*. Significantly, in negligence concerns over diversion of funds away from frontline services go to the duty-of-care question and therefore whether primary legal obligations exist in the first place, rather than to remedial questions.[227] There is a fair argument that it is legitimate for courts to consider wider community concerns, *if they are competent to do so*, in deciding whether to recognise primary legal duties, given deciding whether to institutionalise a primary duty is quintessentially a distributive decision. Further, negligence's function as a social mechanism for allocation of responsibility for loss naturally implicates wider concerns.[228] Also, in negligence the question of whether an authority owes duties for the benefit of individuals generally arises in the context of statutes passed specifically to promote public purposes, such as maintenance of highways or provision of education, and within which Parliament has not expressly provided for individuated duties sounding in liability. This makes judicial recognition of individuated duties at common law rather contentious, and implicates an inquiry into the compatibility of imposing liability with fulfilment of statutory public goals; if there is any conflict public goals must prevail.

[224] (n 1) [56], [75]; *Wilkinson* (n 84) [48]ff; H Woolf, 'The Human Rights Act 1998 and Remedies' in M Andenas and D Fairgrieve (eds), *Judicial Review in International Perspective* (Kluwer, 2000) 433.

[225] Harlow (n 124) 11.

[226] B Markesinis et al, *Tortious Liability of Statutory Bodies* (Hart Publishing, 1999) 45, 92.

[227] eg *Hill v Chief Constable of West Yorkshire* [1989] AC 53, 63; *Van Colle v Chief Constable Hertfordshire Police* [2009] 1 AC 225, [133]; *X* (n 91) 750–51; *Mitchell v Glasgow CC* [2009] 1 AC 874, [28]. Note, however, that when it comes to financial considerations courts have focused more on costs that may be incurred by authorities in defending negligence claims, rather than depletion of public resources caused by damages awards. But see: *Stovin* (n 109) 933E, 934E, 939B, 952E, 955B, 958B–C; *Michael v Chief Constable of South Wales* [2015] 2 WLR 343, [122].

[228] See chs 2.II.B, 3.I.D.

All of this is important as it would be all too easy to argue that because concerns with public funding are given weight in public authority negligence cases, it is legitimate for such concerns to enter judicial analysis of human rights damages claims against authorities. This would be sloppy reasoning. Negligence is fundamentally different in nature to vindicatory actions, while Parliament has expressly enacted the rights under the HRA and a damages action. In negligence policy concerns go to the open-ended distributive question of whether a legal duty should be recognised in the first place, whereas in human rights law we are concerned with a different situation in which an already recognised primary legal entitlement has been denied. Negligence sets no precedent for taking policy concerns into account in the latter context; where the tort is proven full damages follow. In any case there has been strong criticism of the judicial approach to novel duty cases. Some observe, with justification, that judicial reliance on policy concerns not generally disciplined by empirical evidence means the duty analysis collapses into 'an open-ended and unsubstantiated debate over value judgments',[229] which in turn has plunged the field into incoherence. Further, it is increasingly, though not consistently, being recognised that the starting point in duty analysis is that the public policy which has the first claim upon the law's loyalty is that wrongs should be remedied, with weighty countervailing concerns being required before courts countenance departure from that starting point.[230] There is also some evidence, in the negligence context, of courts growing to accept their limited capacity to competently evaluate policy considerations.[231] These developments contrast with the approach in *Anufrijeva* which weighted the balancing calculus overwhelmingly in favour of protection of the public interest and placed policy-type considerations at the forefront of the analysis.

As a matter of law, it is a well-established principle of English law that the same loss should not lead to different damages according to the relative means of defendants,[232] while we saw above that the ECtHR has disapproved of domestic courts justifying less than effective redress on the basis of protection of public funds.[233] The principle that levels of damages for non-pecuniary loss should command public respect is recognised at common law as mandating moderate or reasonable awards: it is important that

[229] Markesinis et al (n 226) 3.

[230] But note that this proposition suffers from a problem of circularity in negligence, as the very question being addressed in the duty calculus is whether a primary duty exists (there can be no legal wrong if there is no legal duty). See, eg, *X* (n 91) 663, 749; *Jones* (n 92) [113]; *Crawford Adjusters v Sagicor General Insurance (Cayman) Ltd* [2014] AC 366, [73].

[231] eg *Michael* (n 227) [121], [182]–[186]; *Van Colle* (n 227) [48]ff, [73]; *Sagicor* ibid [72]–[73]; *Zurich Insurance PLC UK Branch v International Energy Group Ltd* [2015] UKSC 33 per Lords Neuberger and Reed.

[232] *Wells v Wells* [1999] 1 AC 345, 373.

[233] Text to n 55 above.

awards are not so large as to constitute a windfall, and not meagre so as to trivialise protected interests.[234] In some cases the scarce resources of authorities, among other factors, have been cited in support of this principle.[235] However, the rule that full compensatory damages are available as of right has never been varied because a defendant is publically funded. A recent example is the Supreme Court decision finding Birmingham City Council liable for wage-discrimination, which resulted in the Council facing compensation pay-outs totalling at least £757 million; it made no difference that awards would be paid from public funds, notwithstanding the huge sums involved.[236] As the High Court of Australia has said,

> the course of development over the last two and a half centuries of the law respecting Crown liability in tort does not support attention to the financial means of the miscreant public officers as a significant and limiting determinant of the quantum of liability.[237]

And this is notwithstanding that it is typically the Crown that defends such cases and pays awards.[238] Even in respect of exemplary damages, for which it is permissible to take into account the defendant's (whether public or private) means, given awards are punitive, the courts have generally not reduced awards where the defendant is an authority,[239] and maintained: 'the proceeds of taxation represent the price paid for maintaining respect by public officials for the observance of the rule of law, to the benefit of taxpayers and society as a whole'.[240]

On a normative level, some may argue that a *sui generis*, restrictive approach should be taken to human rights damages because awards entail the courts *redistributing* public resources to private individuals. One finds something close to this in the Law Commission's argument that authorities ought to be subject to different liability rules than others, influenced by a prominent American article: an award to the claimant is viewed as a private 'gain', and simultaneously entails 'loss' to general welfare.[241] Analysed in this way damages awards have an air of illegitimacy in that the general public has been made to suffer for one person's gain, while this analysis may also implicate that judges are illegitimately being drawn into redistributive decisions.

[234] eg *John v MGN Ltd* [1997] QB 586, 611; *Prison Service v Johnson* [1997] ICR 275, 283; *Kemeh v MOD* [2014] ICR 625, [52]–[59].

[235] *Heil v Rankin* [2001] QB 272, [11], [32]–[38], [95]; *Thompson v Commissioner for the Metropolis* [1998] QB 498, 513, 517. In the human rights context see: *Bernard* (n 186) [58]–[59].

[236] *Abdulla v Birmingham* CC [2013] 1 All ER 649; 'Birmingham City Council Liable for £757m Equal Pay Claims' www.bbc.com/news/uk-england-birmingham-20294633.

[237] *NSW v Ibbett* [2006] HCA 57, [55]; *Sharp* (n 109) 266.

[238] *Ibbett* ibid [41].

[239] *Muuse v SOSHD* [2010] EWCA Civ 453, [84]; *Thompson* (n 235) 517.

[240] *Ibbett* (n 237) [48]; *cf R(WL (Congo)) v SOSHD* [2010] 1 WLR 2168, [122].

[241] Administrative Redress Consultation Paper (n 155) [A21]–[A22]; Levinson (n 154) 412.

Clearly damages awards against authorities can[242] involve transfers of money from the public purse to individuals. But viewing these as mere transfers, and assessing their validity as such, ignores a fundamental point—such payments are made in satisfaction of legal wrongs; they are not mere allocations away from the common good for private gain. The claimant has a legal right that the defendant act a certain way, so that his basic interests are protected. In the case of breach, there is a failure by the authority to do what was lawfully required, and damages restore the claimant to a position equivalent to that which he is entitled to have been in. Thus, damages confirm, give effect to and restore (albeit in a second-best way) a *pre-existing* distribution of entitlements, consistent with the aims of public welfare as sanctioned by the legislature in the terms of the rights-charter. An award does not constitute a 'gain' for the claimant. Rather, it restores 'parity', returning the claimant to the position he was legally entitled to be in, and requiring the authority to offer a second-best form of performance in lieu of its failure to fulfil its primary obligations.

Given this perspective it is the interest-balancing approach which in fact entails dubious redistributions. Denying an award for wrongdoing entails granting 'an undeserved windfall' to 'an unworthy beneficiary',[243] given the authority will have escaped their primary legal obligations (as well as any remedial obligation), and a loss for the claimant, given they are denied their lawful entitlement, that entitlement is not restored, and they are left to bear the consequential negative effects the defendant's wrong has imposed. Whereas provision of damages for wrongs gives effect to and is consonant with the distribution of primary entitlements made by Parliament in the Act, an interest-balancing approach will frequently cut across and distort those primary distributive choices by not requiring authorities that wrongfully deny legal entitlements to restore those entitlements and thus make good Parliament's original distribution. As Hogg says, albeit in a different context, '[a] compensation regime should not work at cross-purposes to the redistributive choices that are made by democratic legislative bodies'.[244] Not only this, but these remedial choices, which cut across Parliament's allocations, are to be based in judges' opinions, unmediated by any particular legal principle, as to how public monies are best distributed.

Notwithstanding the foregoing preliminary points, it is understandable that there may nonetheless be anxiety over the pecuniary burden that damages may impose. However, is it appropriate for courts to take fiscal impact into account? And, if so, how should courts go about analysing fiscal impact? The remainder of this subsection argues that if courts are to consider this factor they should take an evidence-based approach; there are constitutional

242 See s 2.V.A.i below.
243 *Hounga v Allen* [2014] 1 WLR 2889, [56].
244 (n 111) 11.

and practical concerns with courts weighing competing demands on public resources, which counsel against courts considering this factor at all; and, notwithstanding the position in private law, despite interest-balancing being billed as a distinctive public law approach, there is no or little precedent in public law for courts considering financial implications of relief.

i. The Importance of a Robust, Evidence-Based Approach

In *Anufrijeva* the Court did not consider whether awards would *in fact* deplete resources earmarked for funding frontline services, the degree to which damages would impact those funds, or whether any depletion would *in fact* undermine the authority's ability to perform. In proposing that awards be depressed in the case before it, the Court relied on the simplistic proposition that payment of substantial damages would deplete resources available to fund services.[245] Unfortunately such superficial approach is not confined to human rights damages. As Sunkin and Richardson record in the judicial review context, 'many judges remain undeterred by the absence of reliable data from making assumptions about the effects of their intervention'.[246] In the different context of public authority negligence Markesinis et al similarly record that lawyers and judges' consideration of consequential economic effects is 'essentially intuitive',[247] depending on 'unproved and, perhaps, unprovable policy propositions',[248] and that 'policy arguments' cannot be sustained 'on the strength of hunches rather than verifiable evidence'.[249]

The problem with judges basing assessments of consequential effects on intuition is that they may be wrong, so victims are denied redress on the basis of unfounded concerns. By not inquiring into empirical reality courts also encourage defendants to strategically assert hardship; as Lord Reid recognised some time ago, '[m]en can exaggerate the extent of their interests and so can the Crown'.[250] Further, if courts do not discipline decision-making by critically analysing claims of financial hardship and/or requiring evidence before denying awards on this basis, the factor could be invoked indiscriminately, with the weight given to this factor influenced more by unstated judicial value-judgements than hard facts.

Thus, if a court is to rely on fiscal impact to deny or reduce awards it ought to take a rigorous and evidence-based approach. We need to know, for example, which funds damages will be paid from, which will in turn help to identify the possible impact, if any, damages may have on service provision.

245 *Anufrijeva* (n 1) [75].
246 M Sunkin and G Richardson, 'Judicial Review: Questions of Impact' [1996] *PL* 79, 82.
247 Markesinis et al (n 226) 1–3; Sunkin and Richardson, ibid 83.
248 Markesinis et al ibid 45.
249 ibid 40.
250 *Chandler v DPP* [1964] AC 763, 811.

Contrary to common judicial assumption, it is relatively unusual for awards to be paid from funds earmarked for frontline services. Awards are much more likely to be covered by insurance, or paid out of legal, 'unplanned items', contingency or reserve funds which are separate from day-to-day operating budgets, so funds allocated to frontline services are insulated. There are other possibilities too, generally reserved for extreme cases: awards may be covered or partially covered by appropriations from central government, by raising of tax revenues or through borrowing.[251] Put simply, it is wholly unlikely that there will be a simple, 1:1 correlation between money spent on damages and depletion of funds reserved for services.

As Halliday et al conclude in their empirical study of public management of liability risks in the UK and Ireland, the issue of how liability impacts on authority finances is complex and 'we should be wary of an easy calculus':[252] there is 'no direct relationship between liability costs and service budgets'.[253] This study found little evidence of typical concerns judges associate with liability including that public services will be undermined by damages liability, or that insurers will bully authorities into cutting back services to mitigate liability risks. The study also shows that the common assumption that an increase in an authority's liability costs will lead to increased insurance premiums (which could in turn impact public funds) is simplistic. While insurers consider an authority's claims-history in setting premiums, (i) insurance contracts are 'fairly comprehensive and liability is a relatively small area of coverage within the policy', such that liability costs 'could easily be marginal for the price of future premiums';[254] and (ii) the factor which most influences premiums is the stock market, such that power to affect premiums largely lies beyond the authority's control.[255] We may add that public authority insurance contracts are valuable for insurers and often up for renewal, so that authorities hold significant bargaining power in negotiating premiums.

Even if damages were paid from funds earmarked for service provision, in order to gauge the likely impact of an award, the court would need certain information, such as the size of the annual operating budget from which damages are paid, and need to establish, in the light of evidence, how seriously (or not) the putative award would impact authority performance.

[251] For such an example see: 'Birmingham City Council £200m Short to Pay Equal Pay Bill' www.bbc.com/news/uk-england-birmingham-21242834.

[252] S Halliday et al, 'The Public Management of Liability Risks' (2011) 31 *Oxford Journal of Legal Studies* 527, 548 [Halliday et al 2011]; see also D Cohen, 'Responding to Government Failure' (1995) 6 *National Journal of Constitutional Law* 23, 28–29.

[253] Halliday et al, ibid.

[254] ibid.

[255] ibid; R Lewis and A Morris, 'Tort Law Culture: Image and Reality' (2012) 39 *Journal of Law and Society* 562, 585, recording that observed increases in liability insurance premiums in certain sectors are due to non-tort factors.

It is important to observe that these complexities suggest that judges should be open to the possibility that it may often be impossible to determine with any confidence what impact awards will have. In such instances the only course is to treat fiscal impact as neutral.

An approach resembling that propounded here has, at times, been taken to analogous questions in other contexts, while one would expect an evidence-based approach to factual questions within legal proceedings. In tort the House of Lords—albeit higher courts have been far from consistent—has held that if an authority argues it should not be exposed to liability on the basis that this would so interfere with performance of its duties, it is for the authority to establish that this will in fact be the consequence of liability and the courts will not presume such effects (some judges conjecturing that such argument would only be established exceptionally).[256] Similarly, across other contexts, including reasonableness review,[257] legitimate expectations[258] and substantive human rights law,[259] where defendants seek to rely on consequentialist claims to justify their acts courts may require evidence in support of those claims and reject arguments if no evidence is supplied. The ECtHR has similarly taken a robust approach; for example where defendants argue that the Court ought not to find a violation as this would cause the state severe financial hardship, the Court has rigorously scrutinised evidence in support of such claims.[260] Where exemplary damages are claimed, in which context it is permissible to consider the defendant's means, courts will not assume damages would cause a defendant authority hardship but consider, for example, the size of the award relative to the authority's budget.[261] Whereas in certain contexts juries are to be informed if exemplary awards will be paid from public funds, they are not given this instruction if awards would be met by insurance.[262]

Some English judges have expressed scepticism as to whether it is realistic and practically feasible to require authorities to produce evidence of likely impacts on frontline services.[263] If this is accepted (see further below in this section), then one must also accept that courts cannot know, with any confidence, the likely impact of awards on service provision, and fiscal impact ought to be treated as neutral.

256 *Phelps v Hillingdon LBC* [2001] 2 AC 619, 653; *Spring v Guardian Assurance Plc* [1995] 2 AC 296, 326. And see those references in n 231 above.

257 *R (Litvinenko) v SOSHD* [2014] EWHC 194, particularly [68]–[72].

258 *Paponette v Attorney General of Trinidad and Tobago* [2012] 1 AC 1, [38], [41]–[43].

259 *Smith and Grady v UK* (2000) 29 EHRR 493, [99]-[100]; *R (Quila) v SOSHD* [2012] 1 AC 621, [44]–[59], [74]–[77]. Specifically in respect of public funds see: *MOH v Atkinson* [2012] 3 NZLR 456, [170]–[171].

260 *Jeličić v Bosnia and Herzegovina* (2008) 47 EHRR 13, [41]–[46].

261 *Muuse* (n 239) [84].

262 *Thompson* (n 235) 517.

263 eg *R v Cambridge HA, ex p B* [1995] 1 WLR 898, 906 (contrast the High Court decision: (1995) 25 BMLR 5).

Lastly, while judges may naturally be anxious about fiscal impact, it is important to maintain perspective. While we do not know the overall amount of compensation paid by the UK Government per annum because of incomplete information (see below in this section), figures from other jurisdictions suggest that arguments against liability based on fiscal impact can be overstated, and at worst blown out of all proportion. For example Cohen records that in the 1990 fiscal year the total paid in compensation by the Canadian Federal Government was $16 million, while the total Government Budget was $132 billion. Thus 0.012 per cent of total Government budget went to damages.[264] Cohen records that this figure may be an underestimate. But even if doubled, tripled or quadrupled the figure pales in comparison to overall expenditure, and it is unlikely that reduction of total budget by such relatively small amount could seriously compromise government's ability to fulfil its primary functions. Similar percentages are recorded in other jurisdictions, such as Germany, where a thorough empirical study found that the financial burden imposed by state liability across all types of claim amounted to 0.015 per cent of total budget.[265] These figures are a little out of date, and there are contextual differences between jurisdictions. However, the statistics offer a sense of perspective, which is sometimes missing in debates over public liability.

ii. Constitutional, Institutional and Practical Concerns

Thus, if courts consider fiscal impact, they ought to take a rigorous approach. However, there are strong arguments that courts should not consider this factor at all.

In *Anufrijeva* the Court offered no criteria against which to decide whether the interest in safeguarding public funds should trump that in vindicating rights. Formulation of criteria is fraught with difficulties. For example, what degree of fiscal impact or detriment to public services ought courts to tolerate before denying relief? Is it acceptable to trade one unit of health funding to compensate a patient unlawfully denied treatment in breach of human rights? Is it acceptable to award damages to the estate of a victim unlawfully killed by police if this would deplete the Metropolitan Police budget such that there are two less police officers on the beat in London at any given time? If fiscal impact is taken seriously then these are the sort of questions that must be confronted. However, the problems are manifest: these are inherently subjective questions which raise complex issues of politics, morality and economics. As the courts acknowledge in judicial review

[264] Cohen (n 252) 29.

[265] Markesinis et al (n 226) 61–62 citing *Zur Reform des Staatshaftungsrechts* (1976) 5, 71. See also: B Markesinis and J Fedtke, 'Damages for the Negligence of Statutory Bodies: the Empirical and Comparative Dimension to an Unending Debate' [2007] *PL* 299.

challenges to executive decisions allocating scarce public resources, such decisions 'could not be measured by any yardstick available to the court';[266] the courts do not possess 'objective criteria' against which to assess competing financial claims.[267]

Ultimately, the courts lack the constitutional legitimacy to decide between competing demands on public finances. This is quintessentially a function of the political branches as it concerns, in the words of the higher judiciary, 'matters of political judgment';[268] as Harlow says, '[l]egislators remain the legitimate arbiters between collective and individual interests where resources are at issue'.[269] As the courts repeatedly maintain in other contexts: if there are concerns as to how public money should be spent 'persuasion should be offered not to the judges, who are not qualified to listen, but to the department, the Minister, all members of parliament and ultimately to the electorate';[270] 'discretionary choice[s] about resources' are 'pre-eminently a matter for the Government rather than the Courts';[271] 'the allocation of resources is not a matter for the Court';[272] '[t]he court has never engaged in determining how a finite pot is to be distributed between competing demands'.[273] Specifically in respect of damages it has been said that, 'it is not part of the judicial function to depress the level of awards on policy grounds. The Courts have no mandate to entertain any such policy'.[274] Of course judicial decisions often have implications for public expenditure. However, these decisions are not made by explicitly weighing competing financial demands but through dispassionate application of legal rules.[275]

There are further, practical impediments to courts considering fiscal impact. It is highly unlikely that damages awarded in one case would seriously compromise an authority's ability to function. The real issue is whether establishment of damages liability in one case will lead to further similar awards, which could start to add up. However, it would be difficult for a court to reliably predict ex ante whether imposition of liability in one

[266] *R (Javed) v SOSHD* [2002] QB 129, 152.

[267] *R v SOS for the Environment, ex p Hammersmith and Fulham LBC* [1991] 1 AC 521, 593; *R (Howard League for Penal Reform) v Lord Chancellor* [2014] EWHC 709, [49]–[52]; *R(SG) v SOS for Work and Pensions* [2013] EWHC 3350, [100]; (n 179) [44]; *R (Patel) v Lord Chancellor* [2010] EWHC 2220, [38]–[39]; *R (L) v West London Mental Health NHS Trust* [2014] EWCA Civ 47, [79]; *R (Rotherham MBC) v SOS for Business, Innovation and Skills* [2015] UKSC 6; *R v Chief Constable of Sussex, ex p ITF Ltd* [1999] 2 AC 418, 430.

[268] *R v SOS for the Environment, ex p Nottinghamshire CC* [1986] AC 240, 247; *Howard League* ibid [52].

[269] Harlow (n 124) 122.

[270] *Nottinghamshire* (n 268) 267.

[271] *R (Walker) v SOSJ* [2008] 1 WLR 1977, [67]; *Rotherham* (n 267) [22]–[23].

[272] *Fletcher v Governor of HMP Whatton* [2014] EWHC 3586, [67].

[273] *R (London Borough of Islington) v Mayor of London* [2013] EWHC 4142, [399].

[274] *Barrell Insurance Pty Ltd v Pennant Hills Restaurants Pty Ltd* (1981) 34 ALR 162, 185.

[275] W Bishop, 'The Rational Strength of the Private Law Model' (1990) 40 *University of Toronto Law Journal* 633, 665.

case will lead to similar follow-up litigation, and, importantly, what the aggregate financial consequences are likely to be.

The difficulty in trying to assess the aggregate financial burden that may flow from liability is demonstrated by the Law Commission's study on administrative redress. The Commission was unable to quantify the likely financial impact of its proposals for reform of public authority liability, as it was unable to collate a dataset on current liabilities.[276] This was despite much consultation with HM Treasury and establishment of a Government Contact Group to investigate the matter. One significant impediment was that public bodies, in their financial reporting, do not generally disaggregate money spent on compensation from other allocations.[277] Given the Commission was unable to predict the financial ramifications of its proposals, it seems improbable that a court would fare better in predicting financial impacts on a case-by-case basis. This explains why courts have, when presented with differing financial predictions on review, stressed that 'prediction' is an area 'into which the courts cannot venture'.[278]

Overall, it is not the courts' constitutional role to determine how public money is best spent, while there are real difficulties in trying to predict flow-on effects of imposing liability in particular cases. Further, by concerning itself with public expenditure the judiciary 'relieves the government of the need to make important decisions about how public money should be allocated as between making amends for past failings and improving matters for the future'.[279] The courts should focus on questions that fall within their constitutional competence and which they are capable of resolving rigorously. Thus, if 'it seems consistent with sound *legal* principles to expand the public law of damages, the courts should do so and leave it to the executive and the legislature to react if they think that public law damages liability has become too extensive'.[280] Authorities and central government are far better placed to monitor the financial impact of specific awards ex post and overall damages liability, over time, and have the constitutional legitimacy to decide between competing demands on resources.

iii. Financial Impact in Other Parts of Public Law

While the interest-balancing approach is premised on the view that public law requires a different remedial approach to private law, it is difficult to identify precedent *in public law* for conditioning remedies upon a financial

[276] Administrative Redress Report (n 109) [1.5], [1.37], [4.32]ff, [6.14]–[6.16]; Administrative Redress Consultation Paper (n 155) Pt 6.

[277] Administrative Redress Report [4.47], and [6.14]–[6.16].

[278] *Howard League* (n 267) [52].

[279] P Cane, 'Damages in Public Law' (1999) 9 *Otago Law Review* 489, 515.

[280] ibid 515–16 (emphasis added); Bishop (n 275) 665; Administrative Redress Consultation Paper (n 155) [6.17].

calculus. We have already seen that the ECtHR has held domestic courts should not take financial impact into account in determining damages.[281] Importantly, it is also the case that traditional remedies on judicial review are granted routinely regardless of financial implications, while the Ombudsman too does not take account of fiscal impact in recommending awards.

Traditional review remedies are non-monetary. But, while 'a non-monetary remedy will not expressly require the expenditure of financial resources' this 'may only mean that its resources implications are hidden at the time the remedy is awarded'.[282] Quashing orders are the standard review remedy. The administrative task of retaking a decision following quashing of the original decision is far from costless; administrators must invest time and resources in retaking the decision, while the authority will likely seek legal advice. There may also be 'knock-on'[283] costs, such as the cost of new measures to guard against unlawful conduct in future, including retraining staff, redrafting internal guidelines, design and implementation of more sophisticated decision-procedures which make provision for legal review of draft decisions etc. Where a court quashes a governmental decision to close a care home in order to enforce a person's substantive legitimate expectation that they can remain in the home, notwithstanding that the government's own analysis concludes that this is not financially viable, the resulting financial burden may be sizeable and ongoing.[284] Where courts find that an authority's public consultation was carried out in breach of common law procedural fairness, the cost of a fresh consultation could run into tens of millions of pounds. Even a simple declaration may have massive ramifications. In *Osborn* the Supreme Court declared the Parole Board's failure to hold an oral hearing breached its common law duty of procedural fairness and Article 5(4).[285] As a result the Parole Board estimates that it will need to hold three times as many hearings, at an added cost of £10 million per annum for the Board (this excludes associated costs including legal representation and attendance of prison and probation staff).[286]

That remedies which can have substantial resource implications have been 'freely available'[287] in common law review—a field not concerned principally with protection of fundamental rights but rather preservation of the public interest—makes it difficult to justify a remedial approach in human rights law which affords even greater priority to the public interest in preservation of funds. In administrative law, courts have refused relief on the

[281] Above n 55.
[282] Cane (n 279) 496.
[283] ibid.
[284] See *R v North and East Devon HA, ex p Coughlan* [2001] QB 213.
[285] *Osborn v Parole Board* [2014] AC 1115.
[286] 'Parole Hearings "to Treble" After "Fairness" Ruling' at www.bbc.com/news/uk-28272742.
[287] Cane (n 279) 496.

basis of possible negative administrative impacts. However, relief has very rarely been denied on the basis of financial impact. The principal bases for refusal directed to protection of administration are that relief would cause 'administrative chaos', for example if quashing a policy would compromise many decisions made pursuant to that policy; prejudice third parties who had relied on the impugned decision; or entail a pointless rerunning of the decision process;[288] while courts have dismissed arguments for refusal of relief based on financial impact as 'without force'.[289] Thus, the principal concerns are finality, certainty and guarding against unnecessary disruption to administration, rather than financial considerations. Of course damages do not give rise to these types of concerns, or do so less obviously, because damages do not entail invalidation of decisions. More generally courts have at times required evidence to prove consequentialist arguments for denial of relief,[290] while the higher courts increasingly reiterate that the ordinary course will be to grant relief.[291] So even within a field in which the public good dominates, we do not find the marked emphasis on public interest concerns that characterises *Anufrijeva*.

The Parliamentary Ombudsman often recommends that government pay compensation to individuals who have suffered loss as a result of maladministration. The Ombudsman only has recommendatory power. However, its recommendations are generally implemented;[292] '[i]n practice ... it may be just as difficult for a government to reject a recommendation of an ombudsman that damages be paid as to ignore a judicial award'.[293] In some cases governmental implementation of Ombudsman reports has entailed payment of very significant sums, in circumstances where government was not the primary cause of losses.[294] It is significant that such practice has developed outside cases of legal rights, 'maladministration' covering a wide array of non-legal wrongs;[295] complaints often pertain to matters as prosaic as poor service or use of confusing official language.[296] Of significance, the Ombudsman's *Principles for Remedy*—which echo the Treasury's guidelines

[288] eg *R v Monopolies and Mergers Commission, ex p Argyll* [1986] 1 WLR 763, 774–75; *R v Dairy Produce Quota Tribunal for England and Wales, ex p Caswell* [1989] 1 WLR 1089; *R (Hurley) v SOS for Business Innovation and Skills* [2012] HRLR 13, [99]; *Walton* (n 84) [103], [130]–[131]; *R (Core Issues Trust) v Transport for London* [2014] PTSR 785, [42].

[289] *R v IRC, ex p MFK Underwriting Agents Ltd* [1990] 1 WLR 1545, 1575.

[290] eg *R v SOSHD, ex p Oyeleye* [1994] Imm AR 268, 274; *R (Holder) v Gedling BC* [2014] EWCA Civ 599, [31].

[291] See text to n 552. Note that there may be a gap between statements of principle and practice in this respect.

[292] *The Ombudsman in Question*, HC 1081 (2006) Appendix.

[293] Cane (n 279) 515.

[294] See n 128 above.

[295] The Ombudsman only has jurisdiction where no legal remedy is available: Parliamentary Commissioner Act 1967, s 5(2).

[296] *Bad Language: the Use and Abuse of Official Language*, HC 17 (2009) [37]–[39].

on managing public money—provide that 'finite resources should not be used as an excuse for failing to provide a fair remedy', and that the governing principle is *restitutio in integrum*.[297] That significant monetary redress is often recovered for interference with interests that are not even legally protected would suggest that judges should not be so circumspect in awarding damages for violations of fundamental legal rights.

B. Moral Status of the Victim

The balancing approach endorsed in *Anufrijeva*, coupled with the mirror approach, has laid the foundation for English courts to follow the Strasbourg Court's[298] widely criticised practice under Article 41 of considering the victim's moral status or character in deciding whether to make awards and quantum. In particular, domestic courts have adopted this practice in claims by prisoners against the Parole Board for failure to provide a speedy hearing as required by Article 5(4). Courts have denied damages partly because the victim was serving a sentence for past criminal offending.[299] For example, in *Downing* the Judge said:

> I am entirely satisfied that is a factor which must be taken into account as part of the wide discretion which I have, in particular in the light of the quotations from [*Anufrijeva*] above emphasising the role of the public interest in the exercise of my discretion.[300]

As we saw in chapter 5, in other HRA damages claims brought by prisoners courts have not mentioned moral character, or raised the factor but questioned its relevance.[301] This illustrates the first problem with considering moral worthiness. It is inherently subjective and virtually certain to be invoked and applied inconsistently.

At common law the 'illegality defence' may deny individuals ordinary rights and remedies in certain circumstances where the loss claimed is linked to their own wrongdoing, criminal or otherwise. In this context similar problems have arisen. Lord Sumption, speaking extra-judicially, has observed, '[f]or as long as I can remember, the English courts have been endeavouring to rationalise [the defence]'; the case law is characterised by 'a large degree

[297] PHSO (n 147) 3; *cf Equitable Life* (n 127) 392.

[298] See O Ichim, *Just Satisfaction under the European Convention on Human Rights* (CUP, 2015) 168–70; D Shelton, *Remedies in International Human Rights Law* 2nd edn (OUP, 2005) 260–65, 312–13, 345–46, 348; *McCann v UK* (1996) 21 EHRR 97, [219]; *A v UK* (2009) 49 EHRR 29, [251]; Law Commissions Report (n 19) [3.55]–[3.57].

[299] *R (Biggin) v SOSJ* [2009] EWHC 1704, [35]; *Downing v Parole Board* [2008] EWHC 3198, [29], [31].

[300] *Downing* ibid [29].

[301] ch 5.2.II.C.ii.

of incoherence and unpredictability' and 'complexity, capriciousness and injustice'.[302]

However, there are important differences between the approach to moral status at common law and under the HRA. In particular there have been more recent moves to place the common law illegality defence on a more principled footing. The emergent approach at common law offers a benchmark against which to test the defensibility of the approach under the HRA.

At common law, given the seriousness of denying an individual their rights, courts take a robust approach, requiring a strong nexus between the claimant's wrongdoing and the defendant's wrong before the defence may succeed. Courts variously require an 'inextricable' link between the claim and the claimant's wrongdoing,[303] that the claimant must necessarily have to rely on or plead her own wrongdoing to advance her claim,[304] or that the damage was directly 'caused by the criminal act of the claimant';[305] 'It is not sufficient if the criminal activity merely gives occasion for tortious conduct of the defendant'[306] or the claimant's wrongdoing is 'collateral' to the claim.[307] The defence plays a 'slighter role' in tort 'because the interests traditionally in issue are basic—liberty, life and limb, property'.[308] Courts observe that '[c]ases where an action in tort has been defeated by the [illegality defence] are exceedingly rare',[309] and that 'quite extreme circumstances' are required 'before the test will exclude a tort claim'.[310] Similarly, in equity a remedy may be declined under the 'clean hands' doctrine. However, the maxim 'must not be taken too far':[311] 'Equity does not demand that its suitors shall have led blameless lives';[312] the claimant's impropriety must have 'an immediate and necessary relation to the equity sued for'.[313]

While identifying a justification for the defence has proven difficult, clarity is emerging. That we are able to identify a clear and convincing rationale is crucial if the defence is to be relied on to deny basic rights, but also because without a clear understanding of the doctrine's purpose—along with its confinement by refined legal tests—its application may come to turn

[302] 'Reflexions on the Law of Illegality' (Chancery Bar Association, 23 April 2012) 1, 5, 20 (www.supremecourt.uk/docs/speech_120423.pdf); see similarly *Hounga* (n 243) [25], [54]; *Les Laboratoires Servier v Apotex Inc* [2015] AC 430, [14].

[303] *Cross v Kirkby* [2000] EWCA Civ 426, [76], [103].

[304] *Tinsley v Milligan* [1994] 1 AC 340; *Stone & Rolls Ltd v Moore Stephens* [2009] 1 AC 1391.

[305] *Gray v Thames Trains Ltd* [2009] 1 AC 1339, [54].

[306] *Vellino v Chief Constable of the Greater Manchester Police* [2002] 1 WLR 218, [70], quoted in *Gray* ibid [53].

[307] *Hounga* (n 243) [58].

[308] Weir (n 87) 261.

[309] *National Coal Board v England* [1954] AC 403, 428–29.

[310] *Hall v Woolston Hall Leisure Ltd* [2001] 1 WLR 225, [79].

[311] *Grobbelaar v News Group Newspapers Ltd* [2002] 1 WLR 3024, [70].

[312] *Loughran v Loughran* 292 US 216, 229 (1934).

[313] *Dering v Earl of Winchelsea* (1787) 1 Cox Eq 318, 319.

on the untrammelled subjective view of the claimant's worthiness, which would lead down a dangerous path. The Supreme Court has now clarified that the illegality defence is a *rule* not a discretion, based on specific public policies, 'not on the perceived balance of merits between the parties', or 'subjective judgments about how badly [the claimant] had behaved and how much it mattered'.[314] Consensus is emerging around the idea that the defence 'preserve[s] the integrity of the legal system' in a narrow sense: the system is threatened where a person profits from wrongful conduct, evades a criminal penalty, or where allowing liability would encourage 'nefarious' conduct.[315] The overarching idea is consistency: the law should not condone what it otherwise condemns, should not reward what it otherwise punishes.[316]

The approach at private law is very different from the 'woolly' approach under the HRA. HRA damages have been denied to claimant prisoners because they did something wrong at some point in the past, in circumstances which have no direct connection to the rights-violation. That there is, in these cases, a tenuous connection between the claimant's past wrongdoing and the rights-violation for which damages are claimed is clear if we apply those tests governing the illegality defence at common law. For example where awards have been denied on the basis of past wrongdoing in human rights law the cases are not ones in which the claimant must rely on or plead their prior criminal conduct; in the Parole Board delay cases the prisoner only need point to the Board's unlawful delays. Nor are the prisoner's losses in such cases caused by their prior criminal conduct: their distress and frustration is caused by the excessive amount of time the Parole Board has taken over their case. At a very great stretch one might say that the prisoner's prior wrongdoing provided the occasion for the rights-violation because they would not have been in prison and suffered delays before the Parole Board but for their original offence. But this is insufficient basis for establishing a causal link in law, as made clear in the illegality cases: 'It is not sufficient if the criminal activity merely gives occasion for tortious conduct of the defendant'.[317] As Lord Sumption observes, that the claimant was positively engaged in illegal activity *at the time of* the wrong is not even sufficient for the defence to succeed at common law: 'The Claimant's illegal act must be the basis of his claim'.[318]

It is also informative to test the Article 5(4) cases against the policy rationales given for the illegality defence. Would an award to a prisoner in an Article 5(4) delay case encourage criminal wrongdoing? It would be

[314] *Apotex* (n 302) [14], [21], [29].
[315] eg *Hounga* (n 243) [42]–[44]; *Stone & Rolls* (n 304) [26], [226].
[316] *Hounga* ibid [43], [55], [67], the Supreme Court drawing on *Hall v Herbert* [1993] 2 SCR 159, 169; *Apotex* (n 302) [24].
[317] *Vellino* (n 306) [70], approved in *Gray* (n 305) [53]–[54].
[318] Sumption (n 302) 17.

fanciful to claim that individuals would be encouraged to commit crimes, so that they may be jailed, and thus have a chance of claiming damages for delays before the Parole Board. Does liability allow the claimant to profit from his criminal conduct? The claim of a rights-violation is far removed from and not founded in the prisoner's original criminal conduct.[319] Would an award enable the claimant to avoid a penalty? No, as an award does not affect a prisoner's sentence.

Against this backdrop, why should damages for breach of basic rights be denied in human rights law on the basis of past wrongdoing, whereas damages liability would not be so denied in other fields such as tort? Usually no rationale is offered in the HRA cases, other than generic appeals to the public interest or the seriousness of the original offence.[320] One more specific purported rationale is that making awards would undermine 'public confidence in the administration of justice'.[321] But if that is correct would the same not also be true in tort? Yet awards are routinely made to prisoners in tort. It is worth observing that precisely this sort of test—a 'public confidence' test—has been rejected at common law on the basis that it is too imponderable, would reduce remedies to open-ended discretion, could be invoked indiscriminately and involves subjective judgement.[322] Instead, there has been a judicial move to think hard about and make clear the exact evils that the common law illegality defence is designed to counter and tailor legal rules to avoidance of those evils. In human rights law the lack of a clear rationale for denying awards for past wrongdoing or a meaningful test to govern when awards should be denied raises the spectre of decision-making based in subjective assessments of the claimant's worthiness. At this point, we are beyond decision-making according to law, and the legal system's integrity is truly undermined. Further, another reason for closely confining the defence is that relieving defendants of liability may compromise the legal system's integrity by signalling that those in the defendant's position may commit wrongs with impunity.[323]

It is worth considering briefly how the Convention and fundamental principles bear on this matter. In *Huonga* the Supreme Court held that if application of the common law illegality defence placed the UK in breach of international commitments this would be an important factor counselling against applying the defence, as well as indicating that the public policies encapsulated in human-rights-type treaties are of such importance that

[319] See by analogy, *Hounga* (n 243) [44](a).

[320] See those cases cited above at n 299 and *DSD v Commissioner for Police* [2015] 1 WLR 1833, [37]–[39]. In contrast at common law application of the illegality defence does not depend on the court's value judgement as to the significance of the illegality: *Apotex* (n 302) [18].

[321] *R (Faulkner) v SOSJ* [2009] EWHC 1507, [39].

[322] *Tinsley* (n 304); *Hounga* (n 243) [28]; *Apotex* (n 302) [14]ff.

[323] *Hounga* (n 243) [44](d).

they may outweigh the public policies underpinning the illegality defence.[324] These concerns are even more acute in the HRA context as the Act was specifically intended to give effect to Convention protections.

Denying victims effective redress because they are imprisoned for past wrongdoing could fall foul of Article 13. The ECtHR has said that 'prisoners in general continue to enjoy all the fundamental rights and freedoms guaranteed under the Convention save for the right to liberty, where lawfully imposed detention expressly falls within the scope of Article 5';[325] the remedial right survives imprisonment. This is consonant with the common law tradition: 'under English law, a convicted prisoner, in spite of his imprisonment, retains all civil rights which are not taken away expressly or by necessary implication'.[326] As such,

> [t]hat a prisoner has a right to sue in respect of torts committed against him in prison is beyond doubt ... If he is assaulted by a prison officer he may sue for damages, and if he is negligently cared for whereby he sustains injury to his health he may likewise sue.[327]

The Convention clearly contemplates that those deprived of liberty will be awarded compensation where wronged. Article 5(5) provides, '[e]veryone who has been the victim of arrest or detention in contravention of the provisions of this article shall have an enforceable right to compensation'.

The ECtHR has, within its Article 41 remedial jurisdiction, expressly considered the applicant's wrongdoing in determining just satisfaction, and been observed by commentators to be less likely to award compensation to criminals.[328] But the Court's explicit reliance on moral status has generally been confined to extreme cases of victim wrongdoing, such as commission of terrorist acts, and where there is a close nexus between wrongdoing and violation.[329] As recognised in *Faulkner*, the ECtHR has often made awards to prisoners in Article 5(4) delay cases.[330]

In addition we should note the right against discrimination in enjoyment of one's rights (Article 14), which reflects the basic principle of equality before the law.

Lastly, it is encouraging that in the Supreme Court decision in *Faulkner*, which concerned prisoner damages claims for breach of Article 5(4), the Court did not consider the claimant's past wrongdoing. However, neither did the Court address and condemn lower courts' reliance on this factor

[324] ibid [46]ff.
[325] *Hirst v UK* (2006) 42 EHRR 41, [69].
[326] *Raymond v Honey* [1983] 1 AC 1, 10; *R v Board of Visitors of Hull Prison, ex p St Germain* [1979] QB 425, 455.
[327] *R v Deputy Governor of Parkhurst Prison, ex p Hague* [1992] 1 AC 58, 176; see also Law Commissions Report (n 19) [4.53] ('the status of the claimant is irrelevant in a claim for damages in tort').
[328] Above n 298.
[329] eg *McCann* (n 298).
[330] *Faulkner* (n 67).

(while in subsequent decisions the Court has taken an exceptionally restrictive approach to HRA damages claims by prisoners).[331] Until the higher courts squarely address this matter lower courts remain unconstrained by authority to continue to consider the victim's moral character, and have done so.[332] Perhaps a lead could be taken from New Zealand. Thomas J, in the damages case of *Dunlea*, said 'the right has a real value to the recidivist offender as well as to the model citizen',[333] while the Chief Justice in *Chapman* rejected treating 'those tried for criminal offences as not entitled to vindication of rights on the same basis as others'.[334]

C. Pragmatic Political Concerns

In *Anufrijeva* one reason given in support of making only modest awards to the claimants, who were asylum seekers, was that it 'could bring the HRA into disrepute' if 'the impression is created that asylum seekers whether genuine or not are profiting from their status'.[335] It is conceivable that such concerns could also influence the decision whether to award damages.

It is right that courts should avoid developing the law in a way that would bring it into disrepute. However, it is difficult to see how properly compensating individuals for loss suffered through wrongful conduct could undermine confidence in the administration of justice. Further, compensation does not constitute profit; it restores the claimant's pre-breach position. Thus, if the media or public were under the impression that a compensatory award constituted a windfall, that would be erroneous. Rather than pander to mistaken impressions, judges should instead actively seek to expel such impressions in the terms of their judgments or, for example, through judicial speeches or press releases from senior members of the judiciary. The government, and particularly the Lord Chancellor, also has a role to play in this respect, and it is regrettable that a mooted Governmental campaign to better inform civil society of the functions of the HRA never materialised.[336] In any case, that a given judgment may give rise to a particular impression does not seem a particularly weighty reason for taking the serious step of undercompensating victims of violations of fundamental rights. Indeed, I am not aware of any other legal field where a remedy could be denied for a legal wrong on the basis that its grant could give a certain 'impression'.

[331] *Shahid v Scottish Ministers* [2015] 3 WLR 1003, [87]–[90].
[332] *DSD* (n 320) [37]–[39].
[333] *Dunlea* (n 153) [67].
[334] *Chapman* (n 25) [71]. See also Crown Liability (n 115) [70].
[335] (n 1) [75]. A similar attitude is arguably reflected in the Supreme Court's view that awarding damages on common law principles for human rights breaches would entail 'gold-plating the claimant's Convention rights': *Michael* (n 227) [125].
[336] Department for Constitutional Affairs, *Review of the Implementation of the Human Rights Act* (2006) 2, 42.

As the ECtHR has said, offence to public opinion is not a sound basis upon which to deny rights within the field of human rights protection, 'where tolerance and broadmindedness are the acknowledged hallmarks of democratic society'.[337]

There are more general reasons why courts should be circumspect about denying or reducing awards on the basis of negative media reaction. First, the anticipated reaction may not materialise. Second, these are questions of law and judges are best placed to decide them; all the evidence points to limited public awareness and understanding of the HRA, and that misperceptions of the Act are not uncommon due to negative media reporting and government statements.[338] As Saunders J said in rejecting the principle that damages may be denied to prisoners:

> True it is that some, perhaps most, members of the public would be outraged at the idea of payments of money by the State to people who have committed terrible crimes because they have had to wait for a decision as to whether they should be released [in breach of Article 5(4)]. It has, however, to be borne in mind that the public are not necessarily in the best position to make an informed opinion because they may only be aware of the issue through sensational reporting. Are they in the best position to decide what is or is not just and appropriate?[339]

Third, treating one group, such as asylum seekers, differently from others according to populist-type concerns undermines the rule-of-law principle that all are equal before the law, rubs against Article 14 ECHR and draws the courts into ordinary politics, undermining judicial independence.

Lastly, one reason often given for adoption of bills of rights is to ensure protection of vulnerable or unpopular minorities, marginalised in society and the political process;[340] it is 'one of the essential roles of the courts in a democracy' to protect 'the rights of minorities, including unpopular minorities'.[341] It is therefore concerning that the courts have reduced the practical protection of the rights of asylum seekers and prisoners, two groups that are particularly vulnerable given their reliance on the state, that are unpopular, and for whom it is nearly impossible to influence public decision-making. These developments are deeply troubling. The higher courts should show leadership and expunge such practice forthwith.

337 *Hirst* (n 325) [70].

338 EHRC, *Public Perceptions of Human Rights* (2009) ch 3.4–3.5 (www.equalityhumanrights.com/sites/default/files/publication_pdf/public_perceptions_of_human_rights_ipos_mori.pdf) [EHRC Public Perceptions Report]; EHRC, *Human Rights in Britain Since the Human Rights Act 1998: A Critical Review* (2008) ch 6 (www.equalityhumanrights.com/sites/default/files/documents/human_rights_in_britain_since_the_human_rights_act_1998_-_a_critical_review.pdf) [EHRC Human Rights Review].

339 *R (Degainis) v SOSJ* [2010] EWHC 137, [19].

340 JH Ely, *Democracy and Distrust* (Harvard, 1980).

341 *R (Chester) v SOSJ* [2014] 1 AC 271, [88].

D. Chilling Effects

Lord Woolf, speaking extra-judicially, has cautioned against replicating 'the dangers of "defensive medicine" by creating dangers of "preventive administration"' through human rights damages.[342] Courts elsewhere, in fashioning their approach to human rights damages, have similarly placed weight on the potential 'chilling effects' that liability may have on administrative decision-making,[343] while the factor has often been invoked to deny novel duties in negligence.[344] Albeit this factor has not so far featured prominently in HRA jurisprudence it is the sort of consideration that is bound to be taken into account under interest-balancing to justify restricting awards and depressing quantum.

Undoubtedly there is a public interest in 'encouraging officials to act promptly, decisively, and without excessive self-regard or calculation' and 'to accomplish the public's business in socially efficient, cost-minimising ways'.[345] These interests may be undermined if the threat or imposition of liability causes officials to act with excessive caution. Nonetheless it is strongly arguable that courts should not consider this factor in determining human rights damages claims: courts lack capacity to reliably assess whether awards will in fact precipitate defensive practices.

i. An Empirical Void

Courts seldom examine empirical studies of the impacts of liability.[346] Judicial predictions of defensive administration occur in an empirical void, being based on 'untested speculation and intuition' which provides 'an unreliable basis for deciding what to do'.[347] It is not uncommon to find one judge in a given case claiming that liability will have negative impacts whereas another judge in the same case claims it will have positive or no effects, with neither basing their claims in evidence.[348] It is clearly unacceptable that decisions affecting basic rights should rest on 'hunches', 'speculation', 'intuition', and

[342] Woolf (n 224) 433.

[343] eg *Ward* (n 6) [38]ff; *Chapman* (n 25) [166], [172]; *Scheuer v Rhodes* 416 US 232, 240 (1974); *Butz v Economou* 438 US 478, 497, 506 (1978); *Ashcroft v Iqbal* 129 S Ct 1937, 1953–1954 (2009).

[344] eg *Rowling v Takaro Properties Ltd* [1988] AC 473, 502; *Hill* (n 227) 63; *X* (n 91) 750; *Van Colle* (n 227) [73]ff, [108], [132]; *Yuen Kun Yeu v Attorney-General of Hong Kong* [1988] AC 175, 198; *Brooks v Commissioner for the Metropolis* [2005] 1 WLR 1495, [4], [5], [30]; *Elguzouli-Daf v Commissioner for the Metropolis* [1995] QB 335, 349; *Calveley v Chief Constable Merseyside Police* [1989] AC 1228, 1238.

[345] Schuck (n 144) 21.

[346] There are rare exceptions: *Michael* (n 227) [185].

[347] P Cane, 'Consequences in Judicial Reasoning' in J Horder (ed), *Oxford Essays in Jurisprudence, Fourth Series* (OUP, 2000) 42, 49 [Consequences].

[348] *Stovin* (n 109) 941C, 958B–C; *Van Colle* (n 227) [49], [73]ff, [108], [132].

'unproved' and 'unprovable'[349] propositions. Such practice also raises issues of transparency; if predictions are not evidence-based the suspicion may arise that consequentialist arguments mask unstated normative assumptions, not tested in legal argument nor justified in judgments. If this is to be the judicial approach to assessing consequentialist arguments, then it is best that courts not consider such arguments at all.

ii. Empirical Evidence and Difficulties of Prediction

Even if courts considered empirical evidence it would still be very difficult, if not impossible, to predict ex ante what effect, if any, damages liability would have on bureaucratic behaviour. First, there is a dearth of empirical research into the administrative impacts of liability, while impact studies are generally 'modest in scope and hedged about with numerous qualifications and caveats';[350] one must 'be cautious in generalising about the determinants of decision-making beyond the particular bureaucratic cultures which were investigated'.[351] Second, there are very substantial risks of error in predicting future events because one does so in the face of myriad uncontrollable and unknowable variables. It is part of the human condition that this reality does not prevent us from irrationally overestimating our predictive capacities;[352] however, we should not give in to irrationality.

The Law Commission, in its administrative redress project, reviewed the literature on impact of liability on authorities, finding such research is 'extremely limited' in the UK.[353] On the basis of what research exists, as well as theories of bureaucratic behaviour and impact studies of judicial review, the Commission concluded: '[i]t is ... simply not possible to make an accurate general statement as to the likely outcome of any given change in liability on a range of public bodies'.[354] Whether an authority reacts to a damages judgment appropriately or inappropriately, or has no reaction 'is heavily context-, indeed organisation specific'.[355]

Impact depends on multiple variables. Impact may vary according to the nature of the legal norm at issue,[356] and whether implementation of the norm rubs against engrained administrative values, organisational goals

[349] Markesinis et al (n 226) 1–2, 40, 45, 78–81.

[350] P Cane, 'Understanding Judicial Review and its Impact' in M Hertogh and S Halliday (eds), *Judicial Review and Bureaucratic Impact* (CUP, 2004) 40.

[351] S Halliday, 'The Influence of Judicial Review on Bureaucratic Decision-making' [2000] *PL* 110, 113.

[352] NN Taleb, *The Black Swan: the Impact of the Highly Improbable* (Penguin, 2008).

[353] Administrative Redress Consultation Paper (n 155) [B.2].

[354] ibid [B.83].

[355] ibid [B.82].

[356] G Richardson, 'Impact Studies in the United Kingdom' in Hertogh and Halliday (n 350) 117–21.

or established practices, which may operate to 'neutralise' impact:[357] 'each administrative body is characterised by a certain inner rationality and a degree of autonomy from external influences'.[358] Impact varies with an authority's idiosyncratic litigation experiences.[359] Impact may be dynamic: authorities may initially react defensively to a legal decision as it rubs against prevailing organisational culture, but over time view the decision positively and it may contribute to improved administration.[360] Within organisations individual officials may react differently to the threat of liability according to their risk-characteristics—eg whether they are risk-averse, risk-neutral or risk-takers—and, on a broader level, their cognitive understandings and normative attitudes.[361] Impact may vary according to the task performed by officials.[362] It may vary according to whether there are organisational 'feedback loops', so that lessons learned from litigation are fed back into administrative process,[363] and vary with the way internal legal guidance is framed.[364] Impact may differ across organisational units within an authority, and/or across an organisation's hierarchy.[365] For example, a department's executive management team may react positively to a liability judgment by distributing revised policy guidance which seeks to ensure legal norms are considered in street-level decision-making. However, officials may resist top-down change,[366] while information may take a long time to trickle down, may become distorted in the process, and/or be ignored because officials are inundated with policy circulars.[367]

[357] eg ibid 112–15, 121–23, 125–28; Halliday (n 351) 113–18; B Canon, 'Studying Bureaucratic Implementation of Judicial Policies in the United States: Conceptual and Methodological Approaches' in Hertogh and Halliday (n 350) 95–96. In the human rights context see: D Feldman, 'Changes in Human Rights' in M Adler (ed), *Administrative Justice in Context* (Hart Publishing, 2010) 102–06, 117.

[358] D Galligan and D Sandler, 'Implementing Human Rights' in S Halliday and P Schmidt (eds), *Human Rights Brought Home: Socio-Legal Perspectives on Human Rights in the National Context* (Hart Publishing, 2004) 51–54.

[359] eg Halliday (n 351); M Sunkin and V Bondy, 'The Use and Effects of Judicial Review: Assumptions and the Empirical Evidence' in J Bell et al (eds), *Public Law Adjudication in Common Law Systems: Process and Substance* (Hart Publishing, forthcoming 2016).

[360] Some such examples are given in Sunkin and Bondy ibid; CR Epp, *Making Rights Real* (Chicago, 2009) 217.

[361] Galligan and Sandler (n 358) 29–30, 51–52; EHRC, *Evaluating the Impact of Selected Cases under the Human Rights Act on Public Services Provision* (2009) 106–07 (available: www.equalityhumanrights.com/sites/default/files/publication_pdf/evaluating_the_impact_of_selected_cases_under_the_human_rights_act_on_public_services_provision.pdf) [EHRC Evaluating Impact].

[362] Richardson (n 356) 107.

[363] Epp (n 360) 161; Halliday (n 351) 116; EHRC Evaluating Impact (n 361) 108–10.

[364] eg Feldman (n 357) 102–03 (circulars which stress liability risks—rather than congruence between human rights and administrative values—are more likely to engender defensive behaviours); EHRC ibid 114–15.

[365] eg Halliday (n 351) 118–19.

[366] See, eg, ibid; Epp (n 360) 161–62. On intra-institutional dynamics see further: Schuck (n 144) ch 6.

[367] Schuck ibid 4–6, 130–31; J Hartshorne et al, '"*Caparo* Under Fire": a Study into the Effects upon the Fire Service of Liability in Negligence' (2000) 63 *MLR* 502, 518–19.

In any case there is no straightforward interrelationship between 'legal conscientiousness', ie the degree to which officials care about legal compliance and are cognisant of legal rules, and actual legal compliance; legal conscientiousness may be high but unlawfulness rife.[368] Legal compliance and impact may also depend on the incidence and strength of non-legal accountability mechanisms in a given administrative context, while such mechanisms may be far more influential in shaping administrative behaviour than economic incentives associated with liability.[369] Such mechanisms include hierarchical institutions such as the National Audit Office, which may demand action to mitigate liability risks; market mechanisms such as insurance contracts, the terms of which vary among authorities;[370] and professional networks, which may reinforce the importance of legal obligations.[371] The media, public opinion and activists may also affect compliance in different ways.[372]

As the Law Commission records, once one moves beyond simplistic microeconomic models of rationality, and considers, inter alia, socio-legal and/or behavioural law and economics[373] approaches and empirical studies, which better capture the nuances of human and organisational behaviour, it becomes clear that 'a wide range of factors, operating at the level of the individual and the organisation' and beyond 'act to make the picture much more complex'.[374] While the Commission records that it is possible to offer hypotheses regarding circumstances where legal concerns will be marginal, it concludes that 'empirical evidence does not yet allow us to state with confidence how these circumstances are distributed within and between policy sectors'.[375] All of the factors discussed, which affect impact, make it very difficult to accurately predict what effect a given decision, series of decisions or the threat of liability will have on administrative behaviour. Reflecting this, studies record myriad impacts, ranging from litigation improving administrative decision-making to having no effect to paradoxically reducing the extent to which agencies engage in self-scrutiny. In terms of legal compliance, imposition of liability may, inter alia, engender full compliance, tokenistic, defensive compliance, or be met with outright defiance.

Though it is impossible to reach general conclusions as to likely effects of imposing liability, two recent studies specifically into the effects of damages

[368] Halliday (n 351); S Halliday, *Judicial Review and Compliance with Administrative Law* (Hart Publishing, 2004).

[369] Halliday et al 2011 (n 252) 543–44; Epp (n 360).

[370] See Markesinis et al (n 226) 81–86.

[371] S Halliday, 'The Governance of Compliance with Public Law' [2013] *PL* 312; Halliday et al 2011 (n 252).

[372] Epp (n 360).

[373] eg C Jolls et al, 'A Behavioral Approach to Law and Economics' (1998) 50 *Stanford Law Review* 1471.

[374] Administrative Redress Consultation Paper (n 155) [B.53].

[375] ibid [B.82].

liability on public administration warrant attention, especially given a general 'dearth of empirical evidence about how public authorities manage the liability risks inherent in public service provision'.[376]

One study examined how local authorities in Scotland and Ireland manage liability risks associated with negligence in the context of road maintenance. Echoing the foregoing analysis Halliday et al found that 'mundane complexities of public administration' 'mediate the significance of liability risks ... in a host of ways' and make it difficult to reach generalised conclusions as to the 'promise or threat' of liability.[377] In their road maintenance case study the authors found that '[t]here is much in the messy and prosaic quality of public administration which militates against tort law having the presumed negative and unintended effects that constitute compensation culture fears'.[378] They found only 'limited evidence' of typical concerns associated with liability, including over-caution.[379] The findings are particularly significant because provision of roads is amongst the riskiest activities undertaken by local authorities, with roads-claims accounting for the highest aggregate financial pay-out by such authorities.[380] If one would expect significant chilling effects in any context it would have been this one.

Epp's study of the bureaucratic impact of damages liability in the US, across the areas of policing, sexual harassment and playground safety, is highly significant as it shows that even if liability engenders 'fear' among bureaucrats, this is not necessarily negative. Rather, fear may drive necessary improvements.

Epp describes how, beginning in the 1970s, damages lawsuits coordinated by activists began to produce negative publicity for authorities. Litigation proved an extraordinarily powerful strategy because damages claims allowed activists to maintain sustained pressure on authorities, while large damages awards and shocking stories of wrongdoing exposed through damages claims consistently caught headlines. Over time managers within authorities recognised that successful damages claims, and associated negative press, were a real threat to their public and professional legitimacy. These claims 'forced agencies to face up to long-ignored problems of abuse and injury'.[381] Driven by fear not of the financial implications of liability but rather of damage to professional reputation, these managers sought to align bureaucratic practice with legal norms through reforms, including written rules, formal training and internal oversight mechanisms, leading to 'real lasting change in bureaucratic practice'.[382] Damages claims came

[376] Halliday et al 2011 (n 252) 528.
[377] ibid 549.
[378] ibid.
[379] ibid 529.
[380] ibid.
[381] Epp (n 360) 1.
[382] ibid 3.

to be welcomed enthusiastically by reform-minded managers who utilised liability risk as a 'lever' to implement reforms necessary to facilitate legal compliance, while more generally authorities viewed reform as an opportunity to regain legitimacy. In turn, professional networks reinforced the reform-movement, and the new accountability model became dominant, the result being emergence of a new administrative fidelity to legal norms. However, aspects of the new administrative accountability model which 'intrude more deeply into organizational practices are less widely adopted than the model's less intrusive elements'.[383]

When these two landmark studies are added to research into the impact of judicial review, the general thrust of which is that review has a 'limited ability ... to influence administrative decision-making',[384] as well as more recent research revealing that review may improve public administration in ways welcomed by officials,[385] the over-arching picture is not one of officials living in fear of court challenges to the detriment of public administration.

No study has examined the impact of HRA damages. There is some material on bureaucratic impact of the HRA more generally, although this is scarce and patchy. That evidence which exists does not suggest overly-cautious administration is a major problem associated with the Act. Indeed, some evidence indicates cavalier approaches to compliance.

The 2006 Government review of the HRA documents anecdotal evidence of some overly-cautious official behaviour based in misapprehensions about the Act, anecdotal evidence of the HRA having a positive effect on decision-making, as well as instances where authorities have revised policies in response to litigation.[386] The Joint Committee on Human Rights found little if any evidence of the HRA precipitating risk aversion in the Home Office, despite Government assertions to this effect.[387] An Audit Commission report, in the Act's early years, records that in many cases public authorities responded to the HRA with a 'wait and see what happens' or 'let's defend a challenge' approach,[388] had not taken positive action in response to the Act,[389] and that most authorities made no arrangements to ensure compliance by contracted-out providers.[390] One empirical study, which surveyed responses to the HRA of roughly 30 per cent of all UK local authorities in the early 2000s, found that awareness of the Act was initially high.

[383] ibid 8.

[384] Richardson (n 356) 112.

[385] See n 611 below, and see J King, *Judging Social Rights* (CUP, 2012) 70–76, interpreting the impact literature on judicial review in a more optimistic light.

[386] DCA (n 336) ch 3.

[387] *The Human Rights Act: the DCA and Home Office Reviews*, HC 1716/HL 278 (2006) [101]–[104].

[388] Audit Commission, *Human Rights: Improving Public Service Delivery* (2003) [6].

[389] ibid [12], [21]–[23], [29].

[390] ibid [13], [24]–[27].

However, a significant proportion of authorities subsequently regarded the Act as a 'non-event', akin to the 'millennium blip'.[391] The authors found it striking that so many authorities considered the Act would make no difference to prevailing administrative practices.[392] The findings reinforce the Audit Commission's conclusions that many authorities have adopted a passive non-implementation policy,[393] while they also mirror the conclusions of judicial review studies which find legal norms are often side-lined relative to organisational values.

More recently, an important review of the HRA by the Equality and Human Rights Commission in 2009 reaches 'the central finding ... that a culture of respect for human rights has largely failed to take root among public authorities in England'; outside the Ministry of Justice 'efforts to embed human rights by ... departments have been, at best, piecemeal'; 'well over half the number of public authorities could not demonstrate that they had taken proactive steps to comply with the HRA'; human rights are not taken seriously but are a matter of 'tick-box compliance'; and there are low levels of awareness of the HRA among public service staff.[394] Reasons for the lack of penetration of human rights norms included lack of leadership at senior levels of government, including failure to communicate the importance of human rights and how they can be implemented so as to benefit public administration, entrenched organisational cultures and lack of awareness among service users of human rights and avenues for complaint. Another important study by the Commission into the impacts of human rights litigation on authorities, far from finding legal challenges precipitate defensive behaviours, found successful challenges had often had little impact at all, albeit some beneficial impacts were observable.[395] The study of one case, *Bernard*,[396] in which £10,000 HRA damages were awarded against a housing authority, found little impact. In respect of the damages award in particular the Commission recorded that managers of housing authorities felt awards could not be ignored but none thought 'the £10,000 penalty in *Bernard* to be significant in the context of authorities with multi-million pound budgets', while one director of housing 'said a fine of this order "was not much of a threat"'.[397] So much for bald assertions that damages precipitate defensive administration.

[391] L Clements and R Morris, 'The Millennium Blip: The Human Rights Act 1998 and Local Government' in Halliday and Schmidt (n 358) 228.
[392] ibid 228.
[393] ibid 229.
[394] EHRC Human Rights Review (n 338). See also EHRC, *Human Rights Review 2012: An Assessment of How Well Public Authorities Protect Human Rights* (2012).
[395] EHRC Evaluating Impact (n 361).
[396] (n 186).
[397] EHRC Evaluating Impact (n 361) 102.

iii. Limitations of Courts

Impact studies and behavioural research raise difficult issues, and it is doubtful whether courts have the time, resources or institutional competence to engage rigorously with a complex literature. For example, there are ongoing disputes as to what is meant by 'impact',[398] and how we gauge whether a judgment has 'caused' observed behavioural changes.[399] Terms such as 'defensive administration' lack 'any widely-accepted definition'.[400] What separates 'appropriate' or 'positive' administrative responses from 'negative' ones is a difficult question, and one of degree: 'one [person's] excessive caution is another's prudent practice'.[401]

There are also difficult practical issues. If our aim is to discern how a damages judgment affects the degree of defensive behaviour within an organisation, we must know what the level of defensive behaviour was prior to the judgment;[402] 'it seems clear [such matters] might be very difficult to resolve in a rigorous way'.[403] Difficult issues also arise in connection with behavioural models and compliance theories which might be used to predict bureaucratic responses absent concrete evidence. This literature can throw up 'competing accounts, rather than clear conclusions'.[404] For example, 'enforcement' theories of compliance assume that decisions whether to comply depend on rational weighing of costs and benefits, while 'managerialist' theories maintain institutions have a general propensity to comply and the 'principal source of non-compliance is not wilful disobedience but the lack of capability or clarity or priority'.[405]

On top of institutional and practical issues, judicial acceptance of chilling effect arguments 'gives normative weight to what appear to be illogical reactions to legal liability rules'.[406] Overly-cautious behaviour is by

[398] See M Sunkin, 'Conceptual Issues in Researching the Impact of Judicial Review on Government Bureaucrats' in Hertogh and Halliday (n 350); Sunkin and Richardson (n 246). It may be difficult to separate conceptual and methodological issues from wider normative debates: Cane (n 350).

[399] See, eg, the high-profile debate between 'positivists' and 'interpretivists': M McCann, 'Causal Versus Constitutive Explanations (Or, on the Difficulty of Being so Positive)' (1996) 21 *Law & Social Inquiry* 457.

[400] Administrative Redress Consultation Paper (n 155) [B.28]. Also, one's definition of defensive behaviour is sensitive to subjective attitudes to risk: Consequences (n 347) 45.

[401] Markesinis et al (n 226) 80.

[402] See Consequences (n 347) 51.

[403] ibid.

[404] Administrative Redress Consultation Paper (n 155) [B.54]. For example, there are many different accounts and theories of how bureaucracy operates or should operate: eg J Mashaw, *Bureaucratic Justice* (Yale, 1985); RA Kagan, 'The Organisation of Administrative Justice Systems' in M Adler (ed) *Administrative Justice in Context* (Hart Publishing, 2010); S Shapiro, 'Why Administrative Law Misunderstands How Government Works: The Missing Institutional Analysis' (2013) 53 *Washburn Law Journal* 1; Schuck (n 144).

[405] A Chayes and AH Chayes, *The New Sovereignty: Compliance with International Regulatory Agreements* (Harvard, 1995) 22; EHRC Evaluating Impact (n 361) 107–08.

[406] Consequences (n 347) 45; *Barrett v Enfield LBC* [1998] QB 367, 380, endorsed on appeal: [2001] 2 AC 550, 568.

definition irrational in that it involves more caution than necessary or appropriate; 'the law never imposes an obligation to behave defensively, a person could never incur liability for failing to do so'.[407]

Overall, notwithstanding public interests in vigorous administration, it would be difficult, if not impossible, for courts to predict reliably whether granting an award would precipitate defensive administrative behaviours. In any case, English courts do not generally consider empirical studies or behavioural theory, while there are well-founded concerns over courts considering such material. All of this indicates that chilling effect arguments are not a reliable basis for judicial decision-making. The prudent approach is to decide cases according to accepted legal principle, and government may respond if liability *in fact* leads to widespread defensive practices, seriously compromising public interests.

In response some might argue, while acknowledging that a cautious approach should be taken to consequentialist arguments,[408] that if liability effects are difficult to predict because of lack of empirical knowledge then courts are in no worse position than the political branches.[409] This argument may have some force, ex ante. However, government has significant institutional advantages ex post. Government has the benefit of hindsight, and the ability to monitor unfolding events and commission studies on actual impact after liability has been imposed. It has many means of response open to it, as discussed below. Importantly, the political branches have the constitutional legitimacy to determine difficult policy questions which may, if they cannot be resolved by empirical research, call for contentious value-judgements.

Furthermore, that courts may be in no worse position than the political branches does not prove the case for courts determining damages claims according to guesswork. If it is impossible to predict reliably the consequences of liability then courts should refrain from consequentialist reasoning. Instead they should 'develop criteria for good decision-making which do not depend on knowledge of likely consequences'.[410] In this respect there are some encouraging signs in other fields of liability.[411]

E. Floodgates and 'Litigation Culture'

Traditionally it was taken as read that

> if men will multiply injuries, actions must be multiplied too; for every man that is injured ought to have his recompence. Suppose the defendant had beat forty or

[407] Consequences ibid 45–46; *Van Colle* (n 227) [52].

[408] J Morgan, 'Policy Reasoning in Tort Law: the Courts, the Law Commissions and the Critics' (2009) 125 *LQR* 215, 220.

[409] ibid 220, 222.

[410] Consequences (n 347) 43; Bishop (n 275) 663.

[411] eg *Van Colle* (n 227) [102]; *Michael* (n 227) [121], [130], [184].

> fifty men, the damage done to each one is peculiar to himself, and he shall have his action.[412]

However, today an increasingly common argument against imposing liability is that it may result in a flood of claims that could, inter alia, clog up the civil justice system, entail large-scale expenditure on litigation, and unduly burden defendants.[413] It is also commonly argued that expansion of liability could contribute to a 'compensation' or 'litigation culture'. Lord Woolf, specifically addressing HRA damages, has warned against promotion of a 'public law damages culture',[414] while judges adjudicating such claims have justified a restrictive approach on the basis that '[i]t is manifestly not the intention of the law to create a "get rich quick" litigation culture'.[415]

Overall, while potential for a flood of claims and development of a compensation culture are common concerns, there are good reasons why courts should not consider these factors or at least approach them with extreme caution.

In the first instance, it is, in general, difficult to predict ex ante whether imposition of liability in one or a number of cases will precipitate a large number of claims. As the Law Commission observes, the empirical picture is incomplete and complex:

> there is limited empirical evidence available upon which to ground estimates of the likely impact of increased public liability. It is, however, well-known in the socio-legal literature that decisions to litigate are not just influenced by the absence or presence of a monetary remedy. There may be an increase in litigation even when there has been no change in the liability regime. The relationship between a liability regime and the propensity to litigate is by no means straightforward.[416]

This gives credence to more recent judicial scepticism towards defendant incantations of the floodgates argument, Lord Wilson in *Sagicor* querying: 'how powerful is this argument in the absence of empirical evidence in support of it?'[417]

A striking example of the complex, often counter-intuitive, relationship between liability rules and propensity to litigate is the story of the Australian High Court's adoption in *Beaudesert*, and eventual abandonment, of a broad

412 *Ashby* (n 89) 955.

413 The floodgates argument is commonly considered by courts in deciding whether to recognise a duty of care in negligence, although the courts' reliance upon this consideration and the weight given to it is far from consistent: eg *X* (n 91) 750–51; *Elguzouli-Daf* (n 344) 349; *Phelps* (n 256) 672; *Arthur JS Hall & Co v Simons* [2002] 1 AC 615, 681–82. The floodgates argument has also been invoked as a reason against imposing liability for violations of constitutional rights: see, eg, *Bivens v Six Unknown Named Agents of Federal Bureau of Narcotics* 403 US 388, 428, 430 (1971).

414 Woolf (n 224) 433.

415 *DSD* (n 320) [41].

416 Administrative Redress Consultation Paper (n 155) [B.12].

417 *Sagicor* (n 230) [72](e); *Arthur Hall* (n 413) 682.

liability principle, that 'a person who suffers harm or loss as the inevitable consequence of the unlawful, positive and intentional acts of another is entitled to recover damages from that other'.[418] The principle's scope was exceptionally broad and the threshold for establishing liability very low. This led to concerns that a flood of claims would eventuate, particularly against authorities that had acted ultra vires: if an authority intentionally did an act, which turned out to be beyond powers, and the inevitable consequence was the causing of harm to X, this was sufficient for X to recover. However, some 30 years after *Beaudesert* the Court, in abandoning the principle, observed that there was no reported case in which *Beaudesert* had been applied and that it could not be said that the decision had led to any great inconvenience.[419]

There are further issues with deploying the floodgates argument to deny human rights damages. First, courts are not well-placed to observe macro-trends in litigation, while deciding whether to award damages or not on a case-by-case basis is not exactly a precision instrument for managing levels of litigation. The government is well-placed institutionally to observe and analyse litigation trends, and implement systematic reform if levels of litigation are unacceptably high. It can tailor solutions to meet specific problems. For example, analysis may reveal that an increase in litigation has been caused by a spate of claims relating to a particular subject-matter or instance of government wrongdoing. Government may set up an ad hoc, low-cost claims-process separate from courts with the power to determine such claims, or transfer such cases from courts to another institution, such as a tribunal.[420] Another option may be not to remove claims from courts but to establish a quick, low-cost procedural route for such claims.[421] Of course methods beyond procedural reform are open. These may be as diverse as reducing costs of medical reports for particular injuries in respect of which many fraudulent claims are made, or prescribing that courts must dismiss claims where a claimant has lied about his injuries.[422] Government has all such options at its disposal. A court does not.

[418] *Beaudesert Shire Council v Smith* (1966) 120 CLR 145, 156.

[419] *Northern Territory v Mengel* (1995) 185 CLR 307, 338.

[420] As has occurred with immigration judicial review cases: *Jurisdiction of the Upper Tribunal under s 18 of the Tribunals, Courts and Enforcement Act 2007 and Mandatory Transfer of Judicial Review Applications to the Upper Tribunal under s 31A(2) of the Senior Courts Act 1981*, Practice Direction given in accordance with Part 1 of Schedule 2 to the Constitutional Reform Act 2005 and s 18 of the Tribunals, Courts and Enforcement Act 2007 (21 August 2013); Crime and Courts Act 2013, s 22.

[421] See, eg, the procedure established for low-value claims for road traffic accidents: Civil Procedure Rules SI 1998 No 3132, Pt 8, Practice Direction 8B and Pre-Action Protocol for Low Value Personal Injury Claims in Road Traffic Accidents [CPR].

[422] 'Fee Cut for Whiplash Medical Reports' at www.gov.uk/government/news/fee-cut-for-whiplash-medical-reports; Criminal Justice and Courts Act 2015, s 57.

Second, reducing litigation is not a good in and of itself. Overly-restrictive measures will prevent meritorious claimants from obtaining relief. Thus, deciding what level of litigation is 'acceptable' may require difficult moral, economic or political judgements, which are quintessentially for the political branches.[423]

Third, if we wish to reduce litigation or claiming, should we not, for example, first look to reduce minor claims concerning interests of less than fundamental status? For example studies of local authority liability show that roads represent the sector which attracts the most claims and highest aggregate financial pay-out, while most such claims concern very small amounts for minor vehicle damage caused by potholes.[424] As Harlan J said in *Bivens*, court resources may be increasingly scarce, but 'when we automatically close the courthouse door solely on this basis we implicitly express a value judgment on the comparative importance of classes of legally protected interests'.[425]

Fourth, there is no evidence that introduction of HRA damages liability has resulted in a worryingly high number of claims, nor do we have evidence as to levels of HRA damages litigation relative to other types of damages claims. For what it is worth a 2003 report—considering a time-period prior to the restrictive decisions in *Anufrijeva* and *Greenfield*—found 'little evidence that the introduction of the [HRA] has led to a significant increase in the use of judicial review'.[426] There was, from 2000 to 2011, an increase in cases initiated via review more generally, but this was largely due to one problem area (immigration cases); if these cases are subtracted the rate of applications was largely constant,[427] which may be surprising given the effect enactment of the HRA was expected to have on levels of litigation. In New Zealand the Chief Justice observed in 2011 that,

> [t]he number of cases in which [human rights] damages have been sought from the State since 1994 [the year in which damages liability was established] is small, suggesting that early predictions of a flood of claims to vex the administration are well astray, as such predictions usually are.[428]

423 A Morris, 'Spiralling or Stabilising? The Compensation Culture and Our Propensity to Claim Damages for Personal Injury' (2007) 70 *MLR* 349, 377 [Morris 2007].

424 Halliday (n 371) 317; Halliday et al 2011 (n 252) 529; S Halliday et al, 'Street-Level Tort Law: The Bureaucratic Justice of Liability Decision-Making' (2012) 75 *MLR* 347, 348–49 [Halliday et al 2012].

425 *Bivens* (n 413) 411.

426 Public Law Project, *The Impact of the Human Rights Act on Judicial Review: An Empirical Research Study* (2003) 31. See similarly J Raine and C Walker, 'Implementing the Human Rights Act into the Courts in England and Wales: Culture Shift or Damp Squib?' in Halliday and Schmidt (n 358).

427 J Bell et al, 'University of Cambridge Centre for Public Law Response to Ministry of Justice Consultation Paper, "Judicial Review: Proposals for Reform"', University of Cambridge Faculty of Law Research Paper (23 January 2013) 4–5 (papers.ssrn.com/sol3/papers.cfm?abstract_id=2205830).

428 *Chapman* (n 25) [5].

Human rights cases (but not human rights damages cases, of which there have been relatively few) take up an increasing proportion of the Supreme Court's time[429] but studies of apex courts tell us next to nothing about general litigation trends as they miss the bulk of the action.

The concept of 'litigation' or 'compensation culture' is not easily defined. The terminology tends to denote a 'host of bads' that arise when people too easily resort to litigation or legal claims.[430] These 'bads' include: 'high insurance, inefficiency, fragmentation, homogenization and the decline of community, dignity, spontaneity, and self-reliance', as well as significant costs to the taxpayer, clogging up the court system, and spread of defensive behaviours.[431] These bads are said to arise not from people resorting to litigation where they have arguable claims, but because those with unmeritorious claims too easily resort to legal action.[432] This practice can be encouraged by certain phenomena including inaccurate media reporting suggesting significant compensation is readily recoverable, and advertising by lawyers and claims management companies.[433]

The relevant question here is whether these matters warrant a judge denying damages for harm suffered through a human rights violation? The clear answer is 'no'. It would be illogical to deny damages in a meritorious case, on the premise that unmeritorious claims should be deterred.

Further, problems associated with litigation culture can be and *are* addressed through other mechanisms. Civil procedure rules are based squarely on policies of keeping cases out of court, early settlement and dissuasion of unmeritorious claims.[434] Unmeritorious claims will not be legally aided. Alternative, less expensive routes to redress can be established for classes of claim that are problematic.[435] Tighter professional regulation and regulation of fees and costs can help to ensure that lawyers and claims-services do not exacerbate problems;[436] recent research suggests such measures are effective.[437]

[429] S Shah and T Poole, 'The Impact of the Human Rights Act on the House of Lords' [2009] *PL* 347.

[430] J Hand, 'The Compensation Culture: Cliché or Cause for Concern?' (2010) 37 *Journal of Law & Society* 569, 571; A Morris, '"Common Sense Common Safety": the Compensation Culture Perspective' [2011] *Journal of Professional Negligence* 82, 84–85 [Morris 2011].

[431] Hand ibid 571, 573.

[432] Taskforce (n 130) 3, 5–6.

[433] See ibid 3, 16–17; Department for Constitutional Affairs, *Effects of Advertising in Respect of Compensation Claims for Personal Injuries* (2006); W Haltom and M McCann, *Distorting the Law: Politics, Media, and the Litigation Crisis* (Chicago, 2004).

[434] Text to nn 197ff above.

[435] See, eg, Young (n 130) 22–23. See also the fast-track scheme for low-value personal injury claims arising from road accidents: above n 421.

[436] See, eg, Young (n 130) 20–21; Compensation Culture (n 130) 23–26; Compensation Act 2006, Pt 2 (regulating claims management companies); LASPO, ss 56–60 (regulating referral fees for legal services); Criminal Justice and Courts Act 2015, ss 58–61 (regulating inducements to litigate).

[437] Faculty and Institute of Actuaries, *Report of the Third Party Working Party (Short Version)* (2014) (www.actuaries.org.uk/sites/all/files/documents/pdf/short-version-2014-report-third-party-motor-claims.pdf).

Courts lack capacity to predict reliably whether denial or reduction of damages in any one case would make any difference to individuals' propensity to litigate or claim in future. As Lord Hoffmann acknowledged in response to arguments that imposing liability would lead to an '"unacceptable" increase in claims': '[t]hese are questions on which it is difficult to offer any concrete evidence and I am simply not in a position to form a view one way or the other'.[438] Indeed, there is an air of unreality in contentions that denial or reduction of awards in human rights law would slow development of a compensation culture (if one is developing), given how ever many human rights claims were made the number would be dwarfed by the number made in other established fields, particularly personal injury.

More generally, it is questionable whether courts should attempt to discern whether a compensation culture is developing or exists, and restrict damages on this basis. Notwithstanding definitional and empirical difficulties, whether one considers such culture to exist depends on subjective 'individual *political* views on risk, responsibility, resource allocation and so on'.[439]

Much empirical research on compensation culture focuses on trends in the propensity to claim. In general these studies find a significant gap between the perception of spiralling claims and reality. Claim rates (the number who *do* claim relative to the number who suffer actionable injury and *could* claim) 'remain low for most injuries',[440] while volume of claims across significant areas of personal injury liability have in recent times either stabilised or decreased[441] (albeit one field—road traffic accidents—had emerged as a problem area, but recent reforms have reduced claims).[442] Studies specifically focussed on claims against government have reached similar conclusions.[443] The overall conclusion, based in empirical evidence, is that 'it is difficult to support complaints that tort in recent years has become a burden as a result of increasing numbers of claims'.[444]

[438] *White v Chief Constable South Yorkshire Police* [1999] 2 AC 455, 510.

[439] Morris 2011 (n 430) 85 (emphasis added); Morris 2007 (n 423) 377–78.

[440] Lewis and Morris (n 255) 586.

[441] See Hand (n 430); R Lewis et al, 'Tort Personal Injury Claims Statistics: Is There a Compensation Culture in the United Kingdom?' (2006) 14 *Torts Law Journal* 158; Morris 2007 (n 423); Lewis and Morris (n 255) 579ff.

[442] On trends in claiming for traffic accidents see the report at n 437 above.

[443] Halliday et al 2011 (n 252) 536–37. See also the following studies which have found a similar gap between perception and reality in US constitutional tort litigation: T Eisenberg and SJ Schwab, 'The Reality of Constitutional Tort Litigation' (1987) 72 *Cornell Law Review* 641; T Eisenberg and SJ Schwab, 'Explaining Constitutional Tort Litigation' (1988) 73 *Cornell Law Review* 719; T Eisenberg, 'Section 1983: Doctrinal Foundations and an Empirical Study' (1982) 67 *Cornell Law Review* 482, 522ff; YS Lee, 'Civil Liability of State and Local Governments: Myth and Reality' (1987) 47 *Public Administration Review* 160.

[444] Lewis and Morris (n 255) 583. See the official statistics: *Compensation Recovery Unit Statistics* (2015) (available at www.gov.uk/government/uploads/system/uploads/attachment_data/file/424356/cases-registered-cru-2014-15.csv/preview).

In respect of *litigation* specifically, empirical studies show that assertions of 'litigation explosion' have no basis in reality *whatsoever*. Rather the concern is the inverse: a concern over the 'vanishing trial', that is, there is *not enough* court litigation.[445] The number of civil trials in England is at historic lows and in long-term decline, though that process may now be 'bottoming out' (while volume of criminal trials[446] has, over a long period, remained relatively stable).[447] In addition, Government predicts that implementation of the recent Jackson reforms is likely to result in further 'net reduction in demand for legal services'.[448] It has been suggested that only one per cent of tort claims go to court, while hardly any decisions are appealed.[449] This trend is consonant with other research finding most compensation claims settle, and where the defendant is insured (very often), claimants often accept the insurer's first offer;[450] '[w]hen faced with a justiciable event most people simply want to solve the problem'.[451] As we saw above, there are similar trends in judicial review. More generally, total costs associated with the UK tort system compare favourably with other countries.[452]

Thus, as the Better Regulation Taskforce concluded in its study of compensation culture, it is not the existence of such culture but the perception of one which is problematic, and it is that perception which must be addressed.[453] For example, the inaccurate *perception* that compensation is readily recoverable may encourage spurious claims, while the *perception* that one may be sued for innocuous mistakes may chill beneficial conduct. There are more effective and nuanced ways of addressing these problems than limiting redress for genuine claims of violation of basic rights, such as tighter regulation of advertising and professional standards, and education, while government and judges should take a lead by themselves avoiding sensationalism and claims unsupported by evidence.

[445] M Galanter, 'The Vanishing Trial' (2004) 1 *Journal of Empirical Legal Studies* 459.

[446] See HM Kritzer, 'Disappearing Trials? A Comparative Perspective' (2004) 1 *Journal of Empirical Legal Studies* 735.

[447] Ibid; R Dingwall and E Cloatre, 'Vanishing Trials: An English Perspective' [2006] *Journal of Dispute Resolution* 51.

[448] Ministry of Justice, *Overarching Jackson Proposals: Impact Assessment*, MOJ 044 (2010).

[449] Lewis and Morris (n 255) 570.

[450] ibid 569–71; Genn (n 221).

[451] Genn (n 221) 254.

[452] The figure (costs as a percentage of GDP) for the UK is 0.6%. Contrast Australia (1.1%), Germany (1.3%), Italy (1.7%) and the US (1.9%). Only Denmark, of the countries analysed, had a lower figure than the UK (0.4%): Tillinghurst—Towers Perrin, *US Tort Costs 2000. Trends and Findings on the Costs of the US Tort System* (2002) (cited in Taskforce (n 130) 15).

[453] Taskforce (n 130) ch 3.

F. Leaving the Political Branches to Respond: Is it Realistic?

This section's core argument has been that courts ought to adjudicate damages claims according to ordinary legal principle and not base decisions on public interest considerations which they lack constitutional legitimacy to determine and/or institutional competence to analyse rigorously;

> if principle inexorably requires a decision which entails a degree of policy risk, the court's function is to adjudicate according to principle ... If principle leads to results which are thought to be socially unacceptable, Parliament can legislate to draw a line or map out a new path.[454]

This is not to say that wider concerns are unimportant, but that such matters are primarily for the political branches.

A critic might respond that it is unrealistic to expect government to act given many political priorities rank ahead of issues raised by damages.[455] However, examples and case studies discussed herein show that the political branches have acted, and are quite willing to act. In any case, it would be difficult to criticise courts for awarding damages notwithstanding possible implications for government finances or administrative behaviour, if imposition of liability does not even cause government—which has direct interests in preservation of funds and vigorous administration—sufficient concern to act.

The Westminster Parliament has passed many statutes within the province of tort; 'legislation is a vital and inherent part of, and influence upon, the law of tort'.[456] For example, limitation periods have been imposed,[457] the legislature has intervened in negligence law,[458] including in response to judgments,[459] reformed defamation and related procedures,[460] while legislation governs contributory negligence,[461] and survival of actions following death.[462] Parliament has created actions,[463] abolished or circumscribed liabilities[464] and enacted statutory schemes to regulate fields of

[454] *McLoughlin v O'Brian* [1983] 1 AC 410, 430; *Airedale NHS Trust v Bland* [1993] AC 789, 880; *Cattanach v Melchior* (2003) 215 CLR 1, [137]; *Zurich* (n 231) per Lords Neuberger and Reed; Lord Hoffmann, 'Constitutionalism and Private Law' (Cambridge Freshfields Annual Lecture, 28 January 2015) (www.privatelaw.law.cam.ac.uk/Documents/freshfields-annual-law-lecture-2015-constitutionalism-and-private-law).

[455] eg Morgan (n 408) 219–20.

[456] TT Arvind and J Steele, 'Introduction: Legislation and the Shape of Tort Law' in TT Arvind and J Steele (eds), *Tort Law and the Legislature* (Hart Publishing, 2012) 1.

[457] Limitation Act 1980. The common law imposed no limitation period.

[458] Compensation Act 2006, Pt 1.

[459] ibid s 3, in response to: *Barker v Corus* [2006] 2 AC 572.

[460] Defamation Act 2013; Defamation Act 1996.

[461] Law Reform (Contributory Negligence) Act 1945.

[462] Law Reform (Miscellaneous Provisions) Act 1934; see also Fatal Accidents Act 1976.

[463] eg Consumer Protection Act 1987; Copyright, Designs and Patents Act 1988; Protection from Harassment Act 1997; Equality Act 2010.

[464] Enterprise and Regulatory Reform Act 2013, s 69.

liability.[465] Parliament has removed immunities,[466] relieved government of liability in response to judgments,[467] immunised certain acts from particular liabilities,[468] and immunised institutions, including public entities—but often with an exception specifically preserving HRA damages claims.[469]

The political branches have been similarly active in the sub-field of damages. Parliament has passed legislation governing deductions for welfare benefits,[470] abolishing particular heads of recoverable damage,[471] empowering courts to order periodical payments,[472] making tortfeasors liable to reimburse the NHS for funds expended on claimants' care,[473] and altering availability of punitive damages on public policy grounds.[474] We should also recall those reforms discussed above which alter the rules of the tort litigation game, such as changes in rules governing costs and procedure, as well as regulation of claims advertising, referral fees and claims management companies. Further, much of the Law Commission's time over the last 20 years was spent investigating sub-topics in the damages field, including damages claims against authorities.[475] In other jurisdictions, such as Australia[476] and New Zealand,[477] tort and damages reforms have been far more extensive.

The political branches are thus active players in setting the rules of tort law, the limits of liability and the law of damages, consider the implications of liability in establishing public bodies, including providing for immunities, and actively monitor[478] the implications of significant liability judgments, demonstrating capacity and willingness to respond.

[465] Occupiers' Liability Act 1957; Occupiers' Liability Act 1984; Animals Act 1971.

[466] Crown Proceedings Act 1947, s 2.

[467] A classic example is the War Damage Act 1965, in response to: *Burmah Oil v Lord Advocate* [1965] AC 75.

[468] Civil Aviation Act 1982, s 76; Planning Act 2008, s 158; Companies Act 2006, s 956.

[469] eg Financial Services and Markets Act 2000, Sch 1, para 19 (HRA exception: Sch 1, para 19(3)(b); Companies Act 2006, s 961 (HRA exception: s 961(3)(b)).

[470] Social Security (Recovery of Benefits) Act 1997.

[471] Administration of Justice Act 1982, s 1.

[472] Damages Act 1996.

[473] Health and Social Care (Community Health and Standards) Act 2003, Pt 3.

[474] Crime and Courts Act 2013, ss 34–38.

[475] eg *Structured Settlements and Interim and Provisional Damages*, Law Com 224 (1994); *Personal Injury Compensation: How Much Is Enough: A Study of the Compensation Experiences of Victims of Personal Injury*, Law Com 225 (1994); *Damages for Personal Injury: Non-Pecuniary Loss*, Law Com 257 (1999) [Personal Injury Report]; *Damages for Personal Injury: Medical, Nursing and Other Expenses; Collateral Benefits*, Law Com 262 (1999); *Aggravated, Exemplary and Restitutionary Damages*, Law Com 247 (1997); Law Commissions Report (n 19); Administrative Redress Report (n 109).

[476] See the case studies below in this section.

[477] Royal Commission to Inquire into and Report upon Workers' Compensation, *Compensation for Personal Injury in New Zealand* (1967); Accident Compensation Act 2001.

[478] For example, in response to recent litigation in tort and human rights law in respect of military operations both the Commons Defence Committee and Ministry of Defence have been considering various options including introduction of statutory immunities: *UK Armed Forces Personnel and the Legal Framework for Future Operations: Government Response to*

In public law Harlow and Rawlings document numerous instances of government and Parliament 'striking back'—removing or minimising a judgment's effects—or 'clamping down'—taking steps to protect governmental or public interests by changing the rules of the game so as to blunt legal action, such as procedural or structural reforms.[479] Various methods have been employed including statutory reversal, legislative direction, immunities, retaking impugned decisions the same way, ouster clauses, removal of judicial competence over specific matters, strict limitation periods, ramping up court fees and winding back legal aid, curtailment of appeal-rights, limiting claimant costs-protections, restricting remedies, disobedience, and particularly in the supranational context, retaliation and threats. Further, government is perfectly capable of developing and coordinating litigation strategies which make litigation work in its interests. Thus, striking back and clamping down are significant features of the working constitution. Importantly, as Harlow and Rawlings stress, striking back or clamping down is not always achieved through high-visibility means such as legislation but, for example, through informal administrative techniques out of the public eye, some such tactics verging on the underhand. Thus, the judiciary need not take it upon itself to safeguard governmental pecuniary or administrative interests, and thereby undermine their own constitutional legitimacy. Put simply, government is not helpless; far from it, government occupies the privileged position of a defendant that can alter the rules of the game in its interests. Nor is government apathetic; it is perfectly willing to safeguard its and the public's interests, and it suffers no shortage of techniques. To think otherwise is simply naïve.

i. Case Studies

Let us move from the general to more specific examples. The following case studies, drawn from Australia, New Zealand and the UK, illustrate starkly governmental capacity and willingness to respond to judgments establishing public authority liability, including specifically in the context of human rights damages and prisoner claims.

In the wake of a perceived insurance crisis in Australia in the early 2000s almost all States passed large-scale tort reform.[480] These Civil Liability Acts [CLA] largely addressed negligence, restricting liability and

the Defence Committee's Twelfth Report of Session 2013–14, HC 548 (2014), especially 1, 9; *UK Armed Forces Personnel and the Legal Framework for Future Operations*, HC 931 (2013), especially 35–38.

[479] C Harlow and R Rawlings, '"Striking Back" and "Clamping Down": An Alternative Perspective on Judicial Review' in Bell et al (n 359).

[480] A special Panel of Eminent Persons was constituted to examine reform: *Review of the Law of Negligence: Final Report* (2002); for an overview of the reforms see Spigelman (n 132); see also, P Cane, 'Reforming Tort Law in Australia: A Personal Perspective' (2003) 27 *Melbourne University Law Review* 649.

quantum.[481] The Acts clamped down on public authority liability. For example, provisions enumerate relevant factors for courts in determining whether authorities owe duties of care and/or breach,[482] including that authorities have limited resources, and restrict negligence liability of authorities for failing to, or failing to consider whether to exercise a power.[483] In a paradigm example of strike-back New South Wales (NSW) added a further provision, in direct response to the NSW Supreme Court decision in *Presland*,[484] which held the health service liable for loss caused by failure to detain the claimant under mental health legislation. The amendment provides that an authority's exercise of or failure to exercise a 'special statutory power' can only generate negligence liability if *Wednesbury* unreasonable, affording authorities significant protection.

Awards to prisoners in particular have caught the attention of politicians. Following a 'media frenzy' over prisoner pay-outs the NSW legislature inserted Part 2A into its CLA.[485] This Part applies to damages for personal injury or death suffered by prisoners, as a result of the negligence of 'protected defendants', or any tort (whether negligence or otherwise) of a person for whose tort the 'protected defendant' is vicariously liable. Protected defendants include officials, government departments and the Crown.[486] Under this Part prisoners may only recover for death or if physical injury results in 'a degree of permanent impairment of … at least 15%'.[487] Quantum is subject to restrictions, while more recent reforms bar exemplary and aggravated awards against vicariously liable protected defendants.[488]

In 2005 NSW passed further reforms[489] following a newspaper campaign concerning victims' rights which focused on a child sex offender who recovered damages for injuries suffered in prison.[490] Any damages for personal injury awarded to a prisoner are paid into a victim trust fund. The prisoner's past victims may then claim against this fund in respect of losses caused by the prisoner's wrongdoing.[491]

[481] eg Civil Liability Act 2002 (NSW) [CLA].
[482] CLA, s 42.
[483] CLA, ss 44, 45.
[484] *Presland v Hunter Area Health Service* [2003] NSWSC 754 (later overturned: (2005) 63 NSWLR 22); CLA, s 43A; GS Watson, 'Section 43A of the Civil Liability Act 2002 (NSW): Public Law Styled Immunity for the Negligence of Public and Other Authorities?' (2007) 15 *Torts Law Journal* 153.
[485] Civil Liability (Offender Damages) Act 2004 (NSW); GS Watson, 'Civil Claims and Civil Death: "Offender Damages" and the Civil Liability Act 2002 (NSW)' (2008) 16 *Torts Law Journal* 81, 90–91, 95–96.
[486] CLA, ss 26A, 26B.
[487] CLA, s 26C–26D.
[488] See CLA, s 26X, and see: CLA, s 21.
[489] Civil Liability (Offender Damages Trust Fund) Act 2005 (NSW); CLA, Pt 2A, Div 6.
[490] Watson (n 485) 98–99.
[491] The prisoner need not have been convicted of an offence against the victim: it is sufficient that the prisoner caused the victim personal injury through conduct which, on the balance of probabilities, constitutes an offence: CLA, s 26K.

In New Zealand a similar series of events took place in response to the High Court decision in *Taunoa*,[492] in which prisoners, whose human rights were violated due to poor prison conditions, were awarded New Zealand Bill of Rights Act 1990 (NZBORA) damages. Following a media outcry and in direct response Parliament passed the Prisoners' and Victims' Claims Act 2005 [PVCA]. The original Act included sunset clauses[493] (extended a number of times) as it was only intended to deal with the follow-on claims to *Taunoa*. However, the Act was considered such a good thing it was made permanent.[494] The Act provides that awards to prisoners for human rights violations (or breaches of other specified rights, but not common law rights) be paid, via the Justice Secretary, into a victim trust account.[495] Victims may then make claims. The Act also restricts the courts' power to award prisoners human rights damages; for example damages may be denied if the claimant has not made 'reasonable use' of other complaint mechanisms.[496] The Act enumerates general considerations to guide courts in making awards and quantum.[497] These include the importance of deterring violations, steps taken in mitigation by either party, importance of the right, claimant conduct and the nature of the violation.

Human rights awards to prisoners have also prompted legislative reform in the UK. In *Napier v Scottish Ministers*[498] Lord Bonomy held that the conditions in which Napier was imprisoned at HMP Barlinnie, Glasgow, breached Article 3. The aspect of prison life which tipped the scales in favour of a violation was the practice of 'slopping out'. The Court awarded £2,450 for distress, psychological symptoms and resurgence of the prisoner's eczema caused by stress induced by prison conditions. Many other prisoners were subject to similar conditions, and a raft of claims followed. The Scottish Justice Secretary reported that, as of 5 March 2009, 3,737 cases had been settled at a total cost of £11.2 million, a further 1,223 cases were being processed, approximately 200 new claims were being raised per month, and the Scottish Prison Service had set aside £66.7 million to cover its liabilities, and established an administrative scheme to process claims.[499] The Scottish Executive considered it was 'faced with a continuing and substantial liability that shows no sign of abating' and resolved that too much public

[492] *Taunoa v Attorney-General* (2004) 7 HRNZ 379 (liability); (2004) 8 HRNZ 53 (damages).

[493] Prisoners' and Victims' Claims Act 2005 (NZ), ss 16, 17 [PVCA] (these sections subsequently repealed or amended).

[494] Prisoners' and Victims' Claims (Continuation and Reform) Amendment Act 2013 (NZ).

[495] PVCA, ss 17–18.

[496] PVCA, s 13.

[497] PVCA, s 14.

[498] [2005] 1 SC 229 (affirmed: [2005] 1 SC 307).

[499] Scot Parl Deb cols 15604–05 (11 March 2009) Mr Kenny MacAskill; see also *Scottish Prison Service Annual Report and Accounts 2009–2010*, SG/2010/108 (2010) 48–49 [SPS Report 09–10].

money, which could have been spent otherwise, had gone to prisoners.[500] To 'draw a line'[501] under the Government's liability the Scottish Parliament passed legislation[502]—since superseded by Westminster legislation to identical effect[503]—introducing a one year time limit for human rights claims in Scotland, the Law Lords in *Somerville*[504] having previously held that the time limit under the HRA did not apply in Scotland.[505] It was estimated that the reform could save up to £50 million.[506] The numbers of claims settled and still outstanding have fallen drastically year-on-year since.[507] A very large proportion (nearly 80 per cent) of those funds initially set aside to meet potential liabilities were released following enactment of the time limit.[508]

Thus, the political branches have demonstrated willingness to reform tort and damages, and to strike back in response to specific judgments, including in the field of human rights damages. Regardless of whether one considers specific reforms justifiable, the legislature has the legitimacy to make broad value-judgements on behalf of the community concerning contentious moral, economic and political issues such as whether a prisoner's past wrongdoing should disqualify them from relief, or how resources should be allocated between remedying wrongs and funding services.

The Scottish example clearly demonstrates government's institutional advantages: government can observe the effects of a judgment ex post and over time, with access to relevant information such as estimates of aggregate financial burden likely to result from liability. On top of this, government possesses power and resources to commission reviews of difficult issues by, for example, ad hoc working groups, such as the Ipp Panel,[509] which investigated tort reform in Australia. The political branches can tailor solutions to specific public interest concerns. They have capacity to institute systemic reforms, such as the Australian tort reforms, procedural reforms, such as the Scottish Parliament's introduction of a time limit for HRA claims, and devise elaborate schemes, such as those under victim and prisoner legislation.

[500] Scot Parl Deb cols 15604–07 (11 March 2009) Mr Kenny MacAskill.

[501] Scot Parl Deb col 15606 (11 March 2009) Mr Kenny MacAskill.

[502] Convention Rights Proceedings (Amendment) (Scotland) Act 2009 (repealed). The UK Government had to secure an amendment to the Scotland Act to empower the Scottish Parliament to pass legislation amending the same Act: Scotland Act 1998 (Modification of Schedule 4) Order SI 2009 No 1380 (repealed).

[503] Scotland Act 2012, s 14; Scotland Act 1998, s 100(3A)–(3E).

[504] *Somerville v Scottish Ministers* [2007] 1 WLR 2734.

[505] It had been thought that the Prescription and Limitation (Scotland) Act 1973, s 6 (which imposes a five year limitation period) might apply to HRA claims. However, *Docherty v Scottish Ministers* held otherwise: [2011] CSIH 58.

[506] Scot Parl Deb col 15606 (11 March 2009) Mr Kenny MacAskill.

[507] *Scottish Prison Service Annual Report and Accounts 2010–2011*, SG/2011/101 (2011) 12; *Scottish Prison Service Annual Report and Accounts 2011–2012*, SG/2012/103 (2012) 57; *Scottish Prison Service Annual Report and Accounts 2012–2013*, SG/2013/102 (2013) 60; *Scottish Prison Service Annual Report and Accounts 2013–2014*, SG/2014/8 (2014) 18.

[508] SPS Report 09–10 (n 499) 10.

[509] Above n 480.

A note of caution is required. While the reforms discussed herein have a degree of *formal* legitimacy, in that they were instituted by those branches with institutional and constitutional legitimacy to address difficult policy-political issues, it does not follow necessarily that the reforms are justifiable on their merits. For example, as discussed above, there are strong arguments against restricting remedies for prisoners, given the universality of human rights, Articles 5, 13 and 14, and the fundamental principle of equal application of law. Particular aspects of legislative reforms discussed here are especially objectionable. For example the prisoner compensation reforms in Australasia generally apply retrospectively, as does the NSW CLA[510] and the limitation period introduced in Scotland.[511]

Lastly, given the significance of the individual and public interests at stake it is important that where political branches respond to human rights judgments they announce their response publically, offer reasoned justification, take an evidence-based approach, and allow time for adequate and informed debate. If the executive does not utilise its relative institutional expertise and information and resources at its disposal, and/or MPs do not take seriously their representative law-making function, not only will bad decisions follow but the legitimacy of these institutions will be undermined.

Regrettably, the political branches have not always taken such a rigorous approach.

For example, the Scottish Parliament passed the legislation establishing the one-year limitation period via the Emergency Bill Procedure within one day, leaving little time for public or parliamentary scrutiny, while there was no impact assessment. While the PVCA took seven months to pass the New Zealand Parliament (including the summer recess) it was rushed through the Introduction stage[512] and its final stages[513] under urgency, while, remarkably, the Attorney-General did not issue a human rights report to Parliament—as required where provisions appear incompatible with the NZBORA.[514] The Bill making the PVCA permanent passed the Second Reading and Committee of the Whole House stage under urgency,[515] while the Select Committee report on the Bill was pitiful,[516] and completely

[510] CLA, s 2 (the Act was passed in June 2002 but provides that it should be taken to have commenced in March 2002).

[511] Convention Rights Proceedings (Amendment) (Scotland) Act 2009, s 1 (repealed); Scotland Act 2012, s 14(5), (8).

[512] NZ Parl Deb vol 622 page 17685 (14 December 2004) Hon Dr Michael Cullen.

[513] NZ Parl Deb vol 626 page 20925 (1 June 2005) Hon Dr Michael Cullen.

[514] NZBORA, s 7. The failure to so report was subsequently criticised by a later Attorney-General: *Attorney-General's Report on the Prisoners' and Victims' Claims (Redirecting Prisoner Compensation) Amendment Bill* (2011) [4]–[5] (available at: www.parliament.nz/resource/en-nz/49DBHOH_PAP22229_1/64f0948fa4738d3a421c491fcc444fd2d4c201c2).

[515] NZ Parl Deb vol 689 page 9656 (08 May 2013) Hon Gerry Brownlee.

[516] *Report of the Justice and Electoral Committee on the Prisoners' and Victims' Claims (Continuation and Reform) Amendment Bill (92-1)* (2013).

ignored criticisms by international human rights bodies.[517] On the positive side other proposed reforms to prisoner compensation, which would have struck even more profoundly at effective redress, were reported by the Attorney-General as contrary to the NZBORA, and subsequently abandoned following a period of reflection and consultation.[518]

The NSW reforms concerning negligence liability of authorities and prisoner compensation were the product of the Government's desire to find a 'quick-fix' to concerted media campaigns, rather than reasoned deliberation. Indeed, the Government announcement that the law would be reformed following *Presland* was made only two days after the judgment, and the statutory reforms passed within three weeks;[519] ironically *Presland* was later overturned on appeal.[520] Unsurprisingly—legislate in haste, repent at leisure—the *Presland* reforms have proven problematic.[521] There has been much criticism of the Australian tort reforms in general, on the basis that they were reactionary and piecemeal, rushed, have gone too far in limiting liability, have set the law on an unprincipled basis, and that it was never proven that the insurance crisis, which prompted the tort crackdown, was in fact caused by the tort system.[522] This has led some to conclude that '[w]hat the Australian experience does clearly illustrate is the danger of sacrificing balance and principle when implementing law reform in a crisis'.[523] By contrast the English Law Commission's project on administrative redress, which investigated public authority liability, commenced with a discussion paper in 2004 and ended with a full report in 2010, allowing much time for discussion, deliberation, detailed analysis and reflection, and incorporated a full consultative process including publication of a scoping paper, consultation paper and paper responding to consultee responses, as well as a seminar series.[524] Albeit any prospect of reform was ultimately kyboshed by Government, such 'Rolls Royce' approach is illustrative of the sort of process apt for issues of such importance and complexity.

[517] eg UNCAT, *Concluding Observations: New Zealand*, CAT/C/NZL/CO/5 (2009) [14].

[518] Prisoners' and Victims' Claims (Redirecting Prisoner Compensation) Amendment Bill 2011 (Bill No 328-1) (NZ) (discharged); Attorney-General (n 514); NZ Parl Deb vol 686 page 7368 (1 December 2012) Hon Judith Collins.

[519] See Watson (n 484) 155–56.

[520] Above n 484.

[521] See, eg, the discussion in: *Curtis v Harden Shire Council* [2014] NSWCA 314; *Grant v Roads and Traffic Authority of NSW* [2014] NSWSC 379, [117]ff; *Sydney Water Corporation v Turano* [2009] HCA 42, [24]–[26]; M Aronson, 'Government Liability in Negligence' (2008) 32 *Melbourne University Law Review* 44.

[522] Administrative Redress Consultation Paper (n 155) [6.66]–[6.71]; H Luntz, 'The Australian Picture' (2004) 35 *Victoria University of Wellington Law Review* 879; B McDonald, 'The Impact of the Civil Liability Legislation on Fundamental Policies and Principles of the Common Law of Negligence' (2006) 14 *Torts Law Journal* 268; P Underwood, 'Is Ms Donoghue's Snail in Mortal Peril?' (2004) 12 *Torts Law Journal* 1; K Burns, 'Distorting the Law: Politics, Media and the Litigation Crisis: An Australian Perspective' (2007) 15 *Torts Law Journal* 195.

[523] Administrative Redress Consultation Paper (n 155) [6.71].

[524] All material available at: 'Administrative Redress: Public Bodies and the Citizen' at www.justice.gov.uk/lawcommission/administrative-redress.htm.

VI. RULE-OF-LAW AND OTHER CONCERNS RAISED BY THE DISCRETIONARY NATURE OF THE INTEREST-BALANCING APPROACH

A significant drawback of interest-balancing approaches generally is that their operation will likely undermine rule-of-law principles, specifically legal certainty and consistency.[525] Such concerns are exacerbated in the human rights damages context as judges have adopted an unstructured approach to balancing with no set starting-point, and emphasised the power to award damages entails 'wide',[526] 'broad'[527] or 'very wide'[528] discretion.

The interest-balancing approach produces significant uncertainty. Ex ante it will be difficult to predict what factors a judge will consider relevant, what weight she will apportion factors, and how she will go about striking the balance. That many factors considered under the HRA are highly subjective only exacerbates this uncertainty.

Furthermore, the law may not become more certain over time. The reason is that the aim of discretionary balancing approaches is to strike a balance and do justice *on the facts of the case*, and no two cases are identical. Such approaches are 'not intended to settle down', but are 'kept fresh for the next exercise'.[529] As Millett LJ has observed of judicial discretions,

> [r]eported cases are merely illustrations of circumstances in which particular judges have exercised their discretion ... Since they are all cases on the exercise of a discretion, none of them is a binding authority on how the discretion should be exercised. The most that any of them can demonstrate is that in similar circumstances it would not be wrong to exercise the discretion in the same way. But it does not follow that it would be wrong to exercise it differently.[530]

Uncertainty is not only uncomfortable for those it affects, but also has wider ramifications. Legal uncertainty undermines lawyers' ability to meaningfully advise clients. In turn, this may further discourage deserving claimants from pursuing their claim. In terms of settlements, we know that the vast majority of tort claims—including against authorities[531]—are settled with the defendant's insurer, that a majority accept the insurer's first offer, and that '[d]elay, uncertainty, financial need, and other pressures cause claimants to accept sums much lower than a judge would award'.[532] The risks of

[525] Other principles such as government under law and equality have been discussed above: s 1.III.

[526] *Anufrijeva* (n 1) [56].

[527] *Dobson v Thames Valley Utilities Ltd* [2009] 3 All ER 319, [43].

[528] *Downing* (n 299) [12].

[529] P Birks, 'Three Kinds of Objection to Discretionary Remedialism' (2000) 29 *University of Western Australia Law Review* 1, 7, 13.

[530] *Jaggard v Sawyer* [1995] 1 WLR 269, 288.

[531] Halliday et al 2011 (n 252) 535; Halliday et al 2012 (n 424) 348.

[532] Lewis and Morris (n 255) 574.

unfairness can only be exacerbated by gross legal uncertainty as to remedies. In fields characterised by a reasonably high degree of remedial certainty, such as personal injury—damages are as of right and there is detailed guidance on quantum—claimants may feel confident negotiating or challenging inadequate insurer offers, as there are clear benchmarks against which to vet offers (and yet even in these conditions there is relatively little negotiation). In a field marked by gross remedial uncertainty—where damages and quantum are subject to wide discretion—it seems virtually certain that claimants will *systematically* end up 'lumping' insurer assessments, whatever the fairness of those assessments, because there are no firm benchmarks against which to scrutinise offers. Furthermore, there is the possibility that insurers or authorities, jealous of their pecuniary interests but also because of efficiencies associated with standardised systems of claims-adjudication,[533] will adopt a working assumption that no compensation or only token amounts should be paid, as it is far from clear a court would award damages under interest-balancing. Insurers would be encouraged in this by there being little chance of claimants challenging assessments: there are multifarious barriers to litigation (cost, time etc), these being exacerbated by great difficulties in gauging the likelihood of victory, given the outcome depends on open-ended judicial discretion. Of course, uncertainty may also inconvenience government; for example it may undermine officials' ability to reliably assess liability risks associated with policy options.

The interest-balancing approach is liable to produce inconsistency. As has been observed of remedial discretion within common law review, which inspired the approach in *Anufrijeva*,[534] different judges consider different factors and apportion different weight to factors, even on similar facts.[535] Such variations mean that recovery may depend on the judge one is allocated; we saw in chapter 5 that there are signs of such inconsistency in the HRA damages jurisprudence.[536] Not only does this undermine equality before the law, but it may diminish faith in the courts in a field in which they play an important constitutional role.[537] One might hypothesise that such inconsistencies would be weeded out eventually. But experience suggests that this is unlikely. Consider the judicial discretion whether to grant a review applicant permission to proceed to full hearing. In common with

[533] Halliday et al 2012 (n 424) 365–67.

[534] See ch 4.2.I–III.

[535] eg J McLean, 'Roadblocks, Restraint, and Remedies: The Idea of Progress in Administrative Law' in G Huscroft and M Taggart (eds), *Inside and Outside Canadian Administrative Law* (Toronto, 2006) 233; Harlow and Rawlings (n 209) 724; *cf* D Feldman, 'Error of Law and Flawed Administrative Acts' (2014) 73 *CLJ* 275.

[536] ch 5.2.II.C.ii.

[537] Even if a balancing approach does, no matter how unlikely, abide the principle of equal treatment, it may be difficult to maintain the *appearance* of equality: A Scalia, 'The Rule of Law as a Law of Rules' (1989) 56 *University of Chicago Law Review* 1175, 1178.

the *Anufrijeva* interest-balancing test, this entails weighing a number of factors,[538] and is imbued with 'public interest' concerns.[539] Inconsistency has been a 'running sore'.[540] Three significant studies of this discretion between 1992 and 2008 all concluded that uncertainty and inconsistency are serious concerns; the rate at which different judges granted permission varied significantly.[541]

There are further significant concerns raised by discretion. Wide discretions afford greater room for decision-making based in personal preference, given they afford scope for choice[542] or 'decisional manoeuvre'.[543] There is an acute risk of this where individual factors implicate morality and ordinary politics. Linked to this, discretion may free judges 'from the shackles of traditional legal rationality'.[544] For example, some suggest rightly that the sorry state of the Article 41 jurisprudence follows from the ECtHR's discretionary approach,[545] while irrationality and incoherence characterise domestic damages jurisprudence which follows the ECtHR's approach.[546] Tellingly adoption of a wide discretionary approach in *Anufrijeva* was coupled with guidance that a 'broad-brush approach' should be taken to assessment, without close examination of facts or authorities.[547]

The trend in other fields is away from open-ended discretion, towards structured discretion or rules; in some instances this has been driven by supranational courts finding broad discretions incompatible with rule-of-law requirements.[548] The trend is observable in fields a defining characteristic of which has been broad discretion, such as criminal sentencing[549] and equity.[550] There have even been recent attempts to bridle remedial discretion in common law review, a field with a 'discretionary heart'.[551] In recent

538 M Sunkin and A Le Sueur, 'Applications for Judicial Review: the Requirement of Leave' [1992] *PL* 102, 119–25.

539 ibid 104–07; Harlow and Rawlings (n 209) 671.

540 Harlow and Rawlings (n 209) 693.

541 See Sunkin and Le Sueur (n 538); L Bridges et al, *Judicial Review in Perspective* 2nd edn (Cavendish, 1995) chs 7–8; V Bondy and M Sunkin, 'Accessing Judicial Review' [2008] *PL* 647.

542 *SOS for Education and Science v Tameside MBC* [1977] AC 1014, 1064.

543 J Jowell, 'The Legal Control of Administrative Discretion' [1973] *PL* 178, 179–80.

544 Birks (n 529) 17.

545 *Dobson* (n 527) [43]; ch 5.2.II.A.

546 ch 5.2.II.C.

547 (n 1) [81].

548 *European Commission v UK* [2014] 3 WLR 853; *Uniplex (UK) Ltd v NHS Business Services Authority* [2010] 2 CMLR 47.

549 T Bingham, *The Rule of Law* (Allen Lane, 2010) 51–54. See the detailed sentencing guidelines published by the Sentencing Council (www.sentencingcouncil.org.uk).

550 While equitable remedies are formally discretionary, the discretions are generally weak, structured and ruled-based; for example, we may readily predict when specific performance will or will not be granted, or when an injunction to restrain a continuing trespass or nuisance will or will not issue or damages will be awarded in lieu.

551 Lord Cooke, 'The Discretionary Heart of Administrative Law' in CF Forsyth and I Hare (eds), *The Golden Metwand and the Crooked Cord* (OUP, 1998).

times the Law Lords have held that the discretion to refuse relief is 'very narrow'[552] and 'exceptional'.[553] Albeit, it is not difficult to locate cases in which relief is denied, and there are signs of retreat from these statements.[554] Nonetheless, that courts have sought to narrow and structure discretion is significant in itself given the discretion has been an important tool for protecting effective administration, existence of wide discretion being consonant with the traditional public interest ethos of English administrative law.[555] If we find retreat from wide remedial discretion even in fields with a discretionary heart and a primary concern for public interests, it is difficult to rationalise wholesale endorsement of very wide remedial discretion in human rights law.

In any case, there may be specific reasons why discretion is justified for some remedies but not others. Prohibitory or mandatory orders or injunctions are more intrusive than damages awards, in the sense of 'how much freedom the addressee ... has in deciding how to react to the remedy'.[556] Because such orders can seriously limit freedom of action into the future, and raise separation of powers concerns—as they entail courts prescribing how administrative powers should be exercised—one can more easily see the case for discretion.

So far the discussion's focus has been the decision to award damages. However, Lord Woolf in *Anufrijeva* also held that a balance had to be struck between interests in assessing *quantum*,[557] while courts in other jurisdictions similarly consider that factors unconnected to loss—such as deterrence, good governance and financial concerns—should be taken into account in setting quantum.[558] Thus, different claimants who suffer identical losses may receive different awards depending on the balance of interests in their case; from a claimant's perspective this is something of a lottery. Making quantum dependant on balancing also makes it incredibly difficult, if not impossible, to formulate guidelines or tariffs according to particular types of violations and/or harms. The absence of guidelines would almost certainly lead to inconsistency and unpredictability. This is especially problematic in the damages context, as it is generally accepted that for damages for non-pecuniary loss to be legitimate awards must be consistent, particularly given lack of an objective basis for assessment.[559] This is why concerted efforts

[552] *Berkeley v SOS for the Environment, Transport and the Regions (No 1)* [2001] 2 AC 603, 608.

[553] ibid 616.

[554] eg *R (Edwards) v Environment Agency (No 2)* [2008] 1 WLR 1587, [63]–[65]; *Walton* (n 84) [103], [130]–[131]; *R (Moseley) v Haringey LBC* [2014] 1 WLR 3947, [33].

[555] H Woolf, 'Droit Public—English Style' [1995] *PL* 57, 60–61; see further ch 4.2.I.

[556] Cane (n 279) 493.

[557] See also *DSD* (n 320) [40] [125]–[127], [138].

[558] eg *Taunoa* (n 6) [258], [318]–[319]; *Ward* (n 6) [53].

[559] *Damages for Personal Injury: Non-Pecuniary Loss*, Law Com Consultation Paper 140 (1995) [2.21]; *Wright v British Railways Board* [1983] 2 AC 773, 777.

have been made in tort to ensure consistent awards, including phasing out jury assessment and introduction of tariff-style guidance. Welcoming such developments Lord Woolf, speaking of tort damages for personal injury, emphasised:

> Consistency is important, because it assists in achieving justice between one claimant and another and one defendant and another. It also assists to achieve justice by facilitating settlements. The courts have become increasingly aware that this is in the interests of the litigants and society as a whole, particularly in the personal injury field.[560]

Is consistency any less important in human rights law?

VII. REFINING THE INTEREST-BALANCING APPROACH

If, despite arguments made above, an interest-balancing approach were adopted, the approach propounded in *Anufrijeva* requires refinement. In particular, the idea of striking a balance between individual and public interests entails a false dichotomy. Further, English courts have not directly addressed the weight to be accorded to particular interests in the balancing calculus, particularly the interest in vindicating the right, nor has balancing been disciplined by a set starting-point or structure.

A. Individual versus Public: Avoiding a False Dichotomy

In *Anufrijeva* the Court said that in deciding whether to award damages, and how much, 'there is a balance to be drawn between the interests of the victim and those of the public as a whole'.[561] Such dichotomy is problematic in that it suggests that the victim's interests and those of the public invariably pull in opposite directions, that is, individual interests are balanced *against* public interests. Reinforcing this, the Court only considered public interests that told against awards or for reduced awards. Such approach excludes the possibility that vindicating rights not only serves claimant interests, but that there is also a '*public interest* in effective remedy for breach of rights'.[562]

First, at a general level one reason why we afford strong protection to fundamental individual interests is because this promotes wider interests.[563] For example, protection of property facilitates commercial interaction. Without protection of free expression and public protest true democracy is impossible. Without protecting privacy, beneficial social interaction may be

[560] *Heil* (n 235) 294.
[561] (n 1) [56].
[562] *Chapman* (n 25) [56] (emphasis added).
[563] For discussion see, eg, J Raz, *Ethics in the Public Domain* (Clarendon, 1994) ch 3.

stymied.[564] Certain rights, such as freedoms of religion and assembly, have a group element in that they enable people to come together in community to practice their faith, protest or exchange ideas. If we do not make explicit the wider benefits served by protecting fundamental rights, it seems inevitable that the interest in protecting and vindicating rights will be undervalued. Further, we should not forget that remedies uphold a distribution of entitlements that Parliament has sanctioned as lying in the common good, and vindicate rights that Parliament has designated as fundamental to British society.

Second, the damages remedy in particular can serve discrete public interests.

Most obviously damages may deter unlawful conduct in a way that non-monetary relief may not;[565] notably, empirical research into the administrative impact of HRA challenges against authorities resulting in traditional relief or miserly damages finds some beneficial impacts, but in general impact is limited.[566] Damages operate as a sanction for breach, making non-compliance costly, and dissuading the defendant from committing similar wrongs again. Making awards also signals to other potential defendants that violations will sound in damages. The prospect of incurring other costs on top of damages may enhance deterrence effects. For example, the Audit Commission has emphasised that authorities should take human rights responsibilities seriously because of the potential financial burden of having to defend legal claims, pay damages awards, deal with copycat claims and rewrite policy guidance in response to judgments, while successful actions may result in negative media reporting leading to poor public perception of authorities and low staff morale.[567] Reputational costs associated with sizeable damages awards in particular have been shown to significantly affect authorities' incentives structures.[568]

Damages awards may not only cause authorities to cease rights-violating conduct. Awards may spur authorities to take *positive steps* to implement systematically their human rights obligations. As we saw above, Epp's important study of the impact of damages claims on public administration in America documented how damages claims, which caught media headlines, placed sustained pressure on administrators to change bureaucratic practices so as to safeguard their public and professional legitimacy, culminating in introduction of positive organisational measures designed to internalise

[564] D Feldman, 'Privacy-related Rights and their Social Value' in P Birks (ed), *Privacy and Loyalty* (Clarendon, 1997).

[565] The potential for damages to deter has been emphasised by lawyer-economists in particular: see, eg, Schuck (n 144); G Calabresi, *The Costs of Accidents* (Yale, 1970); S Shavell, *Economic Analysis of Accident Law* (Harvard, 1987).

[566] EHRC Evaluating Impact (n 361).

[567] Audit Commission (n 388) 4.

[568] Epp (n 360).

legal norms, such as written rules, training, and oversight mechanisms.[569] Epp investigated one British case study: the rise of tort litigation against police from the 1980s.[570] This study reached similar conclusions. Increased damages litigation in respect of discriminatory and abusive police practices, which garnered significant media attention and caused police persistent embarrassment, drove significant national policy reforms. However, fidelity to legal norms was not absorbed into police practice to the same extent as it was within American police forces. Epp argues that a key reason for this was that the English Court of Appeal, in 1997, acceded to the Metropolitan Police's request that damages be restricted. Lord Woolf, for the Court, ruled that exemplary damages should be capped, and reduced the scale of compensatory damages below what London juries had been awarding.[571] Because it is generally large awards that garner media attention the result was that '[a]lthough isolated cases still draw attention in the media, the wave of media coverage associated with the litigation campaign declined along with damage awards'.[572] In turn pressure for reform dissipated.

Thus deterrence of unlawful conduct and driving positive administrative reform are important wider benefits which may be lost if awards are denied or miserly. If awards had these effects within the human rights field then this would be no bad thing given there is significant variation in the seriousness with which authorities have engaged with their human rights responsibilities.[573]

Damages awards may serve 'fire alarm' functions.[574] The administrative state is vast and it can be difficult for Parliament and its committees, as well as central government, to detect administrative policies which violate legislative goals encapsulated in the HRA. Damages actions and awards, while a 'blunt and imperfect tool',[575] can pinpoint areas of the administration where something has gone seriously awry. Damages claims may thus facilitate political consciousness of and accountability for wrongdoing; for example damages may spur mobilisation of political forces and pressure from the centre, and instigation of external monitoring mechanisms, to ensure wrongdoing is not repeated.[576] Indeed courts have used the occasion

[569] ibid.
[570] ibid ch 7.
[571] *Thompson* (n 235).
[572] Epp (n 360) 156–57.
[573] See the material at nn 386–397 above. See also F Butler, *Improving Public Services: Using a Human Rights Approach* (IPPR, 2005).
[574] MD McCubbins and T Schwartz, 'Congressional Oversight Overlooked: Police Patrols versus Fire Alarms' (1984) 28 *American Journal of Political Science* 165.
[575] AM Linden, 'Tort Law as Ombudsman' (1973) 51 *Canadian Bar Review* 155, 168.
[576] On the use of liability to secure accountability, and the limits of tort in this respect see, eg, ibid; Harlow (n 124) 49–53. More generally, there are many examples of litigation being used to exert political pressure: C Harlow and R Rawlings, *Pressure Through Law* (Routledge, 1992).

of significant awards to highlight serious shortcomings in administrative process and call for urgent investigation by the political branches.[577]

The case studies discussed above provide concrete examples of the 'fire alarm' and compliance-control functions of damages actions. In the wake of the first instance decision in *Taunoa*, in which the New Zealand High Court awarded significant damages to prisoners for rights-violations caused by the draconian 'Behaviour Management Regime' operated at Auckland Prison, the Regime was disestablished. Although the Government sought, through legislative reforms, to narrow the circumstances in which prisoners could be awarded human rights damages, those reforms were coupled with a review and reform of prisoner complaints-procedures 'so that any breaches can be dealt with at the earliest opportunity'.[578] As a result of the damages actions, the review and other high profile incidents involving the Department of Corrections,[579] Government requested that the Ombudsman 'enhance their presence in the prison sector by directly investigating all deaths in custody and selected serious incidents', making extra resources available.[580]

Following *Napier* slopping out is 'a thing of the past' in Scotland.[581] This cannot be attributed solely to *Napier* and the follow-on claims. For example the Chief Inspector of Prisoners had, before *Napier*, consistently drawn attention to slopping out and prison conditions, counselling reform.[582] The Scottish Prison Service too had stated its commitment to ending slopping out 'as soon as practicable'.[583] However, the Chief Inspector, just before *Napier* was decided, while recording 'some progress' towards ending slopping out, concluded, '[n]evertheless, hundreds of prisoners are living in profoundly unsatisfactory conditions'.[584] Against this backdrop, *Napier* and its progeny served as a jolt—an exogenous shock—that provided impetus to finally and

[577] *Muuse* (n 239) [86]–[87].

[578] NZ Parl Deb vol 622 page 17986 (14 December 2004) Hon Phil Goff; Ministry of Justice, *Review of Prisoner Complaints Processes* (2005); 'Improvements to be Made in Prison Complaints System' www.beehive.govt.nz/node/22909; Corrections Act 2004 (NZ), Pt 2, Subpart 6.

[579] See 'Ombudsmen's Bigger Role in Prison Complaints' at www.stuff.co.nz/national/14035; 'Prison Ombudsman Major Victory for Greens and Justice' at www.scoop.co.nz/stories/PA0710/S00464.htm.

[580] *Agreement Between the Chief Executive of the Department of Corrections and the Chief Ombudsman* (2009) [6]. Most recent agreement available at www.ombudsman.parliament.nz/system/paperclip/document_files/document_files/367/original/corrections_protocol_2012.pdf?1347065662.

[581] *HM Chief Inspector of Prisons for Scotland Annual Report 2012–2013*, SG/2013/81 (2013) 19–20.

[582] eg *HM Chief Inspector of Prisons for Scotland Annual Report 2001–2002*, SE/2002/191 (2002) 8, 49–50; *HM Chief Inspector of Prisons for Scotland Annual Report 2002–2003*, SE/2003/287 (2003) 4 [Inspector 02–03].

[583] *Scottish Prison Service Annual Report and Accounts 2002–2003*, SE/2003/190 (2003) 8.

[584] Inspector 02–03 (n 582) 4.

swiftly eradicate slopping out. From April 2004[585]—when it was clear that the practice of slopping out was on borrowed time due to initiation of proceedings in *Napier* and other cases—to March 2005—several months after *Napier* was decided—the percentage of prisoners slopping out dropped significantly from 19 per cent to nine per cent.[586] In his 2006–2007 Report the Chief Inspector said: 'It has been a pleasure to report regularly in the last two or three years'—that is the years since *Napier*—that '"slopping out has ended" in prison after prison'.[587] In his 2007–2008 Report he observed that eradication of slopping out was an 'enormous improvement', 'over the last few years',[588] again showing *Napier* and the follow-on claims to have been the driver of swift change across prisons. Reinforcing that *Napier* and subsequent claims had a crucial role in this 'domino effect' was that the Prison Service's Annual Reports consistently explicitly linked the drive to improve facilities with *Napier* and subsequent claims,[589] while fresh measures to reduce the incidence of slopping out were announced immediately following *Napier*.[590] It is worth noting that imposition of damages liability led to mobilisation or strengthening of other accountability mechanisms, which reinforced that reform of estate facilities was a matter of urgency. For example the Chief Inspector placed weight on *Napier* to reinforce his calls for abolition of slopping out,[591] while the significant potential liabilities implicated by the judgment led the Scottish Auditor-General to issue special reports bringing those liabilities to Parliament's attention, again placing further pressure on the Prison Service to mitigate its liabilities by ending the unlawful practice.[592] Thus, while slopping out had been in slow decline over the 30 years preceding *Napier*,[593] it was *Napier* and the follow-on claims which precipitated its sudden and complete eradication.

[585] This date precedes the date of judgment in *Napier*, but the proceedings had already been heard at this point, so the Prison Service was aware that the practice was precarious: *Scottish Prison Service Annual Report and Accounts 2003–2004*, SE/2004/131 (2004) 17 [SPS Report 03–04].

[586] *HM Chief Inspector of Prisons for Scotland Annual Report 2004–2005*, SE/2005/17 (2005) 1.

[587] *HM Chief Inspector of Prisons for Scotland Annual Report 2006–2007*, SE/2007/183 (2007) 5.

[588] *HM Chief Inspector of Prisons for Scotland Annual Report 2007–2008*, SE/2008/162 (2008) 6 [Inspector 07–08].

[589] eg *Scottish Prison Service Annual Report and Accounts 2004–2005*, SE/2005/137 (2005) 54, 78 [SPS Report 04–05]; *Scottish Prison Service Annual Report and Accounts 2005–2006*, SE/2006/151 (2006) 34; *Scottish Prison Service Annual Report and Accounts 2006–2007*, SE/2007/99 (2007) 8; *Scottish Prison Service Annual Report and Accounts 2007–2008*, SG/2008/108 (2008) 9.

[590] *HM Chief Inspector of Prisons for Scotland Annual Report 2003–2004*, SE/2004/207 (2004) 6.

[591] ibid 2, 6–7.

[592] SPS Report 03–04 (n 585) 74–76; SPS Report 04–05 (n 589) 77–78.

[593] Inspector 07–08 (n 588) 6.

Damages may serve as a 'carrot' for victims to sue, the prospect of damages helping to overcome those very significant hurdles and disincentives to litigating. This is the very reason why the Jackson Report on costs recommended and the courts implemented a ten per cent increase in general damages across tort.[594] If claimants lack capacity or incentives to litigate where legal obligations are breached, this could undermine the integrity of the legal system and the rule of law, as legal obligations may be infringed with impunity and thus be rendered hollow. Another risk is that victims may routinely be forced to lump unfair settlements leading to systemic injustice. Furthermore, there are many public goods served by litigation in itself.[595] Such goods include that litigation allows citizens an opportunity for participation in the public sphere, and courts to resolve outstanding and important questions of human rights law, and thus give concrete meaning to broad values constitutive of society and set rules and precedents to guide behaviour.

Damages awards may promote principles of good administration, good public service lying in the interest of all.[596] Let us utilise the Parliamentary Ombudsman's *Principles of Good Administration* as criteria against which to assess this claim. Availability of damages can help to ensure authorities abide the administrative principle of acting 'in accordance with the law and with regard for the rights of those concerned',[597] by offering an inducement to individuals to enforce legal obligations against authorities, by incentivising compliance with legal obligations, and because awards symbolically reinforce fundamental rights. Incentivising engagement with human rights may reinforce principles that authorities act 'fairly and proportionately'[598] and treat people with 'sensitivity';[599] at a general level Convention rights 'represent a distillation of common sense and common humanity',[600] while fair process and proportionality are important aspects of human rights law. Indeed, an approach to administration informed by human rights has been found to facilitate responsiveness to user needs, offer a sophisticated approach to resolving complex policy issues, and precipitate renewal of a

[594] See text to n 220 above.

[595] D Luban, 'Settlements and the Erosion of the Public Realm' (1995) 83 *Georgetown Law Journal* 2619; O Fiss, 'Against Settlement' (1984) 93 *Yale Law Journal* 1073.

[596] A number of official publications have similarly observed compliance with human rights norms can promote good public administration: eg DCA (n 336) 35; Audit Commission (n 388) 3–4, 8; EHRC, *The Impact of a Human Rights Culture on Public Sector Organisations: Lessons from Practice* (2009) ch 7; EHRC Human Rights Review (n 338); see also Butler (n 573) ch 2.

[597] Parliamentary and Health Service Ombudsman, *Principles of Good Administration* (2009) 2, 4.

[598] ibid 7.

[599] ibid 5.

[600] Feldman (n 357) 119.

public interest ethos within public organisations.[601] The practical operation of damages actions, including discovery and oral evidence, can promote the administrative principle of transparency[602] by shedding light on important information about the operation of public authorities, and which may facilitate public and political accountability.[603] More generally damages actions may be the only vehicle for securing accountability;[604] Epp found that one reason for the rise in tort claims against British police from the 1980s onwards was the failure of internal and official mechanisms to hold police to account.[605]

Payment of compensation most obviously gives effect to administrative principles of 'putting things right'[606] and public bodies 'taking responsibility'[607] for their actions, while damages actions may spur 'continuous improvement'[608] of public services. Indeed, Government has stated that at a 'fundamental level' provision of redress for administrative wrongdoing 'is to ensure that public bodies learn from their mistakes and provide a better and more consistent service, thus benefiting the public as a whole',[609] while the Parliamentary Ombudsman observes that '[i]t is frequently the payment of compensation that focuses the minds of public servants and leads to real learning and real improvements in public services'.[610] Epp's study, discussed above, starkly illustrates that given the right conditions damages actions may have extraordinary transformative effects on administration. Research on the impact of judicial review and human rights challenges also reveals that judgments may enable change, lead to improvements in performance, and be an important resource for administrators, providing valuable guidance as to their legal duties and resolving conundrums or

601 EHRC Human Rights Review (n 338) ch 3.

602 PHSO (n 597) 6.

603 For example the *Lumba* litigation brought to light that the Government had been operating a secret policy in respect of detention of foreign prisoners which was at variance with its public policy. Furthermore, as the case climbed the appellate hierarchy more and more information as to the internal workings of the defendant Home Office was revealed: contrast *Abdi v SOSHD* [2008] EWHC 3166, [205] and *Lumba* (n 192) [150]–[168]; see also *R (Anufrijeva) v SOSHD* [2004] 1 AC 604, [24].

604 This being one important reason, recognised by courts, as to why they should hear such claims and grant remedies: *Belhaj v Straw* [2015] 2 WLR 1105, [119]; *Muuse* (n 239) [75], [77].

605 (n 360) ch 7.

606 PHSO (n 597) 3, 8.

607 ibid 2, 6

608 ibid 3, 9.

609 Law Commission, *Administrative Redress: Public Bodies and the Citizen: Analysis of Consultation Responses* (2010) [5.1]. The Head of the Home Civil Service has similarly emphasised the role of public law principles in 'improving policy development and decision-making in the public service' (Treasury Solicitor's Department, *The Judge Over Your Shoulder* 4th edn (2006) 3, and see 7).

610 Law Commission, ibid [4.7]–[4.8].

uncertainties which they face.[611] It is thus unsurprising that researchers find that both review and damages claims may be welcomed by officials.[612]

To the foregoing we may add that, as discussed above, provision of damages for governmental wrongdoing can promote trust and confidence in and the legitimacy of the administration and judiciary, as well as reinforcing and promoting basic constitutional precepts such as government under law and the principle of equality.

Thus, it is not only claimant interests served by awards. If wider interests served by awards are not factored into a balancing exercise, the exercise will be 'unbalanced'. Rather than balancing individual against public interests, courts should balance interests (individual and public) in favour of awards, against those which tell against.

Some courts recognise this and have taken a more 'balanced' approach than that taken in *Anufrijeva*. For example the Court of Appeal in *Faulkner* considered a number of factors in favour of damages such as the 'high value' of 'personal liberty' and importance of compensating wrongs, as well as wider factors including the importance of disapproving unlawful executive action, and that damages 'will—or ought to—concentrate the mind of the wrongdoer, especially where the latter is a public authority which is capable, unless it changes its ways, of repeating its error'.[613] In other jurisdictions public interest factors have been considered on both sides of the balancing equation. In New Zealand these have included the importance of deterring future violations, incentivising compliance being said to lie in society's interest, as well as marking society's disapproval of wrongful conduct.[614] Similarly, in Canada factors in favour of awards include the 'societal purpose' of deterring future violations,[615] which in turn promotes 'good governance',[616] and the somewhat more abstract (and unelaborated) idea that rights-violations harm society as a whole.[617] South African courts also have regard to deterrence effects as well as the idea that rights-violations inflict societal harm; here the idea of societal harm denotes simply that if violations are not remedied this could undermine wider public interests including

[611] Sunkin and Bondy (n 359); L Platt et al, 'Judicial Review Litigation as an Incentive to Change in Local Authority Public Services in England and Wales' (2010) 20 (suppl 2) *Journal of Public Administration Research & Theory* i243; EHRC Evaluating Impact (n 361). See also Audit Commission (n 388) (particularly ch 4) which draws out lessons for public authorities derived from human rights litigation; EHRC, *Human Rights: Human Lives: A Guide to the Human Rights Act for Public Authorities* (2014).

[612] Sunkin and Bondy ibid; Epp (n 360); see also EHRC Human Rights Review (n 338) ch 3.2.2.

[613] *Faulkner v SOSJ* [2011] EWCA Civ 349, [12]; *Bernard* (n 186) [59]; *Greenfield* (n 18) [19].

[614] *Taunoa* (n 6); *Combined Beneficiaries Union Inc v Auckland City COGS Committee* [2009] 2 NZLR 56.

[615] *Ward* (n 6) [29].

[616] ibid [38].

[617] ibid [28].

'impair[ing] public confidence and diminish[ing] public faith in the efficacy of the protection' afforded by constitutional rights: 'one invasion discounted may well lead to another'.[618]

This section has so far assumed that it is appropriate for courts to consider the public interest factors discussed herein, on the basis that if courts insist upon considering contentious countervailing public interests, such as preservation of public funds or chilling effects, they should also consider public interests in favour of awards. However, I argued that there were powerful constitutional, institutional and other arguments against courts taking into account the sorts of *countervailing* public interests discussed above. The same sorts of arguments tell against courts considering certain public interest factors which *favour* liability; in turn, this reinforces the case against interest-balancing. If courts are nonetheless intent on considering such factors, they should take a cautious, evidence-based approach.

Take the example of deterrence effects. It would be difficult, if not impossible, for a court to reliably predict ex ante whether awarding damages in a particular case will effectively deter future breaches. Whether damages successfully deter specific defendants or classes of potential defendants depends on myriad variables, including whether defendants have resources and/or expertise to implement measures to ensure future compliance, whether rights-consistent decision-making is consonant with a defendant's organisational culture, whether awards lead to media and political criticism, incentives set by insurance arrangements, how the defendant funds damages, and so on.

In considering deterrence effects many are influenced by stylised economic models of liability, which predict that damages will have strong deterrence effects by rendering non-compliance more costly. However, the interrelationship between liability and compliance is not so straightforward. Several empirical studies have found deterrence effects are not as strong as commonly asserted and not uniform.[619] Some studies show that other factors have far greater influence on authorities' propensity to comply than economic costs of liability, such as strong professional networks and non-legal accountability mechanisms.[620] Others theorise that government responds to political rather than economic incentives, meaning damages may be beside the point.[621] We know that at least one study—by Epp[622]—tends to support

[618] *Fose v Minister of Safety and Security* [1997] 3 SA 786, [82].

[619] eg GT Schwartz, 'Reality in the Economic Analysis of Tort Law: Does Tort Law Really Deter?' (1994) 42 *UCLA Law Review* 377; D Dewees et al, *Exploring the Domain of Accident Law* (OUP, 1996).

[620] Halliday et al 2011 (n 252).

[621] Levinson (n 154); L Rosenthal, 'A Theory of Governmental Damages Liability: Torts, Constitutional Torts, and Takings' (2007) 9 *University of Pennsylvania Journal of Constitutional Law* 797.

[622] (n 360).

the proposition that it is not economic incentives that matter for governmental compliance so much as threats to public and professional legitimacy. But Epp's study equally demonstrates that it would be wrong to dismiss the transformative potential of damages on the basis that authorities do not respond to economic costs of liability. His study shows that sizeable awards against authorities precipitated the *reputational* costs which threatened authorities' public and professional legitimacy and stimulated administrative reform. Similarly, the New Zealand and Scottish prison case studies discussed above show that damages actions can precipitate swift eradication of unlawful practices.

The key point is that although we know damages *may* have positive compliance-control effects, there is no straightforward interrelationship between liability costs and legal compliance so that a court would find it very difficult to accurately predict the effects of a single award. In any case, even if we could be sure that damages deter it would be difficult for judges to ascertain what quantum would produce optimal incentives given judges would need to quantify variables which are difficult to estimate, such as the probability that the defendant would repeat a rights-violation and/or the likelihood that other rights-violators will escape detection.[623]

B. Starting-Point, Structure and Weighting of Factors

If interest-balancing is adopted, the interest in protecting and vindicating the right ought to be given primacy, and structure ought to be imposed on the balancing exercise.

Gewirtz observes that one danger of balancing is that it may 'open the way for judges hostile to the right to dilute its force by excessively diluting the remedy in particular cases'.[624] He also suggests that 'psychologically, judges may systematically undervalue individual rights if allowed to balance them against broad social interests'.[625] For example, if a judge is faced with the submission that awarding compensation to a hardened criminal for interference with an intangible interest and associated moderate distress could undermine crucial public services and lead to multiple repeat claims, it is not difficult to see how the judge might undervalue the importance of protecting the right. Gewirtz meets this concern with an empirical claim, that there is no reason to doubt judicial capacity to properly balance interests.[626] However, the experience under the HRA, especially in the leading case of *Anufrijeva*, suggests that in this jurisdiction there are good reasons for such

[623] See Shavell (n 565) ch 6.
[624] (n 86) 607.
[625] ibid 607–08.
[626] ibid 608.

doubts. The Court in *Anufrijeva* did not consider public interest factors for awarding damages, only addressing countervailing factors, while individual interests in redress were largely ignored, as they often have been under the Act. The Court also emphasised that damages are a last resort and of secondary, if any, importance. The result of such approach, in combination with the mirror approach, has been relatively few successful HRA damages claims, with scales well below tort, and the more general marginalisation of damages, outside a few select areas. In other jurisdictions too, courts, under the umbrella of balancing approaches, have nearly completely subordinated interests in redress to countervailing public concerns.[627]

Such judicial discounting of the importance of protecting rights runs against a core purpose of adopting a bill of rights, which is to elevate fundamental rights 'above the hurly-burly tradeoffs of day-to-day public life'.[628] Gewirtz, himself a tentative supporter of remedial balancing, though only for specific relief, argues that if such approach is adopted and is to be at all justifiable 'the social benefit of the right and the interest in undoing effects of its violation must be given exceptional weight in the balance; otherwise the Constitution's allocation of rights would be subject to a de novo utilitarian re-evaluation in particular cases'.[629] Similarly, under the HRA Parliament created a set of legal entitlements to protect those interests considered fundamental; the courts should not undermine this distribution or the primary policy goals of protection and vindication by too lightly denying effective relief. The 'default setting' should be that that distribution is given practical effect through remedies, so that remedies ought to maintain, or restore entitlements (albeit in a second-best way) where they are threatened or wrongfully denied; under the HRA the current default is the near-inverse. Similarly, even those who support remedial discretion in private law fields nonetheless maintain that there is an 'unbreakable relationship' between right and remedy, acknowledging that 'the nature of the obligation breached is the starting point and generally the most important factor (while not necessarily the only one) determining the appropriate remedy in any particular case'.[630]

The argument for effective redress to be the default response to rights-violations is made all the more powerful by the contentious nature of public interest factors which would form the basis of any decision to deny damages. Many reasons invoked for denying relief, such as chilling effects or

[627] In respect of New Zealand see: ch 4.2.I.B, IV; JNE Varuhas, 'The Development of the Damages Remedy under the New Zealand Bill of Rights Act 1990: From Torts to Administrative Law' [2016] *New Zealand Law Review* (forthcoming). In respect of the US see text to nn 9–12 above, and see ch 7.III.

[628] Gewirtz (n 86) 677.

[629] ibid 607.

[630] M Tilbury, 'Remedies and the Classification of Obligations' in A Robertson (ed), *The Law of Obligations: Connections and Boundaries* (UCL, 2004) 26.

floodgates, rest on consequentialist predictions which judges are not well-placed to make. Because of the high chance of error in making such predictions it is right that remedial balancing should be stacked heavily in favour of redress, with redress denied only if there are very strong reasons, based in evidence, to believe that relief would precipitate significant negative effects. In this way the chance that relief is denied according to baseless concerns is minimised. Lord Kerr's observations in *Sagicor*, made in the course of deciding whether to recognise a novel tort, echo this view:

> As a general observation ... it is right to recognise that conclusions on matters of policy in the legal context are not usually the product of empirical research. Customarily, they are formed instinctually and constitute, at most, informed guesswork about the impact that the selection of a particular policy course will have. While, therefore, policy considerations can, and on occasions must, underlie decisions as to how law should develop, it is necessary to recognise the inherent impossibility of making an infallible prediction about the outcome of a policy choice. Where possible, therefore, such a choice should be aligned with principle. In my view, fundamental principle has a large part to play in the resolution of the debate in this case. And the pre-eminent principle at stake here is that for every injustice there should be remedy at law.[631]

In other fields where courts conduct balancing the interest in remedying legal wrongs is afforded primacy. When courts determine whether a novel duty of care should be recognised in negligence they weigh public policy factors for and against. In that context it is increasingly said that 'the public policy consideration which has first claim on the loyalty of the law is that wrongs should be remedied and very potent considerations are required to override that policy'.[632] If an otherwise 'perfectly good cause of action' is to be defeated on public policy grounds this may only be in 'clear cases in which the potential harm to the public is incontestable', and whether the harm is likely to occur 'must be determined on tangible grounds instead of on mere generalities', the burden of proof lying with those who seek to evade enforcement of a liability that prime facie exists.[633] Significantly in negligence this approach has been applied to decide whether a primary legal obligation should be recognised in the first place; the normative imperative for righting wrongs is clearer and stronger where a legal wrong has been proven. Similarly, in determining whether immunities ought to be recognised in tort courts observe that '[t]he general rule that where there is a wrong there should be a remedy is a cornerstone of any system of justice. To deny a remedy to the victim of a wrong should always be regarded as

[631] (n 230) [94]. See to similar effect his Lordship's judgment in *Michael* (n 227) [182]–[186] (dissenting).

[632] *X (Minors) v Bedfordshire CC* [1994] 2 WLR 554, 571; (n 91) 749; *Van Colle* (n 227) [56]; *Gorringe* (n 132) [2]; *cf Stovin* (n 109) 949D.

[633] *Spring* (n 256) 326.

exceptional ... any justification must be necessary and requires [to be] strict and cogent';[634] '[t]he onus lies fairly and squarely on the respondent to justify the immunity behind which she seeks to shelter'.[635]

Of course, if we accept that rights-protection should be afforded primacy one may question why interest-balancing is justified at all. If we wish to ensure this interest is given primacy it would make more sense to erect a rule or presumption in favour of relief, coupled with narrow exceptions or defences for exceptional cases, with the onus on the defendant to prove defences. Such approach has important benefits. For example, it better guards against judicial undervaluing of rights and is more faithful to the distribution of entitlements encapsulated in the HRA, does not undermine formal rule of law values in the way open-ended discretionary approaches do, reduces the chance that redress will be denied according to unsafe assessments of consequential effects, and, yet, provides scope for denial of relief where it is clear—according to weighty evidence—that awards would seriously undermine important interests. The defendant should bear the onus of proving defences because, inter alia, the claimant has already, by proving a rights-violation, established a prima facie case for redress; it is the defendant who is seeking release from the ordinary obligation to right one's wrong; placing the onus on the defendant is consonant with the overarching structure of human rights law and serves the goal of ensuring maximal protection of basic interests; and the defendant will generally have better access to evidence relevant to public interest defences.

Even if one maintains a preference for balancing, the legal tests adopted should institutionalise the primacy of protecting rights. One precedent that might be drawn upon is structured proportionality, which is the test of lawful justification for interference with certain rights.[636] This test makes the right the analytical starting-point and requires weighty reasons before justification may be established. Such approach *may* make remedial balancing less objectionable, as proportionality has built-in features which militate against undervaluing rights, and other problematic features of balancing. Under proportionality the matter is one of *law*, not discretion, while balancing is *structured* around several distinct inquiries. Relief could only be denied if there was a *rational connection* between denial and preserving countervailing interests, and only if denial was *strictly necessary* to preserve those interests, while only the *most important and pressing* public interests could justify denial, and those interests would be *construed narrowly*. Reasons for denial would be *anxiously scrutinised*, and the defendant would

[634] *Jones* (n 92) [113].

[635] ibid [51].

[636] Or perhaps the approach to balancing should vary with the right at stake. For example, perhaps for absolute rights, such as the right to life, there should be no or very little scope to refuse damages, but proportionality balancing should apply for qualified rights.

be required to prove the factual premises of arguments for denial. These features, *if taken seriously*, may help to ensure that rights-protection is given primacy and a robust approach is taken to countervailing arguments. However, caution is required. When one moves from formal features to how proportionality has operated in practice, there is less scope for optimism. Despite proportionality's formal structure and promise of analytical rigour, it has too often (wrongly) collapsed into unstructured balancing,[637] attended by all of the typical problems with such approach.

There are precedents for a more structured (and balanced) approach. Although the New Zealand case law on NZBORA damages has more recently been heavily influenced by *Anufrijeva*, there are statements within this jurisprudence which support the approach propounded here. In *Baigent* Hardie Boys J said that

> the terms of the Bill of Rights Act itself require a rights-centred response to infringements. That is not to exclude other objectives: to ensure compliance, and to secure the wider public interest. *But the primary focus has been on providing an appropriate remedy to a person whose rights have been infringed.*[638]

In *Chapman*, the Chief Justice, albeit in the minority, took as her starting point that: 'Observance of [the] general principle [that wrongs are to be remedied] is axiomatic where the wrong in issue is breach of the rights and freedoms contained in the [NZBORA]'.[639] From this it followed that a strict approach should be taken to refusal of relief: '[i]f effective vindication of the Bill of Rights Act requires the availability of a direct remedy in damages … any [countervailing] policy [arguments] would have to be overwhelming to justify an exception'.[640] The Canadian Supreme Court in *Ward* elaborated a four-step approach to the damages inquiry, which holds out the prospect of a structured and more balanced approach.[641] First, a rights-violation must be established. Second, the court considers individual and public factors for an award. Third, the court considers countervailing factors or other reasons for denial such as availability of alternative remedies. The defendant bears the burden of establishing these factors and negating the case for an award. Fourth, if the defendant fails to justify denial, the court moves to quantum. However, it should be noted that in the first major post-*Ward* Charter damages case adjudicated by the Supreme Court, *Henry*, the majority did not apply this structured, step-by-step approach, with the consequence that

637 See M Elliott, 'Proportionality and Deference: The Importance of a Structured Approach' in CF Forsyth et al (eds), *Effective Judicial Review* (OUP, 2010).

638 *Baigent* (n 134) 702–03 (emphasis added).

639 (n 25) [67].

640 ibid [60] and see also [183].

641 *Ward* (n 6). But note the appearance of balance arguably belies a public interest focus: ch 4.2.I.B.

individual and social goals served by imposing liability were lost sight of in a sea of countervailing policy factors.[642] This is a stark illustration of the dangers discussed above; formal structures may be ineffective in bridling balancing approaches so as to mitigate their worst features.

SECTION 3. CONCLUSIONS

The interest-balancing approach reflects understandable concerns. For example, there are obvious public interests in authorities having financial capacity to perform their primary functions and in vigorous administration. However, it does not follow necessarily that interest-balancing should be adopted. Indeed, there are strong arguments against such approach.

In terms of positive law, it is difficult to reconcile balancing with the terms of the HRA. Such approach will likely lead to violations of Article 13, as well as substantive human rights, and undermines fundamental tenets of English law including *ubi ius, ibi remedium* and the equality principle.

On a normative level the interest-balancing approach is problematic. First, such approach would leave many victims without effective redress, undermining the normative importance of human rights and the vindicatory and protective policies that underpin the field. Second, it is difficult to justify why human rights law in particular ought to be singled out for departure from ordinary damages principles. Third, given many countervailing interests are already protected by substantive human rights law, ordinary damages principles, procedural rules and non-legal phenomena one may question why interest-balancing is necessary. Fourth, many public interest factors which would be taken into account under balancing are inappropriate for judicial consideration. Moreover, detailed examination of public interest factors shows it is far from clear-cut that damages would undermine relevant public interests; the interrelationship between public interest factors and damages awards is often complex and unpredictable. Difficult policy issues, such as resource allocation, are best left to political institutions, which have institutional capacity and constitutional legitimacy to determine them, and a range of tools to address well-founded concerns where they arise. Case studies show the political branches are willing and able to act. If courts are, nonetheless, to take public interest factors into account, then a rigorous, principled and evidence-based approach should be taken. Fifth, interest-balancing, particularly where unstructured and discretionary, will significantly undermine formal rule-of-law values.

642 *Henry v British Columbia* [2015] SCC 24. In contrast the Chief Justice, who penned the decision in *Ward*, entered a minority judgment in *Henry* (with Karakatsanis J), faithfully (and perhaps pointedly) applying the *Ward* structure.

If, despite powerful arguments against interest-balancing, such approach were nonetheless adopted then the approach in *Anufrijeva* would require significant refinement so as to mitigate its worst features. In particular, in deciding whether to make awards courts should consider not only countervailing public interests but also public interests which favour awards. The interest in protecting the right should be accorded primacy in any balancing-calculus, balancing ought to be structured, and criteria for justifying refusal of relief ought to be strict and the defendant should bear the justificatory burden. Alternatively, and preferably, courts could adopt a rule in favour of relief that could be overridden in exceptional cases where enumerated defences are proven.

Quantum should not be subject to interest-balancing. This would lead to intolerable uncertainty, unpredictability and inconsistency. Furthermore, it is hard to justify departure from the near-universal compensatory principle in human rights law, while the ordinary principle that awards should be moderate guards against excessive awards. Neither the terms of the HRA nor ECtHR jurisprudence provide support for a balancing approach to quantum.

Let us conclude with two general observations.

First, if we put to the side those competing policy considerations, both for and against awarding damages, which are complex and difficult to assess because of messy empirical realities, and/or inappropriate for judicial consideration because of constitutional and institutional constraints on courts, we are left with the powerful argument of legal principle advanced in Part 1 of this book for a vindicatory, tort-based approach to human rights damages. That argument rested on ordinary techniques of legal reasoning such as analogical reasoning, and appeal to established legal principle, and to coherence and consistency. A critic may retort that the tort-based approach is not value-free but based on a *policy*-rationale of affording strong protection to fundamental interests. This is correct. But what distinguishes the argument for the tort-based approach is that it takes its 'policy direction' not from highly contested conceptions of the good or public law or arguments that rest on disputed or incomplete empirical foundations, but from the nature of the primary rights, as evidenced by significant features of human rights doctrine and the intention of the Parliament that passed the HRA. Rather than superimposing a competing and exogenous policy vision at the remedial stage that appeals to one's subjective tastes, the tort-based approach is faithful to the policy that underpins the primary rights and gives effect to the distribution of entitlements sanctioned by Parliament. If the policy that underpins primary rights were to change, for example because human rights were no longer considered fundamental by the political community, then a vindicatory approach may become inapt. However, empirical evidence indicates the rights protected by human rights legislation are those most important to British people.[643]

[643] EHRC Public Perceptions Report (n 338).

Second, at the heart of the balancing approach propounded in *Anufrijeva* lies the idea, discussed in chapter 4, that the dominant concern of human rights law, being a field of public law, is protection of the public interest. If this is one's conception of human rights law then one may readily accept denial of individual redress where grant of remedies may undermine public interests, foremost among these interests, for protagonists of the public interest conception, being that in effective administration. As Beatson observes, the 'public interest view of public law litigation makes it difficult to see how an individual interest could ever outweigh communal interests in a balancing approach'.[644] On the other hand, if one is alert to the distinctive nature of human rights law, in particular that the primary obligations are individual, personal rights underpinned by a policy of protection and vindication of basic personal interests, one will recognise that a remedial approach which often leaves rights-holders without adequate remedy and systematically prioritises public interests ahead of individual interests, is out of place and at odds with the field's animating concerns. As McLean says, '[t]he existence of a discretion to grant a remedy is much more difficult to justify when the focus is on positive individual rights against government rather than on public wrongs'.[645]

[644] J Beatson, '"Public" and "Private" in English Administrative Law' (1987) 103 *LQR* 34, 59 (specifically addressing Lord Woolf's public interest conception of public law: see ch 4.2.

[645] McLean (n 535) 219, 222, 233.

7

Other Methods of Limiting Human Rights Damages

THE INTEREST-BALANCING APPROACH proposed in *Anufrijeva* is not the only device that could be used to temper or limit public authority liability for human rights violations. This chapter considers a number of limiting devices that have been employed in supranational and comparative constitutional contexts, and which have been or could potentially be read across to English human rights law: (1) it is a core feature of the Strasbourg Court's approach under Article 41 that it limits compensation for non-pecuniary loss to cases where consequential non-pecuniary losses reach a minimum level of intensity; (2) in EU law individuals may only recover damages for loss caused by state violation of EU law where that breach is 'sufficiently serious'; and (3) in US constitutional tort law public officials are protected from suit by myriad immunities.

The basic objections to importation of such devices are the same as those applicable to interest-balancing. Why should such limitation devices apply where fundamental rights are at stake, so as to deny effective remedies, especially if such devices do not apply to limit liability for wrongful interference with lesser interests in other fields, including those not underpinned by policies of protection and vindication? Furthermore, adoption of such devices under the Human Rights Act 1998 (HRA) would likely rest on public policy justifications of the sort considered in detail in chapter 6, such as chilling effects or a concern that awards will cripple public services. However, it is not clear that such arguments in fact justify restriction of liability, and if such concerns did happen to materialise then the executive and legislature are well-placed to address them. In any case judges should be slow to adopt such limiting devices on their own motion given they lack the constitutional legitimacy to make the sorts of contentious value-judgements required and/or the necessary institutional expertise and information to assess complex policy considerations competently. Further, many public interests are already accounted for in substantive human rights law, the ordinary law of damages and civil procedure rules, and protected by operation of legal and non-legal phenomena, while it is not clear that concerns over chilling effects etc are unique to human rights law so as to justify a *sui generis* approach to liability. On top of all of this, such limiting devices—especially blanket immunities for officials—could violate the terms of the Convention. And it is questionable whether there is any *express* basis for adoption of such devices in the terms of the HRA, which would be required given such devices undermine fundamental principles of government under law, equality and *ubi ius, ibi remedium*.

As this chapter argues, on top of these general objections there are more specific reasons for resisting incorporation of these particular limiting devices into the English law of human rights damages.

I. DEGREE OF LOSS UNDER ARTICLE 41, ECHR

The Strasbourg Court often holds that degree of loss suffered as a result of a violation is insufficient to justify a monetary award.[1] For example, it might conclude the applicant has suffered anxiety and frustration as a result of the violation but this is not 'of such intensity that it would in itself justify an award of compensation for non-pecuniary damage';[2] put another way,

> [i]n some situations ... the impact of the violation may be regarded as being of a nature and degree as to have impinged so significantly on the moral well-being of the applicant as to require something further [than a finding of violation].[3]

Where loss does not reach the requisite intensity the European Court of Human Rights (ECtHR) holds the finding of violation is sufficient to afford just satisfaction: 'The Court has a wide discretion to determine when an award of damages should be made, and frequently holds that the finding of a violation is sufficient satisfaction without any further monetary award'.[4] The English courts, including the Supreme Court,[5] have endorsed the Strasbourg practice, according to the mirror approach, and denied damages on this basis in a high proportion of the damages claims determined under the HRA.[6]

[1] *Damages Under the Human Rights Act 1998*, Law Com 266/Scot Law Com 180 (2000) [3.44] [Law Commissions Report].

[2] eg *Silver v UK* (1983) 6 EHRR 62, [10]; *Faulkner v UK* (2002) 35 EHRR 27, [18]; *Campbell v UK* (1985) 7 EHRR 165, [141]; *Schönenberger v Switzerland* (1989) 11 EHRR 202, [36]; *A v France* (23 November 1993) App no 14838/89, [42] (ECtHR); *Koendjbiharie v Netherlands* (1991) 13 EHRR 820, [34]; *Schenkel v Netherlands* (2006) 43 EHRR 31, [45]; *Yildiz v Austria* (2003) 36 EHRR 32, [51]; *S v UK* (2009) 48 EHRR 50, [134]; *Firth v UK* (12 August 2014) App no 47784/09, [18] (ECtHR Fourth Section).

[3] *Varnava v Turkey* (18 September 2009) App no 16064/90, [224] (GC).

[4] *A v UK* (2009) 49 EHRR 29, [250].

[5] *R (Faulkner) v SOSJ* [2013] 2 AC 254, [13](15), [62]–[66]; *R (Osborn) v Parole Board* [2015] AC 1115, [115]; *Shahid v Scottish Ministers* [2015] 3 WLR 1003, [87]–[90].

[6] On degree of loss see: *R (Biggin) v SOSJ* [2009] EWHC 1704, [36]; *R (KB) v South London and South and West Region MHRT* [2004] QB 936, [73]; *R (Degainis) v SOSJ* [2010] EWHC 137, [17]–[18]; *R (Bernard) v SOSHD* [2005] EWHC 452, [61]; *R (Baiai) v SOSHD* [2006] EWHC 1035, [37], [38]–[46], [49]; *R (Shaw) v SOSHD* [2013] EWHC 42, [45]; *CM v State Hospitals Board for Scotland* [2014] CSIH 71, [104]. On a finding as just satisfaction

There are several significant drawbacks to adopting such a threshold for recovery which suggest English courts should discontinue this practice.

The first problem is such approach completely ignores the normative dimensions of a violation, focusing solely on consequential non-pecuniary losses. Thus there are examples of the ECtHR and English courts,[7] denying claims for compensation for relatively serious rights-violations on the basis of the chance factor that the individual did not suffer significant mental distress in consequence.[8] Contrast the approach at common law. In *Iqbal* the Court of Appeal, adopting the orthodox approach to damages for vindicatory torts, affirmed that even for a brief false imprisonment a court must generally award substantial (rather than nominal) damages given the fundamental importance of liberty.[9] Lord Neuberger MR expressly rejected the idea, adopted by the trial Judge, that for a brief false imprisonment a declaration that the victim had been falsely imprisoned afforded substantial 'just satisfaction', meaning substantial damages need not be awarded.[10] In defamation too the courts have explicitly rejected the idea that the terms of the judgment could afford adequate vindication.[11] Thus substantial damages have routinely been awarded within vindicatory torts for wrongs described as 'trivial' and where no factual loss has been suffered; claimants are entitled to have their most important rights 'vindicated by a substantial award of damages'.[12] In contrast, as Cooke P said in *Baigent*, '[a] mere declaration would be toothless'.[13]

see: *R (Greenfield) v SOSHD* [2005] 1 WLR 673, [8]–[9], [19], [26], [29], [31]; *Re P (A Child)* [2007] HRLR 14, [58], [71]; *R (H) v SOSHD* [2004] 2 AC 253, [30]; *Austin v Commissioner of the Metropolis* [2005] EWHC 480, [597]; *Downing v Parole Board* [2008] EWHC 3198, [31]; *Dobson v Thames Water Utilities Ltd* [2011] EWHC 3253, [1092]–[1104]; *R (Negassi) v SOSHD* [2011] 2 CMLR 36, [33]; *A v Essex CC* [2011] 1 AC 280, [169].

[7] For example, in *Baiai*, ibid, an administrative scheme to prevent sham marriages violated the claimants' Article 12 right to marry and Article 14 right against discrimination—the Judge finding *no* reasonable or objective justification for these violations, even affording the Minister 'substantial deference', yet no award was made. In *Shahid* a prisoner had been kept in solitary confinement continuously for the extraordinary period of five years in violation of Article 8 yet the Supreme Court refused to make any award of damages for mental suffering, ruling that a declaration and award of costs constituted sufficient remedy: (n 5) [87]–[90].

[8] For example the case of *Silver* (n 2), in which compensation was denied, entailed multiple violations, including breaches of Articles 6(1), 8 and 13, caused by government interference with prisoner correspondence, relatively far-reaching controls on prisoner correspondence, prisoners being prevented from seeking legal advice, and there being no effective remedy to address these violations.

[9] *Iqbal v POA* [2010] QB 732, [44]–[49], [83]–[84], [104]; *Karagozlu v Commissioner of the Metropolis* [2007] 1 WLR 1881, [25]. But note: *R (Lumba) v SOSHD* [2012] 1 AC 245, discussed in ch 2.III.C.iii.

[10] *Iqbal* ibid [47].

[11] *Cairns v Modi* [2013] 1 WLR 1015, [30]ff.

[12] eg *Plenty v Dillon* (1991) 171 CLR 635, 645, 654–55; *NSW v Abed* [2014] NSWCA 419. See further ch 2.III.B–C.

[13] *Simpson v Attorney-General [Baigent's Case]* [1994] 3 NZLR 667, 676.

Second, while the Strasbourg Court's approach *may* be a defensible one for a subsidiary, supranational institution—it is not the job of an international supervisory court charged with maintaining basic standards across Europe, and completely swamped with cases, to adjudicate small claims for compensation—it is questionable whether it is appropriate for domestic institutions to adopt such approach given they are charged with primary responsibility for protecting rights.[14] Even members of the Strasbourg Court have questioned whether a finding of violation can afford just satisfaction, let alone an effective remedy domestically.[15]

Third, the idea of a threshold for recovery of damages for non-pecuniary loss was firmly rejected by the Law Commission in the context of personal injury damages, in its report, *Damages for Personal Injury: Non-Pecuniary Loss*.[16] The Commission acknowledged certain arguments for a threshold: it would reduce the cost of tort compensation in terms of damages and legal costs, and there is less of a case for compensating minor injuries than serious ones.[17] As the Commission noted, such arguments tended to be pragmatic rather than principled.[18] Further, such arguments do not take one very far. For example, there is an intuitive appeal in the idea that if we are to limit compensatory awards to certain classes of case we should limit awards to cases where the claimant has suffered the greatest loss.[19] However, such argument begs the question of why we should limit availability of awards in otherwise meritorious cases in the first place, and poses a difficult question of where we should draw the line as between cases in which damages should be awarded and those in which they should not. The answer to these questions is likely to rest on contentious value-judgements as to allocation of scarce resources and also consequentialist, practical claims, such as whether introduction of a threshold would significantly reduce costs associated with the liability system, and whether this is the best way of reducing costs, which judges are not well-placed to analyse robustly. As such it is not surprising that the issue of thresholds, and also caps, has generally been left to policy

[14] See ch 5.2.I.

[15] See the dissenting judgments in: *Engel v Netherlands* (1979–80) 1 EHRR 706, 710; *TW v Malta* (1999) 29 EHRR 185, 207–09; *Nikolova v Bulgaria* (2001) 31 EHRR 3, 91–94 (eg 'I consider it wholly inadequate and unacceptable that a court of justice should "satisfy" the victim of a breach of fundamental rights with a mere handout of legal idiom'); *Kingsley v UK* (2002) 35 EHRR 10, 196–97; *Disk and Kesk v Turkey* (29 April 2013) App no 38676/08 (ECtHR Second Section) (Judges Ziemele and Karakas).

[16] Law Com 257 (1999) [2.25]–[2.28] [Law Commission 1999]; see also, *Damages for Personal Injury: Non-Pecuniary Loss*, Law Com Consultation Paper 140 (1995) [4.23]–[4.26].

[17] Law Commission 1999 ibid [2.25].

[18] ibid.

[19] Albeit, if we have to limit incidence of compensation there may be alternative, more principled bases on which to do so. For example perhaps we should limit awards to breaches of those rights we consider most important. See: N McBride, 'Tort Law and Criminal Law in an Age of Austerity' in M Dyson (ed), *Unravelling Tort and Crime* (CUP, 2014).

bodies such as the Law Commission—to which the courts should defer on such matters—while where thresholds have been introduced, it has been via primary and/or secondary legislation, as an aspect of an overall statutory scheme or set of reforms.[20]

The Law Commission ultimately rejected the idea of a threshold because 93 per cent of consultees opposed it[21] and according to several strong arguments—which apply with equal, if not greater force in human rights law:[22]

— Even if the tort system is too expensive, costs can be reduced via other methods without interfering with basic principles. For example, summary judgment and strike-out procedures can save costs of a full trial where there is no arguable case, the doctrine of abuse of process might be relied upon to exclude trivial claims,[23] and various procedural reforms have been implemented to bring down costs.
— A minimum threshold may lead to claimants exaggerating loss suffered. The Commission recorded that many consultees, including judges of the Queen's Bench and Family Divisions, saw this risk as a decisive factor telling against a threshold, and cited the experience of the Criminal Injuries Compensation Board as an example.[24]
— As minor injuries usually do not cause pecuniary loss, to refuse non-pecuniary damages would mean some wrongs go uncompensated. This point is particularly pertinent in human rights law as many rights-violations will only cause non-pecuniary harm.
— There already exist very strong disincentives to bringing small claims. As discussed in chapter 6,[25] there are many hurdles a human rights claimant must negotiate to mount a successful claim—in particular it is wholly unlikely legal aid would be granted for a small claim—while it is highly likely claimants and government/insurers would settle small claims rather than engage in expensive litigation. Indeed, it is uncommon for small tort claims to make it to court; this only typically occurs where a significant point of principle arises.[26]

[20] eg Civil Liability Act 2002 (NSW), ss 12, 15–17 [CLA]; Financial Services and Markets Act 2000, ss 214(1)(j), 229(4)–(7); Race Relations Act 1976, s 56(2) (repealed); Race Discrimination Act 1975, s 65(2) (repealed); Ministry of Justice, *Criminal Injuries Compensation Scheme* (Stationery Office 2012), [31], [32](b), [36](c), [37], [50], [60], [77], [84].

[21] Law Commission 1999 (n 16) [2.27]–[2.28].

[22] ibid [2.26]. The Law Commission also addressed the Pearson Commission's recommendation that a threshold should be adopted. The Law Commission (at [2.26]) observed that that recommendation must be understood in light of the Pearson Commission's view that tort damages should be supplementary to a state-run, no-fault compensation scheme: *Report on Civil Liability and Compensation for Personal Injury*, Cm 7054 (1978) vol I, [382]–[389].

[23] eg *Tamiz v Google Inc* [2013] EWCA Civ 68, [48]–[51].

[24] Law Commission 1999 (n 16) [2.27].

[25] See ch 6.2.IV.

[26] eg *Iqbal* (n 9); *Austin* (n 6) (see the appeal: [2009] 1 AC 564); *Hounga v Allen* [2014] 1 WLR 2889, [4].

In addition to these points, consultees submitted the public would view a threshold as unfair, and that it would lead to injustice and inconsistency.[27]

One can see the unfairness argument. Assume that the threshold is 10 units of distress. If someone suffers 10.1 units they will receive full compensation for non-pecuniary losses. Yet if they suffer 9.9 units—which may be a not insubstantial level of harm—they will receive nothing. It seems inevitable victims will view such approach as arbitrary.

One can also see the inconsistency argument. Individual judges are likely to vary in their assessment of what level of loss is sufficiently serious. Such variation will be marked where the threshold applies, as it does in human rights law, to non-pecuniary loss given there is no objective method of measuring distress and anxiety. Perhaps unsurprisingly judges have generally relied on subjective intuition in determining whether distress is such to warrant an award, often adopting conclusory reasoning: 'the evidence of the distress suffered does not justify a further award ... None of the other heads of damage listed in the schedule in my judgment call for any award of damages ... to ensure just satisfaction';[28] 'In my view, accepting what is said in the statement of the claimant, the intensity of distress in this case is not such as to justify an award'.[29] It would be very difficult to formulate a minimum threshold for non-pecuniary loss with any precision. It is therefore not surprising that the Strasbourg Court's practice as to when the threshold is met has been criticised as inconsistent.[30] We find similar problems even in jurisdictions where minimum thresholds have been introduced by statute and thresholds appear precise and objective, holding out the prospect of consistent decision-making. For example in Australia the New South Wales Civil Liability Act provides that, in respect of damages for personal injury, '[n]o damages may be awarded for non-economic loss unless the severity of the non-economic loss is at least 15% of the most extreme case', while the Act also prescribes how quantum should be assessed according to a scale of 15 per cent to 100 per cent of the extreme case.[31] Despite the veneer of scientific objectivity associated with use of numerical figures, there is no scientific method in play here. Courts openly admit that determining what the most extreme case is, and how the case before them relates to the putative extreme in percentage terms, is a matter

[27] Law Commission 1999 (n 16) [2.27].
[28] *Shaw* (n 6) [45].
[29] *Biggin* (n 6) [36].
[30] eg Law Commissions Report (n 1) [3.39]–[3.41]; *Degainis* (n 6) [17]. Complicating the picture is the fact that the ECtHR is also influenced by factors other than degree of loss, such as the victim's moral status, in deciding whether to award compensation, but may not have *express* regard to such factors: D Shelton, *Remedies in International Human Rights Law* 2nd edn (OUP, 2005) 260–65; ch 6.2.V.B.
[31] CLA, s 16.

'of opinion, impression, speculation and estimation'.[32] Further, there is, as one might predict, stark evidence of judges reasoning backwards, that is determining the relevant percentage—and thus whether the case falls below or above the minimum threshold—according to whether they subjectively consider the case is a worthy one meriting compensation.[33] The result is very little hope of consistent decision-making. Inconsistency is obviously undesirable in itself. But when coupled with the fact that 'a small variation in the assessment [of percentage] may have significant consequences for the amount of damages'[34]—it could make the difference between a claimant receiving a substantial sum or nothing—there is significant potential for unfairness, actual or perceived.

Australian courts suggest judges 'used to awarding damages for non-economic loss over the years' would no doubt 'baulk before' finding suffering comes below a minimum threshold so that damages should be denied.[35] Not so in English human rights law. The idea of a minimum threshold has been adopted without the batting of an eyelid, nor any mention of the incongruity between such approach and common law, and led to systematic denial of awards. The Supreme Court decision in *Faulkner* is a paradigm example of adoption of a minimum threshold within human rights law, and demonstrates the problems with such thresholds. In that case Lord Reed, for the plurality, held damages could be awarded for distress and frustration suffered by a prisoner whose parole hearing was delayed to such an extent as to constitute breach of Article 5(4), which requires a speedy hearing. However, damages should only be awarded if the distress suffered was 'sufficiently serious'.[36] Injecting some objectivity into the otherwise open-ended inquiry into sufficient seriousness, Lord Reed said that where the rights-violating delay is of more than three months it could generally be assumed that suffering was sufficiently severe; for delays below three months awards should generally be denied.[37] It was possible to articulate such guidance because the violation in issue had a temporal dimension. But a more objective criterion of this sort, to which the 'sufficiently serious' inquiry may be tied, will not be available for most types of violation. Further, while addressing one problem—the open-ended nature of the 'sufficiently serious' test and potential for inconsistency—the guidance gives rise to others, namely concerns over unfairness. Why should someone who suffers an unlawful delay of just over three months receive compensation for the full extent of the distress occasioned by the violation over that entire three month period, but

[32] *Dell v Dalton* (1991) 23 NSWLR 528, 533–34; *Southgate v Waterford* (1990) 21 NSWLR 427, 440; *Clifton v Lewis* [2012] NSWCA 229, [56].

[33] *Concrite Pty Ltd v Rogerson* [2003] NSWCA 306.

[34] *Clifton* (n 32) [56]–[57].

[35] *Kurrie v Azouri* (1998) 28 MVR 406, 413–14.

[36] *Faulkner* (n 5) [66], [13](15).

[37] ibid [66], [13](15).

someone who suffers a delay of two months and 27 days receive nothing at all? The plurality judgment does not attempt a normative justification for the choice of three months, only saying it was supported by Strasbourg jurisprudence; but given that jurisprudence does not in fact articulate such bright line guidance,[38] let alone entail a normative rationale, this is no justification at all. That it is difficult to locate any defensible justification for the choice of three months rather than any other time period—two and a half months, four and three quarter months, one month and 25 days, and so on—is made patent by the manner of the plurality's determination of one of the appeals in *Faulkner*: '[t]he frustration and anxiety occasioned by a delay of six months cannot in my view be regarded as insufficiently severe to warrant such an award'.[39] There is no justification here other than: 'in my view'.

One might retort that if a line has to be drawn, then the decision as to where it should be drawn will always entail an element of arbitrariness. Very well. But my point is we should not engage in such practice in the first place, and one of the key reasons for resisting such practice is its arbitrariness, and the unfairness it engenders.

Lastly, if the aim of adopting the Strasbourg approach is to limit impact of awards on the public purse, it is not clear that it would be particularly effective. To deny awards where the loss is not 'serious' would be to deny damages where awards would be at their lowest, and impose the least financial burden.[40] On the other hand, where the violation has a serious impact, awards will be higher and potentially impose a much heavier burden. In this respect it is worth observing that in 2002 insurers estimated only one per cent of all cases in the tort system resulted in a payment of £100,000 or more. However, these few cases accounted for 32 per cent of the total damages paid out by the system.[41]

II. EU LAW, *FRANCOVICH* LIABILITY AND THE 'SUFFICIENTLY SERIOUS' CRITERION

In *Anufrijeva* Lord Woolf cited the approach to damages for state infringements of EU law, first established in the European Court of Justice's (ECJ) decision in *Francovich*,[42] as supporting his view that damages ought to play a different role in public law.[43] It has been suggested by commentators,

[38] See ch 5.2.II.D.

[39] *Faulkner* (n 5) [97].

[40] Although, providing monetary redress for less than serious violations which cause loss to a large class could result in a sizeable burden on public resources. See the 'slopping out' case study in ch 6.2.V.F.i.

[41] Lord Chancellor's Department, *Courts Bill: Regulatory Impact Assessment* (November 2002) Table 1.

[42] *Francovich and Bonafaci v Italian Republic* [1991] ECR 5357.

[43] *Anufrijeva v Southwark LBC* [2004] QB 1124, [54].

including Lord Woolf, speaking extra-judicially, that English courts might draw on the rules of state liability developed in EU law in fashioning their approach to HRA damages.[44] It has also been argued that these rules could provide a good model were damages to be introduced as a remedy in domestic administrative law, for breach of common law duties of legality, procedural fairness and rationality.[45] More generally, the EU liability rules merit consideration given they are rules specifically formulated to govern state liability.

A. The *Francovich* Criteria

In EU law a Member State will be liable to pay damages to individuals who suffer loss as a result of non- or mis-implementation of a Directive or any other breach of EU law by a national authority, including the legislature[46] and judiciary,[47] if:[48]

1. The rule of law infringed was intended to confer rights on individuals;
2. The breach was sufficiently serious; and
3. There was a direct causal link between the breach of the obligation and the damage suffered by the individual claimants.

The most significant feature of this test—that feature which is determinative in the vast majority of claims[49]—is the 'sufficiently serious' criterion. In general state violation of an EU law which confers rights on individuals will not give rise to liability per se. Rather it is a necessary condition that the breach must be of sufficient seriousness to warrant liability; this 'hurdle ... is a high one',[50] requiring that the breach be 'grave and manifest'.[51]

[44] H Woolf, 'The Human Rights Act 1998 and Remedies' in M Andenas and D Fairgrieve (eds), *Judicial Review in International Perspective* (Kluwer, 2000) 433; D Fairgrieve, 'The Human Rights Act 1998, Damages and English Tort Law' in D Fairgrieve et al (eds), *Tort Liability of Public Authorities in Comparative Perspective* (BIICL, 2002) 86–87.

[45] See for example, PP Craig, 'Once More Unto the Breach: the Community, the State and Damages Liability' (1997) 113 *LQR* 67, 89–94. The Law Commission's proposals (ultimately not taken forward) for reform of public authority liability included a 'serious fault' requirement, which was based on the 'sufficiently serious' test: *Administrative Redress: Public Bodies and the Citizen*, Law Com 322 (2010) [2.80], [3.32]–[3.34] [Administrative Redress Report]; *Administrative Redress: Public Bodies and the Citizen*, Law Com Consultation Paper 187 (2008) [4.143]ff [Administrative Redress Consultation Paper].

[46] See *Brasserie du Pecheur SA v Germany* [1996] QB 404; *R v SOS for Transport, ex p Factortame Ltd (No 5)* [2000] 1 AC 524.

[47] *Köbler v Republik Österrich* [2004] QB 848.

[48] *Brasserie* (n 46) [51].

[49] T Lock, 'Is Private Enforcement of EU Law Through State Liability a Myth? An Assessment 20 Years After *Francovich*' (2012) 49 *CML Rev* 1675, 1688–89.

[50] *Negassi* (n 6) [25].

[51] *Brasserie* (n 46) [55]; *Dillenkofer v Germany* [1997] QB 259, [25].

In *Brasserie* the ECJ held that whether the threshold is met depends upon several factors: the clarity of the rule breached; the measure of discretion left by that rule to national authorities; whether the infringement and damage caused were intentional or involuntary; whether any legal error was excusable or inexcusable; and whether the position taken by an EU institution may have contributed to breach.[52] There are a few categories of case in which the fact of breach is conclusive of sufficient seriousness, and successful damages claims have generally been limited to such cases:[53] where the breach persists despite a judgment finding breach; where it is clear from settled case law that the relevant conduct constitutes an infringement;[54] and where the measure breached leaves the Member State no discretion, as in cases where the Member State does not transpose a Directive within the prescribed time-limit for transposition.[55] Over time the degree of discretion left to the Member State—which implicates an inquiry into the clarity and precision of the rule breached[56]—has emerged as the key factor in determining whether the breach is sufficiently serious, with the other *Brasserie* factors treated as ancillary.[57] Thus the touchstone of sufficient seriousness is whether the state manifestly and gravely disregarded the limits on its discretion. Where the state enjoys no or very limited discretion, say because the norm breached enunciates a clear rule with no exceptions, the court will likely conclude the breach was sufficiently serious. But where the rule breached is other than crystal clear, as will often be the case, practice shows it is very unlikely that a court will reach a conclusion of sufficiently serious breach.[58]

B. Should the *Francovich* Criteria Govern Human Rights Damages?

There are strong arguments which tell against importing the EU test into domestic human rights law, so that damages would be limited to cases of 'sufficiently serious' breach.

i. Different Interests

This restrictive approach may be more justifiable in the EU context because EU law protects a vast range of interests, most of which have traditionally

[52] *Brasserie* ibid [56].
[53] Lock (n 49) 1693–97.
[54] *Brasserie* (n 46) [57].
[55] *Dillenkofer* (n 51) [25]–[26]; *R v Ministry of Agriculture, Fisheries and Food, ex p Hedley Lomas* [1997] QB 139, [28].
[56] eg *R v HM Treasury, ex p British Telecommunications Plc* [1996] QB 615, [42].
[57] eg *Laboratoires Pharmaceutiques Bergaderm SA v Commission* [2000] ECR I-5291, [43]–[44]; *R (Chester) v SOSJ* [2014] 1 AC 271, [76]–[79].
[58] See Lock (n 49) 1693–97.

been economic in nature,[59] which are in general[60] less fundamental than those protected by human rights law. For example claims have been made in the fields of insolvency and pensions,[61] export licences for livestock,[62] package travel holidays,[63] financial regulation,[64] and procurement procedures for public utilities.[65] By analogy, in tort law it is common for torts that protect merely economic interests to require something more than interference with the underlying interest before liability is established.[66]

Of course it is important to observe that within the EU system the EU Charter on Fundamental Rights has recently been given direct legal force, now having the same legal value as the Treaties, so that the *Brasserie* criteria in principle govern liability for breaches of human rights within the province of EU law.[67] However, the test of EU liability was developed well before human rights had the central place within the EU system which they now occupy, and is thus not a test developed with human rights norms in mind. This point has not been lost on commentators, who have been quick to observe:

> There is something inherently unsettling about reliance on EU damages liability as the touchstone for determining the circumstances in which compensation will be paid for breach of the Charter ... almost all of the cases concerning damages for breach of EU law ... have arisen in the context of commercial or economic law. This immediately raises the question of whether these rules are appropriately adapted to secure compliance with rules of law that are central to the rights of European citizens, and which form the heartland of EU constitutional principle.[68]

It may be that the Charter prompts rethinking of the *Francovich/Brasserie* criteria, specifically as they apply to human rights breaches. Possible EU accession to the European Convention on Human Rights (ECHR) may also

[59] C Harlow, 'Francovich and the Problem of the Disobedient State' (1996) 2 *European Law Journal* 199, 211.

[60] Of course some norms, such as the four freedoms, are viewed as equivalent in status to fundamental human rights, and indeed may take priority over human rights (eg *International Transport Workers' Federation v Viking Line ABP* [2008] 1 CMLR 51; *Laval un Partneri Ltd v Svenska Byggnadsarbetareforbundet* [2008] 2 CMLR 9). However, the point is the test for state liability is a *general* one that also applies to breach of myriad norms which fall below fundamental status and that this inevitably affects the liability rules adopted.

[61] *Robins v SOS for Work and Pensions* [2007] 2 CMLR 13.

[62] *Hedley Lomas* (n 55).

[63] *Dillenkofer* (n 51).

[64] *Paul v Germany* [2004] ECR I-9425; *Three Rivers DC v Bank of England (No 3)* [2003] 2 AC 1.

[65] *British Telecommunications* (n 56).

[66] See generally ch 2.I–II.

[67] See for example A Ward, 'Damages under the EU Charter of Fundamental Rights' (2012) 12 *ERA Forum* 589; *Chester* (n 57) [75]–[83] (*Francovich* criteria applied in case concerning the right to vote); *McGeoch v Scottish LAB* [2013] CSOH 6, [87]–[88] (*Francovich* in principle applies to breach of Charter).

[68] Ward ibid 603.

be a catalyst, given the demands of Article 13 ECHR. In any case, as is discussed further below (section II.B.iv), in specific contexts in which EU law protects basic interests akin to those protected by human rights the ECJ has enunciated more stringent remedial requirements.

ii. A Marginal Remedy

Given the strictness of the criteria governing *Francovich* liability, it is unsurprising that very few claims have been successful. An empirical study of EU state liability claims brought in Germany and England over the 20-year period following *Francovich* found few claims have been made, and that very few have been successful.[69] In England there has been, on average, just over one claim decided by English courts per year, and only 36 per cent of claims (nine out of 25) have been successful. In Germany approximately two cases have been decided by national courts per year, with a success rate of 22 per cent (eight out of 37). So much for predictions of a flood of claims that invariably followed the *Francovich* decision; yet again[70] idle speculation rubs up against reality.[71] Significantly, the study finds the 'vast majority of claims fail because the national court was unable to establish a sufficiently serious breach' and that this is the 'most difficult condition for a claimant to establish'.[72] Similarly, a study published in 2011 found that since the founding of the European Community there have been only 20 successful claims for damages against EU institutions for breach of EU law, the rules governing such claims being analogous to those governing state liability.[73]

These studies show *Francovich* damages to be a damp squib, a remedy rarely sought and very rarely granted. Adoption in domestic human rights law of a test limiting damages to cases of flagrant breach, with the result that damages would hardly ever be claimed or awarded, would achieve a mean feat: it would render damages even more marginal than they currently are under the HRA. Marginalisation of the damages remedy would be particularly pronounced if, as is the recent trend in EU law, the touchstone of sufficiently serious breach were whether the norm violated sets forth a clear rule, given the outcome in many human rights cases depends not on clear

[69] Lock (n 49).

[70] See ch 6.2.V.

[71] The paucity of claims is not explained by there being few breaches of EU law by German and UK authorities. For example, for the time period studied the author records the number of infringement proceedings initiated by the Commission against England and Germany, and decided by the ECJ, was almost five times higher than the number of *Francovich* cases decided in English and German courts, while it is well-known, for example, that Member States regularly violate their duties to transpose Directives in time.

[72] Lock (n 49) 1688, 1693–97.

[73] P Aalto, *Public Liability in EU Law* (Hart Publishing, 2011) 148ff.

rules but fact-dependant weighing of factors, as under proportionality. It is very difficult to justify such restrictive approach where basic interests are at stake, especially as damages are often awarded for innocuous violations of equivalent or less significant interests in English law.

iii. Range of Institutions Potentially Liable

State liability in EU law attaches not only to administrative acts, but also acts and omissions of the legislature.[74] The idea of constraining legislative action through threat of imposition of liability is far more contentious than constraining administrative action in this way given the very strong democratic interest in the legislature not being shackled in terms of what primary legislation it may or may not pass.[75] Furthermore, the class of persons that may be negatively affected by legislative action or inaction may be vast. For example following the ECJ's decision in *Dillenkofer*, in which liability was imposed for the German legislature's failure to transpose a Directive, around 7,800 individuals were paid compensation totalling 10 million Euros.[76] Also, while in domestic law government and legislature can respond to imposition of liability by passing legislation narrowing or removing that liability, there is no such option in the context of EU law. It is therefore unsurprising EU liability rules allow defendant states substantial 'wriggle-room'.

iv. Different Contexts: EU Law versus Domestic Human Rights Law

To fully understand the ECJ's approach to state liability, it is imperative to consider the distinctive nature of the EU context, which is very different from the domestic human rights context.

a. Structure of Juridical Relationships and Nature of Obligations

The juridical relationships between the various players may be quite different. In domestic human rights law there is a direct relationship between the rights-bearer and the defendant authority; the rights-bearer has a right in

[74] See n 46 above.

[75] *British Telecommunications* (n 56) [40]; *Brasserie* (n 46) [43]ff.

[76] Lock (n 49) 1681. Another illustrative example is the legislative ban on prisoner voting in Britain, which has been challenged in human rights and EU law. Huge numbers of claims have been made, given the ban affects a large class of individuals. For example the ECtHR disposed of 1,015 applications in *McHugh v UK* (10 February 2015) App no 51987/08 (ECtHR Fourth Section), while the English High Court recorded over 500 claims had been filed domestically: *Tovey v MOJ* [2011] EWHC 271, [3]. No HRA damages have been awarded as legislative acts are insulated from liability under the HRA, while damages claims in EU law failed on their merits: *Chester* (n 57).

respect of X vis-à-vis the authority and the authority has a duty in respect of X vis-à-vis the rights-holder. This is not necessarily so in the Union context. Take, for example, cases concerning failure to implement a Directive into domestic law or failure to implement Directives properly, which make up a large proportion of state liability claims. Where a state is liable to compensate individuals who have suffered loss in consequence of such failure, the causative event, giving rise to liability, is not that the state breached legal duties owed to those specific individuals. Rather, the state has violated an obligation that is contractual in nature, that is, an obligation owed to other Member States of the Union to transpose and implement the Directive. Individuals have suffered as a result. But they have not suffered in consequence of breach of a duty owed directly to them, but rather as third party beneficiaries of these contract-like duties owed to other states. These individuals would have had realisable legal rights had the Directive in fact been transposed into domestic law, but those rights are only putative or potential rights before transposition.[77] In any case it is not breach of those rights that constitute the violation upon which the *Francovich* claim is based in cases of non- or mis-implementation of a Directive; rather the relevant 'wrong' is breach of a duty to implement the Directive in time and properly. Therefore, at least in non- or mis-implementation cases, the proximity between the state and individual 'victims' is much more remote and indirect than in domestic human rights law; individuals in these cases cannot be said to have suffered a personal legal wrong. Further, the nature of the duty breached is distinct from the nature of duties in human rights law, being a legal obligation generated by promise rather than one correlative to fundamental right.

b. Political and Legal Context

The ECJ's assertion of state liability was highly contentious, legally and politically, for reasons peculiar to the Union context. In turn it was always going to be necessary for the ECJ to limit recoverability of damages so as to render state liability palatable for Member States; as Dougan observes, 'the [ECJ] is as much concerned to avoid treading on domestic toes as it is committed to pursuing its own agenda of effective judicial protection'.[78]

An important aspect of the EU context, which helps to explain adoption of a restrained approach, is that there is no express textual basis in the

[77] Though Directives may be directly effective and enforceable against public institutions if certain criteria are met, despite not having been transposed.

[78] M Dougan, 'The Francovich Right to Reparation: Reshaping the Contours of Community Remedial Competence' (2000) 6 *European Public Law* 103, 120 [Dougan 2000]; see generally M Dougan, 'The Vicissitudes of Life at the Coalface: Remedies and Procedures for Enforcing Union Law Before the National Courts' in P Craig and G de Búrca (eds), *The Evolution of EU Law* 2nd edn (OUP, 2011) [Dougan 2011].

Treaties[79] for imposition of state liability, which made assertion of such liability contentious.[80] The ECJ, in *Francovich* and *Brasserie*, asserted that the principle of state liability was 'inherent in the system of the [EC] Treaty',[81] and sought to justify its adoption by reference to some fairly open-textured norms of EU law, including: the principle that Community law be effective;[82] Article 5 EEC (now Article 4 TEU) which requires member states to take all appropriate measures to fulfil EU obligations;[83] and the 'general principle familiar to the legal systems of the member states that an unlawful act or omission gives rise to an obligation to make good the damage caused', reflected in Article 215 EC (now Article 340 TFEU), governing liability of Union institutions.[84] Given the absence of any express authority in the Treaties, and given this was an instance of state liability imposed from without rather than from within the domestic order, therefore cutting across the principle of national procedural autonomy, it was always going to be necessary for the ECJ to impose limits on liability so as to avoid serious political backlash from Member States. Indeed, despite the restrictive approach adopted the political reaction was still not favourable.[85]

On top of this it would have undermined the legitimacy of the EU order if the rules governing state liability were less restrictive than those liability rules applied to EU institutions: 'a judgment which imposed a much stricter liability on the states than on the Community itself would have provided ammunition to those eager to limit the Court's powers'.[86] It is therefore not surprising that the three-pronged test 'exactly mirrors' the liability formula for Union institutions.[87]

c. A Minimum Standard

The principle of national procedural autonomy is a cornerstone of the EU legal order and holds that procedure and remedies are principally for Member States, founded on the idea that procedure and remedies reflect values and traditions peculiar to each Member State. The corollary of this principle is that the ECJ's role in respect of remedies is generally a supervisory and

[79] As acknowledged by the ECJ: *Brasserie* (n 46) [27].

[80] See RC Smith, 'Remedies for Breaches of EC Law in National Courts: Legal Variation and Selection' in P Craig and G de Búrca (eds), *The Evolution of EU Law* (OUP, 1999) 288–90.

[81] *Brasserie* (n 46) [31]; *Francovich* (n 42) [35].

[82] *Francovich* ibid [32]–[34].

[83] ibid [36].

[84] *Brasserie* (n 46) [28]–[29].

[85] C Harlow, *State Liability* (OUP, 2004) 65–67; J Tallberg, 'Supranational Influence in EU Enforcement: the ECJ and the Principle of State Liability' (2000) 7 *Journal of European Public Policy* 104, 113ff.

[86] Craig (n 45) 79; Smith (n 80) 305.

[87] Harlow (n 59) 203; *Brasserie* (n 46) [42], [53]; *Bergaderm* (n 57) [41]ff. On the interrelationship between the two systems see further: Aalto (n 73).

subsidiary one. Given this, the three-pronged test for *Francovich* liability, imposed as it is from the supranational plane, is not intended to be a *model* remedial approach for domestic courts adjudicating claims for remedies for breach of EU norms. Rather, *Francovich* represents a 'minimum standard' erected by a supranational court with a principally supervisory responsibility for redress; a 'default action' 'intended to supplement the relief already available under national law'; a 'minimum Community-wide framework of liability'.[88] As the ECJ has repeated time and again, that the three criteria governing the *Francovich* action are sufficient to found a claim for damages 'does not mean that the State cannot incur liability [for breach of EU law] under less strict conditions on the basis of national law'.[89] In other words the *Francovich* criteria represent a 'floor'—a basic level of protection below which national remedial standards may not drop[90]—rather than a 'ceiling', or a model approach for national courts.

It is important to observe that beyond the minimum *Francovich* framework for liability, that is to apply *generally* as a default for all state breaches of EU law, in *specific* contexts, particularly where *basic interests* are at stake, and there is an *express provision* within a Directive addressing remedies, the ECJ has set the minimum higher, and come closer to articulating a vindicatory remedial framework. For example, in a series of cases concerning the Directive on sex equality the ECJ adopted an expansive interpretation of a procedural clause guaranteeing access to judicial process for victims of discrimination, holding it to entail an entitlement to effective redress for breach of equality guarantees.[91] The ECJ set down detailed requirements of an effective remedy, these requirements being shaped by the Directive's goal and its normative importance: 'to arrive at real equality of opportunity'.[92] States were required to adopt an appropriate system of sanctions for breach of the right of equal opportunity, which produce real deterrent effects, and those remedies had to be capable of fully 'restoring' equality.[93] This meant that where, for example, an individual was subject to discriminatory dismissal from employment national courts were required to either: (i) order the individual's reinstatement, so as to secure actual enjoyment of the right; or (ii) grant compensation for loss and damage sustained, which made good the losses 'in full', offering a second-best equivalent to actual enjoyment of the individual entitlement.[94] Any cap on recovery would be unlawful as inconsistent with the goal of ensuring real equality, given it would prevent

[88] Dougan 2000 (n 78) *passim*.

[89] *Brasserie* (n 46) [66].

[90] eg ibid [70]–[74].

[91] *Von Colson v Land Nordrhein-Westfahlen* [1986] 2 CMLR 430; *Johnston v Chief Constable Royal Ulster Constabulary* [1987] QB 129; *Marshall v Southampton and SW Hampshire AHA (No 2)* [1994] QB 126.

[92] *Von Colson* ibid [18]; *Johnston* ibid [17][19]; *Marshall* ibid [22]–[26].

[93] *Von Colson* ibid [22]–[23], [28]; *Marshall* ibid [24]–[25].

[94] *Marshall* ibid [22]–[38].

full restoration of the equality entitlement through damages, while interest on damage must be awarded, otherwise the entitlement would be undervalued given 'effluxion of time'.[95]

d. Different Goals

As counsel submitted in *Anufrijeva*, '[d]amages under the [HRA] should not be developed by analogy with [*Francovich*] damages, so as not to be payable unless the breach involves a grave and manifest breach, *since the rationale for such damages is different*'.[96] This is a persuasive argument. The rationale for state liability in EU law is contested. But the most convincing view[97] is that the principal concern is an integrationist one: to further the project of European integration by incentivising state compliance with EU norms, particularly duties to implement Directives.[98] This goal is far removed from the principal goal of domestic human rights law, which is protection and vindication of basic human interests. In turn this suggests that it would be inapt to read across damages criteria from EU law to the very different context of human rights law.

Along with rulings that unimplemented Directives may be directly effective against emanations of the state,[99] adoption of doctrines of indirect effect[100] and incidental horizontal effect,[101] and the decision in *Mangold* that general principles of EU law may have direct effect,[102] assertion of state liability is part of a concerted effort by the ECJ to secure the effectiveness of EU law and the penetration of EU norms into the domestic order.[103] This concern

95 ibid [30]–[32].

96 *Anufrijeva* (n 43) 1133 (Clayton QC, emphasis added).

97 See, eg, Harlow (n 59) 204ff; (n 85) 57–58; R Caranta, 'Judicial Protection Against Member States: A New *Jus Commune* Takes Shape' (1995) 32 *CML Rev* 703, 710; T Tridimas, 'Liability for Breach of Community Law: Growing Up and Mellowing Down?' in Fairgrieve et al (n 44) 149–50; Smith (n 80) 303.

98 *Francovich*, which established state liability, concerned Italy's failure to implement a Directive, and it is in the context of such breaches that most successful state liability claims have been brought.

99 *Van Duyn v Home Office* [1974] ECR 1337; *Pubblico Ministero v Ratti* [1979] ECR 1629; *Marshall v Southampton and SW Hampshire AHA* [1986] ECR 723.

100 *Von Colson* (n 91); *Marleasing SA v La Comercial Internacional de Alimentacion SA* [1990] ECR I-4135.

101 *CIA Security International SA v Singalson SA* [1996] ECR I-2201.

102 *Mangold v Helm* [2005] ECR I-9981.

103 See, eg, J Steiner, 'From Direct Effects to *Francovich*: Shifting Means of Enforcement of Community Law' (1993) 18 *European Law Review* 3. As Tridimas observes, the ECJ's approach in *Francovich* 'incorporated all signs of constitution-building' ((n 97) 149), while Harlow considers *Francovich* 'must ... be seen as an assertion of power or even act of defiance by the ECJ' ((n 85) 58), observing the ideology of the Court is 'self-avowedly integrationist' ((n 59) 200). See also Smith (n 80), tracing how the ECJ has, over time, 'tightened the screw' on Member States through decisions on remedies, though that trend has now abated somewhat given a fear of overreach: Dougan 2011 (n 78); A Arnull, 'The Principle of Effective Judicial Protection in EU Law: An Unruly Horse?' (2011) 36 *European Law Review* 51.

has continued to underpin subsequent developments in state liability. For example it seems clear that a key motivation for confirming applicability of *Francovich* liability to judicial acts in the ECJ's 2004 decision in *Köbler* was to ensure national courts comply with their obligation to make references to the ECJ for preliminary rulings.[104] The reluctance or failure of national courts to do so has the potential to undermine effectiveness of EU law: national courts may adopt conservative interpretations of EU norms; adopt varied interpretations of EU law so that the same norm is not applied uniformly across EU member states; while the ECJ's capacity to shape Union law in accord with the goals of the European order may be diminished, as it is denied the opportunity to rule on important legal matters.

That compliance is the principal concern is reflected in significant features of the *Francovich* action, particularly the sufficiently serious criterion. A state will almost certainly suffer the sanction of damages if it deliberately or recklessly violates a clear norm of EU law. However, if a state demonstrates a genuine attempt to comply with a somewhat ambiguous rule but nonetheless fails, or was, for example, led into legal error by erroneous guidance from EU institutions, it is very unlikely to be held liable. In this way liability rules are calibrated to incentivise and reward behaviour orientated towards bona fide compliance.

The ECJ has invoked the lofty language of 'rights-talk' in this area, arguing damages liability affords protection to the individual rights of citizens of Member States. For the cynic the ECJ's appeal to rights is a rhetorical device to sure up justification for creation of a remedy with no basis in the text of any Treaty, while an appeal to individual rights has often been utilised by the ECJ as a technique to enhance the legitimacy of the EU order more generally.[105]

But, even giving the Court the benefit of the doubt, that there may be some concern expressed for individual rights does not undermine the claim that integration is the Court's core concern. If the Court is concerned to protect individuals through imposition of liability this is *because* this carries forward the project of European integration. We see this linkage in the Court's dictum in *Brasserie* that 'the full effectiveness of Community law would be impaired if individuals were unable to obtain redress when their rights were infringed by a breach of Community law';[106] provision

[104] *Köbler* (n 47). The Court held non-compliance with the duty to refer was a factor going to the sufficiently serious inquiry (at [55]), while the facts of the case raised that matter squarely (eg at [117]–[118], [123]). Further, in theory imposing liability for manifestly incorrect judicial interpretations of EU law incentivises national courts to refer where in doubt as to the correct interpretation.

[105] eg J Coppel and A O'Neill, 'The European Court of Justice: Taking Rights Seriously?' (1992) 12 *Legal Studies* 227, 245; A O'Neill, 'The EU and Fundamental Rights' [2011] *Judicial Review* 216, 222.

[106] *Brasserie* (n 46) [20].

for individual reparation is premised on the principal aim of ensuring full effectiveness.

Further, any concern to protect individual rights is only given effect *to the extent* this carries forward the primary integrationist goal. Individual harm, including very significant harm, suffered as a result of a violation, will go uncompensated if the state has demonstrated some commitment to compliance, or its non-compliance is excusable, so the violation is not grave and manifest. Further, none of the factors identified in *Brasserie* which go to the seriousness inquiry are orientated to or responsive to the needs of individual claimants who have suffered harm. Nor do those factors address whether the norm breached protects fundamental interests. The principal focus is on the degree of discretion afforded to the Member State by the measure breached; even in cases concerning infringement of basic rights, such as the right to vote, the sole focus is on discretion and compliance concerns, with the importance of the right never mentioned, let alone afforded weight.[107] Given these features, it is hard to see how it could be maintained that individual redress or protection could be the *principal* focus of *Francovich* liability. Further telling against this conception is that, as we saw above, claimants have only rarely secured compensation. Again, this is largely due to operation of the sufficiently serious criterion, which is squarely based in integrationist concerns. As commentators conclude, state liability 'is there to penalise the very wayward state rather than to be concerned with redress for individuals. For, if it were the latter, there would be little justification for such a restrictive test'.[108] In addition, the remedial focus is seemingly on compensating material losses,[109] subject to standard counterfactual analysis, while English courts have, where there is some degree of doubt over causation, readily denied the claim;[110] there is no indication of a normative, vindicatory dimension to damages, or of any presumptions of loss that operate for the claimant's benefit.

Lastly, though the matter can only be broached in passing, there is a fair argument that the *Francovich* 'experiment' has failed on its own terms.

[107] *Chester* (n 57) [76]–[80]

[108] D Chalmers et al, *European Union Law* 2nd edn (CUP, 2010) 307.

[109] There have been very few cases in which recoverable heads of damage and method of quantification have been directly addressed, such matters being for the forum state. Where heads of damage have been considered the focus has been on factual loss, and specifically economic loss, given the economic nature of many norms in EU, while there has been a reluctance to recognise heads of non-pecuniary loss of any kind, including aggravated damages. See: *R v SOSHD, ex p Gallagher* [1996] 2 CMLR 951; *R v SOS for Transport, ex p Factortame Ltd (No 6)* [2001] 1 WLR 942; *Negassi* (n 6). This is all consonant with a tendency in English law to analogise *Francovich* to the tort of breach of statutory duty, which is a loss-based tort (P Giliker, 'English Tort Law and the Challenge of *Francovich* Liability: 20 Years On' (2012) 128 *LQR* 541); in *Factortame (No 6)* the Court refused to draw an analogy with vindicatory torts which protect dignitary interests. Exemplary damages may be available: *Brasserie* (n 46) [89]–[90].

[110] eg *Negassi* (n 6) [30]; *Chester* (n 57) [81]–[83].

The aim is to incentivise compliance. We lack direct evidence on how the threat of liability influences Member State behaviour. However, what indicators we have suggest liability has not been particularly effective in engendering compliance. We know Member States continue regularly to violate duties to transpose Directives in time, for example. We also know the Commission brings far more public infringement proceedings against Member States than there are *Francovich* actions, and such proceedings succeed at far higher rates than *Francovich* actions.[111] As such, 'in the overall picture of enforcement, *Francovich* type cases are only of limited importance'.[112] Furthermore, there have been exceptionally few *Francovich* cases, and even fewer successful claims, which makes it difficult to see how Member States could view liability as a credible threat, in terms of both reputational and pecuniary costs. The reality is the sufficiently serious criterion makes it all too easy for states to evade liability for loss-causing violations. In addition, Dougan observes that despite the intention that *Francovich* serve as a minimum standard or default action, there is evidence that its adoption may have precipitated dilution of national remedial standards, ironically undermining effectiveness of EU law.[113] Consonant with the theme of chapter 6, the experience with *Francovich* reinforces the view that courts should be extremely cautious about calibrating liability criteria according to expected consequential effects.

C. Conclusion

There are good reasons counselling against adoption of the 'sufficiently serious' test within domestic human rights law. EU state liability rules have been developed to govern damages liability for interference with interests which are less than fundamental. These liability rules have resulted in exceptionally few cases and even fewer successful claims, suggesting these rules would be too restrictive for human rights law; such approach would leave many victims of not insignificant violations of basic rights without remedy. Importantly, the context in which the 'sufficiently serious' test has developed is very different from the domestic human rights context. The nature of juridical relationships in EU law may be different, such that, unlike in human rights law, compensation may be awarded to individuals who have suffered no personal legal wrong, and for breach of contract-like norms. Further, the restrictive liability rules adopted by the ECJ were, at least in some measure, influenced by the distinctive political context in which it

[111] Lock (n 49) 1685–88.
[112] ibid 1687.
[113] Dougan 2000 (n 78).

operates. Those rules are intended as a minimum EU-wide standard, not a best practice model for domestic law. Most importantly, the chief rationale for damages liability in EU law is not vindication of fundamental rights, but incentivising state compliance so as to secure deeper integration, and the liability rules reflect this goal.

The liability rules asserted in *Francovich* and refined in *Brasserie* may be explicable in the EU context. They might, as the Law Commission thought, offer a viable starting point for development of a monetary remedy for breach of duties within common law judicial review, given the narrow remedial concern in that field with guiding and regulating power so that it is exercised properly.[114] However, the sufficiently serious criterion would be out of place in human rights law, given the distinctive concerns of that field.

III. IMMUNITIES FROM SUIT IN US CONSTITUTIONAL TORT LAW[115]

The US Supreme Court has taken a different tack in limiting damages liability for breaches of rights under the US Constitution. It has recognised immunities that are available to officials as a shield to constitutional tort actions;[116] these are not defences but immunities from suit. The Supreme Court has held that there ought to be no difference in the approach to immunities depending on whether the damages claim is made against state officials, under 42 USC § 1983, or federal officials, according to the *Bivens*[117] cause of action.[118]

There are two forms of immunity.[119] *Absolute immunity* affords complete protection from damages suits. Such immunities are considered exceptional and have been held to apply to prosecutors, judges, legislators and the President.[120] In deciding which officials should enjoy absolute immunity the courts have been guided by which officials have traditionally enjoyed immunities at common law and the interests protected by such immunities,[121]

[114] See ch 4.2.I–II. Although, the justifiability of such a remedy depends on whether it would in fact promote compliance. The *Francovich* experience counsels caution.

[115] For background on the US constitutional torts see: ch 3.V.

[116] See generally JL Mashaw et al, *Administrative Law: The American Public Law System* 6th edn (West, 2014) ch 8; PH Schuck, *Suing Government: Citizen Remedies for Official Wrongs* (Yale, 1983) ch 2, apps 2–3; SH Nahmod et al, *Constitutional Torts* 4th edn (LexisNexis, 2015) chs 7–8.

[117] *Bivens v Six Unknown Named Agents of Federal Bureau of Narcotics* 403 US 388 (1971).

[118] See *Butz v Economou* 438 US 478, 499–501 (1978).

[119] For an excellent critical analysis of these different rules see: JC Jeffries, 'The Liability Rule for Constitutional Torts' (2013) 99 *Virginia Law Review* 207 [Jeffries 2013].

[120] See, eg, *Butz* (n 118) 508ff; *Harlow v Fitzgerald* 457 US 800, 810–11 (1982). Deciding which immunity should apply to which class of officials is not an easy exercise and the Supreme Court has been criticised for its allocations: Schuck (n 116) 89–92; AA Burris, 'Qualifying Immunity in Section 1983 and *Bivens* Actions' (1992) 71 *Texas Law Review* 123.

[121] *Butz* (n 118) 508.

as well as policy considerations.[122] The scope of such immunities is defined functionally, so the immunity attaches to the task, not the office.[123] Thus a federal prosecutor is immune in respect of prosecutorial tasks, but not administrative tasks undertaken in the course of employment.[124] Officials not afforded absolute immunity typically enjoy *qualified immunity* in exercise of their discretionary powers; if absolute immunity is the exception, qualified immunity is the 'general rule'.[125] Qualified immunity shields officials from suit where the constitutional right that was violated was not 'clearly established' by past case law.[126] Even if the right is clearly established the official will still enjoy immunity if her conduct was 'objectively reasonable' in the light of established legal principle.[127]

Immunities of this sort have not been a significant feature of the law of human rights or constitutional damages in other common law jurisdictions. However, there are signs that courts may reach for such immunities as a means of limiting damages. For example the New Zealand Supreme Court has within the last few years established a limited set of absolute immunities from *Baigent* liability;[128] now that the cat is out of the bag such immunities show signs of creep,[129] and Crown counsel are pushing for their expansion.[130] The Supreme Court of Canada has also recognised qualified immunities from Charter damages claims, albeit in the special and specific context of claims in relation to administrative acts pursuant to statutes subsequently found unconstitutional.[131] Though it seems the Supreme Court may be open to recognition of further immunities in future.[132]

A. The Importance of Context

Before considering qualified immunity in detail several more general observations require to be made, so as to contextualise the pervasiveness of immunities within US constitutional tort doctrine. As we shall see,

[122] *Harlow* (n 120) 814. Defendants bear the burden of proving immunities: ibid 506.

[123] *Harlow* (n 120) 810–11.

[124] *Buckley v Fitzsimmons* 509 US 259 (1993). Drawing the line between primary and administrative tasks has proven difficult: Mashaw et al (n 116) 1214–15; Burris (n 120) 126–27.

[125] *Butz* (n 118) 508.

[126] *Harlow* (n 120) 818.

[127] *Anderson v Creighton* 483 US 635, 640–41 (1987).

[128] *Attorney-General v Chapman* [2012] 1 NZLR 462 (judicial immunity).

[129] *Siemer v Attorney-General* [2014] NZHC 3175, [127]–[131] (extension of immunity to Court Registrars).

[130] *Currie v Clayton* [2014] NZCA 511 (attempt by Crown counsel to extend immunity to prosecutors).

[131] *City of Vancouver v Ward* [2010] 2 SCR 28, [39]–[41]; *Mackin v New Brunswick* [2002] 1 SCR 405.

[132] *Ward* ibid [42]; *Henry v British Columbia* [2015] SCC 24 (establishing a special zone of protection—within which the threshold for establishing liability is very high—for Crown failures to disclose).

the American legal context in which these immunities have developed has features which distinguish it from the English context, these differences in turn telling against any Trans-Atlantic legal transplant.

i. Constitutional Concerns

Both the § 1983 and *Bivens* actions implicate constitutional concerns peculiar to the American context. One motivation for adoption of widespread immunities, among other control devices, has been to meet these concerns.

Imposition of damages liability by federal courts on state actors under § 1983 gives rise to federalist concerns. In the seminal case of *Monroe*, which awoke § 1983 from its long sleep, the majority was unpersuaded by the argument that a plaintiff needed to show state law remedies were inadequate before they could rely on § 1983; Congress's intention was to give individuals remedies specifically for breaches of *federal* rights under the Constitution, and such an action was to operate in parallel to existing state remedies.[133] In contrast, Frankfurter J, in a lone dissent, would have afforded primacy to state law, and required a plaintiff to demonstrate state remedies, for example in state tort law, were inadequate before allowing recourse to § 1983. His reasoning was founded upon a federalist concern that too easily allowing recourse to § 1983 would threaten the primacy of state law in affording redress for injuries caused by state actors:

> The jurisdiction which Article III of the Constitution conferred on the national judiciary reflected the assumption that the state courts, not the federal courts, would remain the primary guardians of that fundamental security of person and property which the long evolution of the common law had secured to one individual as against other individuals.[134]

Despite Frankfurter J's view representing a minority position in *Monroe* the federalist concern has, over the decades since *Monroe*, assumed ascendency. It has operated as a background concern, underpinning steps by the Supreme Court over time to reel in § 1983 liability, and in turn ameliorate the perceived incursion upon state law.[135] Assertion of myriad immunities, and subsequent steps to strengthen those immunities, has formed a central element of this trend.[136]

Similar federalist concerns have more recently shaped the *Bivens* jurisprudence, with the Supreme Court identifying the availability of alternative remedies in state tort law as a reason for restricting constitutional damages

[133] *Monroe v Pape* 365 US 167 (1961).
[134] ibid 237.
[135] For a recent example see: *Connick v Thompson* 131 S Ct 1350 (2011).
[136] See, eg, SH Nahmod, 'The Long and Winding Road from *Monroe* to *Connick*' (2012) 13 *Loyola Journal of Public Interest Law* 427, especially 443–45.

liability of federal actors.[137] However, the separation of powers has been the predominant constitutional concern in this field. The Court's unease derives from there being no express provision for damages claims in the text of the Constitution, the *Bivens* action being an implied cause of action. The concern originally found expression in the dissents in *Bivens*, the dissenters arguing that recognition of the damages remedy was, in the absence of an express basis in the Constitution or statute, a legislative act and that the decision whether to provide a constitutional damages action was properly for Congress.[138] As in the § 1983 context, views originally aired in dissent have, in time, assumed ascendency. Over the last 30 years a Supreme Court dominated by Justices generally hostile to the *Bivens* remedy has repeatedly invoked separation-of-powers concerns to justify not extending the *Bivens* remedy to new constitutional rights, contexts or defendants.[139] Some members of the Court openly call for *Bivens*, and immediately subsequent cases which extended the remedy, to be limited to the precise circumstances in which they were decided on the basis that the Supreme Court now considers it impermissible to create actions by implication.[140] Symptomatic of the concern that *Bivens* constitutes an illegitimate incursion upon the competence of other branches, the Court has capitalised upon every opportunity presented to it to further marginalise the remedy, and thus ameliorate the perceived constitutional transgression. This has included strengthening immunities. Developments in the realm of immunities may not often have been justified explicitly by reference to separation-of-powers concerns. However, such concerns are a powerful consideration which loom large whenever *Bivens* claims reach the Court, and fundamentally shape the Court's general approach to legal questions in this context.

These aspects of the American context mark it out from the English and UK contexts. Although federalism-type issues are currently in the legal and political spotlight in the UK, the precise federalist concern, underpinning moves to restrict the § 1983 action, is not translatable to the UK (at present). The specific separation-of-powers concern driving marginalisation of *Bivens* does not arise in the UK; the HRA expressly provides for damages. Although it cannot be discussed in detail here, there is also a fair argument that the separation-of-powers concern is overstated even in the American

[137] eg *Minneci v Pollard* 132 S Ct 617 (2012); AA Reinert and LN Mulligan, 'Asking the First Question: Reframing *Bivens* After *Minneci*' (2013) 90 *Washington University Law Review* 1473.

[138] *Bivens* (n 117) 411–12, 427–28, 430. To similar effect see *Carlson v Green* 446 US 14, 29, 53–54 (1980); *Davis v Passman* 442 US 228, 252 (1979).

[139] *Minneci* (n 137); *Ashcroft v Iqbal* 129 S Ct 1937, 1948 (2009); *Wilkie v Robbins* 551 US 537, 549ff (2007); *Correctional Services Corp v Malesko* 534 US 61, especially 66–71 (2001); *FDIC v Meyer* 510 US 471 (1994); *Schweiker v Chilicky* 487 US 412 (1988); *Bush v Lucas* 462 US 367 (1983).

[140] *Minneci* (n 137) 626; *Wilkie* ibid 568; *Malesko* ibid 75.

context (while damages have been recognised as a remedy in other jurisdictions despite the lack of express provision for them in the relevant charter of rights).[141] Congress has ratified the *Bivens* action,[142] and while it has placed severe restrictions on damages claims against officials and government in tort,[143] it has taken no such steps to curtail *Bivens*, and indeed specifically preserved *Bivens* where other types of claims have been ousted.[144] The Supreme Court's recognition of the remedy did not rest on contentious policy calculations best left to Congress but on longstanding *legal* principles that where there is a right there ought to be a remedy and that where federal rights are invaded courts may use any available remedy to make good the wrong. Indeed it has been the rule 'from the beginning' that courts ought to be alive to adjust their remedies so as to grant necessary relief for breaches of federal rights;[145] in other words, within the separation of powers fashioning of remedies is properly the judiciary's role,[146] while there is nothing radical in awarding damages given '[h]istorically, damages have been regarded as the ordinary remedy for an invasion of personal interests in liberty' and are a remedy 'normally available in the federal courts'.[147] Further, the right-remedy principle has justified assertion of a range of remedies to protect constitutional rights which have no express basis in the Constitution,[148] such as injunctive relief,[149] and some of which are far more controversial in separation-of-powers terms, such as striking down unconstitutional statutes.[150] There is also a strong argument that the federalist concerns that inform § 1983 jurisprudence are overstated given the action does, after all, attach to *federal* constitutional rights, while Congressional power to create such action through statute against state officials has been held consistent with federalism.[151] But the key point for present purposes is that restrictions

[141] eg *Baigent* (n 13); *Ward* (n 131).

[142] Federal Employees Liability Reform and Tort Compensation Act 1988 (28 USC § 2679(b)(2)(A)). On the significance of Congressional ratification for the separation-of-powers concerns often associated with *Bivens* see: Reinert and Mulligan (n 137); JE Pfander and D Baltmanis, 'Rethinking *Bivens*: Legitimacy and Constitutional Adjudication' (2009) 98 *Georgetown Law Journal* 117; CM Vazquez and SI Vladeck, 'State Law, the Westfall Act and the Nature of the *Bivens* Question' (2012) 161 *University of Pennsylvania Law Review* 509.

[143] See the next section.

[144] 28 USC § 2679(b)(2)(A).

[145] See *Bell v Hood* 327 US 678, 684 (1946); *Bivens* (n 117) 392, 395–97.

[146] In the English context see similarly: *R v Governor of Brockhill Prison, ex p Evans (No 2)* [2001] 2 AC 19, 48 ('The constitutional role of the courts is to decide disputes and grant remedies').

[147] *Bivens* (n 117) 395, 397. See similarly, in the Canadian charter damages context: *Ward* (n 131) [21] (damages 'employ a means well-recognized within our legal framework. They are appropriate to the function and powers of a court').

[148] See Mashaw et al (n 116) 1183 ('No provision of the Constitution ... expressly authorises any remedy, judicial or administrative for official conduct that violates constitutional rights').

[149] *Bell* (n 145) 684.

[150] *Marbury v Madison* 1 Cranch 137, 163 (1803) (drawing on Blackstone's statement of the right-remedy principle).

[151] *Monroe* (n 133).

on constitutional damages, including pervasive and broad immunities, are in significant measure the product of constitutional concerns peculiar to the American context.

ii. Widespread Governmental and Official Immunities

Another important contextual difference is that governmental and official immunities from suit have been and continue to be a pervasive feature of the American legal system. Sovereign immunity of the federal government (and state sovereign immunity)[152] is a bedrock feature of the legal system. Congress has increasingly waived this immunity across various contexts. Nonetheless 'the doctrine of sovereign immunity is in no danger of falling out of official favor any time soon',[153] being the analytical starting point of claims against federal government.[154] It has been observed to have a 'persisting influence' to the extent that '[e]ven when the government has waived sovereign immunity through legislation, the doctrine influences the manner in which the courts interpret and apply such statutes';[155] purported statutory waivers have traditionally been construed narrowly in favour of the sovereign by the Supreme Court,[156] which has approached this field with an 'enthusiasm for sovereign immunity'.[157] Furthermore, the general waiver of federal sovereign immunity in respect of damages claims in tort pursuant to the Federal Tort Claims Act has been given a 'grudging construction',[158] and was heavily qualified such that '[t]aken as a whole, the FTCA denied—and continues to deny—relief for much, perhaps most, governmental misconduct'.[159] For example it remains the case that the Federal government enjoys extensive immunities, often broadly construed by courts, from liability in tort in respect of, inter alia, intentional torts (except in the law enforcement context) and performance or failure to perform discretionary functions.[160]

[152] See *Hans v Louisiana* 134 US 1 (1890); VC Jackson, 'The Supreme Court, the Eleventh Amendment, and State Sovereign Immunity' (1988) 98 *Yale Law Journal* 1; E Chemerinsky, 'Against Sovereign Immunity' (2001) 53 *Stanford Law Review* 1201.

[153] LH Tribe, *American Constitutional Law* 3rd edn (Foundation Press, 2000) 520.

[154] eg *Meyer* (n 139) 475; *US v Mitchell* 463 US 206, 212 (1983); *Federal Housing Administration v Burr* 309 US 242, 244 (1940).

[155] GC Sisk, 'A Primer on the Doctrine of Federal Sovereign Immunity' (2005) 58 *Oklahoma Law Review* 439, 400 (2005).

[156] eg *Federal Housing Administration v Nordic Village Inc* 503 US 30, 34 (1992); ibid. But the jurisprudence may now be turning a corner: Mashaw et al (n 116) 1165–70; GC Sisk, 'Twilight for the Strict Construction of Waivers of Federal Sovereign Immunity' (2014) 92 *North Carolina Law Review* 1245.

[157] JC Nagle, 'Waiving Sovereign Immunity in an Age of Clear Statement Rules' [1995] *Wisconsin Law Review* 771, 806.

[158] Mashaw et al (n 116) 1165.

[159] Schuck (n 116) 41.

[160] Federal Tort Claims Act 1946 (28 USC §§ 1346(b), 2671–80); Mashaw et al (n 116) 1139–65; Schuck (n 116) ch 2, apps 2–3.

Importantly, it is not only governments that have enjoyed significant tracts of immunity. Until the middle of the twentieth century, albeit there were a number of immunities for certain classes of federal official such as judges and high-ranking government officials, it was generally the case that ordinary tort law would apply equally to officials as to other individuals. However, in the course of the twentieth century the Supreme Court, on its own motion, began to expand the application of and ultimately generalise those immunities. Following the pivotal 1959 decision in *Barr*[161] absolute immunity was 'accorded to virtually any administrative officer who could show that the conduct that was the basis for the common law tort suit fell generally within the scope of his or her assigned responsibilities'.[162] Subsequently, following a prompt from the Supreme Court in the late 1980s in a decision which threatened to reel in absolute immunity,[163] Congress passed legislation affording absolute immunity to federal officials from common law tort claims so long as they are acting within the scope of their employment, subject to limited exceptions.[164]

Against this backdrop the development of—and judicial enthusiasm for—widespread official immunities within US constitutional tort doctrine is not exceptional. Indeed, what proved controversial was not the mainstreaming of immunities within constitutional tort law but rather adoption of qualified instead of absolute immunity for most classes of officials; there was a strong view among some Justices that qualified immunity did not go far enough.[165]

In contrast in England, it has been, and continues to be, a fundamental feature of the rule of law that officials are subject to the same law as everyone else, this principle of equality being a cornerstone of the constitution and adherence to it has ensured that ordinary fields of law, such as tort, have operated as important checks on abuses of public power;[166] as Lord Denning MR observed, in this jurisdiction it is 'unthinkable' that an 'injured person would be left without a remedy' simply because the defendant is an official.[167] There are of course deviations from the principle, such as statutory immunities in some contexts, and it is more common now for the Crown or a public authority, rather than an individual officer, to be defendant where a wrong is committed through exercise of public power. But it remains a general proposition at common law that individual officers may be sued for their wrongs committed when acting in an official capacity,

[161] *Barr v Matteo* 360 US 564 (1959).
[162] Mashaw et al (n 116) 1181.
[163] *Westfall v Erwin* 484 US 292 (1988).
[164] Federal Employees Liability Reform and Tort Compensation Act 1988 (28 USC § 2679).
[165] See the minority opinions in *Butz* (n 118).
[166] See chs 3.I.A, 6.1.III.B.
[167] *Ministry of Housing and Local Government v Sharp* [1970] 2 QB 223, 266.

no matter their rank, and there is no generally applicable immunity for officials as in America; such immunity would be anathema given a constitutional tradition of equality. In this way the analytical starting point for public liability is the inverse of that in America, where federal officials are presumptively immune.

Of course the Crown enjoyed immunity traditionally, and this immunity undoubtedly operated to cause injustice. But the immunity has been rolled back, as far as tort is concerned, and given way to the principle of equality. The legislature, through the Crown Proceedings Act 1947, adopted the general principle that the Crown should be subject to the same liabilities in tort as any private person—without the types of broad exceptions within the Federal Tort Claims Act—and in this way signalled a choice on behalf of the polity to prioritise government under law over governmental interests in immunity. The courts have not shied away from giving effect to the Act,[168] and the Crown is regularly held liable for the acts of its servants. Further, not only is the Crown liable on the same footing as any private person, but the Crown and public authorities have, again in consequence of legislative policy choices, over time been made subject to additional liabilities, for example under the HRA and in EU law.

Whereas the US Supreme Court has, on its own motion, developed extensive blanket immunities for officials, and been protective of sovereign immunity, the English courts have adopted a generally sceptical attitude, given such immunities transgress the rule of law and the right-remedy principle. The 'correct starting point' for analysing immunities is, 'every wrong should have a remedy'.[169] Because immunities transgress fundamental principle they are to be exceptional and strictly limited. In *Darker* Lord Cooke said

> [a]bsolute immunity is in principle inconsistent with the rule of law but in a few, strictly limited, categories of cases it has to be granted for practical reasons. It is granted grudgingly ... The protection should not be given any wider application than is absolutely necessary.[170]

In the same case Lord Clyde said

> immunity may cut across the rights of others to a legal remedy and so runs counter to the policy that no wrong should be without a remedy, it should be only allowed with reluctance, and should not readily be extended. It should only be allowed where it is necessary to do so.[171]

[168] eg *M v Home Office* [1994] 1 AC 377.
[169] *Jones v Kaney* [2011] 2 AC 398, [108].
[170] *Darker v Chief Constable West Midlands* [2001] 1 AC 435, 453 (drawing on: *Rees v Sinclair* [1974] 1 NZLR 180, 187); see also *Chapman* (n 128) [57], [77].
[171] *Darker* ibid 456–57.

Features of English law reflect judicial hostility to immunities.[172] English courts have been willing to abolish common law immunities, including those that are longstanding.[173] They have repeatedly refused to extend common law immunities,[174] and maintained narrow readings of common law doctrines which immunise public actors or authorities, such as combat immunity or act of state;[175] it has been observed judicially that 'the tide is running against wide immunities'.[176] As such it is generally for Parliament to establish new immunities or extend old ones. The courts have been especially reluctant to oust liability where constitutional rights, such as that in liberty, or fundamental international human rights norms are at stake, and where grant of immunity would undermine the principle of equality.[177] When it comes to statutory provisions purporting to oust private rights or immunise officials the courts have held that express language or necessary implication is required to achieve such ends, while, where recognised, immunities will be construed narrowly.[178] These maxims are reinforced where human rights are at stake, and indeed strengthened, such that purported immunities may be read down to the point of being ineffective where they would immunise authorities from human rights claims, including claims for damages.[179] Where courts conclude that a statutory provision does not confer immunity or that the claim before them does not fall within the scope of an official immunity, that conclusion is 'arrive[d] at with a measure of satisfaction'.[180]

Given this legal context it would run wholly against the grain for English courts, absent any express provision for immunities, to read into a human rights instrument widespread immunities from suit for public actors. Further, the HRA expressly confers a type of immunity from damages actions in respect of judicial acts and also excludes legal liability for administrative acts required by primary legislation and for legislative acts;[181] that Parliament expressly provided for caveats on liability further tells against courts implying immunities, and thus upsetting the balance of rights and interests

[172] A counter-example likely to be invoked in response to this claim is the courts' reluctance to impose positive duties on public authorities in negligence in certain contexts (see ch 3.I.D). But these cases concern whether primary obligations exist in the first place, rather than decisions as to whether public authorities should be immunised from liability for breaches of existing rights: *Michael v Chief Constable South Wales* [2015] 2 WLR 343, [44], [116].

[173] eg *Arthur JS Hall & Co v Simons* [2002] 1 AC 615; *Jones* (n 169).

[174] eg *Smith v MOD* [2014] AC 52, [90], [92]; *Darker* (n 170).

[175] *Smith* ibid [90]; *Bici v MOD* [2004] EWHC 786.

[176] *An Informer v A Chief Constable* [2013] QB 579, [110].

[177] eg *Bici* (n 175); *Smith* (n 174); *Hounga* (n 26); *Belhaj v Straw* [2015] 2 WLR 1105; *M* (n 168).

[178] eg *Morris v Beardmore* [1981] AC 446; *ID v Home Office* [2006] 1 WLR 1003, [120]; *Lumba* (n 9) [53]; *M v Hackney LBC* [2011] 1 WLR 2873, [100].

[179] HRA, s 3; *M* ibid [66]; *Baigent* (n 13); *R (GC) v Commissioner for the Metropolis* [2011] WLR 1230.

[180] *ID* (n 178) [121].

[181] HRA, ss 6, 9(3).

prescribed by Parliament in the terms of the Act. More generally, as the courts have recognised, to imply into the HRA exceptions to the actionability of breaches of human rights would be impermissible as it would clearly undermine the Act's central purposes.[182] Indeed the courts have held that if, before entry into force of the HRA, certain matters were non-justiciable at common law, the HRA supplants the common law position to the extent that those matters are implicated in human rights claims.[183] It should also be borne in mind that Parliament is perfectly capable of immunising specific authorities or officials through legislation. Where it has immunised public actors it has in general expressly excluded HRA claims from the scope of immunities.[184] This legislative pattern further tells against courts immunising authorities from human rights claims on their own motion. We must also recall the requirements of Article 13[185] and Article 6.[186]

Even in the American context, characterised by a judicial penchant for official immunity, one must question the legitimacy of reading widespread immunities into § 1983 in particular. Such immunities have no basis in the statutory text.[187] The immunity doctrines, the courts say, represent an attempt to strike a balance between 'the interests in vindication of citizens' constitutional rights and in public officials' effective performance of their duties'.[188] But if, as the Supreme Court now strongly maintains, it is generally impermissible to imply actions into legislation or the Constitution where there is no express basis for such actions, how can it be permissible to imply immunities into a provision establishing a cause of action which provides no textual basis for immunities? As Rudovsky says,

> a serious question exists whether the Court should use the qualified immunity doctrine to impose a judicially crafted balance of these factors [ie vindication versus good administration]. Normally the legislature should decide the policy

[182] *Serdar Mohammed v MOD* [2014] EWHC 1369, [409]ff; see also *R (Al Skeini) v SOS for Defence* [2008] 1 AC 153, [57].

[183] *Serdar* ibid; *R (Gentle) v Prime Minister* [2008] 1 AC 1356, [60]; *R (Carlile) v SOSHD* [2015] 1 AC 945, [30] ('when it comes to reviewing the compatibility of executive decisions with the Convention, there can be no absolute constitutional bar to any inquiry which is both relevant and necessary to enable the court to adjudicate').

[184] Financial Services and Markets Act 2000, Sch 1, para 19(3)(b); Companies Act 2006, s 961(3)(b).

[185] Text to n 203 below.

[186] eg *Osman v UK* (2000) 29 EHRR 245.

[187] There was initially a dubious attempt by courts to justify immunities on the basis that Congress had not intended to deviate from common law immunities applicable to public officials in state tort law at the time § 1983 was passed, in the second half of the nineteenth century. However, this purported rationale fell away, the Supreme Court eventually acknowledging qualified immunity was distinct from common law defences (good faith and probable cause), and that immunities superimposed on § 1983 were the product of judicial policy calculations. See: D Hassel 'Living a Lie: The Cost of Qualified Immunity' (1999) 64 *Missouri Law Review* 123, 125–134.

[188] *Davis v Scherer* 468 US 183, 195 (1983); *Butz* (n 118) 503; *Anderson* (n 127) 639.

questions inherent in this process, particularly if it has the means of protecting the very interests that an immunity defence would serve.[189]

Yet it is the Supreme Court that has exercised that 'policy judgment'—in favour of governmental interests.[190]

iii. Relevant Defendant

Constitutional tort actions can only typically be brought against individual officers such that liability is personal,[191] while constitutional tort jurisprudence vehemently rejects vicarious liability.[192] Indeed so entrenched is the aversion to imposing liability on the federal government that even where statute expressly waives immunity for a federal agency, the Supreme Court refuses to recognise agency liability under *Bivens*.[193] That constitutional torts impose individual liability is fundamental as it goes to the core of the legal rationale for immunity doctrines. The rationale for qualified immunity is twofold: (1) there is an injustice in subjecting an individual officer to liability, particularly in the absence of bad faith, where that officer must, because of the legal obligations of her office, exercise discretion;[194] and (2) there is a danger that the threat of liability could deter an officer's willingness to perform her function 'with the decisiveness and the judgment required by the public good';[195] there is a 'public interest in encouraging the vigorous exercise of official authority'.[196]

Perhaps these concerns are understandable: one may feel aggrieved if required to pay damages out of one's own pocket for simply making a mistake in the course of one's employment (although people routinely do pay damages for such mistakes in tort), while it is not implausible that the possibility that officials may have to pay large awards out of their own savings could lead to overly-cautious administration. However, both arguments are problematic. The Supreme Court has operated in an 'empirical void',[197] not citing any empirical evidence which demonstrates over-caution is a real problem. There is no systematic study of the effects of constitutional tort

189 D Rudovsky, 'The Qualified Immunity Doctrine in the Supreme Court: Judicial Activism and the Restriction of Constitutional Rights' (1989) 138 *University Pennsylvania Law Review* 23, 36, 74; Administrative Redress Consultation Paper (n 45) [6.17].

190 Rudovsky ibid 36, 39, 77.

191 The most important caveat is that municipalities can be liable for § 1983 violations in their own right, albeit in limited circumstances: *Monell v NYC Department of Social Services* 436 US 658 (1978); *Connick* (n 135).

192 *Meyer* (n 139); *Ashcroft* (n 139) 1948–49; see also *Connick* (n 135).

193 *Meyer* (n 139).

194 *Scheuer v Rhodes* 416 US 232, 240 (1974); *Butz* (n 118) 497, 506.

195 *Scheuer* ibid 240; *Butz* (n 118) 497, 506.

196 *Butz* (n 118) 506; see also *Harlow* (n 120) 814; *Ashcroft* (n 139) 1953–54.

197 T Eisenberg and SJ Schwab, 'The Reality of Constitutional Tort Litigation' (1987) 72 *Cornell Law Review* 641, 695.

litigation on officials' morale or performance.[198] Further, severely undermining both rationales for qualified immunity, it is a fact that in respect of § 1983 and *Bivens* actions the relevant government generally stands behind their officials and pays damages awards and costs; this fact has led commentators to observe regularly that the whole rationale for qualified immunity is a myth.[199] That empirical research which does exist demonstrates significant divergence between (judicial) perceptions, and the empirical reality of constitutional tort litigation: there are surprisingly few constitutional tort claims, such claims making up an exceptionally modest percentage of court dockets, and the direct costs of constitutional tort litigation 'appear modest'.[200] In turn such studies conclude that absent further evidence that evidence which does exist 'could not support new legislative or judicial restrictions on constitutional tort litigation in the name of reducing the federal docket or decreasing the fiscal drain on state and local defendants'.[201] Importantly such studies considered data sets from an era just prior to the Supreme Court's turn to a hostile approach to constitutional torts, which resulted in many more restrictions on constitutional tort liability; the studies show there was little rationale for this from a policy perspective.

Whether qualified immunity can be justified in the US or not, its purported rationales could not justify adoption of immunities under the HRA, given damages claims are made against *public authorities*, not individual officers.[202] This means that the individual injustice rationale does not apply, while the chilling effect argument, evaluated as an intuitive rather than empirical claim, is nowhere near as powerful given individual officials do not pay awards. One must also recall Article 13 ECHR, which requires effective remedies for rights-violations notwithstanding that those violations were committed by persons acting in official capacity. Under Article 13, even if a *personal* immunity may be justified on policy grounds for particular officials, such as judges, *the state* nonetheless remains obliged to afford effective redress.[203]

Many American commentators have long argued that the relevant defendant in constitutional tort cases ought to be agencies, not individuals.[204]

[198] Mashaw et al (n 116) 1199–200.

[199] CTL Pillard, 'Taking Fiction Seriously: The Strange Results of Public Officials' Individual Liability Under *Bivens*' (1999) 88 *Georgetown Law Journal* 65; JC Jeffries, 'In Praise of the Eleventh Amendment and Section 1983' (1998) 84 *Virginia Law Review* 47, 49–50.

[200] SJ Schwab and T Eisenberg, 'Explaining Constitutional Tort Litigation' (1988) 73 *Cornell Law Review* 719; Eisenberg and Schwab (n 197).

[201] Schwab and Eisenberg (n 200) 780–81.

[202] HRA, ss 6, 7.

[203] *McFarlane v Ireland* (2011) 52 EHRR 20, [121].

[204] Schuck (n 116) chs 3–5; WE Dellinger, 'Of Rights and Remedies: the Constitution as a Sword' (1972) 85 *Harvard Law Review* 1532, 1556; DJ Levinson, 'Making Government Pay: Markets, Politics, and the Allocation of Constitutional Costs' (2000) 67 *University of Chicago Law Review* 345, 408; see also D Cohen, 'Regulating Regulators: The Legal Environment of the State' (1990) 40 *University of Toronto Law Journal* 213, 219–30.

First, pitching liability at agency level makes it less likely that street-level officials will be deterred from vigorous decision-making as they will not have to pay.[205] Second, the positive deterrence potential of damages actions is limited where individuals are defendants given 'much official wrongdoing is ultimately rooted in organisational conditions and can only be organisationally deterred'.[206] Third, if liability was pitched at agency level, immunities would no longer be required to protect vigorous decision-making,[207] meaning many deserving claimants would receive compensation who otherwise would not.[208] As Schuck concludes, the status quo is doubly troubling: officials work in the shadow of potentially devastating liability, which may undermine vigorous decision-making, while immunities deny compensation to many deserving victims.[209] 'This reality in turn dims the remedy's moral luster, its capacity to project and affirm the values that justify our legal order'.[210] Despite the apparent sense of these arguments, they 'have fallen on deaf congressional and Supreme Court ears'.[211]

iv. Instrumentalist Conception of Liability

Embedded in modern American legal thinking is an instrumentalist conception of damages liability, in large part due to the peculiar influence in the US of Law and Economics since the middle of the twentieth century. In *Bivens* the majority gave several rationales for recognising the constitutional damages remedy, including vindication of important interests and constitutional policies, and individual redress for wrongs. Deterrence of official wrongdoing was also one rationale, albeit Justice Harlan observed, the 'appropriateness of according … compensatory relief does not turn simply on the deterrent effect liability will have'; damages may be 'entirely appropriate' even if their award would have 'no substantial deterrence effects'.[212] However, over time, arguably reflecting, inter alia, the influence of economic accounts of liability which emphasise behavioural effects, the US Supreme Court has narrowed its conception of constitutional liability: 'The purpose of *Bivens* is to deter individual officers from committing constitutional violations'.[213]

[205] Schuck (n 116) chs 3–4.
[206] ibid 98; Dellinger (n 204) 1553.
[207] For example, municipalities do not enjoy immunity against § 1983 claims, while the Supreme Court seems to accept that if constitutional tort liability were imposed on federal agencies, immunities would not apply: *Meyer* (n 139) 485.
[208] Schuck (n 116) 98.
[209] ibid 98–99.
[210] ibid.
[211] Mashaw et al (n 116) 1200.
[212] *Bivens* (n 117) 408.
[213] *Malesko* (n 139) 70; *Minneci* (n 137) 627.

This is significant because if damages liability is only analysed in terms of consequential effects, then it follows that we should deny liability where we consider that on balance those effects will not be beneficial or are unnecessary. So, for example, where the Supreme Court refused to impose *Bivens* liability on a federal agency for which Congress had waived sovereign immunity, the principal reason given was an assertion that imposing liability on an agency—as opposed to individual officers—would not produce the desired deterrence effects.[214] Similarly the Supreme Court has justified marginalisation of the damages remedy through recognition of widespread immunities on the basis that the mere *threat* of liability (rather than *actual* imposition of liability) is sufficient to deter official wrongdoing, while opening up availability of damages would result in negative consequences such as undermining public administration.[215]

What is missing in these analyses is any concern whatsoever for redressing harm suffered by wronged individuals, or any concern to reinforce the importance of and ensure strong protection of basic interests. The purposes of tortious liability are not so narrowly conceived in English law nor in other common law jurisdictions, where economic analysis has failed to make the same impact it has in the US. Nor is it at all clear why the rationale should be so narrow, nor has the Supreme Court attempted to justify why the original rationales articulated in *Bivens* have been (quietly) dropped. We might also add that all of the Supreme Court's analysis of consequential behavioural effects is based in broad brush speculation rather than disciplined by empirical evidence; this is staggering given that if the whole rationale for liability (and its denial) is based in consequential reasoning we would surely want to know that liability (or its denial) would in fact have the claimed effects, otherwise the whole rationale for the relevant liability rules falls away. Further, this lack of recourse to actual evidence makes it all too easy for a Court hostile to constitutional damages to strategically assert whatever consequentialist claims will allow it to justify marginalising the remedy.

Adoption of widespread official immunities within constitutional tort doctrine has been heavily dependent on factors peculiar to the US. The foregoing analysis strongly tells against legal transplantation: immunities would cut across significant features of the English legal system, and in the English context would lack the foundations which support their adoption in America. Immunities are in part a product of constitutional concerns particular to the US context. Judicial assertion of immunities in constitutional tort doctrine is unexceptional given a tradition of blanket immunities for officials across other liability fields, a tradition which runs counter to English constitutional orthodoxy. The rationale for widespread immunities

[214] *Meyer* (n 139) 485.
[215] *Malesko* (n 139) 70.

in constitutional tort law is wholly dependent on the relevant defendants being officials. However, under the HRA claims are made against public authorities—and there are good reasons why authorities ought to be defendants—such that the same concerns do not arise. Lastly, adoption of immunities and other restrictions on constitutional tort liability in part rest on a narrow deterrence-based conception of damages liability which does not enjoy general acceptance in the laws of other common law jurisdictions, while the normative and empirical bases for such conception of damages are obscure.

B. The Qualified Immunity Doctrine

On top of these general points, the qualified immunity doctrine—which applies to most officials—has proven deeply problematic. The doctrine has been described by American commentators as, 'in a perpetual state of crisis',[216] 'notoriously unstable in application',[217] 'complicated, unstable, and overprotective of government officers',[218] and 'one of the most significant and problematic defences to claims of civil rights violations'.[219] Several issues stand out, and reinforce strongly that the American model ought not to be imported.

i. The 'Clearly Established' Element

According to qualified immunity doctrine, if a constitutional right is *not* 'clearly established' then an official who violates that right shall be immune from suit.[220] The matter of whether a right is clearly established has proven problematic.

'Clarity' is an elastic concept and difficult to define with precision (ironically); the result has been uncertainty, divergence in judicial approach and inconsistency in decision-making. So, for example, there is marked variation in the level of generality or particularity at which courts will require a right to be clearly established before they will hold the criterion fulfilled.[221] Some courts have applied an extraordinarily strict approach, requiring that for a right to be clearly established there must be a legal ruling as to the meaning

[216] C Saiman, 'Interpreting Immunity' (2005) 7 *University of Pennsylvania Journal of Constitutional Law* 1155, 1155.

[217] JC Jeffries, 'Reversing the Order of Battle in Constitutional Torts' [2009] *Supreme Court Review* 115, 136 [Jeffries 2009]; "What's Wrong with Qualified Immunity" (2010) 62 *Florida Law Review* 1, 2 [Jeffries 2010].

[218] Jeffries 2013 (n 119) 250.

[219] Rudovsky (n 189) 36.

[220] *Harlow* (n 120) 818–19; *Anderson* (n 127).

[221] Rudovsky (n 189) 45–47; Jeffries 2010 (n 217) 4–8.

of the right in the context of facts analogous to those giving rise to the constitutional damages claim. Other courts have been far less strict, pitching the inquiry at a much higher level of abstraction or generality, finding the right clearly established where the basic framework of rules and principles governing the right have been mapped out in previous case law. Other courts have required that the right be clearly established at levels of generality/particularity in between these poles. The fact is that it is very difficult to formulate a test with sufficient precision that it will satisfactorily discipline the level of generality at which the inquiry should be pitched. As a result it has been observed that the clearly established element 'allows the judge a great deal of latitude'—an 'almost unfettered judgment'—such that 'widely different outcomes' are possible in analogous cases; of course all norms afford some scope for divergent approaches and inconsistent application but the point is qualified immunity 'provides exceptionally loose parameters'.[222] Not only does this give rise to problems of inconsistency, but it also means the clearly established criterion can be manipulated easily to reach particular results, so that the reasoning as to whether the right is clearly defined or not may 'camouflage' the true, unstated basis of the decision.[223]

If there is a trend in American jurisprudence it is, consistent with the thrust of Supreme Court pronouncements,[224] towards requiring that the right be clearly established with greater particularity. However, this has not done much to promote certainty and consistency.[225] Further, this trend gives rise to other problems: the notion of particularity has in many cases been taken to an extreme, with courts requiring a precedent on near-identical facts before concluding that a right is clearly established. The result is hyper-legalistic analysis and that the clearly established inquiry may be virtually impossible to fulfil, such that qualified immunity in practice collapses into absolute immunity. Motivating judicial moves to require precedents directly on point is a concern to enable courts to resolve constitutional tort claims at an early stage in proceedings and before trial so as to avoid costs of discovery and litigation for defendants; the clearly established element raises a question of law and does not necessitate the making of factual findings.[226] However, the result is to effectively eviscerate constitutional torts.

The American trend towards requiring more particularised precedents before a right may be clearly established raises further concerns. It cuts across

[222] Hassel (n 187) 137, 139, 145.

[223] ibid. We find similar problems in the *Francovich* case law on whether a rule breached was clear and precise. If one is intent on finding a rule ambiguous, it is not difficult to identify some ambiguity.

[224] *Anderson* (n 127) 640.

[225] Jeffries 2013 (n 119) 257 ('the degree of precedential specificity required for clearly established law is hard to state precisely').

[226] Questions of law can be determined conclusively through procedures such as summary judgment or motions to dismiss, so that full trial is avoided.

the reality of common law method. Courts do not generally give guidance by reference to specific situations in which officials might find themselves, as if their judgments were part of a pocket guide book for administrators. Rather courts give guidance in the form of generalised legal tests or principles, which are to be applied on a case-by-case basis.[227] Applications of such tests in particular cases may not afford a great deal of guidance, because the outcome will often depend on the factual nuances of that particular case; this is particularly so where legal tests are heavily fact-dependant, such as requirements of reasonableness or proportionality, which are pervasive in human rights law.

Even if these issues could be resolved, issues arise as to which sources of law count for the purposes of the 'clearly established' test. Would a right be clearly established if it is clearly defined in a consistent line of ECtHR decisions but no domestic court has ruled on the matter? What if the Supreme Court clearly defined the right, but a subsequent ECtHR decision casts doubt on that definition? Similarly, what if both Northern Irish and Scottish courts have reached the same clear definition of a particular Convention right but the matter has not arisen in England—should an English court conclude that the right is clearly established? American courts have struggled with analogous issues and failed to settle on a common approach, leading to further uncertainty and inconsistency.[228]

There is a further problem.[229] Some rights lend themselves more readily to clear rules, such as criminal due process rights which are often stated as a series of reasonably concrete prescriptions or proscriptions, whereas other rights do not, such as those which require balancing. In the context of the latter class some American courts have 'come close to saying the law could never be clearly established'.[230] It seems rather odd that whether damages should issue for particular constitutional wrongs or not should depend on the happenstance of whether the right breached is capable naturally of being expressed as a narrow rule.

The requirement that an official may only be liable if the right violated was clearly established by past case law appears to be premised on the rationale that it would be unfair to find someone liable for conduct which they could not, at the relevant time, have known was unlawful.[231] This is an understandable concern. On the other hand this may be to oversimplify the matter; for example there may be acts which we would all know to be unlawful even if the courts had not rendered a concrete ruling to this effect on a particular fact pattern. Also, there is an air of unreality in the idea that officials keep up to date with the latest judicial pronouncements,

[227] See Jeffries 2010 (n 217) 4–5.
[228] ibid 8–9.
[229] ibid 9ff.
[230] Hassel (n 187) 140–41.
[231] eg *Anderson* (n 127) 639–40, 646; *Hope v Pelzer* 536 US 730, 739 (2002).

consciously looking out for and then memorising cases decided on all fours with factual scenarios they envision they might face in the course of their employment, and then recalling those decisions as they confront those factual scenarios as they exercise their powers. In any case, accepting the concern for fairness, it is not peculiar to the human rights or constitutional law context, which in turn calls into question why a special approach is warranted in this context. It is common across all fields of law for courts to impose legal liability on both public and private entities in cases which change substantive law; every novel duty of care situation in negligence provides an example. Such practice has led some to argue for prospective overruling.[232] If this doctrine is accepted it should be accepted in principle across the legal system; or at least it is not clear why it should be limited to one narrow subfield such as human rights damages. However, in England the doctrine is highly contentious and the courts maintain that if they were to apply this doctrine it would be confined strictly to exceptional cases.[233] Importantly, there is an even greater reluctance to apply it where interpretation of statute is concerned,[234] which is of significance in the HRA context given determinations as to the meanings of rights are determinations as to the meaning of statutory terms. Similarly the courts are reluctant to apply such doctrine where basic rights are at stake; in *Evans* Lord Hope opined that if ever there was a case to maintain orthodoxy—so that the claimant were not denied the fruits of their victory and protection of their rights—it was in a case concerning individual liberty.[235]

ii. The 'Objective Reasonableness' Element

According to qualified immunity doctrine, even where the right breached is clearly established the defendant may still enjoy immunity if a reasonable officer could have believed that the defendant's actions were lawful given clearly established law.[236] The inquiry is objective and does not depend on the defendant's subject beliefs about the lawfulness of their actions.[237] There are several problems with this criterion.

232 M Zander, *The Law-Making Process* 6th edn (CUP, 2004) 397–403.

233 *National Westminster Bank Plc v Spectrum Plus Ltd* [2005] 2 AC 680. Within common law judicial review courts have refused to quash decisions, thus preserving unlawful acts, or suspended the effect of quashing orders. However, this is due in part to the nature of the remedy, quashing a decision having the potential to cause significant administrative disruption, while it is significant that common law review is a field shot through with concerns for the public interest and protection of administrative process: see ch 4.2.I–II.

234 *National Westminster Bank* ibid [125].

235 *Evans* (n 146) (prospective overruling discussed at 26–27, 29, 35–37, 47–49).

236 *Harlow* (n 120) 815–19; *Anderson* (n 127) 639, 641.

237 *Anderson* (n 127) 641. Originally qualified immunity had subjective and objective limbs. However, the subjective limb was abandoned as it implicated a factual inquiry which prevented immunity from being determined on summary judgment: *Harlow* (n 120) 814–19; Rudovsky (n 189) 43–44.

First, it sends a perverse signal for courts to on the one hand maintain the fundamental importance of constitutional rights, but on the other hold actions which breach clearly-established constitutional rights, and in respect of which no lawful excuse has been proven, to be objectively reasonable actions for a public officer to take. Bearing in mind qualified immunity, if successfully pleaded, affords complete immunity from suit, this is to take protection of the interest in vigorous administration to the extreme of effectively affording officials the 'discretion to act in illegal ways' in a field which protects fundamental rights.[238] And that discretion is intended to be a wide one, so that only instances of gross incompetence or malicious violation are capable of generating liability.[239]

Second, the reason for the clearly established requirement is to ensure that officials have fair warning as to which acts are unlawful. If the clearly established requirement is fulfilled then in the eyes of the law the official has been fairly warned; given this it is difficult to see how, in a case of clearly established rights, courts could conclude that an official could reasonably believe that their unlawful acts were lawful. Such proposition becomes even more difficult to sustain the more stringently courts frame the clearly established inquiry. If courts go so far, as indeed they have, as to require a previous ruling on analogous facts before a right is clearly established, then it is all the more incongruous to maintain that a reasonable official could have thought their rights-violating actions were lawful.

Third, as with the clearly established requirement, the objective reasonableness 'prong provides ample opportunity for wide discretion in the imposition of this element of the defence'.[240] This further exacerbates problems of uncertainty and inconsistency.

Fourth, because the test is purely objective there is no inquiry into the official's subjective intent or motivations.[241] It follows that a court could find an official's conduct reasonable even though the official in fact knew her actions were unlawful.

Fifth, at root the Supreme Court's aim in adopting the objective reasonableness test is to afford officials a margin for error, so that every violation of clearly established rights does not result in liability. However, as in US constitutional law,[242] the substantive law of human rights in England already affords public authorities latitude. The permissible leeway afforded in human rights law is, in general, narrower than in other contexts because we are here concerned with fundamental rights, but there is generally some margin afforded to decision-makers nonetheless. Interferences with most

[238] *Anderson* (n 127) 653.

[239] *Malley v Briggs* 475 US 335, 341 (1986), cited: *Anderson* (n 127) 638; Jeffries 2013 (n 119) 257–58.

[240] Hassel (n 187) 143.

[241] eg *Anderson* (n 127) 641, 646.

[242] ibid 661 (Stevens J dissenting).

rights are open to justification, for example, on the basis of the proportionality test. On top of this the courts will, in determining whether there has been a violation, afford 'appropriate weight to the judgment of a person with responsibility for a given subject matter and access to special sources of knowledge and advice'.[243] If the defendant authority has demonstrated human rights learning and genuinely sought to engage with its human rights obligations in taking the relevant action, its view that the action is justified may be accorded greater weight by courts in deciding whether the interference was justified in law.[244] Provision of reasons for the decision may also make it more likely that the court accords the authority's view weight in its analysis, so that a finding of unlawfulness may be less likely. In other words human rights law, through its operation, affords officials some room for manoeuvre, which may be enlarged if the authority has applied its institutional knowledge and learning to develop its own considered view on human rights questions. The common law of damages also takes into account the defendant's conduct. For example, if the violation was committed in good faith then aggravated damages would not be awarded.

Sixth, the rules governing each human rights duty have been carefully calibrated to afford due protection to the relevant protected interests in the light of, inter alia, the particular circumstances in which the right is likely to be implicated, the need to accommodate important public and third party interests, the relative importance of the protected individual interests, and the nature of the obligation (for example, whether it is negative or positive). Adding a further layer of legal rules to the existing legal framework may distort the careful balancing of interests struck in the substantive law of human rights, so that assertion of qualified immunity across the board effectively entails 'redefining substantive constitutional law'.[245] It may be right, as a matter of principle, in respect of some rights that interferences can be justified on the basis that the official's conduct was 'reasonable'. For example, Article 5(1)(c) ECHR provides an individual may be deprived of their liberty where they are lawfully detained for the purpose of bringing them before a court given a reasonable suspicion that they have committed an offence. In the context of other rights legality of official action may depend on the proportionality test, more particularised justifications,[246] on whether restrictions are arbitrary,[247] and for a narrow class of rights upon mental elements such as intention,[248] or knowledge.[249]

[243] *Huang v SOSHD* [2007] 2 AC 167, [16].

[244] *Belfast CC v Miss Behavin' Ltd* [2007] 1 WLR 1420 per Baroness Hale.

[245] Rudovsky (n 189) 27; Jeffries 2010 (n 217) 9ff; *Anderson* (n 127) 668 (Stevens J dissenting).

[246] eg ECHR, arts 2(2), 4(3).

[247] eg *Saadi v UK* (2008) 47 EHRR 427, [67]ff (Art 5).

[248] For example, torture is '*deliberate* inhuman treatment causing very serious and cruel suffering': *Ireland v UK* (1979–80) 2 EHRR 25, [167] (emphasis added).

[249] *Osman* (n 186).

To add a general reasonableness test 'across the board'[250] would distort the deliberate, intricate balancing of interests inherent in the substantive law of human rights, and run against the grain of the generally strict nature of human rights obligations which is, in turn, strongly linked to the underlying goal of protection. Indeed supplementing human rights law with a general reasonableness test would seriously undermine the principal goals of human rights law by entrenching a system-wide privileging of governmental interests in vigorous administration—including administration so vigorous it breaches clearly established rights—ahead of protection of basic rights. Take the example of Article 5(1)(c) again. The starting point of analysis within Article 5 is that no one should be deprived of their liberty. However, if the defendant acts reasonably (as well as meeting certain other criteria, such as non-arbitrariness) it shall have a defence; in this way the law strikes a balance between preservation of liberty and interests in legitimate law enforcement, and allows margin for official error. If the law then provides for a further reasonableness criterion so as to protect vigorous administration, the law will be 'count[ing] the law enforcement interest twice and the individual's ... interest only once'; the defendant is afforded 'two layers of insulation from liability'.[251] In this way qualified privilege institutionalises subordination of fundamental rights to governmental concerns.

iii. Avoidance of Substantive Constitutional Issues

The third problematic aspect of qualified immunity is it affords courts an opportunity to avoid ruling on whether constitutional rights have been violated. Rather than considering the merits and then going on to consider immunity, if necessary, US courts have generally bypassed the merits and progressed straight to qualified immunity, typically dismissing the claim on the basis that the claimed right is not clearly established. In 2001 the Supreme Court addressed this issue, ruling that lower courts must consider merits before moving to qualified immunity.[252] However, given criticism from lower court judges that this required them to make 'unnecessary' merits decisions and imposed costs,[253] the Supreme Court backtracked in 2009, ruling that while the merits-first approach 'is often appropriate', 'it should no longer be regarded as mandatory'.[254]

The problems with allowing courts to dismiss claims according to qualified immunity without consideration of the merits are several. If courts routinely dismiss cases on the basis that no clearly established right exists without determining the merits then courts pass up the opportunity to

250 *Anderson* (n 127) 642, 645.
251 ibid 659, 664 (Stevens J dissenting); Jeffries 2010 (n 217) 11–12.
252 *Saucier v Katz* 533 US 194 (2001).
253 *Pearson v Callahan* 129 S Ct 808, 817–19 (2009).
254 ibid 818; see Jeffries 2009 (n 217) for a full discussion of this saga.

develop constitutional doctrine by determining novel legal issues thrown up by novel fact patterns; constitutional doctrine stagnates. By following such practice courts also forgo the opportunity to clarify ambiguous rights, which leads to ongoing uncertainty and makes it unlikely that damages will ever be successfully recovered for breach of the claimed right—because a court will not have the opportunity to clearly establish the right through a ruling on the merits. This may have the further knock-on effect that 'for rights that depend on vindication through money damages, abandoning merits adjudication will reduce constitutional protections to the least-common-denominator understanding of their meaning'.[255] This is because as the right is not clearly established it will be open to a number of possible interpretations, and the incentive for officials is to conduct their affairs according to that interpretation which least interferes with their tasks. That lowest-common-denominator interpretation is unlikely to be questioned in court as long as claims based on the uncertain right continue to be dismissed without consideration of the substance of claims. Thus, judicial avoidance leaves officials 'free to continue in potentially unconstitutional conduct'.[256] All of these concerns have been exacerbated by developments which make it easier for courts to dismiss constitutional tort claims at an early stage, including heightened pleading standards.[257] Lastly, the practice of dismissing claims without reaching their merits suggests that all that is important to claimants is whether they receive damages. But claimants may care just as much or even more about obtaining a public finding that their rights have been violated, or establishing a point of legal principle.[258] That a claimant happens to have included a damages claim—perhaps to make the litigation financially viable whereas they could not afford it otherwise—should not rob them of this opportunity.

Overall, bringing all of the foregoing analysis together, qualified immunity 'makes the essential issue of a civil rights claim the question of whether it would be too much of an inhibitor of government action to require a particular defendant to pay damages to the plaintiff'.[259] Adoption of such immunities in human rights law would turn the field on its head: instead of the focus being upon human rights, it would be on protecting governmental interests.

[255] Jeffries ibid 121.

[256] Rudovsky (n 189) 55.

[257] *Ashcroft* (n 139); M Windsor, '(Pro)motion to Dismiss? Constitutional Tort Litigation and Threshold Failure in the War on Terror' (2012) 1 *British Journal of American Legal Studies* 241.

[258] eg *Savage v South Essex Partnership NHS Foundation Trust* [2010] EWHC 865, [97]; *R (Bernard) v Enfield LBC* [2003] LGR 423, [17]; *Ashley v Chief Constable Sussex Police* [2008] 1 AC 962, [70]; Administrative Redress Consultation Paper (n 45) [3.12].

[259] Hassel (n 187) 156.

C. Conclusion

Significant differences between American and English legal contexts tell against transplantation of the myriad immunities that characterise American constitutional tort law into English human rights law, while close examination of qualified immunity shows it to be a seriously flawed doctrine.

More generally, the history of constitutional torts, and particularly *Bivens*, has been a sorry tale. Over the past 25 to 30 years a Supreme Court dominated by Justices hostile to *Bivens* has taken every opportunity to dismantle the remedy. It has consistently refused to extend the remedy to new constitutional rights, the remedy only having been extended to new rights twice and not extended since 1980.[260] It has consistently refused to extend the remedy to new classes of defendant, refusing to extend it to private entities or employees performing public functions,[261] or to federal agencies for which Congress has waived sovereign immunity.[262] The Court has 'to a considerable extent, converted [qualified immunity] into the functional equivalent of absolute immunity in an attempt to minimise the costs of defending',[263] procedural hurdles to recovery have been bolstered,[264] and supervisory liability apparently eliminated.[265] Dissenters on the Court claim that the 'driving force' behind majority decisions 'is a disagreement with the holding in *Bivens* itself', and admonish them for revising settled law on the basis of their own notions of policy.[266] Put simply, the trend has been to marginalise the remedy as far as can be done without overruling the original decision in *Bivens*. One leading commentator observes *Bivens* is 'on life support with little prospect of recovery',[267] while another questions whether the action is even 'sufficiently alive that it is capable of being reinvigorated',[268] while yet others observe *Bivens* has 'proved to be a surreptitiously progovernment decision'.[269] Thus, it is not at all surprising that doctrine in this field, including qualified immunity, is in a troubled state, as

[260] See *Malesko* (n 139) 67ff. Damages may be claimed for breach of the Fourth Amendment (*Bivens* (n 117)), the due process clause of the Fifth Amendment (*Davis* (n 138)), and the cruel and unusual punishments clause of the Eighth Amendment (*Carlson* (n 138)).

[261] *Malesko* (n 139).

[262] *Meyer* (n 139).

[263] Nahmod (n 136) 444.

[264] *Ashcroft* (n 139).

[265] ibid 1957; see also: *Connick* (n 135), cutting back liability of municipalities under § 1983 for failure to train.

[266] *Malesko* (n 139) 82–83.

[267] LH Tribe, 'Death by a Thousand Cuts: Constitutional Wrongs Without Remedies After *Wilkie v Robbins*' (2007) 23 *Cato Supreme Court Review* 23, 26.

[268] RH Fallon et al, *Hart and Wechsler's Federal Courts and the Federal System* 6th edn (Foundation Press, 2009) 740.

[269] Pillard (n 199) 65.

these are hardly conditions—that is where the apex court does not believe the remedy should even exist—conducive to development of a coherent and principled jurisprudence of damages for breach of basic rights.

The net result of these doctrinal trends is that claimants 'are rarely allowed recovery for deplorable violations of their civil rights'.[270] Empirical studies show success rates for constitutional torts to be low relative to rates for other types of civil claims.[271] Figures emanating from within government suggest that out of approximately 12,000 *Bivens* claims filed between 1971 and 1985 claimants only received a damages award that survived appeal in four cases,[272] while in 1999 the Director of the Torts Branch of the US Department of Justice estimated claimants obtain a damages judgment in a fraction of one per cent of *Bivens* cases and a monetary settlement in less than one per cent of cases.[273] Viewed alongside more detailed studies of civil litigation the prevailing view is that *Bivens* claims are by far the least successful claims filed in federal courts.[274] However, it is important to note that a recent empirical study into *Bivens* claims casts doubt on the dominant view.[275] But even on the most generous measure adopted by the study's author, it is still the case that success rates in *Bivens* claims are moderate compared to success rates for other constitutional tort claims and relatively low compared to other classes of civil litigation (on the least generous measure they are very low). This evidence shows the evolution of *Bivens* to be doubly troubling. Claimants have low success rates in claiming damages for constitutional injuries, while '*Bivens* litigation is fruitless and wasteful, because it does not provide the remedies contemplated by the decision, and it burdens litigants and the judicial system'.[276]

The fraught nature of American constitutional tort law suggests it is not likely to offer a principled way forward for the development of human rights damages.

[270] Burris (n 120) 126–27.

[271] Schwab and Eisenberg (n 200); Eisenberg and Schwab (n 197); T Eisenberg, 'Section 1983: Doctrinal Foundations and an Empirical Study' (1982) 67 *Cornell Law Review* 482.

[272] Pillard (n 199) 66.

[273] ibid 66 fn 6.

[274] See the overview in AA Reinert, 'Measuring The Success of *Bivens* Litigation and Its Consequences for the Individual Liability Model' (2010) 62 *Stanford Law Review* 809, 827.

[275] ibid.

[276] Pillard (n 199) 66; Burris (n 120) 125, 127–28, 186.

8

Conclusion

Several conclusions follow from the foregoing analysis.

On the public law—private law divide. The distinction between public and private law is an unsound foundation on which to rest legal development, including the decision over what approach should be taken to human rights damages. Indeed, nothing of legal significance should ever be allowed to rest on this distinction alone.

The distinction lacks an anchor in English law, and there is longstanding and increasing difficulty in distinguishing public and private spheres. It is thus not surprising that the distinction has proven unworkable when put into practice.

Even if we could draw the distinction between private and public with surgical precision it is not clear what the implications of this would be for human rights damages. The idea of public law is bound up in interminable theoretical disagreement. Furthermore contemporary public law is not a monolith characterised by a single set of norms, functions or ideas, which could be relied upon to guide legal development across the field, but rather an umbrella doctrinal category comprised of distinct sub-categories of doctrine, each characterised by discrete normative concerns.

Attempts to rest the approach to human rights damages on the distinction have proven problematic. In England (as elsewhere) the use of the distinction and appeal to a unitary conception of public law, developed principally by reference to common law judicial review, has led to an approach to human rights damages which is fundamentally at odds with the underlying nature of human rights law. A remedial approach suited to fields characterised by public duties owed to the public at large for the good of the community as a collective has been imported into a field characterised by rights personal to particular individuals, conferred so as to protect their basic individual interests. In turn the result of 'shoehorning' human rights damages into this 'public interest' conception of public law is to produce incoherence within human rights law and suppress the field's distinctive protective and vindicatory aims at the remedial stage.

Rather than subordinating human rights damages to abstract notions of public law which one subjectively finds appealing, the answer to the question of what approach should be taken to human rights damages lies in

considering the distinct goals that underpin creation of the primary rights in human rights law.

On the mirror approach. The mirror approach to damages under the Human Rights Act 1998 (HRA) ought to be abandoned forthwith. The normative foundations of such approach are obscure. It cannot be justified by reference to the terms of the Act. It cannot be supported as a matter of principle: the subsidiary, supranational context within which the European Court of Human Rights (ECtHR) awards just satisfaction is fundamentally different from the domestic legal context where English courts have primary responsibility for ensuring rights-violations are effectively remedied. The mirror approach is not required by Convention law: the ECtHR has explicitly stated on numerous occasions that domestic courts are free to, and indeed encouraged to develop their own remedial approach, consonant with domestic traditions and conditions.

The mirror approach cannot be supported on a practical level. The Strasbourg jurisprudence is riddled with problems. It lacks principle, coherence, consistency and is largely unreasoned. Domestic courts have struggled to interpret and apply the Strasbourg jurisprudence, and very little meaningful guidance can be divined from it. As a result of the higher courts' continued attachment to such approach a deeply problematic domestic damages jurisprudence is emerging under the Act, which mirrors many of the problems associated with the Strasbourg jurisprudence. Further, the methodology applied by domestic courts to give effect to the mirror approach is confused, inconsistent and open to gaming, allowing domestic courts to 'massage' the unreasoned Strasbourg jurisprudence one way or the other to reach particular results. An approach which requires domestic courts to replicate mechanistically Strasbourg practice relieves domestic courts of evaluating or justifying the merits of the legal norms derived from Strasbourg. In addition, despite the formal proscription under the mirror approach on domestic courts looking to domestic rules and principles, courts have, on an ad hoc basis, had recourse to domestic principles and modes of reasoning, demonstrating the artificiality of the 'ban' and calling into question the viability of maintaining strict separation between tort and human rights damages.

Altogether the experience with the mirror approach has been a tortured one, and has led to significant unfairness for victims, who are, for example, systematically undercompensated relative to domestic scales. Ideally section 8(4) of the HRA should be repealed so that domestic courts are not legally required to pay regard to the Article 41 jurisprudence. Replacement of the HRA with a British Bill of Rights would offer such opportunity. However, even if the provision is not repealed it does not stand in the way of an approach to HRA damages that takes common law principles as its starting point; such approach is consonant with the terms and scheme of the Act.

On interest-balancing. The interest-balancing approach propounded in *Anufrijeva*, and adopted in other jurisdictions, may be intuitively attractive as it is underpinned by understandable concerns, such as ensuring authorities have sufficient resources to fulfil public goals, ensuring administrators are able to vigorously discharge their functions, and protecting against development of a damaging litigation culture. However, that the concerns underlying such approach are understandable does not in itself justify adoption of such approach.

In terms of positive law, it is difficult to reconcile the approach with the terms of the HRA, its operation would invariably lead to violations of the Convention, and it undermines fundamental and longstanding principles of English law including the principle of equality and *ubi ius, ibi remedium*.

On a normative level the case for the interest-balancing approach is not straightforward and there are strong arguments against: (1) It would entail denying effective remedies to those who have suffered violation of their fundamental rights, thus undermining practical protection of basic rights and their normative importance within the polity, all of which runs counter to the underlying functions of human rights law; (2) It is difficult to justify why human rights law should be singled out for such *sui generis* approach, given many public interest concerns which underlie balancing are equally applicable in other legal contexts where damages issue as of course for wrongfully-inflicted damage; (3) Many public and other interests are already protected by human rights law, ordinary damages law, procedural law and extra-legal phenomena. As such, introducing a balancing approach at the remedial stage would strike the overall balance of the law too far away from human rights law's central goals of protecting and vindicating rights; (4) The discretionary nature of interest-balancing will operate to undermine important rule of law values; (5) There are significant concerns about the manner in which countervailing public interest factors have been taken into account under the HRA, with courts denying or reducing awards on the basis of consequentialist arguments which have not been scrutinised rigorously or proven by reference to evidence. In-depth examination of each of these public interest concerns showed some to be unfounded and others questionable. Importantly, there are strong arguments that some factors, such as preservation of public funds, are inappropriate for judicial consideration at all given constitutional and institutional constraints on courts.

More generally, courts ought to develop the law of human rights damages by reference to legal principle and orthodox techniques of legal reasoning, and leave complex and contentious questions of policy and politics, such as bare allocative questions over how money should be distributed between redressing wrongs and frontline public services, to the political branches. Government and Parliament have the constitutional legitimacy to strike difficult balances between competing policy considerations and determine issues which raise contentious matters of morality, economics and politics.

Further, the political branches are well-placed institutionally to observe and assess the impacts of liability on the public purse and administrative behaviour and take appropriate action where necessary, while they have many tools at their disposal for this purpose. In this respect consideration of several case studies showed that the political branches are both willing and able to act, when necessary, so as to protect important governmental and public interests in the context of public authority liability. The courts need not risk their own constitutional and institutional legitimacy in order to safeguard the government's pecuniary interests; government is perfectly capable of protecting itself.

Despite the powerful arguments against, if an interest-balancing approach were adopted it ought to be one which is structured, prioritises the interest in vindicating the right, and takes account not only of public interests that tell against awarding damages but also public interests served by protecting and vindicating rights through awards. Preferably there would be a presumption in favour of relief, coupled with a set of narrow defences reserved for exceptional cases, while consequentialist arguments for denial of relief must be thoroughly scrutinised and substantiated by evidence. Quantum should not be subject to balancing given this would represent significant deviation from the near-universal principle of full compensation, applied across legal fields in domestic and international law and in the context of non-legal wrongs. Such approach would generate intolerable uncertainty and inevitably lead to inconsistent awards, while the common law principle that awards must be moderate protects against excessive awards. These modifications would make the balancing approach less objectionable by stripping its worst features. However, it remains questionable why such deviation from the orthodox common law approach is justified for breach of the most fundamental of rights. Further, there remain significant concerns over the capacity of courts to competently predict whether damages would have consequential negative effects if awarded, and the constitutional propriety of courts weighing how public monies are best allocated, especially given the political branches are well-placed to respond to public interest concerns, if they eventuate.

On alternative control devices. The case for adoption of alternative limiting devices such as the minimum intensity test under Article 41 of the European Convention on Human Rights, the 'sufficiently serious' test in the EU law of state liability, and immunity doctrines in US constitutional law, is far from convincing and such principles suffer from many of the same sorts of drawbacks as the interest-balancing approach. Furthermore, these principles have been developed in contexts which have their own peculiarities and are far removed from the English human rights context, while there are specific, not insignificant problems associated with each device.

On a vindicatory, tort-based approach. This book's central conclusion is that the approach to human rights damages ought to be modelled on that developed within torts actionable per se (TAPS).

A tort-based approach is consistent with the terms of the HRA. While courts must have regard to the principles applied by the ECtHR under Article 41 of the Convention according to section 8(4) of the Act in deciding whether to award damages and quantum, that section does not tell against an approach which takes tort as its starting point. The few broad principles identifiable in the Strasbourg jurisprudence, such as *restitutio in integrum*, are consonant with common law principles and it is, in any case, open to English courts to depart from Strasbourg principles where appropriate given the Act only requires domestic courts to have regard to such principles. Under the Convention domestic courts are free to fashion a remedial approach consonant with domestic traditions and, unlike other approaches, a tort-based approach would ensure compliance with Article 13, which requires rights-violations to be effectively remedied.

As a matter of principle the approach to human rights damages should follow that developed within vindicatory torts. Both human rights law and TAPS perform similar functions in protecting the most fundamental of interests, as evidenced by their near-identical legal structures. A vindicatory approach to damages accords with and gives effect to the policies of protection and vindication of fundamental interests that underpin the primary obligations in human rights law at the remedial stage.

A tort-based approach would ensure coherence and consistency across English law. Both human rights and TAPS protect similarly basic interests, and it is difficult to justify adoption of a more restrictive approach to damages for interference with such interests in the human rights context. Furthermore, to take a more restrictive approach to human rights damages would be to devalue the fundamental interests that human rights law protects, undermine the place of human rights within the normative hierarchy of legally protected interests and compromise protection of rights.

The law of damages in tort provides a rich resource of reasonably coherent, fair and rational principles and rules and offers an analytical methodology for the assessment of quantum, all of which could readily and naturally be read across and adapted to human rights law. Further, the vast body of common law precedent provides significant and reasoned guidance as to scales of awards.

On top of these positive arguments in favour of a tort-based approach, such approach does not suffer from some of the significant shortcomings of other approaches, such as balancing approaches. For example the tort-based approach is consonant with long-standing principles of the common law, such as *ubi ius*, *ibi remedium* and the principle of equality. Its operation would provide a strong symbolic reinforcement of the rule of law principle of government under law, and such approach would not give rise to the formal rule of law concerns associated with other approaches, which tend to be discretionary. Furthermore, the tort-based approach does not require judges to consider matters which they are not institutionally well-placed to analyse in a robust manner, and which they lack the constitutional legitimacy to determine. On top of this the rationale for the tort-based approach is based in legal principle, and is not premised on contested conceptions of the good or public law or consequential arguments which lack a firm empirical foundation. The vindicatory approach takes its lead from and remains faithful to the policy that underlies the primary rights, as evidenced by the internal structure of human rights law and the HRA, and the intention of the Parliament that passed the Act, as well as giving practical effect to and vindicating the distribution of primary entitlements encapsulated in the HRA.

The implications of a vindicatory, tort-based approach are severalfold.

In principle a full range of damages should be available to vindicate a rights-violation, including nominal, compensatory, aggravated and exemplary damages (and possibly gain-based damages); we need not recognise the novel head of 'vindicatory damages' as it adds nothing to existing remedies. All of these types of damages ought to be available on the same basis upon which they are presently available within vindicatory torts, or at least this should be the starting point.

Compensatory damages ought to be awarded wherever relevant damage and/or loss is suffered by a claimant through a proven rights-violation, where other remedies granted by the court—such as specific relief or damages in tort—are not capable of remedying the violation. A fundamental feature of a vindicatory approach to compensatory damages is that such damages are not only available to redress factual losses consequential upon the wrong, ie negative psychological, physical or economic effects suffered by the claimant, but also for the wrongful interference with the underlying protected interest in itself. Thus, even if the claimant suffers no consequential factual losses, damages ought to be awarded for interference with the right in and of itself, as in TAPS. In this way the law 'restores'—at least notionally—the entitlement that was denied, so the claimant is, in a second best way, placed in the position they were lawfully entitled to be in: one in which their fundamental interests were maintained inviolate. Such 'normative damages' give direct effect to the underlying functions of the law. They afford strong and direct protection to the interests that are the very object of the law's protection, in that one may recover damages for the wrongful interference with those interests in itself. They provide a powerful vindication of the right and the allocation of entitlements encapsulated in the HRA, symbolically reinforcing and affirming the importance of the protected interests, their inherent value and that they ought to be respected and maintained inviolate. Damages for this normative injury are assessed objectively, with quantum dependant on the seriousness of the violation and importance of the protected interest, and consideration of past awards, so as to ensure consistency of treatment. In contrast damages for consequential non-pecuniary losses are assessed subjectively, according to the actual loss, for example distress or frustration, the claimant has suffered, to be proven through direct evidence or inferred from the facts. As with assessment of damages for normative damage, judges would look to past awards for consequential non-pecuniary loss so as to ensure claimants are treated consistently, and appellate courts would likely develop detailed guidelines to facilitate consistency. Pecuniary losses would need to be specifically pleaded and proven by reference to concrete evidence, as at common law.

Quantum should be calibrated to domestic scales, which reflect domestic economic conditions, so that victims of human rights violations are no longer unfairly undercompensated relative to claimants in tort for identical heads of loss, and fundamental human rights no longer relegated to second-class rights.

If it transpires that operation of the tort-based approach is undermining important public interests in a particular context then it would be open to the government and/or Parliament to take appropriate action. As Sir Alfred Denning said in his Hamlyn Lectures, 'if the hands of the judges are tied, the hands of Parliament are not' and where the courts have struck the balance too far in favour of individual rights, 'Parliament has repeatedly intervened so as to give the public good its proper place'.[1] However, the political branches must take an approach apt for matters of such importance. Where fundamental rights are at stake the political branches must announce publically any proposed response and offer reasoned justification, allow time for adequate and informed debate, and take an evidence-based approach, making use of their relative institutional advantages, as well as considering whether alternative courses of action, which would not entail limiting remedies for victims, could secure the protection of the public interest. All relevant factors must be taken into account, including important public interests served by protecting rights through the imposition of damages liability, and factors must be scrutinised rigorously.

Overall, the answer to the riddle of what approach ought to be taken to human rights damages was in front of us all along. It lies in the law of damages developed within TAPS, which have for centuries played a crucial constitutional function in protecting those rights fundamental to English civil society through imposition of damages liability. We need look no further than the common law for all of the resources which we need to fashion an approach to human rights damages which is principled, coherent and rational, and gives effect to the policy of protection and vindication of fundamental interests that underpins human rights law.

[1] *Freedom under the Law* (Stevens, 1949) 71.

Index

www.ingramcontent.com/pod-product-compliance
Lightning Source LLC
Chambersburg PA
CBHW051149180926
51611CB00001B/3
9781509924448